PREACH THE WORD

PREACH THE WORD

A Pauline Theology of Preaching Based
on 2 Timothy 4:1–5

STEPHEN OLIVER STOUT

FOREWORD BY
Darryl A. Bodie

RESOURCE *Publications* • Eugene, Oregon

PREACH THE WORD
A Pauline Theology of Preaching Based on 2 Timothy 4:1–5

Copyright © 2014 Stephen O. Stout. All rights reserved. Except for brief quotations in critical publications or reviews, no part of this book may be reproduced in any manner without prior written permission from the publisher. Write: Permissions. Wipf and Stock Publishers, 199 W. 8th Ave., Suite 3, Eugene, OR 97401.

Resource Publications
An Imprint of Wipf and Stock Publishers
199 W. 8th Ave., Suite 3
Eugene, OR 97401

www.wipfandstock.com

ISBN 13: 978-1-62564-899-0

Manufactured in the U.S.A.   11/07/2014

Consent was obtained from the Buswell Library of Covenant Theological Seminary to use the original D.Min. project as the basis of this book.

Unless otherwise noted, the quotations from the English Bible are taken from the New American Standard Bible (NASB). Copyright © The Lockman Foundation 1960, 1962, 1963, 1968, 1971, 1972, 1973, 1975, 1977, 1988, 1995. Used by permission.

Unless otherwise noted, the quotations from the Greek NT are taken from the BibleWorks, v.9 database (BGT/BNT) of the United Bible Society 4th edition/ Nestle-Aland 27th edition of the *Greek New Testament*, edited by Barbara Aland, Kurt Aland, Johannes Karavidopoulos, Carlo M. Martini, and Bruce M. Metzger in cooperation with the Institute for New Testament Textual Research, Münster/Westphalia. Copyright © 1993 Deutsche Bibelgesellschaft, Stuttgart. Copyright © 1998–2008 *BibleWorks*, LLC. BibleWorks, v.9.

Citations from the Hebrew Bible are taken from the Groves-Wheeler Westminster Morphology and Lemma Database. Copyright © 2010 (release 4.14) by the Westminster Theological Seminary, and used by arrangement with Westminster Theological Seminary, Glenside, Pennsylvania. The Hebrew text has been corrected to the latest available facsimiles of Codex Leningradensis. Copyright © 1998–2008 BibleWorks, LLC.

Unless otherwise noted, the quotations from the Septuagint, the Greek Translation of the OT, are taken from the database of Rahlfs' Septuagint (Copyright © 1935 by the Württembergische Bibelanstalt/Deutsche Bibelgesellschaft, Stuttgart). Copyright © 1998–2008 BibleWorks, LLC.

Scripture quotations marked CSB or HCSB are been taken from the Holman Christian Standard Bible®. Copyright © 1999, 2000, 2002, 2003, 2009 by Holman Bible Publishers. Used by permission. Holman Christian Standard Bible®, Holman CSB®, and HCSB® are federally registered trademarks of Holman Bible Publishers.

Scripture quotations marked DBY are from The English Darby Bible 1884/1890, a literal translation by John Nelson Darby (1800–1882), ASCII version Copyright © 1988-1997 by the Online Bible Foundation and Woodside Fellowship of Ontario, Canada. Licensed from the Institute for Creation Research. Used by permission.

Scripture quotations marked ERV are from the English Revised Version (1885). The electronic text is Copyright © 2002 by Larry Nelson, Box 1681, Cathedral City, CA 92235. All rights reserved. Used by permission.

Scripture quotations marked ESV are from the Holy Bible, English Standard Version, copyright © 2001 by Crossway Bibles, a division of Good News Publishers. Used by permission. All rights reserved.

Scripture quotations marked KJV, KJA, KJG are from the 1769 Blayney Edition of the 1611 King James Version of the English Bible. Copyright © 1988–1997 by the Online Bible Foundation and Woodside Fellowship of Ontario, Canada. Licensed from the Institute for Creation Research. Used by permission.

Scripture quotations marked NET are from *The NET Bible, Version 1.0*, Copyright © 2004, 2005 Biblical Studies Foundation. Used by permission in conformity with the stipulations listed at *www.netbible.org*.

Quotations designated NIV/NIB are from THE HOLY BIBLE: NEW INTERNATIONAL VERSION®. NIV®. Copyright © 1973, 1978, 1984 by International Bible Society, www.ibs.org. All rights reserved worldwide.

Quotations marked NRS are from the *New Revised Standard Version Bible*. Copyright © 1989, Division of Christian Education of the National Council of the Churches of Christ in the United States of America. Used by permission. All rights reserved.

Scripture quotations marked YLT are from The English Young's Literal Translation of the Holy Bible 1862/1887/1898, by J. N. Young. ASCII version Copyright © 1988–1997 by the Online Bible Foundation and Woodside Fellowship of Ontario, Canada. Licensed from the Institute for Creation Research. Used by permission.

All emphases in Scripture quotations have been added by the author.

Note on Style

This book follows the SBL *Handbook of Style* with a few exceptions: in contrast to SBLH 4.3, distinction in gender reflects its use in each biblical text, particularly with regard to Divine Names as well as the general masculine emphasis of the minister, with all due deference to women in ministry. Also, in contrast to SBLH 4.4.8, pronouns referring to Divine Names and Titles shall be capitalized, in conformity to the primary English version of use, the NASB, and in respect of the Father, Son, and Holy Spirit.

Contents

Dedication and Acknowledgments | xi
Foreword by Darryl A. Bodie | xiii
Introduction | xv
Abbreviations | xxiv

CHAPTER 1   The Preacher's Commission: "I Charge You!" | 1

CHAPTER 2   The Preacher's Reason: "Before God and Jesus Christ!" | 12
                    Because Jesus is God | 14
                    Because Jesus is Judge | 19
                    Because Jesus is Revealer | 22
                    Because Jesus is King | 26

CHAPTER 3   The Preacher's Content: "The Word!" (*Ho Logos*) | 32
                    Preaching the Revealed *Logos* | 33
                    Preaching The *Logos* of Old Testament *Graphē* | 38
                    Preaching The *Logos* of the Kingdom of God | 42
                    Preaching The *Logos* of the New Covenant | 43
                    Preaching The *Logos* of Truth | 47
                    Preaching The *Logos* unto Salvation | 49
                    Preaching The *Logos* unto Edification | 59

CHAPTER 4   The Preacher's Activities: "Preach, . . . Reprove, Rebuke, Exhort!" | 69
                    The Activity of Preaching: Speaking | 59
                    The Activity of Preaching: Evangelizing | 71
                    The Activity of Preaching: Instructing | 84
                    The Activity of Preaching: Defending | 89
                    The Activity of Preaching: Governing | 93
                    The Activity of Preaching: Caring | 104

Contents

CHAPTER 5	The Preacher's Motives: "Be Ready!" | 108
CHAPTER 6	The Preacher's Setting: "In Season; Out Of Season!" | 113
CHAPTER 7	The Preacher's Delivery: "Exhort in All Patience!" | 118
CHAPTER 8	The Preacher's Structure: "Exhort in all . . . Doctrine!" | 126
	The Structure of Paul's Sermons in the Book of Acts | 127
	The Structure of Paul's Epistles as Sermons | 148
CHAPTER 9	The Preacher's Audience: "Tickled Ears" | 158
	Preaching and the Hearing of the Audience | 160
	Preaching and the Hearing of an Unbelieving Audience | 160
	Preaching and the Hearing of a Believing Audience | 166
CHAPTER 10	The Preacher's Character: "But As For You!" | 170
	The Character of the False Preacher | 171
	The Character of Fellow-Preachers | 173
	The Character of Paul as an Example for Preachers | 174
	The Character of the Godly Preacher | 177
CHAPTER 11	The Preacher's Manner: "Be Sober in All!" | 189
CHAPTER 12	The Preacher's Hardships: "Endure Hardship!" | 195
	The Hardship of Intentional Opposition | 196
	The Hardship of Impersonal Trials | 199
	The Hardship of Personal Weaknesses | 202
CHAPTER 13	The Preacher's Work: "Do Work!" | 204
	As a Worker Working the Work: *Ergatēs Ergazetai to Ergon* | 204
	As one Doing is Doing: *Ho Poiōn Poieī* | 209
	As one Practicing is Practicing: *Ho Prassōn Prassei* | 209
	As a Laborer is Laboring at Labor: *Ho Kopon Kopizei Kopos* | 210
	As a Servant is Servicing the Service: *Diakonos Diakonei Diakonia* | 212
	As a Slave is Slaving: *Doulos Douleuei* | 213
	As a Minister is Ministering: *Hupēretēs Hupēretei* | 214
	As one Liturgizing the Liturgy: *Latrueō ē Latreia* | 215
	As the one Striving: *Sunathleō* | 216
	As one Agonizing the Agony: *Agōnizomai ton Agōna* | 217
	As a Soldier Soldiering the Strategy: *Stratiotēs Strateuei Strateian* | 218
	As a Builder Building the Building: *Ho Oikodomōn Oikodomei tēn Oikodomēn* | 218

CONTENTS

CHAPTER 14	The Preacher's Offices: "Do the Work of an Evangelist!"	220
	The Offices of Proclamation	220
	The Offices of Teaching	228
	The Offices of Revelation	242
	Table 1: A Comparison of the Lists of the Twelve Apostles	253
	Table 2: A Synthesis of the Twelve Apostles	255
CHAPTER 15	The Preacher's Dynamic: "Fulfill Your Ministry!"	257
	The Dynamic of Fulfillment	258
	The Dynamic of the Gospel	260
	The Dynamic Energy	262
	The Dynamic of Mediation	263
	The Dynamic of *Charisma*	272
	The Dynamic of Prayer	282
CHAPTER 16	The Preacher's Ministry: "Your Ministry" (*Diakonia*)	284
	Descriptions of *Diakonia*	285
	Applications of *Diakonia*	286
	The Source of *Diakonia*	288
	The Authority of *Diakonia*	288
	Spheres of *Diakonia*	289
	Attitudes of *Diakonia*	292
	Completion of *Diakonia*	293
CHAPTER 17	Conclusions and Applications	295

Bibliography | 303

Author Index
Scripture Index
Subject Index

Dedication and Acknowledgments

THIS BOOK IS DEDICATED to the memory of my colleague in ministry, Marshall St. John, who endured several trips from Charlotte to St. Louis in my 1980 Nissan pickup truck for our D.Min. courses together at Covenant Seminary. Marshall made sure I persevered to the end of my studies, so I was saddened when I heard that he had finished his course, being called home on September 2, 2011 at the early age of 63. Marshall was one of the first pastors to welcome me to my new Charlotte pastorate in 1977, and his pleasant demeanor made my studies an enjoyable process. As an encourager of my ministry, Marshall was an example of one who faithfully preached the Word.

This book is also dedicated to my family, including my dear and patient wife Marlene; our children, Deirdre and Adam Mumpower; Danielle and Daniel Renstrom; and Lydia and David Poole; and our grandchildren, Brock, Macie and Jack Mumpower, and Bennett, Eden and Mercy Renstrom, and Daphne Poole, plus any others God may provide to fill our quiver.

A special thanks is extended to the faculty and staff of Covenant Theological Seminary for their biblical fidelity and scholarly excellence in my course of study. My particular thanks goes to my major professors, Dr. David Jones and Dr. Robert Raymond—of whom I was one of his last doctoral students before his untimely homegoing. It was under their careful direction that I wrote the original project of this book as my D.Min. project, and it is with the consent of the CTS Library that I use that project as the basis for this book.

Thanks is also extended to the faculty of Carolina Graduate School of Divinity, Greensboro, N.C., and Charlotte Christian College and Theological Seminary, Charlotte, N.C., who push me on toward academic excellence; to the Officers and Congregations of the Prosperity Presbyterian Church, Charlotte, N.C. and the Shearer Presbyterian Church (PCA), Mooresville, N.C., who graciously permitted me the study time away from pastoral duties to complete my studies and write this book. Hopefully, their patience will be rewarded in the improved preaching and pastoring of their minister.

Dedication and Acknowledgments

Special thanks is also given to my students at CGSD, Gary Baldwin, Wesley McCarter, and Robert Yost, who spent many tedious hours proofreading the first draft and making helpful suggestions for clarity of reading. Plus, they wanted a good grade in their D.Min. course on the Theology of Preaching. I hope the effort made them better preachers.

Particular acknowledgment of thanks is given to my proofreader Lynn Haddock. Her keen eye for good English composition has made this work far more readable than when I first typed it into my word processor. She has made me realize how effective communication is a matter of having the author's thoughts agree with what is written, spoken and eventually read or heard by another who might have some interest in the topic.

I am also highly appreciative of my friend and colleague Dr. Darryl Bodie, who kindly wrote the Foreword to this book. Darryl and I attended college and seminary together, and then he asked me to teach with him at CGSD, where I have observed his passion to train others for the preaching ministry.

Supreme thanks must also be given to the One who called me to preach His Gospel and instructed me from the preaching of His herald, the Apostle Paul. My prayer continues that through this book "the proclamation might be fully accomplished, and that all the Gentiles might hear."

—Stephen O. Stout
Charlotte, N.C.

Foreword

EVERY SUNDAY, PREACHERS ACROSS the world stand at the pulpit, in front of people and for a period of time speak on a variety of subjects. While some simply tell stories or moral tales, many open the pages of ancient scripture and preach from its pages. They preach, in part because that is an element of the job description and has become expected by church folk. With guidelines which have been established by local tradition or more likely from personal experience, preachers head each week into the pulpit. Very few have worked through a biblical understanding of what it means to preach from the Word of God. (Who has the time in school while studying for all those classes and who has time once out of school with the pressures of ministry?)

From my days in Bible College and then in Seminary preparing for pastoral ministry, I heard numerous professors encourage us to take hold of the Word of God and preach its truths. That is where the challenge stopped. As students, we were not given a clear biblical understanding of why we were to preach and what would be accomplished by that task. We did not understand how the Lord would use us in this particular part of our ministry nor what was required beyond the mechanics on our part to bring a sermon to the people each week. We learned about hermeneutics and exegesis (the theory of text interpretation), homiletics (the application of the general principles of public speaking), but never an extended lesson or class on a biblical theology of preaching.

As a young man, I had to step behind the pulpit twice a week. I had read numerous books on preaching by famous authors, but a clear understanding of a theology of preaching evaded me. Since I did not have that foundational understanding, I chose to emulate the things I saw well known preachers of that era doing. Evidently I was not the only one who followed such a practice. I remember hearing Charles Swindoll remark a number of years ago, that when he started preaching he was sounded a bit like the seven headed dragon in Revelation looked. He was part one preacher, and parts of six others. I am afraid that was close to how I sounded in the pulpit too in those early years.

Over the years, my understanding of the task of preaching grew as I interacted with the text of the New Testament. A gradual self-developed biblical theology of preaching (including my calling, the task and why of preaching, etc.) provided a stronger foundation of confidence which allowed me to be free to become myself and allow the Holy Spirit use my "voice" to present sermons from the pages of the Bible. I wish this book had been penned in those days, for it would have provided the structured theology of preaching that I needed.

Using the Apostle Paul's famous passage on preaching in 2 Timothy 4:1-5, this book explores the concepts that make up a biblical formulation for this ministry of preaching. Steve has taken that text to be the framework for examining the Scripture to discover what this ministry involves. To that outline, he masterfully intersperses elements from Paul's other epistles as well as the early church found in the book of Acts to amplify and enhance understanding. He tracks down meaning and use in the New Testament words found in that passage and gives a clear understanding of the imperatives the Apostle uses to communicate to Timothy the task he was called to perform and the person he was called to become as a representative of the Lord.

I have been given the privilege of writing this forward for a unique book on preaching by my longtime friend and colleague Steve Stout. That assignment means I was among the first few to view its content and interact with the concepts that he has crafted into this read. It is my assessment that this book will provide help to preachers of all experiences.

Those who are new to the pulpit (within the last few years) will find this book will help you better understand the task of preaching. You would eventually gather this on your own over your years if you systematically worked through the New Testament books. Dr. Stout has provided you with a gift that will enhance your understanding of your duty as you stand in front of the people whom God has placed under your charge. By grasping the truths provided in this theology, you will be years ahead in the process of personal development. Such knowledge will help you as you define your own "voice" to preach the Word.

Those who are seasoned in the task of preaching will find this book providing clear perspective. It will tidy up the fragmented pieces of the truths of theology of preaching that you have found over the years. The organized, concise arrangement of the truths will bring clarity to your personal understanding along with encouragement and challenge to you heart as you face the challenge of speaking in the climate of today.

As you read this book, may the Lord strengthen your resolve to Preach the Word.

—Darryl A. Bodie

Director of Doctoral Studies
Billy and Viola Britt Professor of Ministry
Carolina Graduate School of Divinity

Introduction

THIS BOOK IS A revision of my D.Min. project submitted to Covenant Theological Seminary, St. Louis, Mo., back in 1988 under the persistent guidance of Dr. David Jones and Dr. Robert Raymond. The bound copy, however, collected dust on my bookshelf for more than twenty-five years until I was asked by the Carolina Graduate School of Divinity to teach a D.Min. course on the Theology of Preaching. I was hard pressed to find a comprehensive work on Paul's view of preaching,[1] so I dusted off this study of 2 Timothy 4:1–5, which provided the title for this book in the opening command, "Preach the Word." The topic seems to be more pertinent now than a generation earlier, since preaching has fallen on hard times. The original study was prompted by the question, "What to Preach?" and the answer is supplied in large part by the apostle Paul in his sermons and letters as recorded in the NT. So, here I present to the preachers of Jesus Christ a Pauline Theology of Preaching in hopes that it will help them formulate a more systematic reason why and what to preach—the Word.

Thesis

The thesis of this work is that the central governing activity of the ministry of the Apostle Paul is the oral proclamation of the Gospel of Christ. All other activities in his ministry are subservient to this over-riding concern, and they find meaning only if preaching is primary.

In order to prove this thesis, this study develops a Pauline Theology of Preaching, taking the words of Paul seriously when he encourages future preachers to follow his teaching, conduct and purpose (2 Tim 3:10).[2] While the preacher must distinguish

---

1. A recent effort is that of John Beaudean, *Paul's Theology of Preaching*, but it only studies the critically accepted epistles of Paul and is quite influenced by existential theories, detracting from its benefits.

2. While it is academically fashionable to deny Pauline authorship of 2 Timothy, an unexpected defense of Pauline authorship of the Pastoral Epistles appeared from the otherwise quite critical scholar Robinson, *Redating the New Testament*, 67–85. Also, Johnson, *The Writings of the New Testament: An Interpretation*, 423–31, examines the supposed reasons for denying Pauline authorship and

between his own preaching and Paul's apostolic commission, it is evident that Paul serves as the model preacher of the NT. If one desires to preach biblically, he should seek to preach like Paul. This thesis, explaining why Paul thought it paramount that Timothy "Preach the Word," will govern the procedure of this book.

Methodology

In order to establish this thesis, it is the conviction of the author that preaching is as much a discipline of systematic and biblical theology as any other aspect of the Christian faith, agreeing with D. W. Ford, "Preaching can be defended only by the steady build up of a theology of preaching, establishing it as a form of discourse which is *sui generis*; that is, it stands in a class by itself."[3]

Accordingly, it will be the approach of this study to use the preaching charge of the Apostle Paul in 2 Tim 4:1–5 as the basic outline of this study, locating and studying the appropriate passages and terminologies that describe the preaching ministry of Paul as they are recorded in his letters as well as in his sermons in the Book of Acts. In so doing, a Pauline theology of preaching will emerge.

Outline of This Study

For many good reasons, the primary passage of study in this book, 2 Tim 4:1–5, is often cited or preached at ordination services—perhaps more than any other text. Truly, it provides a logical framework for developing Paul's theology of preaching, and so a rather wooden translation of the passage furnishes the outline that this book shall follow:

1. The Preacher's Commission: I solemnly charge (you)
2. The Preacher's Reason: before God, even Christ Jesus,
    The One about to be judging living and dead;
    And (before) His appearance
    And (before) his Kingdom!
3. The Preacher's Content: The Word
4. The Preacher's Activities: Preach! Reprove! Rebuke! Exhort!

---

frankly acknowledges that the Pastorals are written in Paul's name and "seek to communicate teaching which is recognizably Pauline" (ibid., 424). He calls for the Pastorals to be "restored to separate but equal statues within the Pauline collection" (ibid., 430). From a conservative perspective, William Mounce, *Pastoral Epistles*, lxxxxiii–cxxix, ably defends Pauline authorship of the Pastoral epistle as he chronicles the concurrence of the church Fathers toward Pauline authorship and suggests that the large number of *hapax legomena* in this letter were necessitated due to the refutation of a new heresy. He also observes that the issue of authorship relates more to methodology than with the text itself.

3. Ford, *The Ministry of the Word*, 17.

5. The Preacher's Motives: Stand by
6. The Preacher's Setting: (in) good timeliness
    (or in) bad timeliness;
7. The Preacher's Delivery: Exhort in all patience
8. The Preacher's Structure: and doctrine;
9. The Preacher's Audience: For time shall be when they shall not hear sound doctrine
    But rather, according to their own lusts,
    They shall heap up teachers, (having) itching ears;
    And indeed, away from the truth they shall turn their ears,
    And unto myths they shall be turned aside;
10. The Preacher's Character: But You—
11. The Preacher's Manner: Be keeping a sober watch in all things;
12. The Preacher's Hardships: Be enduring hardships;
13. The Preacher's Work: Do work
14. The Preacher's Offices: Of an evangelist;
15. The Preacher's Dynamic: Fulfill
16. The Preacher's Ministry: Your ministry.

These major headings will serve as the basic outline of this book, as noted in the Table of Contents.

Limits of This Study

While the very nature of this study demands exegetical and theological endeavor, it needs to be noted that the primary limits of this book are pastoral, homiletical, practical, and admittedly, personal, as the author asked himself, Why am I preaching? This quest for an answer led him to determine a biblical method of preaching, as this is the task to which he has been ordained by the Church of Jesus Christ. It has been his painful observation that far too many young preachers are thrust into pulpits (and upon their congregations) without ever having been challenged to develop a biblical theology of preaching. So, this book began first as a personal search, and if God seems pleased to use it to guide other preachers in their desire to preach the gospel, then may He receive the praise for any benefit derived from it.

INTRODUCTION

Assumptions

This book makes several assumptions, some of which will be taken for granted because proof lies beyond the scope of this study, having been defended far more adequately by other esteemed scholars and theologians. Such assumptions include the following:

1. The nature of God as essentially communicative and revelatory will be assumed. This assumption refutes the notion of skeptical criticism that denies that which the Bible announces from its opening page, that God speaks (Gen 1:3); instead, this book will assume, "The Lord God has spoken! Who can but prophesy?" (Amos 3:8).

2. The verbal inspiration and inerrancy of Scripture as defined by the *Chicago Statement on Biblical Inerrancy* will be assumed, namely, that ". . .being wholly and verbally God-given, Scripture is without error or fault in all its teaching."[4] This doctrine has been assailed on many fronts, as when Worley comments, "There is no normative or absolute theological basis of all Christendom."[5] If this non-standard is true, then no preacher has any basis from which to preach; instead, flowing from the assumption of the revealing God, inspiration implies that God has spoken though the prophets and apostles so that what they preached and wrote came not from their own speculative imagination (2 Pet 1:21), but rather as a "thus says the Lord." Furthermore, since God reveals Himself as the unlying God whose word is truth,[6] then a necessary consequence of inspiration is inerrancy, that the original manuscripts were penned without error.[7] This doctrine will be assumed throughout this book, building upon the foundation of previous evangelical writers.[8]

3. The Pauline and Lukan authorship of those NT books historically credited to them shall also be assumed,[9] although many scholars deny traditional authorship

---

4. A full copy of the *Chicago Statement on Biblical Inerrancy*, as drafted by the International Council on Biblical Inerrancy in 1978 is available at http://library.dts.edu/Pages/TL/Special/ICBI_1.pdf.

5. Worley, *Preaching and Teaching in the Earliest Church*, 137. His statement is actually self-contradictory, for it is an absolute assertion—a norm—that there is no norm, except, apparently, for his illogical dogmatism.

6. "God . . . cannot lie" (Titus 1:2); "Thy word is truth" (John 17:17).

7. "When ye received from us the word of the message, *even the word* of God, ye accepted *it* not *as* the word of men, but, as it is in truth, the word of God (καθὼς ἐστιν ἀληθῶς λόγον θεοῦ), which also worketh in you that believe" (1 Thess 2:13 ERV).

8. Some of the classic evangelical defenses of inspiration include Warfield, *The Inspiration and Authority of the Bible*; Gaussen, *Theopneustia*; Harris, *Inspiration and Canonicity of the Bible*; Lindsell, *The Battle for the Bible*; Montgomery, *God's Inerrant Word*; Pache, *The Inspiration and Authority of Scripture*; Young, *Thy Word is Truth*; Carson and Woodbridge, *Scripture and Truth*. For a recent discussion, see the article by Frame, "Inerrancy: A Place to Live," *JETS* (March 2014): 29–39.

9. It is not within the scope of this study to explore the authenticity of the Pauline and Lukan corpora, since extensive studies on that topic currently exist; for example, see Köstenberger et al., *The Cradle, the Cross, and the Crown: An Introduction to the New Testament*. It is the opinion of this

INTRODUCTION

due to what McDonald labels as "the principle of skepticism—assuming the historical tradition to be guilty of inauthenticity, as it were, until proven innocent."[10] To the contrary, this study shall assume the truthfulness of the texts, as Luke insists in his prologue[11] and as Paul asserts in 1 Tim 2:7, "I am telling the truth, I am not lying."[12] The concept of truth as found in Christian Scripture is utterly incompatible with the theories of myth and historical emendation supposedly perpetrated by biblical writers, since a pious fabrication is still a lie condemned by Scripture, no matter how noble the intent.[13] Furthermore, if the concept of biblical truth is gutted, the preacher has nothing left to proclaim, since no honest person can preach for very long what he doubts.

4. Although much benefit can be garnered from the science of public speaking, this book will assume that the Bible is the authoritative guide to teach the Christian preacher how to preach. Weirsbe and Perry note, "The NT has something to say to us about preaching, about its essential nature, its central and controlling message, its aims, its evangelistic and interpretive state."[14] While their observations are quite true (and this book shall develop these themes), the statement itself fails to note that the Bible is itself the authoritative text for preaching. Anyone who wants to learn to preach must first submit himself to the instructions and examples of preaching as recording in Scripture. To this end, a faithful biblical preacher is an unabashed imitator, in that his sermons should only be expositions and explanations of the sermons of the prophets and apostles.

---

writer that the arguments supporting traditional authorship are convincing and can stand the tests of inquiry. That being the case, this study will assume the Pauline authorship of the thirteen letters bearing his signature, as well as the Lukan authenticity of the recorded sermons of Paul in the book of Acts. Furthermore, this study will also assume the apostolic authority of those writings as binding upon believers, as asserted in 2 Tim 3:16–17, that "All Scripture *is* given by inspiration of God, and *is* profitable for doctrine, for reproof, for correction, for instruction in righteousness, that the man of God may be complete, thoroughly equipped for every good work." In other words, this study will follow a textual approach within the traditional canon of the Christian Bible.

10. McDonald, *Kerygma and Didache*, 20.

11. The Gospel of Luke begins with this prologue: "Inasmuch as many have undertaken to compile an account of the things accomplished among us, just as those who from the beginning were eyewitnesses and servants of the word have handed them down to us, it seemed fitting for me as well, having investigated everything carefully from the beginning, to write *it* out for you in consecutive order, most excellent Theophilus; so that you might know the exact truth about the things you have been taught" (Luke 1:1–4).

12. See Porter, "Pauline Authorship and the Pastoral Epistles: Implications for Canon," 105–23, who calls for a "begrudging" acceptance of the Pastorals in formulating a full Pauline theology. This study follows his advice quite willingly in developing a total picture of Paul's thinking by embracing 2 Timothy as a genuine letter of the Apostle.

13. See the penetrating analysis in Wilder, *Pseudonymity, the New Testament, and Deception*.

14. Weirsbe and Perry, *Wycliffe Handbook of Preaching and Preachers*, 16.

INTRODUCTION

Argument

Even in a time when preaching has fallen on hard times (or deaf ears), there lurks a danger of exalting preaching beyond its biblical limits. While Neo-Orthodox theology rightfully elevated the role of preaching, rescuing it from the sterility of liberalism, it confused preaching with revelation; for example, Robert Mounce, a devotee of Karl Barth, insists that preaching continues the saving events, so that apart from preaching, there is no salvation.[15]

While this opinion may seem to reflect Rom 10:14 ("How shall they hear without a preacher?"), Mounce credits more to preaching than does the Bible, for no gospel preacher should ever confuse his own sermons with the saving events proclaimed in the sermon. Still, Neo-Orthodoxy made a refreshing rediscovery of the Reformed distinctive of preaching as a means of grace, and this aspect of preaching will be explored in further detail. Thus, an aim of this work will be to maintain a balance between the preaching of the text of Scripture and the empowerment of the Holy Spirit who speaks dynamically through His Word—and He does so, quite remarkably, through the preaching of men of unclean lips (Isa 6:5).

Chapter Summaries

This book divides into sixteen chapters, following the outline of the primary passage of study, 2 Tim 4:1–5. The first chapter studies the Preacher's Commission, when Paul "solemnly charges" Timothy "before the presence of God and of Christ Jesus, the one about to judge the living and the dead, and before His appearing and His kingdom"; in other words, the Christian preacher has a divine mandate to preach. This role is thrust upon him by Jesus Christ Himself, who appoints preachers of His gospel and then validates them through the tests given in Scripture and given by the Church.

Chapter 2 concern the Preacher's Reasons for preaching, as Paul stands Timothy "before God and Jesus Christ," whose earthly calling was also as a preacher but now prepares to return as Judge in the revelation of His Kingdom. While it should seem obvious, the Christian preacher has one primary reason for preaching—to proclaim Christ (Col 1:28).

The third chapter explores the content of Christian Preaching, the revealed Word (*Logos*) of God, which Paul elsewhere describes as the *rhēma*, the *mustērion* and even *Christos* as the revealed Word. The depository of this *Logos* is found in the "sacred writings" (2 Tim 3:15), which for Paul included the *Graphē* of the OT, plus the *Logos* of the New Covenant, found for Paul in his concepts of Prophecy, Tradition (*Paradosis*) and the Deposit (*Parthēke*) of truth. This *Logos* is to be preached to the unsaved in the form of the Gospel (*Euangelion*), the Message (*Akoē*), Proclamation (*Kērygma*), and Reconciliation (*Katallagē*). Then the Word is preached to believers as Edification

---

15. Mounce, *The Essential Nature of New Testament Preaching*, 153–54.

INTRODUCTION

(*Paraklēsis*), Comfort (*Paramuthia*), Teaching (*Didachē* and *Didaskalia*), Commandment (*Parangelia*), Reading (*Anagnōsis*), and Defense (*Apologia* and *Bebaiōsis*), showing the many facets of the content of the Word that are to be preached.

The fourth chapter concerns the Preacher's Activities, expressed in the imperatives Paul uses in this charge, "Preach, Reprove, Rebuke, Exhort!" These are certainly not the only verbs Paul uses to describe the speaking of the Word: besides proclaiming (*kerussō*), the preacher is also to be evangelizing by announcing good news (*euangelizō*), pronouncing (*angelizō*), explaining (*ektithēmi*), reasoning (*dialegomai*), proving (*sumbibazō*), disputing (*suzēteō*), boldly speaking (*parrēsiazomai*), solemnly testifying (*diamarturomai*), declaring (*apophthengomai*), ambassadoring (*presbuō*), and persuading (*peithō*). In his preaching to the gathered church, the preacher is to be active in instructing by teaching (*didaskein*), reading (*angnōsein*), relating (*exēgeomai*), discipling (*mathēteō*), and catechizing (*katēchein*). He is also to defend the Word by apologizing (*apologeomai*), witnessing (*martureō*), heeding (*epiekhō* and *prosekō*), and watching (*grēgoreō*). In addition, he is to proclaim the Word in his various pastoral activities of the church, including his governing, exhorting godliness upon believers, and caring for their well being. In these various aspects of the preached Word, the preacher shows the activities of preaching.

Chapter 5 explores Paul's command for Timothy to "be ready," as it examines the motives of the preacher toward God, his message, others and himself; and chapter 6 explores the significance of the preacher's setting, defined to Timothy as "in season; out of season;" that is, in convenient and in inconvenient times and places. The actual delivery of the Word is echoed in the command, "Exhort with all patience," in which chapter 7 looks at the homiletics of Paul in his rhetoric, elocution, emotions, and gestures as pictured in the book of Acts, showing that the Word is to be incarnated in the personality of the preacher.

The actual structure of a preacher's sermon is explored in chapter 8, as implied in the command, "Exhort in all Doctrine!" Here, the sermons of Paul as recorded in Acts are examined, plus his letters are analyzed as written sermons he intended to be "preached" to their recipient churches. In this manner, repeated patterns that would assist a modern preacher in the structuring of his own sermons will be suggested.

The ninth chapter examine the audience of the sermon, yet the one Paul describes in 2 Tim 4:3–4 is not ideal at all, as it possesses "tickled ears," preventing by false preachers from hearing the truth. Timothy needs to preach persuasively, that his audience may believe and bear with sound teaching–all which requires a supernatural intervention of God in opening ears so they may hear and believe.

The tenth chapter concerns the preacher's character, expressed in the differentiation Paul makes between the false preachers (2 Tim 4:4) and Timothy (4:5) with the contrastive, "But You!" Paul teaches that the character of a true preacher should express the qualities of godly motives, emotions, and conduct as outlined in the requirements listed in 1 Tim 3:1–15 and Titus 1:5–9, character that is to be tested by other leaders but enabled by the Holy Spirit, who works godliness in the life of the preacher.

Chapter 11 concerns the next command, "Be Sober in all!" It describes the Preacher's Manner, that he should preach with a clear mind, but also with boldness, watching and heeding his deportment as he preaches the Word authoritatively. This soberness is necessary because of the Preacher's hardships, expressed in the command studied in chapter 12, "Endure Hardship!" These hardships come from intentional opposition, impersonal trials, and the preacher's own personal weaknesses.

Due to these difficulties, he must devote his efforts to do the work of ministry, as Paul instructs Timothy, "Do Work!" a concept explored in chapter 13, studying the many verbs Paul uses to express the Preacher's work, that he is the one doing work (*ho poiōn poieī*); the practitioner practicing (*ho prassōn prassei*); the laborer laboring in labor (*ho kopon kopizei kopos*); the servant serving in service (*diakonos diakonei diakonia*); the slave who is slaving (*doulos douleuei*); the minister who is ministering (*hupēretēs hupēretei*); the liturgist who is "liturgizing" (*latrueō ē latreia*); the one striving (*sunathleō*), even agonizing in the struggle (*agōnizomai ton agōna*); the soldier soldiering in strategy (*stratiotēs strateuei strateian*); and the builder building the building (*ho oikodomōn oikodomei tēn oikodomēn*). Even though these works are done along with other fellow workers to lighten the load, these various pictures show that the preacher's work is a labor in the Lord.

Chapter 14 investigates Paul's command to Timothy to "Work as an Evangelist," plus it looks at the other offices a preacher occupies toward the unsaved world, such as a Herald, an Ambassador, and a Witness. Then it will examine the offices a preacher has with reference to the church as a Teacher, an Overseer, a Shepherd, a Minister, and as a Steward, plus it will consider the relationship of the preacher to the offices of Apostle and Prophet.

Chapter 15 discusses how the preacher's task would be overwhelming if it were not for the spiritual dynamic implied in the command to "fulfill the ministry," which relates to Paul's understanding of the fullness of God and His infilling in the life of the believer through the Holy Spirit and the dynamic of the gospel message. In this regard, the preacher mediates the grace of God, but only through the gifts (*charismata*) given to him by the Holy Spirit that are activated in the dynamic of prayer.

The final chapter (16) studies Paul's concept of the preacher's ministry that Timothy is to fulfill, looking at his sphere as a shepherd to the flock. Thus, in these studies, the preacher should be able to arrive at a "theology" of preaching as expounded by the apostle Paul himself.

Perimeters

So, the channels of this book have been charted. On one hand, it will steer the course mapped by the sufficiency and authority of the biblical text itself, yet, on the other hand, it must sail between the Scylla and Charybdis of hard questions: How does God use the "foolishness of preaching" to save those who believe while also confounding the wise of this world (1 Cor 1:21)? What does it mean that preaching has been considered a means of grace, which, when mixed with faith, is able to edify the hearers and give them the inheritance among all who are sanctified (Acts 20:32)? Has preaching justified its lofty position at the center of Protestant worship? Can the thesis of this book be defended, that preaching is the central governing feature of Pauline ministry, and therefore, of the ministry of every following minister of the Gospel of Christ? Is preaching paramount over pastoring, counseling, ruling, and all the other biblical tasks to which a pastor is called to perform?

As the Lord said to Isaiah, "Come let us reason together," and let us discover why Paul claims, "'I believed, therefore I spoke,' we also believe, therefore also we speak" (2 Cor 4:13).

Abbreviations

Acts	The New Testament Book of the Acts of the Apostles
AT	Author's Translation of the Greek or Hebrew text of the Bible
BDAG	*Greek-English Lexicon of the New Testament and Other Early Christian Literature.*
BDB	*Hebrew-Aramaic and English Lexicon of the Old Testament.*
BDF	*A Greek Grammar of the New Testament and Other Early Christian Literature.*
BW	*Bible Works for Windows.* Copyright © 2008 Bible Works, and updates to Version 9.0.00.
BYZ	*The New Testament in the Original Greek: Byzantine Textform (2005).* Public domain.
CSB	The Holman Christian Standard Bible®. Second edition.
DLZ	Delitzsch Hebrew New Testament (1877). Public domain.
DNTT	*Dictionary of the New Testament Theology.* Edited by Colon Brown.
EDNT	*Evangelical Dictionary of the New Testament.*
ERV	The English Revised Version (1885).
ESV	The English Standard Version.
HB	The Hebrew Bible.
HCSB	The Holman Christian Standard Bible.
KJV	The King James Version of the English Bible.
L&N	*Greek-English Lexicon of the New Testament: Based on Semantic Domains.* Edited by J. P. Louw and E. A. Nida.
LXX	The *Septuagint*, the Greek Translation of the OT.

Abbreviations

MT	Masoretic Text of the Hebrew Bible (see HB and OT).
NASB	The New American Standard Bible
NET	The NET Bible
NIV/NIB	The New International Version of the Bible
NRS	The New Revised Standard Version Bible.
NT	The New Testament of the Christian Scriptures.
OT	The Old Testament of the Hebrew Bible (HB).
TDNT	*The Theological Dictionary of the New Testament.* Edited by Gerhard Kittel. Translated by Geoffry W. Bromiley. 10 vols. Grand Rapids: Eerdmans, 1964–1976.
TWOT	*Theological Wordbook of the Old Testament.*
VGNT	*The Vocabulary of the Greek Testament: Illustrated from the Papyri and Other Non-Literary Sources.* Edited by James H. Moulton and George Milligan.
YLT	Young's Literal Translation of the Holy Bible

CHAPTER 1

The Preacher's Commission: "I Solemnly Charge You"

Who Commissioned You to Preach?

"I SOLEMNLY CHARGE YOU: . . . Preach!" So reads Paul's terse commission to Timothy in the closing chapter of what has traditionally been considered the last epistle of the apostle (2 Tim 4:1–2),[1] as the aging evangelist impresses upon his disciple Timothy what is most important in the gospel ministry—preaching. This commission is emphasized not only by the imperative mode of the following verbs telling Timothy how to preach ("Be ready! Reprove! Rebuke! Exhort!"), but also by the solemn adjuration implied in the verb, *diamarturomai*.[2]

Paul's commission to Timothy raises the immediate question of the authority of preaching, which is perhaps the most important consideration pertaining to the public proclamation of the gospel. Who or what gives the preacher the right to tell others what to believe and how to think? Is it not the height of presumption for a mortal man

---

1. The writer is well aware that some may dismiss this study as unscholarly because it treats all thirteen of Paul's signed epistles as actually penned by Paul himself, so an appeal is extended to those who reject apostolic authorship to acknowledge that these letters certainly purport to be Pauline. See Wilder, *Pseudonymity, the New Testament, and Deception: An Inquiry into Intention and Reception*, 222–27, where he observes that the invocation of apostolic authority (1 Tim 1:1; 2:7; 5:21), the notice of an impending personal visit (1 Tim 3:14–15; 4:13), and the inclusion of insignificant personal details (1 Tim 5:23) means that someone went to a great deal of trouble to make the Pastorals appear to be genuinely Pauline. If the letter is a forgery, then such efforts make the claim of the forger, "I am telling the truth, I am not lying" (1 Tim 2:7) to be especially audacious—unless it is Paul himself making this claim; otherwise, the ethics of even non-deceptive pseudonymity (2 Thess 2:2) suggest that pseudonymous writings ought to be excluded from the canon (ibid., 255). If, however, Paul did in fact author his signed epistles, then it would be remiss not to include all pertinent material in a study on Pauline theology, as argued by Towner, "Christology in the Letters to Timothy and Titus," 220. See also the discussion in James Aageson, *Paul, the Pastoral Epistles, and the Early Church* (2007).

2. Strathmann, "μαρτύρομαι," *TDNT* 4:511, defines this verb as follows: "The first meaning is 'to invoke some one (god or men) as witness with reference to something'; 'to declare with an appeal to a witness'; and then secondly, 'to declare emphatically,' whether with reference to facts or truth or in the sense of a summons, admonition, or warning." It is in this last sense that the word is used in 2 Tim 4:1.

to explain the immortal God to another?[3] No preacher can be effective unless he is assured of a legitimate commission to preach, that his authority comes from one who is empowered to delegate it.

For example, who is Paul to commission Timothy, or any other believer, for that matter? This command to preach is not isolated; the Pastoral Epistles are replete with examples of Paul commanding other preachers to teach various doctrines,[4] even adjuring his readers by using the same verb *diamarturomai*.[5] Luke also uses this same verb to show the solemn authority that marked the preaching of the early church.[6] Clearly, the gospel is intended to be a message of authority, but who gives the preacher the authoritative right to the message?

Commission from Jesus

The answer is found in the Lordship of Jesus Christ, who by virtue of His death and resurrection has been granted the Name above every name, that every tongue should confess that Jesus Christ is Lord (Phil 2:9–11). Only by coming under the sovereignty of Jesus over all is a person enabled to speak by the authority of His Lordship. Thus, surrender to Jesus as Lord is the beginning point of the commissioning of the preacher.

It is quite evident that Jesus intended to extend His authority to delegated spokesmen; in fact, He gives His preachers His very own authority when He states, "He who hears you, hears me" (Luke 10:16). This promise is astounding, because it displays the fact that when the gospel is faithfully preached, the Lord Himself speaks through His

---

3. For ease of writing, this work follows the general tenor of Scripture in describing preachers as men, as has been the general practice of the church until fairly recent times. Since Paul notes in 1 Cor 11:5 that a woman may prophesy—such as Philip's four daughters (Acts 21:9)—and Acts 18:26 reports that Priscilla clearly had a teaching ministry, this study in no way intends to diminish nor offend any sister in Christ who is called as a fellow-worker in the gospel (Phil 4:3). However, the general thrust of the NT addresses men as preachers, and so this study shall reflect similar language of the masculine gender. Hopefully, any "elect lady" (2 John 1:1) who happens to read this work will make her own applications helpful in developing her own theology of ministry.

4. "This command I entrust to you" (1 Tim 1:18); "Prescribe and teach these things" (1 Tim 4:11; 5:7; 6:2); "These things speak and exhort and reprove with all authority" (Titus 2:15).

5. "We also . . . solemnly warned *you* that no man should transgress and defraud his brother (1 Thess 4:6); "I solemnly charge you in the presence of God and of Christ Jesus and of *His* chosen angels, to maintain these *principles* without bias" (1 Tim 5:21); "Solemnly charge *them* in the presence of God not to wrangle about words" (2 Tim 2:14).

6. "With many other words he solemnly testified . . . , saying, "Be saved from this perverse generation!" (Acts 2:40); "When they had solemnly testified and spoken the word of the Lord" (Acts 8:25); "Paul *began* devoting himself completely to the word, solemnly testifying to the Jews that Jesus was the Christ" (Acts 18:5); ". . . solemnly testifying to both Jews and Greeks of repentance toward God and faith in our Lord Jesus Christ" (Acts 20:21); ". . . to testify solemnly of the gospel of the grace of God" (Acts 20:24); "As you have solemnly witnessed to My cause at Jerusalem, so you must witness at Rome also" (Acts 23:11); "He was explaining to them by solemnly testifying about the kingdom of God" (Acts 28:23).

messenger, as Paul notes in 2 Cor 5:20, "We are ambassadors for Christ, as though God were entreating through us."

Thus, the preacher derives his authority to preach on the basis that the Lord Jesus orders the propagation of His message. Peter states, "Jesus ordered us to preach to the people, and solemnly to testify (*diamarturomai*) that this is the One who has been appointed by God as Judge of the living and the dead" (Acts 10:42). The parallel between this statement and Paul's charge in 2 Tim 4:1 is unmistakable, as both verses show the delegation of authority that has been passed from Jesus to His apostles and then on to the next generation of preachers. Likewise, the chain of command continues as the Lord appoints other men to preach the Word by apostolic commissioning under the supervision of the Word and the eldership (*presbuteroi*; 1 Tim 4:14).

Commission of Paul

It is important to note that Paul's authority is apostolic, meaning that he speaks as one sent by another authority to deliver the message verbatim.[7] Paul never tires of reminding his readers of his own commission to preach the gospel: the appearance of the risen Christ to him on the Damascus Road was not only a call to salvation, but also a call to preach. For that matter, one is hard pressed to find Paul making a distinction between saving grace and appointing grace.[8] Paul was approved to be entrusted (*episteuthen*) with the gospel (1 Tim 1:11) by divine appointment (*tithēmi*, 1 Tim 2:7), and it is from this personal commissioning by the resurrected Lord that Paul derives his commission as one legitimately sent as an apostle of Jesus Christ.

Commission by Appointment

Paul's apostolic call illustrates the principle stated in Heb 5:4, "No one takes the honor to himself, but receives it when he is called by God, even as Aaron was." The concept of a divine call is not only biblical—it is essential, as Christ called the Twelve "as He desired" (Mark 3:13), and as the Holy Spirit said, "Set apart for Me Barnabas and Saul for the work to which I have called them" (Acts 13:2). Such a call comes by the sovereign summons of the Triune God.

Paul expresses his belief in this divine call repeatedly, stating that it was "God who set (*ethetō*) in the church, first apostles, second prophets, third teachers" (1 Cor 12:28). Paul also claims that it was God (the Father) who "gave (*didōmi*) us the

---

7. The delegated authority is implied in the word *apostolos* as derived from *apostellō*. VGNT § 502 ἀποστέλλω cites P Oxy I. 8718 (A.D. 342) ἀπαντῆσαι ἅμα τοῖς εἰς τοῦτον ἀποσταλῖα[σ]ι [ὁ] φ(φικιαλίοις), "to proceed with the officers sent for this purpose," which may illustrate the frequent NT sense of "commissioning." See also the discussion in Schmidals, *The Office of Apostle in the Early Church*, 40–41.

8. For the entrusting of Paul with the gospel, see Rom 15:15; Gal 1:16; 2:7; Eph 3:6–9; Phil 1:16; Col 1:23–25; 1 Thess 2:4; 1 Tim 1:11; 2 Tim 1:11; and Titus 1:3.

ministry of reconciliation and . . . has committed (*tithei*) to us the word of reconciliation" (2 Cor 5:18–19), and he reminds the Ephesian elders that it was "the Holy Spirit who made (*tithei*) overseers" (Acts 20:28). In addition, Paul is ever mindful of his own divine appointment, for he gives thanks to "Christ Jesus our Lord who . . . considered me faithful, putting (*tithēmi*) me into service" (1 Tim 1:12).[9]

Another interesting concept used to convey divine appointment is found in the risen Lord's explanation to Paul at his conversion, "For this purpose I have appeared to you, to appoint (*procheirizō*) you a minister and a witness" (Acts 26:16). This verb *procheirizō* etymologically means "to lay hands on beforehand," thus showing the personal apprehension of Paul by the risen Lord in order to place him into a specific ministry.[10] In like manner, a minister ought to have such a strong conviction that his vocation (or "calling," as the word means[11]) has been appointed by God. No one should cavalierly presume he has been appointed to the ministry without this deep sense of divine appointment.

Commission by Virtue of the Message

The gospel message itself is authoritative, since it is the word of the risen Lord to whom all authority in heaven and earth has been given; on this basis, He commands His disciples to go and teach all nations to observe all that He commanded them (Matt 28:18). While popular methods of evangelism speak of the "gospel Invitation" (and it does exist, Matt 11:28), it might be more proper to speak of the "gospel Command," because the invitation is actually an imperative: "Believe in the Lord Jesus, and you shall be saved, you and your household" (Acts 16:31).

The gospel message is inherently authoritative, as it commands rebel subjects to submit to the authority of the King, as pictured in the Parable of the Wedding Banquet (Matt 22:2–14). In that account, the king issues royal decrees he expects to be obeyed, picturing how God as sovereign is not offering alternatives to be accepted or rejected at the whim of the listener; instead, when He gives an order, sinners must cease their unbelief and submit to His rule.

Clowney points out that the titles given to preachers also imply the authority of the message: as a herald of the King, he announces the *kērygma*; as an evangelist, he pronounces good news of God; as a witness, he calls others to the truth of

---

9. BDAG § 7362.3 defines τίθημι, "to assign to some task or function, *appoint, assign*" in 1 Tim 2:7 and 2 Tim 1:11, both of which include the identical phrase, ἐτέθην ἐγὼ κῆρυξ καὶ ἀπόστολος, "I was appointed a preacher and apostle." The basic meaning of τίθημι is "to put or place in a particular location," but the NT uses the word frequently of divine appointment so that it intends "the thought of God settling what shall be by sovereign decision" (Packer, "Determine," *DNTT* 1:477).

10. Paul uses the same verb in his testimony on the Temple steps when he quotes Ananias, "The God of our fathers has appointed (*procheirizō*) you to know His will, and to see the Righteous One, and to hear an utterance from His mouth" (Acts 22:14). See the study by Michaelis, "*procheirizō*," *TDNT* 6:862.

11. *Merriam-Webster's Collegiate Dictionary*, 11th edition, defines "vocation" as "a divine call," 1400.

God's covenant; as a teacher, he delivers entrusted traditions.[12] Even though no living preacher can claim the sort of personal divine calling received by Paul (in the sense that Jesus visually and audibly appointed him as an apostle), every preacher should claim that his authority to preach rests on the apostolic message commissioned by the risen Lord.

Commission By Reason of Necessity

The authority of the gospel lies not only in the delegation by the risen Lord, but also in the ultimate necessity of it, since there is "no other name under heaven that has been given among men, by which we must be saved" (Acts 4:12). The sobering fact is that where the gospel is not preached, people will not come to salvation.

This reality is the gist of Paul's string of questions in Romans 10:14–15, "How then shall they call upon Him in whom they have not believed? And how shall they believe in Him whom they have not heard? And how shall they hear without a preacher? And how shall they preach unless they are sent?" The expected answer to each question is simply, "They will not." They will not call on Him nor believe in Him if they have not heard of Him, so the third question necessitates a preacher, while the fourth question implies that no preacher is self-appointed: he must be sent (presumably by both God and the church), because the authority to go is latent in the message, not in the messenger. No preacher should preach unless he knows he is sent (*apostellō*), being delegated with authority. Paul's point in Rom 10:15 is that the preacher ought to have a sense of this authority and be driven by divine necessity: he must speak if others are to call on the Lord.

Commission as Selection

The three common systems of church government, episcopacy, presbyterianism, and congregationalism, are distinguished from one another in various ways, notably in the manner of selecting ministers. Customarily, a bishop appoints ministers under the Episcopal order; the congregation elects ministers under the Congregational system, and a body of elders (the Presbytery) approves elected ministers under the Presbyterian method. All three systems appeal to Scripture for support of their positions, and quite frankly, all three methods can be found therein![13]

For example, Paul, acting like a bishop, instructs his apostolic legate Titus to "set in order" what remains of the church in Crete and "to appoint elders in every city as I directed you" (Titus 1:5). The verb "to appoint" (*kathistēmi*) describes legal

---

12. Clowney, *Preaching and Biblical Theology*, 54–59.
13. See the studies by Stewart, *The Original Bishops: Office and Order in the First Christian Communities* (2014).

commissioning,[14] and it is also used of the appointment of the High Priest (Num 3:10 LXX; Heb 5:1) and of the first deacons (Acts 6:3, as these seven men seem to be). Clearly, there are times when an overseeing authority must intervene to appoint officers over a congregation; for example, it appears that Paul addresses an emergency situation in Crete in which the leadership was either non-existent or unable to function. Circumstances today that may necessitate an episcopal appointment of leaders would include times when all church officers have resigned (or died!) or when there are no qualified local candidates to fill the positions of leadership. In such cases, leaders from another congregation might be appointed to fill the vacancies until home-grown leaders from within that congregation can be trained.

Another appointive example is found in the experience of the new churches established by Paul and Barnabas in the region of Cilicia. Returning to the cities of Lystra, Iconium, and Antioch, the apostles "appointed elders for them in every church" (Acts 14:23). Closer examination reveals that the word translated "appointed" is *cheirotoneō*, which etymologically means "to vote by stretching out the hand."[15] Apparently, the apostles did not arbitrarily designate elders without congregational consent; if anything, these particular elders were appointed because the congregation had initially designated their preferences. It may be deduced then, that while the NT does in fact allow for episcopal oversight, it does not do so to the exclusion of the congregation's right and responsibility to approve its own leaders.

The pattern for this method was established early in church history with the selection of what appears to be the first deacons in Acts 6:1–6. The Twelve apostles, who had been serving as the leaders of the Jerusalem congregation, summoned the body of believers and instructed them to "select from among you, brethren, seven men of good reputation, full of the Spirit and of wisdom, whom we may put in charge of this task" (Acts 6:3). The verb "to select" (*episkeptomai*) comes from the same root word as *episkopos* ("bishop or overseer," Acts 20:28; Phil 1:1; 1 Tim 3:2; Titus 1:7), indicating that the congregation is charged with oversight of its own affairs, particularly the determination and election of qualified officers.[16]

Furthermore, the record shows that "the whole multitude" then elected (*eklegō*) the seven nominated men. This same verb (*eklegō*) is used in Acts 15:22, where "it seemed good to the apostles and the elders, with the whole church, to choose (*eklegō*) men from

---

14. See the examples cited by VGNT § 2068 καθίστημι and of the appointment of civil judges in Exod 18:21.

15. BDAG § 7912 "χειροτονέω, lit. 'stretch out the hand' in voting." See also Packer, "Determine," DNTT 1:478. The verb is used elsewhere only in 2 Cor 8:19, where Paul describes an unnamed brother who along with Titus "has also been appointed by the churches to travel with us in this gracious work."

16. Beyer, "ἐπισκέπτομαι," TDNT 2:605, shows how the word is used to appoint to an office, and that the process in Acts 6 is of decisive significance because it marks the first time the congregation elects its own officers apart from special revelation. Luke may have included this episode as a precedent for the manner by which leaders would generally be chosen for the duration of the church age—it certainly has been used for that purpose.

among them to send to Antioch with Paul and Barnabas" to deliver the instructions of the Jerusalem Synod to the churches of Antioch. The verb *eklegō* is also used elsewhere of sovereign election to salvation (Eph 1:3), so its use in the Book of Acts indicates that it is the sovereign right of the congregation to choose their own officers.

However, NT church polity does not seem to be strictly congregational either. The newly elected deacons were brought before the apostles for the laying-on of their hands (Acts 6:6), indicating an ordination by the body of leaders. This same custom of hand-laying upon new leaders presumably derived from the OT ceremony (Num 8:10; Deut 34:9),[17] and it was practiced when Barnabas and Paul were commissioned by the leaders at the Antioch Church for their mission work (Acts 13:3).[18] Paul later encourages Timothy not to "neglect the spiritual gift within you, which was bestowed upon you through prophetic utterance with the laying-on of hands by the presbytery" (*presbuteroi*, 1 Tim 4:14), a group among whom Paul included himself (2 Tim 1:6, "I remind you to kindle afresh the gift of God which is in you through the laying-on of my hands."). Apparently, a council or senate of other leaders (whether apostles, elders, prophets or teachers) approved the election of other leaders by what Heb 6:2 calls "a foundation of . . . laying-on of hands." While chapter 15 will explore the connection between the laying-on of hands and impartation of ministerial gifts by the Holy Spirit, suffice it to say here that the ritual certainly shows that the new leader places himself under the authority of those imposing their hands upon him. This relationship seems to be the thrust of Peter's admonition to the younger men to "be subject to your elders" as those who have special responsibilities of mentoring and then approving new leaders for the church—yet "all of you, clothe yourselves with humility toward one another" (1 Pet 5:5).

Combining all these concepts, the selection of a leader to the ministry involves episcopal oversight (thus ensuring that those being considered meet the expected standards), congregational assent (its choice by some manner of hand-raising), and presbyterial approval by laying-on of their hand upon those chosen. This process prevents opposing errors: on one side, it keeps a congregation from choosing unqualified leaders, as Israel chose Saul as king out of bad motives, "that we may be like all the nations" (1 Sam 8:19–20); and it also restrains a bishop from "lording it over the flock" as did Diotrephes, "who loved to be first" (3 John 9; 1 Pet 5:3). No one should assume an office in the church of Christ without this joint approval of the leaders and the congregation.

---

17. Numbers 8:10, "Present the Levites before the LORD; and the sons of Israel shall lay their hands on the Levites"; Deut 34:9, "Now Joshua the son of Nun was filled with the spirit of wisdom, for Moses had laid his hands on him."

18. Acts 13:3, "When they had fasted and prayed and laid their hands on them, they sent them away."

The Commission as Ordination

As noted above, the official recognition of a preacher's calling to the ministry is signified in the NT by the laying-on of hands of the eldership (the *presbuteroi*; Acts 6:6; 13:3; 1 Tim 4:14; 5:22; 2 Tim 1:6). This ceremony has its background in the OT ritual of the consecration of the Levites (Lev 8:12), in the designation of Joshua as the successor of Moses (Deut 34:9), and in the anointing of kings (1 Sam 16:13).[19] Old Covenant imposition of hands was an investiture ceremony whereby a man was initiated into an office to minister on behalf of Israel's God. It was often accompanied with a special anointing of the Spirit of God in order to equip the anointed one to perform his tasks (Isa 61:1–2).

Similarly, the ritual of laying-on of hands is prominent in the NT, particularly concerning the healing ministries of both Jesus (Luke 4:40) and His disciples (Acts 9:17) and with the conveying of the Spirit by the apostles (Acts 8:17–18; 19:6). However, the early church also used hand-laying as a public ceremony performed by the body of leaders (Acts 13:1–2) and accompanied with prayer and fasting (Acts 6:6; 13:3), whereby another person would be set aside to some office of ministry.

Like other New Covenant ceremonies, the laying-on of hands has also attracted extremes: some say hand-laying is merely symbolic and conveys nothing of substance; others insist that it is sacramentally necessary and conveys the gifts of ministry. At the very least, the ceremony is symbolic; the imposition of hands indicates the favor and approval of the ordaining body, as the laying-on of hands often speaks of divine favor (Ps 139:10; Rev 1:17). Furthermore, it indicates the authority delegated to the new minister as joining and continuing the ministry shared by other ministers (Acts 6:3–6). For this reason, Timothy is not to lay hands hastily on a man before determining if he is sufficiently qualified for the ministry (1 Tim 5:22).

Yet the ordination service is more than symbolic, as Paul reminds Timothy "to kindle afresh the gift (*charisma*) of God which is in you through the laying-on of my hands" (2 Tim 1:6). He refers to the same event when he urges Timothy, "Do not neglect the spiritual gift (*charismatos*) within you, which was bestowed upon you through prophetic utterance with the laying-on of hands by the presbytery" (1 Tim 4:14). While some argue that the mention of "prophetic utterances" limits this *charismata* to the apostolic period, these "prophecies" need not be understood as special apostolic revelation but rather as prophecies of written Scriptures (in this case, the OT) particularly applied to Timothy as he began his ministry. For that matter, if Paul intended for Timothy's ordination to serve as a precedent for all future ordinations—and it has certainly been used that way throughout church history—then at each ordination service, the Holy Spirit may grant *charismata* for ministry when the

---

19. Leviticus 8:12, "Then [Moses] poured some of the anointing oil on Aaron's head and anointed him, to consecrate him"; Deut 34:9, "Joshua the son of Nun was filled with the spirit of wisdom, for Moses had laid his hands on him"; 1 Sam 16:13, "Samuel took the horn of oil and anointed him in the midst of his brothers; and the Spirit of the LORD came mightily upon David from that day forward."

attending elders impose their hands and apply the prophetic utterances of the apostles now inscripturated in the NT.

While it is quite clear that the imposition of hands begins one's ministry, is it a once-for-all-time ritual in the same way that Eph 4:5 mentions "one baptism"? Apparently not, as Acts 13:1–3 indicates that it would be appropriate for the eldership to lay on hands at the initiation of each new task, since no doubt Barnabas and Saul (as Paul was then called) had been previously ordained as prophets and teachers. Now they were being set aside for a new missionary endeavor with a special hand-laying ceremony, thus giving a precedent for the repetition of such a practice whenever a new ministry is initiated.

In any case, ordination can be viewed as a special anointing of the Holy Spirit accompanying the hand-laying of the eldership whereby a minister receives further confirmation of his gifts and calling. It cannot be ruled out—indeed, it might be expected—that the Spirit might bestow additional *charismata* at that moment. Certainly, the prayer offered for the ordinand ought to request the unction of the Spirit of God to empower the man to perform and complete his ministry. Accordingly, no preacher should assume a ministry apart from some sort of public service of ordination or commissioning.

Commission as Charge

It is appropriate that a formal commission accompany the ordination. Paul frequently referred to his commissioning by the resurrected Lord (Acts 26:16–20; 1 Tim 2:7), and he constantly reminds his fellow-workers of their charge; for example, he concluded his letter to the Colossians with this charge to Archippus, "Take heed to the ministry which you have received in the Lord, that you may fulfill it" (Col 4:17). To Timothy, Paul charges, "This command I entrust to you, Timothy, my son, in accordance with the prophecies previously made concerning you, that by them you may fight the good fight, keeping faith and a good conscience" (1 Tim 1:18–19). It could well be that these charges are the same as the prophetic utterances mentioned in 1 Tim 4:14, giving the particular admonitions Timothy heard at his ordination.

An additional example of specific charges is found when Barnabas and Paul appointed elders, "commending them to the Lord in whom they had believed" (Acts 14:23). They were following the same pattern as the church at Antioch had previously "commended them to the grace of God for the work that they had accomplished" (Acts 14:26). Actually, two different Greek words are translated by "commended" (*paratithēmi* and *paradidōmi*), but both words carry with them the nuance of official delegation, as also seen in Acts 15:40 and 2 Tim 2:2, where the words are used respectively.[20] But now in 2 Tim 4:1, when additional responsibilities necessitate new

---

20. Acts 15:40, "Paul chose Silas and departed, being committed (*paradidōmi*) by the brethren to the grace of the Lord"; 2 Tim 2:2, "The things which you have heard from me in the presence of many

charges, Paul "solemnly charges" Timothy in the presence of God and Christ to remain faithful to his present ministry, indicating that whenever the minister receives a new task, a fellow elder ought to deliver a charge appropriate to the calling.

Commission as Allotment

This study assumes, then, that a man should not undertake an office within the church without an approved call to a specific ministry, for no laborer works without an assigned task. Peter specifies this task as a *klēros* (a "heritage," KJV), as "those allotted to your charge" (1 Pet 5:3).[21] This word also describes the "part" of the apostolic ministry vacated by Judas and later filled by Matthias (Acts 1:17, 25), and of the apostolic "lot" refused to Simon Magus (Acts 8:21). At the hand-laying of Barnabas and Saul, the Holy Spirit directed, "Set apart for Me Barnabas and Saul for the [specific] work to which I have called them" (Acts 13:2), which included the work of fully preaching the gospel of Christ "from Jerusalem and round about as far as Illyricum" (Rom 15:19). Likewise, the call of Titus was to the church on Crete (Titus 1:5); Epaphroditus' call was to the church at Philippi (Phil 2:25); Timothy's to Ephesus (1 Tim 1:3) and Epaphras' to the church at Colossae (Col 1:7; 4:12). In addition, the description of each congregation as a flock implies a pastoral allotment whereby elders should "shepherd the church of God among you" (Acts 20:28).

These various assignments embrace a variety of tasks, whether as a missionary-evangelist (Acts 13:1–3), as a representative of a congregation (Acts 15:3; Phil 2:25), or most generally, as a pastor-teacher, elder, or deacon of a local assembly (Eph 4:11; Acts 6:3; 14:23). No one should assume that he is properly called to a particular ministry without some designated allotment.

Summary: Christ Commissioned the Preacher!

Mounce is correct when he asserts, "We may say that apart from a commission, there exists no preaching at all in the true sense of the word."[22] Although the preacher knows that his authority differs from that of an apostle, he should also know that he falls under the same delegation as does Timothy, as one who is called to preach not new revelation, but the deposit of faith (2 Tim 1:14). While the preacher does not speak as an apostle or prophet, he does so as a minister of the Word commissioned ultimately by Christ Jesus Himself.[23]

---

witnesses, these entrust (*paratithēmi*) to faithful men, who will be able to teach others also" (see also Wegenast, "Teach," *DNTT* 3:773.

21. Foerster, "κλῆρος," *TDNT* 3:764, refutes the notion that this "lot" is a church tax but rather is the portion of the flock entrusted to each individual elder or pastor.

22. Mounce, *Essential Nature of New Testament Preaching*, 56.

23. Clowney, *Preaching and Biblical Theology*, 61.

In those times when authority is questioned, the preacher finds himself under particular scrutiny, as the world demands, "Who appointed you?" The preacher must be convinced that his commission comes from none other than the resurrected Lord Jesus Christ. Only then can he preach with conviction, knowing he has the right to do so, not to abuse that authority but to proclaim the authority of the Lordship of Christ. It is for this solemn reason that Paul proceeds to commission Timothy.

CHAPTER 2

The Preacher's Reason: "The Presence of God and of Christ Jesus"

The Primary Reason to Preach: Christ Jesus

THE IDEA THAT A Christian minister should be involved in preaching is usually assumed rather than proven, yet this very assumption necessitates the question, Why preach at all? What is there about the Christian faith that requires its preaching? Why is the minister placed under the imperative, "Preach the Word!"?

Paul gives the primary reason in 2 Tim 4:1–2 when he prefaces the command to preach with this theological basis: "I solemnly charge *you* in the presence of God and of Christ Jesus, who is to judge the living and the dead, and by His appearing and His kingdom: preach the Word!" The obvious emphasis in this charge is the focal individual of Paul's interest, the one he identifies as "Christ Jesus."[1] Unquestionably, Paul refers to the historical man, Jesus of Nazareth,[2] but he distinguishes Jesus here by the OT title, *Christos*, the promised Messiah.[3] Despite some textual variants in 2 Tim 4:1 that allow for translational differences,[4] Paul places Timothy in the presence of

---

1. Paul refers ninety times to "Christ Jesus" and seventy-nine times to "Jesus Christ." There is no discernable difference in the order of the words, although Paul may have desired to emphasize the man Jesus by placing His name first, or His Messianic title by placing it first, but there is no definitive way of knowing.

2. See the studies on Paul's view of the humanity of Jesus in Stout, *The Man Christ Jesus,* chapter 3.

3. The LXX always uses χριστὸς to translate הַמָּשִׁיחַ (Lev 4:5, 16; 6:15; 1 Sam 24:6, 6, 11; 26:9, 11, 16, 23; 2 Sam 1:14, 16; 19:22; 23:1), or for מְשִׁיחוֹ (1 Sam 2:10, 35; 12:3, 5; 16:6; 2 Sam 22:51; 1 Chr 16:22; 2 Chr 6:42; Ps 2:2; 17:51; 19:7; 27:8; 84:9; 89:38, 51; 105:15; 132:10; 132:17; Isa 45:1; Lam 4:20; Dan 9:26, 27; Hab 3:13), or for שֶׁמֶן מִשְׁחַת (Lev 21:10, 12), but never as a personal name.

4. The NAS translates 2 Tim 4:1, "I solemnly charge *you* in the presence of God and of Christ Jesus, who is to judge the living and the dead, and by His appearing and His kingdom," whereas the NKJ reads, "I charge *you* therefore before God and the Lord Jesus Christ, who will judge the living and the dead at His appearing and His kingdom." These minor differences are due to the family of variants followed by each translation; for example, the NA text reads, Διαμαρτύρομαι ἐνώπιον τοῦ θεοῦ καὶ Χριστοῦ Ἰησοῦ τοῦ μέλλοντος κρίνειν ζῶντας καὶ νεκρούς, καὶ τὴν ἐπιφάνειαν αὐτοῦ καὶ τὴν βασιλείαν αὐτοῦ· The BYZ text adds a few words (in italics): Διαμαρτύρομαι οὖν ἐγὼ ἐνώπιον τοῦ θεοῦ, καὶ τοῦ

four divine realities that surround the historical Jesus: God, Christ, His Appearance, and His Kingdom. By using the preposition *enōpion*,[5] Paul brings Timothy face to face with the reality of the returning Christ to whom he is accountable. This rather lengthy prepositional phrase (twenty words in Greek governed by *enōpion*[6]), then, constructs a bridge linking preaching with a considerable amount of Christology either stated or assumed, for the preacher can only be effective as he understands the eschatological expectations stated in this charge, the return of Jesus Christ appearing as God, Judge, Revealer, and King.

κυρίου Ἰησοῦ χριστοῦ, τοῦ μέλλοντος κρίνειν ζῶντας καὶ νεκρούς, κατὰ τὴν ἐπιφάνειαν αὐτοῦ καὶ τὴν βασιλείαν αὐτοῦ.

Comfort, *New Testament Text and Translation Commentary*, 677, notes on the first variant (οὖν ἐγώ, "therefore I") makes Paul's personal declaration "more emphatic," and he suggests the words were added to strengthen the verb, "I am solemnly charging." However, if "therefore I" is original, it could have been dropped as being unnecessary to the syntax (and perhaps in the interest of saving space on the papyri). At any rate, neither variant effects the meaning.

The second variant, "the Lord Jesus Christ" (BYZ) appears elsewhere in this word order at Acts 28:31; 1 Cor 16:23; 2 Cor 11:31; 13:14; Phil 4:23; 2 Tim 4:1; Rev 22:21, although the NA uses a shorter form "Christ Jesus" in 1 Cor 16:23, 2 Cor 11:31; Rev 22:21. The debate will continue whether it is more reasonable to think that BYZ copyists expanded the fuller title or that the NA scribes shortened it to "Christ Jesus." Regardless, neither variant effects the identity of the one to whom Paul refers.

The third variant (καὶ or κατὰ) is the most significant, as Comfort (ibid.) notes that the NA text is "syntactically awkward," since the nouns ἐπιφάνειαν and βασιλείαν are in the accusative case whereas the governing preposition ἐνώπιον takes the genitive case everywhere else in the NT. The BYZ text has a "smoother" grammatical reading with κατὰ rather than καὶ, "according to His appearance and kingdom." Even so, Comfort suggests that καὶ was the original word and was emended to κατὰ, but frankly, the original could have been the other way around, with κατὰ being changed very early in the copying process to καὶ due to very understandable error of the eye, as the original text (κατὰτὴνἐπιφάνειαν) could easily have been copied as καὶτὴνἐπιφάνειαν. While Metzger, *A Textual Commentary on the Greek New Testament*, 580–1, gives the NA reading (καὶ) a "B" rating because "the text is amply supported by representatives of both the Alexandrian and the Western types of text (ℵ* A C D* F G 33 424c 1739 2495 itd, g, 61 vg copbo *al*)," this study favors the BYZ reading (κατὰ) as providing a better explanation why the nouns ἐπιφάνειαν and βασιλείαν are in the accusative case. Regardless, neither καὶ nor κατὰ significantly effect the meaning of the phrase.

5. BDAG § 2710.2 defines ἐνώπιον as "pert. to being present or in view, *in the sight of, in the presence* of, *among;* . . . [it is] also a favorite expr. in assertions and oaths which call upon God, as the One who sees all." Paul uses *enōpios* seventeen times, but only four times as "before" some human (Rom 12:17; 2 Cor 8:21c; 1 Tim 5:20; 6:12); all the other instances are "before God (or Him = God; Rom 3:20; 14:22; 1 Cor 1:29; 2 Cor 4:2; 7:12; Gal 1:20; 1 Tim 2:3; 5:4; 6:13; 2 Tim 2:14; 4:1) or before (the) Lord (2 Cor 8:21b). The phrase ἐνώπιον κυρίου appears 117 times in the LXX (but only three times in the NT, Luke 1:76, 2 Cor 8:21; Jam 4:10), while the phrase ἐνώπιον τοῦ θεοῦ appears thirty-six times in the *BW* BGT text (Exod 3:6; 22:7, 8; Jda. 21:2; Jdg 21:2; 2 Sam 6:7; Ezra 7:19; Esth 10:3, 3; Jdt. 5:17; 13:20; Ps 55:14; 60:8; 67:4; Ps. Sol. 2:5; Luke 1:19; 12:6; 16:15; Acts 4:19; 7:46; 10:31, 33; Rom 14:22; 1 Cor 1:29; 2 Cor 4:2; 7:12; Gal 1:20; 1 Tim 5:4, 21; 6:13; 2 Tim 2:14; 4:1; 1 Pet 3:4; Rev 3:2; 8:2, 4; 9:13; 11:16; 12:10; 16:19). Clearly, Paul favors ἐνώπιον when referring to the Divine presence. The preposition conjures for Paul not merely a geographical location (standing in front or someone) but a relational presence of the person appearing in the presence of God.

6. BDAG § 2710 apparently cites ἐνώπιον as governing not only the genitive nouns θεοῦ and Χριστοῦ Ἰησοῦ in 2 Tim 4:1, but also the two accusative nouns ἐπιφάνειαν and βασιλείαν.

The Reason for Preaching: Because Christ Jesus is God

The question may well arise: Where in this phrase under consideration is a reference to Jesus as God? Readers of the English text are laboring under a handicap, because the translations make it appear that Paul refers to the appearance of two personages, "God and Christ Jesus." However, the entirety of 2 Tim 4:1 anticipates the coming of one person, and so does the Greek grammar, because Paul uses a grammatical structure known as the Granville Sharp Rule, "when the construction article-substantive-*kai*-substantive (TSKS) involved personal nouns which were singular and not proper names, they always referred to the same person."[7] This particular prepositional phrase meets these criteria: there is one definite article *toū* modifying two nouns linked by the conjunction *kai*, and neither title (*Theoū kaì Christoū* or *Kurioū*) is a proper name.[8] In such a case, this phrase could well be translated, "before the God, even Christ/Lord."[9]

Yet Paul does not spring on Timothy a novel idea by equating Jesus with God—the NT is replete with direct statements[10] and indirect allusions[11] to the deity of Jesus. Recent studies have explored the apparent conundrum that worship of Jesus arose from within Jewish monotheism,[12] wondering how Paul as "a Pharisee, a son of

---

7. See Wallace, *Greek Grammar Beyond the Basics*, 270–71, ftnt 42, where he argues that θεος is not a proper name and thus fits Sharpe's rule. While Wallace questions 2 Tim 4:1 as giving a proper TSKS construction because it "involves [a] dubious textual variant" (ibid., 276), the variant is only the inclusion of τοῦ κυρίου in the BYZ text form. Even if τοῦ κυρίου is not in the original text, the next impersonal title Χριστοῦ precedes Ἰησοῦ in the NA text form, meaning that the Granville Sharpe rule applies in both the NA and BYZ forms.

8. Other examples of the Granville Sharp Rule equating God and Jesus include: Eph 5:5, ἐν τῇ βασιλείᾳ τοῦ Χριστοῦ καὶ θεοῦ ("in the kingdom of Christ and God"); 2 Thess 1:12, κατὰ τὴν χάριν τοῦ θεοῦ ἡμῶν καὶ κυρίου Ἰησοῦ Χριστοῦ ("according to the grace of our God and Lord Jesus Christ"); 1 Tim 5:21, ἐνώπιον τοῦ θεοῦ καὶ Χριστοῦ Ἰησοῦ ("before God and Christ Jesus"); Titus 2:13, δόξης τοῦ μεγάλου θεοῦ καὶ σωτῆρος ἡμῶν Ἰησοῦ Χριστοῦ ("the glory of our great God and Savior, Christ Jesus"); 2 Pet 1:1, δικαιοσύνῃ τοῦ θεοῦ ἡμῶν καὶ σωτῆρος Ἰησοῦ Χριστοῦ ("righteousness of our God and Savior, Jesus Christ"); 2 Pet 1:11, βασιλείαν τοῦ κυρίου ἡμῶν καὶ σωτῆρος Ἰησοῦ Χριστοῦ ("kingdom of our Lord and Savior Jesus Christ"); 1 John 5:20, Ἰησοῦ Χριστῷ. οὗτός ἐστιν ὁ ἀληθινὸς θεὸς καὶ ζωὴ αἰώνιος ("Jesus Christ. This is the true God and eternal life"). Wallace, ibid., 276–77, takes exception to some of these examples, but they are well worth noting from the fact that the apostles place Jesus on equal status with God.

9. Turner, *Syntax*, 181, notes that ". . . the article may be carried over from the first noun to the other(s), especially if they are regarded as a unified whole." He thinks that the unity must be determined on theological rather than grammatical considerations (ibid.), and Paul states this unity between God and Jesus in 1 Cor 8:6, "For us there is *but* one God, the Father, from whom are all things, and we *exist* for Him; and one Lord, Jesus Christ, by whom are all things, and we *exist* through Him."

10. John 1:1; 5:18; 14:9; Rom 9:5; Col 2:9; Heb 1:8; 1 John 5:20.

11. Jesus is given titles of deity, such as Emmanuel, I AM (John 8:59); Son of God; Son of Man, Lord, Savior, Word, etc. He also is credited with divine works, such as creating (Col 1:16) and giving life (John 5:21).

12. For example, see Hengel, *The Son of God: The Origin of Christology and the History of Jewish-Hellenistic Religion*; Newman et al., *The Jewish Roots of Christological Monotheism* (1990); Bauckham, *God Crucified* (1999); Hurtado, *Lord Jesus Christ* (2003); and Bauckham, *Jesus and the God of Israel* (2008).

Pharisees" (Acts 23:6) could maintain belief in the one God of Israel while also elevating Jesus to equal divine status.[13] Bird observes, "Paul is an advocate of what we should call *messianic monotheism*, that is, God is known through Jesus the Messiah, or Jesus is the one who reveals and manifests the person and work of God."[14] However one may regard Paul's Christology, Paul does not view his belief in Christ as God as conflicting with his belief in God as one.[15] As Athanasius later keenly observed,[16] if Christ is not God, he cannot be Savior, but since He is also God, Christ can be preached as Savior who saves all who call upon Him.

God as a Preacher

The biblical revelation of God is that He is the God who speaks ("and God said," Gen 1:3). More precisely, He is the preaching God. Paul states this fact quite remarkably in Titus 1:2–3, "God, who cannot lie, promised (eternal life) long ages ago, but at the proper time manifested (*phanerō*), *even* His word, in the proclamation (*kērugma*) with which I was entrusted." This statement makes evident that God reveals His Word in (or by[17]) the preached message, as *kērugma* implies.[18] While it is true that Paul serves as the mouthpiece, it is still God who is the primary preacher. So, if there is any vocation to which God calls Himself, it is unmistakably that of speaking or preaching. He is the calling God, experiencing in His prophets the frustration of every preacher when the Lord declares, "I called you but you did not answer" (Jer 7:13). Under the New Covenant, God calls His people to salvation through "our gospel," again showing it is God who actually makes the gospel call of the preacher efficacious (2 Thess 2:13–14).

---

13. Lau, *Manifest in Flesh,* 74, notes how Paul in 1 Cor 8:6 ". . . has modified the Jewish religion at its most essential point and redefined the *shema* christologically, indicating a dual referent in θεός and κύριος as well as acknowledging Christ's sharing of the Father's status and functions." See also the study by Brad Young, *Paul the Jewish Theologian: A Pharisee among Christians, Jews, and Gentiles* (1995).

14. Bird, *Introducing Paul,* 125. Italics are in the original.

15. Fee, *Pauline Christology,* 481, comments on Paul's understanding of Christ as a preexistent person by observing that ". . . it is nearly impossible to account for such a Christ devotion by an avid monotheist unless his understanding of the one God now included the Son of God in the divine identity."

16. Athanasius, "On the Incarnation," in *Christology of the Later Fathers*, ed. Edward Hardy, 62–63.

17. The perplexing and fascinating preposition ἐν presents the problem of whether to understand it in Titus 1:3 as a locative dative (the Word is resident "in preaching," Young's version) or as an instrumental dative (the Word is revealed "by or through preaching," as in the ESV and NIV). The first option might steer toward neo-orthodoxy, that the Bible *becomes* the Word of God in preaching, whereas the second view preserves the distinction between meditated revelation—the inscripturated Word—and the preached Word as the responsibility of every preacher. While this author believes that the second view accords better with biblical teaching, he is hesitant to dismiss the other position entirely because preaching has been recognized as a means of grace, as will be discussed.

18. While *kērugma* can refer to the content of a herald's proclamation, BDAG § 4230 places all the appearances of *kērugma* as the public declaration of the herald (2 Chr 30:5; Prov 9:3; Jonah 3:2; Matt 12:41; Mark 16:8; Luke 11:32; Rom 16:25; 1 Cor 1:21; 2:4; 15:14; 2 Tim 4:17; Titus 1:3).

Thus, it can be asserted that the Bible is God's sermon addressed to humanity. He is entreating through His chosen ambassadors that estranged people be reconciled with Him (2 Cor 5:20). What the Scripture reads is the same as if God continues to speak; for this reason, Heb 3:7, quoting Ps 95:7, states, "Therefore, just as the Holy Spirit says...." Hundreds of times the prophets announce such expressions as, "Thus says the Lord," or, "The Word of the Lord came to me," showing that they were not only recipients of divine preaching but also spokesmen for it as well (see the later discussion in chapter 15 on the "Dynamic of Preaching").[19]

It is this undergirding concept of the speaking and preaching God that lies behind the basic theology of preaching. The only difference between the spoken Word of God and the written Word of God is that one is verbal and other is inscribed, but both constitute the singularity of the living and powerful Word of God (Heb 4:12). Since "no word from God shall be void of power"[20] (as the ERV translates the difficult Greek of Luke 1:37), so the writer of Heb 11:3 calls on his readers to "understand by faith that the worlds were prepared by the Word of God, so that what is seen was not made out of things which are visible." When God speaks, His Word shall accomplish what He desires (Isa 55:11). However, many modern skeptics reject the idea that God speaks to humanity, thereby reducing the Bible to absurdity, since the writers assume on nearly every page of the Bible that God does in fact speak coherently to people. It was the renegade prophet Balaam who stated the idea of inspiration most succinctly: "The word that God puts in my mouth, that I shall speak" (Num 22:38; also Exod 4:15). Those spokesmen in whose mouth God placed His Word then inscribed God's words for the future preservation and edification of all who would read and listen to the recorded voice of God as Preacher (2 Tim 3:16–17).

Jesus as the Preacher of the Father

While the Bible maintains that the preaching of God is "incarnate" in the preaching of His prophets and apostles (Eph 3:4–6), the same Word through which all things were created became flesh in Jesus of Nazareth (John 1:3, 14), who came to "exegete" (*exegeomai*) fully the unseen God to humanity (John 1:18). Despite the controversy engendered by His unique claim to be the God-Man, Jesus is *the* Preacher who speaks only the words of the Father[21] in fulfillment of the prophecy of Moses, that the

---

19. See also Young, *My Servants the Prophets*, chapter 9 in particular.

20. The Greek of Luke 1:37 reads, ὅτι οὐκ ἀδυνατήσει παρὰ τοῦ θεοῦ πᾶν ῥῆμα. It is usually translated, "For nothing will be impossible with God" (NAS, NET, ESV), but this translation loses the phrase πᾶν ῥῆμα that is retained in the ERV and ASV, "No word from God shall be void of power."

21. Note these remarkable claims of Jesus: "I speak these things as the Father taught Me" (John 8:28); "I speak the things which I have seen with *My* Father" (John 8:38); "The Father Himself who sent Me has given Me commandment, what to say, and what to speak" (John 12:49); "The things I speak, I speak just as the Father has told Me" (John 12:50).

Lord would raise up a prophet in whose mouth God would put His words (compare Deut 18:18 with Acts 3:23).

It was the Puritan Thomas Goodwin who noted, "God had only one Son, and He made Him a preacher."[22] From the outset of His ministry, "Jesus came preaching" (Mark 1:14), announcing, "I must (*deī*) preach . . . , for I was sent for this purpose" (Luke 4:43). While the miracles of Jesus brought Him the most publicity, those signs were intended primarily to validate His preaching messages, for He did no work without oral explanation or application, at least to His disciples (Matt 13:11).

Also, wherever the title "Christ/Messiah" is used of Jesus (as it is in 2 Tim 4:1), the designation implies the preaching ministry of Jesus. That link is established in the prophecy of Isa 61:1–2, where the mark of the Messiah (*mashiach*) is that "the LORD anointed (*mashach*) Me to preach good tidings to the poor; . . . to proclaim the acceptable year of the LORD."[23] This passage served as the text for the first recorded sermon of Jesus (Luke 4:16–21), and from then on, "He kept on preaching in the synagogues of Judea" (Luke 4:44, AT). Because of His authoritative preaching, Jesus was regarded by the people to be "a prophet mighty in deed and word in the sight of God" (Luke 24:19). It was Jesus' bold preaching that brought Him into deadly conflict with the Sanhedrin, leading eventually to His crucifixion on the charge of blasphemy—false preaching (Matt 26:65). Even when Peter led the first Gentiles to salvation a decade or so later, he referred to the well-known reputation of Jesus as the preacher through whom God "preached peace"(Acts 10:36).

It is apparent that by linking the solemn preaching charge to Christ Jesus, Paul reminds Timothy that the Anointed One also came to preach the Word. In imitation of Jesus as the supreme preacher, Timothy and every future preacher needs the same divine anointing in order to emulate Christ's example as a preacher of the Word.

Paul and the Preaching of Jesus

Many, however, would disagree with any linking by Paul to Jesus as a preacher, because it has been questioned for centuries as to why Paul did not make greater reference to

---

22. Quoted in *50 Days of Prayer for the PCA*, "The Anointed One," n.p. [cited 6 June 2013]. Online: http://pca50daysofprayer.blogspot.com/2009/06/anointed-one.html.

23. The noun *mashiach* (מָשִׁיחַ) appears thirty-eight times in the OT (Lev 4:3, 5, 16; 6:15; 1 Sam 2:10, 35; 10:1; 12:3, 5; 16:6; 24:7, 11; 26:9, 11, 16, 23; 2 Sam 1:14, 16; 19:22; 22:51; 23:1; 1 Chr 16:22; 2 Chr 6:42; Ps 2:2; 18:51; 20:7; 28:8; 84:10; 89:39, 52; 105:15; 132:10, 17; Isa 45:1; Lam 4:20; Dan 9:25, 26; and Hab 3:13). It is applied to priests (Lev 4:3), prophets (Ps 105:15), but mostly to kings (as in 1 Sam 2:10). In the LXX, Χριστὸς translates מָשִׁיחַ in Lev 4:3, 5, 16; 6:15; 1 Sam 2:10, 35; 12:3, 5; 16:6; 24:7, 11; 26:9, 11, 16, 23; 2 Sam 1:14, 16; 19:22; 22:51; 23:1; 1 Chr 16:22; 2 Chr 6:42; Ps 2:2; 18:51; 20:7; 28:8; 84:10; 89:39, 52; 105:15; 132:10, 17; Isa 45:1; Lam 4:20; Dan 9:25–26; and Hab 3:13. Conversely, *christos* translates other words in the LXX at Lev 21:10 ("oil of the Christ"); 21:12 ("anointing oil"); 2 Sam 2:5 (translates אֲדֹנֵיכֶם); 2 Sam 22:7 (translates the verb מָשַׁחוֹ); and Amos 4:13 (God "reveals unto men His Christ," translating "reveals His plans."). See Grundmann, "χρίω, Χριστός, etc.," in *TDNT* 9:493–589.

the preaching ministry of Jesus, especially since the Gospels present Him as such a powerful preacher. Bornkann, for example, is so taken by this absence that he asserts, "Never does Paul make the slightest effort to expound the teaching of the historical Jesus.... The Jesus of history is apparently dismissed."[24]

Such an evaluation ignores what Paul assumes to be true, for while it is a fact that Paul does not comment on the Parables of Jesus, he does call his reader to "agree with sound words, those of our Lord Jesus Christ" (1 Tim 6:3). How else would his readers know the sound words of Jesus unless Paul assumes their knowledge of the Gospel narratives, even if they existed in pre-literary oral traditions? Furthermore, when Paul quotes Isa 57:19 as a reminder that "He [Jesus] preached peace to you" (Eph 2:17), he clearly assumes that his readers have some previous knowledge of Jesus' preaching about peace in particular (such as found in John 14:27; 16:33; 20:19, 21, 26).

Furthermore, Paul concludes his epistle to the Romans (16:25) with a reference to the preaching of Jesus when he writes, "Now to Him who is able to establish you according to my gospel and the preaching of Jesus Christ." Of interest for this study is the second part of the prepositional phrase, *to kērugma Iēsou Christou*, whether this phrase should be understood as an objective genitive ("the proclamation *of* Jesus Christ," NIV) or as a subjective genitive, the preaching proclaimed *by* Jesus. In support of the latter is the parallel with *to euangelion mou*, which is certainly not an objective genitive (Paul is not preaching a gospel about himself!), but rather it refers to the gospel preached by Paul.[25] In Rom 16:25, then, Paul states that his readers are established according to the content of his gospel *and* the content preached by Jesus, meaning—as a logical consequence—that Paul knew Jesus had been a preacher. This realization, of course, agrees with the initial introduction of Jesus' public ministry, "From that time Jesus began to preach (*kērussein*) and say, 'Repent, for the kingdom of heaven is at hand'" (Matt 4:17). He even stated to His disciples that preaching was one of his divine missions when He said, "Let us go somewhere else to the towns nearby, in order that I may preach (*kēruxō*) there also; for that is what I came out for" (Mark 1:38).[26] While Jesus is certainly the primary object of Paul's gospel ("We preach Christ crucified," 1 Cor 1:23), in the context of Rom 16:25, it is also the message preached by Jesus—His

---

24. Bornkamm, *Paul*, 110.

25. The noun κήρυγμα appears twelve times in the NA (2 Chr 30:5; Prov 9:3; Jonah 3:2; Matt 12:41; Mark 16:8; Luke 11:32; Rom 16:25; 1 Cor 1:21; 2:4; 15:14; 2 Tim 4:17; Titus 1:3). In 2 Tim 4:17 and Titus 1:3, Paul uses *kērygma* to refer to the content being preached; however, whenever the noun κήρυγμα is followed by a possessive, it is always a subjective genitive (except for the disputed reading in Mark 16:8, κήρυγμα τῆς αἰωνίου σωτηρίας), describing the activity of preaching. For example, when κήρυγμα is followed by a genitive in Matt 12:41 || Luke 11:32 (τὸ κήρυγμα Ἰωνᾶ), it is not the "preaching about Jonah," but Jonah's preaching; in 1 Cor 2:4 (καὶ ὁ λόγος μου καὶ τὸ κήρυγμά μου), it is not the preaching "about me (Paul)," but Paul's preaching; and in 1 Cor 15:14 (εἰ δὲ Χριστὸς οὐκ ἐγήγερται, κενὸν ἄρα [καὶ] τὸ κήρυγμα ἡμῶν), it is not the "preaching about us," but "our preaching."

26. When used of Jesus, the verb κηρύσσειν describes his preaching activity (Matt 4:17; 9:35; 11:1; Mark 1:14, 38, 39, 45; Luke 4:44; 8:1; 20:1) and does so by explaining his preaching as a messianic sign in fulfillment of Isa 61:1 (Matt 11:5; Luke 4:18–19, 43; Luke 7:22; 16:18).

doctrine—that establishes believers in the Faith. How else would Paul's readers be established in the preaching of Jesus unless they had been previously informed of its content and knew how to access His preaching—by referring to "that form of teaching to which you were committed"? (Rom 6:17).

A more sympathetic explanation regarding the disinterest Paul supposedly holds toward the preaching of Jesus can be found in these observations:

1. living eyewitnesses of the life of Jesus were available to confirm His teaching (1 Cor 15:6);

2. primitive written accounts—often called Q (*Quelle*)—were circulating, according to Luke 1:1, so Paul avoided repetition because these manuscripts were already available; and

3. when Paul does quote Jesus, he appears to cite sayings that are found outside the Gospel corpus of Jesus' teachings for which his readers would have no other means of access (Acts 20:35; 1 Cor 7:10).[27] Hence, the simple explanation as to why Paul does not refer frequently to the content of Jesus' preaching is that His teaching sources were otherwise accessible—just as they are today in the four Gospels.

Summary to Preaching Christ Jesus as God:

The first reason why Timothy should preach the Word is because of the historical appearance of Jesus as the incarnate Word of God. Jesus preached, and so should the preacher, not only in imitation of Christ as a preacher, but also because Jesus as the Christ is the object of preaching itself, as Paul states, "We preach not ourselves, but Christ Jesus the Lord" (2 Cor 4:5 KJV).

The Reason for Preaching: Because Christ Jesus is Judge

In this commission to preach the Word, Paul next confronts Timothy with a second Christological distinction, a particular emphasis of Christ as the One "who is about to be judging the living and the dead" (AT). What is the specific relationship between preaching the Word and the position of Christ Jesus as Judge?

---

27. The reader is referred to these studies on Paul's use of Jesus' teaching: Addley, "The Sayings of Jesus in the Epistles of Paul" (1971); Dungan, *The Sayings of Jesus in the Churches of Paul: The Use of the Synoptic Tradition in the Regulation of Early Church Life* (1971); Wenham, ed., *The Jesus Tradition outside the Gospels* (1984); Calvert, "An Examination of the Criteria for Distinguishing the Authentic Words of Jesus," 209–19; Gerhardsson, *Memory and Manuscript: Oral Tradition in Rabbinic Judaism and Early Christianity* with *Tradition and Transmission in Early Christianity* (1998), 288–323; Kim, "Jesus, Sayings of," in *Dictionary of Paul and His Letters*, 474–92; Lindemann, "Paulus und die JesusTradition" (2008), 281–316; Neirynck, "Paul and the Sayings of Jesus" (1986), 265–321; Resch, *Der Paulinismus und die Logia Jesu*; Stanley, "Pauline Allusions to the Sayings of Jesus," 26–39; Walter, "Paul and the Early Christian Jesus-Tradition," 51–80.

Biblical Justice

This reference to "the one about to be judging" brings the reader to the awesome reality of final accounting before God as Judge, by which Paul assumes the biblical concepts of justice, righteousness, condemnation, and justification. Central to the entire discussion is the question Abraham posed to God, "Shall not the Judge of all the earth deal justly?" (Gen 18:25). The answer is always affirmative, as in Deut 32:4, "The Rock! His work is perfect, for all His ways are just; A God of faithfulness and without injustice, righteous and upright is He!"

In numerous places, the Bible teaches that "we shall all stand before the judgment seat (*bēma*[28]) of God" (Rom 14:10), at which time the righteous will be declared justified and the unrighteous will be condemned (John 5:28–29). All history is moving ever closer to this climatic day of the wrath of God (Rev 6:16–17), and it is this event to which Paul refers in 2 Tim 4:1, at which time all those living or having died shall be called to final tribunal. The time is short, as the active verb tenses (*toū mellontos krinein*) accentuate the immediacy of the appearance of the Judge, which Paul describes in this verse as the *Parousia*.

The recurring NT theme of the impending return of Christ has received skeptical criticism from scholars such as Albert Schweitzer, who insists that the first century writers were mistaken in such a belief.[29] In defense of the NT, it ought to be noted that none of its writers predicted that Christ's return would be within their own lifetimes; in fact, the Beloved Disciple had to correct such a common misunderstanding (John 21:23). If anything, the NT balances the expectation of an impending *Parousia* with the anticipation of a long delay (Matt 24:48; 2 Pet 3:8–9).[30] Paul certainly does not set a date in the passage under consideration: he merely reminds Timothy of the fact of an ultimate accounting before the coming Judge.

Jesus as Judge by Virtue of His Resurrection

Paul's statement to Timothy assumes what is arguably the most important NT teaching about Jesus, that He is a man who died on a Roman cross but is very much alive by virtue of His resurrection from the dead.[31] The idea that judgment has been delegated

---

28. BDAG § 1475.3, defines βῆμα, "a dais or platform that required steps to ascend, *tribunal*."

29. Schweitzer, *Search for the Historical Jesus*, 398.

30. Matthew 24:48 reads, "That evil slave says in his heart, 'My master is not coming for a long time"; 2 Pet 3:8–9 states, "Do not let this one *fact* escape your notice, beloved, that with the Lord one day is as a thousand years, and a thousand years as one day. The Lord is not slow about His promise, as some count slowness, but is patient toward you, not wishing for any to perish but for all to come to repentance."

31. Paul prioritizes the gospel order in 1 Cor 15:3–5, "I delivered to you as of first importance what I also received, that Christ died for our sins according to the Scriptures, and that He was buried, and that He was raised on the third day according to the Scriptures, and that He appeared. . . . "

to a Resurrected Man lies behind the picture of the coming of the Son of Man in Dan 7:13–14.[32] In fact, Jesus was condemned as a blasphemer because he identified Himself as this heavenly figure who represented resurrection and judgment, activities reserved for God alone (Matt 26:64).[33] Jesus had previously linked these similar concepts in John 5:27 when He asserted that the Father had given to Him "authority to execute judgment, since He is the Son of Man."[34]

Paul also argues that judgment is given to Jesus because of His resurrection, as in his address at the Areopagus, "[God] has fixed a day in which He will judge the world in righteousness through a Man whom He has appointed, having furnished proof to all men by raising Him from the dead" (Acts 17:31). Without actually naming the Judge, Paul clearly has Jesus in mind as the Resurrected One before whom every person will give account, a fact he states in 2 Cor 5:10, "We must all appear before the judgment seat of Christ, that each one may be recompensed for his deeds in the body, according to what he has done, whether good or bad." In anticipation of this final accounting, the preacher should prepare his listeners for a confrontation with Jesus as the Risen Judge.

Judgment and Resurrection

Another theme implied in Paul's charge to Timothy is the final resurrection of the living and the dead. According to the astounding claim of Jesus in John 5:28–29, His voice as the resurrected Judge shall summon those living on earth as well as the dead in their tombs to appear for the final reckoning.[35] His mighty summons shall bring about the miraculous physical resurrection of each individual, so that it is not merely disembodied souls who are judged, but souls re-united to their bodies. All humanity shall appear bodily to hear the Judge Himself render the verdict of guilt or innocence, and then each one shall enter heaven or hell respectively (Rev 20:11–15; 21:6–8).

---

32. Daniel 7:13–14, "Behold, with the clouds of heaven One like a Son of Man was coming, And He came up to the Ancient of Days And was presented before Him. And to Him was given dominion, Glory and a kingdom, That all the peoples, nations, and *men of every* language Might serve Him. His dominion is an everlasting dominion Which will not pass away; And His kingdom is one Which will not be destroyed."

33. Matthew 26:64–65, "Jesus said to him, 'You have said it *yourself*; nevertheless I tell you, hereafter you shall see the Son of Man sitting at the right hand of Power, and coming on the clouds of heaven.' Then the high priest tore his robes, saying, 'He has blasphemed! What further need do we have of witnesses?'" See also the discussion by Cullmann, *Christology of the New Testament*, 137.

34. See the studies on the link between Jesus and Son on Man by Matthew Black, "Jesus and the Son of Man," *JSNT* 1 (1978): 4–18; and, "The Son of Man Problem in Recent Research and Debate," *BJRL* 45.2 (March 1963): 305–18.

35. Jesus asserts in John 5:28–29, "Do not marvel at this; for an hour is coming, in which all who are in the tombs shall hear His voice, and shall come forth; those who did the good *deeds* to a resurrection of life, those who committed the evil *deeds* to a resurrection of judgment."

Judgment as the Preacher's Imperative

These realities of the consummate appearing of the Lord Jesus Christ as Judge, the impending bodily resurrection of all humanity to face that judgment, and the final inescapable verdict place an urgent imperative upon the preacher to warn his hearers to flee from the approaching wrath of God (Matt 3:7). The sermon itself becomes a *krisis*, a judgment in which the hearer confronts the awful realities of heaven and hell. The sermon acts as a "pre-trial hearing," as the listener is brought to the realization that at that moment, he faces the condemnation of the Judge and stands in desperate need of a defense attorney who will intercede on his behalf. Remarkably, the gospel also announces that the Judge has also become the Intercessor, in that there is no condemnation to those in Christ Jesus because of His intercession as the One who died and rose again (Rom 8:1, 33–34).

Summary to Preaching Christ Jesus as Judge

By calling Timothy's attention to the coming of Jesus as the resurrected Judge, Paul reminds not only Timothy but also all future preachers that they "shall incur a stricter judgment" from Jesus in the final *Krites,* as James 3:1 ominously warns. Because of this impending reality, the preacher must also summon his listeners to the impending *krisis*. Each sermon should confront the hearers with the inevitable verdict of the Judge—"Well done, good and faithful servant," or, "I never knew you; depart from Me, you who practice lawlessness" (Matt 25:21; 7:23).

The Reason for Preaching: Because Christ Jesus is Revealer

A third aspect of Christology that serves as the reason for preaching is found in the reference to the *epiphaneia* of Jesus, the "bringing of light" upon earth by His appearance as the One revealed as Life, Light and Truth.[36] Gartner observes on the use of *epiphaneia*, "It is not surprising that at the time of Jesus, the word has almost become a technical term for the succoring appearance of an otherwise hidden deity.[37] Now Paul announces that the hidden deity who will appear is the person of Christ Jesus.

Jesus as the *Epiphany* of God

The concept of the Word as a divine appearance is rooted in the OT, which anticipates the visible appearance of God Himself on the "great and terrible day of the Lord" (Joel 2:31; Mal 4:5), at which time the Spirit will be poured out so that the sons and

---

36. The word *epiphaneia* is used in Luke 1:79; 1 Tim 6:14; 2 Tim 1:10; 4:1; 4:8, Titus 2:11, 2:12, and 3:4 in a revelatory sense of God shedding the light of His presence.

37. Gartner, ἐπιφάνεια, *TDNT* 3:317.

daughters of Israel would prophecy (Joel 2:28). When God appears, men cannot stop speaking of that which they have seen and heard of such a notable (*epiphanēs*[38]) event (Acts 2:20; 4:20).

Paul actually views the incarnate appearance of Jesus as an "*epiphany* of the kindness and love of God" (Titus 3:4), although it is the glorious epiphany of Jesus at the end of the age to which he refers here in 2 Tim 4:1. In both appearances, God does not arrive in shrouded darkness: when Jesus as the incarnate Word was "revealed (*phaneroō*) in the flesh" (1 Tim 3:16), the saving purpose of God was revealed (*phaneroō*) by the "appearance (*epiphaneia*) of our Savior Christ Jesus, who abolished death, and brought life and immortality to light (*photizō*) through the gospel" (2 Tim 1:10), which is to be "preached to the nations" (1 Tim 3:16). Preaching the appearing Christ, then, becomes the "**making visible** (*phaneroō*) of the knowledge of God in every place" (2 Cor 2:14). This aspect of preaching as an epiphany of God should be quite staggering to the preacher, for in preaching, the invisible Lord becomes manifest, in the sense that Paul's preaching was such that "Jesus Christ was publicly portrayed *as* crucified before your eyes" (Gal 3:1). It is inadequate to say that Paul only meant that he used vivid language, for when the revealed Word is preached, the Resurrected Lord also appears—not in the eschatological sense, but in the soteriological sense, effectively bringing salvation to those who hear and believe.

Distinguishing Preaching from Revelation

This discussion on the relationship between revelation and proclamation elicits the debate between the advocates of Dialectic Theology and Evangelical Theology.[39] Following Barth, Dialectic Theology insists that God can only be known indirectly, so that the words of Scripture are only witnesses to revelation and not the revelation itself.[40] The Bible may only *become* the Word of God in an existential moment, when it is mingled with faith. In that instant, Christ is revealed to the hearer, so that preaching becomes the actual revelation of God, as Bultmann states, "The word of preaching confronts us as the word of God."[41]

The danger of the existential view is that if preaching and revelation become one and the same, then the consequences must be a minimizing of the written Word, since the words of the preacher are considered as "inspired" as those of Paul. The Dialectic view also overlooks the crucial factor of prophetic apostolicity, because it fails to note

---

38. BDAG § 3072 ἐπιφανής, "pert. to being resplendent, *splendid, glorious, remarkable,* prob. suggesting light whose impact is esp. striking in its sudden appearance, of the day of God's judgment."

39. See the helpful summary by Brown, "Revelation in Contemporary Theology," in *DNTT* 3:325–37.

40. Barth, *Church Dogmatics*, Vol. 1, *The Doctrine of the Word of God*, 109, writes, "The Bible is God's Word to the extent that God causes it to be His Word, to the extent that He speaks through it."

41. Bultmann, "New Testament and Myth," 41.

that the mysteries of the gospel were revealed to the prophets and apostles, the men who were especially designated by God as mediators of revelation (Eph 3:5). When Paul charges Timothy to "preach the Word," he is not telling him to receive new revelation (much less invent his own revelation), but to expound the revelation that Paul previously defined a few verses earlier as "the Holy Scriptures, which are able to make you wise for salvation through faith in Christ Jesus" (2 Tim 3:15 NIV).

Preaching the Revelation as Mystery

Perhaps no other concept of Paul emphasizes the revealed nature of the gospel more than that of *mustērion,* which has been defined as ". . . secret, secret rite, secret teaching, . . . mostly to the mysteries [with] their secret teachings, religious and political in nature, concealed within many strange customs and ceremonies. The principal rites remain unknown because of a reluctance in antiquity to divulge them."[42] The Pauline use of *mustērion,* however, speaks of the "private counsel of God,"[43] the secret plans of God that are beyond human comprehension, but now—and this is Paul's significant insight—they have been revealed. From a survey of Paul's use of *mustērion,* the word appears to be a near-synonym for the gospel itself, emphasizing its supernatural origin as revealed truth. Christianity itself is "the mystery of the faith" (1 Tim 3:9) that is contained in the confession of the mystery of godliness concerning the historical appearance of the Incarnate God (1 Tim. 3:16). The ultimate mystery, then, is Christ Himself (Col 2:2).[44]

---

42. BDAG § 5015 μυστήριον.
43. Ibid.
44. The noun μυστήριον occurs 28 times in the NA, as follows:
   1. The Mysteries of the Kingdom (Matt 13:11; Mark 4:11; Luke 8:10);.
   2. Mysteries in general (1 Cor 13:2; 14:2);
   3. A specific revealed mystery (Rom 11:25; Eph 5:32; 2 Thess 2:7);
   4. The Christian Faith as a mystery (1 Tim 3:9, 16);
   5. Eschatological mysteries (Rev 1:20; 10:7; 17:5; 17:7);
   6. The revealed and preached mystery: Rom 16:25, "Now to Him who is able to establish you according to my gospel and the preaching of Jesus Christ, according to the revelation of the mystery which has been kept secret for long ages past," 1 Cor 2:1, "When I came to you, brethren, I did not come with superiority of speech or of wisdom, proclaiming to you the mystery of God;" 1 Cor 2:7, "We speak God's wisdom in a mystery, the hidden *wisdom,* which God predestined before the ages to our glory; 1 Cor 4:1, "Let a man regard us in this manner, as servants of Christ, and stewards of the mysteries of God;" 1 Cor 15:51, "Behold, I tell you a mystery; we shall not all sleep, but we shall all be changed;" Eph 1:9, "He made known to us the mystery of His will, according to His kind intention which He purposed in Him;" Eph 3:3–4, "by revelation there was made known to me the mystery, as I wrote before in brief, and by referring to this, when you read you can understand my insight into the mystery of Christ," Eph 3:9, "to bring to light what is the administration of the mystery which for ages has been hidden in God,;" Eph 6:19, "Pray on my behalf, that utterance may be given to me in the opening of my mouth, to make known with boldness the mystery of the gospel;" Col 1:26–27,

What is particularly instructive is that the mystery is to be preached to all nations (Rom 16:26).[45] What was once hidden about the gospel in the OT is now an open secret that is to be preached (Eph 3:8–9). Against the denial of Dialectic Theology that humans can speak God's revelation, Paul affirmatively announces, "We speak God's wisdom in a mystery . . . " (1 Cor 2:7).[46]

The preacher, then, is not at liberty to tamper with the content of the mystery: he is called to be a "steward of the mysteries of God," faithfully dispensing what has been entrusted to him, according to 1 Cor 4:1. This verse has been used as a prooftext by both Roman Catholic and Protestant theologians as the tie between preaching and the sacraments as means of grace.[47] The assumption is made that Paul refers to the sacraments by the use of the word *mustērion* (which the Vulgate translates by *sacramentum*), since the secular background of *mustērion* included cultic rites "in which the destinies of a god are portrayed by sacral actions."[48] However, this explanation of *mustērion* as sacrament tends to be dubious at best, especially since Paul elsewhere uses "mystery" to refer to the content of the gospel rather than to its signs. At the least, one could argue that the signs are mysteries in that they are visible representations of the historical events of salvation (Passover → the Lord's Supper → Christ's death; Pentecost → Baptism → Holy Spirit's outpouring), but only so far as they are conjoined with the Word. This bond between Word and Sacrament necessitates that the signs be administered only when accompanied by an explanation from the preached Word.

Paul's usage of *mustērion* clearly shows that the preacher is called to preach revealed truth, as the apostle insists, "I would have you know, brethren, that the gospel which was preached by me is not according to man. For I neither received it from man, nor was I taught it, but *I received it* through a revelation of Jesus Christ" (Gal 1:11–12). Paul makes it clear, in contrast to Dialectic Theology, that the revelation given to the apostles is propositional: it is made up of intelligible words taught by the Holy Spirit (1 Cor 2:13). Admittedly, the actual process of how the Spirit filtered His words through the words of sinful men so that the product remains the Word of God

---

"the mystery which has been hidden from the *past* ages and generations; but has now been manifested to His saints, to whom God willed to make known what is the riches of the glory of this mystery among the Gentiles, which is Christ in you, the hope of glory;" Col 2:2, "the full assurance of understanding, *resulting* in a true knowledge of God's mystery, *that is*, Christ Himself;" Col 4:3, "that we may speak forth the mystery of Christ."

45. Finkenrath, "Secret," *DNTT* 3:504, observes, "Practically everywhere it occurs in the NT *mysterion* is found with verbs denoting revelation or proclamation."

46. Bornkamm, μυστήριον, *TDNT* 4:819, states, "In the Pauline corpus, the term *mysterion* is firmly connected with the *kerygma* of Christ." Even so, Bornkamm denies that mystery is itself revelation (ibid., 4:820), a distinction he finds hard pressed to defend, since he notes that *musterion* is used mostly with terms for revelation.

47. See Grasso, *Proclaiming God's Message,* 70, for a Roman Catholic explanation of mystery; and Calvin, *Institutes*, 4:3.6 for a Reformed perspective.

48. Bornkamm, μυστήριον, *TDNT* 4:803.

is itself not revealed to us, other than to say that the process is miraculous. Surely, a perfect God can keep imperfect men from making mistakes!

Therefore, the preacher must be careful to distinguish his own words from those of the Word of God. He should correct those who might enthusiastically describe his sermons as inspired, because the concept of inspiration is reserved for the Scriptures alone (2 Tim 3:16). As Paul charges Timothy, the preacher is to preach written revelation, the Word, not some supposed new revelation.

Summary to Preaching Christ Jesus as Revealer

By making reference to the return of Jesus as an epiphany, Paul reminds Timothy that the message he is charged to preach concerns the manifestation of Jesus as revealer; in fact, despite the imbalance of Dialectic Theology in confusing preaching with revelation, it does contain an element of truth in that there is an epiphany in the process of preaching: Christ is revealed. His appearance in preaching is due to the dynamic nature of the preached Word, that it is "living and powerful" (Heb 4:12). When the sermon agrees with the written revelation of the Word (as it always should), the preacher can confidently say with the apostle, "For this reason we also thank God without ceasing, because when you received the Word of God which you heard from us, you welcomed *it* not *as* the word of men, but as it is in truth, the word of God, which also effectively works in you who believe" (1 Thess 2:13 NKJ). While the preacher cannot claim apostolicity, he can be confident that it is Christ who speaks though him when he preaches the true Word of God, in the manner Paul asserts, "Christ . . . speaks in me" (2 Cor 13:3). Grasso asserts, "In preaching it is God who speaks: He is the principal subject."[49] The listener needs to be brought into the presence of Jesus as the Revealer of God, who then may enlighten those who hear to understand the mysteries of the Kingdom of God.

The Reason for Preaching: Because Christ Jesus is King

The fourth aspect of Christology Paul cites as a reason for preaching concerns the Kingdom of Jesus: "I solemnly charge you before . . . His kingdom" (2 Tim 4:1 NET). Because Paul rarely describes Jesus as King (only elsewhere at 1 Tim 1:17 and 6:15), the question must be asked, why would Paul make a connection between preaching and the coming Kingdom of Christ?

---

49. Grasso, *Proclaiming God's Message*, 24.

The Coming Kingdom Preached in the OT

The answer to this question is found in the fact that the Kingdom of God is one of the most pronounced subjects in the Bible. The Psalmist declares, "The LORD has established his throne in the heavens, and his kingdom rules over all" (Ps 103:19 ESV). Although God actually reigns always as sovereign, a distinction can be made between His providential rule over His creation and His mediatorial rule whereby God comes to earth to reign in righteousness (Ps 96:10–13[50]). The concept of God as the coming King became more prominent during the rise of the Davidic dynasty, when Isa 33:22 proclaimed, "The LORD is our king; He will save us."[51]

Central to the idea of God's rule is the Covenant made with David, to whom God promised to enthrone one of his descendant unto an eternal kingdom (2 Sam 7:12–16). In this enthronement, the Lord installs His King upon Mount Zion and declares Him as His very Son (Ps 2:6–7).[52] The rising expectation is that there shall be no end to the increase of the government of peace on the throne of David through the Prince of Peace (Isa 9:7), and the extent of this Kingdom will spread to every people, nation, and tongue when the Son of Man is given His everlasting dominion (Dan 7:13–14). It is no wonder that this wonderful message should be proclaimed to the world, so when the prophet sees the approach of the time when the Lord God shall be enthroned as King over all creation, he describes the beauty of the feet of the evangelist who shall announce the good news—the gospel—"Your God reigns!" (Isa 52:7)

The Kingdom Preached by Jesus

It is within this OT backdrop of the proclamation of the Kingdom of God that Jesus' preaching of that Kingdom should be understood. At the outset of the Gospels, Jesus burst onto the villages of Galilee, preaching the Kingdom of God by announcing, "The time is fulfilled, and the Kingdom of God is at hand!" (Mark 1:14). It is the appearance of Jesus as King that signals the arrival of the Kingdom: the providential domination of God that governs the world is now moving toward becoming one with the mediatorial Kingdom in which God will "reconcile all things to Himself, having made peace

---

50. Psalm 96:10–13 declares, "Say among the nations, 'The LORD reigns; Indeed, the world is firmly established, it will not be moved; He will judge the peoples with equity. Let the heavens be glad, and let the earth rejoice; Let the sea roar, and all it contains; Let the field exult, and all that is in it. Then all the trees of the forest will sing for joy Before the LORD, for He is coming; For He is coming to judge the earth. He will judge the world in righteousness, And the peoples in His faithfulness.'" See the discussion in Klappert, "King," *DNTT* 2:375.

51. Klappert, ibid., states, "Yahweh would not have been described as *melek* before the time of the monarchy." While that observation is generally true, the concept of God's kingship predates the Davidic monarchy, as Miriam sang at the Exodus, "The Lord shall reign forever" (Exod 15:18).

52. Ibid., 2:374–75. Psalm 2:6–7 reads, "But as for Me, I have installed My King Upon Zion, My holy mountain. I will surely tell of the decree of the LORD: He said to Me, 'Thou art My Son, Today I have begotten Thee.'"

through the blood of His cross; through Him, *I say*, whether things on earth or things in heaven" (Col 1:20). This expectation becomes the final answer to the Lord's model prayer, "Thy Kingdom come: Thy will be done" (Matt 6:10).

Quite evidently, even with the first arrival of Jesus as the King, the will of man has not become one with the will of the King; for that matter, it was the decision of rebellious men that crucified the King! It is at this point that the interpretive theories of Dispensationalism, popularized by the *Scofield Reference Bible*, greatly influenced evangelical thought in the twentieth century by teaching that the Kingdom has been delayed until the Second Coming of Christ; for that reason, Dispensationalism stresses that Paul anticipates the arrival of Christ's Kingdom at His second *epiphany* but not before that event.[53] The practical effect of this view has been to rob the church of any triumphant mission during the present age, overlooking the Pauline emphasis on the dynamic conquest of the Word (Col 1:5–6).[54] According to Dispensationalism, the church is merely a parenthesis that bides its time until God decides to remove it at the rapture when He will then resume His Kingdom work with Israel once again. Consequently, there is no present Kingdom now that the King has ascended back to heaven.

The Kingdom Preached by Paul

But surely there is a present Kingdom, for it should not be overlooked that Paul plainly teaches the present existence of the Kingdom of Christ when he states that believers have already been "transferred . . . to the Kingdom of the Beloved Son" (Col 1:13). This tension between a present kingdom and a coming kingdom is not an internal contradiction, for Jesus Himself authored the paradox by preaching that the Kingdom is both present ("the kingdom of God is in your midst," Luke 17:21) and yet still future, as He speaks of the Son of Man coming in His kingdom (Matt 16:28). So, is the Kingdom wholly present, or is it wholly future?

The studies of Vos, Dodd, and Ridderbos[55] help to sort out this dilemma with their explanation of "realized eschatology," which maintains that the Kingdom is already present and yet it is also coming. There is an aspect in which God has already called His elect into "His own Kingdom and glory" through the preached message (1 Thess 2:12), and yet there is also the future coming Kingdom that is heavenly and eternal (2 Tim 4:18; 2 Pet 2:11). The difference seems to be one of degree: the present kingdom advances under the spiritual kingship of Jesus until every enemy is subdued (1 Cor 15:24), and then at the personal appearance of the King, the Kingdom itself

---

53. See the arguments in Ryrie, *Dispensationalism Today* (1965).

54. Colossians 1:5–6 reads, ". . . the word of truth, the gospel, which has come to you, just as in all the world also it is constantly bearing fruit and increasing, even as *it has been doing* in you also since the day you heard *of it* and understood the grace of God in truth."

55. Vos, *Biblical Theology* (1948); Dodd, *Apostolic Preaching and its Development* (1949); Ridderbos, *Coming of the Kingdom* (1976).

becomes visible. The difficulty seems to lies in the fact that the long development between the birth of the King and His final conquest was not easily discerned in the OT. What has never been easy for the Jewish people to recognize is that the King must suffer first before entering his glory (Luke 24:26), and so the preaching of the Kingdom becomes concurrent with the preaching of name of Jesus as the King (Acts 8:12; 28:31). To preach Jesus is to preach the Kingdom, for the two are inseparable.[56] This link accounts for the fact that the kingdom concept recedes in the epistles, which places greater emphasis on the death, resurrection, and ascension of Jesus, because these are the events that declared Jesus to be the King and through which sinners are converted (Acts 2:32–36).

Preaching the Kingdom Psalm 110

The idea of Jesus as the exalted King is very plainly preached in the NT, since it appears whenever there is an allusion to the "right hand" of God as presented in Ps 110:1, "The LORD says to my Lord: "Sit at My right hand, Until I make Thine enemies a footstool for Thy feet."[57] Jesus not only quoted this verse during His trial before the Sanhedrin, but it was His application of Ps 110:1 (along with Dan 7:13) to Himself that led directly to His condemnation (Matt 26:64).[58] On the basis of Jesus' reference to Ps 110:1, the apostles found in that verse the spiritual nature of the present Kingdom as being inaugurated at the Ascension of Jesus; in fact, the first Christian sermon includes an explanation of Ps 110:1 as the coronation of Jesus to the Davidic throne when God declared Him to be Lord and Messiah (Acts 2:33–36). Having been exalted to the right hand of God, Jesus now pours out His Spirit upon His people, with the immediate consequence that they proclaim the gospel.

Indeed, the only basis by which the preacher can proclaim the saving majesty of Jesus is to have a clear understanding of the ascension as the coronation of Jesus as King. By overlooking the obvious application of Psalm 110 to the ascension of Jesus, Dispensationalism fails to acknowledge that Jesus has already been crowned with majestic glory and has begun His reign "until He has put all His enemies under His feet" (1 Cor 15:25, quoting Ps 110:1b). The Dispensational distinction between the gospel and the Kingdom crumbles when Jesus states that "this gospel of the kingdom shall be preached in the whole world for a witness to all the nations, and then the end shall come" (Matt 24:14). Significantly, when the Book of Acts closes its segment on

---

56. Schmidt, βασιλεία, *TDNT* 1:589, states, "It is on this decisive fact of the equation of the incarnate, exalted and present Jesus Christ with the future kingdom of God that the Christological *kerugma* depends with its understanding of the Mission of the Messiah as once and for all."

57. The "Right Hand of God" motif is cited in Matt 22:44; 26:64; Mark 12:36; 14:62; (16:19); Luke 20:42; 22:69; Acts 2:33–34; 5:31; 7:55–56; Rom 8:34; Eph 1:20; Col 3:1; Heb 1:3; 1:13; 8:1; 10:12; 12:2; 1 Pet 3:22; Rev 5:1.

58. Matthew 26:64, ". . . I tell you, hereafter you shall see the Son of Man sitting at the right hand of Power, and coming on the clouds of heaven."

Paul's ministry in Rome, it reports that the apostle is "preaching the kingdom of God, and teaching concerning the Lord Jesus Christ with all openness, unhindered" (Acts 28:31). While the concepts of Kingdom and gospel differ, one cannot be explained or understood without the other, meaning that no New Covenant preacher is fully preaching if he does not assume the present Kingship of the ascended Lord.

Preaching as a Gift of the King

Furthermore, the concept of the exaltation of the King would be an encouragement to Timothy to recall the ancient custom whereby a king would bestow gifts to his people at his investiture.[59] In Eph 4:7-10,[60] Paul applies the investiture announced in Ps 68:18 in this manner,[61] as now that Jesus has ascended to the right hand, He gives gifts to His church, notably the "apostles, prophets, evangelists, pastors and teachers" (Eph 4:11). Common to each of these leaders is the gift of proclamation, for now that the King has exalted, He gifts these men to become His heralds. Without such gifting, no preacher would be adequate for the task of preaching.

The concept of the preacher as a herald will be explored later more fully in chapter 14, where it will be shown that the herald of a king publishes the royal decrees to his subjects. By reminding Timothy of the coming kingdom, Paul impresses on him the importance of serving as a herald whose duty is to announce the royal decrees of the King, as the Lord's Great Commission requires ("teaching them to all things I have commanded you," Matt 28:20). The King, then, prepares His message, calls His heralds, equips them for their task, and sends them as royal ambassadors to publish the news, "Your God reigns!" (Isa 52:7). The preacher is given the awesome responsibility of delivering the royal invitation to His subjects, as "the King will say to those on His right, 'Come, you who are blessed of My Father, inherit the kingdom prepared for you from the foundation of the world'" (Matt 25:34).

Summary to Preaching Christ Jesus as King:

It is not incidental that Paul mentions the appearing Kingdom as a reason for his charge to preach the Word. The Kingship of Christ Jesus necessitates a vocal announcement of the realm of the Sovereign Monarch with all His attendant blessings

---

59. As noted by Hendriksen, *Ephesians*, 191.

60. Ephesians 4:7-10 reads, "But to each one of us grace was given according to the measure of Christ's gift. Therefore it says, 'When He ascended on high, He led captive a host of captives, And He gave gifts to men.' (Now this *expression*, 'He ascended,' what does it mean except that He also had descended into the lower parts of the earth?" He who descended is Himself also He who ascended far above all the heavens, that He might fill all things.)."

61. Psalm 68:18 states, "Thou hast ascended on high, Thou hast led captive *Thy* captives; Thou hast received gifts among men, Even *among* the rebellious also, that the LORD God may dwell *there*" (NAS).

and warnings; indeed, apart from the Kingship of Jesus, the preacher has nothing to announce, but since the King has been crowned at the right hand of Majesty, the preacher can confidently announce the reign of the coming Prince of Peace.

Conclusion to the Reason for Preaching

In giving the reason for preaching, Paul presents Timothy with an imperial view of Jesus as God, Judge, Revelator, and King. All four concepts compel verbal proclamation: God, by nature, speaks His creative Word. As Judge, He renders verdicts; as Revelator, He discloses Himself; and as King, He makes royal decrees.

These concepts bring Timothy to the heart of the gospel message, for he is called to preach only what Jesus has authorized. These themes serve as solemn reminders that the Christian faith brings the living and the dead to account before the God who is communicative and revealing: He speaks–or better stated, He preaches, and He does so through His preachers.

The ultimate reason why the preacher preaches, then, is stated in 2 Cor 2:17, ". . . We are not like many, peddling the word of God, but as from sincerity, but as from God, we speak in Christ in the sight of God." Only as Timothy preaches with the awareness that he is standing in the presence of the exalted Lord will he find an adequate reason to preach, and that is just as true for every succeeding preacher of the gospel: the reason for preaching is only found "in the presence of God and of Christ Jesus, who is to judge the living and the dead, and by His appearing and His kingdom" (2 Tim 4:1).

CHAPTER 3

The Preacher's Content: "The Word"

HAVING GIVEN TIMOTHY HIS commission with attached theological reasons, Paul now turns to the actual charge: "Preach the Word." In these three words (*kēruxon ton logon*) is found the primary task of the Christian minister, which is to devote himself to the preaching of the Word of God.

While that duty seems simple enough, apparently it is not so. Debate rages on the nature of preaching as well as the content of the preaching; however, the two aspects cannot be separated. McDonald argues that the kerygmatic Word ". . . almost invariably contains the primary notion of the dynamic activity of preaching, but no context excludes the idea of content."[1] Because the content is "the Word," it begs to be spoken.

Grammatically, the apostle places the activity ("Preach") before the content ("The Word"), but logically, one must discuss them in reverse order, because the preacher must know what he is to preach before he begins to speak. Therefore, this chapter will explore the various aspects of the content of the Word so that the modern reader will have an understanding of what the apostle meant by "The Word" as the content of preaching.

What then is the actual content of this "Word"? Preaching suffers through various trends; for example, Kuiper points out that the preaching of rationalism was in vogue in the 1850's. By the turn of the century, that trend gave way to the preaching of Schliermacher's religious consciousness, which in turn surrendered to Fosdick's "profound religious living."[2] By the mid-twentieth century, favorite topics in both liberal and conservative pulpits included social justice and political involvement, while popular media preachers of the twenty-first century preached a popular "feel good" message. Far worse was the influence of radical criticism that the Bible was no better than any other book, and maybe even worse. That left preachers with nothing much to preach at all.

---

1. McDonald, *Kerygma and Didache*, 2.
2. Kuiper, "Scriptural Preaching," in *The Infallible Word*, 225.

Such trendy preaching can leave the hearers wondering just what the content of Christian preaching ought to sound like. This issue ought to be of utmost importance to every preacher, because no one wants to spend an entire ministry involved in what 1 Cor 15:14 calls "vain preaching." What then is this "Word" that Timothy and every successive preacher is commanded to preach? At some time or another, every preacher has entered the pulpit wondering, what shall I preach? In giving Timothy this commission to preach, Paul also gives him the exclusive content to preach, and this chapter shall search for a definition of this "Word," the *Logos* as Paul himself understood it.

The Content of Preaching: The Revealed *Logos*

The *Logos* as Revealed Word

The simplest definition of the Greek word *logos* is a word or a statement,[3] but it is quite evident that Paul meant far more than Timothy should preach with the use of words. The definite article *ho* indicates that "the" word has a specific content, and it must be assumed that Timothy would have known what particular "word" Paul intended. Of course, the only way modern readers can discover Paul's definition of *ho logos* is to explore his use of this phrase in his letters,[4] as well as its usage in the Book of Acts.[5]

---

3. BDAG § 4605.1.

4. Paul uses the word *logos* 84 times in his signed letters, and of those, he generally uses the anarthous word *logos* (without the definite article) to refer to spoken words or speech in general (Rom 9:28; 14:12; 15:18; 1 Cor 1:5; 1:17; 2:1; 2:4b; 2:13; 4:20; 12:8; 14:9; 14:19; 15:2; 2 Cor 6:7; 8:7; Gal 5:14 ("one word," quoting Lev 19:18); Eph 4:29; 5:6; 6:19; Phil 2:16 ("word of life"); Col 3:17; 1 Thess 1:5; 2:5; 2:15b; 2:15c ("word of God"); 4:15 ("by word of Lord"); 4:18; 2 Thess 2:2; 2:15; 2:17; 2 Thess 3:14; 1 Tim 4:5 ("word of God"); 4:12; 5:17; 6:3; 2 Tim 1:13; Titus 2:8 ("sound words"); or *logos* as a particular matter (Phil 4:15; 4:17; Col 2:23). However, Paul uses the singular ("the word") with a definite article 38 times:

   A. Of Paul's own words: "My word and my message" (ὁ λόγος μου καὶ τὸ κήρυγμά μου: 1 Cor 2:4a); "The word of us" (ὁ λόγος ἡμῶν; 2 Cor 1:18); Paul's "contemptible word" (ὁ λόγος ἐξουθενημένος; 2 Cor 10:10); Paul's "unskilled words" (2 Cor 11:6); "your word" (Col 4:6); "their words" (2 Tim 2:17); "our words" (2 Tim 4:15).

   B. Of a Divine word: 1. "The Word" (Gal 6:6; Phil 1:14; Col 4:3; 1 Thess 1:6; 2 Tim 4:2); 2. the Word of (the) God (ὁ λόγος τοῦ θεοῦ; Rom 9:6; 1 Cor 14:36; 2 Cor 2:17; 4:2; Col 1:25; 2 Thess 2:15a; 2 Tim 2:9; Titus 2:5); 3. The word of promise (ἐπαγγελίας γὰρ ὁ λόγος; Rom 9:9); 4. "in this word" (ἐν τῷ λόγῳ τούτῳ; Rom 13:9, quoting Lev 19:18); 5. the word of the Cross ('Ο λόγος ὁ τοῦ σταυρου; 1 Cor 1:18); 6. The word having been written (ὁ λόγος ὁ γεγραμμένος; 1 Cor 15:5, quoting Hos 13:14); 7. the word of reconciliation (τὸν λόγον τῆς καταλλαγῆς; 2 Cor 5:19); 8. "the word of the truth" (τὸν λόγον τῆς ἀληθείας; Eph 1:13; 2 Tim 2:15); 9. "the word of truth, the gospel" (ἐν τῷ λόγῳ τῆς ἀληθείας τοῦ εὐαγγελίου (Col 1:5); 10. "the Word of the Christ" ('Ο λόγος τοῦ Χριστοῦ; Col 3:16); 11. "the Word of the Lord" (ὁ λόγος τοῦ κυρίου; 1 Thess 1:8; 2 Thess 3:1); 12. "the faithful word" (1 Tim 1:15; 3:1; 4:9; 2 Tim 2:11; Titus 1:9; 3:8); 13. "word of Him" (Titus 1:3); plus, the plural, "the words of the faith" (1 Tim 4:6).

5. The Book of Acts links "the Word of God/ Lord" to the ministry of Paul beginning at 13:5; 7; 44; 46; 48; 49; 15:35; 15:26; 17:13; 18:11; 19:10; 19:20), plus just "the Word" (Acts 14:25; 16:6; 16:32;

This quest to find content to preach is not some mysterious venture, since Paul has previously mentioned "the Word of God" (2 Tim 2:9) and "the word of the truth" (2 Tim 2:15) in this letter to Timothy. It is clear that he refers to divine revelation in contrast to the speculations of men, in the way he draws this same distinction in 1 Thess 2:13, "We also constantly thank God that when you received from us the word (*logos*) of God's message, you accepted *it* not *as* the word (*logos*) of men, but *for* what it really is, the word (*logos*) of God." For Timothy to "preach the Word," then, is to preach divine revelation, which for Paul included the written word of the OT (1 Cor 15:5), the spoken words of Jesus (Acts 20:35), and the message of the gospel (Col 1:5).

This identification of the Word with revelation is not to imply that the preached *logos* is identical with the revealed *logos,* as the existentialists might insist. Instead, Klappert correctly observes, "Paul distinguishes between the historical event of the reconciliation of the world and the speaking event of the word of proclamation concerning this event."[6] This distinction should be maintained if the preacher is to be faithful to the revealed Word, which obviously is of greater importance than the preacher's own words.

At the other extreme is the neo-orthodox view, which denies that any specific proposition of the Bible can itself be *ho logos toū Theoū*. However, such a notion cannot find support with Paul, who maintains that one actually can hear "the word of truth, the gospel of your salvation" (Eph 1:13 ESV), because it actually can be spoken fearlessly (Phil 1:14). One of Paul's clearest expressions linking the revealed word with the content of preaching is Titus 1:3, "God manifested in His own time His Word (*logos*) in preaching, which I was entrusted according to the command of our Savior God" (AT). This verse indicates that the preacher truly handles the Word of God, and other verses show that the Word affects a number of varied actions when it is proclaimed.[7]

Given Paul's Jewish background, behind his understanding of the *logos* must lie the OT concept of the Word of the Lord (*Dabar Yahweh;* דְּבַר־יְהוָה), which appears 270 times in the MT[8] and refers to the speaking voice of the living God. Paul equates the

---

17:11; 18:5; 20:7; 20:38) or "the word of salvation (Acts 13:26); "word of His grace" (Acts 14:3; 20:32); "word of the gospel" (Acts 15:7); "words of the prophets" (Acts 15:15); "much word" (Acts 20:2); and "words of the Lord Jesus" (Acts 20:35).

6. Klappert, "Word," *DNTT*, 3:1112.

7. The various verbal actions concerning the *logos* include being preached (2 Tim 2:2); spoken (Acts 4:29; 8:25; 11:19; 13:46; 14:25; 16:6; 16:32; Phil 1:14); witnessed (Acts 8:25; 14:3); evangelized (Acts 8:4; 15:35; 1 Cor 15:2); taught (Acts 15:35; 16:11); catechized (Gal 6:6); announced (Acts 13:5; 15:36; 17:13); so that it is heard (Acts 4:4; 10:44; 13:7; 13:44; 15:7; 19:10, Eph 1:13) and received (Acts 8:14; 11:1; 17:11; 1 Thess 1:6). Although the Word can be blasphemed (Titus 2:5), it also increases (Acts 6:7; 12:24; 19:20); is glorified (Acts 13:48; 2 Thess 3:1); spreads (Acts 13:49; 2 Thess 3:1); sounds out (1 Thess 1:8); and is fulfilled (Col 1:25).

8. דְּבַר־יְהוָה appears in Genesis 15:1, 4; 24:51; Exod 4:30; 6:28; 7:13, 22; 8:11, 15; 9:12, 20, 21, 35; 16:23; 19:8; 24:3, 7; 34:32; Lev 10:3, 11; Num 3:1; 5:4; 12:2; 15:22, 31; 17:5; 23:17; 27:23; 32:31; Deut 1:21; 2:1; 4:15; 5:4, 5, 22; 6:3, 19; 9:3, 10; 10:4, 9; 27:3; 31:3; Jos 4:8; 11:23; 14:6, 10, 12; 21:45; 23:5, 14, 15; Jdg 2:15; 1 Sam 3:7, 9; 15:10, 13, 16, 23, 26; 16:4; 2 Sam 7:4; 12:9; 1 Kgs 2:27; 5:19; 6:11; 8:20; 12:15, 24; 13:3, 20; 16:1, 7; 17:2, 8; 18:31; 19:9; 21:17, 23, 28; 22:5, 19, 28; 2 Kgs 3:12; 7:1; 9:36; 10:10; 14:27;

Word of God to the OT in Rom 9:6, but his use of *Logos toū Theoū* refers most often to the preaching of the New Covenant. This fact is borne out by Paul's varied descriptions of the *logos* when modified with various propositions of the gospel message, including "the word of reconciliation" (2 Cor 5:19) and "the Word of Christ" (Col 3:16).[9] The most concise statement of Paul's idea of *logos* appears when he enunciates the specific content of "which word (*tini logoi*) I preached to you, . . . that Christ died for our sins according to the Scriptures, and that He was buried, and that He was raised on the third day according to the Scriptures, and that He appeared . . ." (1 Cor 15:2–5). Here Paul lists the content as of "first importance" to be preached, and it includes the *logos* of particular historical events pertaining to Jesus (His death, burial, and resurrection appearances), as explained by previous *logoi*, the *graphē* of the OT. In these matters of "first importance," Paul makes the propositional nature of his *logos* patently specific. The gospel is not merely the speaking of personal experiences with the divine but the retelling the divine events enacted in human history by which the hearer is saved, "if you hold fast the *logos* which I preached to you, unless you believed in vain" (1 Cor 15:2).

The possibility of "vain belief" should remind both the speaker and the hearer of the imperative nature of *ho logos*, that it is to be preached and heard as the revealed Word of God. As the Word of Christ, *ho logos* should indwell the life of the preacher so richly that he will wisely teach and exhort others (Col 3:16) by verbally declaring the full content of "the whole purpose of God" (Acts 20:27).

The *Rhēma* as Revealed Word

Very closely associated with *logos* is the noun *rhēma*. Both words are usually translated by "word,"[10] so that any distinction in Greek is lost on the English reader. Admittedly, it is impossible to insist on an absolute distinction of meaning between *logos* and *rhēma*, although Betz notes, "Whereas *logos* can often designate the Christian proclamation as a whole in the NT, *rhēma* usually relates to individual words and utterances."[11]

15:12; 19:21; 20:16, 19; 24:13; 1 Chr 10:13; 22:8; 2 Chr 6:10; 11:2; 12:7; 18:4, 18, 27; 19:11; 23:3; 34:21; 36:21, 22; Ezra 1:1; Job 42:7; Ps 33:4; Isa 1:10; 16:13, 14; 20:2; 28:13, 14; 37:22; 38:4; 39:5, 8; 66:5; Jer 1:2, 4, 11, 13; 2:1, 4, 31; 6:10; 7:2; 9:19; 10:1; 13:3, 8; 14:1; 16:1, 10; 17:15, 20; 18:5; 19:3; 20:8; 21:11; 22:2, 29; 23:17, 35, 37; 24:4; 25:3; 27:13, 18; 28:12; 29:20, 30; 30:4; 31:10; 32:6, 8, 26; 33:1, 19, 23; 34:4, 12; 35:12; 36:7, 27; 37:6; 39:15; 42:7, 15, 19; 43:8; 44:24, 26; 46:1, 13; 47:1; 49:34; 50:1; Ezek 1:3; 3:16; 6:1; 7:1; 11:14; 12:1, 8, 17, 21, 26; 13:1, 2; 14:2, 12; 15:1; 16:1, 35; 17:1, 11; 18:1; 20:2; 21:1, 3, 6, 13, 23; 22:1, 17, 23; 23:1; 24:1, 15, 20; 25:1; 26:1; 27:1; 28:1, 11, 20; 29:1, 17; 30:1, 20; 31:1; 32:1, 17; 33:1, 23; 34:1, 7, 9; 35:1; 36:1, 16; 37:4, 15; 38:1; Dan 9:2; Hos 1:1, 2; 4:1; Joel 1:1; Amos 3:1; 7:16; 8:12; Jonah 1:1; 3:1; Mic 1:1; Zeph 1:1; 2:5; Hag 1:1, 3; 2:1, 10, 20; Zech 1:1, 7; 4:6, 8; 6:9; 7:1, 4, 8; 8:1, 18; 9:1; 11:11; 12:1; Mal 1:1.

9. Besides "Word of God/Lord/ Christ," *logos* is also described as the word of salvation (Acts 13:26), of grace (Acts 14:3; 20:32), of the gospel (Acts 15:7), of promise (Rom 9:9), of the cross (1 Cor 1:18); of wisdom (1 Cor 12:8), of knowledge (1 Cor 12:8), of reconciliation (2 Cor 5:19), of truth (Eph 1:13, Col 1:5, 2 Tim 2:15), of life (Phil 2:16), of report (1 Thess 2:13), and of faith (Titus 1:9).

10. BDAG § 6501.1 ῥῆμα, "that which is said, *word, saying, expression, or statement of any* kind."

11. Betz, "Word," *DNTT* 3:1121.

An examination of the few times *rhēma* is found in Paul's letters indicates that he appears to use it in contexts stressing the dynamic effect of the revelation of God.[12] This observation is not to imply that *rhēma* is the active Word of God behind the written or spoken Word of God, because Paul actually identifies the preached *rhēma* with the OT Scripture as the faith-engendering *rhēma* when he states, "We are preaching the *rhēma* of faith" (Rom 10:8), and this message comes "though the *rhēma* of Christ" (Rom 10:17). However, *rhēma* does appear to emphasize the dynamic of the Word in that it converts (Rom 10:17), sanctifies (Eph 5:26), and protects (Eph 6:17) believers. To these ends, the preacher should pray that his preaching of the *rhēma* accomplishes what God intends (Isa 55:11[13]) as he realizes that the power of preaching comes not from himself but from the *Logos* as the *Rhēma Theoū*.

The *Mustērion* as Revealed Word

Another aspect of revealed knowledge that Paul preaches is "the mystery (*mustērion*) of God" (1 Cor 2:1).[14] Finkenrath observes, "Practically everywhere it appears in the NT, *mustērion* is found with verbs denoting revelation or proclamation."[15] The content of the mystery might refer to the gospel in general (Eph 6:19) or to a particular doctrinal point revealed to the apostle (Rom 11:25; 1 Cor 15:51). Specifically, the *mustērion* concerns the content of the New Covenant that was preciously hidden from the Old Covenant saints but has now come to light with the appearance of the Messiah (Col

---

12. Paul uses *rhēma* eight times, beginning in Romans 10:8, quoting Deut 30:14, "But what does it say?" The word (*rhēma*) is near you, in your mouth and in your heart'—that is, the word (*rhēma*) of faith which we are preaching"; then in Rom 10:17, "So then faith *comes* by hearing, and hearing by the word (*rhēmatos*) of God"; in Rom 10:18, quoting Ps 19:4, "But I say, have they not heard? Yes indeed: 'Their sound has gone out to all the earth, And their words (*rhēmata*) to the ends of the world'"; in 2 Cor 12:4, "he was caught up into Paradise and heard inexpressible words (*rhēmata*), which it is not lawful for a man to utter"; in 2 Cor 13:1, quoting Deut 19:15, "By the mouth of two or three witnesses every word (*rhēma*) shall be established"; in Eph 5:26, "that He might sanctify and cleanse her with the washing of water by the word" (*rhēmati*); and lastly, in Eph 6:17, "Take the helmet of salvation, and the sword of the Spirit, which is the word (*rhēma*) of God."

13. Isaiah 55:11, "So shall My word (*rhēma*) be which goes forth from My mouth; It shall not return to Me empty, Without accomplishing what I desire, And without succeeding *in the matter* for which I sent it."

14. See the previous discussion in chapter 2, "Preaching the Revelation as Mystery." There the *uses loquendi* of μυστήριον was suggested as follows:
   1. The Mysteries of the Kingdom (Matt 13:11; Mark 4:11; Luke 8:10);
   2. Mysteries in general (1 Cor 13:2; 14:2);
   3. A specific revealed mystery (Rom 11:25; Eph 5:32; 2 Thess 2:7);
   4. The Christian Faith as a mystery (1 Tim 3:9, 16);
   5. Eschatological mysteries (Rev 1:20; 10:7; 17:5; 17:7);
   6. The revealed and preached mystery (Rom 16:25, 1 Cor 2:1; 2:7; 4:1; 15:51; Eph 1:9; 3:3–4, 3:9; Eph 6:19; Col 1:26–27, Col 2:2, Col 4:3).

15. Finkenrath, "Secret," *DNTT* 3:504.

1:26–27). Because Jesus as the incarnate Word has revealed the Father (John 1:18), the *mustērion* is no longer esoteric. What was once a secret should now be proclaimed to the entire world (Rom 16:26), a task relegated especially to the preacher (Eph 6:19).

So then, to preach the *mustērion* is not only to proclaim revealed propositional doctrines (such as listed in 1 Tim 3:16[16]) but above all, it is the proclamation of Christ Jesus, who is the greatest *mustērion* of God (Col 2:2; 4:3). The risen Lord is mediated in the preaching of the *mustērion* of the gospel (Col 1:27), and that means, ultimately, that the supreme content of preaching is Christ Jesus Himself.

Christos as Revealed Word

Even though Paul mentions the person of Christ Jesus as the direct object of preaching only a few times,[17] those references show that, principally, the content of the preacher should be to proclaim Jesus Christ Himself. Such was Paul's message immediately after his conversion, when he began to "proclaim Jesus in the synagogues, saying, 'He is the Son of God'" (Acts 9:20) and "proving that this *Jesus* is the Christ" (Acts 9:22). Here, very early in Christian history, Paul confesses the primary titles of Jesus as the Son of God and as the Christ, although it can be reasonably presumed that these titles were already recognized by the Messianic communities in Damascus and Jerusalem. While critics argue that Paul imposed these titles on an unsuspecting Jesus,[18] the source actually originated with Jesus, as He quoted Himself with the claim, "I am the Son of God" (John 10:36, AT), and He also acknowledged Himself to be the Christ/Messiah on numerous occasions (John 4:25–26; 10:24–25; Matt 26:63).

When Paul proclaims Jesus, he demonstrates that he makes no distinction between the historical Jesus of Nazareth (Acts 22:8, 26:9) and the heavenly Jesus as the ascended Lord (Acts 16:31). He preaches the same Christ as crucified (1 Cor 1:22) and also as "Jesus Christ Lord!" (2 Cor 4:5, AT). It is clear that in preaching Christ, Paul is not only preaching facts about the historical person of Jesus (1 Cor 15:1–5), but he is also presenting Jesus as the resurrected Lord (Rom 14:9). Ellis comments, "Christ crucified is not only the message but also the One who speaks through and in that Word, not only in the historical content of the message, but also the 'wisdom' that is active in it."[19] The concept of the living dynamic of the gospel message will be explored in further detail in chapter 15.

---

16. 1 Timothy 3:16, "And by common confession great is the mystery of godliness: He who was revealed in the flesh, Was vindicated in the Spirit, Beheld by angels, Proclaimed among the nations, Believed on in the world, Taken up in glory."

17. Those references include the following: Acts 9:20, "Immediately [Paul] *began* to proclaim Jesus in the synagogues, saying, 'He is the Son of God'"; Rom 1:3–5, "the gospel . . . concerning His Son"; 1 Cor 1:23, "We preach Christ crucified"; 2 Cor 1:19, "For the Son of God, Christ Jesus, who was preached among you by us"; 2 Cor 4:5, "We do not preach ourselves but Christ Jesus as Lord."

18. Lüdemann, *Paul: The Founder of Christianity*, 214–15.

19. Ellis, "Christ Crucified," 70.

Grasso even insists that when Paul commands Timothy to "preach the Word," he means that Timothy should preach Jesus as the incarnate Word (John 1:14) rather than the written Word.[20] His interpretation is questionable in that it reads Johannine theology into Paul, and it may also tend to divorce the incarnate Word from the inscripturated Word, on the supposed ground that the written Word is fallible, being the words of men, whereas Jesus as the incarnate Word is infallible. However, the NT makes no separation between the historical person of Jesus as the *Logos* of God and the written Scripture as the *Logos* of God, as Clowney notes, "He who preaches the Word must preach Christ."[21] The opposite is also true: he who preaches Christ must also preach the Word. There exists no other revealed explanation of Jesus apart from the written Word, meaning that the content of preaching must be the incarnate Word of God as He is presented in the written Word of God.

The Content of Preaching: The *Logos* of Old Testament *Graphē*

When Paul charges Timothy to "Preach the Word," the intended content would have also included the writings of the OT, to which he has just referred as the "holy Scriptures" (*Hieros Gramma*) a few sentences earlier (2 Tim 3:15). In other places, Paul equates specific quotations from the OT to the *Logos toū Theoū* (as in Rom 9:6–7, quoting Gen 21:12; Rom 13:9, quoting Lev 19:18; and 1 Cor 15:5, quoting Hos 13:14), so it is apparent that the *logos* in Paul's charge to Timothy must have reference to the written *logos toū Theoū* that was accessible in the synagogue readings. Acts 17:2 gives what amounts to a summary statement of Paul's ministry in that he "reasoned with them from the *graphon*," using the written OT Scripture as the source of his preaching.

OT Preaching as the Source of Texts

A reading of Paul's letters shows that his gospel has its roots in the OT; in one sense, there is nothing brand new in the NT, because it is all concealed in seed form in the OT.[22] The mystery of revelation has now been manifested through the Scriptures of the prophets (Rom 16:25–26), so that Paul preaches "the gospel of God which He promised before through His prophets in the Holy Scriptures, concerning His Son . . . Jesus Christ our Lord" (Rom 1:1–4). The OT became the source of Paul's texts for his preaching. His own confession is, "I worship the God of my fathers, believing all things which are written in the Law and in the Prophets" (Acts 24:14).

Even the specific doctrinal tenets of the New Covenant find prooftexts in the OT, as Paul claims, "Christ died for our sins according to the *Graphas*, and that He was

---

20. Grasso, *Proclaiming God's Message*, 5.

21. Clowney, *Preaching and Biblical Theology*, 74.

22. See Fitzmyer, *To Advance the Gospel*, 59, in the chapter titled, "The Gospel in the Theology of Paul."

buried, and that He rose again the third day according to the *Graphas*" (1 Cor 15:3–4). Ellis counts ninety-three times that Paul quotes the OT, including his quotations in the Book of Acts (these will be studied in chapter 8 on Structure),[23] and Hays points out that Paul constantly echoes allusions to the OT in his letters.[24] Clearly, if one removes the OT from Paul's writings, he would have very little to preach.

Paul's use of the OT is extremely varied: he may use a specific OT prooftext for support of a subpoint (as in Gal 3:11 and Eph 5:31), or he may employ an OT quotation to govern an entire paragraph (Eph 4:8), or even to serve as the text for an entire letter (Rom 1:17). Kuist observes, "Paul knew what he taught, the Hebrew Bible. He was able to quote it from memory, relate historical facts (Acts 13:16), give authoritative interpretation (Acts 13:45), refer to the great characters, plus give his own apostolic revelation."[25]

The application is evident: the New Covenant preacher should derive his texts for preaching from the Scripture itself; in fact, he must be able to support every argument with reference to Scripture and be able to tie together the Old and New Covenant Scriptures in the manner displayed by the Apostle Paul.

OT Preachers as Examples for Paul

Paul's quotation of Isa 52:17 in Rom 10:15 ("How beautiful the feet of the ones evangelizing good things!" AT) shows "... that his notion of *euangelion* is heavily dependant on the OT idea of God's herald and his message."[26] This observation is so obvious that Ford's insistence that Israel came into being without preaching seems ludicrous.[27] The OT plainly shows that Moses (through Aaron) delivered the laws of God orally to the captives in Egypt (Exod 4:15–16; 7:11), and without such preaching it is doubtful that the nation of Israel would have ever emerged. Moses later overcame his reticence by preaching personally to the people of God (Deut 1:11), calling on Israel to listen to the coming Prophet (*nabhi*) who like him would speak all that the Lord commanded him (Deut 18:15–18), for "the *Nabhi* was a speaker who declared the [W]ord God had given him."[28]

However, not every OT preacher was a prophet. Clowney distinguishes between the prophetic, mediatorial ministry of conveying God's Word to the people (Exod 20:19) from the regular teaching of the revealed Word.[29] The former duty was con-

---

23. Ellis, *Paul's Use of the Old Testament*, 11. See also Steve Moyise, *Paul and Scripture: Studying the New Testament Use of the Old Testament* (2010).
24. Hays, *Echoes of Scripture in the Letters of Paul* (1989).
25. Kuist, *The Pedagogy of Paul*, 53.
26. Fitzmyer, *To Advance the Gospel*, 159.
27. Ford, *Ministry of the Word*, 39.
28. Young, *My Servants the Prophets*, 60.
29. Clowney, *Preaching and Biblical Theology*, 48–49.

fined to the prophets, whereas the latter was exercised by the judges and elders, who were not to add to the Word but to enact it (Deut 4:2; 12:32). Clearly Ezra and his helpers fall into this latter category (Neh 8:5–8). The distinction between the prophet and the teacher carries across into Paul's thinking because he sees himself as a continuation of the OT prophet—he places himself in company with David in that he delivers the Word of God, as he asserts, "Having the same spirit of faith, according to what has been written, 'I believed, so I spoke,' also we believed and so we are speaking" (2 Cor 4:13, quoting Ps 116:10, AT). However, Paul is also a teacher of the revealed Word, and it is in this connection that Timothy is to understand the exhortation to "preach the Word." As James wants his readers to take the OT prophets as examples of suffering and patience (Jam 5:10[30]), so Paul cites the events of OT redemptive history as "example[s], . . . written for our instruction, upon whom the ends of the ages have come" (1 Cor 10:11).

The application to the New Covenant preacher is very clear. As the OT preachers were faithful in declaring the Word of God, so too should Paul's protégés preach the Word by use of the examples of OT personalities and events, because those prophets "predicted the sufferings of Christ and the glories to follow," as 1 Pet 1:11 explains.

OT Finality of *Graphē*: "It is Written!"

Since the arrival of the New Covenant signals that "the ends of the ages have come" (1 Cor 10:11), the historical completion of redemptive history also determines Paul's understanding of the finality of the Scriptures. Paul states his conviction succinctly: "Now these things, brethren, I have figuratively applied to myself and Apollos for your sakes, that in us you might learn not to exceed what is written. . ." (1 Cor 4:6). By use of the passive verb, *gegraptai*, Paul casts the concept of "what has been written" into permanent form.[31] When he begins a statement with the formula, "It is written," Paul gives the OT perennial validity and appeals to the completeness and authority of Scripture.[32]

---

30. James 5:10, "As an example, brethren, of suffering and patience, take the prophets who spoke in the name of the Lord."

31. The NT uses the perfect passive γέγραπται sixty-seven times, and of those, sixty-five refer to the authoritative nature of the OT (Matt 2:5; 4:4, 6, 7, 10; 11:10; 21:13; 26:24, 31; Mark 1:2; 7:6; 9:12, 13; 11:17; 14:21, 27; Luke 2:23; 3:4; 4:4, 8, 10; 7:27; 10:26; 19:46; 24:46; John 8:17; 20:31; Acts 1:20; 7:42; 13:33; 15:15; 23:5; Rom 1:17; 2:24; 3:4, 10; 4:17; 8:36; 9:13, 33; 10:15; 11:8, 26; 12:19; 14:11; 15:3, 9, 21; 1 Cor 1:19, 31; 2:9; 3:19; 4:6; 9:9; 10:7; 14:21; 15:45; 2 Cor 8:15; 9:9; Gal 3:10, 13; 4:22, 27; Heb 10:7; 1 Pet 1:16). The only two exceptions are Rev 13:8 and 17:8, which refer to the names written in the book of life. BDAG § 1687 notes, "Esp. freq. is the perf. γέγραπται (abundantly attested as a legal expr.: Dssm., B 109f, NB 77f [BS 112ff, 249f]; Thieme 22. Cp. also 2 Esdr 20:35, 37; Job 42:17a; Jos., Vi. 342) as a formula introducing quotations fr. the OT . . . ."

32. The perfect passive γέγραπται appears 31 times in Paul's letters, almost always introducing the fulfillment of an OT quotation (Rom 1:17; 2:24; 3:4, 10; 4:17; 8:36; 9:13, 33; 10:15; 11:8, 26; 12:19; 14:11; 15:3, 9, 21; 1 Cor 1:19, 31; 2:9; 3:19; 4:6; 9:9; 10:7; 14:21; 15:45; 2 Cor 8:15; 9:9; Gal 3:10, 13; 4:22, 27).

It is a similar undergirding that his preaching is grounded on "what has been written" that gives the preacher confidence in his own preaching. Whatever success he might have in preaching, it is only possible because he can claim the same finality for his preaching as certainly as Paul found assurance in Isa 52:16, "As it is written, 'They who had no news of Him shall see, And they who have not heard shall understand'" (quoted in Rom 15:21). Such finality bolsters the concept of the preacher's authority, which has already been discussed in chapter 1.

The Dynamic of OT *Graphē*

While Paul emphatically views the Scripture as complete, it is not a static book. His preaching of Scripture is not merely the retelling of past events, for to Paul, a continuing dynamic of Scripture exists. It not only "has been written" (*gegraptai*, 1 Cor 2:9), but also "it is speaking" (*legei*, Eph 4:8).[33] In this regard, Paul cites the prophets as if they are still speaking although they had been dead for centuries: Isaiah not only "is saying" (*legei*, Rom 10:16, 20; 15:12) but also he "is crying" (*krazei*, Rom 9:27), as David also "is saying" (*legei*, Rom 11:9). Likewise, Moses not only continues to speak (*legei*, Rom 10:19), but he even continues to write (*graphei*, Rom 10:5)! By far, the most dynamic preacher of the OT is the Scripture itself, as Paul asserts, "The Scripture, foreseeing that God would justify the Gentiles by faith, preached the gospel beforehand to Abraham" (Gal 3:8). This fascinating illustration pictures the *Graphē* as itself an evangelist proclaiming the gospel, in that what has been written is also currently speaking.[34] The vehicle through which the Word is speaking is the preacher, and this important concept will be considered in detail in the chapter 15, The Preacher's Dynamic.

Summary to Preaching the Content of OT *Graphē*

Paul's understanding of *Graphē* as being the repository of the Word of God is extremely important for the post-apostolic preacher. By commanding Timothy to "preach the Word," Paul surely means that his colleague is to preach the *Graphē*, the inscripturated Word. This deduction cuts across the neo-orthodox assumption that the *Logos* and the *Graphē* must be sharply distinguished, in the way that Ford insists, "The Bible becomes the Word of God in preaching, and preaching becomes the Word of God

---

33. See this observation by Ellis, *Paul's Use of the Old Testament*, 22–23.

34. This personification of the OT is also shown in Rom 4:3, "For what does the Scripture say?" quoting Gen 3:15; in Rom 9:17, "For the Scripture says to Pharaoh," quoting Exod 9:16; in Rom 10:11, "For the Scripture says," quoting Isa 28:16; in Rom 11:2, "Do you not know what the Scripture says?" quoting 1 Kgs 19:10; in Gal 4:30, "But what does the Scripture say?" quoting Gen 21:10; and in 1 Tim 5:18, "For the Scripture says," quoting Deut 25:4 and Luke 10:7.

when it is informed by the Bible."³⁵ This view robs preaching of all objectiveness and robs the preacher of all confidence, for even Ford admits, "The preacher cannot even be sure that the Word of God will actually be in his preaching."³⁶ How far afield this statement is from Paul's assured command to Timothy, "Preach the Word!" The Word to which he refers has permanent form: the *Logos* is now also the *Graphē*, the recorded Scripture, so that the preacher is bound to the written *Logos* as the *Graphē* for his primary text for preaching.

The Content of Preaching: The *Logos* of the Kingdom of God

This insistence on the content of preaching of the Word as *Graphē* should not to be taken as a separation of the Word from history. The drama of redemption is played out on the stage of human history, appearing in the over-riding concept of the Kingdom of God, which Paul mentions in 2 Tim 4:1 when he charges Timothy to preach the Word because of Christ's "appearing and His kingdom." The link, then, between the Word (*Logos*) and the Kingdom (*Baseleia*) is unmistakable; in fact, the Kingdom becomes the historical framework in which the Word is revealed. Furthermore, the Kingdom concept serves as the bridge between the Old and New Covenants.

The Kingdom of God was previously discussed in chapter 2, where it was shown that the reason why the subject matter of apostolic preaching moved from the Kingdom to the Christ is because the King has now arrived in the Messianic ministry of Jesus. As Mounce notes, "To preach Christ is to preach the Kingdom."³⁷ Due to His death, resurrection, and ascension, "the risen Christ whom the apostles proclaimed is actually the kingdom of God come with power which Jesus proclaimed."³⁸

An exegetical link between Kingdom and Word as the preacher's content appears in Acts 28:31, where Paul was "preaching the kingdom of God, and teaching concerning the Lord Jesus Christ with all openness, unhindered." This conclusion to the Book of Acts serves as a reminder that the gospel content must not be separated from the historical and theological foundation of the Kingdom. The preacher should preach Christ within the confines of the Kingdom as it unfolds progressively, covenantally, and eschatologically, binding the Old and New Testaments under the broad concept of the Kingdom as the sovereign reign of God mediated in Jesus as the Prince³⁹ designated to sit "at the right hand of Majesty on high" (Heb 1:3).

---

35. Ford, *The Ministry of the Word*, 103.
36. Ibid., 107.
37. Mounce, *Essential Nature*, 52.
38. Ford, *Ministry of the Word*, 51–52.
39. Jesus is called *archēgos* in Acts 3:15; 5:31; Heb 2:10; 12:2. BDAG § 1154 translates ἀρχηγός as "Prince" in Acts 3:15 and 5:31; and as "Founder" in Heb 2:10 and 12:2.

The Content of Preaching: The *Logos* of the New Covenant

Of course, the OT *Graphē*, as revealed in the *Baseleia*, is incomplete apart from the fulfillment of the New Covenant, so that the preaching of the Word definitely includes the *Logos* of apostolic doctrine, which today we know as the written New Testament. For that matter, most Christian preaching today is of necessity taken from the books of the NT. Like the OT, the NT also claims to be the revealed *Logos* of God (2 Thess 2:13), and Jesus Himself attributes prophetic authority to its writers (John 16:13). Still, this fact raises the question, whether there is a difference between the prophetic preaching of the apostles and that of post-apostolic preachers who follow after Timothy. Some would insist that there is no difference, that both are pneumatically inspired with the gift of prophecy so that both apostles and preachers speak the Word of God immediately. Yet even Paul, who describes himself as a preacher (1 Tim 2:7; 2 Tim 1:11), never ascribes to himself the title of a prophet,[40] although he claimed to have received prophetic revelation (Gal 1:12; Eph 3:3). What then is the relationship between prophecy and preaching?

New Covenant Prophecy as the Content of Preaching

The NT clearly records that the early church was instructed by those who were endowed with the gift of prophecy,[41] which is listed by Paul among the pneumatic gifts (Rom 12:6; 1 Cor 12:10; 1 Thess 5:20; 1 Tim 1:18; 4:14). Although Paul distinguishes between teaching and prophecy in 1 Cor 14:6,[42] he makes it clear that prophesying is the greatest of the speaking gifts (1 Cor 14:5).[43] Such emphasis raises the question whether God continues to gift His church with such prophets so that a preacher could also consider his preaching as the delivery of prophecy. This question is far more crucial than it may appear: if a preacher possesses a prophetic ability, then his words become as authoritative as that of the original NT prophets. Thus, the NT writings become merely the first of many records of revelation, but is this what Paul meant by telling Timothy to preach the Word? Presumably, he could have charged him,

---

40. The closest Paul comes to claiming himself to be a prophet is found in 1 Cor 14:37, "If anyone thinks he is a prophet or spiritual, let him recognize that the things which I write to you are the Lord's commandment."

41. NT prophets include Agabus (Acts 11:27–28; 21:10); the prophets in Antioch, Barnabas, Simeon who was called Niger, Lucius of Cyrene, Manaen who had been brought up with Herod the tetrarch, and Saul/ Paul (Acts 13:1), Judas and Silas (Acts 15:32), and the four daughters of Philip (Acts 21:9). These prophets will be studied later in chapter 14 on the Preacher's Offices; for now, the issue concerns the prophecy prophesied by these prophets.

42. 1 Corinthians 14:6, "If I come to you speaking in tongues, what shall I profit you, unless I speak to you either by way of revelation or of knowledge or of prophecy or of teaching?"

43. 1 Corinthians 14:1, "Pursue love, yet desire earnestly spiritual *gifts*, but especially that you may prophesy."

'Prophecy the Word," directing Timothy and all succeeding preachers to preach new revelations of the Spirit beyond the written Word.

The issue is not whether God could give continuing revelation—being sovereign, He could certainly do so, if He desired—nor is this a matter of whether the gift of prophecy shall cease, as it eventually will (1 Cor 13:8–10, "If *there are gifts of* prophecy, they will be done away . . . when the perfect comes"). Instead, it should be noted that the prophets of the NT were a specially gifted and limited group. While every apostolic prophet was also a preacher, not every NT preacher was necessarily a prophet. This observation is borne out as one compares the special functions of NT prophets with their OT counterparts: prophets predict the future (Acts 11:28), declare judgment (Acts 13:11), use symbolic actions (Acts 21:11), and interpret previous revelation (Acts 15:32). Clearly, not every first century preacher possessed these abilities—nor have all preachers in the centuries since—and some would argue, not any, for that matter. Furthermore, Paul notes that the church is built upon "the foundation of the apostles and prophets" (Eph 2:20), implying that prophets constitute a foundational office that is not repeated, whereas the offices of teacher (Heb 5:12), pastor (Eph 4:11), and preacher (Rom 10:14) are perpetual. This observation suggests that prophecy was a gift granted exclusively during the inaugural stage of the church, for not even every first generation preacher was gifted with prophecy (1 Cor 12:10), because the gift of prophesying (Rom 12:6) is distinct from the gift of teaching (Rom 12:7), which is a gift required for each one called to preach (1 Cor 14:6). In fact, Paul treats prophesying as a particular sub-set of the gift of teaching in that its purpose "speaks to men for edification and exhortation and consolation" (1 Cor 14:3). Ellis suggests, "For Paul, prophecy apparently is a formal term embracing various kinds of inspired teaching,"[44] indicating that prophecy is immediate revelation whereas teaching is mediate revelation of prophecy that has been previously given.

If this distinction between prophecy and teaching bears out (as it appears to do), then the only way a modern preacher exercises prophecy occurs when he reads or preaches the inscripturated words of the prophets. Not being a prophet nor being gifted with prophesying, the modern preacher is not to add to the words of the prophecy of the Book (Rev 22:18–19); instead, the foundation of his preaching should be the prophecies of the Covenant prophets: his preaching is mediated indirectly through the Prophetic Word, not immediately through the inspiring ministry of the Holy Spirit. The Preacher's task is to teach the prophetic word, not to prophesy new teachings.

New Covenant Tradition (*Paradosis*) as the Content of Preaching

If the New Covenant Preacher is not a prophet nor gifted with prophecy, what constitutes the particular content of his preaching? The answer is located in the

---

44. Ellis, "The Role of the Christian Prophet," 64.

specific content of a neglected but important NT concept of apostolic tradition, or *Paradosis*, the oral instructions mentioned in 1 Cor 11:2, "Hold firmly to the traditions, just as I delivered them to you." It is this *Paradosis* as the spoken *Logos* that lies behind the written *Graphē*.

The terminology Paul uses in 1 Cor 11:2 would be recognized in the first century as a technical expression of "delivering/receiving" authoritative information.[45] Contrary to those who contend that Paul's tradition severs him from the historical Jesus,[46] this study assumes that the concept of *Paradosis* actually requires a continuity of teaching from Jesus to the apostles.[47] To Paul, tradition includes such matters as church rules (1 Cor 11:2; 2 Thess 2:15; 3:6[48]), liturgical guidelines (1 Cor 11:23–25[49]), ethical instructions (Phil 4:9; Col 2:6–7; 1 Thess 4:1; 2 Thess 3:6[50]), and specific doctrinal content (1 Cor 15:1–8; 2 Thess 2:13[51]). In short, apostolic tradition is revealed prophecy that has now become the written New Testament. *Paradosis* and *Graphē* are

---

45. See the article by Büchsel, "παραδίδωμι, παράδοσις," *TDNT* 2:169–173, as well as the examples given by Moulton and Milligan, *The Vocabulary of the Greek Testament*, § 483.

46. Those who posit discontinuity from Jesus to Paul would include such scholars as Baur, Wendt, Windish, and Bultmann, among others. See the excellent historical survey in Furnish, "The Jesus-Paul Debate," *BJRL* 47: 342–81.

47. Those who maintain a continuity between Jesus and Paul include Seeberg, Resch, Dodd, Hunter, Cullmann, and Wenham, plus other evangelical scholars. See the unpublished ThM thesis by Stout, "The New Testament Concept of Tradition," Westminster Theological Seminary, 1977.

48. 1 Corinthians 11:2, "Hold firmly to the traditions, just as I delivered them to you"; 2 Thess 2:15, "So then, brethren, stand firm and hold to the traditions which you were taught, whether by word *of mouth* or by letter from us"; 2 Thess 3:6, "Now we command you, brethren, in the name of our Lord Jesus Christ, that you keep aloof from every brother who leads an unruly life and not according to the tradition which you received from us."

49. 1 Corinthians 11:23–25, "For I received from the Lord that which I also delivered to you, that the Lord Jesus in the night in which He was betrayed took bread; and when He had given thanks, He broke it, and said, "This is My body, which is for you; do this in remembrance of Me." In the same way *He took* the cup also, after supper, saying, "This cup is the new covenant in My blood; do this, as often as you drink *it*, in remembrance of Me.""

50. Philippians 4:9, "The things you have learned and *received* and heard and seen in me, practice these things"; Col 2:6–7, "As you therefore have *received* Christ Jesus the Lord, *so* walk in Him, having been firmly rooted and now being built up in Him and established in your faith, just as you were instructed, and overflowing with gratitude"; 1 Thess 4:1, "Finally then, brethren, we request and exhort you in the Lord Jesus, that, as you *received* from us instruction as to how you ought to walk and please God (just as you actually do walk)"; 2 Thess 3:6, "Now we command you, brethren, in the name of our Lord Jesus Christ, that you keep aloof from every brother who leads an unruly life and not according to the *tradition* which you *received* from us."

51. 1 Corinthians 15:1–5, "Now I make known to you, brethren, the gospel which I preached to you, which also you *received*, in which also you stand, by which also you are saved, if you hold fast the word which I preached to you, unless you believed in vain. For I *delivered* to you as of first importance what I also *received*, that Christ died for our sins according to the Scriptures, and that He was buried, and that He was raised on the third day according to the Scriptures, and that He appeared to Cephas. . . ."; 1 Thess 2:13, "When you *received* from us the word of God's message, you accepted *it* not *as* the word of men, but *for* what it really is, the word of God. . . ."

now one and the same, as the traditions have been inscripturated, and it is this tradition that is to be delivered by the preacher for the hearers to receive.

New Covenant Deposit (*Parthēkē*) as the Content of Preaching

The finality of Tradition is shown when Paul uses another similar concept, that of The Deposit (*Parthēkē*), referring to a possession that is entrusted to another for safekeeping and to be returned upon request.[52] Timothy is to "guard the deposit" (1 Tim 6:20) "through the Holy Spirit" (1 Tim 1:18). Paul is convinced that Christ "is able to guard what I have entrusted to Him until that day" (2 Tim 1:12),[53] and the context[54] suggests that Christ has first entrusted the gospel as a deposit to the apostle who in turn entrusts it back to the Lord and also on to Timothy (2 Tim 1:14[55]). In any case, Paul knows he must hand back the entrusted gospel on the day when Christ demands its return. Likewise, Timothy is to entrust (*paratithēmi*) the things he has heard from Paul to faithful men, who will be able to teach others also (2 Tim 2:2).

Parthēkē stresses the completeness of the content: the preacher is not to search for preaching texts outside of the deposit that has been originally entrusted in "the words spoken beforehand by the holy prophets and the commandment of the Lord and Savior *spoken* by your apostles" (2 Pet 3:2) but are now inscribed in "the sacred Scriptures" (2 Tim 3:15). The New Covenant Preacher serves as a steward of God's mysteries that have been handed down to him (1 Cor 4:1), and this idea of stewardship "implies that the preacher does not supply his own message: he is supplied with it."[56] In this chain of revelation, the Word of the New Covenant is revealed initially by NT Prophecy, which becomes apostolic Tradition to be delivered and received, and then it is inscripturated as The Deposit. The contemporary preacher of the New Covenant, then, stands alongside Timothy, who is to confine his content of preaching to The Deposit of the gospel as it has been revealed to the Covenant apostles and prophets.

---

52. Mauer, παρατίθημι, *TDNT* 8:162; also BDAG § 5640.3, "to entrust for safekeeping, give over, entrust, commend."

53. The NET translates δυνατός ἐστιν τὴν παραθήκην μου φυλάξαι εἰς ἐκείνην τὴν ἡμέραν, "He is able to protect what has been entrusted to me until that day." At issue is how to understand "my deposit," whether as Paul's deposit to Christ or as Christ's deposit to Paul. By use of *parathēkē*, the apostle may have both aspects in mind.

54. Paul mentions in 1 Tim 1:11 that he was entrusted by God with the gospel by use of the passive voice of *pisteueō*, also used in this manner in Rom 3:2; 1 Cor 9:17–18; Gal 2:7; and 1 Thess 2:4.

55. 2 Timothy 1:14, "Guard through the Holy Spirit who dwells in us, the treasure (παραθήκην) which has been entrusted to *you*."

56. Stott, *Preacher's Portrait*, 23.

Summary of Content as New Covenant *Logos*

So then, when Paul commands Timothy, "Preach the Word," the younger understudy would understand his apostolic mentor to refer to the revealed prophecies of the gospel message that were first delivered by the Lord Jesus as oral tradition (*Paradosis*) and then inscribed by the NT apostles[57] and prophets as the written Deposit (*Parthēkē*) through the Holy Spirit's mediation. This process eventually produced the existing New Testament,[58] which, along with the Old Testament, defines the boundaries of preaching: it is not to go beyond what has been revealed, meaning that the preacher does not cull his topics from texts outside the Word of God. He is free to expound on the disciplines of science and the humanities only so far as the Word of God touches on these areas, and only in an illustrative way, in the manner that Paul uses Greek religion and philosophy in his message before the Areopagus (Acts 17:22–34). As Paul brings a "woe" upon himself if he does not preach the gospel (1 Cor 9:16), so the preacher should not discourse on any other topic apart from the Word of God, for to do so would violate his cardinal charge: "Preach the Word!"

The Content of Preaching: The *Logos* of Truth

One may object that such a limitation in preaching shackles the preacher; after all, is not all truth God's truth?[59] If a matter proves to be true in some human endeavor, should it not be preached? Such sentiment is particularly expressed with regard to human psychology, in the way that preachers constantly incorporate into their preaching the most recent theory of behavior, such as the transactionalism fad of the 1970's ("I'm OK: You're OK") to the feel-good messages of various popular TV preachers.[60]

Would Paul have agreed that every claim to truth is gospel truth? Decidedly not, as his repeated warnings against false teaching suggest that what the heretic deems to be true is not at all true for the apostle (Gal 1:8–9; 2 Thess 2:9; 1 Tim 4:2; 6:20). The content of false apostles must be judged by the content of the true gospel (2 Cor

---

57. The identity of the NT apostles will be discussed in fuller detail in chapter 14 on the Preacher's Offices.

58. This point is argued quite persuasively by David Trobisch, *The First Edition of the New Testament* (2000), as he studies the editing evidence of the NT manuscripts, which includes the title of the entire volume (ἡ καινὴ διαθήκη), the consistent titles of each 'chapter' (the individual books), and the general uniformity of these chapters (Gospels, Acts-General Epistles, Paul, and Revelation). All this consistency shows a deliberate editing process, which could have been completed before the end of the first century. Since we know that Timothy had been entrusted with "the parchments" (2 Tim 4:13), which presumably included Paul's copies of his letters plus other New Covenant writings, it is not unreasonable to assume he had a hand in this early editing.

59. This phrase was popularized by Frank Gaebelein's 1968 book, *The Pattern of God's Truth*, 20. While his thesis is quite biblical, others have stretched the concept to mean that even the knowledge of sin is God's truth.

60. See also, for example, Louis Tice, *Investment in Excellence* (1983).

11:13), and for this reason Paul frequently appeals to the content of his message as "the truth"[61] that is being presented "in truth."[62]

Paul's emphasis on truth is especially pertinent when he refers to "the truth of the gospel" (Gal 2:5, 14), so that one is saved by believing upon hearing "the word of the truth of the gospel" (Gal 1:5; Eph 1:13). Timothy the preacher is called upon to "handle accurately the word of truth" (2 Tim 2:15), and this reference can only be understood as objective, propositional truth that Timothy should interpret properly. Clearly, Paul means that the written *Logos* of God is "the Truth," and he leaves no doubt regarding this fact when he describes the OT Law as "the embodiment of the truth" (Rom 2:20). Thus, when Paul writes of truth, it is "essentially the revealed truth of the gospel message," as Thiselton notes.[63]

Concerning the perennial debate over the inerrancy of Scripture,[64] this one consideration should seal the issue, for if the gospel is "the Word of the Truth" (Col 1:5), then logically it cannot contain error. If a preacher is not convinced that he preaches a Bible that is true in every respect, he will soon find other "truths" to proclaim, thus explaining why some preachers feel compelled to wander into extra-biblical subjects. What Boice observed in 1978 still remains relevant: "The current decline in preaching is due . . . to a prior decline in a belief in the Bible as the authoritative and inerrant Word of God on the part of the church's theologians, seminary professors, and those ministers who are trained by them."[65]

Conversely, since the Word is of necessity also the truth, and thus inerrant, then the preacher can takes his text from any portion of the Bible and assert with confidence the truthfulness of the passage, thus "handling accurately the Word of the truth" (2 Tim 2:15, AT). The importance of receiving the Scripture as the Word of Truth cannot be overemphasized when it comes to the content of preaching, for the preacher is called to "speak the truth in Christ" (1 Tim 2:7).

---

61. See Paul's mention of ἡ ἀλήθεια in Rom 1:18, 25; 2:8, 20; 3:7; 9:1; 15:8; 1 Cor 13:6; 2 Cor 7:14; 11:10; 12:6; 13:8; Gal 2:5, 14; 4:16; 5:7; Eph 4:15, 24; 2 Thess 2:10, 12, 13; 1 Tim 2:4, 7; 3:15; 4:3; 6:5; 2 Tim 2:18, 25; 3:7, 8; 4:4; Titus 1:1, 14.

62. As in 2 Corinthians 7:14, "We spoke all things to you in truth." See also general references to "speaking truth" (Rom 9:1); the "truth of God" (Rom 15:8); "bread of sincerity and truth" (1 Cor 5:8); "in word of truth" (2 Cor 6:7); "speaking truth" (2 Cor 7:14; 12:6; Eph 4:25; 1 Tim 2:7a); "truth of Christ" (2 Cor 11:10); "truth is in Jesus" (Eph 4:21); "fruit of the light *consists* in all goodness and righteousness and truth" (Eph 5:9); "gird your loins with truth" (Eph 6:14); "in truth, Christ is proclaimed" (Phil 1:18); "you understood the grace of God in truth" (Col 1:6); "faith in truth" (1 Thess 2:13); "knowledge of truth" (1 Tim 2:4; 2 Tim 2:25; 3:7; Titus 1:1); "a teacher of the Gentiles in faith and truth" (1 Tim 2:7b).

63. Thiselton, "Truth," *DNTT* 3:887.

64. As chronicled in Gregory K. Beale, *The Erosion of Inerrancy in Evangelicalism: Responding to New Challenges to Biblical Authority* (2008). Also, see the articles in *JETS* (March 2014), 5–62.

65. Boice, "The Preacher and God's Word," 125. See also Craig Blomberg, *Can We Still Believe the Bible?*, chapter four, "Don't These issues Rule out Biblical Inerrancy?"

The Content of Preaching: The *Logos* unto Salvation

Once the preacher is convinced that his message is the Truth of God's revelation, he is then in a position to preach; however, he must know the specific content of the Word, especially since the Word of God has a two-fold application, whether it is addressed to the unbelieving world or to the believing community. Chapter 9 will examine the concept of the Preacher's audience in greater depth, but it needs to be observed that the emphasis of content changes somewhat depending on whether the listeners are Christian or not. These broad categories could be classed as evangelism (the word to the unsaved) and edification (the word to the church). Obviously, there is much overlap; the message is the same although the emphasis differs. Accordingly, the following section will examine the content of the gospel preached to the unbelieving world as what Paul calls "the word of salvation" (*ho logos tēs sōtērias tautēs*, Acts 13:26)

The Gospel of Salvation: *Euangelion*

As will be demonstrated in chapter 4, the activity of evangelizing is directed primarily at the unsaved, when an evangelist tells unbelievers the good news of the Lord Jesus (Acts 5:42; 11:20). Evangelizing presents the facts of the Evangel so that the light of the gospel will shine in the hearts of the blinded, producing faith and repentance (2 Cor 4:2–6).

The noun *euangelion* derives from the verb *euangelizein*, which BDAG defines in its basic sense as "announcing good news."[66] The noun, then, refers to "the message of victory or personal news that causes joy."[67] In Paul's letters, the secular use of the term has nearly disappeared and its meaning almost exclusively defines the Christian message: this fact is noted in the number of times that Paul uses the noun without any further description or explanation.[68] Paul makes very clear that the word of the

---

66. BDAG § 3197 εὐαγγελίζω 1. "gener. bring good news, announce good news."
67. Becker, "Gospel," *DNTT* 2:107.
68. The *uses loquendi* of the 70 appearances of εὐαγγέλιον in Paul's letters can be organized as follows:
   1. another (false) gospel (2 Cor 11:14; Gal 1:6);
   2. the gospel, without description (Rom 10:16; 11:28; 1 Cor 4:15; 9:14; 9:18; 9:23; 15:1; 2 Cor 8:18; Gal 1:11; 2:2; Eph 3:6; Phil 1:5; 1:7, 1:16; 2:22; 4:3; 1 Thess 2:4);
   3. the gospel, preceded by some description: the truth word of the gospel (Gal 2:5; 2:14; Eph 1:13); the mystery of the gospel (Eph 6:19); the defense and confirmation of the gospel (Phil 1:10); the furtherance of the gospel (Phil 1:12); the faith of the gospel (Phil 1:27); the beginning of the gospel (Phil 4:15); the word of the truth of the gospel (Col 1:23); the hope of the gospel (Col 1:23); suffering for the gospel (2 Tim 1:8); imprisonment for the gospel (Phlm 1:13); my gospel (Rom 2:16; 16:25; 2 Tim 2:8);
   4. The gospel with a following description: the gospel of us (2 Cor 4:3; 1 Thess 1:5; 2 Thess 2:14); the gospel to the uncircumcised (Gal 2:7); the gospel of your salvation (Eph 1:13); the gospel of peace (Eph 6:15); the gospel of God (Rom 1:1; 15:16; 1 Thess 2:2; 2:8; 2:9); the gospel of His Son (Rom 1:9); the gospel of Christ (Rom 15:19; 15:29?; 1 Cor 9:12; 9:18; 2 Cor 2:12; 9:13;

euangelion has become his primary message when he makes known "the gospel which I preached to you, which also you received, in which also you stand, by which also you are saved, if you hold fast the word which I preached to you, unless you believed in vain, for I delivered [it] to you as of first importance" (1 Cor 15:1–3).

What then is the content of Paul's *euangelion*? Grasso gives the simplest definition, stating, "The content of the Gospel, therefore, is a Person, God in Christ, or simply Christ in whom God reveals Himself and saves."[69] While these observations are generally true, they need some propositional substance, for what Paul proclaims is not only the person of Jesus Christ but also what He did, as stated in 1 Cor 1:23, "We preach Christ crucified." In a more helpful study, Fitzmyer notes that the use of *euangelion* is ". . . almost distinctly a Pauline concept in usage, with the vast majority of uses denoting the content of the apostolic message."[70] However, a perusal of the Paul's use of *euangelion* shows that the concept is far-ranging, and Fitzmyer summarizes the nuances by stating, "The Gospel, par excellence, is Paul's personal way of summing up the significance of the Christ-event, the meaning that the person, life, ministry, passion, death, resurrection and lordship of Jesus of Nazareth had and still has for human history and existence."[71] Noting that Paul uses "gospel" absolutely some twenty-three times without any modifiers, Friedrich observes that ". . . for Paul, the heart of the good news is the story of Jesus and His suffering, death and resurrection. Everything connected with this may be preaching of the Gospel."[72]

While there is a dynamic aspect to the gospel as "the power of God unto salvation" (Rom 1:16),[73] it is not merely the act of preaching that saves, but it is the declared content of the gospel that brings salvation, especially offering the Person of Jesus Christ and His work in history—particularly His death for sins, His burial, His resurrection the third day, and His subsequent appearances, as outlined in 1 Cor 15:3–8. When Christ in these saving activities is preached and believed, then the gospel brings salvation. This being the case, it is then the business of the preacher to devote himself to the content of the *euangelion*: he needs to know what constitutes the gospel so that

---

10:14; 11:7; Gal 1:7; Phil 1:27; 1 Thess 3:2; 2 Thess 1:8); the gospel of the glory of Christ (2 Cor 4:4); the glorious gospel of the blessed God (1 Tim 1:11); the gospel . . . is the power of God for salvation (Rom 1:16).

69. Grasso, *Proclaiming God's Message*, 7.

70. Fitzmyer, "The Gospel in the Theology of Paul," 151. In this article, Fitzmyer identifies these main characteristics in the gospel, that it is revelatory, dynamic, kerygmatic (Rom 1:16; 1 Thess 1:5; 2:13), normative (the gospel stands over the church), promissory (Rom 1:2), and universal (Rom 1:16).

71. Ibid.

72. Friedrich, εὐαγγελίζω, *TDNT* 2:730.

73. For example, Baird, "What is the Kerygma," 188, insists that "to preach the gospel is to preach Christ that He might confront the hearer and call him to decision." This view tends to confuse the act of preaching with the message that is preached, for if preaching alone saved, then salvation would result regardless of content, which is obviously not the case. Even so, the dynamic quality of preaching is an aspect of *euangelion* that will be explored in chapter 15.

he may present it clearly to unbelievers so they may place their faith in Christ as Savior. For that matter, every sermon should at some point present enough of the basic content of the gospel so that anyone would have sufficient information to believe unto salvation. Any minister who so defines and preaches the gospel brings the risen Christ to bear upon the one who hears Him unto salvation.

The Report of Salvation: *Akoē*

Although used less frequently by Paul, a similar word expressing the content of the gospel is *akoē*.[74] Related to the verb *akouō* ("to hear"), *akoē* is actually, "the ear" (Mark 7:35), and so it connotes the act of hearing as well as the report that is heard; in fact, at times it is difficult to determine which nuance is intended, for to mention the ear implies the report heard by the ear.[75]

What is evident is that Paul selects *akoē* when he wants to emphasize the audible effects of the preached gospel when it is heard and received by faith. For example, in answer to the objection that "not all obeyed the gospel," Paul quotes Isaiah's complaint, "LORD, who has believed our report?" (Rom 10:16, quoting Isa 53:1). Paul answers, "So then, faith [is] out of report (*akoēs*) and the report (*akoē*) [is] through word of Christ" (Rom 10:17, AT), thus showing the dynamic effect of the message when it is heard: it engenders faith, as the report itself is mediated through the Word of Christ—as if Christ Himself speaks the report. Similarly, Paul asks the Galatians, "Did you receive the Spirit by the works of the Law, or by report (*akoēs*) of faith?" (Gal 3:2, AT). The answer is obvious: the source of the received Holy Spirit is by the report of faith, which Mundle defines as "the apostolic message which (*sic*) has faith as its content and is spoken and received as God's Word."[76] The equation of the report with

---

74. Paul uses ἀκοή ten times: Rom 10:16, "However, they did not all heed the glad tidings; for Isaiah says, "LORD, who has believed our report?"; Rom 10:17, "So faith *comes* from hearing, and hearing by the word of Christ"; 1 Cor 12:17, "If the whole body were an eye, where would the hearing be? If the whole were hearing, where would the sense of smell be?"; Gal 3:2, "This is the only thing I want to find out from you: did you receive the Spirit by the works of the Law, or by hearing with faith?"; Gal 3:5, "Does He then, who provides you with the Spirit and works miracles among you, do it by the works of the Law, or by hearing with faith?"; 1 Thess 2:13, "And for this reason we also constantly thank God that when you received from us the word of God's message, you accepted *it* not *as* the word of men, but *for* what it really is, the word of God, which also performs its work in you who believe"; 2 Tim 4:3, "For the time will come when they will not endure sound doctrine; but *wanting* to have their ears tickled, they will accumulate for themselves teachers in accordance to their own desires"; 2 Tim 4:4, "They will turn away their ears from the truth, and will turn aside to myths."

75. BDAG § 270, lists these usages of ἀκοή:
 1. the faculty of hearing (1 Cor 12:17);
 2. the act of hearing, *listening* (2 Pet 2:8; Matt 13:14; Acts 28:26; Gal 3:2, 5);
 3. the organ with which one hears, *ear* (Mark 7:35; Acts 17:20; Luke 7:1; Heb 5:11; 2 Tim 4:3);
 4. that which is heard: a. *fame, report, rumor* (Matt 4:24; 14:1; 24:6; Mark 1:28; 13:7); b. *account, report, message* (John 12:38; Rom 10:16–17; Gal 3:2, 5; Heb 4:2; 1 Thess 2:13).

76. Mundle, ἀκοή, *DNTT*, 2:175.

the Word is verified when Paul notes that his listeners had "received from us the word of God's *akoē*" (1 Thess 2:13). The selection of this word *akoē* shows that the gospel is an audible report that needs to be heard—and thus needs to be preached.

The Proclamation of Salvation: *Kērygma*

Another word Paul uses to express the content of the gospel is that of *kērygma*, "public proclamation,"[77] although the word is found only six times in his letters and only that many more times in the rest of the Greek Bible.[78] Despite this infrequency, Dodd claims that *kērygma* should be the primary designation for the preached word, and while his insistence seems a bit overreaching, his mid-twentieth century studies certainly paved the way for reviewed interest in the content of the gospel.[79] Dodd made a helpful distinction between *kērygma* (preaching) and *didachē* (teaching), defining *kērygma* as the "public proclamation of Christianity to the non-Christian world."[80] He insisted that Paul distinguished the fundamental gospel from higher wisdom that he identified with the *didachē*, so that the Pauline *kērygma* is "a proclamation of the facts of the death and resurrection of Christ in an eschatological setting which gives significance to the facts."[81]

A major oversight of Dodd's investigation, however, is that he does not actually examine every instance of *kērygma* in the NT! He lays himself open to Baird's criticism that his thesis seems to be "more a technical term of modern biblical theology than of the Bible itself."[82] In Dodd's defense, some of the difficulty arises because

---

77. BDAG § 4230, defines κήρυγμα as 1. an official announcement and 2. a public declaration.

78. *Kērygma* appears in 2 Chron 30:5, "So they established a decree (*kērygma*) to circulate a proclamation throughout all Israel from Beersheba even to Dan, that they should come to celebrate the Passover to the LORD God of Israel at Jerusalem"; Prov 9:3, "He has sent out her maidens, she calls From the tops of the heights (*kērygma*) of the city"; Jonah 3:2, "Arise, go to Nineveh the great city and proclaim to it the proclamation (*kērygma*) which I am going to tell you"; Matt 12:41 ‖ Luke 11:32, "The men of Nineveh shall stand up with this generation at the judgment, and shall condemn it because they repented at the preaching (*kērygma*) of Jonah"; Mark 16:20, "Jesus Himself sent out through them from east to west the sacred and imperishable proclamation (*kērygma*) of eternal salvation."; Rom 16:25, "Now to Him who is able to establish you according to my gospel and the preaching (*kērygma*) of Jesus Christ"; 1 Cor 1:2, "God was well-pleased through the foolishness of the message preached (*kērygma*) to save those who believe"; 1 Cor 2:4, "And my message and my preaching (*kērygma*) were not in persuasive words of wisdom, but in demonstration of the Spirit and of power"; 1 Cor 15:14, "If Christ has not been raised, then our preaching (*kērygma*) is vain"; 2 Tim 4:17, "But the Lord stood with me, and strengthened me, in order that through me the proclamation (*kērygma*) might be fully accomplished, and that all the Gentiles might hear"; Titus 1:3; "God . . . at the proper time manifested, *even* His word, in the proclamation (*kērygma*) with which I was entrusted according to the commandment of God our Savior."

79. Dodd, *Apostolic Preaching and its Developments* (1947); *According to the Scriptures: the Substructure of New Testament Theology* (1953).

80. Dodd, *Apostolic Preaching*, 7.

81. Ibid., 13.

82. Baird, "What is the Kerygma?", 184.

the word *kērygma* can express either the content or the activity of preaching;[83] for example, Friedrich stresses that *kērygma* is the "act of proclamation, but not excluding the message."[84] Not surprisingly, then, scholars have disagreed whether Paul refers to the act or the content of preaching when he uses *kērygma*, so a closer look at the specific instances is warranted:

Romans 16:25. Here Paul states, "Now to Him who is able to establish you according to my gospel (*euangelion moū*) and the preaching of Jesus Christ (*to kērugma 'Iēsoū Christoū*). . . . " Is this genitive construction subjective (the preaching *by* Jesus) or objective (the preaching *about* Jesus)? Contextually, since Paul places "preaching of Jesus Christ" in parallel with "my gospel," it would appear that he refers to the objective message, because it is not by the mere activity of preaching the gospel that the listeners are established but rather by the content that is preached—in this case, the gospel preached by Paul and the *kērygma* preached by Jesus (Matt 9:35, *kērussōn to euangelion*). This reference, then, shows the close connection between *euangelion* and *kērygma*, so much so that even Friedrich admits, "The gospel of Paul is identified with that which Jesus himself preached during his earthly life."[85]

1 Corinthians 1:21 reads, ". . . God was well-pleased through the foolishness of the message preached (*tou kērugmatos*) to save those who believe." Does Paul refer here to the act of preaching or to the message proclaimed? Obviously, without the message, the act of preaching is utter nonsense, so that Friedrich notes, "The context favors the sense of content ('We are preaching Christ crucified.')."[86] The *kērygma* here then refers to the content that appears to the world to be foolish, but to those who believe, it is the means (*dia*) through which salvation comes.

1 Corinthians 2:4. In 1 Cor 2:4, Paul comments, ". . . My message (*logos*) and my preaching (*kērygma*) were not in persuasive words of wisdom, but in demonstration of the Spirit and of power." While Paul emphasizes the delivery of the message (in Spirit and power), the link with *logos* shows that *kērygma* indicates that content is still primary, so that the better translation would be, "my message" (ESV).

---

83. Coenen, "Proclamation," *DNTT* 3:48, points out that the *kērygma* may show either the act of *kērygsein*, crying aloud, or the content of the announcement.

84. Friedrich, κήρυγμα, *TDNT*, 3:716.

85. Ibid. It should not be overlooked that Paul appeals in Rom 16:25 to the historical preaching ministry of Jesus, an important observation since critics often complain that Paul seldom quotes the teaching of Jesus and supposedly ignores His earthly ministry as irrelevant to his own gospel. To the contrary Paul appeals to the *kērygma* preached by Jesus as that which establishes believers. See Stout, *The Man Christ Jesus*, 105–106.

86. Friedrich, κήρυγμα, *TDNT*, 3:716, fnt. 15.

In 1 Cor 15:14, the apostle claims, "... If Christ has not been raised, then our preaching (*kērygma*) is vain...," and again the NAS rendering appears to mean that the act of preaching would be useless without the resurrection. It is clear, however, that the act of preaching is absurd at any time if the content is not true, so it seems that what Paul intends by *kērygma* here in 1 Cor 15:14 is the content of the message, the resurrection of Christ in particular. This view is implied by the NIRV, "... if Christ has not been raised, what we preach doesn't mean anything," not merely that the act of preaching is vain, but without some historical reality, the *kērygma* itself is empty.

2 Timothy 4:17 is set in the context of admonition under consideration in this study ("Preach the Word!" 4:1), so that Paul's testimony is that "... the Lord stood with me, and strengthened me, in order that through me the proclamation (*to kērygma*) might be fully accomplished, and that all the Gentiles might hear." While Friedrich thinks that the preaching office is in view,[87] Paul is much more concerned to convey the preached content of the gospel as he stood to witness before his accusers (v. 16); thus, the translation "the proclamation" (NAS) is more accurate than "my preaching" (KJV).

Titus 1:3 is the last appearance of *kērygma* in Paul's letters: "... God ... at the proper time manifested, *even* His word (*ton logon*), in the proclamation (*en kērygmtii*) with which I was entrusted according to the commandment of God our Savior." Paul intentionally selects *kērygma* to emphasize the verbal proclamation of the *logos*, because the nature of *kērygma* is that it must be announced. Friedrich, however, confuses the proclamation of the Word with the content being proclaimed when he states, "The *kērygma* is the mode in which the Divine *Logos* comes to us."[88] This view is typical of an existential explanation of the gospel, as it has latched onto *kērygma* as a description of a dynamic, non-historical aspect of NT preaching. For example, Bultmann holds that the NT is so "legend-tinted" that the only way the message can save is by an existential leap of faith beyond the message to the God of that message.[89]

However, the prior discussion of Paul's use of *kērygma* ought to show that he is preaching content, not mere experience. At this point, Dodd is correct in asserting that *kērygma* stresses content,[90] and other scholars have further defined the particularities of that content from the teachings of the NT itself (what other source is there of the gospel?). For example, Mounce delineates the *kērygma* as (1) the proclamation of the death, resurrection, and exaltation of Jesus, seen as the fulfillment of prophecy, with the ministry of Jesus assumed in most cases; (2) the resultant evaluation of Jesus

---

87. Ibid., 3:717.
88. Ibid., 3:716.
89. Bultmann, *Theology of the New Testament*, 33. Brown, *DNTT*, 3:57, gives a historical overview of this debate and takes to task Bultmann's distinction between the kerygmatic Christ and the historical Jesus.
90. Dodd, *Apostolic Preaching*, 7.

as both Lord and Christ; and (3) a summons for the hearer to repent, accompanied with the promise of forgiveness of sins.[91] He concludes that *kērygma* has a two-fold connotation: the content of the message as well as the act of proclamation.[92] Stott simplifies the suppositions of both Dodd and Mounce by defining *kērygma* as the proclamation of Jesus as Savior and Lord, accompanied with an appeal for the unbeliever to come to Him in repentance and faith.[93]

Summary: This brief overview of Paul's uses of *kērygma* indicates that the apostle has in mind not the act of preaching but the content that is preached, the theological interpretation of the life and work of Jesus—despite the rather nonsensical assertion of Grasso, that the *kērygma* is "the pure Christian message, unfiltered by any theological categories."[94] Surely, he does not mean that Paul is devoid of any theology! Instead, Mounce defines *kērygma* as "a systematic theological statement,"[95] and the particularities will be explored in the next section. Baird comments, "The factual character of the proclamation should not come as a surprise, since it has been long held that Christianity is a historical religion. God has acted in history, and the communication of that revelation inevitably involves the announcement of what God has done."[96]

Paul insists that is it is necessary for the preacher to know the apostolic *kērygma* in order that he may proclaim it accurately. What are the essential elements of this *kērygma*?

The Proclamation of Reconciliation: *katallagē kērygma*

These specifics can best be described under the heading of reconciliation (*katallagē*). Even though Paul uses this noun only four times,[97] the concept encompasses the entire Pauline message, as the apostle notes, "God . . . committed to us the word of the reconciliation" (2 Cor 5:19). The word *katallagē* is defined as "the restoration of

---

91. Mounce, *Essential Nature*, 77.
92. Ibid., 55.
93. Stott, *Preacher's Portrait*, 41.
94. Grasso, *Proclaiming God's Message*, 234. Probably he means that the gospel should not be subjected to dogmatic biases besides those given in the NT, but his statement does not make such a distinction.
95. Mounce, *Essential Nature*, 76.
96. Baird, "What is the Kerygma?", 187.
97. Romans 5:11, "We also exult in God through our Lord Jesus Christ, through whom we have now received the reconciliation" (τὴν καταλλαγὴν); Rom 11:15, "If their rejection be the reconciliation (καταλλαγὴ) of the world, what will *their* acceptance be but life from the dead?"; (2 Cor 5:18–19, "God, who reconciled us to Himself through Christ, and gave us the ministry of reconciliation (τὴν διακονίαν τῆς καταλλαγῆς), namely, that God was in Christ reconciling the world to Himself, not counting their trespasses against them, and He has committed to us the word of reconciliation" (τὸν λόγον τῆς καταλλαγῆς).

original understanding between people after hostility or displeasure,"[98] capturing a specific nuance of the gospel in a way that the otherwise less vivid translation of "good news or report" may not.

In describing his message as "the gospel of peace" (Eph 6:15), Paul expresses the nature of the gospel's content as bringing the peace of reconciliation, and in Rom 10:15, he ties this content to that of the evangelist of *Shalom* in Isa 52:7,[99] where the apostle finds many of the themes that characterize his own message, themes that also need to be present when the modern preacher preaches to unbelievers. These themes include the need, the promise, the person, and the appeal of reconciliation:

The Need for Reconciliation: The sinner stands in great need of reconciliation with God, although he may not even be aware of that need, since ". . . our *euangelion* is veiled . . . to those who are perishing, in whose case the god of this world has blinded the minds of the unbelieving, that they might not see the light of the gospel of the glory of Christ" (2 Cor 4:3–4). The unbeliever's need is accented further because the gospel reveals the righteousness of God (Rom 1:16–17) and will expose the secrets of men on the day when God will judge all men "according to the gospel" (Rom 2:16). This sampling of verses shows that the preached content of the gospel must include mention of the judgment of God because the gospel exposes sin and renders it inexcusable. Perhaps the greatest criticism of Dodd's reconstruction of the *kērygma* is that the theme of judgment is lacking in his scheme,[100] whereas it is highly prominent in Paul's gospel.[101] One may well wonder how the threat of judgment can be considered good news; however, if one heeds the warning to escape the coming wrath, the message does indeed become good news. As an example, an alert that one's house is burning will initially be received as very bad news, but later the report would be embraced as good news to those who escaped the inferno. Accordingly, if the preacher is to impart faithfully the content of the gospel, he must not back-peddle from the implications of judgment as a reason expressing the urgent need for reconciliation with God.

The Promise of Reconciliation: A second prominent feature in the content of the gospel Paul preaches is the promise of reconciliation.[102] In his sermon before the

---

98. Vorlander, "Reconciliation," *DNTT* 3:166.

99. Romans 10:15 asks, "And how shall they preach unless they are sent? Just as it is written, 'How beautiful are the feet of those who bring glad tidings of good things,'" quoting Isaiah 52:7, "How lovely on the mountains Are the feet of him who brings good news, Who announces peace and brings good news of happiness, Who announces salvation, *And* says to Zion, 'Your God reigns!'"

100. For example, in his chapter on "The Fundamentals of Christian Theology," Dodd, *According to the Scriptures*," 111–27, gives no hint that the death of Christ is necessitated because of divine judgment on sin.

101. For example, see Rom 3:6; 1 Cor 5:12; 2 Thess 1:5; 1 Tim 5:24; 2 Tim 4:1.

102. The concept of promise (ἐπαγγελία) appears 26 times in Paul's writings in Rom 4:13, 14, 16, 20; 9:4, 8, 9; 15:8; 2 Cor 1:20; 7:1; Gal 3:14, 16, 17, 18, 21, 22, 29; 4:23, 28; Eph 1:13; 2:12; 3:6; 6:2; 1 Tim

synagogue at Pisidian Antioch, Paul states, "We preach (*euaggelizometha*) to you the good news of the promise made to the fathers" (Acts 13:32). Although many of Paul's references pertain to the OT promises now fulfilled in the coming of Jesus as Messiah, the gospel itself is "the promise of life in Christ Jesus" (2 Tim 1:1). Even though all are now "shut up in sin , . . . the promise by faith in Jesus Christ might be given to those who believe" (Gal 3:22). In keeping with this emphasis, the preacher must present the gospel in such a way as to show the historical flow of God's promise, culminating in Christ and offering salvation to "whoever calls on the name of the Lord" (Rom 10:13).

In various circles of Reformed Theology, the "free offer of the gospel" has at times met with some opposition, but it finds no rival in Paul. He indiscriminately preached Christ to Jew and Greek alike, for "the same Lord is Lord of all, abounding in riches to all who call on Him." The "allness" of the gospel promise does not bother Paul whatsoever, although he also prominently teaches that only those whom God particularly calls are in fact saved (Rom 9:11, 23–24). The solution to this mystery lies in the exclamation of Paul, "Oh, the depth of the riches both of the wisdom and knowledge of God! How unsearchable are His judgments and unfathomable His ways!" (Rom 11:33). While it is God's choice to call His elect, the preacher must still extend the promise of salvation to every listener so that "whoever believes in Him will not be disappointed" (Rom 10:11).

The Person of Reconciliation: The focus of the gospel content is, of course, the Person and Work of Jesus Christ Himself. Paul declares that God was pleased "to reveal His Son in me, that I might preach (*euaggelizomai*) Him among the Gentiles" (Gal 1:16), so that he proclaims "the unfathomable riches of Christ" (Eph 3:8). Because God has acted "through Him [Christ] to reconcile all things to Himself" (Col 1:20), Paul's gospel is thoroughly christocentric: he preaches "Christ Jesus as Lord" (2 Cor 4:5). Yet, this content is not a mere rehash of the earthly ministry of Jesus, which Paul mentions primarily by historical allusion throughout his epistles.[103] Rather, Paul focuses on "Christ crucified" (1 Cor 1:23), because reconciliation occurred when God "made peace though the blood of the cross" (Col 1:20). This theological interpretation of the crucifixion of Jesus is essential to the gospel content, as Paul notes that the gospel he preaches includes of "first importance that Christ died for our sins according to the Scriptures" (1 Cor 15:3). While it is beyond the scope of this study to examine the implications of the death of Christ (including the concepts of redemption, propitiation, and justification[104]), Paul's letters make it clear that the substitutionary

---

4:8; 2 Tim 1:1. Also, he uses the verb ἐπαγγέλλομαι (BDAG § 2832 1. "to declare to do someth. with implication of obligation to carry out what is stated, *promise, offer*.") another five times (Rom 4:21; Gal 3:19; 1 Tim 2:10; 6:21; Titus 1:2).

103. Stout, *The Man Christ Jesus*, 188–91, counts 71 separate details about the historical ministry of Jesus in Paul's sermons and letters.

104. The reader is referred to the extensive studies by Leon Morris, *The Apostolic Preaching of the*

sacrifice of Jesus lies at the core of Paul's preaching, and it must also be the core for the modern preacher as well.

In Paul's discussion of the gospel essentials, he presents an unbreakable chain of reconciliation, moving from the death and burial of Jesus to His resurrection appearances (1 Cor 15: 3–8). Clearly, the resurrection is "the ground work" of Paul's message, as Ford describes it.[105] The resurrection was so prominent in Paul's preaching that the Athenians supposed he was "evangelizing Jesus and the *Anastasis*" (Acts 17:18), as if Jesus and the resurrection were consorting deities. For Paul, there was no other Jesus to preach other than the One who was raised from the dead, although it is not the mere historical event that arrests Paul's attention; it is that he shares in the power of Christ's resurrection (Phil 3:10), so that he proclaims Christ who was "raised because of our justification" (Rom 4:25). It is impossible to separate Jesus from the resurrection He experienced on behalf of His people, so that when "Christ is preached," it is the Christ who "has been raised from the dead" (1 Cor 15:12).

The next event in Christ's history was His ascension (Luke 24:50–51), although Paul omits it from the essential content of the *euangelion* in 1 Cor 15:3–8. He does, however, include the ascension in his proclamation of reconciliation, for He preaches the ascended Christ who has been set at the right hand of God as the Lord Christ.[106] For that matter, whenever Paul refers to Jesus as Lord, he implies His ascension, as noted when he states pointedly, "We are preaching (*kerussomen*) Jesus Christ–Lord!" (2 Cor 4:5). Clowney comments, "If a man cannot believe in Christ's ascension, he cannot preach the apostolic gospel or know the power of Pentecost."[107]

The gospel, then, concerns the historical events of the death, resurrection, and ascension of Jesus, but it is history interpreted in terms of reconciliation. Ridderbos observes, "It is precisely this redemptive-historical character of the death of Christ that dominates and directs Paul's preaching as well as his explanation of the atoning power of Christ's death and resurrection."[108] The gospel is not preached unless it is presented with apostolic explanation, so that the preacher must be careful to be faithful, not just to the facts of reconciliation, but also to its meaning as presented in the NT.

The Appeal to Reconciliation: It would appear, however, that even a faithful presentation does not complete the gospel, since Paul preaches in such a way that his listeners would respond to his appeal and in fact trust in Christ: Paul expects a positive

---

Cross (1955) and *The Cross in the New Testament* (1965).

105. Ford, *The Ministry of the Word*, 58.

106. The ascension is implied in Rom 8:34, "Christ Jesus . . . , who is at the right hand of God, who also intercedes for us"; Eph 1:19–20, "The working of the strength of His might which He brought about in Christ, when He raised Him from the dead, and seated Him at His right hand in the heavenly places"; Col 3:1, "If then you have been raised up with Christ, keep seeking the things above, where Christ is, seated at the right hand of God"; and 1 Tim 3:16, that Christ was "taken up in glory."

107. Clowney, *Biblical Theology and Preaching*, 67.

108. Ridderbos, *Reconciliation and Hope*, 89.

response when he begs on behalf of Christ, "Be reconciled to God!" (2 Cor 5:20)[109] The reason for this appeal is because Paul believed that God actually saves through preaching (1 Cor 1:21); however, Stott cautions correctly that the preacher must never issue an appeal without first making the proclamation.[110] Then, the appeal comes in the manner that Paul "solemnly testified (*diamarturomenos*) of repentance and faith unto our Lord Jesus" (Acts 20:21). To this end, Paul keeps declaring (*apaggellōkē*) that "all should repent and turn to God" (Acts 26:20). The appeal is specific: "If you confess with your mouth Jesus *as* Lord, and believe in your heart that God raised Him from the dead, you shall be saved" (Rom 10:9). Dodd notes, "The Kerygma always closes with an appeal for repentance, the gift of the forgiveness, and of the Holy Spirit, the promise of salvation." So, while Schutz' observation is true (that Paul avoids making the gospel message an object of belief),[111] it is faith in the Person of the gospel message that saves. It is Christ Himself who exposes the need for reconciliation, who fulfills the promise of reconciliation, who acts to effect reconciliation, and then who answers His own appeal for reconciliation. Certainly these elements ought to be included in every public preaching of "the word of reconciliation" (2 Cor 5:19).

Summary to Preaching the Content of the *Logos* of Salvation

Having studied the key words Paul uses to express the content of his preaching (*euangelion, akoē, kērygma,* and *katallegē*), it has been seen that Paul preaches a consistent content when evangelizing the unbelieving world. This fact will be explored further when the actual structure of Paul's sermons will be examined (chapter 8), noting how he organizes his content around these elements. The application to Timothy—and modern preachers—is obvious: if one is to preach the Word to the unsaved listener, then he needs to concentrate his content on the basic ideas outlined above (Christ crucified and risen), and he must present the content in such a way that none of its truths are neglected or limited. "We proclaim Him!" announces Paul, for it is only by the crucified and resurrected Lord that the listener will be presented complete in Christ (Col 1:28).

The Content of Preaching: The *Logos* unto Edification

Whereas the sermons of Paul in the Book of Acts give illustrations of his preaching to the unbelieving world (and much helpful research has examined the evangelistic application of the gospel[112]), it is in the letters of Paul where one derives the content of

---

109. Stott, *Preacher's Portrait*, 42.

110. Ibid., 55.

111. Schutz, *Paul and the Anatomy of Apostolic Authority*, 42.

112. Such as the studies of Dodd, *Apostolic Preaching and its Developments*; Mounce, *Essential Nature of New Testament Preaching*; Morris, *The Apostolic Preaching of the Cross*; and Baird, "What is

the Word to be preached to the believing community. While it is beyond the scope of this study to develop a full Pauline Theology,[113] it is within the purpose of this work to examine what Paul called "the word of His grace which is able to edify" (Acts 20:32, AT). To that end, this section will discuss the vocabulary Paul often uses in order to ascertain the basic content of the Word as it is preached to edify the church, specifically the nouns *paraklēsis, paramuthia, didachē, didaskalia, parangelia, anagnōsis, apologia* and *bebaiōsis*.

Edification as Exhortation: *Paraklēsis*

The preacher assumes that his hearers live in the same world of suffering and anxiety as he does, and thus they need words of encouragement of God's care and concern; therefore, a theological concept Paul mentions specifically in his charge to Timothy is for him "to exhort" (*parakalēson*) in such a manner that exhortation and comfort (*paraklēsis*) become important aspects of the content of preaching.[114]

It can be argued that the ministry of *paraklēsis* is directed to those who are believers; in fact, Paul never seems to use the word with reference to unbelievers (they would have no expectation of divine comfort), but a very common expression he uses with regard to believers is, "I urge (*parakaleō*) you, brethren."[115] The basis of past salvation always lies behind this exhortation, as Paul urges ". . . by the mercies of God" (Rom 12:1), while the future of comfort lies in the impending deliverance and everlasting consolation given by grace (2 Thess 2:16). No doubt Paul knew that Jesus had described heaven as a final *paraklēsis* (Luke 16:25), which ". . . expresses the divine aid which is already lavishly granted to the members of the suffering community of Jesus by present exhortation and encouraging event and will reach its goal when the NT people of God is (*sic*) delivered out of all its tribulation."[116] If this assessment

---

the Kerygma? A Study of 1 Cor 15:3-8 and Gal 1:11-17."

113. As others have done so admirably, including: Ridderbos, *Paul: An Outline of His Theology* (1975); Fitzmyer, *Paul and His Theology: A Brief Sketch* (1989); Hay, et al, *Pauline Theology* (1993-97); Pate, *The End of the Age Has Come: The Theology of Paul* (1995); Hawthorne and Martin, eds., *Dictionary of Paul and his Letters* (1993); Dunn, *The Theology of Paul the Apostle* (1998); Gorman, *Apostle of the Crucified Lord: A Theological Introduction to Paul and His Letters* (2004); Schnelle, *Apostle Paul: His Life and Theology* (2005); Schreiner, *Paul: Apostle of God's Glory in Christ* (2006).

114. *Parakaleō* is a favorite verb of Paul, as he uses it fifty-four times in his letters (Rom 12:1, 8; 15:30; 16:17; 1 Cor 1:10; 4:13, 16; 14:31; 16:12, 15; 2 Cor 1:4, 6; 2:7, 8; 5:20; 6:1; 7:6, 7, 13; 8:6; 9:5; 10:1; 12:8, 18; 13:11; Eph 4:1; 6:22; Phil 4:2; Col 2:2; 4:8; 1 Thess 2:12; 3:2, 7; 4:1, 10, 18; 5:11, 14; 2 Thess 2:17; 3:12; 1 Tim 1:3; 2:1; 5:1; 6:2; 2 Tim 4:2; Titus 1:9; 2:6, 15; Phlm 1:9, 10). He also used *paraklēsis* another twenty times (Rom 12:8; 15:4, 5; 1 Cor 14:3; 2 Cor 1:3, 4, 5, 6, 7; 7:4, 7, 13; 8:4, 17; Phil 2:1; 1 Thess 2:3; 2 Thess 2:16; 1 Tim 4:13; Phlm 1:7).

115. Paul uses the first person indicative Παρακαλῶ ("I exhort!") fourteen times (Rom 12:1; 15:30; 16:17; 1 Cor 1:10; 4:16; 16:15; 2 Cor 2:8; 10:1; Eph 4:1; Phil 4:2; 1 Tim 2:1; Phlm 1:9, 10).

116. Schmitz and Stählin, "παρακαλέω," *TDNT* 5:777-99. They add, "*Parakaleō* may be traced back to the saving work the triune God which leads those in need of help as supplicants to the Son of God, which is preached as exhortation in the power of the Spirit of God, and which carries with it

is true—as it appears to be—then *parakaleō paraklēsis* impresses upon believers the comforting truths of the gospel as well as urging the practice of corresponding duties that accompany salvation.[117]

The Meaning of Paraklēsis: The etymological meaning of *paraklēsis* is to "call alongside," but the Bible uses the word most often in the sense of giving comfort.[118] The word was a favorite of Paul, who uses either the noun or the related verb *parakaleō* in every letter except Galatians.[119] He views *paraklēsis* as a spiritual gift (Rom 12:8) that must be evidenced by the elder so he "may be able to exhort in sound doctrine" (Titus 1:9). In this regard, the minister must "exhort with great patience and instruction" (2 Tim 4:2), never in error or impurity or deceit (1 Thess 2:3).

The God of Paraklēsis: Paul uses the noun *paraklēsis* with some frequency,[120] although for him *paraklēsis* begins with "the God of all *paraklēsis*" (2 Cor 1:3). The preacher announces this comfort when he proclaims the "God of *paraklēsis*" (Rom 15:5), referencing this divine attribute as does the prophet Isaiah, who likewise assured Israel that "the LORD will comfort (*parakalesō*) Zion; He will comfort (*paraekalesa*) all her waste places" (Isa 51:3). The Lord's Servant is anointed "to comfort (*parakalesai*) all who mourn" (Isa 61:2) in response to God's call, "Comfort, O comfort (*parakaleite*) My people" (Isa 40:1). For Paul, comfort is such an important attribute of God that he uses *paraklēsis* as a synonym for salvation (*sōterias*) in 2 Cor 1:6.

The Mediation of Paraklēsis: While Jesus specifically labels the Holy Spirit as the *Paraklēte* (John 14:16, 26; 15:26, 16:7), Paul tends to use the word as an application of the ministry, as when he urges Timothy to "give attention to 'the *paraklēsis*'" (1 Tim

---

already in this time the eternal comfort of God the Father" (Ibid.).

117. Paul uses *parakaleō* with other verbs to encourage believers to present their bodies, to strive, to watch, to agree, to imitate, to subject, to love, to walk, to be of the same mind, to please God, to pray, and to be sensible.

118. BDAG § 5590 defines παράκλησις as
   1. act of emboldening another in belief or course of action;
   2. strong request, appeal, request;
   3. lifting of another's spirits, comfort, consolation.

119. Braumann, "παρακαλέω," DNTT 1:570, finds the word used 109 times in the NT and means (a) to summon, invite, ask, implore; (b) to exhort; or (c) to comfort and encourage. It seems that whenever Paul exhorts "to do this or that," the basic meaning of the word is that of a demand. Whenever *parakaleō* is used in the context of suffering or trial, the basic meaning is that of comfort, but it may be used in either sense, depending on the context.

120. *Paraklēsis* is used of or by Paul as follows: *paraklēsis* of the Holy Spirit (Acts 9:31); a word of *paraklēsis* (Acts 13:15); the letter brought joy because of the *paraklēsis* (Acts 15:31); exhort in *paraklēsis* (Rom 12:8; 1 Tim 4:13); the *paraklēsis* of Scripture (Rom 15:4); the God of *paraklēsis* (Rom 15:5; 2 Cor 1:3); prophets speak *paraklēsis* (1 Cor 14:3); *paraklēsis* in trials (2 Cor 1:4–7; 7:4, 7, 13; 8:4, 17); *paraklēsis* in Christ (Phil 2:2); everlasting *paraklēsis* (2 Thess 2:16).

4:13); in fact, Acts 13:15 describes one of Paul's synagogue messages as a "word of *paraklēsis*," and the apostle calls upon fellow believers to encourage one another in *paraklēsis* (Rom 12:8). Although this word is not used of Jesus' preaching, *paraklēsis* does describe the preaching of Peter (Acts 2:40), Barnabas (Acts 11:23), Judas and Silas (Acts 15:32), Titus (2 Cor 7:6–7, 13), and of course, Paul (Acts 14:22; 20:2). *Paraklēsis* is thus mediated by preachers who act as comforters by bringing divine comfort to bear on human need and suffering.[121]

The Source of Paraklēsis: So where is the preacher to find these words of *paraklēsis*? The answer is that the Scripture itself is "The Encouragement" of 1 Tim 4:13,[122] as shown by the fact that spoken encouragement is an application of the written encouragement from the God of *paraklēsis* (Rom 15:4 mentions that "through the *paraklēsis* of the Scriptures we might have hope"). The encouraging God ministers the gift of encouragement when His word of *paraklēsis* is preached, so that the preacher should use the precise words of Scripture as the very encouragement of God.

The Applications of Paraklēsis: What then would be appropriate settings for sermons of *paraklēsis*? Typically, one would think of a funeral as an occasion to comfort one another with words of resurrection, as Paul does for the grieving Thessalonians (1 Thess 4:18). In the face of death, people need encouragement, but mere words alone ("Cheer up!") without any basis for hope are empty and even cruel, as Schmits observes, "For all the consoling descriptions there is at bottom a profound lack of hope or comfort in the world of antiquity."[123] Conversely, the gospel brings substantial reasons for the hope of consolation, particularly "the eternal *paraklēsis* and good hope by grace" given by "the Lord Jesus Christ Himself and God our Father" (2 Thess 2:16).

---

121. Luke offers this interesting observation, that the preached *paraklēsis* came "through many words" (Acts 15:32, διὰ λόγου πολλοῦ) and "in many words" (λόγῳ πολλῷ, Acts 20:2). Luke appears to report this lengthiness as an asset, although when Paul kept on talking late into the night, Euytchus fell asleep and then fell out his window perch (Acts 20:9). The debate will forever rage whether Luke intends to encourage awakened listeners or shorter sermons!

122. When Paul writes, "Until I come, give attention to the *public* reading *of Scripture*, to exhortation and teaching." (1 Tim 4:13), he uses three nouns as indirect objects of the verb *proseche*, so that a fairly literal translation is, "Give attention to the reading, to the encouragement, to the teaching." Paul is not referring to what activities Timothy should give attention to (reading, exhorting, teaching), but rather to the content he should give attention to, namely, the Reading, the Encouragement, and the Teaching. These are terms used elsewhere of "the reading of the Law and the Prophets" (Acts 13:15; of "the encouragement of the Scriptures" (Rom 15:4); and of the "Scripture . . . profitable for teaching" (2 Tim 3:16). In other words, Paul is telling Timothy he should devote himself to these aspects of the written Word of God.

123. As an example, Schmitz, "παρακαλέω," *TDNT* 5:787, quotes Theognis, "Best of all for mortals is never to have been born, but for those who have been born to die as soon as possible." Schmitz finds three senses all related to the *paraklēsis* accompanying salvation, as one asks for help, exhortation, and consolation.

Also, in times of great trial or deep tragedy, 'parakletic' sermons would be much in order, as they encourage listeners of God's comforting amid tribulation (2 Cor 1:4–6). Furthermore, the frequency by which Paul uses the verb *parakaleō* in contexts where he deals with practical exhortations indicates that a parakletic application is needed whenever the listeners require greater obedience to the will of God. Thus, specific areas of application of *paraklēsis* are noted when Paul urges his converts to "remain *true* to the Lord" (Acts 11:23) and "to continue in the faith" (Acts 14:22). Through such applications, the preacher brings encouragement to their hearts of his listeners (Eph 6:22; Col 2:2; Eph 4:8) as he points them to the God who "comforts the heart" (2 Thess 2:17).

Summary of Paraklēsis as Edification: When the minister recognizes that he is an instrument of divine encouragement, he finds that he has a supportive role in bringing the *paraklēsis* of Scripture to bear so that the hearers may have hope amid the discouragements of life (Rom 15:4). He "comes alongside" (as the etymology of *paraklēsis* implies) another person and brings the positive aspect of the Word to bear so that the listener can also rejoice in that encouragement (Acts 15:31). By so doing, the minister will prove that what he speaks is not merely an optimistic outlook, but a ministry of divine encouragement. In this manner, preaching as exhortation assumes that the believing community needs comfort; and so, on the basis of the comfort of salvation, the preacher encourages his hearers as he impresses upon them the comfort of Christ and urges their obedience to the imperative demanded by the call of the gospel.

Edification as Comfort: *Paramuthia*

Another noun very similar to *paraklēsis* is *paramuthia*, which could best be translated as "consolation."[124] Jesus speaks 'paramuthically' to Mary and Martha when they stood weeping before the tomb of Lazarus (John 11:19, 31), showing that the term speaks of the consoling content of the gospel, especially the promise of the Jesus, "[E]veryone who lives and believes in Me shall never die" (John 11:26). Although Paul uses the word in its related forms only four times,[125] his concept is formed by the consolation of Christ's love (Phil 2:1) and that "the one prophesying is speaking edification (*oikodomē*) and exhortation (*paraklēsis*) and consolation" (*paramuthia*, 1 Cor 14:3), a verse that clearly shows the comforting content and effect of the gospel. While all believers are encouraged to "console the fainthearted" (1 Thess 5:14), the minister

---

124. BDAG § 5611 defines παραμυθία as "that which serves as encouragement to one who is depressed or in grief, *encouragement, comfort, consolation.*"

125. Paul uses the word παραμυθία only once (1 Cor 14:3), the related adjective παραμύθιον once in Phil 2:2; and the verb παραμυθέομαι twice, in 1 Thess 2:12 and 5:14. Other than Esther 8:13.5 (LXX, where it is used in a negative sense of evil exhortation that made some partakers of the guilt of shedding innocent blood), these are the only appearances of this word group in the Greek Bible.

should devote at least some part of his preaching as parathumatic, in the manner that a father consoles his own children (1 Thess 2:11).

Edification as Teaching: *Didachē* and *Didaskalia*

Twice in the immediate context of 2 Timothy 4, Paul mentions "instruction," telling his disciple to "exhort with great . . . instruction (*didachē*), for the time will come when they will not endure sound doctrine" (*didaskalia*; 2 Tim 4:2–3). These two virtual synonyms are among the most common words Paul uses to express the content of the Word.[126] In its widest sense, "The Instruction" denotes Christ's message and the early Christian preaching,[127] suggesting that a collected body of doctrine was formed very early in the life of the church. This indication is particularly noted when Paul writes of the "form of doctrine to which you were committed" (Rom 6:17). Most likely he is referring to the same "doctrine (*didachē*) of the apostles" to which the new church devoted itself immediately after its founding at Pentecost (Acts 2:42).

Dodd attempted to distinguish between the *kērygma* (as the gospel evangelized to unbelievers) and the *didachē* (the gospel preached to believers),[128] but the present context in 2 Tim 4:2–3 does not bear out his contention, since Timothy is to "preach" (*kerussō*) the Word by exhorting believers in *didachē* although unbelievers will not endure sound *didaskalia*—presumably he intends the same message despite being directed toward different audiences. Worley is therefore correct when he states that *didachē* and *kērygma* are virtually indistinguishable in terms of content,[129] although it may be that the *kērygma* is the *didachē* applied evangelistically. Mounce describes the *didachē* as expounding in detail what is proclaimed (*kerussein*).[130] Regardless, all Christian *didachē* is based on the Christian *kērygma*, making it doubtful that any *kērygma* ever stands without some measure of explanatory *didachē*.[131]

Yet, just any instruction is insufficient, as Paul often mentions false *didaskalia*, some even engendered by demons (Eph 4:14; Col 2:22; 1 Tim 4:1). In contrast, Paul defines his doctrine as "good" (Titus 2:3) and "sound" (1 Tim 1:10; 4:6; 2 Tim 4:2; Titus 1:9; 2:1). It is to be held "in purity" (Titus 2:7), since the *didaskalia* is "according to godliness" (1 Tim 6:3). It is only the *didachē* of the Lord that brings the amazement of

---

126. The revealed *Didaskalia* is mentioned by Paul nineteen times (at Rom 12:7; 15:4; Eph 4:14; Col 2:22; 1 Tim 1:10; 4:1, 6, 13, 16; 5:17; 6:1, 3; 2 Tim 3:10, 16; 4:3; Titus 1:9; 2:1, 7, 10). It is defined by BDAG § 1955 as 1. the act of teaching, *teaching, instruction* 2. that which is taught, *teaching, instruction*. The revealed *Didachē* is found six times (Rom 6:17; 16:17; 1 Cor 14:6, 26; 2 Tim 4:2; Titus 1:9). It is defined by BDAG § 1958 as 1. the activity of teaching, *teaching, instruction* and as 2. the content of teaching.

127. Wegenast, "Teach," *DNTT*, 3:770.

128. Dodd, *Apostolic Preaching and its Developments*, 7–8.

129. Worley, *Preaching and Teaching in the Earliest Church*, 84.

130. Mounce, *Essential Nature*, 42.

131. Ibid., 43.

conversion (Acts 19:12), yet the content of this instruction is so well assumed by Paul that he may even speak of it without any further description. It is to this *didaskalia* "of our Savior God" (Titus 2:10) that the preacher must give heed (1 Tim 4:13; 5:17; 6:1), as the assembled church is to be addressed "in *didachē*" (1 Cor 14:6) when each one who gathers is to have *didachē* to express (1 Cor 14:26)—no doubt by those gifted in teaching the *didaskalia* (Rom 12:7).

So where is this instruction to be found? The association of the *didaskalia* with the written *Logos/Graphē* is unmistakable: The Scriptures were written "for our *didaskalia*" (Rom 15:4) because "all Scripture is profitable unto *didaskalia*" (2 Tim 3:16). Thus, the elder is to hold fast to the faithful *Logos* according to the *didachē* (Titus 1:9), so that he labors hard "in *logos* and in *didaskalia*" (1 Tim 5:17; 6:1). Such interplay of vocabulary indicates that *didaskalia* and *didachē* are terms describing the doctrinal content of biblical revelation, which today would be found in the written *Graphē* of the Old Testament prophets and the New Testament apostles (Eph 2:20); thus, only as the preacher's doctrine agrees with what Paul claims as "my *didaskalia*" (2 Tim 3:10) can it be said that he preaches true content to the church. In his teaching role, the preacher acts in his office as a teacher by giving formal instruction in the doctrinal content of the Bible, whether systematically, exegetically, or topically. It seems then, that every sermon must be didactic to some degree: revealed information must be communicated. To this end, the preacher needs to have a working knowledge of biblical doctrine that he is to teach in his messages.

Edification as Commandment: *Parangelia*

The nature of the gospel content carries with it divine authority, and so Paul at times describes his preaching content as consisting of "commandments" (*parangelia*[132]). He reminds his readers, "You know what commandments we gave you through the Lord Jesus" (1 Thess 4:2), with the context indicating that he refers to sexual conduct (1 Thess 4:3–5). Twice he reminds Timothy of the nature of the *parangelia*, that ". . . the goal of our *parangelia* is love from a pure heart and a good conscience and a sincere faith" (1 Tim 1:5). He entrusts a *parangelia* to Timothy "in accordance with the prophecies previously made concerning you, that by them you may fight the good fight" (1 Tim 1:18). Thus, by using this word, Paul reminds his readers that his instructions ". . . have the character of authoritative apostolic ordinances behind which stand the full authorization of Christ Himself."[133] By extension, when the preacher preaches the commands of the Bible, he assumes the authority of the redemptive work of Christ; hence, Christian ethics do not appear in a vacuum but flow from the holy character of

---

132. The word παραγγελία appears only five times in the NT (Acts 5:28; 16:24; 1 Thess 4:2; 1 Tim 1:5, 18). BDAG § 5559 defines παραγγελία as "an announcement respecting someth. that must be done, order, command, precept, advice, exhortation."

133. Schmitz, παραγγελία, *TDNT* 5:764.

God, meaning that an important aspect of each sermon is a "parangelic" emphasis of practical application. The preacher must ask of each biblical text, "What moral consequences stem from this *didachē*?" The Word, then, is never merely theoretical: it is intensely practical; therefore, the preacher should include in his preaching the moral implications of the gospel.

Edification as Reading: *Anagnōsis*

One such command appears when Paul directs Timothy, "Give attendance to reading" (1 Tim 4:13, KJV), and a modern reader might wonder why Paul orders Timothy to expand his literary ability. Actually, this rather cryptic reference to "reading" is quite specific in the Greek text, which could be translated, "Give heed to The Reading" (*hē anagnōsis,* 1 Tim 4:13 AT). What Paul refers to is "the public reading of scripture," as the NET translates it. The same word appears one other time in Paul's writings, and that is when he speaks of "the reading (*anagnōsis*) of the Old Covenant" (2 Cor 3:14). Another example appears in Acts 13:15, which refers to "the reading of the Law and the Prophets" during a synagogue service,[134] indicating that "the *Anagnōsis*" had become a technical term for the public reading of the written Word.

By the command "give heed,"[135] Paul does not intend for "The Reading" to be an optional part of public Christian worship, as Paul instructs Timothy to give attention, first, to the *Anagnōsis*, then to the *Paraklēsis*, and then to the *Didaskalia*, each previously noted as particular aspects of the gospel content. At some point in each worship service, there should be the public reading of the passage at hand; in addition, other portions of Scripture deemed appropriate to the situation ought to be read also. The tradition of lexical readings certainly has biblical mandate and also historical precedent in the public reading of Scripture by Ezra (Neh 8:8). Sadly, the practice of Scripture reading has been nearly lost in many non-liturgical fellowships, but undoubtedly, attention to "the Reading" should be considered as important to the public worship service as any other aspect—and perhaps even more so, since without the hearing of the Word, there is nothing to preach and certainly nothing to believe either (Rom 10:17).

Edification as Defense: *Apologia* and *Bebaiōsis*

A final aspect of the gospel content to consider is that of the defense of the Faith, and it is found in the immediate context of 2 Timothy 4 when Paul comments, "At my first defense (*apologia*[136]) no one supported me" (2 Tim 4:16). The tie of defense

---

134. BDAG § 459 defines ἀνάγνωσις as 1. the process of reading someth. written, and 2. the content of what is read.

135. BDAG § 6294.3 defines προσέχω in 1 Tim 4:13, "to continue in close attention to someth."

136. BDAG § 64 defines ἀπολογία as 1. a speech of defense (Acts 22:1; 1 Cor 9:3) and 2. the act of

to the preached message is seen when Paul notes that he has been appointed "for the defense (*apologia*) of the gospel" (Phil 1:16) as well as being a partaker "in the defense (*apologia*) and confirmation (*bebaiōsis*[137]) of the gospel" (Phil 1:7). When Paul speaks before the crowd in Jerusalem, he begins with this appeal: "Brethren and fathers, hear my defense (*apologia*) which I now *offer* to you" (Acts 22:1).

The concept of defense indicates that part of the sermon content, whenever necessary, should include a defense of the truth of the gospel, reasoning from the Scriptures as well as from history and experience, as Paul does in his address in Jerusalem (Acts 22). The preacher should readily anticipate objections to the Christian faith and be able to relate the Word to those questions, giving credible reasons for the veracity of the message he preaches. In this manner, some or perhaps all aspects of a sermon could well be apologetic in nature, depending on the particular preaching circumstance.

Summary to the Reason for Preaching

"Preach the Word," Paul directs Timothy, and this chapter has explored the various facets of the preached content of the Word found in Paul's writings and sermons. The Word (*Ho Logos*) is carefully defined by the apostle as referring to divine revelation, whether viewed in its dynamic effects (*rhēma*) or in its particularities as the New Covenant *mustērion*. Supremely, to preach the Word is to preach Jesus Christ Himself.

However, there is no other explanation of Jesus except what is recorded in the Word as written *Graphē*. So, to preach the Word is to preach the Bible. The preacher is not free to expound on ideas outside the written Word: his texts are limited to the written Scripture. Since the Scripture preaches itself, the preacher becomes the mouthpiece of the Word when he preaches the Bible.

To Paul, the Word is embedded in human history in the appearance of God's Kingdom, showing that preaching cannot be separated from redemptive history as it flows from OT to NT. The divine prophecies relating to both the Old and New Covenants have now become inscripturated, meaning that the preacher finds the content of his preaching in the revealed tradition (*paradosis*) and deposit (*parathekē*), which are distinctly located in the writings of the Old and New Testaments. The preacher's content is thus limited to the written Word as the truth of God, but since his subject matter is the revelation of the eternal God, this limitation is scarcely a restriction.

In broad categories, the content of Paul's message is either evangelistic or edifying, depending on his audience. The *euangelion* becomes a specialized application of the overall *didachē* of the Word, stressing the primary works of Christ's redemption

---

making a defense, a. in court (2 Tim 4:16; Acts 25:16), and b. of eagerness to defend oneself (2 Cor 7:11; Phil 1:7, 16; and 1 Pet 3:15).

137. BDAG § 1448 defines βεβαίωσις as "process of establishing or confirming something, confirmation, validation." The word is found only at Lev 25:23; Phil 1:7, and Heb 6:16.

accompanied with a call to repentance and faith. Preaching the gospel is not merely retelling historical events, but it must also include the apostolic interpretations that elucidate the theological significance of those events; thus, the gospel core is not merely that Christ died, but that "He died for our sins" (1 Cor 15:3). Furthermore, the promise of the gospel is offered to all who believe, so that the preacher should not have any reservations urging all sinners to come to Christ. It is the conviction of the author that the basic truths of the judgment, reconciliation, atonement, resurrection, and appeal ought to be included in every public sermon, interwoven throughout the body of the message. If the Christian sermon is to differ from a moral homily, then it must include these distinctive elements of the *Euangelion*.

Yet, the content is not to be exclusively evangelistic; in fact, Paul's letters are actually much more didactic and exhortative in nature. The doctrines of the gospel bring encouragement (*parakalēsis*) and comfort (*parathumia*) as the doctrines (*didachē / didaskalia*) of Scripture are expounded. These aspects of the gospel indicate that every sermon should include some explanation of the particular doctrinal content contained in the passage(s) under consideration. It then becomes the responsibility of the preacher to call the hearers to obedience to that doctrine of the Word, as shown in the concept of *parangelia*. To those who object to the message, the preacher is called to the *apologia* of the gospel, defending the integrity of the message.

In summation, the Apostle Paul indicates in his writings that the content of a sermon ought to contain at a minimum an exposition of some portion of the written Word whereby its doctrines are explained and applied evangelistically and practically as related to the person and work of Jesus Christ. Whatever else a sermon is intended to do, it needs to be prepared and delivered by a preacher who knows that he is charged to "preach the Word" as his primary content, meaning he must be skilled as an exegete and theologian of the Scripture.[138] Now that this study has provided the knowledge of the content Timothy should preach, we turn our attention to the imperative verb of the passage under study, what it means to "preach" the Word. This consideration brings us to the communicating process of bringing the Word to the listener, to the activity of preaching itself.

---

138. See the forthcoming appeal by Vanhoozer and Strachan, *The Pastor as Public Theologian: Reclaiming a Lost Vision* (2015)

CHAPTER 4

The Preacher's Activity: "Preach, . . . Reprove, Rebuke, Exhort!"

THE INITIAL COMMAND OF Paul to Timothy in the paragraph under analysis (2 Tim 4:1–5) is undoubtedly the one upon which all the others in this charge depend: "Preach the Word!" By this imperative, Timothy is confronted with the primary activity of the Christian minister, that of preaching, and it is the purpose of this chapter to examine the various verbal descriptions that Paul uses for the activity of preaching.[1]

As established in the previous chapter, the *content* of preaching ("The Word") must take precedence over the *act* of preaching, because without content there is nothing to proclaim; however, the nature of Christian revelation as "The Word" is that it must be proclaimed, and that fact produces the activity of preaching as the paramount responsibility of the minister. Ford comments, "The Church came to birth with preaching, and preaching came to birth with the Church."[2]

While the verb *kerussō* ("Preach!") is the one Paul uses in his charge to Timothy, it is by no means the only verb he employs to express the activity of preaching. The variety of verbs used by Paul in his letters (and attributed to him in his speeches in the Book of Acts) is really quite amazing. In addition to the verbs describing the activity of speaking in general, the apostle uses other verbs to picture the activity of evangelizing, instructing, defending, governing, and caring. These categories will serve as the subdivisions of this chapter, as it appears that Paul chooses these verbs to fit various distinct situations.

It should be noted, however, that not all scholars agree with this assessment. Coenen claims, "The wide range of words used [for preaching] indicates that none gained a position of clear dominance or was able to become a technical term."[3]

---

1. Wallace, *Greek Grammar*, 721 comments on this imperative, κήρυξον in 2 Tim 4:2: "The idea here is hardly, 'Begin to preach the word,' but, 'I solemnly charge you to preach the word. Make this your priority!' (as the following context clearly indicates)."

2. Ford, *Ministry of the Word*, 53.

3. Coenen, "Proclamation," *DNTT* 3:54.

While the first part of Coenen's statement is certainly true, the second part should be questioned, because the many varied aspects of preaching undoubtedly required a broadening terminology, much of which appears to be somewhat technical (as this chapter shall show); for example, *noutheteō* is always used in the context of church discipline. It will be the aim of this chapter to show that these verbs are not used in an arbitrary manner, since the specific applications of the gospel content are determined by the audience and its needs. As Reinke observes, "It is the content that characterizes the main aspects of the messenger's activity."[4]

The Activity of Preaching: Speaking

Quite naturally, the New Covenant minister is usually identified in his role as preacher, because the content of Christianity (as "good news!") necessitates the activity of speaking. The use of otherwise quite bland verbs emphasizes the normality of the speaking activity of the preacher.

It should be self-evident that someone called to be a preacher must also be a speaker, although some advocate "silent witnessing by one's life;" whereby a believer merely shows Christ by his deeds but does not need to speak of Him. Of course, every believer should witness of Christ by a godly life (1 Tim 3:7), but it is important to note that every Christian ministry, at some time or another, must explain itself by speaking (as Paul asks in Rom 10:14, "How shall they hear without a preacher?"). For proof of this assertion, one need only to point to the various verbs used repeatedly by Paul to describe the vocalizing ministry.[5]

Of all the words describing the speaking activity, *laleō* ("to talk") may be the most colorless of all,[6] yet by virtue of its connection to the theology of the Word (as *Debar* and *Logos*), it is elevated to importance when referring to the vocalization of the Word of revelation. For example, Paul states, "We speak (*laloumen*) God's wisdom in a mystery, . . . which things we also speak (*laloumen*), not in words taught by human wisdom, but in those taught by the Spirit" (1 Cor 2:7 and 13). Such speaking springs out of a true faith in God ("We also believe, therefore also we speak"; 2 Cor 4:13) and

---

4. Reicke, "A Synopsis of Early Christian Preaching," in *Root of the Vine: Essays in Biblical Theology*, 130. He sub-divides the preaching activity as that which is directed toward conversion (admonition and invitation), toward the converted (instruction and edification), as testament, and as revelation.

5. The most common verb for speaking is *legō*, which appears 2353 times in the NT (by a count of *Bible Works* 9 BGT); however, in the vast majority of times Paul uses the verb, the occurrence is not theologically significant. In fact, only twice does he employ *legō* for speaking some aspect the gospel (1 Cor 15:51 and 1 Thess 2:7).

6. BDAG § 4502 traces λαλέω "in older Gk. usu. of informal communication ranging from engagement in small talk to chattering and babbling. In the NT, it is used "1. to make a sound, *sound, give forth sounds/tones*; and 2. to utter words, *talk, speak*."

issues forth in the speaking of the gospel message ("We had the boldness in our God to speak to you the gospel of God," 1 Thess 2:2).[7]

Although found only in Luke's writings, another less common but linguistically important verb is *homileō*,[8] from which the English word "homiletics" is derived, describing the skill of preparing and delivering sermons, although the basic word meant simply, to address another person.[9] In each NT context, however, *homileō* always describes the activity of discussing divine revelation, as in the manner Jesus "conversed" with His disciples (Luke 24:14–15), as Paul "talked" with the believers at Troas "a long while" (Acts 20:11), and as Governor Felix sent for Paul "quite often and conversed with him" (Acts 24:26), where they had been discussing such subjects as the coming judgment (Acts 24:25)

Clearly, Paul understood the office of the ministry in terms of vocalizing. The obvious task of the minister is to imitate the Lord Jesus, who also "words that are spirit and life" (John 6:63, NET), as did the apostles who "spoke the word of God with boldness" (Acts 4:29–31). Likewise, the minister is charged to "speak the things fitting for sound doctrine" (Titus 2:1) and to "speak . . . with all authority (Titus 2:15). Paul requests prayer that he may "speak boldly, as I ought to speak" (Eph 6:20), and that he may "speak forth the mystery of Christ, . . . that I may make it clear in the way I ought to speak" (Col 4:3–4). No man ought to consider himself to be a preacher of the New Covenant unless he can ". . . speak the Word of God with boldness" (Phil 1:14), knowing that his speaking is uttered "in the sight of God" (2 Cor 2:17, 12:19) in the primary activity of speaking the gospel.

There are, however, various ways that the gospel is to be spoken, as the following studies will show:

The Activity of Preaching: Evangelizing

The initial charge to Timothy is to "preach the Word," and at once Paul brings his friend to the great speaking activity of evangelizing the world through the proclamation of the gospel. In the present age of instant media, it is important for the modern reader to remember that public oratory was a much more common medium of communication in the first century than it is in the twenty-first. McDonald asserts, "The Church began in a cultural environment in which preaching was a basic mode of communication."[10] It is not surprising to find that the verb *kerussō* was only one of

---

7. *Laleō* is used of Paul "speaking" the gospel in Acts 13:42; 14:46; 14:1, 9; 16:6, 13, 14, 32; 17:19; 18:9; 21:39; and 26:26. Of the sixty times Paul uses *laleō*, he employs it of speaking the gospel in Rom 15:18; 1 Cor 2:6, 7; 2:13; 14:2, 3, 4, 5, 6, 9, 13, 18, 19, 21, 23, 27, 28, 29, 39; 2 Cor 2:17; 4:13; 12:19; 13:3; Eph 6:20; Phil 1:14; Col 4:3; 1 Thess 2:2, 4; Titus 2:1, 15.

8. Luke 24:14, 15; Acts 20:11; 24:26; however, *homileō* is also found in the OT verses of Prov 5:19; 15:12; 23:31; Dan 1:19.

9. BDAG § 5282 defines ὁμιλέω, "to be in a group and speak, *speak, converse, address.*"

10. McDonald, *Kerygma and Didache*, 39.

many verbs available to Paul to describe the activity of evangelizing, and so it is the purpose of this section to examine the various verbs he employs to convey the activity of evangelizing the world.

Verbs Expressing the Activity of Evangelizing

The actual activity of evangelizing to the world is expressed by several prominent and common verbs used by both Paul and Luke. Both writers show that these verbs became technical Christian terms to define this activity:

Evangelizing by Proclaiming (kērussein): The verb *kērussein* primarily means to proclaim aloud or publicly,[11] particularly the announcing of a herald (*kērux*) broadcasting some public information.[12] This verb *kērussein* is thus very fitting to describe the primary publication of the Christian preacher, which is to proclaim the good news of the arrival of a Savior and King.[13] Even Jesus explained His ministry as being "anointed to proclaim the gospel to the poor" (Luke 4:18), and so He defined his primary activity as proclaiming to the towns of Galilee, "for unto this I came" (Mark 1:38). He then appointed his disciples to proclaim the gospel first to all nations (Mark 13:10), so that each minister, like Paul, is appointed as a *kērux* (1 Tim 2:7) in order to carry out the task of proclaiming (*kērussein*) the *Kērygma*.

Without exception in the NT, *kērussein* describes an open, public proclamation such as expressed in the contrast between "what you have whispered (*laleō*) in private rooms shall be proclaimed (*kērussein*) on the housetops" (Luke 12:3 ESV). Private evangelism is not so much in view in *kērussein* as much as is open declaration announced to the entire world (Col 1:23), indicating that a minister must develop his speaking skills so that he may "proclaim Christ crucified," for it is by the foolishness of that proclamation that God saves those who believe (1 Cor 1:21–23). The minister

---

11. BDAG § 232 defines κηρύσσω 1. "to make an official announcement, announce, make known, by an official herald or one who functions as such; and 2. to make public declarations, proclaim aloud."

12. *VGNT* § 2301 κῆρυξ, cites a number of examples from extra-biblical Greek literature.

13. The verb *kērussō* is found sixty-one times in sixty verses in the Greek NT, and it is used in the following ways: of the preaching of John the Baptist (Matt 3:1; Mark 1:4; Luke 3:3; Acts 10:37); of the preaching of Jesus (Matt 4:17, 23; 9:35; 11:1; Mark 1:14; 38, 39; Luke 4:18, 19, 44; 8:1; 1 Pet 3:19); of the preaching of the disciples (Matt 10:7; 27; Mark 3:14; 6:12; 16:20; Luke 9:2; Acts 10:42); of the leper (Mark 1:45); of the deaf man (Mark 7:36); of the demoniac (Mark 5:20; Luke 8:39); of the church (Matt 24:14; 26:13; Mark 13:10; 14:9; 16:15; Luke 12:3; 24:47); the preaching of Philip (Acts 8:5); the preaching of Paul (Acts 9:20; 19:13; 20:25; 28:31; 1 Cor 9:27; 15:11); the preaching of Scripture (Acts 15:21; Rom 2:21); the preaching of the Word (Rom 10:8; 2 Tim 4:2); the preaching of the gospel (Gal 2:2; Col 1:20; 1 Thess 2:9); the preaching of circumcision (Gal 5:11); the preaching of preachers (Rom 10:14–15); the preaching of Christ (1 Cor 1:23; 15:12; 2 Cor 1:19; 4:5; 11:4; 11:4; Phil 1:15; 1 Tim 3:16); and the preaching of angels (Rev 5:2). The preacher preaches the *kērygma* (Matt 12:41; Luke 11:32; Rom 16:25; 1 Cor 1:21; 2:4; 15:14; 2 Tim 4:17; Titus 1:3) as a herald (*kērux*, 1 Tim 2:7; 2 Tim 1:11; 2 Pet 2:5).

must be persuaded that without one who is "proclaiming (*kērussontos*) the word of faith" (Rom 10:8, AT), sinners will not be saved. It is for this reason that proclamation is the first charge to the minister, as the apostle actually charges Timothy, "Proclaim (*kērusson*) the Word!" (2 Tim 4:2). For that matter, proclaiming is mentioned in the Great Commission as the first task of the church (Luke 24:47; Acts 10:42). However, as important as is the activity of *kērussein*, it cannot take precedence over the content of the *kērygma*, for the preacher would have nothing to proclaim if it were not for the previous acts of God in Christ. This emphasis needs to be maintained because the existential scholars such as Freidrich insist that ". . . preaching is not impartation of facts: it is event. What is proclaimed takes place."[14]

To say that this view is puzzling is an understatement. Does Friedrich mean that Christ is crucified and risen again in each sermon? He continues, "*Kērussein* does not mean the delivery of a learned and edifying or hortatory discourse in well-chosen words and a pleasant voice: it is the declaration of an event."[15] While one would agree that a polished delivery is not necessarily required for preaching, that which defines Christian preaching is the *Kērygma*, the proclamation of the once-for-all-time historical appearance (1 Tim 3:16) and redemptive work of Jesus Christ (". . . The Son of God, Christ Jesus was preached—*kēruxtheis*—among you by us," 2 Cor 1:19). When Paul told Timothy to proclaim the Word, his understudy would never confuse his own preaching with the great redemptive events enacted by Jesus—nor, for that matter, should any other preacher.

Paul even makes a distinction between the act of proclaiming in 2 Tim 4:2 from the content of proclamation in 2 Tim 4:17, when his stated intent is that "the *kērygma*—the gospel content—might be fully accomplished, and that all the Gentiles might hear"—by proclaiming, no doubt. Note that the proclamation is accomplished not by the mere event of preaching, but by the preacher's faithfulness to the *kērygma*, "the gospel that I [Paul] preach (*kērussein*) among the Gentiles" (Gal 2:2).

Such emphasis on content, however, is not to deny an existential element in preaching—salvation is in fact mediated in proclamation, as Paul observes, "So we proclaim (*kērussomen*) and so you have believed" (1 Cor 15:11 CSB). Coenen says of *kērussein*, "It includes information, but it is always more than instruction of a bare offer."[16] Behind the act of proclaiming is the Risen Proclaimer Himself, the One who energizes His Word and brings sinners to faith in Him. As one who imitates Christ, the preacher ought to view himself also as a proclaimer, devoting himself, first, to the *kērygma* and then to the activity of proclaiming (*kērussein*) as skillfully as God enables him to do so.

---

14. Friedrich, κηρύσσω, *TDNT* 3:711.
15. Ibid., 703.
16. Coenen, "Proclamation," *DNTT* 3:57.

Evangelizing by Announcing Good News (euangelizō): Very close in meaning to *kērussein* is the verb *euangelizō*,[17] generally translated, "preaching the gospel," although this study will transliterate it as "evangelizing."[18] This word also lies in the immediate context of Paul's charge, when he orders Timothy to "do the work of an evangelist" (2 Tim 4:5), for as Jesus came evangelizing (Matt 4:18), so God gave to the church some as evangelists (Eph 4:11)—one such example is Philip (Acts 21:8). Yet by extension, every minister is called to the activity of evangelizing, or "announcing the good news."[19]

In a general sense, "evangelizing" refers to the initial contact with unbelievers so that the evangelist tells the good news of the Lord Jesus to those who have never before heard of Him, or at least, to those who have not understood what they have heard (Rom 15:20, 2 Cor 10:16). The occurrence of the verb *euangelizō* in the Book of Acts exclusively refers to the evangelization of the lost, indicating that the world is the target audience of evangelizing rather than the church (which is not to say that some professing church members do not need to be evangelized!).[20] It is little wonder that Schutz asserts, "Nothing comes closer to suggesting the central missionary nature of apostolic activity than the verb *euangeleethai*."[21]

Upon examining Paul's use of *euangelizō*, one notices that the apostle find its background in an OT prophecy, "How beautiful are the feet of those evangelizing good things" (*tōn euaggelozomenōn [ta] agatha*, Rom 10:15). In this quote from Isa 52:7, the messenger announces salvation and proclaims, "Your God reigns!" The announcement of the reign of God brings into focus the kingdom preaching of Jesus when He came 'evangelizing' the reign of God (Matt 4:18). By virtue of His atoning

---

17. The verb εὐαγγελίζω is used seventy-six times in the Greek Bible, according to BW9, twenty-two times in the LXX (1 Sam 31:9; 2 Sam 1:20; 4:10; 18:19, 20, 26, 31; 1 Kgs 1:42; 1 Chr 10:9; Ps 39:10; 67:12; 95:2; Joel 3:5; Nah 2:1; Isa 40:9; 52:7; 60:6; 61:1; Jer 20:15); once in the Apocryphal books (Pss 11:1); and fifty-four times in the NT (Matt 11:5; Luke 1:19; 2:10; 3:18; 4:18, 43; 7:22; 8:1; 9:6; 16:16; 20:1; Acts 5:42; 8:4, 12, 25, 35, 40; 10:36; 11:20; 13:32; 14:7, 15, 21; 15:35; 16:10; 17:18; Rom 1:15; 10:15; 15:20; 1 Cor 1:17; 9:16, 18; 15:1, 2; 2 Cor 10:16; 11:7; Gal 1:8, 8, 9, 11, 16, 23; 4:13; Eph 2:17; 3:8; 1 Thess 3:6; Heb 4:2, 6; 1 Pet 1:12, 25; 4:6; Rev 10:7; 14:6).

18. One must wonder if "preach the gospel" is the best translation of εὐαγγελίζω, since other objects are often designated as being preached, such as, preaching the promise (Acts 13:32), the Word (Col 1:25); Jesus (2 Cor 4:5); the resurrection (Acts 17:18); and the riches of Christ (Eph 3:8). In fact, in 1 Cor 15:1, 2 Cor 11:7 and Gal 1:11, the object of preaching is "the gospel" itself, rendering the translation, "preaching the gospel of the gospel," which is highly redundant. This fact would seem to indicate that a better translation of *euangelizō* might be the transliteration, "evangelizing," as the word has come over into English with the understanding of preaching the gospel to unbelievers; therefore, this study will use the transliteration "evangelizing" to convey the verb *euangelizō*.

19. BDAG § 3197 defines εὐαγγελίζω "1. gener. bring good news, announce good news; 2. mostly specif. proclaim the divine message of salvation, proclaim the gospel." The verb is always used in the NT of preaching some aspect of the revealed gospel, with the exception of 1 Thess 3:6, "But now that Timothy has come to us from you, and has brought us good news of your faith and love."

20. Luke uses εὐαγγελίζω to describe the initial evangelizing activity of Paul in Pisidian Antioch (Acts 13:32); regions of Lycaonia (Acts 14:7); Lystra (Acts 14:15); Derbe (Acts 14:21); Antioch (Acts 15:36); Macedonia (Acts 16:10); and Athens (Acts 17:18).

21. Schutz, *Paul and the Anatomy of Apostolic Authority*, 36.

death and resurrection, Jesus now reigns as King, and His exaltation is the announcement that lies behind Paul's use of the verb *euangelizō*.

What is of further interest is to observe how often Paul uses the verb *euangelizō* without any direct object at all, thus emphasizing the primary activity of evangelizing, telling good news. This observation must not be construed to suggest that the activity of evangelizing can be separated from the content of the Evangel, despite the fact that Schutz insists that ". . . in almost every instance the content of that preaching remains vague and ill defined."[22] Schutz' statement is an incredible assertion, because Paul defines what he evangelizes without question: "I make known to you the gospel which I evangelized to you, . . . the word which I evangelized to you, . . . that Christ died for our sins, etc." (1 Cor 15:1–3, AT). Paul also contrasts true and false evangelizing in Galatians 1, and the deciding factor there is not in the manner of preaching but in the nature of the message delivered (Gal 1:8–9). By using the verb *euangelizō* without an object, Paul shows that *euangelizō* had become to him a technical term by which the activity is equated with the announcement itself: one cannot be separated from the other.

This fact means that in the activity of evangelizing, the preacher announces the good news of the gospel content to the world in general (Gal 1:16) and to individuals in particular (Gal 1:11). To Paul, evangelizing took precedence, as he states, ". . . Christ sent me . . . to evangelize" (1 Cor 1:17, AT). Likewise, it must be the concern of every minister of the New Covenant to devote himself to the activity of evangelizing: he needs to know how to present the gospel to unbelievers in order that they might place their faith in Christ as Savior. Any minister who shuns the work of an evangelist fails to imitate the divine Evangelist and His apostle; instead, he needs to evangelize by announcing the good news of salvation.

Evangelizing by Pronouncing (verbs based on angellō): Closely related to *euangelizō* are those words based on the same verbal root *angellō* but with different prefixes.[23] Nearly synonymous, these words nonetheless have varying shades of meaning that

---

22. Ibid., 39.

23. The related words are: ἀγγέλλω (found only in John 20:18); ἀναγγέλλω, ἀπαγγέλλω (45 times: Matt 2:8; 8:33; 11:4; 12:18; 14:12; 28:8, 10, 11; Mark 5:14, 19; 6:30; 16:10, 13; Luke 7:18, 22; 8:20, 34, 36, 47; 9:36; 13:1; 14:21; 18:37; 24:9; John 16:25; Acts 4:23; 5:22, 25; 11:13; 12:14, 17; 15:27; 16:36, 38; 22:26; 23:16, 17, 19; 26:20; 28:21; 1 Cor 14:25; 1 Thess 1:9; Heb 2:12; 1 John 1:2, 3); διαγγέλλω (nine times, in Paul only in Rom 9:17, quoting Exod 9:16); ἐξαγγέλλω (only Mark 16:8 and 1 Peter 2:9); ἐπαγγέλλομαι (fifteen times; Mark 14:11; Acts 7:5; Rom 4:21; Gal 3:19; 1 Tim 2:10; 6:21; Titus 1:2; Heb 6:13; 10:23; 11:11; 12:26; Jas 1:12; 2:5; 2 Pet 2:19; 1 John 2:25); εὐαγγελίζω (fifty-four times: Matt 11:5; Luke 1:19; 2:10; 3:18; 4:18, 43; 7:22; 8:1; 9:6; 16:16; 20:1; Acts 5:42; 8:4, 12, 25, 35, 40; 10:36; 11:20; 13:32; 14:7, 15, 21; 15:35; 16:10; 17:18; Rom 1:15; 10:15; 15:20; 1 Cor 1:17; 9:16, 16, 18; 15:1, 2; 2 Cor 10:16; 11:7; Gal 1:8, 8, 9, 11, 16, 23; 4:13; Eph 2:17; 3:8; 1 Thess 3:6; Heb 4:2, 6; 1 Pet 1:12, 25; 4:6; Rev 10:7; 14:6); καταγγέλλω (eighteen times; Acts 3:24; 4:2; 13:5, 38; 15:36; 16:17, 21; 17:3, 13, 23; 26:23; Rom 1:8; 1 Cor 2:1; 9:14; 11:26; Phil 1:17, 18; Col 1:28); παραγγέλλω (thirty-two times; Matt 10:5; 15:35; Mark 6:8; 8:6; 16:8; Luke 5:14; 8:29, 56; 9:21; Acts 1:4; 4:18; 5:28, 40; 10:42; 15:5; 16:18, 23; 17:30; 23:22, 30; 1 Cor 7:10; 11:17; 1 Thess 4:11; 2 Thess 3:4, 6, 10, 12; 1 Tim 1:3; 4:11; 5:7; 6:13, 17); προεπαγγέλλομαι (only Rom 1:2; 2 Cor 9:5); προκαταγγέλλω (only Acts 3:18 and 7:52).

enrich the vocabulary of the activity of evangelizing. The first of these words is *anangellō*, which is used only twice by Paul, but it is found several times in the Book of Acts regarding Paul's preaching ministry.[24] The basic idea of *anangellō* is to give a report,[25] as when Paul and Barnabas "gathered the church together and *began* to report (*anēngellon*) all things that God had done with them" (Acts 14:27). Twice in his address to the Ephesian elders, Paul uses *anangellō* to convey his "declaring . . . anything that was profitable" (Acts 20:20) and "declaring to you the whole purpose of God" (Acts 20:27), even as Titus "reported" the longing of the Corinthians for Paul (2 Cor 7:7). Paul uses the verb in Rom 15:21, "As it is written, 'Those who have never been told (*anēngele*) of him will see,'" a quotation from Isa 52:15, which Paul understands as a prophecy promising that once the news of God's Suffering Servant is announced, then "those who have never heard will understand." Thus, *anangellō* seems to contain the idea of the responsibility of the hearer to embrace "the whole counsel of God" (Acts 20:27), making it critical that the preacher actually report the message as it has been delivered to him and not to be an innovator.[26]

Another related word is *diangellō*,[27] a word Paul uses only once in an OT quotation from Exod 9:16, "For the Scripture says to Pharaoh, 'For this very purpose I raised you up, to demonstrate My power in you, and that My name might be proclaimed (*diangellei*) throughout the whole earth.'" Although the word is not directly applicable to Paul's preaching as such, the OT usage surely influences his understanding, as its emphasis seems to stress the extent of proclamation. Its usage demonstrates that the preacher has a responsibility to evangelize the Name of Christ everywhere.

The verb *katangellō* (usually translated, "to proclaim"), on the other hand, is a prominent word attributed to Paul in the Book of Acts and used by Paul in his letters to express the proclaiming aspect of evangelizing.[28] Without any apparent exception,

---

24. The verb ἀναγγέλλω is found fourteen times in the NT: John 4:25; 5:15; 16:13, 14, 15; Acts 14:27; 15:4; 19:18; 20:20, 27; Rom 15:21; 2 Cor 7:7; 1 Pet 1:12; 1 John 1:5.

25. BDAG § 450 defines ἀναγγέλλω 1. "w. full force of ἀνά, to carry back information, and 2. gener. to provide information, *disclose, announce, proclaim,* teach."

26. Other instances of *anangellō* are highly significant: Jesus uses the verb three times to teach that the Sprit of Truth "will disclose to you what is to come. . . . He shall take of Mine, and shall disclose *it* to you. All things that the Father has are Mine; therefore I said, that He takes of Mine, and will disclose *it* to you." 1 Peter 1:12 tells of "these things which now have been announced (*anangellō*) to you through those who preached the gospel to you by the Holy Spirit," and 1 John 1:5 reports, "This is the message we have heard from Him and announce (*anaggellō*) to you, that God is light, and in Him there is no darkness at all."

27. BDAG § 1832 defines διαγγέλλω: "1. to make someth. known far and wide, *proclaim, spread the news concerning/about* ; and 2. to make a report, *announce, report.*" The word appears only twelve times in the Greek Bible (Exod 9:16; Lev 25:9; Jos 6:10; 2 Macc 1:33; 3:34; Ps 2:7; 58:13; Sir 43:2; Luke 9:60; Acts 21:26; Rom 9:17).

28. BDAG § 3950 defines καταγγέλλω "to make known in public, with implication of broad dissemination, *proclaim, announce.*" The word is found twenty times in the Greek Bible (2 Macc 8:36; 9:17; Acts 3:24; 4:2; 13:5, 38; 15:36; 16:17, 21; 17:3, 13, 23; 26:23; Rom 1:8; 1 Cor 2:1; 9:14; 11:26; Phil 1:17, 18; Col 1:28).

katangellō is used by both Luke and Paul to describe initial evangelistic activities of announcing Christ's Lordship. This practice fits well with its classical usage, in the proclaiming of imperial rule.[29] In the Book of Acts, Paul is viewed as *katangellein* the Word in the synagogues of Salamis (Acts 13:5), Berea (Acts 17:13), and Cilicia (Acts 15:36). The slave girl heaps unwanted praise on the apostles for "proclaiming (*katangellousin*) the way of salvation" (Acts 16:17), although her owners accuse them of proclaiming "unlawful customs" (Acts 16:21). The content of Paul's proclamation is "this Jesus whom I proclaim (*katangellō*) to you" (Acts 17:31), so that the gospel proclamation is succinctly, "We proclaim Christ!" (Col 1:28). Even if others do the proclaiming from improper motives, it brings joy to Paul regardless how Christ is proclaimed (Phil 1:16, 18). So then, in a way beyond the verbalizing of a sermon, the Risen Christ is actually proclaimed to the hearer, with this reality especially prominent in the proclamation of Christ's death at the participation around His Table (1 Cor 10:26). Such fellowship leads Schniewind to comment, "This sense is that of the proclamation or declaration of a completed happening rather than instruction marked off from other by distinctive formulation."[30] He also recognizes that the proclamation of Christ is not exclusively existential, but it also includes and produces the conjoining blessing of salvation by promising, "Though this One is proclaimed (*katangelletai*) to you forgiveness of sins" (Acts 13:38).[31] Thus Schniewind states, "By its very nature, declaring the unique historical reality of Jesus, this word (*katangellō*) must also be instruction, admonition, and tradition, but it is teaching which participates in the eschatological and dramatic character of the message."[32] It is, as Paul says, ". . . the Lord (who) commanded to the ones who proclaim (*katangellousin*) the gospel" (1 Cor 9:14) who then also are "proclaiming to you the testimony of God" (1 Cor 2:1).

Thus, these three related words (*anaggellō, diangellō, katangellō*) show various aspects of evangelizing by open verbal proclamation of Christ. The redemptive event of the Redeemer's death has taken place in human history, and now He is proclaimed to all nations, promising forgiveness and justification to everyone who believes through Him (Acts 13:38).

Evangelizing by Explaining (ektithēmi): Occurring only four times in the NT (all in Acts),[33] *ektithēmi* is used only once of the evangelizing activity of Paul, when "he was explaining (*eisetithēto*) to them by solemnly testifying about the kingdom of God, and trying to persuade them concerning Jesus, from both the Law of Moses and from the

---

29. Schniewind, καταγγέλλω, *TDNT*, 1:70.
30. Ibid.
31. Ibid.
32. Ibid., 1:71.
33. The word *ektithēmi* is found only in Acts 7:21; 11:4; 18:26; 28:23 in the NT; however, it also appears in the LXX in Esth 3:14; 4:3, 8; 8:12, 13, 14, 17; 9:14; 2 Macc 11:36; Job 36:15; Wis 18:5; Dan 5:7; Dat 3:96; 6:9.

Prophets, from morning until evening" (Acts 28:23). The word means, "to set forth" a matter in the sense of explaining it,[34] thus showing that Paul patiently unfolded the facts of the gospel as part of his evangelizing.

In summary, the good preacher should also carefully explain the gospel to his audience, as the use of these verbs shows the importance of the activity of evangelizing, for the preacher is assuredly called to proclaim, announce, pronounce, and explain the gospel to the unbelieving world.

Verbs Expressing the Apologetic of Evangelism

Much of Paul's early preaching recorded in the Book of Acts is directed toward the Jewish community in an effort to convince them from their Holy Scriptures that Jesus of Nazareth is the promised Messiah. Such activity takes on an apologetic emphasis as the apostle attempts to reason, persuade and convince others of this truth; hence, several verbs are used to express this activity.

Evangelizing by Reasoning (dialegomai): The verb *dialegomai* is a word not actually used in Paul's letters, but it is found in the Book of Acts to describe his preaching.[35] In its blandest sense, it means to conduct a conversation,[36] although etymologically, it translates as "through-reasoning," showing that the thrust of the word is an appeal to the mind by giving a rational explanation of the gospel. Fürst

---

34. BDAG § 2437.2 defines ἐκτίθημι, "to convey information by careful elaboration, *explain, expound.*"

35. Besides being used seven times in the LXX (Exod 6:27; Judg 8:1; 1 Esd 8:45; Esth 5:2; 2 Macc 11:20; Sir 14:20; Isa 63:1), διαλέγομαι is used thirteen times in the NT (Mark 9:34; Acts 17:2, 17; 18:4, 19; 19:8, 9; 20:7, 9; 24:12, 25; Heb 12:5; Jude 1:9). It is used of Paul's dialoguing with others as follows: "According to Paul's custom, he went to them, and for three Sabbaths reasoned (διελέξατο) with them from the Scriptures" (Acts 17:2); "He was reasoning (διελέγετο) in the synagogue with the Jews and the God-fearing *Gentiles*, and in the market place every day with those who happened to be present" (Acts 17:17); "And he was reasoning (διελέγετο) in the synagogue every Sabbath and trying to persuade Jews and Greeks (Acts 18:4); "Now he himself entered (διελέξατο) the synagogue and reasoned with the Jews" (Acts 18:19); "And he entered the synagogue and continued speaking out boldly for three months, reasoning (διαλεγόμενος) and persuading *them* about the kingdom of God. But when some were becoming hardened and disobedient, speaking evil of the Way before the multitude, he withdrew from them and took away the disciples, reasoning (διαλεγόμενος) daily in the school of Tyrannus" (Acts 19:8–9); "And on the first day of the week, when we were gathered together to break bread, Paul *began* talking (διελέγετο) to them, intending to depart the next day, and he prolonged his message until midnight" (Acts 20:7); "And there was a certain young man named Eutychus sitting on the window sill, sinking into a deep sleep; and as Paul kept on talking (διαλεγομένου), he was overcome by sleep and fell down from the third floor, and was picked up dead" (Acts 20:9); "And neither in the temple, nor in the synagogues, nor in the city *itself* did they find me carrying on a discussion (διαλεγόμενον) with anyone or causing a riot" (Acts 24:12); "And as he was discussing (διαλεγομένου) righteousness, self-control and the judgment to come, Felix became frightened and said (to Paul), "Go away for the present, and when I find time, I will summon you" (Acts 24:25).

36. BDAG § 1868 defines διαλέγομαι "1. to engage in speech interchange, *converse, discuss, argue;* 2. to instruct about someth., *inform, instruct.*"

comments that *dialegomai* has become "... a technical term for Paul's teaching in the synagogue and approaches the meaning of 'give an address or preach.'"[37] The word especially describes the nature of Paul's preaching in the Jewish synagogues of Thessalonica (Acts 17:2), Athens (Acts 17:17), Corinth (Acts 18:4), and Ephesus (Acts 18:19, 19:8). Because it is used of reasoning with a church congregation on only one occasion (Acts 20:7–9), *dialegomai* appears more properly to describe an evangelistic function of reasoning from the Scriptures (Acts 17:2), so that Paul dialogues from a New Covenant understanding of the Old Covenant in such a way that the word specifies an exposition of Scripture.[38] By making an appeal to the intellect, Paul "aimed to inform the mind, awaken the understanding, stir the reason, quicken the judgment."[39]

Following the example of Paul, the preacher should engage the mind of the unbeliever by skillful use of the Word of God, appealing to the logic of the listener. One must ask how reasoning with someone whose mind has been "blinded by the god of this age" can be the least bit effective (2 Cor 4:6), making it appear that Paul contradicts his own anthropological understanding that the mind of the natural man is "hostile to God, for it does not subject itself to the law of God, for it is not even able *to do so*" (Rom 8:7). The solution is found in that the preacher does not reason with the unbeliever by using natural arguments but with scriptural proofs; that way, the convincing is effected by the dynamic of the living Word of God opening the mind to understand "the things spoken by Paul," as in the conversion of Lydia (Acts 16:14). Obviously, this process is the only way that effective reasoning can take place. For example, Paul's reasoning with Felix brought conviction because of the force of the argument, but sadly, it did not bring about conversion—not because Paul failed to convince by his reasoning, but because of the hardness of Felix' heart (Acts 24:27). Paul could do little in himself to overcome that obstacle apart from the conviction of the Holy Spirit, but he would still reason in such a way that the listener had no defense for his unbelief, as is the case for every evangelist. It is God in His sovereignty who performs the effective reasoning through the skilled reasoning of the preacher, and that is the hope of all evangelism.

Evangelizing by Proving (sumbibazō): Another verb that describes an apologetic activity of evangelizing is *sumbibazō*, which is used once of Paul's ministry, "Saul kept increasing in strength and confounding the Jews who lived at Damascus by proving (*sumbibazōn*) that this *Jesus* is the Christ" (Acts 9:22). This Greek word has the idea of "bringing together parts into a unit,"[40] so that what Paul did was to gather and

---

37. Fürst, διαλέγομαι, *DNTT* 3:821.
38. Ibid.
39. Kuist, *Pedagogy of Paul*, 71.
40. BDAG § 6945 defines συμβιβάζω as follows:
    1. to bring together into a unit, unite (Eph 4:16; Col 2:19) or knit together (Col 2:2);

present appropriate Scripture verses to prove that Jesus had to be the promised Messiah.[41] In like fashion, the preacher needs to be skilled in the discipline of scriptural argumentation so that he can gather its passages together for logical presentation in both personal evangelism and public proclamation.

Evangelizing by Disputing (suzēteō): Another verb used once by Luke to describe Paul's activity of evangelizing is *suzēteō*, meaning to carry on a discussion or a debate (Acts 9:29).[42] Etymologically, the word means "to seek together,"[43] indicating that Paul "was debating with the Greek-speaking Jews" (Acts 9:29 NET) by inviting them to a search of Scripture concerning the identity of Jesus as the Son of God (Acts 9:20). In like manner, the preacher will need to be involved in give-and-take debate with unbelievers in an attempt to evangelize them for Christ—such discussion is yet another aspect of public proclamation of the gospel.

Verbs Expressing the Authority of Evangelism

Other verbs are used primarily by Luke to describe the authority of Paul's evangelizing activity, giving an important legitimacy to the authority of Paul as a delegated messenger of the risen Lord. These verbs include *parrēsiazomai, diamarturomai, apophthengomai, presbeuō, peithō*, which are studied in this next section:

Evangelizing by Boldly Speaking (parrēsiazomai): Used nine times in the NT, *parrēsiazomai* refers to the preaching activity of Paul in every instance but one, and, even there, it refers to the bold preaching of Apollos (Acts 18:26).[44] The etymology

---

    2. to draw a conclusion in the face of evidence, conclude, infer (Acts 16:10);
    3. to present a logical conclusion, demonstrate, prove (Acts 9:22);
    4. to advise by giving instructions, instruct, teach, advise (1 Cor 2:16; Acts 19:33).

    41. Paul uses συμβιβάζω only four times in his letters, three times to express a joining together of the body of Christ (Eph 4:16; Col 2:2, 19), and once as a quotation from Isa 40:13, "For who has known the mind of the Lord, that he should instruct (συμβιβάσει) Him?" (1 Cor 2:16). Obviously, none of these usages suggests preaching.

    42. BDAG § 6922 defines συζητέω variously,
      1. "to carry on a discussion;
      2. to contend with persistence for a point of view,
      3. to ponder various aspects of a matter."

    43. Thayer § 4973a. cites usage of συζητέω in Plato, "to seek or examine together."

    44. The verb *parrēsiazomai* appears as follows: "But Barnabas took hold of him and brought him to the apostles and described to them how he had seen the Lord on the road, and that He had talked to him, and how at Damascus he had spoken out boldly (ἐπαρρησιάσατο) in the name of Jesus" (Acts 9:27); "he was with them moving about freely in Jerusalem, speaking out boldly (παρρησιαζόμενος) in the name of the Lord" (Acts 9:28); "Paul and Barnabas spoke out boldly (παρρησιασάμενοι) and said, "It was necessary that the word of God should be spoken to you first; since you repudiate it, and judge yourselves unworthy of eternal life, behold, we are turning to the Gentiles" (Acts 13:46); "Therefore they spent a long time *there* speaking boldly (παρρησιαζόμενοι) *with* reliance upon the Lord, who was

of the word indicates it is a verbal combination of the preposition *para* ("from") and the noun *rhēma* ("speech"), and it came to mean the freedom to speak.[45] Among the Greek city-states, it signified the democratic right of the full citizen to speak freely in the public assembly.[46] It is not hard to see how this idea transferred to the open preaching of the gospel, as the citizens of the Kingdom of heaven exercise their right of free speech to God and humanity; however, Luke's repetition of the word is certainly not accidental, as he wrote to show the governing officials that the apostles were law-abiding citizens of Judea and/or Rome, and as citizens they had the right to speak out. For this reason, *parrēsiazomai* is found within the content of legal hearings where it would be understood as an appeal to free speech (Acts 26:26). This usage helps to explain why Paul "ought" to speak boldly during his imprisonment, because he had the right to do so as a citizen of both the Roman Empire and the Kingdom of God (Eph 6:19–20). Thus, this word defines the authority of evangelizing activity, meaning that the preacher is granted access by the One who is Head over all rule and authority and thus speaks boldly "in the Name of Jesus" (Acts 9:27).

Evangelizing by Solemnly Testifying (diamarturomai): While preachers commonly implore other believers to be witnessing to the lost of the grace of God, the minister likewise is also to be summoned to be a witness (*martus*) of the truths of the gospel. Paul at his conversion was called by the risen Lord to be "a witness [*martus*] not only to the things which you have seen, but also to the things in which I will appear to you" (Acts 26:16). For that matter, the gospel is described as the "*marturion* of the Christ" (1 Cor 1:6), implying that the minister is summoned to confirm the witness of God to His Son. While the Church is certainly commanded in the Great Commission to the activity of witnessing (Matt 28:19–20), the verb "witnessing" (*marturomai*) is not the word Paul customarily uses to convey this ministry;[47] rather, he resorts to the

---

bearing witness to the word of His grace, granting that signs and wonders be done by their hands" (Acts 14:3); "[Apollos] began to speak out boldly (παρρησιάζεσθαι) in the synagogue. But when Priscilla and Aquila heard him, they took him aside and explained to him the way of God more accurately" (Acts 18:26); "[Paul] entered the synagogue and continued speaking out boldly (ἐπαρρησιάζετο) for three months, reasoning and persuading *them* about the kingdom of God" (Acts 19:8); "For the king knows about these matters, and I speak to him also with confidence (παρρησιαζόμενος), since I am persuaded that none of these things escape his notice; for this has not been done in a corner" (Acts 26:26); "I am an ambassador in chains; that in *proclaiming* it I may speak boldly (παρρησιάσωμαι), as I ought to speak" (Eph 6:20); "After we had already suffered and been mistreated in Philippi, as you know, we had the boldness (ἐπαρρησιασάμεθα) in our God to speak to you the gospel of God amid much opposition" (1 Thess 2:2). This list could also include the noun *parrēsia* when used with other speaking verbs: "We use great boldness of speech" (2 Cor 3:12); "That I may open my mouth with boldness" (Eph 6:19); however, Paul's use of this noun refers more frequently to spiritual boldness (Eph 3:12; 1 Tim 3:13, Phlm 1:8) than to speaking boldly.

45. Hahn, "Openness," *DNTT* 2:734.

46. Ibid., 735.

47. While closely related to the more common verb μαρτυρέω, the word μαρτύρομαι appears only five times in the NT (Acts 20:26, "Therefore I testify (μαρτύρομαι) to you this day, that I am innocent

intensive verb, *diamarturomai*, "to testify solemnly."⁴⁸ This Greek word carries the idea of being called to give a solemn witness of the truths of the gospel with the intent to convince the hearers of the truthfulness of the person and work of Jesus Christ so that the hearer would respond with faith and repentance. *Diamarturomai* is repeatedly used in the Book of Acts, where Luke presents Paul when he is preaching as a legal witness of the gospel; thus, he "solemnly testifies [*diamarturomenos*] to both Jews and Greeks of repentance toward God and faith in our Lord Jesus Christ" (Acts 20:21). He was "solemnly testifying [*diamarturomenos*] to the Jews that Jesus was the Christ" (Acts 18:5), to the Kingdom of God (Acts 28:23), and to the church "of the gospel of the grace of God" (Acts 20:24).

While occasionally it is a civil judge who summons Paul to testify, supremely it is the risen Lord who charges His apostle, "As you have solemnly witnessed [*diemarturō*] to My cause at Jerusalem, so you must witness [*marturēsai*] at Rome also" (Acts 23:11). This citation shows that witnessing is a "binding obligation to make known the message and will of God."⁴⁹ The Lord delivered to Paul a divine summons to testify on His behalf, and the apostle will not be found in contempt of that charge.

In his own writings, Paul uses *diamarturomai* infrequently (1 Thess 4:6; 1 Tim 5:21; 2 Tim 2:14; 4:1) and even then not so much to express evangelizing but to show a pastoral charge, such as he lays upon Timothy (2 Tim 4:1). Because it is God Himself who requires His servants to give a good witness, each minister of the New Covenant should view himself as one who solemnly testifies as a witness to the work of God. This requirement demands that the demeanor of preaching be solemn and serious, because the preacher is under divine summons to testify to the truth of the gospel.

Evangelizing by Declaring (apophthengomai): In the LXX, the declaring activity of a prophet (or sometimes of a false prophet) is described by the verb *apophthengomai*, which is defined by BDAG as "expressing oneself orally,"⁵⁰ but its association with divine

---

of the blood of all men"; Acts 26:22, "And so, having obtained help from God, I stand to this day testifying (μαρτυρόμενος) both to small and great, stating nothing but what the Prophets and Moses said was going to take place"; Gal 5:3, "And I testify (μαρτύρομαι) again to every man who receives circumcision, that he is under obligation to keep the whole Law"; Eph 4:17, "This I say therefore, and affirm (μαρτύρομαι) together with the Lord, that you walk no longer just as the Gentiles also walk, in the futility of their mind"; 1 Thess 2:11, "we were ... imploring (μαρτυρόμενοι) each one of you as a father *would* his own children.").

48. BDAG § 1878 defines διαμαρτύρομαι as follows: 1. "to make a solemn declaration about the truth of someth. testify of, bear witness to" (Acts 8:25; 10:42; 18:5 20:21, 23, 24; 23:11; 28:23; 1 Thess 4:6; Heb 2:6); and 2. to exhort with authority in matters of extraordinary importance, freq. w. ref. to higher powers and/or suggestion of peril, solemnly urge, exhort, warn" (Luke 16:28; Acts 2:40; 1 Tim 5:21; 2 Tim 2:14; 4:1).

49. Coenen, "Witness," *DNTT*, 3:1044.

50. BDAG § 1037 defines ἀποφθέγγομαι, "to express oneself orally, w. focus on sound rather than content, *speak out, declare*"; however, it is clear that inspired content is more than sounds. It appears in the Greek Bible nine times (1 Chron 25:1; Ps 58:8; Mic 5:11; Zech 10:2; Ezek 13:9, 19; Acts 2:4, 14; 26:25).

revelation in 1 Chron 25:1 gives the verb a more pronounced meaning ("The sons of Asaph and of Heman and of Jeduthun *were* to prophesy with lyres, harps, and cymbal"); for example, it is used in Acts 2:4 "as the Spirit was giving utterance" (*apophthengesthai*) to the disciples to speak with other tongues, expressing an inspired assertion.[51] The verb is used of Paul only once, when he states, "Most excellent Festus, I utter [*apophthengomai*] words of sober truth" (Acts 26:25). If Festus recognized the religious connotation of this word, he would know that Paul intended to be understood as speaking—not merely with serious intent—but with prophetic authority as one who had received revelatory content. Since Paul has just testified to his heavenly commission from Christ (Acts 26:16), his choice of *apophthengomai* strengthens this explanation.

Needless to say, the modern preacher is not an inspired apostle like Paul who received direct revelation from the risen Lord; however, when the preacher preaches the revelatory content of the inspired prophets, then he does "utter words of sober truth." Evangelistic preaching in fact impresses upon unbelievers the divine imperative to repent and believe.

Evangelizing by Ambassadoring (presbeuō): Another term used by Paul to describe evangelizing is the verb *presbeuō*,[52] defining preaching in terms of a diplomat who delivers royal decrees as a delegated *presbeia*.[53] This noun is used in Luke 14:32 and 19:14 of official "embassages" sent from one authority to another, and Paul applies this office to himself—rather ironically—during his imperial imprisonment as an "ambassador in chains" who prays that he may speak boldly, as he ought to speak (Eph 6:19–20). Likewise, all ministers speak as "ambassadors [*presbeuomen*] of Christ," official delegates through whom God is entreating humanity to be reconciled to Him (2 Cor 5:20). The preacher needs to be aware that he is the personal legate of Christ so that when he speaks, it is as if Christ Himself speaks, as Jesus said, "The one who listens to you listens to Me" (Luke 10:16). In his activity of "embassing,"[54] the preacher's duty is to deliver the "embassy" and nothing more, which is to say, he is to confine his message to the revealed word of the King.

Evangelizing by Persuading (peithō): One final verb that expresses the activity of evangelizing and brings all these preceding words together is *peithō*, "to persuade," for the primary purpose of evangelism is to persuade others to believe in Christ.[55]

---

51. The prophetic implication of the word is also seen in Peter's explanation of Pentecost when he "took his stand with the eleven, raised his voice and declared (ἀπεφθέγξατο)" to the men of Judea and Jerusalem the arrival of the gospel (Acts 2:14).

52. BDAG § 6137 defines πρεσβεύω to "*be an ambassador/envoy, travel/work as an ambassador.*"

53. Bornkamm, πρεσβεύω, *TDNT* 6:682, shows that by Paul's use of the embassy illustration, he "very impressively sets forth this authoritative and official character of the proclamation."

54. Admittedly, "embassing" is a coined word, but all words have to start somewhere!

55. BDAG § 5754 defines πείθω "to cause to come to a particular point of view or course of action."

Although Paul uses *peithō* primarily in contexts dealing with personal confidence (as in 1 Tim 1:5), and notwithstanding his disclaimer that the power of persuasion in his message and preaching was "not in persuasive (*peithos*) words of wisdom, but in demonstration of the Spirit and of power" (1 Cor 2:4), he still asserts, "Therefore knowing the fear of the Lord, we persuade (*peithomen*) men" (2 Cor 5:11). Luke pictures Paul attempting to persuade others of the truth of the gospel in several instances: "Many of the Jews and of the God-fearing proselytes followed Paul and Barnabas, who, speaking to them, were urging (*epeithon*) them to continue in the grace of God" (Acts 13:43); Paul "was reasoning in the synagogue every Sabbath and trying to persuade (*epeithen*) Jews and Greeks" (Acts 18:4); Paul "entered the synagogue and continued speaking out boldly for three months, reasoning and persuading (*peithōn*) *them* about the kingdom of God" (Acts 19:8); Paul "was explaining to them by solemnly testifying about the kingdom of God, and trying to persuade (*peithōn*) them concerning Jesus, from both the Law of Moses and from the Prophets, from morning until evening" (Acts 28:23). Paul's persuasion was so effective that even King Agrippa admitted, "In a short time you will persuade (*peitheis*) me to become a Christian" (Acts 26:28).

In this sense, *peithō* speaks of the motivation that lies behind the presentation of the gospel—the preacher desires to see others convinced to believe in Christ, so he does not merely present facts of the gospel, but he urges a positive response of faith in Christ from the hearers. This emphasis on persuasiveness shows that the activity of evangelism should be accompanied by great fervency arising from personal conviction in the truth of the gospel (1 Cor 5:11).

Summary to Verbs Expressing the Authority of Evangelism: Paul's final charge to Timothy is to "preach the Word" (2 Tim 4:2), and at once Paul brings his friend to the great speaking activity of evangelizing the world through the proclamation of the gospel. Not surprisingly, the verb translated "preach" (*kērussein*) was only one of many verbs available to Paul to describe the activity of evangelizing (including the verbs *euangelizō, angellō, ektithēmi, dialegomai, sumbibazō, parrēsiazomai, diamarturomai, apophthengomai, presbeuō,* and *peithō*), and so this section has examined these various words that the apostle employs to convey the wide-ranging nuances for the activity of evangelizing the world.

The Activity of Preaching: Instructing the Church

Paul continues his charge to Timothy, "Exhort with . . . instruction" (*didachē*, 2 Tim 4:2), and while the emphasis is certainly on the content of the exhortation, the mention of the *didachē* introduces the instructing activity directed to the church. By necessity,

---

The verb is found only in the NT, 39 times in 38 verses (Acts 5:36, 37, 39; 12:20; 13:43; 14:19; 17:4; 18:4; 19:8, 26; 21:14; 23:21; 26:26, 28; 27:11; 28:23, 24; Rom 2:8, 19; 8:38; 14:14; 15:14; 2 Cor 1:9; 2:3; 5:11; 10:7; Gal 1:10; 5:7, 10; Phil 1:6, 14, 25; 2:24; 3:3, 4; 2 Thess 3:4; 2 Tim 1:5, 12; Phlm 1:21).

the majority of the pastor's ministry is directed toward the covenant community, and so Paul then moves from the evangelizing activity toward the unbelieving world to the instructing activity of the believing church.

As one might expect, Paul selects a varied vocabulary to express the activity of instructing the church; indeed, it is impossible to separate verbal instruction from the gathered church. Ford comments, "The Church came to birth with preaching, and preaching came to birth with the Church."[56] On this basis—that preaching and the church are inseparable—Calvin insisted that the true preaching of the gospel is an essential mark of the true church.[57] Calvin's evaluation has guided the Reformed Churches, but it needs to be examined anew, not because it is faulty, but because it has been neglected, or worse, denied. This section will then investigate the primary vocabulary Paul employs to describe the instructing activity of the preacher to the church.

Instructing by Teaching: *Didaskein*

It was shown in chapter 3 that the content of preaching is to be the *didachē* and the *didaskalia*, the doctrines associated with the New Covenant gospel. That specific content—now recorded in the NT—requires the preacher to be active in teaching (*didaskein*), following the example of Jesus as the Master Teacher.[58] Accordingly, God gives to His church some as teachers (*didaskaloi*, Eph 4:11; 1 Cor 12:28–29), a designation Paul applies to himself (1 Tim 2:7; 2 Tim 1:11). As one who has received the gift of teaching, the preacher is to be involved in the activity of *didaskalōn*, instructing the church through the ministry of teaching (Rom 12:7).

Several times in the Book of Acts, Paul is pictured in his teaching activity; and in each case, the beneficiary of his instruction is the church.[59] This insight suggests that teaching is an activity generally directed toward the church, whereas evangelizing is directed toward the unsaved. This distinction is, of course, not absolute. Unbelievers need scriptural instruction, and professing Christians certainly need evangelizing, but even in Paul's letters, the word *didaskalein* usually describes the didactic ministry of the preacher to the church rather than to the world.

---

56. Ford, *The Ministry of the Word*, 53.

57. Calvin, *Institutes* 4.1.9; 2:1023.

58. Jesus as addressed as "Teacher" (*Didaskale*) thirty-one times (Matt 8:19; 12:38; 19:16; 22:16, 24, 36; Mark 4:38; 9:17, 38; 10:17, 20, 35; 12:14, 19, 32; 13:1; Luke 3:12; 7:40; 9:38; 10:25; 11:45; 12:13; 18:18; 19:39; 20:21, 28, 39; 21:7; John 1:38; 8:4; 20:16).

59. Paul's teaching ministry is seen in the following verses: Barnabas brought Paul to Antioch for an entire year to gather the church and to teach (διδάξαι) considerable numbers (Acts 11:26); after the Council, "Paul and Barnabas stayed in Antioch, teaching (διδάσκοντες) and preaching, with many others also, the word of the Lord" (Acts 15:35); Paul later settled in Ephesus for a year and half, "teaching (διδάσκων) the word of God among them" (Acts 18:11), and he later reminded the Ephesian elders that he had been "teaching (διδάξαι) you publicly and from house to house" (Acts 20:20); and the book ends by reporting that Paul was "teaching (διδάσκων) concerning the Lord Jesus Christ with all openness, unhindered" (Acts 28:31). See Stanley Porter, *Paul in Acts* (2000).

In this case, teaching ought to be the major activity of the minister with regard to the church, since the 'great commission' of the resurrected Lord is to be teaching all things He commanded (Matt 28:20). Several times in the course of his letters, Paul tersely commands Timothy to teach (1 Tim 4:11; 6:2), and to the Ephesisan elders, he points to himself as a model for both public and private teaching (Eph 2:20). The perpetuation of Christian Teaching is ensured as the minister entrusts the gospel to faithful men "who will be able to teach others also" (2 Tim 2:2), thus showing clearly the permanent nature of the teaching ministry as it is passed along to succeeding generations of believers.

There is some debate among biblical scholars whether teaching is the same as preaching; for example, Grasso insists, "Preaching is not teaching,"[60] and for support, he maintains that teaching relates to a system of knowledge whereas preaching transmits a person—Christ.[61] On the other hand, Wegenast declares, "Any distinction between teaching and preaching would seem to be inadmissible."[62] The truth seems to lie between these extremes: against Wegenast's assertion, it should be admitted that there must be some distinction between preaching and teaching, or else the NT writers would not have bothered to use the varied and distinct words. Against Grasso's contention, the dichotomy between the taught knowledge and the preached Person is certainly not ironclad, because the body of knowledge (the *didachē*) concerns the Person of Christ. Practically speaking, there can be no preaching without some teaching of Christian truths, nor can there be any teaching without the preaching of Christ. Thus, the Book of Acts conjoins both teaching and evangelizing several times (Acts 15:35; 28:31), as Paul also reminds his readers that in the hearing of the gospel, it is Christ Himself who does the teaching (Eph 4:21).

Even so, the most important element of teaching is not the method but the content, which the NT variously defines as "the Word of the Lord" (Acts 15:35), the "Word of God" (Acts 18:11), the "things concerning the Lord Jesus" (Acts 28:31), "the traditions" (2 Thess 2:15), and "the things you have heard" (2 Tim 2:2). Thus, the preacher should first dedicate himself to the content of the *Didaskalia*, the inscripturated apostolic doctrines, and then devote himself to the skills required to deliver the teaching and instruction to the church. No man can consider himself to be a minister of the New Covenant unless he functions in the activity of teaching the *Didaskalia*.

Instructing by Reading: *Anaginōskō*

Another speaking activity by which the church is instructed is in reading outloud, as demonstrated in the verb *anaginōskō*, which moves from the basic meaning of reading

---

60. Grasso, *Proclaiming God's Message*, 21.
61. Ibid.
62. Wegenast, "Teach," *DNTT*, 3:764.

aloud[63] to the liturgical reading of the Scriptures. As an example, the Levites read to the gathered Israelites from the law of God, "translating to give the sense so that they understood the reading" (Neh 8:8). Although Paul uses the verb *anaginōskō* only eight times,[64] it is clear that that the activity of reading is ministerially important. Following the pattern of reading Scripture in the synagogue (Acts 13:15), "The Reading" (*hē anagnōsis*, 1 Tim 4:13) became a liturgical term in the early church for the prescribed reading of its sacred literature ("I adjure you by the Lord to have this letter read to all the brethren" 1 Thess 5:27), so that every public gathering of the covenant community should include a reading of some portion of the Word of God.

Paul's command to Timothy to "attend to the reading" (1 Tim 4:13 NAB) shows that the *Anagnōsis* had become a technical expression to describe a separate instructional ministry along with "the exhortation" and "the doctrine," which are also mentioned in this charge. By "the reading," Paul does not mean Timothy is to read just any literature: he specifies to the Colossians what they should read—his own letters (Col 4:16). His injunction becomes an indirect evidence of the authoritative inspiration of his writings, since the apostle places his own epistles on equal footing with other compositions received by the church as Scripture (the OT in particular) and read as part of the prescribed liturgy of the New Covenant community.

"The Reading," then, would be at least a verbatim recitation of some passage of Scripture, and this part of the worship assembly would be immensely important to those who were either illiterate or had no access to the written manuscripts for themselves. It stands to reason that the reading of the Old and New Covenant writings became the basis for expository preaching of those texts, following the example of Ezra, who read from the Law and then expounded upon them (Neh 9:6).[65] In a similar manner, the preacher must train himself to read the Scripture with oratorical skill and conviction. No doubt as a rule he should review and practice his reading of Scripture privately before he does so publicly, and then he should impress upon the listeners that what he is reading is the Word of God.

---

63. BDAG § 459 defines ἀνάγνωσις, "the process of reading someth. written."

64. "For we write nothing else to you than what you read (ἀναγινώσκετε) and understand, and I hope you will understand until the end" (2 Cor 1:13); "You are our letter, written in our hearts, known and read (ἀναγινωσκομένη) by all men" (2 Cor 3:2); "But to this day whenever Moses is read (ἀναγινώσκηται), a veil lies over their heart" (2 Cor 3:15); "And by referring to this, when you read (ἀναγινώσκοντες) you can understand my insight into the mystery of Christ" (Eph 3:4); "And when this letter is read (ἀναγνωσθῇ) among you, have it also read (ἀναγνωσθῇ) in the church of the Laodiceans; and you, for your part read (ἀναγνῶτε) my letter *that is coming* from Laodicea" (Col 4:16); "I adjure you by the Lord to have this letter read (ἀναγνωσθῆναι) to all the brethren" (1 Thess 5:27).

65. Blunck, "ἀναγιγνώσκω," *DNTT* 1:246, states, "The reading had to replace the apostolic preaching, on which all later preaching is based."

Instructing by Relating: *Exēgeomai*

Although not found in Paul's letters, the verb *exēgeomai* is used twice in the Book of Acts to describe the ministry of Paul where he "relates" to the church the things "God had done" through him.[66] Thayer points out that while *exēgeomai* properly means to "lead out," metaphorically it came to describe in classical Greek the revealing of divine secrets.[67] Fittingly, in both Pauline references in the Book of Acts, the word is used to describe his leading of the church into the divine words and works of God, so that all who listened were instructed in divine ways.

By way of application, the preacher is called to instruct the church by relating the works of God for them. The term *exēgeomai* implies the preacher's accountability to the people; he is responsible to impress the works of God upon them by the activity of instructing them in the scriptures along with calling them to increased faith in that God.

Instructing by Discipling: *Mathēteuō*

Another word used in the Book of Acts to describe the instructional ministry of Paul is *mathēteuō*, which is found in the report that after Barnabas and Saul had "preached the gospel to that city and had made many disciples (*mathēteusantes*), they returned to Lystra and to Iconium and to Antioch" (Acts 14:21). Although the noun "disciple" is not found in Paul's letters, this absence does not in any way diminish the importance of making disciples, as the verb *mathēteuō* is translated in Acts 14:21.[68] After all, instructing converts in Christian disciplines is a basic responsibility of ministry, as mandated by the Lord's Great Commission: "Go therefore and make disciples (*mathēteusate*) of all the nations" (Matt 28:19).

The basic idea conveyed by *mathēteuō* seems to be that of a private tutorial relationship between a teacher and a student (Mark 13:52). It is teaching on the most personal one-on-one level. Thus, it should to be within the plan of the minister to disciple his entire congregation so that each one becomes a disciple who is able to teach others also (2 Tim 2:2). The method employed in discipleship should be interpersonal instruction between the minister and a faithful learner, so that every minister of the New Covenant will make it his mission to disciple individual believers in his instructional activity as a discipler of the Word of God.

---

66. "Barnabas and Paul as they were relating (ἐξηγουμένων) what signs and wonders God had done through them among the Gentiles" (Acts 15:12); Paul "*began* to relate (ἐξηγεῖτο) one by one the things which God had done among the Gentiles through his ministry" (Acts 21:19).

67. Thayer § 1950, defines ἐξηγέομαι "1. properly, to lead out, be leader, go before (Homer, et al.) and 2. metaphorically, (cf. German *ausführen*) to draw out in narrative, unfold in teaching; a. to recount, rehearse." It is certainly used of divine revelation in John 1:18, "No man has seen God at any time; the only begotten God, who is in the bosom of the Father, He has explained (ἐξηγήσατο) Him."

68. BDAG § 4661 defines μαθητεύω 1. *to be a pupil,* with implication of being an adherent of the teacher (Matt 27:57; Mark 13:52); and 2. to cause one to be a pupil (Matt 28:19; Acts 14:21). The word is found only these four times in the NT.

Instructing by Catechizing: *Katēchein*

One final verb that refers to the instructional activity of the preacher is *katēcheō*, which has come across into English as "catechizing." Of the eight times it appears in the NT, twice it refers to an informal report (Acts 21:21, 24), but the other six times it refer to a catechizing activity.[69]

Beyer insists that Paul borrows *katēcheō* from Greek pedagogy, since the word is not found in the OT;[70] however, it would be most unusual for Paul's theology to spring from sources other than the OT, and the same could also be said for this concept of catechizing. After all, the idea of instructing others is a very Hebraic concept (Deut 6:7, "You shall teach them diligently to your sons."), and Paul himself addresses Jewish teachers as those who are catechizing out of the Law (Rom 2:18).

By definition, then, this activity of instructing seems to be a much more private encounter than public instruction, whereby the teacher individually meets with a catechumen, as historically this one-on-one method has been preferred way catechism has been taught. Thus, Paul distinguishes between the one who is being catechized in the Word (*katēchoumenos ton logon*) and the one who is doing the catechizing (*tō katēchounti*), meaning that the minister has a duty to be a catechizer (Gal 6:6). Following Paul's pattern to catechize others in the church (1 Cor 14:19), the preacher should also find time to catechize others in the truths of Scripture, and to do so with words that are intelligible and understandable.

Summary to the Activity of Instructing the Church

In his activities of teaching, reading, relating, discipling, and catechizing, the preacher instructs the church in the things of the Word of God, following the example and precepts of Paul by these sort of actions. An unlearned congregation is a poor reflection upon the one who is its teacher, whereas a congregation that is instructed in the knowledge and doctrine of the Scripture is a credit to the teaching ability of its pastor. It is necessary, then, for the preacher to consider himself to be a teacher whose first task is to be instructing the congregation in the facts and duties of the Covenant Scriptures.

The Activity of Preaching: Defending the Church

Because the church of God is constantly under attack from its archenemy Satan (Eph 6:12, 16), it is the duty of the New Covenant minister to defend the flock from evil assaults. While there is a lesser danger from unruly believers, Paul warns the Ephesian elders that a greater threat arises from false brothers who appear as false teachers

---

69. BDAG § 4145 defines κατηχέω, "1. to share a communication that one receives, *report, inform* (Luke 1:4; Acts 21:21, 24); 2. *teach, instruct*" (1 Cor 14:19; Gal 6:6b; Rom 2:18; Acts 18:25; Gal 6:6a).

70. Beyer, κατηχέω, *TDNT* 3:639.

(Acts 20:29–30, see also 2 Pet 2:1). These pseudo-professors attack as either "savage wolves, not sparing the flock" or more insidiously, "from your own selves men will arise, speaking perverse things, to draw away the disciples after them" (Acts 20:29–30). A true pastor must not play the part of the hireling who flees from the wolf because he has no concern for the sheep (John 10:12–13); instead, he must protect the flock as David protected his sheep from the lion and the bear (1 Sam 17:34–37). The vocabulary Paul uses to describe the activity of defending the church is quite varied and includes such verbs as defending, apologizing, watching, and heeding. This section will examine these primary verbs describing this defending activity of the ministry.

Defending by Apologizing: *Apologeomai*

The Book of Acts records several occasions in which Paul defended the gospel from the charges leveled against it. The verb of choice in these contexts is *apologeomai*, from which English derives the word "apology." In its classic form, *apologeomai* means to give a defense;[71] thus, it lent itself to the branch of Christian theology known as Apologetics, "the defense (*apologia*) and confirmation of the gospel" (Phil 1:7).

Because Jesus counseled His disciples not to be anxious nor to prepare beforehand to defend themselves when brought before "the synagogues and the rulers and the authorities" (Luke 12:11; 21:14), Paul cheerfully made his defense (*euthumōs tà perì emautoū apologouai*) when he was arraigned before the Proconsul Felix, turning the charges into an opportunity to preach the resurrection of both the righteous and the wicked while he testified to his own innocence (Acts 24:10, 15). Later, Paul made a similar defense (*apologoumenou*) before the Proconsul Festus (Acts 25:8), and then he proceeded to make the same defense (*apelogeito*) before King Agrippa (Acts 26:1), using the opportunity to defend (*apologeisthai*) his heavenly calling by Christ (Acts 26:2–23) until the governor interrupted his continuing defense (*apologoumenon*) by accusing Paul of an additional (but irrational) charge of insanity (Acts 26:24).

Paul claims that he was "appointed for the defense (*apologia*) of the gospel" (Phil 1:16), making clear one aspect of preaching is to give an apologetic for the message (not that anyone should apologize for the gospel!) Generally speaking, however, Apologetics involves the presentation of rational and historical proofs of the Christian Faith, and certainly in his apologies, Paul argues for the historical certainty of the resurrection of Christ (Acts 26:23). Following Paul's example, the preacher should be skilled in presenting reasonable evidences in support of the gospel message.

It seems, however, that the word *apologeomai* means more basically, to speak in one's own defense,[72] as a certain Alexander attempted to do until he was shouted

---

71. BDAG § 963 defines ἀπολογέομαι, "to speak in one's own defense against charges presumed to be false, defend oneself." The word appears in Jer 12:1; 38:6; Luke 12:11; 21:14; Acts 19:33; 24:10; 25:8; 26:1, 2, 24; Rom 2:15; 2 Cor 12:19.

72. L&N § 33.435 defines ἀπολογέομαι simply, "to defend oneself."

down by the angry Ephesian mob (Acts 19:33–34). Likewise, it is often the preacher himself who comes under attack and must give a defense for his own actions and beliefs, as Paul often had to do (2 Tim 4:16). Such charges imply that the reputation of the gospel is inextricably linked to the reputation of the preacher: not surprisingly, if the skeptical world can discredit the messenger, it feels quite justified in dismissing the message. For this reason, the defense of the gospel becomes a vindication of the actions of the preacher, so that the words dealing with the defense of the Faith also relate to the defense of the conduct of the entire believing community (2 Cor 7:11). By defending the gospel, the church becomes a "partaker of grace" along with the accused apostle (Phil 1:7), so that every believer should always be "ready to make a defense to everyone who asks you to give an account for the hope that is in you, yet with gentleness and reverence" (1 Pet 3:15). It is evident that godly conduct is the best proof that Christian doctrine actually leads to godliness, so that the preacher must not only speak a defense of the gospel but also live out its truths.

Defending by Witnessing: *Martureō*

In evangelical terminology, the concept of witnessing has become synonymous with evangelizing the lost, yet the verb *martureō* is rarely used in that sense in the NT;[73] instead, it can be argued that in every instance in the NT, *martureō* carries an unmistakable connotation of acting as a legal witness to the truth of a matter (John 4:39 may be the lone exception).[74]

Accordingly, Paul "bears witness" on behalf of the reputation of others (2 Cor 8:3; Gal 4:15; Col 4:13), but more importantly, he "testifies on behalf of God" (*emarturēsamen kata tou Theou*) concerning the truth of the resurrection (1 Cor 15:15). He is frequently called to the witness stand to testify to the truth of the Faith. Before King Agrippa, Paul states, "I stand to this day testifying (*marturomenos*) both to small and great, stating nothing but what the Prophets and Moses said was going to take place" (Acts 26:22). In this way, Paul defends the Faith against the various accusations of sedition and heresy leveled at him (Acts 24:5), and in so doing he proclaims the testimony of God Himself (1 Cor 2:1). Likewise, a minister should not be ashamed of the witness "of the testimony (*marturion*) of our Lord" (2 Tim 1:8), who "testified (*marturēsantos*) the good confession before Pontius Pilate" (1 Tim 6:13),

---

73. L&N § 3.262 defines μαρτυρέω, "to provide information about a person or an event concerning which the speaker has direct knowledge—'to witness.'" The verb is found eighty-six times in the Greek Bible (Gen 31:46, 48; Num 35:30; Deut 19:15, 18; 31:21; 2 Chr 28:10; Lam 2:13; Matt 23:31; Luke 4:22; John 1:7, 8, 15, 32, 34; 2:25; 3:11, 26, 28, 32; 4:39, 44; 5:31, 32, 33, 36, 37, 39; 7:7; 8:13, 14, 18; 10:25; 12:17; 13:21; 15:26, 27; 18:23, 37; 19:35; 21:24; Acts 6:3; 10:22, 43; 13:22; 14:3; 15:8; 16:2; 22:5, 12; 23:11; 26:5; Rom 3:21; 10:2; 1 Cor 15:15; 2 Cor 8:3; Gal 4:15; Col 4:13; 1 Tim 5:10; 6:13; Heb 7:8, 17; 10:15; 11:2, 4, 5, 39; 1 John 1:2; 4:14; 5:6, 7, 9, 10; 3 John 1:3, 6, 12; Rev 1:2; 22:16, 18, 20).

74. John 4:39 reads, "And from that city many of the Samaritans believed in Him because of the word of the woman who testified, 'He told me all the things that I *have* done.

Defending by Heeding: *Prosechō* and *Epechō*

Paul uses several words based on the verb *echein*[75] to describe the mental heeding that a minister needs in order to defend the gospel. Thus, he instructs the Ephesian elders, "Be on guard (*prosechete*) for yourselves and for all the flock" (Acts 20:28).[76] This caution suggests a need for mental awareness of the danger that threatens both the elder and his charge so that he may be keenly prepared to guard against "savage wolves" and "men speaking perversely" who will arise to draw away the disciples (Acts 20:30).

In the Pastoral Epistles, Paul uses *prosechō* in a negative manner, telling his co-workers "not to pay attention to myths and endless genealogies" (1 Tim 1:4) nor to "Jewish myths and commandments of men who turn away from the truth" (Titus 1:14). Actually, these commands imply that the minister needs to know enough of these aberrations in order to recognize their deception so he may be able to warn others of their dangers. Positively, the minister should "give attention (*proseche*) to the *public* reading *of Scripture*, to exhortation and teaching" (1 Tim 4:13), no doubt doing more than thinking about these disciplines but actually speaking them to others.

Quite similar to Paul's caution to the Ephesian elders to "pay careful attention to yourselves" (Acts 20:28 ESV) appears when he tells Timothy, "Pay close attention (*epeche*) to yourself and to your teaching; persevere in these things; for as you do this you will insure salvation both for yourself and for those who hear you" (1 Tim 4:16).[77] Such careful scrutiny of oneself as well as other believers becomes an essential part of defending the church against slanderous accusation or preventing detractors from finding substantial basis for any such accusations. To accomplish this task, the preacher must constantly remind himself that false teaching is always lurking in the

---

75. BDAG § 3353 defines the basic meaning of ἔχω as "to have."

76. L&N § 27.59 defines προσέχω, "To be in a continuous state of readiness to learn of any future danger, need, or error, and to respond appropriately–'to pay attention to, to keep on the lookout for, to be alert for, to be on one's guard against.'" The verb is fairly common, appearing 145 times in the Greek Bible (Gen 4:5; 24:6; 34:3; Exod 9:21; 10:28; 19:12; 23:21; 34:11, 12; Lev 22:2; Deut 1:45; 4:9, 23; 6:12; 8:11; 11:16; 12:13, 19, 23, 30; 15:9; 24:8; 32:1, 46; 1 Kgs 7:17; 2 Chr 25:16; 35:21; 1 Es. 1:26; Ezra 7:23; Neh 1:6, 11; 9:34; Esth 8:12; Tob 4:12, 14; 1 Macc 2:68; 7:11; 10:61; 2 Macc 7:25; 3 Macc 2:2; 4 Macc 1:1; Ps 5:3; 9:38; 16:1; 21:2, 20; 34:23; 37:23; 39:2, 14; 54:3; 58:6; 60:2; 65:19; 68:19; 69:2; 70:12; 76:2; 77:1; 79:2; 80:12; 85:6; 129:2; 140:1; 141:7; Odes 2:1; Prov 1:24, 30; 4:1, 20; 5:1, 3; 7:24; 17:4; Eccl 4:13; Song 8:13; Job 1:8; 2:3; 7:17; 10:3; 13:6; 27:6; 29:21; Wis. 8:12; 13:1; 14:30; Sir. 1:29; 4:15; 6:13; 7:24; 11:33; 13:8, 13; 16:24; 17:14; 18:27; 23:27; 28:16, 26; 29:20; 32:24; 35:1; 37:31; Hos 5:1; Mic 1:2; Zech 1:4; 7:11; Mal 3:16; Isa 1:10, 23; 28:23; 32:4; 49:1; 55:3; Jer 6:19; 7:24, 26; 25:4; Dan 9:18; 12:10; Dat. 9:19; Matt 6:1; 7:15; 10:17; 16:6, 11, 12; Luke 12:1; 17:3; 20:46; 21:34; Acts 5:35; 8:6, 10, 11; 16:14; 20:28; 1 Tim 1:4; 3:8; 4:1, 13; Titus 1:14; Heb 2:1; 7:13; 2 Pet 1:19).

77. The verb *epechō* is used only five times in the NT (Luke 14:7; Acts 3:5; Acts 19:22; Phil 2:16, and 1 Tim 4:16). BDAG § 2911.2 defines ἐπέχω, "to be mindful or especially observant."

shadows waiting to entrap him. To guard against being snared by false doctrine, the preacher must preach not only to the church, but to himself as well.

Defending by Watching: *Grēgoreō*

Another command that concerns defending the Faith is addressed to the Ephesian elders in Acts 20:31, "Be on the alert (*grēgoreite*)," as if to "keep zealous watch for men or lurking beasts."[78] Such a task would mean that the minister is to "instruct certain men not to teach strange doctrines" (1 Tim 1:3) and to "silence those who are teaching things they should not *teach*, for the sake of sordid gain" (Titus 1:11). Faithful watching over God's flock may even necessitate that a minister confront a fellow minister in the way Paul rebuked his colleague Peter when he was "not straightforward about the truth of the gospel" (Gal 2:14). A watchful pastor must remain constantly vigilant to confront anything or anyone who would disturb or destroy the church of God.

Summary to the Activity of Defending the Church

Because the church is always under attack (Eph 6:12), the preacher must serve as an apologist by defending the actions of the church against slanderous charges. Interestingly, it does not seem that the NT defends the doctrines of the church as much as it defends the conduct of its adherents. This can be seen in the Book of Acts where the behavior of the apostles is repeatedly brought into disrepute by spurious charges. However, there certainly is a defense of the gospel (Phil 1:7), especially against false gospels that distort the "doctrine according to godliness" (1 Tim 6:3), so the preacher must be ever vigilant to alert the church of these distortions as well as presenting positively the truthfulness of the gospel. Of course, all these activities elucidate yet further aspects of proclaiming the Word so that the public defense of the Faith could well be a part or even the entirety of a particular sermon.

The Activity of Preaching: Governing the Church

How then is Timothy, as a representative parish preacher, to instruct the church "in all patience and teaching"? In his charge to Timothy (2 Tim 4:1–5), Paul moves from an evangelizing activity directed toward the unbelieving world ("Preach . . . the Word!") to three terse imperatives depicting the application of the Word to the church: "Reprove!" (*elegchon*) "Rebuke!" (*epitímeson*) "Exhort!" (*parakaleson*). These three verbs introduce

---

78. Oepke, γρηγορέω, *TDNT* 2:338. The word appears thirty-one times in the Greek Bible (Neh 7:3; 1 Macc 12:27; Ps Sol 3:2; Jer 5:6; 38:28, 28; Bar 2:9; Lam 1:14; Dat 9:14; Matt 24:42, 43; 25:13; 26:38, 40, 41; Mark 13:34, 35, 37; 14:34, 37, 38; Luke 12:37; Acts 20:31; 1 Cor 16:13; Col 4:2; 1 Thess 5:6, 10; 1 Pet 5:8; Rev 3:2, 3; 16:15), and BDAG § 1689 notes that it moves from the primary meaning of "staying awake" to "being in constant readiness."

a group of words used by the apostle to convey the activity whereby the preacher governs the church. It is the task of this section to examine this family of words.

Governing by Exposing Error

The commands to reprove and rebuke bring Timothy to an unpleasant, but necessary, aspect of governing, and that is the difficult task of exposing error in doctrine and behavior. These verbs express this jurisdictional authority of the minister in matters of discipline, although the words serve as a bridge from proclaiming to the unsaved world to speaking to the saved community, since the same sins perpetrated by the world need to be exposed when practiced by the church.

Expose by Reproving: While the basic meaning of *elegchō* is to "bring something to light"[79] (as used in Eph 5:13, "all things become visible when they are exposed—*elelchomena*—by the light"), the NT writers prefer to use this word in the legal sense of bringing conviction to a culprit in the way that the Law imposes an unfavorable verdict upon violators (Jas 2:9).[80] This convicting work is a ministry of the Holy Spirit who comes to "convict the world concerning sin" (John 16:8). Thus, in the NT, the word *elegchō* most often means, "to show someone his sin and to summon him to repentance."[81]

Although Paul uses *elegchō* only eight times,[82] its appearance is sufficient to show that reproving is the responsibility of the covenant community to expose the "unfruitful works of darkness" (Eph 5:11) so that unbelievers would be convicted and brought to give account to God (1 Cor 14:24). In the Pastoral Epistles, however, the act of reproving becomes a particular duty of the church leader—he reproves as an aspect of proclaiming the Word of God (2 Tim 4:2). As an overseer of the church, he is to hold to the faithful word so that he may be able to reprove (*elegchein*) opponents, in the sense of correcting them (Titus 1:9).[83] Titus is commanded to reprove believers severely so they may be

---

79. BDAG § 2483.1. In the NT, the NAS translates ἐλέγχω by "reprove" (Matt 18:15; Luke 3:19; 2 Tim 4:2; Titus 1:13; 2:15: Heb 12:5; Rev 3:19); "expose" (John 3:20; Eph 5:11, 13); "convict" (John 8:46; 16:8; 1 Cor 14:24; James 2:9; Jude 15); "rebuke" (1 Tim 5:20); and "refute" (Titus 1:9).

80. "If you show partiality, you are committing sin *and* are convicted (ἐλεγχόμενοι) by the law as transgressors" (Jas 2:9).

81. Büchsel, ἐλέγχω, *TDNT* 2:474.

82. "But if all prophesy, and an unbeliever or an ungifted man enters, he is convicted (ἐλέγχεται) by all, he is called to account by all" (1 Cor 14:24); "And do not participate in the unfruitful deeds of darkness, but instead even expose (ἐλέγχετε) them" (Eph 5:11); "But all things become visible when they are exposed (ἐλεγχόμενα) by the light, for everything that becomes visible is light" (Eph 5:13); "Those who continue in sin, rebuke (ἔλεγχε) in the presence of all, so that the rest also may be fearful *of sinning*" (1 Tim 5:20); "Reprove!" (ἔλεγξον; 2 Tim 4:2); "holding fast the faithful word which is in accordance with the teaching, that he may be able both to exhort in sound doctrine and to refute (ἐλέγχειν) those who contradict" (Titus 1:9); "For this cause reprove (ἔλεγχε) them severely that they may be sound in the faith" (Titus 1:13); "These things speak and exhort and reprove (ἔλεγχε) with all authority" (Titus 2:15).

83. BDAG § 2483.2.

sound in the Faith (Titus 1:13); likewise, he is to reprove the church "with all authority" (Titus 2:15). These references show that the term *elegchō* involves a solemn endeavor on the part of the minister, since reproving is serious business. Sin appearing in any form must be confronted; in fact, not only is sin to be exposed, but the sinners themselves are to be confronted, whether they are within or without the church.

From what source does the authority to reprove another individual derive? While the minister is the agent of conviction, his authority derives only from the Scripture as the *Elegkmos*, the instrument of divine reproof. It is the Word of God that is "profitable for reproof" (*elegmos*); that is, the standard by which sin is exposed can only be the written *Logos*, not the personal preferences of a preacher (2 Tim 3:16).

Expose by Rebuking: A near synonym to the previous verb is *epitímeō*, which is used in tandem with Paul's charge to Timothy ("reprove, rebuke"), but its appearance should not be considered superfluous because it conveys a sufficient nuance to express another aspect of exposing sin. Trench insists that "in *epitiman* lies simply the notion of rebuking,"[84] perhaps even incorrectly, as when Peter rebuked Jesus (Matt 16:22) or ineffectually, as when the dying thief rebuked his colleague in crime (Luke 23:40), whereas *elegchein* shows an attempt to reprove another "with such effectual wielding of the truth to as to bring him to confession, or at least a conviction of his sins."[85]

One might suppose that Trench is correct in saying that *elegchein* (reprove) is the more forceful of the two words, because Paul uses *epitímeō* (rebuke) only once in his letters, here in this charge to Timothy. However, if *epitímeō* is as sterile as Trench implies, it is hard to understand why Paul would have used the word at all. Furthermore, the Gospels use *epitímeō* repeatedly of the rebuking ministry of Jesus,[86] and surely, His rebukes were quite effective!

Perhaps the use of *epitímeō* in the Gospels helps to explain its difference from *elegchein*, because *epitímeō* is used exclusively of Jesus when He rebukes disease (Luke 4:39), hostile forces of nature (Luke 8:24), sometimes even His disciples (Mark 8:33), but especially demonic forces (Luke 9:42). If anything, *epitímeō* (rebuke) may in fact be the more forceful term than *elegchein* (reprove) as it warns someone in order to prevent a wrong action or to bring a sinful action to an end.[87]

Jesus is pictured as rebuking His chief disciple Peter (Mark 8:33) and commanding His disciples to do the same sort of rebuking to those who sin against them (Luke 17:3). These episodes show that rebuking describes a confrontational activity in which the preacher must privately address an offender, and therein may lie the key difference between these two activities: reproving (*elegchein*) expresses the official duty of the

---

84. Trench, *Synonyms of the NT*, 12–13.

85. Ibid.

86. The reproving by Jesus is noted in Matt 8:26; 12:16; 17:18; Mark 1:25; 3:12; 4:39; 8:30, 33; 9:25; Luke 4:35, 39, 41; 8:24; 9:21, 42, 55; 17:3.

87. BDAG § 3060.1 defines ἐπιτιμάω, "to express strong disapproval of someone."

church officer when dealing with sin in the public arena, whereas rebuking (*epitímein*) deals more with pastoral or ministerial censure. Such rebuke may even be more serious in intent than reproof, especially if the minister detects demonic activity; in such cases, the rebuke is directed at Satan himself rather than to the human being satanically duped, as Paul does to the spirit that possessed the slave girl (Acts 16:18). In either case, reproving and rebuking become specific applications of the verbal ministry of preaching the Word.

Not Expose by Berating: The ministry of exposing error can tend toward censoriousness, so the minister must be careful not to allow a proper censure to become a demeaning castigation. Paul warns against this sort of rebuke when he cautions Timothy, "Do not sharply rebuke an older man" (1 Tim 5:1). In the entire Bible, this verb *epiplēssō* is used only in this verse, although it is found in Greek literature meaning to "strike at someone."[88] Eventually it came to mean to give a verbal denouncing.[89] It appears that Paul uses the word to caution Timothy (and succeeding ministers) not to berate an older man (or any believer, for that matter) with objurgated words. While rebuking another may be necessary, the calm tone of voice and wise choice of words are prudent applications of preaching the Word.

Summary: The preacher must cautiously exert his scriptural authority to "reprove (*elegchon*) and rebuke (*epitímeson*) with all patience" (2 Tim 4:2), but every precaution must be taken to avoid doing so with contempt or prejudice. He is to expose sin by the reproof of the Word of God (2 Tim 3:16), so that in this aspect of his speaking ministry, the minister must point out what is wrong in the life of the believer, as unpleasant as such a ministry usually is (Titus 1:9; 13, 2:15).

Governing by Exhorting Godliness

Yet the Christian ministry is by no means all negative. "Exhort!" is the next imperative to be considered in Paul's charge (2 Tim 4:2), and the verb *parakaleson* stresses the positive application of the instructional activity of the Word with which the preacher encourages the church to godliness. Along with this verb, Paul uses a number of similar words to express the positive application of the Word.

---

88. BDAG § 3004.

89. L&N § 33.420 defines ἐπιπλήσσω: "a figurative extension of meaning of ἐπιπλήσσω 'to strike' (not occurring in the NT) to express strong disapproval as a type of punishment–'to rebuke, to reproach, to denounce.'"

Encouraging: Appearing in eleven of Paul's letters, *parakaleō* is a favorite word of the apostle.[90] While the etymological meaning is "to call to one's side,"[91] the word means more succinctly in the NT "to ask for (earnestly), to request, to plead for, to appeal to, earnest request, appeal,"[92] depending on the context it which it appears. A common introductory remark of Paul is, "I beseech (*parakaleō*) you," found when he begins some applicatory comment.[93] The repeated usage of this verb indicates that whenever it is used in a pastoral context, it encourages the application of the truths of the gospel to the practical life and behavior of "the brethren," so that the term is almost exclusively reserved for address to the church, as when Paul and Silas saw the brethren in the house of Lydia and "encouraged them" (Acts 16:20).

Parakaleō is a pressing for a decision to be obedient to the indicative of the gospel, a "wooing proclamation of salvation in apostolic preaching."[94] Hence, Paul exhorts new converts "to continue in the faith through many tribulations" (Acts 14:22); "to present your bodies a living and holy sacrifice" (Rom 12:1); to agree and be made complete in the same mind (1 Cor 1:10); "to walk in a manner worthy of the calling" (Eph 4:1); to please God (1 Thess 4:1); to pray (1 Tim 2:1); "to be sensible" (Titus 2:6); and so forth. Pastorally, the ministry of encouragement is given to the entire congregation to "comfort one another" (1 Thess 4:18), whether in sorrow (2 Cor 1:4), upon repentance (2 Cor 2:7), and in everyday occurrences of Christian living (1 Thess 5:11). Paul sent his co-workers to visit churches for the express purpose of encouraging them (1 Thess 3:2), and the apostolic command to the preacher is simply to "teach and exhort in these things" (1 Tim 6:2; Titus 2:15) Paul reiterates this imperative strongly in the charge to Timothy ("Exhort!" 2 Tim 4:2), as well as in the duties required of an overseer, "to exhort in sound doctrine" (Titus 1:9).

The proper mood for encouraging is "by the meekness and gentleness of Christ" (2 Cor 10:1), or "as a father *would* his own children" (1 Thess 2:11), or as an appeal of a son to a father (1 Tim 5:1). Of course, it is by "the encouragement (*paraklēsis*) of the Scriptures" (Rom 15:4) that others are encouraged (1 Thess 4:18; see chapter 2 on the Content of Preaching), so that the basis of comfort is not in naive optimism but in faith rooted in the hope of the gospel (1 Thess 2:16–17). The only standard and source of Christian encouragement, then, is to "exhort in sound doctrine" (Titus 1:9).

---

90. Paul uses Παρακαλῶ fifty-four times (Rom 12:1, 8; 15:30; 16:17; 1 Cor 1:10; 4:13, 16; 14:31; 16:12, 15; 2 Cor 1:4, 6; 2:7, 8; 5:20; 6:1; 7:6, 7, 13; 8:6; 9:5; 10:1; 12:8, 18; 13:11; Eph 4:1; 6:22; Phil 4:2; Col 2:2; 4:8; 1 Thess 2:12; 3:2, 7; 4:1, 10, 18; 5:11, 14; 2 Thess 2:17; 3:12; 1 Tim 1:3; 2:1; 5:1; 6:2; 2 Tim 4:2; Titus 1:9; 2:6, 15; Phlm 1:9, 10), plus the Book of Acts describes the exhorting ministry of Paul four more times (Acts 14:22; 16:40; 20:2; and 27:33).

91. BDAG § 5584.1.

92. L&N § 33.168.

93. See such use at Rom 12:1; 15:30; 16:17; 1 Cor 1:10; 4:16; 16:15; 2 Cor 2:8; 10:1; Eph 4:1; Phil 4:2, 2; 1 Tim 2:1; Phlm 1:9, 10.

94. Schmitz, παρακαλῶ, *TDNT* 5:795.

It appears, then, that *parakaleō* comes closest to the purpose and tone of the sermon more than any other term used of preaching. Paul gives "much exhortation" to the churches (Acts 20:2), with the effect that the congregations were comforted with encouragement from God (Acts 20:12; 2 Cor 1:4–6). In these examples, the dynamic of encouragement is seen, as the preached *paraklēsis* is activated by the *Paraklētos* (a Johannine designation for the Holy Spirit, John 16:7), and when mixed with faith, the hearers receive spiritual encouragement from God Himself, who encourages His people through the preacher (2 Cor 5:20). Schmitz notes that *parakaleō* shows that "the address proceeds from the speaker with Almighty power."[95] Because there is a dynamic accompanying the activity of encouraging, it is necessary that the preacher is gifted as "the encourager" (*ho parakalōn*; Rom 12:8). Regardless how ill-treated the preacher may be, he can continue to encourage others because he is energized by the Holy Spirit as the *Paraklētos* of God (1 Cor 4:13).

Clearly, the activity of encouraging believers unto godliness is a most important aspect of the preaching activity: it must be so, because Paul, in his charge to Timothy, specifically charges Timothy be an encourager. The preacher then needs to bring positive and practical applications of the Word of the gospel to the hearts of believers—especially to those who are weak in their faith (1 Thess 5:14) so that they may be encouraged in their walk with God.

Counseling: Another term expressing pastoral governing of the church is the verb *noutheteō*), which is an exclusive Pauline word.[96] If *paralaleō* is an appeal to the heart, *noutheteō* is an appeal to the mind, as the verb means "to put to mind, to exert influence on the mind."[97] It is important to note that the ministry of admonishment is an entreaty to the mind of the hearer to think according to the *nouthesia* of the written Word (1 Cor 10:11).

Generally translated in English versions of the Bible "to admonish," *noutheteō* becomes a "form of spiritual counseling within the church community, where one's mind is addressed to become captive to obedience to Christ."[98] Perhaps a better translation of the word, however, would be "to counsel," as *noutheteō* is first of all an apostolic injunction (1 Cor 4:11); secondly, it is a mutual ministry among the members of the body of Christ (Rom 15:4; Col 3:16), and thirdly, and most particularly, it becomes

---

95. Ibid.

96. The word *noutheteō* is found in the NT only in Paul's message to the Ephesian elders (Acts 20:31) and seven times his letters (Rom 15:14, "You are able also to admonish one another"; 1 Cor 4:14, "I do not write these things to shame you, but to admonish you as my beloved children"; Col 1:28, "We proclaim Him, admonishing every man"; "Col 3:16, "with all wisdom . . . admonishing one another"; 1 Thess 5:12, "appreciate those who . . . give you instruction"; 1 Thess 5:14, "admonish the unruly"; and 2 Thess 3:15, "Do not regard him as an enemy, but admonish him as a brother." It is also found nine times in the LXX (1 Sam 3:13; Job 4:3; 23:15; 30:1; 34:16; 36:12; 37:14; 38:18; 40:4).

97. Selter, "Exhort," *DNTT* 1:568.

98. Ibid.

a ministry whereby an officer of the church admonishes the congregation (1 Thess 5:12). Those entrusted with the rule of the church are to admonish the church so that the proclaimer of Christ may admonish every man in order that every believer may be completed in Christ (Col 1:28).

The importance of rule by admonishment is noted when a factious person is to be rejected "after a second *nouthesia*" (Titus 3:10). One's attitude in the exercise of admonishment is all-important: even an unruly person is to be admonished "as a brother" (2 Thess 3:15), and Paul's testimony is that he did not cease to admonish "each one with tears, day and night" (Acts 20:31), as a father would admonish his beloved children (1 Cor 4:14). An elder should admonish only when his heart is broken and compassionate, but he cannot neglect the activity of governing the church no matter how he may feel, since admonishment is a commanded duty of the preacher.

Commanding: Another such directive to pastors is the activity of commanding the church to pursue godliness, as indicated by use of the verb *parangellō*. It is found in military literature, meaning to give an order.[99] The same meaning is often found in the NT when an authority gives an imperative to obey,[100] as when Paul directs a colleague to command others "not to teach strange doctrines" (1 Tim 1:3) or to live above reproach (1 Tim 5:7).[101] This commanding verb is used when Jesus instructs His disciples (Matt 10:5; Mark 6:8) and when the apostles give commands to the church (1 Thess 4:11). Such commands appear to be "regulations of practical conduct,"[102] as when the verb is used to command believers to work for a living (1 Thess 4:11; 2 Thess 3:4, 6, 10, 12) or to instruct "those who are rich in this present world not to be conceited" (1 Tim 6:17). In fact, the word becomes so nearly a technical term for the commanding aspect of ministry that Paul can simply write, "Command these things" (1 Tim 4:11; 5:7).

Without question, the verb *parangellō* asserts that the preacher is delegated divine authority by the indicative of the gospel to require certain behavior of his hearers. As Paul commands Timothy "in the presence of God" (1 Tim 6:13), so the preacher's message, when appropriate, may command believers to strict observance to the biblical requirements of godliness.

Commending: Meaning "to set forth,"[103] *paratithēmi* is another instructional term, used when Jesus "set forth" a teaching parable (Matt 13:24). Paul uses the verb only

---

99. BDAG § 5560 παραγγέλλω.

100. The verb παραγγέλλω appears thirty-two times in the NT, in Matt 10:5; 15:35; Mark 6:8; 8:6; 16:8; Luke 5:14; 8:29, 56; 9:21; Acts 1:4; 4:18; 5:28, 40; 10:42; 15:5; 16:18, 23; 17:30; 23:22, 30; 1 Cor 7:10; 11:17; 1 Thess 4:11; 2 Thess 3:4, 6, 10, 12; 1 Tim 1:3; 4:11; 5:7; 6:13, 17.

101. Mundle, "Command," *DNTT* 1:340.

102. Schmidt, παραγγέλλω, *TDNT* 5:765.

103. BDAG § 5640.1 παρατίθημι.

twice (1 Tim 1:18; 2 Tim 2:2), but its association with the related noun *parathēkē*, the deposit of the Faith (1 Tim 6:20; 2 Tim 1:12, 14) makes it an important aspect of the governing ministry of the preacher.

The classical usage of the verb meant "to entrust for safekeeping,"[104] but eventually it came to signify "a claim of ownership addressed to the keepers of the records."[105] Thus, when Paul gives a charge to Timothy to "guard what has been entrusted to you" (1 Tim 6:20), it is as if he commends to him the truths of the gospel for safekeeping.

This same commendation of the gospel to others should be the task of every preacher, in the manner that Timothy is to entrust to faithful men the things he has learned from Paul (2 Tim 2:2). This process shows that the governing activity of the pastor is to instruct others so that the deposit of the gospel will be preserved without change. The concept of deposit, then, locks the preacher into one primary source of knowledge, the written Word of God, which is to be passed on to succeeding generations through faithful preaching.

Reminding: Because many in the early church were apparently illiterate, it was important that the doctrines of the gospel be impressed upon the memories of believers so they could recall these truths at will. To this end, Paul describes a teaching ministry directed to the church whereby the gospel is committed to memory, and he does so by use of the verb *hupomimneskō*, "to cause to remember."[106]

While Paul uses this Greek word only twice, the first instance follows a faithful confessional statement (2 Tim 2:11–13) when the apostle commands Timothy, "Remind *them* of these things" (2 Tim 2:14a). Similarly, he commands Titus, "Remind them to be subject to rulers" (Titus 3:1). Such reminders imply repetitive instruction by constantly impressing upon believers the importance of practical Christian doctrines and conduct.

A similar verb Paul also uses only twice is *hupotithēmi*, which means quite literally, "to lay down,"[107] as when he uses the word to signify the laying down of the necks of his coworkers Prisca and Aquila (Rom 16:4). Its other appearance, however, expresses an instructional aspect when Paul writes, "In pointing out (*hupotithēmenos*) these things to the brethren, you will be a good servant of Christ Jesus" (1 Tim 4:6). The word picture behind *hupotithēmi* suggests that the governing activity of the pastor "lays down" a foundation of "the words of the faith and of the sound doctrine which you have been following" (1 Tim 4:6). Paul uses this illustration to remind his readers that the foundational undergirding of the church lies in the truths of the Word of God, and they must constantly be reminded of these truths so that they will not drift into forgetfulness. These two verbs show that the truths of the gospel need to be impressed upon the minds

---

104. Ibid., § 5640.3. See also Maurer, παρατίθημι, *TDNT* 8:162.
105. *VGNT* § 3216 παρατίθημι.
106. L&N § 29.10.
107. BDAG § 7647.1 ὑποτίθημι.

and memories of believers, and it is one of the preacher's tasks to bring these truths to mind so that the church will remember to do what God expects of it.

Summary: In his official capacity as an officer of the congregation, the preacher governs the church by the rule of the Word of God, applying it in the activities of encouraging, counseling, commanding, commending, and reminding believers of the proper response to the grace of God, which is to walk in a manner worthy of His calling to salvation—such matters are yet other nuances of a New Covenant sermon.

Governing by Ruling Activities

It is also the God-given duty of ministers to act as rulers of the congregation, and in this regard, the minister is pictured in the activities as an elder and governor whose responsibility is to command the church to preserve and maintain the order to which God has called it. Specifically, such rule is exercised when the Word of God is applied to those whose unruly lives are detrimental to the testimony of the church.

Ruling as an Elder: Throughout biblical history, the primary officer of the covenant community is that of the *presbuteros*, the household head. Consistently, the rule of God's people in the Old Covenant was delegated to the elders of Israel,[108] and because the New Covenant community is also described as "the household of God" (Eph 2:19), it is quite understandable that the basic designation its ruling officers would assume is that of "the elders of the church" (Acts 20:17). Coenen notes, "In a word, they [the church elders] continue the juridical role of elders in the synagogue in the form of a presiding group."[109] Although the church officer is in view only sixteen of the sixty-six times that the word *presbuteros* appears in the NT,[110] it is evident from those citations that the elder is given the responsibility to rule the congregation.

This observation is verified in 1 Tim 5:27, which refers to "elders who rule well," as well as in 1 Thess 5:12, which describes the leaders as "those who have charge over you in the Lord." In both references, Paul uses the verb *proistēmi*, which combines the

---

108. The elders of Israel are mentioned in Exod 3:16, 18; 12:21; 17:5–6; 18:12; 24:1, 9; Lev 9:1; Num 11:16, 30; 16:25; Deut 27:1; 31:9; Jos 7:6; 8:10; 24:1; 1 Sam 4:3; 8:4; 2 Sam 3:17; 5:3; 17:4, 15; 1 Kngs 8:1, 3; 1 Chron 11:3; 15:25; 2 Chron 5:2, 4; Ezek 14:1; 20:1, 3.

109. Coenen, "Bishop," *DNTT* 1:199.

110. BDAG § 6139 lists the *uses loquendi* of πρεσβύτερος as follows: an older person (Luke 15:25; John 8:9; Acts 2:17; 1 Tim 5:1, 2; 1 Pet 5:5; 2 John 1:1; 3 John 1:1); ancestors (Matt 15:2; Mark 7:3, 5; Heb 11:2); a Jewish official (Luke 7:3); elders of the Sanhedrin (Matt 16:21; 21:23; 26:3, 47, 57; 27:1, 3, 12, 20, 41; 28:12; Mark 8:31; 11:27; 14:43, 53; 15:1; Luke 7:3; 9:22; 20:1; 22:52; Acts 4:5, 8, 23; 6:12; 21:18; 23:14; 24:1; 25:15); elders of the Christian church (Acts 11:30; 14:23; 15:2, 4, 6, 22, 23; 16:4; 20:17; 21:18; 1 Tim 5:17, 19; Titus 1:5; Jas 5:14; 1 Pet 5:1, 5); and the twenty-four heavenly elders (Rev 4:4, 10; 5:5–14; 7:11, 13; 11:16; 14:3; 19:4).

ideas of caring with leading,[111] showing that caring concern for the flock is an obligation of those who lead.[112] The ability to rule is a *charisma* that should be employed with "diligence" (*spoudē*, Rom 12:2). A similar word, *kubernesis*, "administration,"[113] also describes the gift granted by the Holy Spirit so that the order of the church will be maintained (1 Cor 12:28).[114]

The most obvious way that a man knows (and the congregation affirms) that he has the gift of ruling is whether he has fatherly rule over his own household. This indicator is given as a specific qualification required of one who aspires to the "office of overseer" (1 Tim 3:1; 4–5). Such a practical example of godly ruling, however, cannot be separated from the requirement to be a godly speaker. In his role as a church leader, the elder exercises his leadership by directing the church to the Word of God, and he speaks the Word in church matters in the same way as a wise patriarch would speak to his family. Accordingly, then, no man should assume he is called as a New Covenant elder unless he has shown that he possesses the gift of ruling, certainly not by lording over the flock, but by being an example of home- and self-control (1 Pet 5:3). In this fatherly way, he is to rule over the flock of God as a godly elder.

Ruling by Governing: Another word used in the NT for governing the church is *hēgeomai*,[115] although it is not used with that meaning in Paul's letters.[116] However, the writer of Hebrews (who is thought by some to be Paul) does use *hēgeomai* three times to describe "those who led you" (Heb 13:7, 17, 24). The tasks of these leaders are to teach the Word of God (13:7) and to keep watch over souls (13:24), duties that Paul assigns to "pastors and teachers" (Eph 4:12). Although some maintain that there is no connection between these offices,[117] the fact is that the writer of Hebrews divides the congregation between "leaders and saints" (Heb 13:24), showing that these leaders are

---

111. BDAG § 6214 defines προΐστημι not only as exercising a position of leadership, but showing concern for another. The word appears in 2 Sam 13:17; Prov 23:5; 26:17; Amos 6:10; Isa 43:24; Rom 12:8; 1 Thess 5:12; 1 Tim 3:4–5, 12; 5:17; Titus 3:8, 14.

112. Reicke, προΐστημι, *TDNT* 6:701.

113. BDAG § 4438.

114. Coenen, "Bishop," *DNTT* 1:198, The NT uses *kubernesis* of a ship's pilot (Acts 27:11; Rev 18:17), showing that the word describes one who directs and controls.

115. L&N 37.58 defines ἡγέομαι "to rule over, with the implication of providing direction and leadership–'to rule over, to order, to govern, government, rule,'" citing Luke 3:1 and Acts 7:10 as examples of this translation.

116. Paul uses ἡγέομαι eleven times (2 Cor 9:5; Phil 2:3, 6, 25; 3:7, 8; 1 Thess 5:13; 2 Thess 3:15; 1 Tim 1:12; 6:1), and BDAG § 3410.2 notes that the predominant use of the verb in Paul's letters is "to engage in an intellectual process, to think."

117. Büchsel, ἡγέομαι, *TDNT*, 2:907, states, "Whether they have the title of *episkopoi* or *presbuteroi*—all these matters are obscure. The interest of Hebrews . . . is ethical and religious rather than ecclesiastical." One must wonder why the author of Hebrews mentions ecclesiastical matters with such force if he is so disinterested in them!

none other than elders mentioned in Paul's letters whose ruling function is identical with these men (1 Tim 5:17).

The term *hēgeomai* also defines a political governor such as Pontius Pilate (Matt 27:21), but more importantly, it is used of the Messiah as the promised Ruler of God's people (Matt 2:6), so it is evident that the word describes an ecclesiastical function whereby a minister must make ruling decisions. While such rule would involve hearing and deciding disciplinary cases, the elder as "the one leading" (*ho hēgoumenos*) must make many judicial decisions involving the rule of the congregation, such as who is to be recognized as members or whom to appoint to various tasks of ministry. This disciplinary activity is spelled out in several places in Paul's letters; for example, a church ruler may act as a "wise man who will be able to decide between his brethren" (1 Cor 6:5), or even by apostolic example, an elder may excommunicate an immoral (and unrepentant) member (1 Cor 5:5) or re-admit him upon repentance (2 Cor 2:6–8). Also, a leader is charged with the unpleasant task of rebuking publicly another elder who persists in sinning, although he must not receive an accusation against a fellow elder unless there are sufficient witnesses (1 Tim 5:19–20).[118] All these activities involve a speaking activity if the church is to be ruled properly.

Summary to Ruling Activities: By exercising these responsibilities of rule, the New Covenant Minister will prove himself to be a governor of God's commonwealth when he speaks in the juridical rule of God's Word (Eph 2:12). Governing the church, however, should always be exercised from a position of piety, as the saints are called to imitate the faith and conduct of those who govern them (Heb 13:7). For this reason, the pastor must be willing to learn ruling responsibilities while maintaining a servant-like attitude (Luke 22:26). To accomplish this task, he needs to speak as a governor who is aware that he will give a spoken account of himself to the One who is the divine Governor (Matt 2:6).

Conclusion to the Activities of Ruling the Church

The three commands Paul gives to Timothy to "rebuke, reprove, and exhort" bring Timothy to the necessary activity of the preacher in governing the church: exposing error (as shown previously in the verbs "rebuke and reprove"), exhorting to godliness (as examined in the verbs, "exhort, counsel, command, commend, and remind"), and exercising discipline (seen in the words, "rule and govern"). By necessity, each of these activities requires a spoken ministry as an application of the reproof, comfort, and discipline of the Word of God (2 Tim 3:16). In the event of a private offense, these activities must take place in the setting of a private confrontation, but surely the public sermon

---

118. 1 Timothy 5:19–20 reads, "Against a presbyter an accusation do not be receiving, except if not upon two or three witnesses. Those sinning rebuke before all, in order that also the rest should be having fear" (AT).

is the most effective way to bring these truths to the gathered congregation in a general way, yet without using the pulpit as a bludgeon! As a rule, the preacher should plan to include the activities of rebuke, reproof, and encouragement within each sermon, because the Word must be applied to the hearts and minds of the listeners.

The Activity of Preaching: Caring for the Church

Paul's command, "Exhort!" serves as a bridge from the activity of governing to that of pastoral care. Timothy is not merely involved with proclaiming a message: he must also minister to people, and so the responsibility of the minister takes on a relational aspect when the Word is ministered in interpersonal situations. In this regard, Paul shows throughout his letters that the minister is assigned duties of shepherding, visiting, comforting, encouraging, and equipping.

As Jesus is the Great and Good Shepherd who shepherds His flock (John 10:11; Heb 13:20; 1 Pet 2:25), so the apostolic writings describe the minister as a shepherd (*poimen*) who shepherds (*poimnainei*) the flock of God (*to poimnion toū Theoū*). While the specific appearances of these words are not all that common in the Pauline epistles,[119] the concept of shepherding as a model for leadership is used consistently throughout the NT;[120] in fact, it can be argued from Acts 20:28 that a principal designation of the preacher is to be identified as a pastor (*poimen*), because Paul there reminds the overseers (*episcopoi*, a title 1 Peter 2:25 joins with Jesus as the shepherd of our souls) that the Holy Spirit appointed them first of all to the primary task of shepherding (*poimainein*) the flock of God. Likewise, when Paul lists the offices given for the edification of the church, he defines the teacher quite pointedly as a pastor (*poimen*, Eph 4:11)

The shepherding concept seems especially close to Peter, for in his advice to the elders to "shepherd the flock of God, . . . proving to be examples to the flock" (1 Pet 5:2–3), he is certainly obeying the personal commission given to him by the resurrected Lord, "Shepherd My sheep" (John 21:16). It would be quite advantageous for a minister to study the tenth chapter of John to discover the characteristics of a faithful shepherd as one who knows his sheep by name, leads them out to pasture, and goes before them. Above all, a good shepherd lays down his life for the sheep just as the Lord Jesus did. If a man is to be a good pastor of the New Covenant, he must view his task in terms of shepherding, gently caring for the flock over which he has been

---

119. The noun "shepherd" (ποιμήν) appears eighteen times in the NT (Matt 9:36; 25:32; 26:31; Mark 6:34; 14:27; Luke 2:8, 15, 18, 20; John 10:2, 11, 12, 14, 16; Eph 4:11; Heb 13:20; 1 Pet 2:25); the verb "to shepherd" (ποιμαίνω) appears eleven times (Matt 2:6; Luke 17:7; John 21:16; Acts 20:28; 1 Cor 9:7; 1 Pet 5:2; Jude 1:12; Rev 2:27; 7:17; 12:5; 19:15); and "flock" (ποίμνη) appears five times (Luke 12:32; Acts 20:28, 29; 1 Pet 5:2, 3).

120. The minister is called a shepherd only at Eph 4:11; the task of pastoring is mentioned at John 21:16; Acts 20:28; 1 Pet 5:2), and the church is likened to a flock only at Luke 12:32; John 10:16; Acts 20:28–29, and 1 Pet 5:2–3.

appointed. His shepherding care is exhibited when he tenderly speaks the consoling truths of the gospel to the flock.

Caring by Visiting

As Jesus visited His people as the Bishop (*episkopos*) of our souls (1 Pet 2:25), so too the minister is called to be a guardian (*episkopos*) by the appointment of the Holy Spirit (Acts 20:28).[121] His charge is described as a visitation (*episcopē*; Acts 1:20; 1 Tim 3:1), and his task is to "take oversight" (*episkopeō*) of his charge (1 Pet 5:2) so that he is "overseeing" (*epikeptomai*) the affairs of the church (Acts 6:3).

Although these verbs *episkopeō* and *epikeptomai* are generally translated "to visit," the meaning is far deeper than mere socializing. Instead, they imply that taking oversight is to see that the physical needs of a person are being met (Matt 25:36; Jas 1:27). For this reason, when Paul planned "to visit" the churches that he and Barnabas had planted earlier, his intent was to determine both their physical and spiritual needs (Acts 15:36).[122]

In this activity of visiting, the preacher as Bishop (*episkopos*) must make it his business to know how his people are faring. He must visit in their homes in order to inquire of their well-being (as Paul taught house to house, Acts 20:20) so he may attempt to meet any needs that may arise or alert the church to meet those needs. Visiting, accordingly, implies a speaking ministry in which the pastor as Bishop conducts an inquiry into the affairs of his people.

Caring by Comforting

In the way that the Lord Jesus comforted (*paramutheomai*) Mary and Martha in their time of grief (John 11:19, 31), so the minister is to share words of consolation (*paramuthia*) to those who are grieving (Acts 14:3). Paul uses the verb *paramutheomai* only twice, reminding his converts that he "comforted" them as a father would his own children (1 Thess 2:11), and he encourages his readers to "comfort the fainthearted" (1 Thess 5:14). Although these few references may suggest that *paramutheomai* is not a common concept, the example and command of Paul shows that the minister must be a man of a sensitive heart, one who is able to minister the gospel in times of tragedy and death.[123] He will need to know the appropriate Scriptures that deal with grief,

---

121. The church leader is designated *episcopos* in Acts 20:28; Phil 1:1; 1 Tim 3:2; and Titus 1:7. BDAG § 3025 explains ἐπίσκοπος as "one who has the responsibility of safeguarding or seeing to it that someth. is done in the correct way." It also cautions that "the loanword 'bishop' is too technical and loaded with late historical baggage for precise signification of usage of ἐπίσκοπος and cognates in our lit., esp. the NT," and for those reasons it translates ἐπίσκοπος as "guardian."

122. Coenen, "Bishop," *DNTT* 1:191.

123. Stallin, παραμυθέομαι, *TDNT* 3:35.

sorrow, and the comfort of God, so he may point the sufferer to the One who sympathizes in all our weaknesses (Heb 4:15).

Caring by Restoring

In the way that a doctor sets a broken bone, so the minister serves as one who restores the ruptures caused by sin.[124] God gave the pastor-teacher to the church for the purpose of equipping (*katartismos*) the saints,[125] so that the prayer of a minister should be for the completion (*katartisis*) of believers (2 Cor 13:9). The ministry of restoration is especially required of those who are spiritual (elders, presumably), who should "restore (*katartizō*) such a one in a spirit of gentleness; *each one* looking to yourself, lest you too be tempted" (Gal 6:1). This verb *katartizō* can refer to the tedious task of net-mending (Matt 4:21), so the minister ought to view himself as called to the time-consuming and heart-wrenching duty as a restorer of those who lives are broken by sin. As the minister is himself being restored from sin unto godliness, so he is to be the instrument of the Holy Spirit in the restoration of others. Such a task can only be accomplished by an "incarnational" ministry whereby the specific portions of the Word of God are taught by the minister to equip what is lacking in faith (1 Thess 3:10) and to mend what has been disrupted in the lives of others (1 Cor 1:10).

Summary to the Activity of Caring

The ministry of care combines the comfort of the Scriptures with the comfort supplied by the minister, who acts as the shepherd of God's flock and as the bishop whose task is to watch over the sheep in ministries of encouragement and comfort so that each believer will be restored to the image of God. This work of what the Puritans called the "cure of the soul" is at the heart of the pastoral ministry,[126] and it should certainly affect the tone of the sermon to make it genuinely warm, caring, and sympathetic because the minister is called to "deal gently with the ignorant and misguided, since he himself also is beset with weakness" (Heb 5:2). The preacher should consider the speaking activity of caring as an essential aspect of the New Covenant ministry and preaching.

Summary to the Activity of Preaching

With the command, "Preach the Word!" Paul brings Timothy and every succeeding preacher to the primary activity of the gospel ministry, which is the verbalizing of the Word of God. This chapter has examined in some detail the many verbal forms that the

---

124. Schipper, "Right," *DNTT* 3:35.
125. BDAG § 4052 καταρτισμός cites two entries by Soranus where the word is used as medical term meaning the 'setting of a bone.'
126. See John McNeill, *History of the Cure of Souls* (N.Y.: Harper Collins, 1977).

apostle uses (or is attributed to him in the Book of Acts) to express the varied activities involved in the spoken proclamation of the Word of God. The first activity studied was that of evangelizing, whereby the gospel is preached to the unsaved world. Although this aspect of ministry is more extensively covered in Paul's letters than in Acts (as would be expected of him as a missionary and church-planter), it is clear that as much or more of his energy (at least in writing) concerned the instructing, defending, governing and caring for the church. Clearly, the speaking ministry of the preacher is twofold: evangelizing the lost and edifying the saved. It is no wonder, then, that Paul's request is that God may open a door for the preaching of the Word so that he may speak forth the mystery of Christ. This task is the primary activity of the preacher (Col 4:3), and to the accomplishment of this task, Paul next exhorts Timothy to be ready!

CHAPTER 5

The Preacher's Motives: "Be Ready!"

Now that Timothy has been instructed in the content of preaching, he must preach that message from motives that are honoring to God. Does the heart of Timothy pound to preach, so that, like Jeremiah, he cannot be silent (Jer 4:19)? Or is preaching for him nothing more than a preoccupation? While it is impossible to know another person's motive—as 1 Cor 2:11 asks, "For who among men knows the thoughts of a man except the spirit of the man, which is in him?"—yet it is imperative that the preacher knows his own motives: preaching must be an activity he longs to do, or, as Paul puts it, "Woe is me if I do not preach the gospel" (1 Cor 9:16).

The Apostle Paul serves as a good example of the preacher whose motives should never be questioned, even though skeptics cannot imagine anyone serving God without an ulterior motive. Throughout his letters, the apostle defends and explains his motives in ways that must have been quite painful for him as he bore his soul to unsympathetic critics. His anguish has left behind a telling record of what the motives of the preacher should be, and they are captured in Paul's charge that Timothy should "preach the word; be ready in season and out of season" (2 Tim 4:2 ESV).

The Preacher's Motive of Readiness

Paul seems to touch on the motives of the preacher by using the aorist imperative *epistēthi*, translated by the KJV as "be instant," a rendering that admittedly means very little to modern readers.[1] When the verb *epistēthi* is used elsewhere in the NT, it refers to someone standing nearby (as in Luke 24:4), or approaching with suddenness (Luke 2:9, 38).[2] Paul may have borrowed this command from his many encounters with shipping captains, who even to this day order their sailors to "Stand by!" Upon

---

1. The various English versions translate ἐπίστηθι "be persistent" (NAB); "be prepared" (NIV); "be urgent" (RSV), but most versions use "be ready" (ESV, NAS, NKJ, NET).

2. BDAG §3344 gives for the primary meaning of ἐφίστημι "to stand at or near a specific place, *stand at/near*, of living entities and oft. w. connotation of suddenness."

hearing the command, the sailor is alerted to be ready to discharge with immediate willingness to discharge his tasks. Fairbairn comments, "When used here in the moral sense with reference no doubt to what goes before—the preaching of the word—it implies an ever wakeful, ready attitude."[3]

Using a similar word, Paul announces to the Romans, "I am ready (*prothumos*) to preach the gospel to you" (Rom 1:15, KJV). The adjective *prothumos* also carries the same nuance of a "promptness of spirit, an inner willingness of readiness."[4] In order to deflect the charge that one preaches only "at regularly scheduled times," the preacher should exhibit a ready willingness to share the gospel at any given moment, even if it is not advantageous for him to do so at that time (as the modifying adverbs "in season and out of season" indicate).[5]

By comparing Paul's various remarks regarding his own motives, one discerns several broad categories in which the preacher must constantly examine the readiness of his motives. These categories include his motives toward God, toward the message, toward others, and toward himself.

The Preacher's Motive toward God

The reason for preaching has previously been discussed, when Paul charges Timothy "in the presence of God and Jesus Christ" (2 Tim 4:1). Truly, this reason of the divine presence also serves as a motive for Paul's preaching. The apostle distinguished himself from those he called "peddlers (*kapēleuō*) of the word of God (2 Cor 2:17 ESV)."[6] Instead, he preaches from sincerity (*eilikrineia*),[7] "as if we are speaking from God in the presence of God in Christ" (2 Cor 2:17, AT). In 2 Cor 12:19, Paul piles up prepositional phrases to emphasize that every sermon is preached in the presence of the hearing God, an idea he reaffirms to the Corinthians because his motives had been savagely attacked by some there. Thus he insists, it is "in the sight of God that we have been speaking in Christ; and all for your upbuilding, beloved."

Similar charges were leveled at Paul by the Thessalonians, gauging from the amount of ink he uses in his first letter when he defends his actions to them. He reminds them, "Our exhortation does not *come* from error or impurity or by way of deceit; but just as we have been approved by God to be entrusted with the gospel, so we speak, not as pleasing men but God, who examines our hearts" (1 Thess

---

3. Fairbairn, *Pastoral Epistles*, 383.

4. BDAG §6207 defines πρόθυμος "being eager to be of service, ready, willing, eager."

5. More precisely, εὐκαίρως means "in good times," or conveniently, whereas ἀκαίρως is "no time;" when it may be untimely to both the speaker and the listener. See BDAG §3441 and § 240.

6. BDAG §3922 καπηλεύω notes, "Because of the tricks of small tradesmen . . . the word almost comes to mean adulterate."

7. BDAG §2265 defines εἰλικρίνεια as "purity of motives." The same word is found in 1 Cor 5:8, "Let us celebrate the feast . . . with the unleavened bread of sincerity," and in 2 Cor 1:12, "the testimony of our conscience, that in holiness and godly sincerity . . . we have conducted ourselves."

2:3–4). Here again, Paul envisions that he is speaking and preaching in the all-hearing of God which in reality He is, omnipresently and omnisciently (Ps 139:4, 7) or to coin a word, omniaudiously. Every message should be preached as if God was the only member of the audience.

The importance of this truth that God hears all cannot be overstated. The preacher must speak with the awareness that there is One listening who is also the author and finisher of the faith to be engendered by the sermon. The preacher should ask himself often, "Will this sermon pass the inspection of the unseen God? Will He approve of it?" To be pleasing to God had to be the primary motive of Paul the preacher (2 Cor 5:9), and it should be the primary motive of every other preacher as well.

The Preacher's Motive toward the Message

Closely linked with the preacher's motives toward God is his motive toward the message of God's gospel. Quite naturally, if the preacher is not convinced that the gospel message is of God, then he will find himself to be a crass peddler of the Word (2 Cor 2:17) by proclaiming Christ out of selfish ambition, or worse, under the guise of pretense (Phil 1: 17–18).[8] Paul is quick to deny any such hidden motives concerning his preaching, as when he asserts that his exhortation never came from error, impurity or deceit (1 Thess 2:3). Nor did he ever come with words of flattery or with a "pretext for greed—God is witness" (1 Thess 2:5).

Instead Paul insists, "We spoke all things to you in truth" (2 Cor 7:14). He wants to "cause no hindrance to the gospel of Christ,"[9] so he is willing to endure all things in order to present the gospel in its revealed form, making certain that he is faithful to its message (1 Cor 9:12). In fact, Paul wants to be so bound to his message that he asserts, "I do all things for the sake of the gospel, that I may become a fellow partaker of it" (1 Cor 9:23). There ought to be no differentiation between the message and the messenger, as the messenger should embody—even incarnate—the message itself, so that the truth of the gospel becomes the truth of the evangelist.

Naturally, such a motive implies personal faith in the message itself, and so the motive of faith becomes tremendously important; in fact, Paul preached only from a position of belief: "Having the same spirit of faith, according to what is written, 'I believed, therefore I spoke,' we also believe, therefore also we speak" (2 Cor 4:13). It is quite obvious if the preacher doubts the message, he cannot be an effective persuader, but as he truly believes that the message is the truth of God, then he can persuade others to believe from a motive of sincere faith.

---

8. BDAG §3123 defines ἐριθεία as "selfishness, selfish ambition," and BDAG §6369 defines πρόφασις, "for a pretext, for appearance' sake."

9. Stahlin, ἐγκοπή, *TDNT* 3:855, shows that the word for hindrance comes from the military practice of making slits in the streets to hold up a pursuing enemy; hence, the basic idea of the word is "to block the way."

The Preacher's Motive toward Others

The cynical evaluation made by the circus promoter P. T. Barnum, "A sucker is born every minute," implies that people can easily be deceived and manipulated at will. Such an attitude toward those in need of the gospel is completely beneath the motives of Paul. In his relationships with others, his words flowed from faith and love in Christ Jesus (2 Tim 1:13), so much so that Paul implored each listener as a father would his own children (1 Thess 2:11), even admonishing them with tears (Acts 20:31).

Especially pertinent are the instructions he gives to Timothy when dealing with personal encounters with others: "The Lord's bond-servant must not be quarrelsome, but be kind to all, able to teach, patient when wronged, with gentleness correcting those who are in opposition" (2 Tim 2:24–25). How many people have turned away from the Faith because of an insensitive preacher who values winning an argument more than winning a soul?

Of course, governing the preacher's entire presentation of the gospel must be the love of God extended toward his fellow man, as Paul admits, "If I speak with the tongues of men and of angels, but do not have love, I have become a noisy gong or a clanging cymbal" (1 Cor 13:1). Apparently, a loveless sermon is worse than a cacophony of babble. The preacher must never treat others as mere objects at which to preach, but as individuals to direct to Christ as gently as possible without compromising the truth of the gospel. The well-being of the listener must direct the preaching, so that Christ is proclaimed in all wisdom in order to present every person complete in Him (Col 1:28).

The Preacher's Motive toward Self

The preacher must also have an honest evaluation of himself if he is to preach the gospel with sincere motives, because the Bible warns that the heart is deceitful and unknowable (Jer 17:9). Self-deception is a great enemy of the truth of God, and the preacher must constantly examine his own motives, prompted by an "incentive to be worthy of God's truth," as Stott puts it.[10]

Surely the passage where Paul exposes his own motives most vividly is 1 Cor 9:16–18.[11] There he notes that he is "under obligation" to preach, meaning that he has a divine stewardship entrusted to him.[12] Because of Christ's commission, Paul's own motives matter nothing: he preaches because he must do so, yet that obligation has

---

10. Stott, *The Preacher's Portrait*, 23.

11. 1 Corinthians 9:16–18 reads in full, "For if I preach the gospel, I have nothing to boast of, for I am under compulsion; for woe is me if I do not preach the gospel. For if I do this voluntarily, I have a reward; but if against my will, I have a stewardship entrusted to me. What then is my reward? That, when I preach the gospel, I may offer the gospel without charge, so as not to make full use of my right in the gospel."

12. BDAG § 456 defines ἀνάγκη in this context as "necessity or constraint."

become so much the nature of his being that he preaches voluntarily.[13] Still, there may be times when preaching is against his will, as every preacher can attest, yet Paul is driven by the stewardship entrusted to him.

Although it is clear that Paul is eager to preach, the idea of his obligation to preach actually is more prominent, as he expresses in Rom 1:14, "I am under obligation both to Greeks and to barbarians, both to the wise and to the foolish." In one sense, Paul had no choice but to preach because of the divine obligation laid upon him—no doubt given by the risen Lord on the road to Damascus when He described Paul as "a chosen instrument of Mine, to bear My name before the Gentiles and kings and the sons of Israel"(Acts 9:15). Paul's personal motives were secondary. He states this fact quite plainly in his message to the Ephesian elders when he claimed, "I do not consider my life of any account as dear to myself, in order that I may finish my course, and the ministry which I received from the Lord Jesus, to testify solemnly of the gospel of the grace of God" (Acts 20:24). Paul emptied himself of any personal self-motivation and was consumed instead by the motivation imposed upon him by the risen Lord—and frankly, this same motive should govern how every preacher views himself.

Summary to the Motive for Preaching

The novelist Sinclair Lewis gave the world the deceptive Elmer Gantry, a charlatan who disguised himself as an evangelist, preaching only for love of money and sex. Sadly, Lewis' portrayal often parallels reality, as sinful men are overcome by the temptation to abuse their calling and use the gospel as a cloak for covetousness. Such charges cannot be laid at the feet of Paul, because he strove constantly to present himself as an example to every preacher in the way he examined his own motives toward God, the message, others, and himself. Likewise, the preacher must have a deep conviction that he must speak (*deī me lalēsai*, Eph 6:20), knowing that he is "under obligation," entrusted with a stewardship to preach the Word.

Knowing this, Timothy—and every future preacher—should "stand ready" to preach, realizing that he has not chosen this occupation for himself. Rather, he has been commissioned to preach from motives that are honoring to the God who has called him to preach.

---

13. L&N § 25.65 explains ἑκών, as "pertaining to being willing to do something without being forced or pressured–'willing, willingly, of one's own free will.'"

CHAPTER 6

The Preacher's Setting: "In Season, Out Of Season"

HAVING BEEN COMMISSIONED TO preach, reminded of the reasons and content to preach, and impressed with the proper motives to preach, Timothy is now charged with the setting in which to preach the Word: "Be ready in season *and* out of season" (2 Tim 4:2). These two adverbs *eukairōs* and *akairōs* convey a sense of urgency—Conveniently! Inconveniently!—and they raise the questions, Where is the preacher to preach and under what circumstances? Obviously, the idea is that the Word itself takes priority over the setting, whether the moment is convenient or not, but even so, the preacher must still consider the setting in which he finds himself with an opportunity to share the Scripture.

The first adverb *eukairōs* translates quite literally, "good time," and so it refers to "a favorable occasion for some event."[1] The preacher should be prepared for such times, as when Philip came upon the Ethiopian eunuch reading Isaiah (Acts 8:30), or when the jailer asked Paul, "What must I do to be saved?" (Acts 16:30). If every believer should always be ready to "make a defense to everyone who asks you to give an account for the hope that is in you" (1 Pet 3:15), how much more should the one called to preach look for the good times to tell the good news of Christ?

The second adverb *akairōs* gives the opposite setting: "no time," or when the time is inconvenient.[2] One needs to ask if Paul means when the time is inconvenient to the hearer or to the preacher,[3] but since the context is a charge addressed to the preacher, it seems more natural to assume that Paul intends an inconvenient time for the preacher. Surely, a sensitive preacher would not want to alienate his listeners by "forcing" the message at a time when they are preoccupied with other interests. It is far better to have the hearer's full attention rather than a distracted focus, even though that moment may come at an inopportune time for the preacher.

---

1. L&N § 67.6.

2. L&N § 67.8 defines ἀκαίρως as "pertaining to the lack of a favorable opportunity for doing something—'unfavorable, when the time is not right.'"

3. Delling, καίρως, *TDNT* 3:462.

Setting of Paul's Preaching

Having traveled with the apostle, Timothy would have been reminded of the many convenient and inconvenient settings in which he had heard Paul preach. In a fascinating study, Howard Kuist lists the varied settings of Paul's preaching as narrated in the Book of Acts:[4] in synagogues (Acts 9:20; 13:5), by a river side (Acts 16:13), in a prison (Acts 16:25), in a marketplace (Acts 17:17), on a hilltop (Acts 17:22), in a formal academy (Acts 19:9); in an upper apartment (Acts 20:6), on a staircase (Acts 21:40), in a council chamber (Acts 22:30), in a courtroom (Acts 25:6), on board a ship (Acts 27:21), and in his own lodging (Acts 28:23). He taught in public and in private (Acts 20:20), to individuals (Acts 16:27), to small groups (Acts 19:7), to large crowds (Acts 14:11), to men (Acts 15:4), to women (Acts 16:13), and to families (Acts 21:5). He taught on the Sabbath Day (Acts 13:14), on the first day of the week (Acts 20:7), from morning until evening (Acts 28:23), until midnight (Acts 16:25), to the break of day (Acts 20:7), and for a year and half (Acts 18:11). Clearly, Paul needed no formal pulpit, because he was quite adaptable to every setting. It is no exaggeration when he claimed, "My circumstances have turned out for the greater progress of the gospel" (Phil 1:12), a statement he wrote while imprisoned for preaching the gospel outside the walls of his confinement. For Paul, any setting was a good time to preach.

The Synagogue Setting

Lest one surmise that Paul cared little for a formal setting to preach, it needs to be noted that the most common place for him to preach (in the initial stages of his missions) was the pubic worship service of the synagogue. The synagogue setting was certainly not unusual: Paul was following his own public worship habits as well as that of the Lord Jesus.[5] Probably originating with the public reading and exposition of Scripture under the guidance of Ezra (Neh 8:8), the synagogues attained a prominent setting for local Jewish worship long before Christians described their own meetings as a "synagoguing (of) the church" (*sunagagontes tēn ekklēsian*; Acts 14:27; James 2:2 even calls a Christian gathering a *sunagogē*).[6] The Jewish synagogues scattered across the Greek and Roman world provided an ideal opportunity for Paul, particularly because it was customary to ask a visiting brother to address the synagogue with a word of exhortation (Acts 13:14–15). Paul took full advantage of such invitations, as shown in the Book of Acts;[7] in fact, his synagogue preaching became the launching point of

---

4. Kuist, *The Pedagogy of Paul*, 49–50.

5. See Matt 4:23; 12:9; 13:59; Mark 1:21; 23, 39; 3:1; 6:2; Luke 4:15, 16, 20, 28, 44; 6:6; 13:10; John 6:59; 18:20 for the attendance of Jesus in local synagogues.

6. Oesterly, *Jewish Background of the Christian Liturgy*, 42. See also the discussion in Daniel Block, *For the Glory of God: Recovering a Biblical Theology of Worship*, chapter 7, "Hearing and Proclaiming the Scriptures in Worship."

7. Paul's first proclamation of Jesus took place in the Synagogues of Damascus, when he

his strategy to evangelize a region. While it is doubtful that this plan should be practiced by modern day (Gentile) preachers, it is clear that the local assembly of believers when they "gather together" (*synegmenōn*) is undoubtedly the most common setting for preaching in the present time, following the pattern of Acts 20:7.[8] Even so, one might want to caution the preacher about prolonging his message until midnight as Paul did that evening!

The House Church Setting

Naturally, the first Christians, being converted Jews, continued to gather in the synagogue pattern, even after they were beaten and expelled by their fellow countrymen, just as Jesus predicted would happen (Matt 23:34; John 16:2). Such ill treatment made it all the more surprising that the early church would call their own assemblies a "synagoguing" together,[9] even embracing the same liturgical forms inherited from Judaism, such as the reading and preaching of sacred Scripture (1 Tim 4:13). Initially, the new believers met "house to house" (Acts 2:46; 5:42), and so private homes became an increasingly important setting for Paul's preaching, as he reminds the Ephesian elders that he taught them both "publicly and from house to house" (Acts 20:20). Because the house church conveyed the idea of the church as the household of God (Eph 2:19),[10] it is reasonable to assume that most of Paul's in-house preaching was not evangelistic but exhortative, as implied in his prolonged message when Eutychus became the first (but certainly not the last!) listener to fall asleep during a lengthy sermon (Acts 20:7–11).

Without argument, preaching found a natural setting in the public gathering of believers (as pictured in 1 Cor 14:26[11]), thus giving biblical warrant for the continuing practice of the Lord's Day sermon. Unlike the present day when most sermons are preached in some sort of designated sanctuary, the Book of Acts closes with Paul confined to his private quarters, unable to speak in the varied settings to which he was accustomed but still "preaching the kingdom of God, and teaching concerning the Lord Jesus Christ with all openness, unhindered" (Acts 28:30–31). The practice

---

announced—no doubt to everyone's shock—"He is the Son of God" (Acts 9:20). The Book of Acts often mentions Paul's synagogue preaching (Acts 13:5, 14; 42, 43; 14:1; 15:21; 17:1, 10; 18:4, 19; 19:8, and 24:12).

8. Acts 20:7 reads, "And on the first day of the week, when we were gathered together (συνηγμένων) to break bread, Paul *began* talking to them, intending to depart the next day, and he prolonged his message until midnight."

9. See the *"synagō"* terminology at Acts 11:26 (συναχθῆναι ἐν τῇ ἐκκλησίᾳ); Acts 14:27 (συναγαγόντες τὴν ἐκκλησίαν); Acts 15:30 (συναγαγόντες τὸ πλῆθος); Acts 20:7 (συνηγμένων ἡμῶν κλάσαι); 1 Cor 5:4 (ἐν τῷ ὀνόματι τοῦ κυρίου [ἡμῶν] Ἰησοῦ συναχθέντων ὑμῶν).

10. Goetzmann, "House," *DNTT* 2:250. See also the study by Robert J. Banks, *Paul's Idea of Community: The Early House Churches in their Cultural Setting* (1994).

11. 1 Cor 14:26 reads, "When you assemble, each one has a psalm, has a teaching, has a revelation, has a tongue, has an interpretation. Let all things be done for edification." See the discussion in Fee, *Paul, the Spirit, and the People of God* (1996).

of the early church could not be confined merely to one setting, because the Lord was opening many opportunities for the proclamation of the Word. In like manner, the modern day preacher should look for opportunities to preach outside the comfortable confines of the believers' assembly.

The Open Door Setting

It is by use of the figurative imagery of an opened door that Paul came to describe his opportunities to preach the Word. Four times he speaks of these doors of opportunity being opened to him (Acts 14:27; 1 Cor 16:9; 2 Cor 2:12; Col 4:3),[12] plus he requests prayer that "that words may be given to me in opening my mouth boldly to proclaim the mystery of the gospel" (Eph 6:19 ESV). The image of an opening door implies that someone else besides the speaker is doing the opening, and, of course, the reference underscores the sovereignty of God in opening the door of salvation to those for whom that door would otherwise be closed.[13] The fact that God is the One who opens the door emphasizes that He superintends both the setting for the gospel as well as its success. Only God can open closed hearts, so the preacher should follow Paul's example by praying that God will in fact open doors so that the lost will hear and believe, just as He opened the heart of Lydia "to respond to the things spoken by Paul" (Acts 16:14). Due to this divine opening, the gospel is applicable to every circumstance, because it is the Risen Christ who has set before His church an open door which no one can shut (Rev 3:8).

Summary to the Preacher's Setting

Where then is the proper setting for a sermon? For the Christian preacher, there is no exclusive or ideal location for preaching. When John Wesley shocked the establishment of Georgian England by preaching from his father's gravestone, he was well within biblical precedence because any and every place serves as a setting for the presentation of the gospel. Because it is the sovereign Lord who directs circumstances for the furtherance of the gospel, then any setting is appropriate for preaching—even if it

---

12. Acts 14:27 ("He had opened a door of faith to the Gentiles."); 1 Cor 16:9 ("A wide door for effective *service* has opened to me"); 2 Cor 2:12 ("When I came to Troas for the gospel of Christ, . . . a door was opened for me in the Lord"); Col 4:3 ("Pray at the same time for us as well, that God may open up to us a door for the word.").

13. Jeremias, θύρα, *TDNT* 3:174, notes of the open door, "In relation to God the expression finds a place in missionary usage in the twofold sense that God opens a door for the missionary through which he can enter, by giving him a field in which to work, and also that he opens a door of faith to those who come to believe." The latter expression put matters in reverse order, since God opens a door not in response to those who come to believe, but rather He opens a door so that others will actually come to faith. The difference is one of possibility verses actuality, for God opens doors in order that missionaries will not just possibly but actually bring the lost to faith, because, as with Lydia, it is the sovereign God who opens the heart to respond to the things spoken by an evangelist (Acts 16:14).

is on a hillside dedicated to the worship of all gods, where Paul finds himself in Athens (Acts 17:19). So then, if Timothy—or any other preacher—is to be a keen preacher, it is necessary that he keep a sharp lookout for whatever door God happens to open at any given moment. If the preacher is ready "in season—out of season," then that door will prove to be the preacher's setting.

CHAPTER 7

The Preacher's Delivery: "Exhort in All Patience"

ALTHOUGH THE BIBLE IS certainly not a textbook on how to deliver a sermon, it includes enough sermons that one can readily develop a biblical theology of homiletics from the accounts of preaching it contains. However, a perusal of works explaining homiletics reveals a dearth of biblical examples on how sermons are to be delivered. Instead, these modern homiletic works concentrate on whatever communicative ideas are in vogue at the time rather than searching for a biblical structure of the message. For example, Marshall McLuhan's dictate, "The medium is the message," dominated the media industry in the late twentieth century by insisting that the packaging was more important than the product.[1] McLuhan's influence is seen in the slick—and sometimes misleading—advertising whereby the appeal is to the emotions rather than to the reason.

Sadly, some media preachers follow suit by preaching sermons with little substance but lots of flash. Paul's warning against teachers who tickle the ears in accordance with their own desires surely censures any ministry that sacrifices the content of sound doctrine to gaudy showmanship (2 Tim 4:3). Paul's indictment, however, is not to suggest that Timothy should ignore the delivery of how he preaches his sermons. This implication is made when Paul commands, "Preach the Word; . . . exhort with all patience" (2 Tim 4:2). The prepositional phrase *en pasē makrothumia* explains how Timothy is to exhort (with all patience),[2] and "patience" definitely describes the demeanor by which the preacher should preach the Word.[3]

---

1. McLuhan introduced the phrase in his book, *Understanding Media: The Extensions of Man* (N.Y.: New American Library, 1964).

2. The preposition ἐν could be understood as a locative dative ("Exhort *in* all patience") or as an instrumental dative ("Exhort *with* all patience."). The latter makes more sense in this context, as Paul is telling Timothy the way to preach effectively, with all patience. See the discussion in Wallace, *Greek Grammar*, 372–75.

3. BDAG § 4684.2 defines μακροθυμία in 2 Tim 4:2 as meaning the "state of being able to bear up under provocation, *forbearance,* patience toward others."

If the most effective way to learn comportment is by imitation, then Timothy certainly had an enviable example in Paul, whose preaching he had personally witnessed on numerous occasions. Thankfully, the Book of Acts gives us glimpses of the preaching delivery of Paul, and the apostle himself gives various indications of his own preaching methods. These methods will be explored in greater depth as the chapter unfolds.

Delivery and the Homiletics of Paul

The word "homiletics" comes from the Greek word *homoleō*, which means etymologically to "speak of like things," although the Bible uses the word to refer to private conversations.[4] In Acts 20:11, the word is used to describe Paul's conversation with the believers in Troas when he "talked (*homilēsas*) with them a long while, until daybreak." *Homoleō*, however, has come into English with the meaning, "the art of preaching."[5]

Paul left no information concerning the methods he used to compose and deliver his sermons, but the Book of Acts has recorded in part four of Paul's sermons (Acts 13:16–41; 14:14–17; 17:22–31; 20:17–35), plus five legal defenses (22:1–21; 24:10–21; 26:1–23; 28:17–20, 23–28) and brief snippets of several other sermons (Acts 9:20, 22; 17:3; 18:4–5; 19:4; 20:7; 27:21–26). From these examples, a good sampling of how Paul composed and delivered his sermons can be ascertained. Furthermore, it could be said that the letters of Paul are actually sermons in print, because he commanded them to be read publicly (Col 4:16), and he makes no distinction whether he delivers apostolic traditions by word or by epistle (*eite dia logou eite di' epistolēs hemōn*, 2 Thess 2:15). His spoken sermons often became letters, making his letters written sermons (See further studies in chapter 8 on "The Preacher's Structure").

McDonald contends that Paul composed his sermons on the pattern of a Cynic diatribe, which was a "discourse on a moral subject given by a preacher to an audience [while] retaining the mannerisms and devices of animated conversation."[6] The characteristics of such diatribes included rhetorical questions, questions and answers, conditional clauses, and repetition.[7] The outline of a diatribe followed

1. a positive exposition of the theme,
2. a negative presentation, and
3. a concluding statement of meaning.[8]

---

4. BDAG § 5282 defines ὁμιλέω "to be in a group and speak, *speak, converse, address.*" The word appears nine times in the Greek Bible (Prov 5:19; 15:12; 23:31; Dan 1:19; Luke 24:14, 15; Acts 20:11; 24:26).
5. *Merrian-Webster's Collegiate Dictionary*, 595.
6. McDonald, *Kerygma and Didache*, 40.
7. Ibid., 41.
8. Ibid., 42.

McDonald identifies these three patterns in Paul's sermon on Mars Hill (Acts 17:22–34), which should certainly come as no surprise, because Paul was addressing Greek intelligentsia who would have dismissed his subject matter out of hand had Paul violated their accustomed structures of rhetoric.

However, Paul adjusts smoothly from a Greek audience to a Jewish congregation when he enters the synagogue, as his sermon in Pisidian Antioch (Acts 13:16–41) follows a very different structure than the one preached on Mars Hill. McDonald points out that Paul's synagogue sermon resembles a typical Jewish *midrash* as a commentary (*haggadah*) on the Davidic Covenant, following a pattern instituted by Moses when he gave his sermon (*halachah*) on the Law now recorded in the Book of Deuteronomy.[9]

Such textual sermons are commonly recorded in the Book of Acts, as quite naturally the apostle's Christological understanding of the OT would lend itself toward public discourses on various prophetic texts and themes. Paul's sermon in Acts 13 might more popularly be called today a topical sermon, whereas Peter's message in Acts 2:22–36 is more of a textual exposition of Joel 2:28–32. There seems to be no clear-cut distinction between these two approaches, although the sermons in the Book of Acts often employ a string of texts tied together by a common Messianic theme. Today this approach might be called preaching along the lines of biblical theology, which, no doubt it is!

It is reasonable to assume that after his conversion, Paul read the OT with new insight. He had come to believe that Jesus was the "Amen to the promises of God" (2 Cor 1:20), leading him "preach the Word" as fulfillment of Messianic prophecy. This emphasis is seen in Paul's sermons in the Book of Acts, and, if they are typical of Paul's homiletics, then one can assert that above all else, his sermon delivery was primarily an exposition of the Scriptures.

Delivery and the Rhetoric of Paul

The word "rhetoric" has acquired a dubious connotation of showy, empty speech, perhaps because of its association with a wordy attorney named Tertullus who accused Paul before Governor Felix (Acts 24:1). Tertullus is actually called a *rhētor*,[10] someone who made his living by spinning clever words (*rhēmata*). Yet, because God also speaks with *rhēmata* (Gen 15:1), there is nothing inherently evil about using carefully constructed words, and so the preacher is called to be a rhetorician, as Paul was certainly a speaker skilled in the use of words.

Paul himself, however, might challenge this statement. He denies that he preaches in "cleverness of speech" (1 Cor 1:17), "with superiority of speech" (1 Cor 2:1) or

---

9. Ibid., 68.

10. BDAG § 6505 defines ῥήτωρ originally as a "public speaker, orator" but then more specifically as "a speaker in court, advocate, attorney." The word is found only in Acts 24:1, and clearly Luke intends for it to have a derogatory implication.

in "persuasive words of wisdom" (1 Cor 2:4). He even insists that he is "unskilled in speech" (2 Cor 11:6), probably meaning that he had no formal training in rhetorical methods. Although some have thought that his denial must be understood as a rejection of any theatrical use of words that characterized the public speaking of his time, it is better to understand Paul as rejecting the pseudo-sophisticated attitudes of his opponents who claimed great speaking skills, because in other places, Paul does in fact use persuasion to bring others to Christ (2 Cor 5:11).[11] Obviously, what is in view is not the use of words but the motives behind the words: are they used to impress others or to convert them? Paul feared that some might even be swept away by impressive delivery rather than converted by the saving content, and that outcome would prove self-defeating to the gospel.[12]

The gospel cannot be separated from spoken words, nor does Paul intend to do so. He often links words and deeds together as inseparable to the gospel ministry (as in Rom 15:18; Col 3:17; 2 Thess 2:17), and he requests prayer that he may be given a word to say while being imprisoned for the cause of Christ (Eph 6:19). Surely Paul took his own advice; he chose each word "as is good for edification according to the need *of the moment*, that it may give grace to those who hear" (Eph 4:29).

The preacher's rhetoric, then, rests on a foundation of a "logology," the study of words. As the incarnate *Logos* exegetes the Father (John 1:18), so the preacher's words (his *logoi*) reveal his thoughts. He ought then to select his words carefully in order to convey his intended thoughts. From a practical standpoint, the best way to ensure using the proper word is to write out one's thoughts and then edit them in an effort to find the words that best explain the mysteries of the gospel. By making use of this method, one learns from Paul's rhetoric to utter "words of sober truth" (Acts 26:25).

Delivery and the Elocution of Paul

Elocution is defined as "the quality of forceful expressiveness,"[13] and surely, every preacher realizes his need to improve consistently in his speaking skills. What can be learned from the actual delivery of Paul's sermons and writings?

First, it can be noted that Paul invited and maintained the attention of his listeners by using various elocutionary devices: he addresses them directly ("Brethren," Acts 13:15, 26; 22:1; 23:1; 28:17; "Men of Athens," Acts 17:22; "Men," Acts 14:15; 27:21) and

---

11. Wilckens, σοφία, *TDNT* 7:527, instead holds that Paul's attack in these passages is not against the form of speech as against the content being taught—the theological positions of the Corinthians adversaries. It may be that these opponents used various philosophical buzz-words, much as cults do to the present time, and it is such "empty words" Paul rejects (Eph 5:6).

12. Benjamin Franklin admitted to being awed but not converted by the rhetorical skills of George Whitfield. In this case, the fault must lie with the hearer, since none doubted Whitfield's sincerity or his message. See excerpts from Franklin's autobiography at http://nationalhumanitiescenter.org/pds/becomingamer/ideas/text2/franklinwhitefield.pdf [accessed June 18, 2014].

13. *Merriam-Webster Dictionary*, 405.

even employs dramatic illustrations, such as tearing his robe in protest (Acts 14:14). He arrests the attention of a mob by speaking to them in their own language (Acts 22:2) or by appealing to their own writers (Acts 17:28). His letters abound with similes ("as a good soldier") and metaphorical illustrations taken from everyday life, such as warfare (1 Tim 1:18), architecture (1 Tim 3:13), agriculture (1 Tim 4:10), athletics (1 Tim 4:7), law (1 Tim 1:6), medicine (1 Tim 6:2), seafaring (1 Tim 1:19), business (1 Tim 6:5), and hunting (1 Tim 3:7). Paul repeatedly communicates by using metonymy ("the cup," 1 Cor 10:21);[14] synecdoche ("the uncircumcision," Rom 2:26);[15] personification ("O death," 1 Cor 15:55);[16] apostrophe ("You who judge," Rom 2:1);[17] contrast ("You who teach others, do you teach yourself?", Rom 2:2);[18] paradox ("We look at things not seen," 2 Cor 4:18);[19] and hyperbole ("You abound in everything," 2 Cor 8:7).[20] Also, Paul might address his readers with irony ("You reign as kings!" 1 Cor 4:8); sarcasm ("Beware of dogs," Phil 3:2); sympathy ("Lest I have sorrow upon sorrow," Phil 2:27); passion ("I am perplexed about you," Gal 4:20); indignation ("It is actually reported that there is immorality among you!" 1 Cor 5:1); forgiveness ("I urge you to reaffirm your love," 2 Cor 2:8); and in a variety of other ways.[21]

There is little doubt that Paul must have been an effective communicator, particularly when his messages proved to be persuasive in bringing others to Christ, even some in an otherwise skeptical audience (Acts 17:23–34). Paul may not have thought much of his own preaching skills (what good preacher does?), but the evidences he left behind certainly show he was a man of eloquent delivery.

---

14. *Miriam-Webster's Collegiate Dictionary*, 11th edition, defines "metonymy" as "a figure of speech consisting of the use of the name of one thing for that of another of which it is an attribute or with which it is associated" (loc. cit.). In 1 Cor 10:21, "the cup of the Lord" refers not only to the actual cup used in the Lord's Supper but to the saving significance it represents.

15. Ibid., loc. cit., defines "synecdoche" as " a figure of speech by which a part is put for the whole." Thus Paul uses "circumcision" and "uncircumcision" (referring to a part of the body) to refer to the whole group of Gentiles and Jews.

16. Ibid., loc. cit., defines "personification" as the "attribution of personal qualities," generally given to inanimate objects, as Paul addresses "death" in 1 Cor 15:55 as a hearing person.

17. Ibid., loc. cit., defines "apostrophe" as "the addressing of a usu. absent person," as Paul addresses a rhetorical audience in Rom 2:1 as "you who judge."

18. Ibid., loc. cit., defines "contrast" in this sense as "a person or thing that exhibits differences when compared with another." In Rom 2:2, the "one who teaches others" is asked in contrast, "Do you teach yourself?" The implied answer is, No, you don't teach yourself.

19. Ibid., loc. cit., defines "paradox" as "a statement that is seemingly contradictory or opposed to common sense and yet is perhaps true." In 2 Cor 4:18, it seems contradictory to look at things that cannot be seen, yet on the spiritual plane, it is true that the believer sees by faith what the physical eye cannot see.

20. Ibid., loc. cit., defines 'hyperbole" as an "extravagant exaggeration." In the context of 2 Cor 8:7, Paul defines "abounding in all things" as applying to "faith and utterance and knowledge," not to "all things" without distinction.

21. See Kuist, *Pedagogy of Paul*, 59 and 102–104 for other examples.

Delivery and the Emotions of Paul

Preachers are generally caught between those who say he speaks with too much emotion and those who say he lacks emotion. It must be noted, however, that biblical preaching, by the very nature of the gospel imperative to implore others to believe, must certainly be invigorated by the preacher's emotions. Paul reminded the Ephesian elders that he admonished each one with tears (Acts 20:31), and his letters are permeated with feelings towards his readers.

Paul might address his readers with an endearing appellative ("O beloved brethren," 1 Thess 4:1), or with an ardent expression ("You man of God," 1 Tim 6:11). His language is filled with affectionate utterances ("I long to see you," Phil 4:1) or sympathetic expressions ("Our comfort is abundant through Christ," 2 Cor 1:5; "my joy would be *the joy* of you all," 2 Cor 2:3; "For indeed in this *house* we groan," 2 Cor 5:2; "knit together in love," Col 2:2) while also expressing deep passion ("I have great sorrow and unceasing grief in my heart," Rom 9:2), bringing to bear severe warnings ("Become sober-minded as you ought, and stop sinning; for some have no knowledge of God. I speak *this* to your shame," 1 Cor 15:34). He also rises to fervent climaxes of confidence ("I am convinced that [nothing] shall be able to separate us from the love of God," Rom 8:38–39), with urges of affection ("Greet one another with a holy kiss," Rom 16:16), or with intensifying joy ("I rejoice and share my joy with you all," Phil 2:17).

Paul's words emote in vivid descriptions of endearment ("Night and day for a period of three years I did not cease to admonish each one with tears," Acts 20:31), heartfelt sympathy ("having the same spirit of faith," 2 Cor 4:13), peaceful contentment ("I have learned to be content in whatever circumstances I am," Phil 4:11), and poignant longing ("We were all the more eager with great desire to see your face," 1 Thess 2:17). He asks pointed questions that express desire ("King Agrippa, do you believe the prophets? I know that you do!" (Acts 26:27); shame ("Dare to go to law before the unrighteous?" 1 Cor 6:1); wonder ("Do you not know that we shall judge angels?" 1 Cor 6:3); reverence ("Do you not know that your bodies are members of Christ?" 1 Cor 6:15); edification ("What is *the outcome* then, brethren?" 1 Cor 14:26); indignation ("I am not speaking these things according to human judgment, am I?" 1 Cor 9:8); concern ("Who is led into sin without my intense concern?" 2 Cor 11:29); and even exasperation ("Are you so foolish?" Gal 3:3).

Paul's language demonstrates sweeping emotional ranges from worshipful thanksgiving (Eph 3:14) to triumphant testimonies (2 Tim 1:12; 4:6–8) to prayerful vigilance (Col 4:2). Paul clearly reveals that he is an emotional man: he even sings (Acts 16:25) and weeps (Acts 20:31) in his delivery of the gospel.[22] To say that one should preach unemotional sermons finds no company with Paul, for when a man is touched by the gospel, by human suffering, by his own weaknesses, and by the majesty of the grace of God, there is no way his heart can remain unmoved.

---

22. These many observations are credited to Kuist, *Pedagogy*, 108–112.

Delivery and the Gestures of Paul

It is well known that one communicates with the entire body, and both Luke and Paul give passing glimpses of gesturing that accompany the apostle's preaching. As is most natural in personal conversation, Paul sat while evangelizing several women in Philippi (Acts 16:13), but while addressing a large crowd, he stood (Acts 13:16; 17:22). In order to arrest attention, Paul motioned[23] with his hand (Acts 13:16, 21:40), or even stretched out[24] his hand (Acts 26:1).

These gestures are details that could have easily been omitted by Luke; in fact, one wonders why he included them if only to show that Paul was an animated speaker whose very presence attracted attention. In addition, Paul knew that his message could be illustrated by physical gesturing, a very important lesson preachers need to learn to guard from becoming static and motionless.

Another physical contrivance Paul used was eye contact. Several times Luke mentions that Paul "fixed his gaze" on someone,[25] either in righteous indignation (Acts 13:9), with sympathetic pity (Acts 14:9), or in a deliberative manner (Acts 23:1). Kuist observes, "His gaze was searching, attention-commanding, and scrutinizing."[26] In like manner, the preacher needs to fix his eyes upon his audience in ways appropriate to his message.

Vocal modulation also varied with Paul. Several times Luke mentions the impact of Paul's voice, such as when he "cried out"[27] to the crowd that attempted to sacrifice to him (Acts 14:14), or when he spoke to the lame man "with a loud voice" (*megalei phonei*, Acts 14:10). While facing another riotous mob in Jerusalem, Paul commanded their silence when he addressed them in their own Hebrew dialect (Acts 21:40, 42).[28] Kuist makes this comment on Paul's effective vocalization: "It was a voice that carried conviction (Acts 13:46, "Paul spoke boldly."), courage, and persuasion (Acts 26:28). At times it became sharp and generous (Acts 23:3–4), at times loud and commanding (Acts 14:10), at other times earnest and deliberative."[29] It should be noted that the times Paul raised his voice were dictated by the seriousness of the moment; it is not

---

23. BDAG § 4054.2 defines κατασείω in Acts 13:16 "to signal by a gesture or to make a sign," in this instance for the crowd to be silent. One can imagine Paul raising a hand with an outward palm.

24. BDAG § 2432.1 defines ἐκτείνω in Acts 26.1 "to cause an object to extend to its full length in space, *stretch* out. In this instance, Paul's palm was probably extended with an outward palm lowered, indicating submission and openness to the court.

25. BDAG § 1245 defines ἀτενίζω "to look intently at, stare at."

26. Kuist, *Pedagogy*, 56.

27. BDAG § 4381.2 defines κράζω in Acts 14:14, "to communicate someth. in a loud voice, call, call out, cry."

28. BDAG § 6353 defines προσφωνέω to call out or speak to, call out, address." The compound word prefixes the preposition πρός to the verb φωνέω, implying the casting forth of sound toward someone, indicating that the quality of Paul's voice attracted the attention of the crowd, as they were startled that he would speak to them in their own dialect.

29. Kuist, *Pedagogy of Paul*, 55–56.

that Paul shouted out every sermon, as some preachers are apt to do; rather, he raised his voice for emphasis.

Although it does not pertain precisely to gesturing, the duration of Paul's delivery indicates some physical stamina: he never quit preaching at noon. In the worship service described in Acts 20:7–11, "he prolonged his message until midnight." As he continued talking "still longer" (ESV translation of *epi pleion*[30]), Eutychus interrupted the service by falling out of the window and was "picked up dead." After the excitement of raising Eutychus from his apparent death, Paul then resumed his "homily" (*homileō*) "with them a long while, until daybreak" (Acts 20:11). Altogether, this sermon may have lasted well over seven hours! Granted, the reason for the length was that Paul intended to depart the next morning for Assos (Acts 20:13), and he presumed that he would never see these friends in Troas again, so perhaps Luke gives this detailed account about the length of this sermon because it was so extraordinary; after all, how many sermons are interrupted by a resuscitation from the dead? Even so, this brief display indicates the physical endurance and gesturing that accompanied the preaching of Paul.

Summary to the Preacher's Delivery

Judging from the homiletical devices Paul employed, it is apparent that he was an effective public and private communicator. This study of his homiletics, rhetoric, elocution, emotion, and gestures has shown that he communicated with his entire person. If the preacher is to "exhort with all patience," he needs to develop similar skills of delivering the message of Christ effectively. There is certainly no premium in speaking sloppily when one preaches the most important message given to humanity, the gospel of our salvation.

---

30. BDAG § 46061 translates πλεῖον in Acts 20:9, "at length."

CHAPTER 8

The Preacher's Structure: "Exhort . . . In All Doctrine"

NEXT IN HIS CHARGE, Paul encourages Timothy to "exhort . . . in all doctrine" (*parakaleson en pasę . . . didachę*; 2 Tim 4:2) and when our previous study (in chapter 2) explored the *didachē* ("doctrine") as the instructional content of the gospel, it was demonstrated that the *didachē* is revealed in the form of Tradition and Deposit. These varying aspects of the gospel imply an orderly and organized structure in which the *didachē* is to be presented; thus, it is the purpose of this chapter to examine the structure of Paul's sermonic material in order to determine if he gives any guidelines that would be helpful–or even normative—for the preacher in structuring his own sermons.

A perusal of books on homiletics reveals that modern preachers have rarely been challenged to integrate their sermonic structure with biblical sermon structure. For example, in their excellent survey of the history of preaching, Wiersbe and Perry note that the NT has something to say about preaching—"its essential nature, its message, its aims"—but they say nothing about structure.[1] Homiletical textbooks give many helpful guidelines for the preparation of sermons based on the science of communication, and these suggestions should be embraced; however, they rarely raise the question of whether the Bible ought to be the starting point for developing a normative structure of sermon organization in the same way that it is normative for each particular doctrine that is to be preached. Such inquiry is another way of asking if the NT should be just as normative in sermon structure as it is in the doctrine of salvation, although certainly Soteriology is far more important than Homiletics in the scheme of redemption. Still, it is a serious problem if bad preaching keeps some away from the Word of salvation, because "faith comes from hearing the Word of Christ" (Rom 10:17)—implying that the Word needs to be preached properly for the listener to come to faith.

This chapter will insist that Paul's sermons display a common core of structure with which he presents his message, and such structure ought to guide Timothy and

1. Wiersbe and Perry, *Wycliffe Handbook of Preaching and Preachers*, 16.

each succeeding preacher as they prepare to preach the Word. The data for such an assertion is not scarce; in fact, it is abundant. First, there are the speeches in the Book of Acts, many of which are public sermons,[2] and secondly, there are the epistles of Paul that were intended to be read out loud to the addressed congregations (Col 4:16).[3] It is the contention of this chapter that common elements of structure can be rather easily identified, serving as patterns by which the modern preacher should structure his own sermons. It is therefore the purpose of this chapter to search for these structures and to suggest possible guidelines for the structuring of biblical sermons.

The Structure of Paul's Sermons in the Book of Acts

According to Acts 16:1–4,[4] Timothy became Paul's traveling companion on his missionary journeys, meaning that he undoubtedly heard the apostle preach on many occasions. As is the case with any student, Timothy would have imitated his teacher. So, when Paul writes to him, "The things which you have heard from me in the presence of many witnesses, these entrust to faithful men" (2 Tim 2:2), Timothy would have naturally assumed Paul intended for him to present the *Didachē* in much the same manner as did the apostle. The modern preacher may also learn from this same teacher through the sermons of Paul recorded in the Book of Acts, and it is the purpose of this section to examine those speeches.

Paul's Sermons: Fact or Fiction?

First, one needs to determine if the Book of Acts has given an accurate account of these speeches: are they historically accurate or mythical fiction?

---

2. The Book of Acts records the following speeches: those of Peter (1:16–22; 2:14–36; 4:8–12; 5:29–32; 10:34–43; 11:5–7; 15:7–10); those of James (15:14–21; 21:20–25); that of Stephen (7:2–59); those of Paul (13:16–41; 14:14–17; 15:22–31; 17:2–21; 20:18–35; 23:1, 6; 24:10–21; 26:2–27; 28:17–28); that of Gamaliel (5:35–39); that of an unnamed scribe (19:35–40); of Tertullus (24:2–8); of Festus (25:14–21, 24–27), as well as prayers, letters (15:23ff.), and court briefs (23:20). Footnotes in this chapter provide observations for homiletical outlines of these sermons.

3. Of Paul's thirteen letters, nine were written to congregations: Romans, 1 and 2 Corinthians, Galatians, Ephesians, Philippians, Colossians, and 1 and 2 Thessalonians. Add to that number the eight other epistles addressed to churches (Hebrews, James, 1 and 2 Peter, 1, 2, 3 John, Jude and the Revelation), totaling two-thirds of the NT writings being originally addressed to churches and intended to be read vocally to them.

4. Acts 16:1–4 reads, "And [Paul] came also to Derbe and to Lystra. And behold, a certain disciple was there, named Timothy, the son of a Jewish woman who was a believer, but his father was a Greek, and he was well spoken of by the brethren who were in Lystra and Iconium. Paul wanted this man to go with him; and he took him and circumcised him because of the Jews who were in those parts, for they all knew that his father was a Greek. Now while they were passing through the cities, they were delivering the decrees, which had been decided upon by the apostles and elders who were in Jerusalem, for them to observe."

The Sermons as Fiction: Following the assertions of Martin Dibelius, one school of thought is that the speeches in Acts are cleverly devised revisions of history intended to convince both Jews and Greeks of the claims of Christianity.[5] Dibelius supposed that the similarities between the Book of Acts and other ancient writings are to be understood less from a historical perspective than from the propaganda intent of the Book of Acts to explain the rejection of Jesus as Messiah by the Jews and how this rejected faith found fertile expansion among Gentiles. Some, like Worley, are totally skeptical of the value of the speeches in Acts, stating that they ". . . cannot be used as authentic material representing the preaching of the earliest Christian community. . . . It is certain that they do not represent the primitive central outline of preaching of the earliest Christian community."[6] While Cadbury, for example, does not follow Worley into his complete skepticism, he tempers his own doubts by suggesting that the speeches in Acts have some historical value "even though [they are] devoid of historical basis in genuine tradition. . . ."[7] In other words, because the Book of Acts is the only available record of first-century Christian history, one must make the best with its flawed accounts and hope to uncover from them how the early church interpreted its own shadowy beginnings—without conceding that much of what it reports actually happened.

Other scholars, however, have examined the contention that the author of Acts (traditionally credited to Luke) followed an acceptable custom of ancient historians of revising or inventing history and found it to be wanting; for example, Gasque exposed this assumption as historically dubious by showing that ancient historians were quite careful in documenting what actually happened.[8] In like manner, F. F. Bruce conducted a study of the Greek historian Thucydides (*History of the Peloponnesian War*) and concluded it was not at all the practice of secular historians to revise history, noting rather that their record of speeches followed "as closely as possible the general sense of what really was said."[9]

The problem, then, appears not to be a matter of ancient historical research but of modern philosophical assumptions. McDonald quips, "The overriding factor [seems to be] that of preserving what may be called the principle of skepticism—assuming the historical tradition to be guilty of inauthenticity, as it were, until it is proven innocent."[10] Rather than surrender to doubt, why not rather assume that the record of the Book of Acts reports what its prologue in Luke 1:4 claims to prove, that Theophilus "might

---

5. Dibelius, *Studies in the Acts of the Apostles*, 174ff.
6. Worley, *Preaching and Teaching in the Earliest Church*, 84.
7. Cadbury, "The Speeches in Acts," in *The Beginnings of Christianity*, 5:426. Despite the importance of this study in Acts, one must wonder what value the speeches have if they are "devoid of historical basis," other than to find what the early church may have believed about its own origins. Evidently, Cadbury can find some meaning by this leap into fiction, but it is hard to tell what or why.
8. Gasque, "The Speeches in Acts: Dibelius Reconsidered," in *New Dimensions in NT Studies*, 139.
9. Bruce, "The Speeches in Acts: 30 Years After," in *Reconciliation and Hope*, 6.
10. McDonald, *Kerygma and Didache*, 20.

know the exact truth about the things you have been taught"? Because Paul insists that he speaks "words of sober truth" in his testimony before Proconsul Felix (Acts 25:25), why not accept the Book of Acts as a true testimony of apostolic Christianity? What benefit would there be for Luke to produce a faulty record that could easily be disproved by any contemporary reader who compared its claims to the court records to which it appeals (such as the letter of Lysias to Felix concerning Paul quoted in Acts 23:25–30)? Why not rather assume that even the differences in the style of each speech are due to the adaptation of the speakers to that which was familiar to the original audience? In this regard, Mounce reminds, "We need a sympathetic understanding of the purpose and movement of thought in each speech."[11] Thus, in accordance with the claim and purpose of the Book of Acts, this study will take the Book of Acts at face value and assume that it is reporting actual historical events.

The Sermons as Fact: This study agrees with the evaluation of Reinke, that ". . . there are good reasons for assuming that the speeches in the Book of Acts are good evidences for the way in which the apostles preached, giving us a fairly good idea of apostolic preaching to Jews as well as to Greeks."[12] It is far better to assume the truthfulness of the accounts, taking at face-value what they constantly affirm (as Paul claims in 1 Tim 2:7, "I am telling the truth, I am not lying."), because the concept of biblical truth is utterly incompatible with the theories of myth and historical emendation supposedly perpetrated by NT writers. A pious fabrication is still a lie, no matter how pious the product may appear to be.[13]

Furthermore, these skeptical assumptions fly in the face of the opening assertion of Acts 1:3, that the risen Lord "presented Himself alive, after His suffering, by many convincing proofs," a fact verified by many eyewitnesses (Acts 2:32; 3:15; 5:32; 10:39–41; 13:31). The Book of Acts is carefully documented with names, places, and events, so that the first century reader could easily check the sources of the writer. Only a fool would deceitfully misquote such well-known contemporary figures as Gamaliel, the Herodian kings, Gallio, Felix, and Festus, and assume that he could dupe his readers without any detection of his fraud. How much better it is to assume that Luke intended for his readers to check his sources.

The most damaging effect of the skeptical approach is that it leaves the preacher in a moral dilemma—how is he to preach fraudulent texts as if they were true? If a preacher agrees with Dibelius that Paul's sermons are not actually Paul's after all, and that "Luke is not a historian but a preacher,"[14] then he would suppose that homileti-

---

11. Mounce, *Essential Nature*, 76.

12. Reinke, "A Synopsis on Early Christian Preaching," in *Root of the Vine*, 140.

13. See the detailed study by Terry Wilder, *Pseudonymity, the New Testament, and Deception: An Inquiry into Intention and Reception*, chapter 2, on the ethics of literary property. He demonstrates that the issue of truth was a major concern for the early Christians.

14. Dibelius, *Studies in Acts*, 183. This statement implies that no preacher can be a historian, or

cal ethics gives a preacher an acceptable license to tamper with historical accuracy, because the greater goal is to win others to the truth of Christ. It seems odd that scholars who attribute revisionism to ancient historians would never tolerate such a practice on their own works (nor should they!). The practical effect of imposing revisionism on Acts is that it will eventually destroy preaching at its root because the undergirding intent of preaching is to proclaim a message that claims to be true. If the preacher consider Acts to be untrustworthy, he will not be able to proclaim for very long what he deems to be false without feeling quite deceitful.

However, if the speeches in the Book of Acts are in fact historically accurate—as they purport themselves to be—then their content and structure can serve as patterns for contemporary preaching. This view summarizes the findings of this study, based upon the claims of the Book of Acts and the supporting research by evangelical scholars over the centuries.

Paul's Sermons: Verbatim or Edited?

Even if the sermons recorded in Acts are regarded as historically accurate, the question remains whether they are recorded *verbatim* or if they are edited renditions of the original speeches. The reality is that the original sermons no longer exist, so nothing remains with which to compare the copies; for that matter, Luke freely admits that Peter kept on exhorting "with many other words" (Acts 2:40) and that Paul was in the habit of preaching at length (Acts 20:7–11). It would appear, then, that the speeches in the Book of Acts are not verbal reproductions but editorial condensations of much longer messages that are nonetheless faithful to the essence of the original. After all, Luke did not hear some of the recorded sermons first-hand, certainly not before injecting himself into the narrative in Acts 16:10. He is citing other witnesses, perhaps even the preachers themselves, so it is quite possible that the substance of the speeches was approved by the speakers before Luke published them, much as the letter of the Jerusalem Council was drafted and approved (Acts 15:23–29). Bruce comments, "We need not suppose that the speeches in the Book of Acts are *verbatim* reports in the sense that they record every word used by the speakers on the occasions in question. Paul, we know, was given to long sermons."[15] Bruce's observation concludes that the speeches are "at least faithful epitomes, giving the gist of the arguments used."[16]

Barclay also suggests the obvious: Luke assumes the readers have a great deal of background knowledge regarding the message contained in Paul's sermons because much of the gospel content is implied rather than explicitly stated.[17] Furthermore, the setting of each speech determines the extent of the content that is included in each

---

worse, that every preacher is a liar, even if a pious one.

15. Bruce, "Speeches in Acts," 27.
16. Ibid.
17. Barclay, "A Comparison of Paul's Missionary Preaching and Preaching to the Church," 168.

message. Clearly, Paul in Acts preaches differently as a missionary than he writes as a pastor in his epistles. Even so, his sermons and letters differ in approach and content because "he begins where his audience was;"[18] however, each sermon or letter proclaims the same gospel despite any differing applications that Paul makes of that same gospel. Bruce concludes, "Taken all in all, each speech suits the speaker, the audience and the circumstances of delivery."[19]

Although the speeches in Acts show signs of being condensed, this observation should not be taken to mean that the recorded speeches do not contain any direct quotations—they obviously do when OT passages are cited. Furthermore, the speeches were written as if they are quoted verbatim, even though Luke provides what may be only an abstract of a full sermon. If such reduction is the case, then Luke apparently quotes the pertinent points of a message while omitting secondary comments. There is certainly nothing unethical with such a literary procedure: the quotations are accurate, even if the entire sermon is not transcribed word-for-word.

Assuming such condensing to be typical of Luke's literary style, this study will treat the speeches in the Book of Acts as if they are excerpts of historical sermons, whereby Luke quotes aspects of the original messages that were essential to the overall structure and content being preached. What he records was actually spoken, even if he did not record every word uttered on that particular occasion.

Paul's Examples: 1st Century Sermon Structure

The sermons in the Book of Acts did not appear in a historical vacuum, as studies in form criticism have demonstrated that ". . . much NT material, especially when preserved in oral form, employed the precise forms of narration and teaching in current use in the non-Christian world."[20] Therefore, this study will briefly explore these literary structures in both the Greek and Jewish cultures that were familiar to Paul.

Classical Structures: One of the structures common to hortatory in classical Greek literature that have been noted in the speeches in the Book of Acts is the Cynic Diatribe, which was a ". . . discourse on a moral subject, given by a preacher before an audience but retaining the mannerisms and devices of animated conversation."[21] The characteristics of these diatribes included devices such as rhetorical interrogation, questions and answers, conditional clauses, and repetition.[22] Such a discourse would begin with a positive exposition of the theme, follow with a rebuff of a negative presentation, and

---

18. Ibid., 166.
19. Bruce, "Speeches in Acts," 27.
20. Bradley, "The *Topos* as a Form in the Pauline Paraenesis," 240.
21. McDonald, *Kerygma and Didache*, 40.
22. Ibid., 41.

then conclude with a statement of meaning.²³ McDonald notes the close similarity of the Cynic Diatribe with Paul's address on the Areopagus, showing that Paul couched his message in a structure commonly heard by the learned classes of Athens.²⁴

Bradley finds another classical structure employed in Paul's letters, the *topos*, which he defines as "a treatment of a topic of a popular thought or action."²⁵ He particularly locates such treatment in the practical exhortations of Paul's epistles that are introduced by the common use of the preposition *perí* with a genitive object (such as used in 1 Cor 7:1, 2 Cor 9:1; 1 Thess 4:9; 5:1). By using these two literary devices found in the oration and writing skills of the Roman and Greek masters, Paul shows evidence of classical training in his own preaching and writing skills.

Jewish Structures: Paul was also educated "at the feet of Gamaliel" (Acts 22:3), a renowned first-century rabbi, ²⁶ and so it is not surprising that he presents his message in forms familiar to the Jewish community. It is quite evident that the early church followed the liturgies common to the synagogue, and Bowker points out that certain words relating to the exposition of Scripture appear in Acts almost exclusively in contexts where synagogue practices are specifically mentioned.²⁷ These customs would include the lexical readings for the Sabbath, after which the reader would give a *midrash*, a running commentary on the text, following the pattern given in Deuteronomy as an exposition of the Law. Known as a *proem*, these comments would begin with an introductory text linguistically linked to the synagogue reading, which would then be bolstered by several other related texts bearing the same theme, a technique known *harusin*, or "stringing of pearls."²⁸ Such homilies often began with the comment, "Let our teacher instruct us," in the manner that the synagogue rulers invited Paul and his companions, "Brethren, if you have any word of exhortation for the people, say it" (Acts 13:15).

In light of these synagogue customs, Paul's sermon recorded in Acts 13:16–41 resembles a rabbinical *proem* based on 1 Sam 13:14, "The LORD has sought out for

---

23. Ibid.
24. Ibid., 42.
25. Bradley, "The *Topos*," 240.
26. Gamaliel, the grandson of the rabbi Hillel, is known to have been the first president of the Great Sanhedrin of Jerusalem and thought to be the source of "the oldest written Targum of which anything is known." See "Gamaliel I," *Jewish Encyclopedia.com*. Cited 19 June 2014. Online: http://www.jewishencyclopedia. com/articles/6494-gamaliel-i.
27. Bowker, "Speeches in Acts: A Study in Proem and *Yellammedenu* Form," 109. Among these "synagogue" words are "the reading (*anagnōsis*) of the Law and the Prophets" (Acts 13:15; Luke 4:16; 2 Cor 3:14); "reasoned (*dialegomai*) from the Scriptures" (Acts 17:2; 17; 18:4, 19; 19:8, 9; 20:7, 9); "explaining" (*dianoigō*, Acts 17:3; Luke 24:32); "spoken boldly" (*parresiazomai*, Acts 9:27, 28; 13:46; 14:3; 19:8); "declaring" (*ektithēmi*, Acts 28:23); "giving evidence" (*paratithēmi*, Acts 17:3); "examining" (*anakrinō*, Acts 17:11); and "word of exhortation" (*paraklēsis*; Acts 13:15).
28. Ibid., 101.

Himself a man after His own heart" (paraphrased by Paul in Acts 13:22[29]), which he introduces with a brief survey of Israel's history (13:17–21) and then supports by a "pearl-stringing" (a *harusin*) that includes Isa 44:28, 2 Sam 7:12, Ps 2:7, Isa 55:3, and Ps 16:10. Bowker suggests that Paul's concluding remark ("Take heed therefore, so that the thing spoken of in the Prophets may not come upon you," 13:40) echoes the *Seder* reading for the Sabbath from Deut 4:25–26,[30] although Paul actually ends with a quote from Hab 1:5, "Behold, you scoffers, and marvel, and perish; For I am accomplishing a work in your days, A work which you will never believe, though someone should describe it to you."

Paul's preaching similarities with Greek and Jewish forms do not mean slavish imitation, nor do they negate the idea that the structure of Christian preaching is rather consistent. Paul is free to embellish the basic forms with oratorical devices commonly known to both Jews and Gentiles, as he follows his own principle, "I have become all things to all men, that I may by all means save some" (1 Cor 9:22). Friedrich points out the difference in Paul's structure from that of a Hermetic sermon, although the vocabulary may be nearly identical: "*Kērussein* does not mean the delivery of a learned or edifying or hortatory discourse in well-chosen words and a pleasant voice. It is the declaration of an event."[31] The content of the gospel is always the distinctive element in Christian preaching, not the structure, although all of Paul's sermons show remarkable similarity in development, and it is to this observation that this study now turns.

Observations on Paul's Sermons in the Book of Acts

The sermons of Paul are as varied as the situations he encountered. He is pictured as preaching inside a Jewish synagogue (Acts 13:14–43), within a private conversation with a Greek jailer (Acts 16:25–34), on a hillside before an Athenian academy (Acts 17:16–34), to a meeting of the Ephesian elders (Acts 20:17–38), and before five groups of accusers (chapters 22, 23, 24, 26, 28). These situations illustrate the types

---

29. Paul's comment in Acts 13:22 reads as follows: "[God] raised up David to be their king, concerning whom He also testified and said, 'I have found David the son of Jesse, a man after My heart, who will do all My will.'" The primary reference is to 1 Sam 13:14 ("The LORD has sought out for Himself a man after His own heart."), where Paul identified the "man" as "David the son of Jesse" (2 Sam 23:1) with a linguistic echo to Ps 89:20, "I have found David My servant." Admittedly, the phrase, "who will do all My will" (Acts 13:22) is not found in the OT, so it seems to be Paul's interpretive explanation of "a man after my heart."

30. Bowker, "Speeches in Acts," 103. Deuteronomy 4:25–26 reads, "When you become the father of children and children's children and have remained long in the land, and act corruptly, and make an idol in the form of anything, and do that which is evil in the sight of the LORD your God *so as* to provoke Him to anger, I call heaven and earth to witness against you today, that you shall surely perish quickly from the land where you are going over the Jordan to possess it. You shall not live long on it, but shall be utterly destroyed."

31. Friedrich, κηρύσσω, *TDNT*, 3:699, 703.

Paul's Sermon in Pisidian Antioch (Acts 13:14-43)[32] is the only recorded sermon of the many Paul preached in a synagogue (as noted in Acts 14:1; 17:1, 10, 17; 18:4, 19; 19:8), and as would be expected, his appeal to the Jewish Scriptures is very prominent, as he brings to light the fulfillment of OT promises in Jesus. While this message contains more allusions to the ministry of Jesus than found in any other sermon, the emphasis of this sermon clearly centers on the resurrection of Jesus as fulfillment of Scripture (Acts 13:33). Paul concludes the sermon with a promise of forgiveness as well as a warning from Hab 1:5. The sermonic structure reveals this general order: OT texts cited → redemptive history → prophetic promise → fulfillment in resurrection → promise upon belief → warning to heed. The structure plainly follows an outline based on the flow of redemptive history.

Paul's Plea to the Crowd at Lystra (Acts 14:15-17): Paul's speech to the crowd at Lystra (14:15-17)[33] is more of an emotional plea for rationality than it is a well-ordered sermon, because it comes in reaction to the crowd's intent to sacrifice to Paul and Barnabas after they healed a lame man. While priests of the god Zeus invite the audience to a pagan ritual, Paul instead appeals to God's witness of "natural revelation" throughout human history, although the apostle supports this concept with allusions

---

32. Paul's Sermon in Pisidian Antioch (Acts 13:14-43) outlines as follows:
   1A. Setting: Paul and companion are asked by the synagogue leaders to speak a word of exhortation (v.15);
   2A. Introduction: review of OT History from the exodus to David (vs.16-22);
   3A. Primary Text quoted (v.22b, from 1 Sam 16:18);
   4A. Gospel Proclaimed (vs.23-37);
      1B. Ministry of Jesus as son of David (vs.23-25);
      2B. Death of Jesus (vs.26-29);
      3B. Resurrection of Jesus (vs.30-37);
         1C. Eyewitness testimony vs.30-32);
         2C. OT testimony (Ps 2:7; Isa 55:3; Ps 16:10);
   5A. Promise: Forgiveness and Justification (v.38-39);
   6A. Warning from Hab 1:5 (vs.40-41);
   7A. Results: Follow-up conversations (vs.42-43).
33. Paul's Plea to the Crowd at Lystra (Acts 14:15-17) outlines as follows:
   1A. Setting: Healing of a lame man leads to attempt of the crowd to sacrifice to Paul and Barnabas (vs.9-13);
   2A. Gospel Proclaimed (vs.14-17);
      1B. A call to turn from vain things;
      2B. A call to turn to the living God as Creator;
      3B. OT Texts cited (Exod 20:11; Ps 146:5; Ps 81:12);
      4B. Appeal to natural revelation (v.17, "God did good and gave you rains from heaven and fruitful seasons, satisfying your hearts with food and gladness.");
   3A. Result: "they with difficulty restrained the crowds from offering sacrifice to them" (v.18).

to the special revelation of OT Scriptures. His appeal to the crowd is that they turn from idols as being incompatible with the living God. Once again, the structure flows from God's witness in history to a call for conversion.

Paul's Conversation with the Philippian Jailer (Acts 16:25-34): The episode of Paul's conversation with the Philippian jailer (Acts 16:25-34)[34] is better classified as an example of "crisis evangelism" than a sermon, because it takes place in a crumbling jailhouse after an earthquake had shaken it to the foundations, prompting the desperate question of the jailer, "What must I do to be saved?" (Acts 16:30). It can be assumed that the jailor possessed some previous information about Christ, because Paul moves directly to the gospel command, "Believe in the Lord Jesus" (16:31a). The jailor would have known the charges against Paul and Silas of the "unlawful customs" about Jesus they were proclaiming, plus he would have heard the apostles "praying and singing hymns of praise to God" (16:25). Paul follows the command with the gospel promise, "You shall be saved, you and your household" (16:31b), leading to the conversion of the jailer and the baptism of his household after the apostles "spoke the word of the Lord to them" (16:32). Despite the brevity of this conversation (only 26 quoted words in the Greek text), the same structure appears: first, there is gospel information → next, gospel command and promise → then a gospel response.

Paul's Sermon on the Areopagus (Acts 17:16-36)[35] is an example of Paul's preaching before a pagan audience, and his appeal is not directly to the OT Scriptures but to

---

34. Paul's Conversation with the Philippian Jailer (Acts 16:25-34)
  1A. Setting: Paul and Silas are imprisoned: an earthquake opens the doors, and the jailer is about to commit suicide when Paul assures him, "Do yourself no harm, for we are all here!" (vs.25-28);
  2A. The Lead-in question of the jailer: "What must I do to be saved?" (vs.29-30);
  3A. The Gospel Command: "Believe in the Lord Jesus" (v.16:31a);
  4A. The Gospel Promise: "You shall be saved, you and your household" (v.16:31b).
  5A. Results: Paul spoke the word of the Lord to his household, and they were baptized (vs.32-34).
35. Paul's Sermon on the Areopagus (Acts 17:16-36) outlines as follows:
  1A. Setting: Paul is invited to speak by philosophers about "this new teaching which you are proclaiming" (vs.19-21);
  2A. Introduction: "Men of Athens, I observe that you are very religious in all respects" (v.22);
  3A. Text cited: "TO AN UNKNOWN GOD'" (v.23);
  4A. Gospel Proclaimed (vs.23c-29);
      1B. God as Creator and Lord (echoes 1 King 8:27; Isa 42:5; Deut 32:8);
      2B. Man's purpose to seek God (echoes Isa 55:6; Job 12:10);
      3B. Support from Epimenides and Aratus (vs.28c-29);
      4B. Spiritual nature of God (Isa 40:8 ff.);
  5A. Gospel command: repent (v.30);
  6A. Gospel warning: God will judge the world (v.31a);
  7A. Gospel basis: a Man God raised from the dead (v.31b);
  8A. Results: some sneered, others believed (vs.32-34).

the general revelation of God in creation. Paul also weaves in a saying found in the *Cretica* attributed to the 6th century B.C. Greek writer Epimenides[36] ("In Him we live and move and have our being"), and then he quotes directly from Aratus (ca. 310–245 B.C.) *Phaenomena* 5 ("We are his offspring") in order to illustrate Christian truths,[37] showing that he had "probably made acquaintance of Stoics in Tarsus, where the stoic Athenodorus had a great influence."[38] Once Paul established common ground with his audience, he then moved directly to special revelation—without directly quoting Scripture, but by giving a call to repentance based on the biblical truths of divine judgment and the resurrection of Jesus. Thus, while there considerable difference in the content presented in this sermon from that in the synagogue sermon, the skeletal structure is remarkably similar: a text is cited → the revelation of God is given → a gospel appeal is offered → the resurrection of Jesus is proclaimed.[39]

Sermon of Paul to the Ephesian Elders (Acts 20:17-38): Luke reports that Paul preached many times to believing audiences (Acts 15:35), but the message to the Ephesian elders (Acts 20:17-38) is the only recorded sermon of Paul given to a Christian audience.[40] This gathering differs from the Lord's Day meeting of believers described

---

36. What is known of Epimenides derives from Diogenes Laertius, *The Lives and Opinions of Eminent Philosophers* (London: Henry G. Bohn, 1853). Several quotations attributed to Epimenides appear in various classical Greek works (see Kathleen Freeman, *Ancilla to the Pre-Socratic Philosophers: A Complete Translation of the Fragments in Diels, Fragmente der Vorsokratiker* (Cambridge, Mass.: Harvard University Press, 1948); also see "Epimenides of Crete: Fragments," in http://demonax.info/ doku.php?id=text:epimenides_of_crete_fragments. Cited June 20, 2014. Epimenides' work *Cretica* is quoted twice in the NT, in Acts 17:28 and Titus 1:12. According to http://www.princeton.edu/~achaney/tmve/wiki100k/docs/Epimenides.html (cited June 20, 2014), "Its only source is a 9th-century Syriac commentary by Isho'dad of Merv on the Acts of the Apostles, discovered, edited and translated (into Greek) by Prof. J. Rendel Harris in a series of articles in the *Expositor*" (Oct. 1906, 305–17; "A Further Note on the Cretans"; April 1907, 332–37; Apr. 1912, 348–353).

37. See the primary text of Aratus' *Phaenomena* in *Callimachus, Hymns and Epigrams. Lycophron. Aratus*. It is available on the *Loeb Classical Library Online* vol. 129 at http://books.google.com/books?id=bqVfAAAAMAAJ&pg=PR7&source =gbs_selected_pages&cad=2#v=onepage&q&f=false. Cited June 20, 2014. See also the article by R. Faber, "The Apostle and the Poet: Paul and Aratus," *Clarion* 42, No. 13 (1993): 291–305.

38. Bruce, "Speeches in Acts," 22.

39. Pattison, *History of Christian Preaching*, 39, outlines this sermon: (1) purpose (Acts 17:23); (2) plan (vs.24–31); and (3) sequel (vs.32–34).

40. The Sermon of Paul to the Ephesian Elders (Acts 20:17-38) outlines as follows:
   1A. Introduction: Paul's reflections on his ministry (vs.17–21);
   2A. Paul's prospect of his continued ministry (vs.22–27);
   3A. Paul's Charge: "Be on guard for yourselves and for all the flock" (v.28);
   4A. Paul's Warning: Entrance of "savage wolves" (vs.29–30);
   5A. Paul's personal example of alertness in the ministry (v.31);
   6A. Paul's Commendation to "God and to the word of His grace" (v.32);
   7A. Paul's Closing remarks about practical ministry (vs.33–34);
   8A. Text Cited: "It is more blessed to give than to receive" (vs.33–35);
   9A. Results: Prayer, tears, departure (vs.36–38).

in Acts 20:7 in that it is a requested assembly of elders from the area surrounding Miletus, making it much like a called presbytery meeting. Bruce suggests that "... this Miletian speech is a sample of the sort of thing that Paul was accustomed to say to Christian audiences;"[41] in other words, this message can be considered fairly normative of the structure of Paul's sermons.

The discourse abounds in parallels and vocabulary present in Paul's epistles, and it even shares the same basic sermonic structure found throughout the Book of Acts, although arranged differently.[42] While its structure does not seem to have a tight organization, it is not a collection of rambling thoughts but a discourse united by a central theme, that of the ministry of giving for the sake of Christ's gospel. The message is climatically illustrated with the closing quotation from the oral teachings of Jesus, "that He Himself said, 'It is more blessed to give than to receive'" (Acts 20:35).[43] Apparently, this quote serves as the "text" for the sermon, although it appears as the closing application. Paul expounds on the text by referencing to his own various personal ministries among the elders (20:18–27), leading to his ministerial charge for them to "be on the alert" for "savage wolves" (20:28–31) before making his concluding remarks. McDonald views this entire message as a *paraneia* on this specific teaching of Jesus on giving, because the sermon focuses on the proper way to give oneself in service, with Paul using himself as an example for the elders to follow.[44] In this manner, the message gives the structure of a *topos*[45] as it discusses a common subject of moral concern—service to others—except that the rationale springs not from general ethics but from the teaching of the Mediator of the New Covenant, the Lord Jesus.

Apparently, the needs of the audience tailored the structure of the message to some extent. Paul speaks as an elder to other elders on the respective duties of ministering, particularly concerning speaking and doing the Word. The key words dealing with deeds of giving are serving, ministering, shepherding, and working, while the key words dealing with the spoken Word include declaring, teaching, testifying, preaching, and admonishing. The unifying concept of ministry is the message of the "gospel of the grace of God" (Acts 20:24), which Paul defines as "repentance toward God and faith in our Lord Jesus Christ" (Acts 20:21). Clearly, the distinction of Christian giving

---

41. Bruce, *Commentary of the Book of Acts*, 413.

42. Other messages develop from text to comment, whereas this one moves from comment to text.

43. This quote from Jesus is one of the few found in Paul's teachings (Others include Rom 14:14; 1 Cor 7:10; 9:14; 11:23–24, 1 Thess 4:15; 1 Tim 5:18; plus many other likely allusions, as in Rom 12:1–15.). See the discussion in Stout, *The Man Christ Jesus*, 90–105, which concludes that Paul, rather than often quoting Jesus directly, as he does here in Acts 20:35, instead assumes the common knowledge of Jesus' teachings shared between himself and his listeners. Thus Paul uses echoes of Jesus' teachings, as he frequently does with the OT (as demonstrated by Hays, *Echoes of Scripture in the Letters of Paul*). Besides, Paul could not quote from the written Gospels for the simple fact that they had not yet been written, so he had to rely on oral tradition or collections of written *logia* used for catechetical purposes.

44. McDonald, *Kerygma and Didache*, 70.

45. Bradley, "The *Topos* as a Form in the Pauline Paraenesis," 240.

flows from the truths of the gospel, as implied in the giving of Christ Himself, when "He purchased [the Church] with His own blood" (Acts 20:28).

What can the modern preacher learn from the structure of Paul's sermon to the Ephesian elders that might help him in the preparation of his own sermons? The primary lesson lies in the statement of the central theme of some passage or text of Scripture, which is then developed by use of personal illustration and doctrinal confirmation, especially with reference to the historical acts of salvation. The theme (in this case, giving) is then applied to the hearers, with adjoining assurances of the promises of God. There does seem to be great latitude in the organization and arrangement of these particulars; for example, the text may even be cited last of all, a device rather contrary to the general rule of homiletics, which is to state one's text first. Paul's message, then, shows that it is not so much logical development that unites a sermon, but rather, it is the unifying theme, which may be presented in a way appropriate to the setting and the audience.

Such observations should not be construed to mean that sermon organization is unbiblical or un-Pauline! The apostle shows thoughtful development of his theme, so that in the final analysis, his address to the elders becomes what could be classified as a textual sermon, with the structure of the message developing as follows: gospel content ("repentance toward God and faith in our Lord Jesus Christ") → redemptive history in Paul's experience, Acts 20:22–26) → gospel charge (20:27–32) → gospel text (20:33–35).

Testimony of Paul to the Jews in Jerusalem (Acts 22:1–21):[46] Paul's testimony to the Jews in Jerusalem (Acts 22:1–21) is the first of five apologies Paul gives as defenses of the Faith. All five testimonies are quite similar in content with varying subtleties of detail, mainly concerning the events surrounding Paul's Damascus Road encounter with the risen Jesus. Bruce points out that the structure in each address differs because the audience differs: in Acts 22, Paul speaks as a Jew (in Hebrew) to Jews, whereas in Acts 26 he speaks as an accused Roman citizen in a Roman court.[47] He comments that the defenses ". . . are so subtly adapted to their respective audiences that we must assume a remarkably astute composer, or conclude that we have substantially faithful

---

46. The Testimony of Paul to the Jews in Jerusalem (Acts 22:1–21) follows this outline:
   1A. Setting: As Paul worships at the Temple, Jews from Asia stir the crowd with charges that Paul has brought in a Greek, causing a riot, but Paul asks the Roman commander for permission to address the crowd (vs.27–40);
   2A. Introduction: Paul speaks from the steps in Hebrew (vs.1–2);
   3A. Text cited: general reference to "the law of our fathers" (v.3);
   4A. Gospel proclaimed in Paul's testimony (vs.4–21);
      1B. His career as a zealous Jew (vs.3–5);
      2B. His Damascus road encounter with Jesus (vs.6–11);
      3B. His commission and baptism from Ananias (vs.12–16);
      4B. His Temple vision from Jesus (vs.17–21);
   5A. Results: The riot resumes (vs.22–23), but Paul is released for a later hearing (v.30).
47. Bruce, "Speeches in Acts," 23.

The Preacher's Structure: "Exhort . . . In All Doctrine"

reports of what Paul really said."⁴⁸ The structure of his first defense follows this pattern: an account of redemptive history (in Paul's life, 22:1–7) → appeal to texts, in this case given by spoken revelation (in Christ's appearance, 21:8–10) → a gospel charge (20:11–15) → a gospel response (21:16–21).

Paul's Defense before the Sanhedrin (Acts 23:1-6):⁴⁹ Paul barely began his defense to the Sanhedrin (Acts 23:1–6) before he was interrupted and nearly torn to pieces by his accusers; but, even so, the development of his brief defense follows this structure: appeal to redemptive history (in Paul's life before God, 23:1) → text of the Law cited (Exod 22:28) → gospel revelation proclaimed (resurrection, 23:6).

Paul's Defense before Felix (Acts 24:10-21):⁵⁰ In this defense before the Roman procurator Felix (Acts 24:10–21), Paul again appeals to Scripture ("believing everything that is in accordance with the Law, and that is written in the Prophets," 24:14) as being fulfilled in resurrection of Jesus (24:15, 21) and verified by a personal application of redemption in his own life (24:16–20). Once again, the common structure is present: gospel text → gospel promise → gospel basis (resurrection).

Paul's Defense before King Agrippa (Acts 26:1-29):⁵¹ In his defense before King Agrippa (Acts 26:1–29), Paul begins with an appeal to the king, and then he recounts

---

48. Ibid., 25.
49. Paul's Defense before the Sanhedrin (Acts 23:1–6) follows this outline:
   1A. Setting: Paul appears to give testimony before the Sanhedrin (v.1a);
   2A. Introduction: Paul's assertion of a good conscience (v.1b);
   3A. Paul interrupted by being struck (v.2);
   4A. Paul's appeal to the Law (v.3);
   5A. Paul's citation of Exod 22:28 (vs.4–5);
   6A. Paul's proclamation of "the hope and resurrection of the dead!" (v.6).
   7A. Result: a "great dissension" among the Sanhedrin (vs.7–10);
50. Paul's Defense before Felix (Acts 24:10–21);
   1A. Setting: The attorney Tertullus charges Paul on behalf of the High Priest (vs.1–8);
   2A. Paul cheerfully makes his defense (vs.9–21);
      1B. Protestation of his innocence (vs.9–13);
      2B. Text cited: appeal to the Law and the Prophets (v.14);
      3B. Gospel presented: "a resurrection of both the righteous and the wicked" (v.15);
      4B. Explanation of the charges (vs.16–21);
   3A. Results: Felix recesses the court for a later hearing (vs.22–23).
51. Paul's Defense before King Agrippa (Acts 26:10–21) follows this outline:
   1A. Setting: Arrival of King Agrippa to pay respect to the new Proconsul Festus (vs.13–27);
   2A. Introduction: Paul appeals to King Agrippa (vs.1–3);
   3A. Paul's review of his previous life (vs.4–5);
   4A. Text cited: "the promise (of resurrection) made by God to our fathers" (vs.6–8); also "what the Prophets and Moses said was going to take place" (v.22);
   5A. Paul recounts his conversion testimony (vs.9–15);
   6A. Paul appeals to his Heavenly Commission (vs.16–20);

139

redemptive history in his personal experience (26:4–5), illustrating the redemptive promise of resurrection in OT history (26:6–8). This citation of OT prophecy leads Paul to explain the special revelation of Jesus' appearances, confirming His risen status (26:9–16) and issuing forth in the gospel proclamation to Paul (26:16–20). His closing appeal is to the general text of Scripture that "the Christ was to suffer, *and that by reason of His* resurrection from the dead He should be the first to proclaim light both to the *Jewish* people and to the Gentiles" (26:23). Once again, the same sermonic elements are noted in the structure of this message, although they are arranged differently, as well as containing various classical literary locutions, such as "proverbial sayings, superlatives, classical *isasin*, and interrogative clauses."[52] By use of these rhetorical devices, Paul is no doubt attempting to impress his distinguished audience, even though the basic gospel content remains consistent.

Paul's Defense to the Jews in Rome (Acts 28:23–31):[53] Paul's defense before the Jews in Rome (Acts 28:23–31) is his final sermon recorded in Acts, and although the content is greatly compacted, the same structure is noted: the gospel revelation is proclaimed, based on the Law and the Prophets (28:23). Similar to the other sermon addressed to Jews in Acts 13, this one concludes with a warning from Scripture (28:25–27, quoting Isa 6:9–10). The structure unfolds as follows: gospel revelation → OT texts → gospel warning.

Characteristics of Sermon Structure in the Book of Acts

The noticeable characteristics of sermon structure in the Book of Acts have attracted the attention of many scholars, such as C. H. Dodd in his groundbreaking study on apostolic preaching.[54] He summarizes the basic structural content of the gospel *kērygma* as follows:

1. fulfillment of the Covenant (both Abrahamic and Davidic) has dawned through
2. the death and resurrection of Jesus, who is

7A. Gospel proclamation (vs.21–23);
8A. Results: Appeal to Festus and Agrippa to believe (vs.24–32).
52. As noted by Bruce, "Speeches in Acts," 24.
53. Paul's Defense to the Jews in Rome (Acts 28:23–31) outlines as follows:
1A. Setting: Paul arrives in Rome and explains the reason for the charges against him (vs.17–22);
2A. Gospel proclaimed (v.23);
   1B. testifying about the Kingdom of God (v.23a);
   2B. persuading them concerning Jesus, from both the Law of Moses and from the Prophets (v.23b);
3A. Response: "some were persuaded by the things spoken, but others would not believe" (v.24);
4A. Gospel Warning: citation of Isa 6:9–10 (vs.25–28);
5A. Result: Paul preaches the Kingdom of God and teaching the Lord Jesus (v.31).
54. Dodd, *Apostolic Preaching and its Developments* (1936).

3. now exalted so that He
4. pours forth the Holy Spirit,
5. leading to the messianic age that will be consummated at Christ's return and
6. issuing forth in an appeal to repent and believe.[55]

Dodd compares this structure with Mark 1:15 ("The time is fulfilled, and the kingdom of God is at hand; repent and believe in the gospel.") and concludes that the apostolic *kērygma* is identical with the preaching of Jesus.[56]

Kerr also observes that the sermonic structure emphasizes these characteristics:

1. the prophetic proclamation of the coming Messiah;
2. the story of the earthly life of Jesus;
3. the death of Christ and
4. His resurrection, concluding with
5. a call to repentance.[57]

Stevens notices that the structure is

1. built on the OT, with the primary question whether Jesus corresponded to the OT picture of the Messiah; it is
2. presented with an apology along with
3. the delivering of didactic material of truth and facts, although it is
4. often leveled with accusations and
5. accompanied by predictions of judgment.[58]

Whereas the basic framework observed by these scholars may differ to some degree, it is quite apparent that the sermons in the Book of Acts show remarkable similarity, not only in content but also in structure as well. Kerr observes, "Apostolic preaching is definite, concrete, substantial, factual, almost formulated in the method and message. The first sermons of the Christian church cover the same ground, present the same facts, make the same demands and reach the same conclusions."[59]

These observations lead to the following outline of the basic structure of an apostolic sermon:

1. the historical death and resurrection of Jesus as the fulfillment of OT prophecy for salvation;
2. the ascended status of Jesus as Lord, Prince, Judge and Savior;

---

55. Ibid., 21–23.
56. Ibid., 48–51.
57. Kerr, *Preaching in the Early Church*, 32–39.
58. Stevens, *The Message of the Apostles*, 37–39.
59. Kerr, *Preaching in the Early Church*, 43.

3. the promise of the Holy Spirit, bringing salvation;

4. the command to repent, turn and believe in Christ for salvation;

5. the offer of salvation made to "all the ones believing in Him" (Acts 10:43; 13:39), who are evidently the same as "many as had been appointed unto eternal life" (Acts 13:48), so that

6. genuine salvation is evidenced by baptism and a life-response of leaving the old-life patterns and opinions (Acts 17:32–43; 19:18).

A synopsis of all the sermons in the Book of Acts reveals a structure that follows this basic outline:

> Introductory remarks
> History of Salvation Explained
>> OT text(s) cited
>> Some revelation of God proclaimed
>
> Fulfillment of Salvation Announced
>> In the Ministry of Jesus
>> In the Death of Jesus
>> In the Resurrection of Jesus
>>> OT prophecy cited
>>> Eyewitness testimony cited
>>
>> In the Exaltation of Jesus as Lord
>
> Promise of Salvation Extended
>> Accompanied by the Holy Spirit
>> Resulting in forgiveness and justification
>> Verified by Scriptural prooftexts
>
> Command unto Salvation Given
>> To repent and to believe
>>> With a warning about unbelief
>>> And a call to baptism

This outline emphasizes what is a prominent theme in the Book of Acts as measured by the occurrence of related words, which is the salvation God revealed in history, culminating in Jesus as the Savior (*sotēr*) who promises salvation (*sotēria, sotērios*) so that believers may be saved (*sozō*).[60] Each of these primary segments of salvation will now be explained briefly.

---

60. While Jesus is labeled "savior" (*sotēr*) only twice in Acts (5:31; 13:23), the noun "salvation" (*sotēria*) appears six times (Acts 4:12; 7:25; 13:26, 47; 16:17; 27:34; also once more in the noun *sotērios*, 28:28), while the verb "to be saved" (*sozō*) appears thirteen times (Acts 2:21, 40, 47; 4:9, 12; 11:14; 14:9; 15:1, 11; 16:30, 31; 27:20, 31). If there is a theme verse climaxing the Book of Acts, it may well be 16:31, "Believe in the Lord Jesus, and you shall be saved, you and your household," although it appears half-way through the book

History of Salvation Explained: The structure of the sermons in the Book of Acts is rooted in the concept that God has progressively revealed salvation in the history of Israel. To a Jewish audience (and presumably also a Christian audience), the initial appeal of these sermons begins with an appeal to OT history, particularly with regard to the Messianic prophecies, so that the primary question is whether Jesus corresponds to the OT portrayal of the Messiah.[61] Even when preaching to a biblically illiterate audience, Paul alludes repeatedly to biblical truths, especially concerning the person and attributes of God.

This observation suggests to the modern preacher that his sermon structure should be careful to ascertain the point of salvation history in which his text appears and then relate that text to its fulfillment in the Messiah. Kaiser coins a phrase to express such exegesis, "epangelical theology," which has as its unifying principle "the plan of God announced and continually expanded."[62] While Kaiser admittedly seeks to synthesize covenant and dispensational hermeneutics, his emphasis that the sermon structure should pay close attention to the historical setting of the salvation God promises offers great merit. The actual structure of the sermon should not be artificially imposed upon a text; instead, it must serve as the bedrock upon which the text lies, so that the sermon is presented within the natural flow of the history of salvation.

Fulfillment of Salvation Announced: The structure next moves to the fulfillment of salvation history in the Person and Work of Jesus of Nazareth. There is a "positive message of truth and fact to deliver,"[63] so that the text at hand is interpreted Christologically, showing how it relates to Jesus in His ministry and particularly in His death. The listeners are confronted with the accusation of their own culpability in the crucifixion of Jesus, but the hostile intent of sinners against God's anointed One is circumvented by the resurrection of Jesus. His raising from the dead is presented with an apologetical defense, complete with supporting evidence from both the OT and the eyewitness confirmation that Jesus in fact appeared quite alive after His death. His resurrection culminates in His exaltation as Lord, inaugurating the Messianic age and guaranteeing the day of His return in judgment but also coming as the Savior of His people.

The announcement of salvation indicates that the structure of a Christian sermon ought to include some indication how the text under consideration relates to Jesus Christ. The preacher should ask in his sermon preparation, How does this text point toward Christ in His mission to "seek and save the lost"? (Luke 19:10). Does the

---

61. Stevens, *The Message of the Apostles*, 37. The origination of the messianic understanding of the OT can be traced to the interpretive principle of Jesus recorded in Luke 24:27, "And beginning with Moses and with all the prophets, He explained to them the things concerning Himself in all the Scriptures."

62. Kaiser, *Use of the Old Testament in the New*, 180. He developed his ideas from his earlier work, *Toward an Exegetical Theology: Biblical Exegesis for Preaching and Teaching* (1981).

63. Stevens, *The Message of the Apostles*, 39.

text apply to His person, to His ministry, to His atonement, to His resurrection, to His Exaltation, or to His return? These questions are not incidental to the structure of the sermon, because the application of the sermon is determined by the particular aspect of Christology fulfilled in the text, leading to an announcement of salvation.

Promise of Salvation Extended: On the basis of Jesus' historical ministry, death, and resurrection as fulfillment of "everything that is in accordance with the Law, and that is written in the Prophets" (Acts 24:14), and based on the present exaltation of Jesus as the ascended Lord, Prince, Judge and Savior, the promise of salvation may now be extended to all humanity, so that the facts of salvation history are accompanied with the promise of salvation. The exaltation of Christ means that the gift of the Holy Spirit is granted (Acts 2:38), that the blessing of salvation is extended (Acts 16:31), and that forgiveness of sins and justification before the Law may be proclaimed and received (Acts 13:38–39; 26:18). Such promises show that sermon structure should include application as a necessary aspect of the delivery. Its inclusion helps to correct the problem that plagues many preachers who present only doctrine: the promises of the gospel also need to be proclaimed, so that in preparation the preacher will want to ask himself what promises the text offers and then include those promises in his presentation.

However, caution needs to be urged upon the preacher so that he extends the promise of salvation on the right basis; for example, nowhere in the Book of Acts (or in the epistles) is an unconverted hearer urged to believe "because Christ died for your sins," an appeal used commonly in modern evangelism. Instead, the unconverted are commanded to repent and believe in Jesus because of His exalted status as Lord, Prince, Judge, and Savior (as shown in Acts 2:38; 3:19; 5:31; 10:43; 13:39; 26:18).[64] A closer look at the apostolic preaching shows that forgiveness is not set forth as an enticement to believe but as a promise to be received upon belief ("everyone who believes in Him receives forgiveness of sins," Acts 10:43). If anything, the preacher goes beyond Scripture if he tells an unconverted person he can be forgiven *because* Christ died for him; instead, he ought to preach that Christ died and rose from the dead to extend forgiveness to all

---

64. "Forgiveness" (*aphesis*) is mentioned five times in Acts, in 2:38, "Repent, and let each of you be baptized in the name of Jesus Christ for the forgiveness of your sins; and you shall receive the gift of the Holy Spirit"; in Acts 5:31, "He is the one whom God exalted to His right hand as a Prince and a Savior, to grant repentance to Israel, and forgiveness of sins"; in Acts 10:43, "Of Him all the prophets bear witness that through His name everyone who believes in Him receives forgiveness of sins"; in Acts 13:38–39; "Let it be known to you, brethren, that through Him forgiveness of sins is proclaimed to you, and through Him everyone who believes is freed from all things, from which you could not be freed through the Law of Moses"; and in Acts 26:18, "that they may turn from darkness to light and from the dominion of Satan to God, in order that they may receive forgiveness of sins." A similar idea is presented in Acts 3:19; "Repent therefore and return, that your sins may be wiped away, in order that times of refreshing may come from the presence of the Lord." In each instance, it should be noted that the promise of forgiveness is extended because Christ is exalted as Lord (Acts 2:36), as Prince and Savior (Acts 5:31); as Judge of the living and the dead (Acts 10:42); as "He whom God raised" (Acts 13:37), and as self-identified, "I am Jesus" (Acts 26:15).

who believe in Him, so if the hearer believes, he shall in fact receive that forgiveness. The difference may seem quite subtle, but the NT does not extend the atoning work of Christ to those who disbelieve, but only to those who believe.[65]

Of course, one may rightly point out that Paul does in fact proclaim, "Christ died for our sins" (1 Cor 15:3), that "Christ died for the ungodly" (Rom 5:6) and that "Christ died for us" (Rom 5:8), but it should be noted, however, that these statements properly apply to repentant sinners, certainly not to rebellious transgressors! The same can be said of the love of God, which rather tellingly is not even mentioned in the Book of Acts at all, much less used as a basis of the gospel promise.[66] This omission does not mean God does not love sinners, for He unquestionably loves the world so much that He gave His Son, as John 3:16 asserts, but the fact remains that the apostolic gospel never appeals to God's love as a reason why a sinner should repent and believe. Instead, salvation is extended to "whoever calls on the name of the Lord" (Acts 2:21) in recognition that Jesus of Nazareth has been enthroned as the rightful Lord of all—faith in Him is the proper response for one to make, receiving Him as Savior and confessing Him as Lord. The promise of the gospel can be compared with an amnesty offered to a rebel, but only on the condition that he lays down his arms and surrenders to rightful authority of the conquering king, who is this case is the Lord Jesus.

Command unto Salvation Given: Because the offer of redemption requires surrender, it actually comes in a series of imperatives: "Repent!"[67] "Turn!"[68] and "Believe!"[69] The

---

65. The importance of believing is shown in that the verb "to believe" (*pisteuō*) is used thirty-seven times in Acts (2:44; 4:4, 32; 5:14; 8:12, 13; 9:26, 42; 10:43; 11:17, 21; 13:12, 39, 41, 48; 14:1, 23; 15:5, 7, 11; 16:31, 34; 17:12, 34; 18:8, 27; 19:2, 4, 18; 21:20, 25; 22:19; 24:14; 26:27; 27:25). It seems clear that there is no benefit of the work of Christ to anyone who remains in unbelief, as stated in John 3:36, "He who believes in the Son has eternal life; but he who does not obey the Son shall not see life, but the wrath of God abides on him."

66. Acts does include repeated references to the grace of God (Acts 4:33; 6:8; 11:23; 13:43; 14:3, 26; 15:11, 40; 18:27; 20:24, 32), especially that the gospel is "the word of His grace" (Acts 14:3; 20:32) and "the gospel of the grace of God" (Acts 20:24), so that the disciples are described as those who "believed through grace" (Acts 18:27). However, even the grace or love of God is not used as an appeal to unbelievers to come to Christ.

67. The verb "to repent" (*metanoeō*) appears five times in Acts 2:38; 3:19; 8:22; 17:30; 26:20, and it is defined by BDAG § 4853 more generally as to "change one's mind, but more specifically as to feel remorse, repent, be converted (in a variety of relationships and in connection w. varied responsibilities, moral, political, social or religious." The related noun *metanoia* appears six times (Acts 5:31; 11:18; 13:24; 19:4; 20:21; 26:20) and is defined by BDAG § 4854 by "repentance, turning about, conversion."

68. The verb *epistrephō* appears ten times in Acts, and, according to BDAG § 3041, ἐπιστρέφω means first of all, 'to turn around,' as Peter turned toward the body of the young girl (Acts 9:40), as Paul turned toward the demonized woman (Acts 16:18), or as Paul intended to 'return' the cities previously visited (Acts 15:36). In the other references, however, *epistrephō* refers to a turning away from sin (Acts 26:18) and a turning "to the Lord (Acts 3:19; 9:35; 11:21; 15:19; 26:20). The noun ἐπιστροφή appears only once, "describing in detail the conversion of the Gentiles" (Acts 15:3).

69. Interestingly, the imperative "Believe!" (πίστευσον) is used only three times in the Greek Bible, in Sirach 2:6, "Believe in him [the Lord], and he will help thee; order thy way aright, and trust in him"

command to the Philippian jailer articulates the mandate most succinctly: "Believe in the Lord Jesus, and you shall be saved, you and your household" (Acts 16:31). Such a command springs from the solemn testimony "of repentance toward God and faith in our Lord Jesus Christ" (Acts 20:21). Thus, the promise of salvation is valid only to "everyone who believes in Him" (Acts 10:43; 13:39), although Acts 13:48 defines those who believe "as many [who] had been appointed to eternal life." Saving faith is not a casual affimation of various facts about Christ, but it must be personal trust in Him, accompanied by a life-response of repentance, which includes the abandonment of old-life habits (Acts 19:18) and opinions (Acts 17:32–34), resulting in obedience evidenced in baptism and association with the believing community.

A fresh look needs to be taken at the way the apostles invited unbelievers to come to Christ, especially because the modern invitational system is assumed to be a given in Scripture. However, what the Book of Acts reports is that the apostles gave no equivalent to what is commonly labeled as an "altar call." Unbelievers were not asked to "come forward" and "accept Christ." Instead, after their gospel presentations, the apostles conducted private audiences with interested listeners (Acts 13:42; 17:4, 11, 34). This observation may come as a startling revelation to those who measure evangelistic success by the number of converts who respond to a gospel invitation. A careful examination needs to be applied to the altar-call practice in light of what the Scripture actually teaches regarding evangelistic methods. While the apostles certainly called on unbelievers to repent and believe, one should pay closer attention to the nature of the call to salvation.

First, the preacher should assume that behind his weak and ineffective preaching lies the dynamic voice of the speaking God, who sovereignly, graciously, and effectively calls His elect to saving faith ("as many as had been appointed to eternal life believed," Acts 13:48). Preaching only "succeeds" because of God's effectual call, so that those who respond are "as many as the Lord our God shall call to Himself" (Acts 2:39). The preacher may (and should) issue a call to repent and believe because he knows it is God who saves and calls "with a holy calling, not according to our works, but according to His own purpose and grace which was granted us in Christ Jesus from all eternity" (2 Tim 1:9). This eternal plan unfolds in human experience when the living God calls a sinner "into fellowship with His Son" (1 Cor 1:9) by beckoning that person to "take hold of the eternal life to which you were called" (1 Tim 6:12). Because this effective call brings the sinner "out of darkness into His marvelous light" (1 Pet 2:9), it also urges him to "walk in a manner worthy of the calling with which you have been called" (Eph 4:1) by producing a walk "worthy of the God who calls you into His own kingdom and glory" (1 Thess 2:12). Because God's converting is also

---

(KJA); in Luke 8:50, "But when Jesus heard *this*, He answered him, "Do not be afraid *any longer*; only believe, and she shall be made well"; and in Acts 16:31, "And they said, "Believe in the Lord Jesus, and you shall be saved, you and your household."

a preserving call, the true believer is given the following promise: "Faithful is He who calls you, and He also will bring it to pass" (1 Thess 5:24).

Armed with this certain knowledge, the preacher also knows that God calls the "through our gospel" (2 Thess 2:14); that is, the sinner is called to faith through the message revealed to Paul and the other apostles, so if a message is not a calling by the grace of Christ, it is a different gospel—not one that saves at all (Gal 1:6). The question that the preacher must constantly ask himself is whether the call to salvation that he extends would be honored by God Himself as the genuine gospel by which God effectually calls sinners to salvation.

These insights into the biblical concept of divine calling bring the preacher to the structure of the gospel call as an imperative based upon the proclamation of the life, death, resurrection, and exaltation of Jesus in fulfillment of OT prophecy. On the basis of those historical acts within salvation history—and those alone—can the preacher extend the promise of forgiveness and eternal life in the Name of Christ by commanding all to repent, turn, and believe on Him. Because these responses are matters to life and death, such a call may need to be accompanied with a warning against unrepentance and unbelief as being highly offensive to God in light of His gracious work of redemption, making the theme of judgment an important part of the structural call of the gospel ("God is now declaring to men that all everywhere should repent, because He has fixed a day in which He will judge the world in righteousness through a Man whom He has appointed, having furnished proof to all men by raising Him from the dead," Acts 17:30–31). The person who refuses to repent and believe has no other recourse but to face the certainty of final judgment, making the command to believe eternally significant.

Summary to Sermon Structure in the Book of Acts

While it is obvious that the structure of a sermon is not nearly as important as the content it proclaims, it has been observed that Paul's sermons in the Book of Acts do in fact follow a similar structural outline. This consistent structure is particularly observable in evangelistic presentations, but even the message preached to a Christian gathering (to the Ephesian elders) reveals similar parallels, as will be noted. Essentially, the messages are explanations of a text or theme of Scripture as it appears in the context of the history of redemption and then as it is expounded in light of its fulfillment in Jesus as Messiah. Based on the completion of God's work in Christ Jesus, the promise of salvation is offered and the command to salvation is extended. At times, this outline is rearranged, abbreviated, or even compacted, with much of its doctrinal content being assumed by Paul in his speeches or by Luke in his narratives. The structure is often embellished with biblical quotations, enhanced by secular references, illustrated by personal testimonies, strengthened by theological assertions, and set within historical references; in other words, great flexibility is allowed in the presentation, according to the particular needs of the listeners. Even so, the basic gospel elements as outlined above are present or assumed in some form or another within the sermons in Acts.

It is important that that modern preacher have an understanding of this biblically based structure in his own proclamation of the apostolic gospel. All too often, appeals are made to trust Christ without a sufficient explanation of the truths of salvation, and so the listener responds (or fails to respond) to an incomplete gospel. A commitment by the preacher to this basic apostolic structure as revealed in the Book of Acts should prevent the preaching of a truncated version of the gospel.

This section, then, has shown that the Book of Acts gives the consistent apostolic structure of the gospel proclamation that ought to serve as a normative guide for preparing messages, particularly those that are primarily evangelistic. While this structure is not 'etched-in-stone' as prescriptive (if it were, all the sermons in the Book of Acts would be identical), the preacher should normally frame his own evangelistic presentations around the structure given in the Book of Acts. It is the contention of this writer, however, that every Christian sermon should include an evangelistic appeal within the course of the delivery, if not as the final application then certainly interwoven within the message as a natural outflow of the text (as Paul does in Acts 20:21, 28). The fulfillment of redemption in Jesus as Messiah ought to be clearly proclaimed, and the ensuing gospel promise appropriate to the text should be announced, along with a call to repent and believe in Jesus as Savior and Lord. It is hard to imagine an address being distinctly Christian without some reference to this basic core of the gospel. Surely, Luke intended for the readers of his history of the apostolic church to note this oft-repeated structure of the apostolic gospel. In this way, Luke shows how the same general structure became customary and serves as a pattern for future preachers to organize their own evangelistic presentations so vital to the preaching ministry.

The Structure of Paul's Epistles as Sermons

Admittedly, most of the sermons in the Book of Acts are directed to unbelieving audiences, while the modern preacher finds himself in a different situation, since most of his sermons will be addressed to professing Christians. When Paul commands Timothy to "exhort in all doctrine" (2 Tim 4:2), does he give his younger colleague any indication of the structure of his church exhortations that are didactic in nature rather than evangelistic in approach? The answer is decidedly yes, though not in specific discussion but rather by inclusion in the framework of the letters Paul intended to be read to his congregations, as indicated in his request of the Colossians, "When this letter is read among you, have it also read in the church of the Laodiceans; and you, for your part read my letter *that is coming* from Laodicea" (Col 4:16). It is the intent of this section to explore the structure of the letters he addressed to local congregations to discover how they assist the modern preacher in the structuring of his sermons.

Paul's Letters as Written Sermons

It is helpful to think of the original autographed letters of Paul as being verbally dictated to a scribe rather than being inscribed by his own hand, thereby making them originally spoken discourses.[70] It appears that Paul normally wrote only his closing signature accompanied by some variation of his apostolic benediction as the authenticating mark of his letters;[71] otherwise, he verbally dictated the actual writing of the letter to a secretary (usually called an amanuensis[72]) such as Tertius.[73]

One can imagine Paul pacing his prison cell verbally preaching the message for his secretary to transcribe, pausing here and there to change a word or to improve a phrase. After reviewing and editing the manuscript, Paul would sign his imprimatur to the finished product, expecting the letter to be read aloud to the congregation (Col 4:16). For that matter, Paul actually places no difference between his verbal teaching and his epistolary instructions, when he reminds the Thessalonians to "hold to the traditions which you were taught, whether by word *of mouth* or by letter from us" (2 Thess 2:15).

Another evidence of the sermonic composition of his letters can be noted by the numerous times Paul writes the expression, "I say to you" (using some form of the verb, *legō*)[74] rather than, "I write to you," suggesting that he was speaking the content at that time rather than writing it. One reference in particular to note is Phlm 1:21, where Paul places no distinction between what he writes and what he says;[75] in fact,

---

70. Paul mentions his own writing ("I wrote, I am writing") in Rom 16:22; 1 Cor 4:14; 5:9, 11; 14:37; 2 Cor 1:13; 2:3, 4, 9; 7:12; Eph 3:3; Col 4:18; 2 Thess 3:17; 1 Tim 3:15; Phlm 1:21.

71. Paul pointedly adds "in my own hand" in the following verses: 1 Cor 16:21 ("The greeting is in my own hand— Paul."); Gal 6:11 ("See with what large letters I am writing to you with my own hand."); Col 4:18 ("I, Paul, write this greeting with my own hand."); 2 Thess 3:17 ("I, Paul, write this greeting with my own hand, and this is a distinguishing mark in every letter; this is the way I write."); and Phlm 1:19 ("I, Paul, am writing this with my own hand."). The *sēmeion* he makes in each letter—when all his epistles are compared—appears to be some variation of the benediction, "Grace be with you" (Rom 16:20; 1 Cor 16:23; 2 Cor 13:14; Gal 6:18; Eph 6:24; Phil 4:23; Col 4:18; 1 Thess 5:28; 2 Thess 3:18; 1 Tim 6:21; 2 Tim 4:22; Titus 3:15; Phlm 1:25).

72. *Merriam-Webster Dictionary* defines "amanuensis" as "one employed to write from dictation or to copy manuscripts." Paul's amanuensis were probably literate friends rather than professional secretaries.

73. Romans 16:22, "I, Tertius, who write this letter, greet you in the Lord." When Paul brings salutations from others beside himself (such as Sosthenes in 1 Cor 1:1; Timothy in 2 Cor 1:1; Phil 1:1; Col 1:1; 1 Thess 1:1; 2 Thess 1:1, along with Silvanus in 1 Thess 1:1; 2 Thess 1:1), it is evident that the letters are not co-written; Paul is the primary author, while one of the other named persons may well have served as the secretary, as Tychicus may have done so for Paul's epistle to the Ephesians (Eph 6:21). It seems more likely that Paul wrote in full the letters of 1 Timothy, 2 Timothy, Titus, and Galatians, which he apparently dashed out in his own hand due to the urgency of the situation (Gal 6:11).

74. Paul writes *legō* ("I say") in the present tense forty-one times (Rom 3:5; 6:19; 9:1; 10:18, 19; 11:1, 11, 13; 12:3; 15:8; 1 Cor 1:12; 6:5; 7:6, 8, 12, 35; 10:15, 29; 15:51; 2 Cor 6:13; 7:3; 8:8; 9:4; 11:16, 21; Gal 1:9; 3:15, 17; 4:1; 5:2, 16; Eph 4:17; 5:32; Phil 3:18; 4:11; Col 2:4; 1 Tim 2:7; 2 Tim 2:7; Phlm 1:19, 21), plus he uses the similar verb *phēmi* in the first person ("I say," or "I affirm"; BDAG § 7713) another four times (1 Cor 7:29; 10:15, 19; 15:50).

75. Philemon 1:21 reads, "Having confidence in your obedience, I write to you, since I know that

the authority behind the writing of Paul is his verbal preaching. The spoken word came first, and then it became the written word.

In this sense, Paul's letters can be considered transcribed sermons, because he communicates primarily as a preacher rather than as an author. Barclay notes that Paul's letters ". . . are sermons far more than they are theological treatises."[76] Reinke observes that ". . . great parts of the epistles are obviously influenced by oral discourse such as were commonly delivered by the apostles, and may often be regarded as literary substitutes for personal addresses (cf. 2 Cor 10:10–11 ["What we are in word by letters when absent, such persons *we are* also in deed when present."]). So, it is legitimate to use the epistles for the study of apostolic preaching."[77]

Paul's Letters as Sermon Structure

Knowing that Paul intended for his letters to be read outloud as written sermons, one may reasonably assume that he employed a similar structure in his letters that can be found in his sermons in the Book of Acts. What observations on structure can be noted from the organization of the letters Paul addresses to local congregations?

Sermonic Structure of Romans: A sermonic outline of Romans—arguably Paul's most carefully organized letter—might develop as follows:

1. Introduction: Gospel Summary and Blessing (1:1–7);
2. Prayer (1:8–15);
3. Theme and Text ("The Just shall live by faith," Hab 2:4); Rom 1:16–17;
4. Doctrinal Development of the theme, interspersed with supporting Scriptural arguments (1:18–11:36);
5. Practical Exhortations based on the theme (12:1–15:33);
6. Final Applications (chapter 16);
7. Benediction (16:25–27).

One can almost hear Paul preach this carefully crafted message, although it would be rather weighty for modern readers.[78] What is of interest for this study is the logical development of the letter, flowing from the basic historical facts of the gospel. From the events of salvation in Christ (Rom 1:1–7) come the doctrinal implications (Rom 1:18–11:36), leading to the ethical applications that derive from "the mercies of God" (Rom

---

you will do even more than what I say."

76. Barclay, "A Comparison of Paul's Mission Preaching," 170.

77. Reinke, "A Synopsis of Early Christian Preaching," 145.

78. The author has preached through Romans twice with over fifty sermons in each series, yet he feels that he barely scratched the surface of its meaning and application.

12:1–15:33). This development shows the same type of structure that was noted in the evangelistic sermons of Paul, although the doctrine and applications found in the Book of Acts are directed toward unbelievers for the purpose of their conversion. In Romans, however, the teaching is directed "to those who are called saints" for the purpose of their holy living (Rom 1:7). Still, the epistle stands rather simply as an exposition of Hab 2:4 ("But the righteous man shall live by faith."), introducing the theme, Who is the just man (Romans 1–11) and how shall he live (Romans 12–16)? The uniting link between being righteous and living is "by faith," specifically faith that rests in the Just One, the Lord Jesus (Rom 5:17–18), with whose preaching the letter/ sermon ends (Rom 16:25). Thus, the structure moves from gospel content to gospel application.

Sermonic Structure of 1 Corinthians: Because of the agitating problems tearing apart the Corinthian church, Paul's first letter to the Corinthians is far weightier on immediate application than on doctrine, therefore, 1 Corinthians resembles a treatise on ethical case studies dealing with specific issues, as demonstrated in the following outline:

1. Prayer and gospel summary (1:1–9);
2. Exhortations on unity (1:8–17);
3. Discourse on church unity (1:18–4:21);
4. Exhortations on various issues: on immorality (chapter 5), on lawsuits (chapter 6); on marriage (chapter 7); on idolatry (chapter 8); on apostleship (chapter 9); on church order (chapters 10–11); on spiritual gifts (chapters 12–14); on resurrection (chapter 15);
5. Personal notes (16:1–12);
6. Closing applications (16:13–14);
7. Greeting and benediction (16:15–24).

While not giving carefully reasoned arguments such as found in Romans, 1 Corinthians reveals a very deliberate development of topics, following the same basic structural framework as seen in the Book of Acts: gospel facts → ethical implications.

Sermonic Structure of 2 Corinthians: Of all Paul's letters, 2 Corinthians is the most personal, as Paul responds not to doctrinal or practical matters but to a personal attack on his apostolicity. It is not surprising to find that the structure of the letter is more rambling in nature:

1. Prayer of worship (1:1–7);
2. Personal experience of Paul's ministry (1:8–6:13);
3. Exhortations (6:14–9:15);
4. Paul's defense of his apostleship (10:1–13:10);

5. Closing exhortations and benediction (13:11–14).

Because Paul answers individual objections to his ministry, 2 Corinthians constantly moves from gospel content to personal experience, one illustrating the other. Paul proves that he does not behave in a spiritual vacuum: his actions spring from his theological convictions and apostolic call; therefore, his message is presented in a way that stresses his own weaknesses and the strength of Christ. Paul's message flows from the same general structure as found in his sermons: from doctrinal content to personal testimony and then to practical application.

Sermonic Structure of Galatians: Paul probably wrote the entire letter to the Galatians with his own hand, due to his exasperation with the congregation's problems, but even as he writes, he still pictures himself as preaching the content (Gal 3:15; 4:1; 5:2, 16). As a sermon, Galatians shows this structure:

1. Gospel presentation (1:1–4);
2. Testimony to the theme of freedom of the gospel (1:5–2:15);
3. Gospel presentation (2:16–21);
4. Doctrinal elaborations (chapters 3–4);
5. Applications (5:1–6:10);
6. Closing personal remarks and benediction (6:11–18).

Although Paul wrote this letter during moments of great mental anguish, Galatians is carefully organized, with deliberative development of the theme of gospel freedom discussed throughout the letter. Once again, the structure follows the framework seen in the Book of Acts: gospel facts → gospel living, sandwiched between an opening prayer and a closing benediction.

Sermonic Structure of Ephesians: Like Romans, Ephesians is a carefully structured letter, sermonically outlining itself as such:

1. Gospel salutation (1:3–14);
2. Prayer (1:15–21);
3. Doctrine (chapters 2–3);
4. Applications (chapter 4:1–6:20);
5. Closing remarks and benediction (6:21–34).

By now, a distinct pattern in Paul's letter emerges, especially in the more doctrinal letters: the gospel (or some aspect of it) is stated, expounded upon, and applied. In Ephesians, the theme is the relationship of the church to Jesus as its Head, and this theme permeates every aspect of the structure, even into the prayers. The clear structural form moves from gospel content (chapters 1–3) → gospel application (chapters 4–6).

Sermonic Structure of Philippians: Like 2 Corinthians, Philippians is more experiential rather than doctrinal in nature, and so the outline is less structured:

1. Prayer (1:3–11);
2. Personal testimony (1:12–26);
3. Appeal for unity (1:27–2:18);
4. Personal news (2:19–20);
5. Gospel illustrated in Paul (chapter 3);
6. Applications (4:1–9);
7. Closing personal notes and benediction (4:10–22).

This letter was at first spoken ("I tell you now even weeping," Phil 3:18), and it reflects the emotional intensity of a man grateful for assistance and burdened by disturbing news. Because Paul meets his distress with thankfulness, the theme of joyful gospel harmony occurs throughout the letter as Paul pours out his own experience in an appeal for his readers to press on to know Christ. Set in this crucible of joy amid the burdens, the structure resembles more of an acceptance speech than a sermon, but a sermon it remains, as the basis for Paul's thanks springs from his hope in the gospel message. Due to that truth, the basic structure once again shows the typical gospel framework: gospel truth → gospel implications for personal and corporate experience.

Sermonic Structure of Colossians: Another carefully structured letter that was intended to be read audibly (Col 4:16), Colossians reveals the following homiletical outline:

1. Prayer (1:3–12);
2. Gospel facts: Supremacy of Christ (1:13–23);
3. Personal testimony (1:24–2:2);
4. Doctrinal discussion of salvation (2:3–19);
5. Applications (2:20–4:6);
6. Personal notes (4:7–17);
7. Benediction (4:18).

Of all of Paul's letters, Colossians contains the most developed theology of preaching: in it, the apostle mentions the dynamic of the gospel (Col 1:6, "it is constantly increasing"); the preacher's commission (Col 1:25, "I was made a minister according to the stewardship from God bestowed on me for your benefit, that I might fully carry out the *preaching of* the word of God"); the content of the word of God (Col 3:16); the aim of preaching (Col 1:28, "We proclaim Him, admonishing every man and teaching every man with all wisdom, that we may present every man complete in Christ."); the enabling for preaching (Col 1:29, "I labor, striving according to His power, which mightily works within me."); prayer for preaching (Col 4:3, "praying at the same time for us as well, that God may open up to us a door for the word, so that we may speak forth the mystery of Christ."); the manner of preaching (Col 4:6, "Let your speech always be with grace, seasoned with salt."); and the fulfillment of preaching "which you have received in the Lord" (Col 4:17). The opening prayer concerns the advance of preaching, and the doctrinal section reveals Christ as the primary object of preaching. Paul's personal testimony concerns his own experience of preaching ("that I might fulfill the word of God," Col 1:25), while many of the doctrinal implications and applications concern the verbal expression of the Faith ("with all wisdom teaching and admonishing one another with psalms *and* hymns *and* spiritual songs," Col 3:16). Once again, the typical Pauline structure appears in Colossians: gospel prayer → gospel content → gospel living → gospel fellowship → gospel benediction.

Sermonic Structure of 1 Thessalonians: Paul's first letter to the Thessalonians was written to give follow-up information to new converts about holy living (1 Thess 4:1), and so it contains more practical admonition than doctrinal content, thus providing a preaching outline that emphasizes personal application:

1. Prayer (1:1–8);
2. The Gospel (1:9–10);
3. Testimony of ministry (2:1–3:10);
4. Prayer (3:11–13);
5. Applications (4:1–5:22);
6. Closing prayer and benediction (5:23–28).

Quite clearly, the same structural development is noted in 1 Thessalonians that typifies Paul's other letters: Gospel content → Gospel testimony → Gospel application.

Sermonic Structure of 2 Thessalonians: The last of Paul's letters addressed specifically to a congregation once again reveals the same general development in structural outline:

1. Prayer (1:1–12);
2. Doctrinal Content on the Day of the Lord (2:1–14);
3. Application of the doctrine (2:15–3:15);
4. Benediction (3:16–18).

Despite the brevity of 2 Thessalonians, this letter reveals clearly the typical Pauline structure: gospel doctrine → gospel application.

Observations on Paul's Sermonic Structure: Should any significance be placed on the structure of Paul's letters to congregations? Baird believes not, stating, "Paul seems to imply a distinction between the form in which he proclaimed the gospel and its essential content—the living Christ."[79] In other words, Baird seems to think that the form of the gospel was man-made whereas the essence of the gospel came from God, so that the form is somewhat inconsequential.

Granted, the form in which the gospel is presented is not deemed absolute in Paul's letters, because they flow from doctrine to application—and back again—several times even within the same letter, but the structure invariably follows a typical pattern, moving from gospel content to gospel application. The apostle consistently shows a two-fold aim, that his readers know right doctrine and live right conduct, and so the structure of his letters generally follows this rather simple structure: "since this is so (the doctrinal indicative), therefore do this (the applied imperative)."

Based on a broad composite of Paul's letters to the churches, a more elaborate sermonic structure could follow this suggested pattern:

1. An opening prayer, emphasizing the theme of the message;
2. A statement of the theme (or text) of some aspect of the gospel (*Euangelion, Kērygma*);
3. An explanation of the theme (*Didaskalia, Didachē*);
4. An application of the theme (*Paraklēsis*);
5. A Sharing of the Theme (*Koinonia*);
6. A closing prayer and benediction summarizing the theme.

While several letters show the above form rather clearly (notably, in Romans, Ephesians, Colossians, 2 Thessalonians), other letters move back and forth between doctrine and application, illustrated frequently by personal testimonies or anecdotes of the preacher and supported by various biblical quotations, allusions, and echoes. Such development may be likened to the subpoints of the primary theme; however, what is identical in each of Paul's church letters is the opening in prayer, the proclamation and application of some aspect of the gospel, and the closing with some reference to fellowship and benediction.

---

79. Baird, "What is the Kerygma?" 191.

Summary to the Preacher's Structure

The previous sections in this chapter have outlined the basic structure of apostolic sermons, beginning with the evangelistic sermons in the Book of Acts. There, the structure

1. starts by proclaiming the historical death and resurrection of Jesus as the fulfillment of OT prophecy and
2. announces the present status of Jesus as Savior, Lord, Prince and Judge. Next,
3. it promises the Holy Spirit, who brings forgiveness and eternal life; and then,
4. it issues forth in a command to repent, turn and believe in Christ. Finally,
5. it concludes by calling for evidence of true faith in baptism as a life-response of leaving old-life habits and embracing new-life patterns by associating with the community of believers.

For an evangelistic sermon to be considered faithful to apostolic preaching, it should include these essentials of the gospel content within the same basic structural outline.

Next, this chapter examined the structure of Paul's letters by viewing them as written sermons. These letters take up where the evangelistic messages of the Book of Acts end, adding further explanations and applications of the doctrinal truths of the gospel. While Paul exercises wide latitude of structural arrangements in his letters and sermons, this chapter has observed that there is a distinct structure found in his exhortative sermons addressed to believers. First, the messages always open with an appropriate prayer, then Paul addresses a gospel theme or expounds on a specific scriptural text with the use of illustrations and applications to emphasize either a promise or a command. Without exception, Paul's letters to Christian audiences conclude with personal reminiscences and with a benediction of God's blessings.

So what is the modern preacher to learn from these observations? He ought to recognize that there exists an apostolic and therefore a normative structure by which he should organize his sermons. Having selected a biblical text or theme, he should then develop each point based on that organizational theme/text and elaborate on how it unfolds in the history of redemption. He should note any doctrinal implications the theme makes and then suggest how it applies practically to the experience of believers within the fellowship of the congregation. The message should be introduced with prayer appropriate to the theme and then concluded with a prayer and a benediction assuring the hearers of God's enabling to do that which He requires.

By fitting the apostolic content into the framework of apostolic structure, the modern preacher not only proclaims the gospel as it was originally preached in the first century but he also preaches it in much the same way. The discipline of planning a sermon using the apostolic structure should be of utmost importance to the preacher who desires to maintain biblical fidelity and uphold his charge to "Preach the Word."

Too often, it seems, so-called "gospel messages" contain little of the content of apostolic preaching because their structure is not consistent with apostolic examples. Also, messages preached to the gathered assembly of believers often bear little resemblance to the doctrinal exposition and application so typical in Paul's letters. Instead, the preacher who fulfills his charge to "exhort in all doctrine" will come closer to doing so when he brings the outline of his sermons into conformity with these general observations on the structure of Paul's messages.

CHAPTER 9

The Preacher's Audience

PREACHING HAS NEVER BEEN an easy occupation. Moses, knowing that God's people did not take kindly to being told what to believe and what to do, asked God about his audience, "What if they will not . . . listen to what I say?" (Exod 4:1). Also, when the Lord commissioned Isaiah to "Go and tell this people," He predicted that the prophet's audience would "Keep on listening, but not perceive; keep on looking, but . . . not understand" (Isa 6:9). For that matter, Isaiah's preaching would ". . . make the heart of this people dull, and their ears heavy, and blind their eyes; lest they see with their eyes, and hear with their ears, and understand with their hearts, and turn and be healed" (Isa 6:10 ESV). Ezekiel actually saw greater success in preaching to dry bones than to a living audience (Ezek 37:4–10). Even the first recorded sermon of Jesus caused so much rage among His hometown audience that they nearly hurled Him from a nearby cliff (Luke 4:28–30). When Paul instructs Timothy to "Preach the Word," he had just reminded his colleague to recall his "sufferings, such as happened to me at Antioch, at Iconium, and at Lystra," persecutions he endured because of his missionary preaching (2 Tim 3:10–11, alluding to Acts 14:19). This constant repetition of audience rejection hardly makes preaching an appealing profession!

Because audience reaction can be so fickle, when Paul commissions Timothy to "preach the Word," he explains why his colleague must preach "with all patience," and that is because ". . . the time will come when they will not endure sound doctrine; but *wanting* to have their ears tickled, they will accumulate for themselves teachers in accordance to their own desires; and will turn away their ears from the truth, and will turn aside to myths" (2 Tim 4:2–4). How sobering it had to be for Timothy to realize that more almost half of Paul's charge reminds him of the difficulty, indifference, and apostasy that will resist his preaching.[1] Apparently, successful preaching is not necessarily measured by great crowds thronging to hear sound biblical preaching! If

---

1. The full charge of 2 Tim 4:1–5 consists of eighty-one Greek words in the BGT, and of those, thirty-three words (41%) are included in the warning of vs. 3–4.

anything, Timothy, along with every other preacher, must make a realistic appraisal of the likely audience opposition he will confront if he is faithful to his charge.

Paul is indefinite in identifying whether the hostile audience he describes is inside or outside the church. He does seem to confirm the prophecy of Jesus, "At that time many will turn away from the faith and will betray and hate each other, and many false prophets will appear and deceive many people" (Matt 24:10–11 NIV). Paul had given a similar prophecy to Timothy in his previous letter when he wrote, "But the Spirit explicitly says that in later times some will fall away from the faith, paying attention to deceitful spirits and doctrines of demons" (1 Tim 4:1). While these sobering predictions may well allude to a final great apostasy (a dismal expectation emphasized particularly by Dispensationalism[2]), they need to be balanced with Paul's very positive expectation that the word of truth, the gospel, is "also constantly bearing fruit and increasing in all the world" (Col 1:6; see chapter 15 on the Preacher's Dynamic). Even so, when Paul refers to "they" in 2 Tim 4:3–4, is he referring to professing Christians, so that he gives an end-time prophecy (as Ryrie thinks[3]), or is he referring to non-Christians and giving a characteristic description of the present age in which the preacher will find himself until the return of the Lord?

Because Paul is rather imprecise by stating when "the time will come," perhaps it is just as well not to draw any definite conclusions nor make any sharp distinctions between the present age and the end of the age. In every situation and in every audience, the preacher will find himself speaking to true believers, to people who merely profess faith, and to unbelievers who may or may not be aware of their own spiritual status. The wise preacher will mentally prepare himself for potentially adverse confrontations that may be engendered by the message he preaches. While it is true that apostates have come from the covenant community (such as Judas Iscariot), and that the unbelieving world has produced plenty of its own anti-christs (1 John 2:18), the true church has always responded to the preached Word with faith and obedience. One way or another, the preacher should make every effort to discern his audience so that his message is tailored to their particular needs without compromising the gospel. The demand for balance between the needs of the audience and faithfulness to the gospel message requires the following discussion on what the Bible teaches about the preacher's audience.

---

2. For example, Ryrie, *Dispensationalism Today*, 153, writes, "The Bible does definitively clearly teach that there was, is, and will be apostasy in the professing church." This Dispensational pessimism needs to be balanced with the optimism of the Lord's promise, that the gates of hell shall not prevail against his church (Matt 16:18). The Bible also definitely, clearly teaches that there was, is and will be victory for the faithful church because of the preserving work of the Holy Spirit.

3. Ibid.

Preaching and the Hearing of the Audience

Just as preaching implies a "logology," a theology of the words spoken, it also implies an "akoulogy," a theology of the ears listening.[4] Because God speaks to the ears of men and women,[5] they are individually responsible to hear His words. The command to hear was a requirement given to Adam and Eve when "they heard the sound of the Lord God walking in the garden" (Gen 3:8) up until the very closing address of Scripture "to everyone who hears the words of the prophecy of this book" (Rev 22:18).

Naturally, the preacher wants his audience to lend their ears to his words, but as Paul indicates to Timothy, many will "turn their ears away." This deliberate deafness is quite devastating to the message, because "faith *comes* from hearing, and hearing by the word of Christ" (Rom 10:17). If one does not hear, whether by absence of the message or by absence of comprehension, then faith will not result, as Paul notes in Rom 10:14, "How shall they believe in Him whom they have not heard? And how shall they hear without a preacher?" It is no wonder that Kittel comments, "The hearing of man represents correspondence to the revelation of the Word, and in biblical religion it is thus the essential form in which this divine revelation is appropriated."[6] If the only one who has an ear can hear what the Spirit says (Rev 2:7), then it is important for the preacher to know what sort of ears his audience has.

Preaching and the Hearing of an Unbelieving Audience

Quite obviously one can hear sounds without discerning meaning, as Paul asks rhetorically in 1 Cor 14:9, "Unless you utter by the tongue speech that is clear, how will it be known what is spoken?" An even worse scenario occurs when the preacher's audience has a hearing problem with regard to the gospel.[7] Such deafness is the problem addressed in Isa 6:9–10,[8] a passage that figures prominently in the NT, as it is cited in conjunction with the parable of the sower (Matt 13:13–23); at the end of Jesus' public ministry as an explanation of why Israel rejected Him (John 12:39–40); by Paul to the Jews in Rome, telling why the gospel promised in the OT is now going to Gentiles (Acts 28:26–27); and again by Paul in his explanation of Israel's hardening against the

---

4. "Akoulogy" is a coined word based on the Greek word, ἀκούω, which is defined by BDAG § 278, "to have or exercise the faculty of hearing."

5. The hearer's duty is implied in the oft-repeated command of Jesus, "He who has ears to hear, let him hear" (Matt 11:15; Mark 4:9; 23; 7:16; Luke 8:8; 14:35).

6. Kittel, ἀκούω, *TDNT* 1:216.

7. Mundle, "Hear," *DNTT* 2:172, observes, "Hearing covers not only sense perception but also the apprehension and acceptance by the mind of the content of what is heard."

8. Isaiah 6:8–10 records this dialogue between the prophet and Lord, "I heard the voice of the Lord, saying, "Whom shall I send, and who will go for Us?" Then I said, "Here am I. Send me!" And He said, "Go, and tell this people: 'Keep on listening, but do not perceive; Keep on looking, but do not understand.' "Render the hearts of this people insensitive, Their ears dull, And their eyes dim, Lest they see with their eyes, Hear with their ears, Understand with their hearts, And return and be healed."

gospel (Rom 11:8). Even when the audience continues to hear the words of the gospel, they will not actually hear in the sense of understanding.[9] Fallen man has stopped up his ears, spiritually speaking, so that even what he hears he has already chosen not to understand. The preacher's dilemma regarding his unbelieving audience has not changed since Jeremiah lamented, "To whom shall I speak and give warning, that they may hear? Behold, their ears are closed, and they cannot listen. Behold, the word of the LORD has become a reproach to them; They have no delight in it" (Jer 6:10).

Hearing False Teachers

Spiritual deafness, however, does not mean that unbelievers cannot hear anything at all: they have itching ears like the Athenians of Paul's day who spent "their time in nothing other than telling or hearing something new" (Acts 17:21). In order to pander to their own lustful desires, the unsaved heap up to themselves teachers who will turn them further from the truth and plunge them deeper into myths (2 Tim 4:3–4).[10] Many times in his sermons and writings, Paul refers to such false teachers, sometimes by name ("Hymenaeus, Alexander, and Philetus," 1 Tim 1:20; 2:17) and always in most uncharitable terms: they are "savage wolves" who will speak "perverse things, to draw away the disciples after them" (Acts 20:29–30); they cause "dissensions and hindrances contrary to the teaching which you learned," using "smooth and flattering speech [to] deceive the hearts of the unsuspecting" (Rom 16:17–18), "deluding others with persuasive arguments" (Col 2:4) and "taking others captive through philosophy and empty deception, according to the tradition of men" (Col 2:8). Paul can find no compliments for such men who "teach strange doctrines' (1 Tim 1:3), even "doctrines of demons" (1 Tim 4:1), describing them as "rebellious men, empty talkers and deceivers" (Titus 1:10).

The effect of deafened sinners piling up deaf teachers for themselves is that the two groups turn each other away from the truth. So, while it may be that Paul has in mind apostates who once professed Christ, there seems to be more indication for supposing that he refers to unbelievers in general whose false teachings turn other unbelievers further from the truth of the gospel into far greater deception. Regardless

9. As in the English use of "hearing" so the Greek word ἀκούω can describe either sense perception of hearing (L&N § 24.52) or the mental perception of understanding what is heard (L&N § 32.1).

10. Existential theology, popularized by Bultmann, "New Testament and Mythology," 1–44 in *Kerygma and Myth: A Theological Debate,* made a rather poor selection by describing the gospel accounts as mythical, especially since the NT pointedly distances itself from "fables," as the KJV translates *mūthos* (μῦθος). Believers are not to occupy themselves with myths (1 Tim 1:4) nor have anything to do with "worldly fables fit only for old women" (1 Tim 4:7) nor to "pay attention to Jewish myths and commandments of men who turn away from the truth" (Titus 1:14). Peter specifically insists that his account of the Transfiguration of Jesus (Mark 9:2) did "not follow cleverly devised *mūthoi*" (2 Pet 1:16). Bultmann's view imposes alien mythology upon the NT, which itself categorically denounces such an imposition, as does Paul in 2 Tim 4:4 by contrasting myths with the truth of the gospel. See Bruce, "Myth," *DNTT* 2:645–47.

of what may be explicitly meant in Paul's reference, the effect is still the same: the "hearers" deafness becomes a chronic condition. Either way, the preacher must not only preach to a deaf audience, but one that listens to lies and is convinced of them by the influence of other prevaricators.

Because of the inability of the lost audience to hear the gospel properly, the initial reaction to the gospel might be resentment or even the sort of hostility that happened to Paul when he was stoned by angry mobs (Acts 14:19; 2 Cor 11:25). Mounce notes, "Wherever the apostolic kerygma was proclaimed there was either a revival or a riot."[11] Because gospel preaching brought unwanted notoriety to Christianity as a controversial religion, Luke is careful to show that the negative reactions to the gospel came from its offence in exposing the vanity of the religions and philosophies of man, not that its preachers were intentionally inciting riots.[12] Still, knowing that the sufferings of the preacher were caused by the violent reactions of rebellious sinners would not make the opposition any less painful to endure, especially since false teaching is so much easier for unbelievers to hear than the difficult statements of the gospel (John 6:60).

Divine Prevention of Hearing

The preacher faces yet another barrier that prevents effectual hearing, and that is his audience is not only unable to hear because of their deafened ears and deceptive teachers, but also because God has responded to their willful deafness with a judicial deafening, so they cannot hear what God demands of them. Paul interprets Isa 20:10 in this manner, "God gave them ... ears to hear not" (Rom 11:8). Such inability to hear renders the one who is not of God so handicapped that he "cannot hear the Word" (John 8:43, 47). It is a total deafness that appears to make the task of preaching utterly impossible, because the preacher is commissioned to preach to those who will not hear the message by choice and cannot hear the message by divine decree!

Preaching and the "Hearing of Faith" (*aloēs pisteuō*)

What may seem like an impossible task—getting deaf people to hear—is overcome by the fact that some lost sinners do in fact hear the gospel and are saved. Paul reminds the Galatians that they received the Spirit by the "hearing of faith" (*aloēs pisteuō*; Gal 3:2), indicating that some in the audience obviously have the ability to hear. If they could not hear, the frequent command of Jesus ("He who has ears to hear, let him

---

11. Mounce, *Essential Nature*, 58,

12. The Book of Acts chronicles these various reactions to preaching: hatred (9:30); stoning (14:19); false charges (16:20–21); beating (16:22); imprisonment (16:23); sneering (17:32); hardening (19:9–10); clamor (23:6); terror (24:24–25); astonishment (26:24); and disagreements (28:24–25).

hear.") would be gobbledygook.[13] So, how does the preacher know who has ears to hear and who does not?

Frankly, he does not know. He faces the same dilemma confronted by the prophet Ezekiel when the Lord asked him, "Son of man, can these bones live?" (Ezek 37:3). The logical answer seems to be, "Of course not: dry bones cannot live." Ezekiel falls back on God's omniscience in his reply, "O Lord God, Thou knowest," an answer that admittedly may be only a theological excuse for his uncertainty, because the Lord had to say to his prophet again, "Prophesy over these bones, and say to them, 'O dry bones, hear the word of the LORD'" (Ezek 37:4). It should not be overlooked that God commands Ezekiel to order dry bones to do something impossible, to hear. For such hearing to happen, a supernatural miracle must occur, and it does, as the Lord God speaks directly to the bones, "Behold, I will cause breath to enter you that you may come to life" (Ezek 37:5). Based on that promise, Ezekiel "prophesied as He commanded me, and the breath came into them, and they came to life" (Ezek 37:10).

This entire dry bones episode illustrates how the preaching of a preacher is used by God to bring life to a deaf (actually, a dead) audience. In the way Ezekiel preached to dry bones, so the preacher appeals to the hearing of a deaf audience, but he does so believing that God will grant to some the ability to hear. The preacher's duty is to preach to all, not to speak only to those he figures will listen. Instead, the preacher should mimic the sower in Jesus' parable and broadcast the seed of the Word indiscriminately, all the while knowing that perhaps only one of four seeds will germinate into fruit (Mark 4:3–9). Following Paul's practice, the preacher calls on unbelievers to listen (Acts 13:16; 22:1; 26:3), although he knows full well that they cannot hear. Despite the deafness of his audience, Paul always extends the gospel invitation, as Kuist notes, in that ". . . he taught whenever the occasion presented itself, wheresoever he happened to be, to whomsoever came within the sphere of his influence."[14] Paul spoke to deaf people expecting them to hear. His confidence is either delusion, insanity, or faith that God will grant hearing to a deaf audience.

Instead, Paul quite realistically acknowledges, "All did not give heed (*hupēkousan*) to the *euangelion*, for Isaiah says, 'Lord who believed our report (*akoē*)?'" (Rom 10:16, citing Isa 53:1). What is it that overcomes the deafness of the ear so that saving faith will actually result from hearing? The answer is supplied in Rom 10:17 (ESV), "Faith *comes* from hearing (*akoēs*), and hearing (*akoē*) through the word of Christ;" that is, faith is engendered by the opening of the ear mediated through the power of the preached Word—in much the same manner as Jesus spoke to the deaf man, "'Be opened,' and his ears were opened" (Mark 7:34–35).

---

13. Matthew 11:15; 13:9, 43; Mark 4:9, 23; 7:16; 8:18; Luke 8:8; 14:35. A variation is found in Rev 2:7, 11, 17, 29; 3:6, 13, 22, "He who has an ear, let him hear what the Spirit says to the churches."

14. Kuist, *The Pedagogy of Paul*, 50. He also notes that Paul addressed Jews, Gentiles, Romans, barbarians, friends, family, strangers, philosophers, occultists, orators, prisoners, slaves, the sick, soldiers, sailors, women, rulers, magistrates, kings and queens. Hardly a broader scope of society could be imagined.

Why is it that among equally deaf sinners some hear and respond while others hear and reject? Clearly, the answer is not found in a greater natural ability for some to hear (because all "are not able to hear My word." John 8:43, AT) nor in an inbred moral sensibility (as the Lord said to Israel, "I spoke to you, but you would not listen," Deut 1:43). The reason anyone hears the preacher and responds with faith must lie in the sovereign grace of God, who is under no obligation to save any rebellious sinner but graciously opens the heart of some—those whom the Bible describes as God's elect—so that they will respond positively to the things spoken by the preacher (Acts 16:14). Divine election, despite its unpopularity, is not a doctrine imposed upon the Bible, since Scripture often describes believers as those who are the "*eklectoi* of God" (Col 3:12).[15] Quite naturally, some object that the doctrine of election would destroy preaching ("Why preach if the elect will be saved anyway?"), whereas Paul sees himself as "an apostle of Jesus Christ, for the faith of those chosen (*elektōn*) of God" (Titus 1:1). The preacher's confidence that anyone will respond to the truth of his preaching is solely "because God has chosen [them] from the beginning for salvation through sanctification by the Spirit and faith in the truth" (2 Thess 2:13); that is, the Holy Spirit affects the end of divine election by granting unbelieving sinners saving faith, and the preacher supplies the means by which deaf sinners hear unto salvation by faith in the truth he is preaching. Divine election, then, becomes the only source of success for the preacher, for in being commanded to preach to those who are deaf by reason of the deadness of sin, he must believe that through his preaching "the dead shall hear the voice of the Son of God; and those who hear shall live" (John 5:25).

Thus, sovereign grace is the salvation of preaching: the one who listens to the preacher listens to the risen Lord (Luke 10:16), because it is God who is "entreating through us, as begging on behalf of Christ, be reconciled to God" (2 Cor 5:20). By the divine call coming through the preacher's call, the audience hears the Word of the

---

15. In the OT, Israel is described as God's chosen (בָּחִיר, 1 Chr 16:13; 105:6, 43; 106:5, Isa 43:20; 45:4; 65:9, 15, 22), as well as Moses (Ps 106:23), Saul (2 Sam 21:6), David (Ps 89:4) and the Servant of the Lord (Isa 42:1). The NT describes God's people as His chosen (ἐκλεκτοί) in Matt 22:14; 24:22, 24, 31; Mark 13:20, 22, 27; Luke 18:7; 23:35 (referring to Jesus); Rom 8:33; 16:13; Col 3:12; 1 Tim 5:21(elect angels); 2 Tim 2:10; Titus 1:1; 1 Pet 1:1; 2:4, 6 (Christ as the choice stone), 9; 2 John 1:1, 13; Rev 17:14. These elect are "those whom He (God) chose" (Mark 13:20); the verb ἐκλέγω is found 163 times in the Greek Bible, so it can scarcely be called a rare usage (Gen 6:2; 13:11; Num 16:5, 7; 17:20; Deut 1:33; 4:37; 7:7; 10:15; 12:5, 11, 14, 18, 21, 26; 14:2, 23-25; 15:20; 16:2, 6, 7, 11, 15, 16; 17:8, 10, 15; 18:5, 6; 26:2; 30:19; 31:11; Jos 9:27; 24:22; Jda 10:14; Jdg 5:8; 10:14; 1 Sam 2:28; 8:18; 10:24; 12:13; 13:2; 16:8, 9, 10; 17:8, 40; 2 Sam 6:21; 16:18; 19:39; 24:12, 13, 14; 1 Kgs 3:8; 8:16, 44, 48; 11:13, 32, 34, 36; 14:21; 18:23, 25; 2 Kgs 21:7; 23:27; 1 Chr 15:2; 16:41; 19:10; 21:10, 11; 28:4, 5; 2 Chr 6:5, 6, 34, 38; 7:12, 16; 12:13; 33:7; 35:19; 1 Esd 5:1; Neh 1:9; 9:7; Tob 1:4; Tbs 1:4; 1 Macc 6:35; 7:37; 9:25; 10:32; 2 Macc 5:19; 3 Macc 2:9; Ps 32:12; 46:5; 64:5; 77:67, 68, 70; 83:11; 104:26; 131:13; 134:4; Prov 24:32; Job 29:25; 34:33; Sir 45:4, 16; Joel 2:16; Zech 3:2; Isa 7:15, 16; 14:1; 40:20; 41:8, 9, 24; 43:10; 44:1, 2, 12; 49:7; 56:4; 58:5, 6; 65:12; 66:3-4; Bar 3:27; Ezek 20:38; Dan 11:35; Dat 11:35; 12:10; Mark 13:20; Luke 6:13; 9:35; 10:42; 14:7; John 6:70; 13:18; 15:16, 19; Acts 1:2, 24; 6:5; 13:17; 15:7, 22, 25; 1 Cor 1:27, 28; Eph 1:4; Jas 2:5).

risen Lord and are taught in Him, as "the truth is in Jesus" (Eph 4:21), and those who hear actually do receive the Sprit by the hearing of faith (Gal 3:2).

Preaching and the Persuasion of the Audience

Because of the truth that Jesus calls the dead to life through His calling Word, Paul charges Timothy to "exhort with all patience and doctrine," for despite all opposition, the Word of God will not return void (Isa 55:11). While there are many negative reactions to preaching, some listeners will be persuaded to make a positive response of saving faith.[16]

Effectual hearing of the gospel is that which persuades a sinner to believe. This fact is plainly taught in Eph 1:13, where the apostle notes, "In Him, you also, after listening [*akousantes*] to the message of truth, the gospel of your salvation—having also believed, you were sealed in Him with the Holy Spirit of promise." The aorist participles, *akousantes* ("having heard") and *pisteusantes* ("having believed") express coincidental action:[17] to hear effectually is to believe savingly, leading to the sealing work in the Spirit.[18]

Implied in Paul's view of effectual hearing is the effectual call of God through the gospel ("He called you through our gospel," 2 Thess 2:14). God's life-giving call goes forth through the preached Word and opens deaf ears, so that the listener hears and then responds to the things spoken by the preacher (Acts 16:14). Because of this dynamic, Paul has a very positive outlook about the success of his preaching: he aspires to preach the gospel on the basis that "it is written, 'They who had no news of Him shall see, and they who have not heard shall understand'" (Rom 15:21, quoting Isa 52:15). As Timothy pays close attention to his doctrine, he will ensure salvation not only for himself but also for those who hear him (1 Tim 4:16). The confidence of both Paul and Timothy is valid because Jesus said that His sheep would hear His voice (John 10:27), and it is through the preaching of His undershepherds that the flock of God hears the voice of the great

---

16. Besides noting the negative reactions to the gospel, Acts also records these positive responses to the same message: wonder (Acts 9:20; 13:44–44); gladness (13:46, 46, 52); surprise (14:9–10); calmness (14:14–18; 15:7); hospitality (16:14); curiosity (17:17–20); baptism (19:5); affection (20:36–38); astonishment (26:24); and of course, belief (13:13, 48; 14:1; 15:7; 16:14, 34; 17;12, 34; 18:8).

17. Wallace, *Greek Grammar*, 625, ftnt. 33, states that "the overall context [of Eph 1:13] leads me to believe that the aorist participle is contemporaneous here."

18. Sealing in (or by) the Spirit should be viewed as a separate ministry of the Holy Spirit that flows from the "washing of regeneration and renewing by the Holy Spirit" (Titus 3:5), although a more consistent translation would be "renewing *of* the Holy Spirit," because the grammatical construction is in the genitive case (ἀνακαινώσεως πνεύματος ἁγίου). When Jesus compares the regenerating work of the Spirit to the mystery of the wind, He intimates that new birth takes place beyond human comprehension (John 3:8); sealing, however, indicates a distinct mark of identification (BDAG § 7197.3), suggesting that sealing applies to the conscious mind and feeling heart (2 Cor 1:22) whereby the believer comes to know the anointing to the Spirit ("But you have an anointing from the Holy One, and you all know," 1 John 2:20).

Shepherd of the sheep. Therefore, some will hear effectually because Jesus promised, "Everyone who is of the truth hears My voice" (John 18:37).

The effectiveness of preaching is shown in one of the most common words used in Acts to describe Paul's preaching, and that is "persuasion." The verb *peithō* means in the active voice, "to persuade or convince,"[19] with the best-known example being the remark of King Agrippa, "In a short time you will persuade me to become a Christian" (Acts 26:28). Even as a prisoner, Paul answered him with unequalled optimism, "I would to God that whether in a short or long time, not only you, but also all who hear me this day" (Acts 26:29). Paul expected a favorable response, so he preached in order that others would trust Christ, because he believed that "God was well-pleased through the foolishness of the message preached to save those who believe" (1 Cor 1:21).[20]

Thus, Paul preached to persuade. Upon entering the synagogue in Iconium, he "spoke in such a manner that a great multitude believed, both of Jews and of Greeks" (Acts 14:1). He looked for strengthening from the Lord so that "through me the proclamation might be fully accomplished, and that all the Gentiles might hear" (2 Tim 4:17). Paul had such firm confidence in the power of the gospel to save that it drove him to proclaim Christ where He had never been named, because the apostle knew that God would bring some to saving faith (Rom 15:20–21). Fitzmyer notes, "Paul makes it clear that people listen to the gospel (Eph 1:3), welcome it (2 Cor 11:4), obey it (2 Thess 1:8), and believe in Christ Jesus preached in it (Rom 1:5). Thus the gospel is understood to exercise a certain authority over human beings, playing a normative role linked to its kerygmatic character."[21] Because of the divine authority of the gospel, the preacher ought to preach to persuade his unbelieving audience to believe in the Lord Jesus.

Preaching and the Hearing of a Believing Audience

It is this same authority of the gospel that causes Paul's preaching to be persuasive even when he addresses an audience consisting primarily of believers, the gathered church. If Timothy finds stated in this charge (2 Tim 4:3–4) the negative reasons why he must exhort in all patience and instruction, he should presume the unstated positive reasons. The following section explores the positive characteristics of a believing audience, that it will endure sound doctrine; it will gather teachers according to God's desires; and it will turn away from myths unto the truth. Based on this understanding of effectual hearing the preacher speaks in the hearing of a believing audience.

19. BDAG § 5754.1 a, b. Paul "persuaded many to continue in the grace of God" (Acts 13:43); he was "trying to persuade Jews and Greeks" (Acts 18:4); "he entered the synagogue, . . . persuading *them* about the kingdom of God." (Acts 19:8); and he was "trying to persuade them concerning Jesus, from both the Law of Moses and from the Prophets, from morning until evening" (Acts 28:23). Because of Paul's efforts, some were in fact persuaded to believe in Christ (Acts 17:3; 28:24).

20. See Stott, *Preacher's Portrait*, 42.

21. Fitzmyer, "The Gospel in the Theology of Paul," 155.

Preaching so the Audience May Bear Sound Doctrine

If the time will come when unbelievers will not endure sound doctrine (2 Tim 4:3), the time must ever be present for believers to bear up (*anechō*) true, "healthy doctrine."[22] Because this verb *anechō* often carries the idea of putting up with an unpleasant person ("How long shall I put up with you?" Matt 17:17) or with some oppressive treatment ("When we are persecuted, we endure," 1 Cor 4:12),[23] it may be that Paul rather ironically borrowed this word from those who used it to demean sound doctrine as burdensome. In other contexts, he prefers to use the similar word *katechō*, which is based on the same root *echō* and can mean, "to adhere firmly to traditions, convictions, or beliefs."[24] *Katechō* is used for "holding firmly" revealed truth as it has been delivered (1 Cor 11:2; 1 Thess 5:21) and for "holding fast the word . . . preached to you" (1 Cor 15:2). Such usage shows that the believing audience is responsible for taking the preached Word into personal possession.

The reason why the believer must "endure sound doctrine" is that hearing unto salvation includes not only understanding but also "obedience of faith," a concept so important that Paul begins and ends his letter to the Romans with the same prepositional phrase *eis hupokonen pisteōs* (Rom 1:5; 16:26),[25] indicating by conjoining listening and believing that effectual faith produces obedience. Behind the concept of obedient hearing lies the OT verb, *shama*, which involves not only hearing but also obeying,[26] as the Lord declares to Israel, "You have not obeyed My voice" (Jer 3:13).[27] For that matter, one has scarcely heard if one is not obedient. Jesus emphasizes this connection between hearing and doing when He states, "Everyone who hears My words, and acts upon them" will be like a man who builds well upon the solid rock (Luke 6:47–48). Conversely, those who "do not obey the gospel of our Lord Jesus" will be punished (2 Thess 1:8), and those who do not obey the apostle's written instructions should be shunned (2 Thess 3:14). Instead, the true believer becomes "obedient from the heart to that form of teaching to which you were committed" (Rom 6:17).

---

22. "Sound doctrine" (ὑγιαινούσης διδασκαλίας) is an important concept Paul also mentions in 1 Tim 1:10; Titus 1:9; and 2:1, along with "sound words" (1 Tim 6:3; 2 Tim 1:13), as well as being "sound in the faith" (Titus 1:13; 2:2). The basic idea behind the verb ὑγιαίνω is "to be in good physical health" (as in 3 John 2), but the Pastoral Epistles use it in the sense of being "sound or free from error" (BDAG § 7500).

23. BDAG § 633.2 ἀνέχω, "to undergo someth. onerous or troublesome without giving in."

24. BDAG § 4831.2.

25. Etymologically, ὑπακοή prefixes the preposition ὑπό onto the noun, *akoē*, "hearing," so the idea of "hearing under" suggests the idea of obeying (*hupakouō*) authority, and that is how the word is generally used in the NT ("Children, obey your parents in the Lord, for this is right," Eph 6:1). Kittel says of ὑπακούω (*TDNT* 1:244) that it is ". . . a term for religious activity to be thought of within the sphere of a religion which receives the divine word by hearing and translates it into action."

26. BDB § 10097 translates שָׁמַע most commonly as "hear" yet also by "obey."

27. The LXX translates the Hebrew of Jer 3:13, לֹא־שְׁמַעְתֶּם נְאֻם־יְהוָה with τῆς δὲ φωνῆς μου οὐχ ὑπήκουσας λέγει κύριος.

Clearly, a New Covenant preacher, like Paul, should "not presume to speak of anything except what Christ has accomplished . . . , resulting in the obedience (*hupakoēn*) of the Gentiles by word and deed" (Rom 15:18). Clearly, a believing audience gladly bears up preaching of the sound doctrine of the gospel by listening to it and becoming obedient to it.

Preaching so the Audience Hears a Godly Teacher

The identification that Paul makes of himself as a preacher (*kērux*) and "teacher (*didaskalos*) of the Gentiles in faith and truth" (1 Tim 2:7) will be examined in detail in chapter 14, "The Preacher's Office," so suffice it to say at this time in our study that the preacher laboring as a teacher must be the complete opposite of the 'ear-tickling' preachers mentioned in 2 Tim 4:3. He must not teach what the audience wants to hear but rather proclaim "the whole counsel of God" (Acts 20:27). In contrast to teachers accumulated by an audience's self desires, the genuine preacher will turn the ears of his audience away from myths and instead turn them "to God from idols to serve a living and true God" (1 Thess 1:9). Because Paul serves as an apostolic example of a biblical preacher and teacher (2 Tim 2:11), the godly preacher must practice the things he has "learned and received and heard and seen" from Paul (Phil 4:9), so that the things that he has heard (in print!) from the apostle he will also "entrust to faithful men, who will be able to teach others also" (2 Tim 2:2).

If unbelievers honor teachers that they have heaped up to tickle their ears, how much greater esteem is due from the church to its true teachers of the Word who labor diligently among them (1 Thess 5:12)? Because the believing audience has received the "word of hearing" (*logon akoēs*) from faithful preachers, it hears the message of a true teacher "just as it is in truth, the Word of God" (1 Thess 2:13). Therefore, contrary to those who will not endure sound doctrine, the regenerate will welcome sound doctrine; they will not want to have tickled ears but will have ears ready to hear what the Spirit says to the churches; they will not accumulate teachers in accordance to their own desires but will seek after teachers who instruct them the desires of God; they will turn away their ears from myths and pursue the truth. Such are the characteristics of a believing audience to whom Timothy—and every succeeding preacher—is called to preach the Word,

Summary to the Preacher's Audience

Because the gospel is primarily communicated through speaking the Word to the hearing of an audience, this chapter has illustrated how the preacher not only needs to understand his responsibility to "exhort in all patience and doctrine," but he must also have an awareness of his audience to whom he speaks. He should realize that the unconverted audience has a hearing deficiency: it is deaf to the gospel invitation due to a self-inflicted deafness of the sinful nature. Furthermore, the unsaved audience is prone to listen to anything other than the gospel, a situation to which God responds with a judicial deafening. It truly demands a miracle for the gospel to penetrate the ears of a deaf audience so that it will not only hear the truth but receive and believe it.

Yet it is exactly in hope of witnessing such a miracle that the preacher continues to preach, believing that God grants ears of faith to some in his audience. Convinced that God knows His elect, the preacher attempts to persuade his unbelieving audience to do what is impossible, to believe the message of salvation. He can make such a demand because he knows the outcome rests solely in the hands of the Lord who fashioned the ear that hears (Prov 20:12) and who will open the ears of some unbelievers to respond with a "hearing of faith."

When addressing an audience of those who have believingly heard the gospel, the preacher appeals to them as those whose ears have been opened by divine grace and who can, in fact, comprehend the mysteries of the kingdom of God (Luke 8:10). When addressing an believing audience, the preacher exhorts them to be "obedient from the heart to that form of teaching to which [they] were committed" (Rom 6:17), and he cautions them about turning aside to myths but instead encourages them to turn their ears to hear the truth of the Word of God.

These biblical insights about listening means that the preacher needs to be sensitive to the spiritual status of his audience. He should ascertain if his audience requires initial evangelism of the unsaved, or if he should lean more to the didactic because his audience is already believing. He should ask if his message needs to "admonish the unruly, encourage the fainthearted, [or] help the weak" (1 Thess 5:13). While the make up of the audience is important in determining the emphasis of the sermon (whether evangelistic or exhortatory), it must not dictate the basic content of the message, which is that "God made a choice among you, that by [a preacher's] mouth the Gentiles should hear the word of the gospel and believe" (Acts 15:7). Such is how Timothy—and every preacher—is to exhort his audience "with great patience and instruction" (2 Tim 4:2).

CHAPTER 10

The Preacher's Character: "But As For You"

HAVING EXPOSED DECEITFUL TEACHERS who turn their listeners away from the truth of the gospel unto myths (2 Tim 4:3–4), Paul returns his remarks to his younger colleague with the address, "But you (sù dè). . . ." In contrast to those who preach only to tickle the ears of the audience, Timothy is to "be sober in all things, endure hardship, do the work of an evangelist, fulfill your ministry" (2 Tim 4:5). While each of these duties will be explored in following chapters, it is clear that the link between them is the godly character of the preacher, emphasized by the second personal pronoun "you" (sù).[1] In order to capture the emphasis of the grammar and the contrast with the previous verse, the beginning of verse five should be translated as it is by the CSB, "But as for you," or even more emphatically, "But as for yourself."[2] By this emphasis, Paul calls to Timothy's attention the fact that the character of the preacher must be in accord with the truth of the doctrine that he is charged to preach.

This high standard for the preacher's character needs to be understood and observed, not only because of the frequent occurrence of immoral behavior among church leaders, but also because some denominations actually condone behavior that is clearly condemned by the Bible.[3] Once biblical authority is rejected, the void is filled by relativistic ethics, so that the moral qualifications of church officers become nothing more than a matter of personal and private preferences.

The moral teachings of Paul could hardly be more at odds with such thinking. He requires the man of God to "pursue righteousness, godliness, faith, love, perseverance *and* gentleness" (1 Tim 6:11), because he considers "the sound words of the Lord

---

1. BDAG § 6869.

2. Some English translations express the contrast to a lesser extent, such as the NIV and NAS ("but you"), whereas the KJV nearly loses the emphasis entirely ("But watch thou"). The Phillips version is better ("For yourself"); the ESV is a bit better ("As for you"), but the best to express the emphasis and contrast appears to the NEB, "But you yourself" and the CSB, "But as for you."

3. What comes to mind includes the official declaration of various associations to ordain practicing homosexuals to the ministry and the allowance of clergy to perform same-sex weddings. It is hard to imagine how these practices can be squared with traditional biblical ethics.

Jesus" to be also "doctrine conforming to godliness" (1 Tim 6:3). Such a standard demands that the Christian preacher not only conduct himself in the same manner expected of every believer, but also that he meets the higher qualifications of conduct and character required of the church leaders (overseers, elders and deacons), because he is called to greater responsibilities and public duties. James 3:1 sounds the sober caution, "Let not many *of you* become teachers, my brethren, knowing that as such we shall incur a stricter judgment."

It is the purpose of this chapter to formulate a Pauline theology of pastoral character, noting the contrast he draws between false preachers and his fellow preachers; the commendation he makes of godly preachers—including himself; the qualifications he requires of all fellow preachers; and the testing of their character he expects in order to enable them to "obtain for themselves a high standing and great confidence in the faith that is in Christ Jesus" (1 Tim 3:13).

The Character of the False Preacher

Paul is not averse to teaching by contrasting good and evil, and in the matter of pastoral ethics, he is certainly not reluctant to expose the character, and even at times, the names of false preachers.[4] In every letter with the exception of the one to Philemon, Paul makes mention of pseudo-preachers or their deceitful propaganda, and he almost always notes the immoral implications of their false teaching.[5] Such men "teach strange doctrines" (1 Tim 1:3) that advocate ascetic ideals (1 Tim 4:12), which are actually "of no value against fleshly indulgence" (Col 2:23). Paul views such teachings

---

4. Paul names Hymenaeus, Alexander and Philetus in particular (1 Tim 1:20; 2 Tim 2:17; and 4:14), and to this infamous list should be added Simon Magus (Acts 9:9–10) and Elymas the magician (Acts 13:8). Apparently there are times in public discourse when the preacher should give names of false preachers.

5. For example, see Rom 16:17–18 ("Keep your eye on those who cause dissensions and hindrances contrary to the teaching which you learned, and turn away from them. For such men are slaves, not of our Lord Christ but of their own appetites; and by their smooth and flattering speech they deceive the hearts of the unsuspecting."); 1 Cor 15:33 ("Do not be deceived: "Bad company corrupts good morals."); 2 Cor 11:13 ("Such men are false apostles, deceitful workers, disguising themselves as apostles of Christ."); Gal 2:4 (". . . false brethren who had sneaked in to spy out our liberty which we have in Christ Jesus, in order to bring us into bondage."); Eph 4:14 (". . . the trickery of men, by craftiness in deceitful scheming."); Phil 3:18–19 (". . . enemies of the cross of Christ, whose end is destruction, whose god is *their* appetite, and *whose* glory is in their shame, who set their minds on earthly things."); Col 2:18–19, 23 (". . . self-abasement and the worship of the angels, taking his stand on *visions* he has seen, inflated without cause by his fleshly mind, and not holding fast to the head; . . . the appearance of wisdom in self-made religion and self-abasement and severe treatment of the body."); 1 Thess 2:16 (Those who are "hindering us from speaking to the Gentiles that they might be saved; with the result that they always fill up the measure of their sins."); 2 Thess 2:9–10 ("The one whose coming is in accord with the activity of Satan, with all power and signs and false wonders, and with all the deception of wickedness for those who perish, because they did not receive the love of the truth so as to be saved."); 1 Tim 4:3 ("*men* who forbid marriage *and advocate* abstaining from foods."); 2 Tim 4:3 ("Teachers in accordance to their own desires."); Titus 1:10 ("Rebellious men, empty talkers and deceivers.").

as nothing more than "foolish controversies and genealogies and strife and disputes about the Law" that the preacher should avoid entirely because they are "unprofitable and worthless" (Titus 3:9).

The reason why these men teach a false gospel is to give rationalizations for their perverse character. Paul describes such factious men as "perverted and sinning, being self-condemned" (Titus 3:11). They are marked by indulging in lusts rather than repenting from them because they are "slaves not of our Lord Christ but of their own appetites" (Rom 16:18), for their "god is *their* appetite" (Phil 3:19). The repeated issue of sexual immorality is quite pertinent to Paul's exposé of false teachers when he speaks of them as "captivating weak women weighed down with sins, led on by various impulses" (2 Tim 3:6). He accuses such men of proclaiming Christ from motives of selfish ambition (Phil 1:17), "peddling the word of God" (2 Cor 2:17), "teaching things they should not *teach*, for the sake of sordid gain" (Titus 1:11).

The primary characteristic of such men is deceit: they are "false apostles, deceitful workers, disguising themselves as apostles of Christ" (2 Cor 11:13), so that they misguide others "by craftiness in deceitful scheming" (Eph 4:14). They claim to speak the truth of God whereas they are actually "speaking lies" (*pseudologos*) in hypocrisy (1 Tim 4:2). Without any hesitation, Paul describes such as "false brethren" (*pseudadelphos*, Gal 2:4).

Their falseness of character is soon revealed in falseness of speech, and it is at this point that the true preacher must heed, lest he fall into the same pit. The false teacher is skilled in the manipulation of words, as he deceives the heart of the unsuspecting through "smooth and flattering speech" (Rom 16:18).[6] Paul derides this sort of preaching as "empty chatter" (1 Tim 6:20; 2 Tim 2:16), speculation arising from "a morbid interest in controversial questions and disputes about words" (1 Tim 6:4).

The reason why Paul opposes such vain preaching is that it leads to further ungodliness (2 Tim 2:16), "upsetting whole families" (Titus 1:11). From these kind of sermons proceed "envy, strife, abusive language, evil suspicions, and constant friction between men of depraved mind and deprived of the truth" (1 Tim 6:4–5). False character begets false preaching, which in turn leads to false conduct. For such reasons, the man of God must be able to identify the doctrine, character, and conduct of a false teacher so that he may not become one himself, and so he may warn the people of God against such rebellious teachers. Without argument, certain men disqualify themselves from the gospel ministry by their ungodly character.

---

6. This is the only occurrence of *chrēstologias* in the NT, and BDAG § 7976 defines χρηστολογίας as "smooth, plausible speech." Paul uses the other word *eulogia* seven times, but Rom 16:18 is the only time he uses it in a negative sense of "words that are well chosen but untrue" (BDAG § 3255.2).

The Character of Fellow-Preachers

Timothy, however, can find positive examples of godly character, since he had worked with many sincere believing leaders who served Christ out of genuine motives. Paul commends several of these believers, designating them as "fellow-workers,"[7] including Prisca and Aquila, who "risked their own necks" for Paul's life (Rom 16:3–4); Andronicus and Junias, "who are outstanding among the apostles" (Rom 16:7); "Persis the beloved, who has worked hard in the Lord" (Rom 16:12), and Justus, who "proved to be an encouragement to me" (Col 4:11).

A quality Paul especially commends of his co-workers is the abounding affection that Titus showed toward believers (2 Cor 7:15), as well as the "deep concern" Epaphras has for the Colossians (Col 4:13).[8] Paul's fellow-worker and fellow-soldier Epaphroditus is likewise commended for his intense "longing"[9] for the Philippians (Phil 2:25–26). Of this beloved brother, Paul adds that believers should "hold men like him in high regard, because he came close to death for the work of Christ, risking his own life to complete what was deficient in your service to me" (Phil 2:29–30). The distinguishing characteristic Epaproditus shows as a godly preacher is a life-giving devotion to the work of God, even to the point of personal danger.

Although he would never dream of doing so, Timothy could even look to himself as an example of a godly preacher, since Paul describes him also as his fellow-worker (Rom 16:21), one who faithfully preached Christ Jesus as the Son of God (2 Cor 1:19). Paul also includes the witness of Timothy in a personal commendation, when he describes him as "my beloved and faithful child in the Lord" (1 Cor 4:17) who "is doing the Lord's work, as I also am" (1 Cor 16:10). Timothy receives the highest commendation of all of Paul's co-workers when the apostle writes of him, "I have no one else of kindred spirit who will genuinely be concerned for your welfare . . . . You know of his proven worth that he served with me in the furtherance of the gospel like a child serving his father" (Phil 2:20, 22). It appears that Timothy was so trustworthy to Paul that the apostle entrusted him with the follow-up ministry and the delivery of the letters to the Corinthians and Thessalonians (1 Cor 4:17; 1 Thess 3:2). These commendations

---

7. The description of a fellow-worker as *sunergos* is nearly a Pauline exclusive: he uses συνεργός twelve times of the thirteen it is found in the NT (The only appearance outside of Paul's letters is in 3 John 8, "We ought to support such men, that we may be fellow workers with the truth."). Otherwise, Paul lists these as his fellow-workers: Prisca and Aquila (Rom 16:3); Urbanus (Rom 16:9); Timothy (Rom 16:21; 1 Thess 3:2); Titus (2 Cor 8:23); Epaphroditus (Phil 2:25); Aristarchus (Col 4:10; Phlm 24); Mark (Col 4:10; Phlm 24); Jesus who is called Justus (Col 4:11); Philemon (Phlm 1:1); Demas (Phlm 24); Luke (Phlm 24); plus, when he writes, "We are God's fellow workers" (1 Cor 3:9), contextually, Paul refers to Apollos who is mentioned along with Paul as "servants though whom you believed" (1 Cor 3:5–6).

8. The word *ponon* is defined by BDAG § 6076.1 in Col 4:13 as "hard labor," but the word more commonly means "great trouble" or even "pain," as in Rev 21:4, "There shall no longer be . . . pain."

9. BDAG § 3005 defines ἐπιποθέω, "to have a strong desire."

of Timothy's dependability show that the preacher needs to devote quality service to other ministers of God.

With similar admonitions, Paul urges both Timothy and Titus to serve as examples (*tupoi*) to other believers.[10] Paul commands Timothy, "Become a *tupos* of the faithful in word (*logos*, in speech of preaching), in conduct, in love, in faith, in purity" (1 Tim 4:12). To Titus he says, "Concerning all things, show yourself to be *tupos* of good works, pure in the Teaching, dignified, sound in *logos*, beyond reproach" (Titus 2:7–8). These challenges are excellent motivations for any preacher, as they clearly link the spoken message (*logos*) with the quality of character. As a *tupos* is a copy of the original, so the preacher is to be an earthly copy of the heavenly Lord in all that the audience hears and sees. Goppelt notes, "The more a life is molded by the Word, the more it becomes *tupos*."[11] This concept of being a type means that the preacher ought to study the lives of other preachers in order to become like them, as he "observes those who walk according to the pattern (*tupos*) you have in us" (Phil 3:17).

The Character of Paul as an Example for Preachers

Timothy also has Paul as a *tupos* for the character of the godly preacher, a fact which the apostle himself reminds his friend, "You followed my teaching, conduct, purpose, faith, patience, love, perseverance, persecutions, and sufferings" (2 Tim 3:10–11). In other words, Timothy learned from Paul not only how to model the Christian life, but also how to minister and preach, a fact to which Paul alludes when he states, "You are having an example (*hupotupōsis*[12]) of sound words which you heard from me, in faith and love that are in Christ Jesus" (2 Tim 1:12). This statement shows that "the proclamation of Paul is a model of sound preaching."[13]

By Paul's own admission, no one knew the apostle better than Timothy, as he said of him to the Corinthians, "I have sent to you Timothy, who is my beloved and faithful child in the Lord, and he will remind you of my ways which are in Christ, just as I teach everywhere in every church" (1 Cor 4:17). The two men had ministered so closely in tandem that Paul was able to use himself and Timothy as examples to the Thessalonians, when he reminded them, "You are witnesses, and so is God, how devoutly and uprightly and blamelessly we behaved toward you believers" (1 Thess 2:10). Due to the mercy Paul had received, he was convinced "as the foremost, Jesus Christ might demonstrate [in me] His perfect patience, as an example for those who

---

10. Goppelt, τύπος, *TDNT* 8:246, notes that the word *tupos* was used originally of a form that was stamped, thus becoming a copy of the original, or an example.

11. Ibid., 250

12. BDAG § 7649 traces ὑποτύπωσις to τυπόομαι, to "be stamped/marked; thus, a pattern, or a basis for behavioral comparison."

13. Goppelt, τύπος, *TDNT* 8:250.

would believe in Him for eternal life" (1 Tim 1:16), especially as Timothy imitated the apostle's life and preaching.

The Imitation of Paul

Several times Paul uses an interplay between the words "example" (*tupos*) and "imitation" (*mimeomai, mimētes*; Phil 3:17), as he does in 2 Thess 3:9, when he reminds his readers that he and his companions "offered ourselves as a model (*tupon*) for you, that you might follow our example (*mimeisthai*)." Bauder points out that the verb *mimeomai* "... very early was used to express ethical demands made on men. One should take as one's model the boldness of a hero, or one should imitate the good example of one's teachers or parents."[14] Thus, Paul reminds the churches that have witnessed his life to imitate him—perhaps not as a hero—but certainly as a good example of Christian experience and ministry.[15]

It sounds rather audacious to modern ears to hear Paul say, "Be imitators of me" (1 Cor 4:16). It seems prideful that he gives himself as a primary example of conduct and character when the archetype for Christian imitation is Christ Himself—and Paul would quickly agree, as he is qualifies his claim by explaining, "Be imitators of me, just as I also am of Christ" (1 Cor 11:1). Bauder notes, "To be an imitator of the apostle accordingly means laying hold of Christ in the consciousness of one's own imperfection and letting one's life be continually remolded by Christ in obedience to him ... to the kinds of behavior that would be consistent with existence in the sphere of the Lordship of Christ."[16]

While Paul serves as the apostolic *tupos* of Christ, every believer is called to live a life worthy of imitation of God Himself (Eph 5:1). That high standard is particularly required of church leaders, as when Paul reminds the Thessalonians that he, Timothy, and Silas serve as "types" to be imitated (*mimeomai*). Additionally, the author of Hebrews calls for his readers to "... remember those who led you, who spoke the word

---

14. Bauder, "Mimic." *DNTT* 1:490.

15. The pertinent references include: 1 Cor 4:16, "I exhort you therefore, be imitators (μιμηταί) of me"; 1 Cor 11:1, "Be imitators (μιμηταί) of me, just as I also am of Christ"; Eph 5:1, "Therefore be imitators (μιμηταί) of God, as beloved children"; Phil 3:17, "Brethren, join in following my example (Συμμιμηταί) and observe those who walk according to the pattern (τύπον) you have in us"; 1 Thess 1:6, "You also became imitators (μιμηταί) of us and of the Lord"; 1 Thess 2:14, "For you, brethren, became imitators (μιμηταί) of the churches of God in Christ Jesus that are in Judea"; 2 Thess 3:7, "For you yourselves know how you ought to follow our example (μιμεῖσθαι), because we did not act in an undisciplined manner among you"; 2 Thess 3:9, "not because we do not have the right *to this*, but in order to offer ourselves as a model (τύπον) for you, that you might follow our example (μιμεῖσθαι)." The same idea is found in Heb 6:12, "Be not sluggish, but imitators (μιμηταί) of those who through faith and patience inherit the promises"; Heb 13:7, "Remember those who led you, who spoke the word of God to you; and considering the result of their conduct, imitate (μιμεῖσθε) their faith"; 3 John 1:11, "Beloved, do not imitate (μιμοῦ) what is evil, but what is good. The one who does good is of God; the one who does evil has not seen God."

16. Bauder, ibid., 1:492.

of God to you; and considering the result of their conduct, imitate (*mimeisthe*) their faith" (Heb 13:7). Without any disputation, the character of the leader must emulate the message he speaks.

The Testimony of Paul

So what can the preacher learn about ministry from imitating the apostle? Paul points to these character qualities in himself: godly motives (2 Cor 1:12),[17] renunciation of shameful things for the manifestation of the truth (2 Cor 4:2),[18] honorable behavior (2 Cor 8:20–21),[19] gentleness of Christ (2 Cor 10:1),[20] consistency of conduct (2 Cor 10:11),[21] and display of humility (1 Cor 4:9).[22] In no way would Paul want to discredit his ministry, but rather he longed to do everything to bring highest repute to his calling (2 Cor 6:3–7).[23]

As a model of the ministry, Paul shows an intense concern for his charge (2 Cor 11:20).[24] He uses familial language to express the analogies of relationship with his converts, describing himself to a father who will gladly spend and be spent for his spiritual children (2 Cor 12:14). He compares himself to a father of a bride, zealous to betroth his daughter as a pure virgin to Christ as the bridegroom (2 Cor 11:2). He even likens himself to a laboring mother who travails until Christ is formed in his readers (Gal 4:19) and compares himself to a nursing mother who proves to be gentle among

---

17. 2 Corinthians 1:12 reads, "For our proud confidence is this, the testimony of our conscience, that in holiness and godly sincerity, not in fleshly wisdom but in the grace of God, we have conducted ourselves in the world, and especially toward you." Note Paul's concern to gain credibility with both believers and unbelievers.

18. Paul announces in 2 Corinthians 4:2, "We have renounced the things hidden because of shame, not walking in craftiness or adulterating the word of God, but by the manifestation of truth commending ourselves to every man's conscience in the sight of God." Paul flees every appearance of duplicity.

19. 2 Corinthians 8:20–21 explains, "Taking precaution that no one should discredit us in our administration of this generous gift; for we have regard for what is honorable, not only in the sight of the Lord, but also in the sight of men." Paul here displays a two-fold standard, honoring both the customs of men as well as the laws of God, Sadly, many preachers give the impression that they are above the laws of man because they serve God. Paul would not stoop to such depths.

20. In 2 Corinthians 10:1, Paul urges "by the meekness and gentleness of Christ."

21. Paul claims in 2 Cor 10:11, "Let such a person consider this, that what we are in word by letters when absent, such persons *we are* also in deed when present."

22. 1 Corinthians 4:9, "For, I think, God has exhibited us apostles last of all, as men condemned to death; because we have become a spectacle to the world, both to angels and to men."

23. 2 Corinthians 6:3–7a, "... giving no cause for offense in anything, in order that the ministry be not discredited, but in everything commending ourselves as servants of God, in much endurance, in afflictions, in hardships, in distresses, in beatings, in imprisonments, in tumults, in labors, in sleeplessness, in hunger, in purity, in knowledge, in patience, in kindness, in the Holy Spirit, in genuine love, in the word of truth, in the power of God." Notice again the close connection between the message of truth and the morality of character. The two are inseparable.

24. 2 Corinthians 11:29, "Who is weak without my being weak? Who is led into sin without my intense concern?"

his spiritual infants, tenderly caring for her own babies (1 Thess 2:7). Quite obviously, the preacher must apply the message to his listeners with such a fond affection that he imparts not only the gospel but also his very own life as well (1 Thess 2:8).

Accordingly, the preacher who would develop Christ-like character traits in his attitude toward his message and toward his audience needs to study the testimony of Paul and ask the Spirit of God to develop similar godly character qualities in his life. It must be quite intentional that God presented Paul as a model for ministry, for He gave through his servant a very human model of one who imitated the Lord Jesus in his practical ministrations to others.

The Character of the Godly Preacher

Paul not only points to himself and his fellow-workers as examples of Christian character, but he also gives specific instructions on the matter, so that a Pauline "theology" of ministerial character is found quite plainly in his writings, especially—although not exclusively—in the Pastoral Epistles. This section will explore the character aspect of the godly preacher.

Character Quality of Godly Motives

The Preacher's motives have been previously discussed in chapter 5, but in review, it is clear that the primary quality of motive is sincerity in serving Christ rather than any desire to please men. Paul states this contrast clearly in Gal 1:10, "If I were still trying to please men, I would not be a bond-servant of Christ." Because of his desire to seek the favor of God, Paul was "determined to know nothing among you except Jesus Christ, and Him crucified" (1 Cor 2:2). Such a desire means that the preacher must proclaim Christ from "pure motives"[25] (Phil 1:17), knowing that he has a stewardship entrusted to him, of which he must be found trustworthy (1 Cor 4:2; 9:17). The preacher then must always examine his motives to determine if he continues to minister from a sense of obligation to the task that he has been called by Christ (Rom 1:13–15; 1 Cor 9:16).

Character Quality of Godly Emotions

The pastor, of necessity, needs to be a sympathetic man whose emotions display a genuine feeling for his work. With regard to the unsaved, Paul experiences "great sorrow and unceasing grief in my heart" (Rom 9:2), even wishing that he were "accursed, *separated* from Christ for the sake of my brethren, my kinsmen according to the flesh" (Rom 9:3). His "heart's desire and prayer to God for them is for their salvation"

---

25. BDAG § 90 translates the adverb ἁγνῶς as "purely, sincerely."

(Rom 10:1), indicating that a pastor should minister with a broken heart to those who are without Christ.

When Paul ministers to believers, his emotions range from being "filled with comfort and overflowing with joy" (2 Cor 7:4), to being in deep mourning "over those who have sinned in the past and not repented of the impurity, immorality and sensuality" (2 Cor 12:21). To such, he ministered "out of much affliction and anguish of heart" so they would know the love he had especially for them (2 Cor 2:4). Such love should be the all-constraining emotion motivating the preacher (2 Cor 5:14), for even if he has the gift of prophecy but lacks love, he is nothing (1 Cor 13:2). The preacher should constantly pray Paul's prayer and ask God to shape his emotions so that he would long for his flock "with the affection of Christ Jesus" (Phil 1:8). Propelled by this divine emotion, the mouth of the preacher will speak freely from a heart opened wide to others (2 Cor 6:11).

Character Quality of Godly Conduct

The outward behavior of the minister in his relationship with others must also display the character of godly conduct. Paul appeals to his own example when he "conducted himself"[26] in holiness and godly sincerity" (2 Cor 1:12). When it came to his conduct, Paul lived under the strictest standards of what he calls the "law of Christ," even when ministering among those "without the law," who, presumably, would have lacked such principles (1 Cor 9:20–21). Paul took great precautions that no one should discredit his ministry, "for we have regard for what is honorable, not only in the sight of the Lord, but also in the sight of men" (2 Cor 8:20–21). Another important Pauline emphasis enters the discussion at this point, that the man of God in particular should be "equipped for every good work" (2 Tim 3:17).[27] As Timothy cleanses himself from unrighteousness, he will be "a vessel for honor, sanctified, useful to the Master, prepared for every good work" (2 Tim 2:21), and Titus is to show himself "in all things to be an example of good deeds" (Titus 2:7). The truths of redemption need to applied practically by the church officer, so that his life displays a pursuit of "righteousness, faith, love *and* peace" (2 Tim 2:22).

The importance of godly conduct for the preacher cannot be overstated. In 1 Cor 9:27, Paul expresses the concern that if he fails to control his body (i.e., his conduct),

---

26. The verb *anastrephō* is defined here in 2 Cor 1:12 by BDAG § 565.3, "to conduct oneself in terms of certain principles."

27. See Stout, "The Pauline Concept of Ethical *Erga*." While Paul's rejection of "work of law" is quite well known (Rom 3:20, 27, 28; Gal 2:16; 3:2, 5, 10), it is frequently overlooked that Paul never disparages "good works" or "doing good" at all (Eph 2:10; Col 1:10; 1 Thess 2:17; 1 Tim 2:10; 5:10; 6:18; 2 Tim 2:12; 3:17; Titus 2:7, 14; 3:8, 14). Failure to note this distinction has led many to assume that Paul has little concern for practical ethical goodness, but such a deduction is far from the truth.

he could be disqualified from preaching.[28] On the other hand, the true minister of Christ will display the message of faith by his conduct.

Character Qualities of the Godly Preacher

It is this interplay between message and life that is found in the two passages where Paul specifically defines the qualifications of the church officer as overseer (*episkopē*) in 1 Tim 3:1–7 and as elder (*presbuteros*) in Titus 1:5–9. Although Lightfoot demonstrated rather persuasively that Paul refers to the same position in these terms,[29] one must wonder why the apostle uses two different descriptions of the same office, and the answer is found in a comparison of these two passages.[30]

---

28. 1 Corinthians 9:27, "I buffet my body and make it my slave, lest possibly, after I have preached to others, I myself should be disqualified."

29. Lightfoot, "The Synonyms 'Bishop' and 'Presbyter,'" *Philippians*, 95–99.

30. This translation compares the two passages, with phrases shared in common underlined:

1 Timothy 3:2–7	Titus 1:6–9
An overseer then must (*dei oun ton episkopes*)	Appoint elders (*katasteses presbuterous*)
be above reproach (*anepilempton einai*)	if one is above reproach (*ei tis estin anegkletos*)
husband of one wife (*mias gunaikos andra*)	husband of one wife (*mias gunaikos anēr*)
temperate (*nē phaleon*)	having believing children (*tekva echon pista*)
prudent (*sō phrona*)	not accused of dissipation or rebellion (*mē in kategoria asotias e anupotakta*)
respectable (*kosmion*)	For the overseer must be (*dei gar ton episkopon*)
hospitable (*philoxenon*)	above reproach as a steward of God (*anegkleton eivai as theou oikonomon*)
able to teach (*didaktikon*)	not self-willed (*mē authade*)
	not quick-tempered (*mē orgilon*)
not addicted to wine (*mē parionon*)	not addicted to wine (*mē paroinon*)
or pugnacious (*mē plekten*)	not pugnacious (*mē plekten*)
but gentle (*alla episike*)	not fond of sordid gain (*mē aischpokerde*)
uncontentious (*amachon*)	but hospitable (*alla piloxenon*)
free from love of money (*aphilarguron*)	loving what is good (*pilagothon*)
his own household ruling well (*tou idiou oikou kalos proistamenon*)	
keeping children under control (*tekva echonta in hupotage*)	sensible (*sō phrona*)
in all dignity (*meta pases semnotetos*)	just (*dikaion*)

At first glance, these passages appear to be quite similar, but a closer examination shows that they are quite dissimilar—they actually share only seven phrases (out of a combined forty-four) in common and differ markedly in content and structure, as the Table in the footnotes reveals.[31] For example, a comparison reveals that Paul's intent in 1 Timothy 3 is to stress the character of the overseer in relation to his outward testimony, whereas the thrust in Titus 1 is to emphasize the elder in his governing leadership. For this reason, Paul uses *episkopē* in 1 Timothy 3 as a title referring to the shepherding work of the minister,[32] whereas his use of *presbuteros* in Titus 1 addresses the functions and duties of the officer as a ruler of the congregation.[33] Despite these differing emphases, there is obviously much overlap between these two aspects of shepherding and governing, and the commonality is found in the qualities required of a godly preacher. These qualities, mentioned not only in these two primary passages but sprinkled throughout Paul's letters, show that one who preaches the gospel and leads God's people should show sterling character in areas of his doctrine, ethics, reputation, relationships in family and society, and his finances.

Doctrinal Qualities: Many denominations require that those who enter the ordained ministry meet strict academic requirements whereby the ordaining agents confirm that the proper course of instruction has been followed so that the candidate possesses

---

but if one does not know to manage his own household (*ei de tis tou idiou oikou prostenai ouk oiden*)	devout (*hosion*)
how will he take care of the church of God? (*pos ekklesias theou epimelesetai*)	self-controlled (*egkrate*)
not a new convert (*mē neophuton*)	holding fast the faithful word according to the teaching (*antechomenontou kata ten didachen pistou logou*)
that not being conceited he fall into the condemnation of the devil (*hina mē tuphotheis eis krima empese tou diaboulou*)	that he may be able also to exhort (*hina dunatos he kai parakalein*)
and he must also be having a good testimony with those outside (*dei de kai marturian kalen exhein apo ton exothen*)	in sound doctrine (*en te didaskalia hugiainouse*)
that he not fall into reproach and snare of the devil (*hina mē eis oneidismon empese kai pagida tou diabolou*)	and refute those who contradict. (*kai tous antilegontas elegchein*)

31. While both passages outline what it necessary (*deī*) for overseers (1 Tim 3:1; Titus 1:7), of all the requirements listed, the only ones shared in common are "man of one wife, prudent, hospitable, not given to wine or pugnacious" and "having children," and these all appear in different order except "not given to wine or pugnacious." Each passage was evidently intended to stand on its own merit.

32. L&N § 35.43 defines ἐπίσκοπος as "one who has the responsibility of caring for spiritual concerns–'one responsible for, one who cares for, guardian, keeper.'"

33. L&N § 53.77 defines πρεσβύτερος as "a person of responsibility and authority in matters of socio-religious concerns, both in Jewish and Christian societies–'elder.'

"orthodox" doctrinal beliefs. The practice of examining potential preachers is not merely a ritual that evolved out of ecclesiastical necessity; instead, ordination finds biblical basis in "the laying-on of hands by the presbytery" (1 Tim 4:14), a custom signifying not only empowering for ministry (2 Tim 1:6; Num 27:18) but also the conferring of authority to a minister by a body of elders (Acts 6:6; 13:3). The laying-on of hands is the culmination of a probationary period during which time the candidate completes a prescribed theological regimen, because the elder is charged with "holding fast the faithful word which is in accordance with the teaching" (Titus 1:9). Contrary to the doctrinal minimalizing common in some denominations, church leadership should commend its preachers to the "whole counsel of God" as it is found "in the Word of God's grace," as Paul did to the Ephesian elders (Acts 20:27, 32). There is no benefit in believing too little of Scripture; instead, the preacher should believe everything "that is written in the Prophets" from both the Old and New Testaments (Acts 24:14). A wise pastor heeds the rebuke of Jesus directed at "foolish men [who are] slow of heart to believe in all that the prophets have spoken!" (Luke 24:25).

Accordingly, it is the responsibility of the examining presbyters to determine if someone who aspires to an office in the church holds "to the mystery of the faith with a clear conscience" (1 Tim 3:9). The candidate must be asked if he is able to give account for the hope that lies within him in that he trusts Christ Jesus as Savior and serves Him as Lord. Also, does he demonstrate skillful use of the Scriptures in "exhorting in sound doctrine and to refuting those who contradict" (Titus 1:9)? By exhibiting a skillful use of Scripture, the candidate demonstrates that he is able to preach and teach the Word of God to his hearers. At the very least, then, one who aspires to the office of overseer should evidence to the church that the Holy Spirit has granted to him the gift of teaching (Rom 12:7),[34] which is why doctrinal qualifications head the list of requirements, because all the other virtues flow from "doctrine conforming to godliness" (1 Tim 6:3).

Ethical Qualities: The fact that the doctrines of the Word have inherent power to effect moral godliness reminds that the qualifications for the preacher require far more than a theological examination. The ethical qualifications outlined specifically in 1 Timothy 3 and Titus 1 show that the preacher's life should "adorn the doctrine of God our Savior in every respect" (Titus 2:10).

The various qualifications that pertain to one's ethical character are non-negotiable, as both lists begin with the verb *deī*, expressing a moral necessity.[35] Thus, the

---

34. Romans 12:7 reads redundantly, ὁ διδάσκων ἐν τῇ διδασκαλίᾳ, although the repetition of related words is intended no doubt for emphasis. BDAG § 1955.1 rather oddly defines διδασκαλίᾳ here as "the act of teaching," whereas the act is implied in the participle, "the one teaching." Paul stresses here what the one teaching should be teaching, and that is the content of Christian instruction, the specific doctrines of Scripture.

35. L&N § 1.21 defines δεῖ, "to be something which should be done as the result of compulsion, whether internal (as a matter of duty) or external (law, custom, and circumstances)–'should, ought.'"

overseer "must" be the kind of man who is self-restrained,[36] sensible,[37] temperate in the use of wine,[38] gentle,[39] "a lover of good,"[40] one who is just (*dikaios*) in his dealings with others,[41] devout *(hosios)* in his relationship with God,[42] and restraining of his passions.[43] It can be deducted from the stated significance of these virtues, that Paul obviously describes a man who has attained a degree of ethical maturity in his walk with Christ.

Reputational Qualities: Flowing from the inner holiness of character comes the necessity *(deī)* of reputational qualifications; thus, the overseer must be above reproach in his testimony, not only among those within the church but also "he must have a good testimony" *(deī . . . marturian kalen echein)* with those outside the church (1 Tim 3:7). This reputational qualification is the first one listed for the overseer in both 1 Tim 3:2 and Titus 1:6, that he "must be above reproach,"[44] meaning that others must know him

---

36. L&N § 88.87 defines νηφάλιος as 'one who holds himself in' or 'one who always has a halter on himself.' BDAG § 5097.1, however, defines νηφάλιος as being "very moderate in the drinking of an alcoholic beverage," making the qualification of being "not addicted to wine" (μὴ πάροινον) rather superfluous, so it is better the follow BDAG § 5097.2 as defining *nephalios* as being self-controlled or level headed.

37. L&N § 88.94 notes that *sophronon* derives from the stem σωφρο 'to behave in a sensible manner,' so the adjective pertains to "being sensible and moderate in one's behavior."

38. BDAG § 5706 defines πάροινος as "addicted to wine." The adjective is a combination of the preposition παρά ("beside") and the noun οἶνος, "a beverage made from fermented juice of the grape" (BDAG § 5240.1.), which is the same word used of the "best wine" Jesus produced from water at the wedding (John 2:10). The word *paroinos* cannot mean "abstaining from wine," since Paul instructs deacons not to "attend to much wine" (1 Tim 3:8) rather than "not attending to any wine," and he tells Timothy to drink wine for the sake of his stomach (1 Tim 5:23). *Paroinos*, then, prohibits the overseer from "lingering long over wine" (Prov 23:30). For a defense of biblical moderation, see Gentry, *The Christian and Alcoholic Beverages: A Biblical Perspective.*

39. BDAG § 2950 defines ἐπιεικής as "not insisting on every right of letter of law or custom, yielding, gentle, kind, courteous, tolerant."

40. This occurrence of *philagathos* is its only appearance in the Bible, but the combination of *philos* and *agathos* makes the definition unmistakable, "loving what is good." BDAG § 7730 explains that φιλάγαθος was used "in the Gr-Rom. world as a characteristic of an esp. respected and responsible citizen."

41. BDAG § 2003.1 defines the adjective δίκαιος as "being in accordance with high standards of rectitude, upright, just, fair."

42. Paul uses this adjective *hosios* only twice (1 Tim 2:8; Titus 2:8), and L&N § 88.24 defines it as "pertaining to being holy in the sense of superior moral qualities and possessing certain essentially divine qualities in contrast with what is human–'holy, pure, divine.'"

43. Found only in Titus 1:7, the adjective *egkrates* is derived from the verb, ἐγκρατεύομαι, 'to exercise self-control' (L&N § 88.83–84). Paul uses the verb in 1 Cor 7:9 ("If they do not have self-control, let them marry.") and in 1 Cor 9:25 ("Everyone who competes in the games exercises self-control in all things."), showing he means it in the sense of having control over one's bodily passions and emotions.

44. Paul uses synonyms for this meaning, as first, in 1 Tim 3:2, he employs *anepileemptos,* which L&N § 33.415 defines as "pertaining to what cannot be criticized–'above criticism, beyond reproach.'" The word is found only in 1 Tim 3:2, 5:7, and 6:14 in the NT, and it pertains to one's testimony of life. In Titus 1:5–6, Paul uses *anegklētos* twice for emphasis: "If any man be above reproach . . . the

as having a sterling character and recognize him as living an orderly life (*kosmios*).[45] Blemishes of one's reputation must also be avoided—the overseer must not be known as one who is self-willed,[46] not quickly angered,[47] nor pugnacious.[48] On the contrary, he is to be uncontentious[49] and make peace among various feuding factions.

The reasons for a good reputation are obvious; specifically, the Name of Christ and the testimony of His church are discredited when one of its vocal representatives conducts himself disgracefully. Paul alludes to this problem when he points out that if one does not maintain a good reputation, he would "fall into reproach and the snare of the devil" (1 Tim 3:7). The preacher then, should be keenly aware of what others think of him, not with pride in the position he holds or in fear of losing his position, but with the awareness of whether his reputation before the community brings glory and honor to the Name of Christ. Furthermore, it is the responsibility of the examining elders to inquire into the reputation of the candidate for ordination, for a man ought to be delayed in serving until he brings his outward testimony into conformity with the standards of doctrine leading to godliness.

Domestic Qualities: Both 1 Tim 3:2–5 and Titus 1:6 outline similar requirements concerning the home life of the church overseer; for that matter, his relationship to his wife is listed as the very first item of concern after being "above reproach," and that is he is to be a "one-woman-man," as the Greek phrase *mias gunaikos andra* translates quite literally. While there have been a number of explanations of this phrase throughout church history,[50] a "one-woman-man" is one who has been or is faithfully

---

overseer must be above reproach." L&N § 33.433 defines the adjective ἀνέγκλητος as being "without accusation."

45. This adjective κόσμιος is defined by BDAG § 4366 as "having characteristics or qualities that evoke admiration or delight, an expression of high regard for pers., *respectable,* honorable."

46. A translation of the Hebrew word *yahir* (Prov 21:24, "Haughty . . . is his name, who acts with insolent pride."), *authades* is defined by BDAG § 263 as "self-willed, stubborn, arrogant."

47. This is the only appearance of *orgilos* in the NT, although it is found in the LXX at Prov 17:49; 21:19; 22:24; 29:22, describing one who is hot-tempered.

48. The adjective *plēktes* is found only in these lists of overseer qualifications (1 Tim 3:3; Titus 1:7), and it describes someone who is who is pugnacious and demanding, a 'bully, violent person' (L&N § 8.137).

49. Also found only in these lists (1 Tim 3:3; Titus 3:2), *amachos* refers to one who is "not warring," thus, peaceable (L&N § 39.24).

50. This phrase, "one woman-man" (μιᾶς γυναικὸς ἄνδρα/ ἀνήρ) has generated much debate, beginning with whether the Greek words γυνή and ἀνήρ should be translated as "woman" and "man" (as they are usually translated in 1 Tim 2:12) or as "wife" and "husband" (as the reversed phrase appears in 1 Tim 5:9, "one-man-wife"). Kent, *Pastoral Epistles,* 126–130, lists the following five interpretations of the expression *mias gunaikos andra*:
   1. that it refers to a man married to the church as Christ's bride (the Roman Catholic view);
   2. that it prohibits a polygamist from church office;
   3. that it prohibits a remarried widower from church office;
   4. that it excludes an unmarried man from church office;

married to one woman. Clearly, sins of unfaithfulness to one's wife disqualify a man as an overseer, while conversely, Christ-like love toward his wife immensely qualifies a man. The requirements also describe the man's household as containing "children who believe, not accused of dissipation or rebellion" (Titus 1:6). As a commendable father, the overseer must keep his children under good management, controlling them with all dignity, thus leading Paul to ask a parenthetical question, "If a man does not know how to manage his own household, how will he take care of the church of God?" (1 Tim 3:5). This analogy is quite significant, because the family represents a microcosm of the church; for this reason, the examining elders need to give thoughtful consideration as to how a man governs his home as an indication of how he will rule the church. Plainly, the preacher must devote himself to the care and love of his family lest he be disqualified from the eldership as was the priest Eli, who honored his son above the Lord (1 Sam 2:29) and would not rebuke their sins (1 Sam 3:13).

Social Qualities: Many of the items Paul lists as qualifications deal with the preacher's social relationships toward others, with emphasis placed on the requirement that the preacher be "given to hospitality," a virtue appearing in both lists (1 Tim 3:2; Titus 1:8).[51] The idea behind hospitality is the opening of one's home and life to those who are not personally known to the preacher. By showing hospitality (which is also mentioned at Rom 12:13; 1 Tim 5:10; Heb 13:2, 1 Pet 4:9), the overseer demonstrates how to apply the gospel to others by loving them in tangible and practical ways.

Financial Qualities: Both passages also list the importance of having a blameless attitude toward finances, as the overseer must be "free from the love of money"[52] (1 Tim 3:3) and not to be "fond of sordid gain" (Titus 1:7).[53] These cautions address a problem that habitually plagues preachers, sometimes due to impoverished wages, but more often because of poor budgeting or covetous greed. An overseer must avoid any accusation of financial mismanagement, and in the face of promised wealth by proponents of the so-called "health and wealth gospel," he needs to be reminded of Jesus' call to

---

5. that it prohibits a divorced man from church office.

Kent favors the last view, but he overlooks that Paul could have specified a divorced man as he does in 1 Cor 7:15 and that Jesus permits divorce on grounds of *porneia* under the exception clause of Matt 5:32 ("everyone who divorces his wife, except for *the* cause of unchastity"). This author favors a sixth view, that "one-woman-man" requires the church leader to be faithfully committed to his wife, assuming he has one.

51. The word *philoxenos* means etymologically, "lover of strangers," and thus, being hospitable (BDAG § 7760). The word invokes the parable of Jesus recorded in Matt 25:31–46, where He compares himself to a stranger (*xenos*) whom the righteous unwittingly welcomed by inviting in "the least of His brothers" who also were strangers.

52. The adjective *aphilarguros* consists of the alpha privative "not" attached to the nouns *philos* ("love") and *argureos* ("silver"); thus, being not "fond of money or avaricious" (BDAG § 7740).

53. BDAG § 209 defines αἰσχροκερδής as "shamelessly greedy for money."

His disciples, "Sell all that you possess, and distribute it to the poor, and you shall have treasure in heaven; and come, follow Me" (Luke 18:22). Paul modeled this standard by working hard to help others, reminding the Ephesian elders, "I have coveted no one's silver or gold or clothes" (Acts 20:33–34). His is an example every minister of the gospel needs to emulate in order to have a financial reputation beyond reproach.

Summary to Character Qualities: It is imperative that the church leader—whether he goes by the title of overseer, bishop, elder, minister, pastor, or preacher—constantly refers to these passages in 1 Tim 3:1–7 and Titus 1:5–9 in order to examine his life and then to measure himself by these qualities.[54] However, such an inquiry is not merely private: Paul also shows that others must be involved in the examination process to determine if the man qualifies to be a preacher of the gospel of Christ.

Character Testing of the Godly Preacher

For one who aspires to be a deacon of Christ's church, Paul instructs Timothy, "Let these also first be tested; then let them serve as deacons if they are beyond reproach" (1 Tim 3:10). Presumably, a similar test is implied in the case of a presbyter, since he is not to be "a new convert" (*neophutos*).[55] It is not merely the individual who makes his own subjective assessment of his acceptability as an overseer; rather, the church has an obligation to test whether the man's call is from God, from his own delusion, or even worse, from a deceptive heart. In calling for the deacon to be tested (*dokimazesthōsan*), Paul assumes that the man seeking an office will be put under probationary scrutiny to determine if he qualifies for leadership.[56] This scrutiny should not be conducted in a censorious manner because Paul harbors expectation of approval ("Let them be tested and then let them serve"). Even so, Timothy is warned, "Do not lay hands upon anyone *too* hastily and thus share *responsibility for* the sins of others" (1 Tim 5:22). This caution implies that those who are responsible for the testing and ordination (identified in 1 Tim 4:14 as the *presbuterion*) ought to put the candidate carefully and cautiously through a series of tests in order to prove the validity of his call before he is charged with the duty of that call. Paul is following his own advice when he mentions

---

54. For a fine popular study of these qualifications, see Getz, *Measure of a Man*.

55. The word *neophutos* has entered the English vocabulary as "neophyte," one who is a "recent convert" or a novice in the faith. The Greek word consists of the compound νέος prefixed to the noun φυτόν to give the meaning of "newly-planted" (BDAG § 5068). Paul likens evangelism to planting in 1 Cor 3:6, "I planted, Apollos watered, but God was causing the growth." Likewise, believers are said to be "planted with" (σύμφυτοι) Christ in the likeness of His death (Rom 6:5), so the neophyte would one who has recently experienced new birth, evidenced in "receiving the implanted word" (τὸν ἔμφυτον λόγον; James 1:21).

56. The general NT usage of δοκιμάζω implies a test that one will stand as approved (BDAG § 2065), as in 1 Pet 1:7, "that the proof of your faith, *being* more precious than gold which is perishable, even though tested by fire, may be found to result in praise and glory and honor at the revelation of Jesus Christ."

to the Corinthians that he is sending a brother (probably Titus, 2 Cor 8:16) "whom we have often tested and found diligent in many things" (2 Cor 8:22).

Because such testing is an apostolic requirement for approval of one's call, the one who aspires to serve in the ministry and has a sense of God's appointment ought to place himself under the careful examination of a body of church leaders (whether titled elders, deacons, trustees, etc.) in order to test his gifts and qualifications. Under the guidance of older and more experienced elders, a young man is to learn the important lesson of being in subjection to his older brethren, even as all elders are to clothe themselves with humility toward one another as 1 Pet 5:5 commands. The time and duties of such a probationary period—or an internship, as it is popularly called among ecclesiastical circles—should be thoughtfully established by the examining body in order to test the reality of the candidate's claim to ministry. Clearly, he should show the qualities for ministry *before* a congregation approves his claim of divine calling, requiring that he should be assigned various tasks in order to test his gifts, character, and faithfulness throughout the duration of an adequate period of time.[57] The body of elders responsible for his oversight must take this duty very seriously if they are to prove their own qualifications of their calling.

But testing does not cease upon ordination, because elders share mutual discipline for each other throughout their ministries. Although charges against an elder should not be received except on the basis of two or three witnesses (1 Tim 5:19), if these witnesses bring forth substantial charges against an elder who continues in sin, he is to be rebuked "in the presence of all so that the rest may fear" (1 Tim 5:20). This declaration implies the types of disciplinary procedure Paul outlines when he instructs Titus to "reject a factious man after a first and second warning, knowing that such a man is perverted and is sinning, being self-condemned" (Titus 3:10–11). It then remains the responsibility of elders to police themselves and call on other fellow-elders to account for their lives and ministries.

Character Enabling for the Godly Preacher

These high standards required for ministry should be most humbling to the one who aspires to be an overseer in the church of Christ (1 Tim 3:1). How does the aspiring minister acquire these qualifications? How does the pressured pastor continue to show these graces that reflect his Savior?

Paul asks such a question in 1 Cor 2:16, "Who is adequate for these things?" and then he answers it a few verses later, "Not that we are adequate in ourselves to consider anything as *coming* from ourselves, but our adequacy is from God, who also made us adequate *as* servants of a new covenant" (2 Cor 3:5–6). None of the qualifications Paul

---

57. In Gal 1:18, Paul spoke of a three year span after his conversion before he returned to Jerusalem, no doubt spending his time by honing his new skills in Christian ministry, under the care of the disciples in Damascus (Acts 9:19–22).

requires for an overseer are self-produced; rather, they are all spiritually endowed by "the Spirit who gives life" (2 Cor 3:6).

Thus, the enabling of the preacher depends on the various means of grace, particularly the Word, which is able to build him up (Acts 20:32); the cup and bread of the Lord's Table, by which he shares in the blood and body of Christ (1 Cor 10:16); and the dynamic energizing of the Holy Spirit (Eph 3:16), by whom he is strengthened in the inner man. Each of these topics will be discussed in greater detail in chapter 15 under the title of the "Preacher's Dynamic," where it will be seen that the means of grace become actual through the channel of prayer. This fact is noted throughout Paul's letters in the many prayers he offers for his converts (as in Col 1:9–12 and 2 Thess 3:10). He also mentions that his fellow-workers such as Epaphras are laboring in prayer for his readers (Col 4:12–13). If the prayers of the pastor are effective for others, certainly his prayers for himself will be effectual as well, as Paul prayed about the removal of the thorn in his flesh, with the answer from the Lord, "My grace is sufficient for you, for power is perfected in weakness" (2 Cor 12:9).

Summary to the Preacher's Character

Springboarding from Paul's emphasis on Timothy (*sù dè*; 2 Tim 4:5) in contrast to the false teachers who turn the ears of their audience from the truth, this chapter has outlined a Pauline theology of the character of the preacher. The particularities of false teachers were noted, seeing that they are marked with a streak of deceit that issues forth in false preaching. On the contrary, the true preacher must always be on guard that his words and life are in accord with the godly standards inherent in the gospel, because a character shrouded in deceit is completely contrary to the message of the Word of Life.

For example, Paul points Timothy to his godly co-workers, and the apostle even refers his other readers to Timothy as an example of a faithful minister. Because of such commendations, it is of great benefit to the preacher to study the lives and preaching of godly Christian leaders of the past, learning from their mistakes and copying their triumphs.

Next to the infallible example of Jesus as the sinless minister who came to serve, Paul serves as the primary example of a godly preacher, since he wrote under the inspiration of the Spirit that others should imitate him as he imitates Christ (1 Cor 11:1). Timothy not only learned to follow Christ by following Paul's example, but he also learned to preach by hearing the apostle's sermons. Timothy's course in homiletics as taught by Paul has been the endeavor of this chapter in particular, and it would certainly profit the modern preacher to conduct a similar exercise. Specifically, he will find that the apostle gives detailed qualifications for the godly church officer in 1 Tim 3:1–7 and Titus 1:5–9, where he discusses the motives, conduct, emotions, and requirements for the elder, which include godliness in doctrine, ethics, reputation, family life, social hospitality, and attitudes toward finances. He will also discover that it is the duty of other presbyters to examine an aspirant to church office to determine if these qualities are present in him before commissioning him to the task. He will also keep in mind the assumption that if God calls a man to minister, He will endow him with the needed gifts to qualify and exercise his ministry. Accordingly, the preacher constantly needs to examine his life in order to see that it conforms to the biblical standard set by the preeminent preacher, the Lord Jesus.

Once his life exhibits the godly characteristics proclaimed in his message, the preacher can then turn to the question of the manner by which he preaches the Word, and this concern leads to the topic of the next chapter, the Preacher's Manner, how he is to be "sober in all things" (2 Tim 4:5a).

CHAPTER 11

The Preacher's Manner: "Be Sober In All"

IN CONTRAST TO THE false teachers who preach popular myths, the preacher of Christian truth must confront audiences that may well be quite hostile to his message. In the face of such opposition, he will be tempted to be intimidated, which apparently was a possibility with Timothy, as Paul had to remind him that God had not given him a spirit of timidity, so he should not be ashamed of the testimony of the Lord (2 Tim 2:7–8). Now, in his closing charge (2 Tim 4:1–5), Paul gives his colleague four positive imperatives to keep him from any fear, "But you, be sober in all things, endure hardship, do the work of an evangelist, fulfill your ministry" (2 Tim 4:5). The first of these commands, "be sober in all" (*nēphe en pasin*), addresses the matter of Timothy's manner as a preacher, what it means to "Preach the Word"—to do so soberly, boldly, defensively, and authoritatively.

The Manner of Preaching Soberly

The verb Paul uses, *nēphō*, is found six times in the NT, and it is invariably translated, "to be sober."[1] Paul is the only biblical writer to use the related noun *nēphalios* when he calls on the overseer and others to be "temperate" (1 Tim 3:2, 11; Titus 2:2). These words had original reference to sobriety from intoxicating wine, but their use in the NT "indicates the clarity of mind able to resist the subtle attractions of deviant mythologies."[2] To be sober in all things indicates that the preacher must keep a clear mind so that he is in control of his emotions at all times. He must avoid any loss of temper and deny any lust that might discredit his message.

---

1. BDAG § 5098 notes that the NT uses νήφω "only figuratively, to be free from every form of mental and spiritual 'drunkenness', from excess, passion, rashness, confusion, etc. *be* well-balanced, self-controlled." It is found in 1 Thess 5:6, 8; 2 Tim 4:5; 1 Pet 1:13; 4:7; 5:8.

2. Budd, "Sober," *DNTT* 1:514. He adds, "For the NT writers, though the literal is often implied, the figurative is also prominent."

Thus, the preacher must be clear thinking, having "self-control necessary for God's sacral work."[3] He must be able to listen carefully to the teaching of an opponent or the objections of an unbeliever so he may be able to answer wisely, meaning that he must know his own beliefs well enough to respond properly. The better he knows the sound doctrines of the Word, the less likely it will be for him to be intimidated by the latest new myth or some aberration of Christian truth. His manner of preaching will then be characterized by sober thinking in all things.

The Manner of Preaching Boldly

Clarity of mind also implies openness of speech, so that one who is sober is able to respond quickly to danger, and for this reason a very important aspect of the preacher's manner is to present the gospel message openly and boldly. To convey this idea of open boldness, the NT writers consistently use the noun *parrēsia* to express plainness of speech that "conceals nothing and passes over nothing."[4] Such bold speech follows the example of the Lord Jesus, who claimed before Pilate, "I have spoken openly (*parrēsia*) to the world; I always taught in synagogues, and in the temple, where all the Jews come together; and I spoke nothing in secret." (John 18:20)

Hahn points out that *parrēsia* was used historically of "the democratic right of a full citizen of a Greek city-state in the public assembly of the people [where] one may speak out freely one's opinion."[5] Because one of Luke's interests is to defend the apostles against charges of sedition, it would not be coincidental that he begins the Book of Acts with Peter speaking "with *parrēsia*" before his Jewish compatriots (Acts 2:29; 4:13) and then concludes Acts by picturing Paul "teaching concerning the Lord Jesus Christ with all *parrēsia*, unhindered" (Acts 28:31) and exercising his right as a Roman citizen to express his opinions.

Because personal opinions are not always greeted with acceptance, the word *parrēsia* came to signify speaking openly despite opposition;[6] in fact, in every occur-

---

3. Bauernfiend, νήφω, *TDNT* 4:941.
4. BDAG § 5720. It defines παρρησία as
   1. "a use of speech that conceals nothing and passes over nothing, outspokenness, frankness, plainness; . . .
   2. openness to the public, before whom speaking and actions take place; and . . .
   3. a state of boldness and confidence, courage, confidence, boldness, fearlessness, esp. in the presence of persons of high rank."

Parrēsia is found thirty-seven times in the Greek Bible (Lev 26:13; Esth 8:12; Prov 1:20; 10:10; 13:5; Job 27:10; Mark 8:32; John 7:4, 13, 26; 10:24; 11:14, 54; 16:25, 29; 18:20; Acts 2:29; 4:13, 29, 31; 28:31; 2 Cor 3:12; 7:4; Eph 3:12; 6:19; Phil 1:20; Col 2:15; 1 Tim 3:13; Phlm 1:8; Heb 3:6; 4:16; 10:19, 35; 1 John 2:28; 3:21; 4:17; 5:14).

5. Hahn, "Openness," *DNTT* 2:735. He observes that *parrēsia* is a compound word derived from *pan* prefixed to *rhēsis*; thus it means "freedom to say all" (p. 734).

6. Schlier, παρρησία, *TDNT* 5:786, notes that ". . . in Acts, it almost takes on the sense of to preach; to speak with candor or boldness amid opposition."

rence in the Book of Acts where the related verb *parrēsiazomai* is used of the apostles, they are facing some hostility or even threats against their lives because of their preaching of the gospel.[7] For example, a plot against Paul's life was hatched when he returned to Jerusalem because he was "speaking out boldly in the name of the Lord" as he had done previously in Damascus (Acts 9:27–28). When Jewish opponents slandered Paul, he responded by speaking all the more boldly (Acts 13:46, 14:3; 19:8). While on trial on the charge that he "ought not to live any longer" (Acts 25:24), Paul addressed King Agrippa, "I speak to him also with confidence" (*parrēsiazomenos lalō*, Acts 26:26). Even while under house arrest in Rome, Paul taught "concerning the Lord Jesus Christ with all *parrēsia*" (Acts 28:31). He confirms this emphasis on speaking boldly amid opposition when he reminded his converts, "After we had already suffered and been mistreated in Philippi, as you know, we had the boldness (*eparrēsiasametha*) in our God to speak to you the gospel of God amid much opposition." (1 Thess 2:2)

Since the noun *parrēsia* speaks of the right of free speech entitled to a citizen, it is used appropriately of the "boldness and confident access through faith in Him [Christ Jesus our Lord]," showing the right of admission believers have with regard to their heavenly citizenship (Eph 3:11–12). Of course, *parrēsia* in the NT is not a political privilege, but rather "great *parrēsia* in the faith that is in Christ Jesus" (1 Tim 3:13). As a result of having *parrēsia* in Christ (Phlm 1:8), Paul exudes great boldness of speech in his prayers, knowing that his right to make requests of God lies not within his natural abilities but in divine empowering. Such dependence is clearly seen in Paul's request that his Ephesian readers pray "that utterance may be given to me in the opening of my mouth, to make known with boldness (*en parrēsia*) the mystery of the gospel, for which I am an ambassador in chains; that in *proclaiming* it I may speak boldly (*parrēsiasōmai*), as I ought to speak" (Eph 6:19–20). Surely, every preacher should make it his habit to pray Paul's prayer before each opportunity to preach, knowing full well that while some may oppose his message, by the hope of God's glory, he may "use great boldness in speech." (2 Cor 3:12).

The Manner of Preaching Protectively

Because the church of God is under attack from Satan, it is the duty of the elder to "be on guard for all the flock" (Acts 20:28) and to protect it from evil influences. While there is a particular danger from unruly believers, the greater threat comes from false brothers (2 Cor 11:26) who will rise up as false apostles (2 Cor 11:13). Such men may come in as "savage wolves who will not spare the flock" (Acts 20:29) or they may

---

7. L&N § 33.90 notes that παρρησιάζομαι is "derivative of παρρησία 'boldness'" (25.158) and means "to speak openly about something and with complete confidence–'to speak boldly, to speak openly.'" The verb *parrēsiazomai* is found in Ps 11:6; 93:1; Prov 20:9; Job 22:26; Acts 9:27, 28; 13:46; 14:3; 18:26; 19:8; 26:26; Eph 6:20; 1 Thess 2:2.

come from within the ranks of the church "to draw away the disciples after them" (Acts 20:30). A pastor who faithfully shepherds the church of God will not be as a hireling who abandons the sheep and flees from danger as one who has no concern for the sheep (John 10: 12–13); instead, he must protect the flock as David did (1 Sam 16:34–35). To do so, his ministry must involve watching and heeding, concepts Paul uses to describe the protective manner of preaching that the preacher must do.

Protecting by Watching (*grēgoreō*)

A command similar to "sober in all things" (2 Tim 4:5) is the one Paul addresses to the elders in Acts 20:31, "Be on the alert," except to Timothy he uses the verb *grēgoreō*, which has the sense of "keeping zealous watch for men or lurking beasts."[8] Such alertness requires a minister to "instruct certain men not to teach strange doctrines" (1 Tim 1:3) and to silence deceivers who are "teaching things they should not *teach*" (Titus 1:11). As Paul rebuked Peter for his hypocrisy,[9] so a pastor may even confront fellow ministers whose actions are not straightforward toward the truth of the gospel (Gal 2:14).[10] A pastor must constantly remain vigilant to anything or anyone who would disturb or destroy the flock of God, meaning that he must preach to protect the church.

---

8. Oepke, γρηγορέω, *TDNT* 2:338. The word is found twenty-seven times in the Greek Bible (Neh 7:3; Jer 5:6; 38:28; Lam 1:14; Matt 24:42, 43; 25:13; 26:38, 40, 41; Mark 13:34, 35, 37; 14:34, 37, 38; Luke 12:37; Acts 20:31; 1 Cor 16:13; Col 4:2; 1 Thess 5:6, 10; 1 Pet 5:8; Rev 3:2, 3; 16:15), and in the NT, its use generally refers to spiritual alertness.

9. One would like to ask Paul why he first referred to Peter using his Greek name *Petros* (Πέτρος) in Gal 2:7–8 but then switches to his Aramaic name *Kephas* (Κηφᾶς) in Gal 2:9, 11, 14. *Petros/ Kephas* was the name Jesus conferred upon Peter (then named Simon) when his brother Andrew first brought him to Jesus, and the Lord looked at him, and said, "You are Simon the son of John; you shall be called Cephas." John 1:42 conveniently translates *Cephas* as Peter, where NET notes, "This is a parenthetical note by the author. The change of name from *Simon* to *Cephas* is indicative of the future role he will play. Only John among the gospel writers gives the Greek transliteration (Κηφᾶς, *Kephas*) of Simon's new name, *Qêphâ* (which is Galilean Aramaic). Neither Πέτρος (*Petros*) in Greek nor *Qêphâ* in Aramaic is a normal proper name; it is more like a nickname." Later, when Peter confesses Jesus as "the Christ, the Son of the living God" (Matt 16:16), Jesus again confirms His choice of the apostle's name by explaining, "You are Peter (*Petros*), and upon this rock (*petra*) I will build My church" (Matt 16:18), so clearly there is a play on words between πέτρα (which BDAG § 5897 defines as "bedrock or massive rock formations") and Πέτρος, which BDAG § 5898 defines simply as "stone." In the situation Paul addresses, Peter is acting anything but stonelike, as he wavers in his hypocrisy concerning table fellowship with Gentile converts (Gal 2:11–14), so one might wonder if Paul might be reminding Peter the day he first met Jesus and the responsibilities conferred upon him by the Lord as *Cephas*, rock of the church.

10. The verb translated "straightforward," ὀρθοποδέω, appears only here in the Bible, but it consists of two common words, *orthos* and *podeō*, "to walk straight" (BDAG § 5368). The idea is that Peter's conduct had not been heading in the direction required by the truth of the gospel.

Protecting by Heeding (*prosechō*)

Paul also orders the Ephesians elders, "Be on guard (*prosechete*) for yourselves and for all the flock" (Acts 20:28).[11] His command implies a mental awareness of the danger that threatens both the minister and his congregation. Similarly, Paul instructs Timothy to "pay close attention (*epeche*) to yourself and to your teaching; persevere in these things; for as you do this you will insure salvation both for yourself and for those who hear you" (1 Tim 4:16).[12] The minister must constantly "hold fast to the word of life" (Phil 2:16) to make sure he is protecting himself and his listeners from those who "pay attention to myths" (1 Tim 1:4; Titus 1:14), and the way to do so ministerially is to "give attention to the *public* reading *of Scripture*, to exhortation and teaching." (1 Tim 4:13)

The Manner of Preaching Authoritatively (*diabebaioomai*)

Another verb that expresses the manner by which the preacher proclaims the gospel is *diabebaioomai*, a verb that appears only twice in the NT, negatively of false teachers who "make confident assertions" (1 Tim 1:7) and positively of Titus when Paul encourages him, "This is a trustworthy statement; and concerning these things I want you to speak confidently" (Titus 3:8). The word is found in classical Greek where it describes the process of securing an inheritance,[13] but by the Koine period it had come to mean, "to state something with confidence and certainty."[14] The idea behind Paul's statement to Titus is that of an authoritative assertion of the truths of the gospel listed in the previous verses (Titus 3:5–7), including regeneration, renewing of the Holy Spirit, justification by grace, and the hope of eternal life. While the concept of the preacher's commission has been explored in chapter 2, here Paul reminds Titus of the authority he possesses in the actual delivery of the "faithful word," that it should be with bold confidence because of the divine authority that undergirds the gospel and empowers the preacher.

That the emphasis is upon the actual manner of delivery is seen in the only other appearance of the verb, and that is when Paul refutes the Judaizers as those who "do not understand either what they are saying or the matters about which they make confident assertions" (1 Tim 1:7). These false teachers boldly proclaim the Law of God with great authority, yet they speak with a false authority because their understanding of the Law is incorrect. Conversely, the Christian preacher uses his authority with confidence in his preaching, because his authority is legitimately bestowed by divine commissioning.

---

11. BDAG § 6294.1 defines προσέχω "in a state of alert, be concerned about, care for, take care." Paul uses the verb in 1 Tim 1:4; 3:8; 4:1; 4:13, and Titus 4:13.

12. L&N § 27.59 defines προσέχω and ἐπέχω identically, as being "in a continuous state of readiness to learn of any future danger, need, or error, and to respond appropriately."

13. *VGNT* § 974.

14. L&N § 33.322.

Of course, the unbelieving world cannot understand how one can speak authoritatively and also speak lovingly, yet that is the model set before the preacher by the Lord he proclaims: Jesus taught as one having authority (Matt 7:29), yet He also felt great compassion for the multitudes (Matt 9:36). Such a balance is possible for the preacher because his authority is conferred by the same Holy Spirit who also moves him to be controlled by the love of Christ (2 Cor 5:14). In this manner, true Christian preaching never becomes dictatorial, but it always remains ministerial.

Summary to the Preacher's Manner

The preacher does not want to become a liability to preaching, so he must pay careful attention to the manner by which he preaches the Word of God. To this end, Paul charges Timothy to be "sober in all things" so that his message, delivery, and authority reflect the clarity of the gospel. If one is open about his own beliefs, then he ought to preach with openness and boldness, even when faced with opposition. Murphy-O'Conner states, "The most prominent of the side effects of this grace [of preaching] is the virtue of *parrēsia*, audacity . . . to transmit the message unswerved by any considerations other than the will of God."[15] This boldness is certainly not anything akin to rudeness—it is a fresh openness to proclaim what God has done for humanity in Christ Jesus. With this certainty in mind, Paul reminds his readers of his own manner of preaching, "Having therefore such a hope, we use great boldness in *our* speech" (2 Cor 3:12). The faithful preacher will desire to use the same manner in his own preaching of the Word of God, despite the difficulties that may come his way. Such difficulties are found in the next imperative in Timothy's charge, to "endure hardship."

---

15. Murphy-O'Conner, *Paul on Preaching*, 84–85.

CHAPTER 12

The Preacher's Hardship: "Endure Hardship"

"Endure hardship!" is the eighth imperative[1] in Paul's charge to Timothy (2 Tim 4:5b), expressing the hardship that is the lot of the preacher. The Greek is but one terse word, *kakopathēson*, and it is found in Paul's writing only in this epistle, suggesting that Timothy needed to be reminded of the difficulties accompanying the gospel ministry.[2] Michaelis comments, "The word obviously means 'to accept suffering, affliction, adversity', not to be overcome by them, [but] to endure them."[3] If the reader misses the reality of gospel hardship in Paul's short command to Timothy, James repeats it in his letter, telling his readers, "As an example, brethren, of suffering (*kakopathias*) and patience, take the prophets who spoke in the name of the Lord" (Jas 5:10).

Paul was clearly writing from his own personal experience. He informs Timothy that he had been imprisoned (2 Tim 1:8), abandoned (2 Tim 1:15), deserted (2 Tim 4:10, 11, 16), and harmed (2 Tim 4:14), all the while expecting imminent death (1 Tim 4:6–7). He reminds Timothy of the "persecutions, *and* sufferings, such as happened to me at Antioch, at Iconium *and* at Lystra" (2 Tim 3:11), although none of these

---

1. The previous seven imperatives are: "I charge you," "Preach the Word," "Be ready," "Reprove," "Rebuke," "Exhort," and "Be sober."

2. Κακοπαθέω and the related noun κακοπάθεια, are defined by L&N § 24.89, "to suffer physical pain, hardship and distress." Besides here in 2 Tim 4:5, the verb appears in 2 Tim 2:8–9 ("Remember Jesus Christ, risen from the dead, descendant of David, according to my gospel, for which I suffer hardship [κακοπαθῶ] even to imprisonment as a criminal; but the word of God is not imprisoned."); James 5:13 ("Is anyone among you suffering [Κακοπαθεῖ]? Let him pray."). The one appearance in the LXX is in Jonah 4:10, and the LXE translates it, "And the Lord said, Thou hadst pity on the gourd, for which thou has not suffered" (ἐκακοπάθησας)." Since the word appears in the context of Jonah's preaching to Ninevah, one must wonder if Paul had this story in mind when reminding Timothy to endure similar hardships due to his preaching. The related verb συγκακοπαθέω (L&N § 24.84, "to undergo the same type of suffering as others do.") appears in 2 Tim 1:8 ("Therefore do not be ashamed of the testimony of our Lord, or of me His prisoner; but join with *me* in suffering [συγκακοπάθησον] for the gospel according to the power of God.") and in 2 Tim 2:3 ("Suffer hardship [Συγκακοπάθησον] with *me*, as a good soldier of Christ Jesus.").

3. Michaelis, κακοπαθέω, *TDNT* 5:937.

afflictions were caused by any criminal misconduct on Paul's part; it was solely the offense of the gospel that caused such hardships (2 Tim 1:8; 2:8–9).

Such adversities serve as reminders to Timothy—and to modern preachers—that the gospel ministry brings hardship to the minister.

Despite the grandiose promises proclaimed by the "health and wealth" preachers to make not only themselves but their adherents healthy and materially prosperous, Paul's realistic warning to Timothy to endure hardship appears to be incongruous with such inflated claims—and it is! Instead, Timothy is warned to count the cost of preaching in the way he had witnessed the troubles endured by Paul when they ministered together among the Corinthians (1 Cor 4:17; 16:10; 2 Cor 1:19). When writing to that congregation, Paul uses a number of words to describe his own difficulties as the sort of sufferings that the preacher might encounter because of preaching the Word.

For example, Paul endured great suffering in order to promote the gospel and not discredit his ministry, so that in everything he commended himself as a servant of God ". . . in much endurance, in afflictions (*thlipsis*), in hardships (*anagkē*), in distresses (*stenochoria*), in beatings (*plegē*), in imprisonments (*phulakē*), in tumults (*akatastasia*), in labors (*kopos*), in sleeplessness (*agrupnia*), in hunger (*nēsteia*)" (2 Cor 6:4–5). He adds to this list, "I am well content with weaknesses (*astheneia*), with insults (*hubris*), with distresses (*anagkē*), with persecutions (*diogmos*), with difficulties (*stenochoria*) for Christ's sake" (2 Cor 12:10). In order to know what kind of hardships he might suffer, the preacher should understand the significance of these words, so it is the task of this chapter to explore each of these words briefly, as they describe the hardships the preacher may well encounter that come from intentional opposition, from impersonal trials, and from what may be the most difficult to endure, one's own personal weaknesses.

The Hardship of Intentional Opposition

Several of the nouns that Paul lists describe intentional opposition that comes from enemies of the gospel message: suffering, persecution, abuse, beatings, imprisonment, and tumults. Each one tells of physical abuse that may possibly be inflicted on the preacher, presumably, to muzzle his testimony by the threat of pain.

Suffering From Opposition

The verb *kakopatheō*, "to endure affliction," is a compound of the nouns *kakos* and the verb *paschō* (2 Tim 1:12, "I suffer these things."), of which the related noun is *pathēma*, "sufferings,"[4] which is used of the sufferings of Christ[5] but also of the suffering of

---

4. BDAG § 5480. The noun πάθημα appears sixteen times in the NT (Rom 7:5; 8:18; 2 Cor 1:5, 6, 7; Gal 5:24; Phil 3:10; Col 1:24; 2 Tim 3:11; Heb 2:9, 10; 10:32; 1 Pet 1:11; 4:13; 5:1, 9).

5. *Pathēma* is the source of the English word for the "passion" of Christ (1 Cor 1:5; Phil 3:10; Col

persecuted believers (Heb 10:32). Paul uses *pathēma* in 2 Tim 3:11 to describe the sufferings that came to him because of fierce opposition against the gospel "at Antioch, at Iconium *and* at Lystra," referring to the various troubles he encountered in those cities, including expulsion (Acts 13:50), conspiracy (Acts 14:5), and stoning (Acts 14:19). The blessings of such hardships, however, come in "the fellowship of His sufferings" (Phil 3:10), whereby the preacher shares in the sense of forsakenness experienced by Jesus as the preacher of righteousness (Matt 27:46). While such sufferings may well be quite painful, Paul rejoices in his sufferings on behalf of others in the body of Christ (Col 1:24)—a perspective the preacher needs to keep in mind if he is to have a proper assessment of any pains he suffers for the gospel.

Persecution as Opposition

A more common expression for opposition to the gospel is that of persecution (*diogmos*),[6] a word that embodies the image of being pursued by those with hostile intent, which is clearly the way the noun *diogmos* is used in the NT.[7] It is not that the behavior of the Christian should provoke persecution ("Who is there to harm you if you prove zealous for what is good?" 1 Pet 3:13); instead, it is that "persecution arises because of the word" (Matt 13:21), as Jesus observes. Paul distinctly links preaching with persecution when he asks, "If I still preach circumcision, why am I still persecuted?" (Gal 5:11). The implication is that if Paul preached a moralistic message instead of "the stumbling block of the cross," he would not suffer any persecution, a fact he repeats in Gal 6:12, "Those who desire to make a good showing in the flesh try to compel you to be circumcised, simply that they may not be persecuted for the cross of Christ." Clearly, the unbeliever finds the gospel message offensive, because it proclaims that sinners cannot save themselves "on the basis of deeds which we have done in righteousness" (Titus 3:5). Such a radical message offends human pride, and so the preacher needs to prepare himself for the possibility of hostile persecution because of the Word he preaches.

Abuse from Opposition

As Jesus was "spitefully treated" (*hubrizō*) by His enemies (Luke 18:32), so too should the preacher of the gospel expect there to be opponents who will spitefully treat him. This verb *hubrizō* describes the treatment of another in "an insolent or spiteful

---

1:24; Heb 2:9–10; 1 Pet 1:11; 4:13; 5:1).

6. BDAG § 2057 defines διωγμός as "a program or process designed to harass and oppress someone, persecution." The word appears in Prov 11:19; Lam 3:19; Matt 13:21; Mark 4:17; 10:30; Acts 8:1; 13:50; Rom 8:35; 2 Cor 12:10; 2 Thess 1:4; 2 Tim 3:11.

7. Ebel, "Persecution," *DNTT* 2:805.

manner,"[8] and Luke provides an illustration of such abuse directed at Paul when the opponents in Iconium attempted "to mistreat (*hubrisai*) and to stone" the apostles (Acts 14:5). Paul also reviews such abuse when he reminds the Thessalonians, "After we had already suffered and been mistreated (*hubristhentes*) in Philippi, as you know, we had the boldness in our God to speak to you the gospel of God amid much opposition" (1 Thess 2:2).[9] While the preacher should not be surprised by any abuse (*hubris*) he suffers for Christ's sake, he should learn from Paul to be content with his own weakness, but more importantly, to rely on the power of Christ dwelling in him (2 Cor 12:9–10).

Beating as Opposition

Paul's troubles became quite painful due to the numerous beatings he endured as a preacher ("beaten times without number," 2 Cor 11:23). Both his letters and the Book of Acts mention the different types of beating he endured, generally at the hands of local officials: he was "beaten with rods" (*rhabdizō*,[10] Acts 16:22; 2 Cor 11:25); wounded by blows (*derō*,[11] Acts 16:37;), and whipped with stripes (*plegē*,[12] Acts 16:23; 2 Cor 6:5; 11:23). One reason why an authority resorts to punitive beating is to use pain as a deterrent or punishment for a crime. While "spankings" have precedent in biblical parenting (Prov 22:15), when one is beaten without due process, he may appeal such injustice, as Paul does when he claimed his protective rights (Acts 16:37; 22:25). It would seem that Luke wanted to show that Paul's beatings were due to mob violence or incorrect judicial procedure (Acts 16:38) and not because of proper official adjudication. Even so, that fact would not lessen the pain for the apostle! As his Lord had been scourged (*mastigoō*; John 19:1) and had predicted scourging for his preachers (Matt 10:17; 20:19; 23:34), so Paul endured the same mistreatment—and so have many other preachers of the gospel throughout church history.

Imprisonment as Opposition

Because Paul spent an inordinate amount of time in various prisons ("in far more imprisonments,"[13] 2 Cor 11:23), it is no wonder that Luke goes to great lengths to show his readers that Paul's confinements often happened without proper judicial proceedings (Acts 25:27; 28:27). After so many incarcerations, Paul began to identify himself

---

8. BDAG § 7496.

9. Bertram, ὕβρις, *TDNT* 8:305, explains the word here as meaning, "undergoing ignominious punishment."

10. BDAG § 6462.

11. BDAG § 1783 defines δέρω as being whipped.

12. BDAG § 5986 πλήσσω, "to strike with force."

13. BDAG § 7837.3 defines φυλακή as "the place where guarding is done, prison."

as "the prisoner of Christ Jesus" (Eph 3:1).[14] He wanted his readers to know that he had been imprisoned primarily for one reason: it is for "the cause of Christ" that "his imprisonment has become well known throughout the whole praetorian guard and to everyone else, and that most of the brethren, trusting in the Lord because of my imprisonment, have far more courage to speak the word of God without fear" (Phil 1:13–14). Likewise, the modern preacher should be emboldened when he too might be imprisoned for the cause of Christ.

Tumults of Opposition

Paul is rather modest when he notes in passing that he has endured "in tumults" (*akatastasia*;[15] 2 Cor 6:5), a word describing the "disruption of the peace of the community by disputes."[16] Several times, Paul found himself embroiled in civil disturbances, such as the riots recorded in the Book of Acts.[17] These tumults are yet another type of persecution afflicted on those who hold to Christian beliefs, serving as a precaution that the preaching of the gospel may have the adverse affect of unsettling the *status quo* of civil order.

Because Paul is the prototypical example of the Christian preacher, his ministry stands like a signpost pointing to the hardship that could come from intentional opposition to the gospel. Apart from the innate rebelliousness of humanity, it is difficult to understand why anyone would want to harm the gospel preacher who offers the gift of eternal life upon faith in Christ Jesus. Even so, every preacher, like Paul, must expect the hardship of opposition that might emanate because of the faithful preaching of the gospel.

The Hardship of Impersonal Trials

As if intentional opposition is not hardship enough, the preacher is also subject to the impersonal trials that confront every believer living in a creation subjected to the futility of the fall (Rom 8:18–19). Paul uses several words to describe his trials as a preacher, including dangers (*kindunos*), troubles (*thlipsis*), trials/temptations (*peirasmos*), necessities

---

14. Paul is described as a prisoner (*desmios*) in Acts 23:18; 25:14, 27; 28:17, Eph 3:1; 4:1; 2 Tim 1:8; Phlm 1, 9. The bonds (*desmos*) of Paul are mentioned in Acts 16:26; 20:23; 23:29; 26:29, 31; Phil 1:7, 13, 14, 17; Col 4:18; 2 Tim 2:9; Phlm 1:10, 13.

15. BDAG § 254 defines ἀκαταστασία as an "unsettled state of affairs, disturbance, tumult."

16. Oepke, ἀκαταστασία, *TDNT* 3:446.

17. Acts 17:5, "But the Jews, becoming jealous and taking along some wicked men from the market place, formed a mob and set the city in an uproar;" 19:29, "And the city was filled with the confusion, and they rushed with one accord into the theater, dragging along Gaius and Aristarchus, Paul's traveling companions from Macedonia"; 21:30, "And all the city was aroused, and the people rushed together; and taking hold of Paul, they dragged him out of the temple."

(*anagkē*), and distresses (*stenochoria*). This section will briefly explore the meanings of these words and how they apply to the hardships of the preacher.

Trials of Danger

A word that serves as a bridge between intentional persecution and impersonal trials is the noun *kindunos*, usually translated "danger." While not a common word in the NT, *kindunos* describes danger or risk,[18] although Paul uses it particularly when describing the dangers that have come to him because of his preaching ministry. He finds himself "in dangers from rivers, dangers from robbers, dangers from *my* countrymen, dangers from the Gentiles, dangers in the city, dangers in the wilderness, dangers on the sea, dangers among false brethren" (2 Cor 11:26). This list is rather astounding in scope, as it mentions perils that come from widespread sources: disasters, criminals, persecutions, inclement elements, and treachery. The implication is that Paul could have avoided most, if not all of these hazards, if he was not preaching the gospel. It does seem, however, that God set Paul as an example of the worst possible scenario that could befall any preacher, because it is unlikely that any preacher since Paul has found himself at risk in all of these dangers. Even so, no preacher ought to be surprised by any such dangers that come his way because of the gospel.

Trials of Trouble

The hardships that come to the preacher originate more normally from living as a believer in a fallen world of trouble and trials; however, it seems that God places His preachers under extra pressures, as the Lord Jesus mentions that "affliction (*thlipsis*) will arise because of the word" (Matt 13:2). This word *thlipsis* carries the sense of a narrow opening;[19] thus, a squeeze, then a "trouble that inflicts distress."[20]

The Holy Spirit revealed to Paul that his future as a preacher included "bonds and afflictions (*thlipsis*)" that awaited him in every city (Acts 20:23), and such stresses actually came upon him (2 Cor 6:4). His converts in turn "received the word in much tribulation" (1 Thess 1:6), yet in so doing, they come to share in the *thlipsis* of Christ (Col 1:24); for that matter, Paul makes a special link between these troubles and his stewardship of preaching (Col 1:25). This fact stands as a correction to the notion that God grants his servants immunity from the pressures of life; if anything, it seems that God actually destines His ministers to undergo greater stresses (1 Thess 3:3),[21] no

---

18. Budd, "Danger," *DNTT* 1:419. The noun appears in Esth 4:17; Ps 114:3; Rom 8:35; and eight times in 2 Cor 11:26; and the verb κινδυνεύω appears in Eccl 10:9; Jonah 1:4; Isa 28:13; Dan 1:10; Luke 8:23; Acts 19:27, 40; 1 Cor 15:30.

19. *VGNT* § 1932.

20. BDAG § 3588 defines θλῖψις as a "pressing, pressure." See also Schlier, θλῖψις, *TDNT* 3:139.

21. In 1 Thess 3:3, Paul consoles his readers, "Let no man be disturbed by these afflictions; for you

doubt to remove from them any self-reliance and to remind them of the admonition of Paul, "Through many tribulations we must enter the kingdom of God" (Acts 14:22).

Trials of Temptation

In his address to the Ephesian elders, Paul notes that his service for the Lord has been accompanied "with many tears, and temptations (*peirasmos*), which befell me by the lying in wait of the Jews" (Acts 20:19 KJV). This appearance marks the only time in his sermons and letters that Paul uses the word *peirasmos* to describe the trials of the preacher as a "temptation."[22] This rare usage may be due to the fact that the word *peirasmos* can mean either a trial of faith or a temptation to evil,[23] and so it is not the most precise term to use for trials. Perhaps the intention of Paul's enemies was to entice him into a morally compromising situation in order to ruin his reputation. Whatever Paul explicitly means by using *peirasmos*, the preacher should expect the Tempter to entice him to sin (as Paul feared of his converts in 1 Thess 3:5) and thus be ever alert when faced with the hardship of temptations.

Trials of Deprivation

The various trials Paul encountered inevitably led to deprivation of personal necessities, and he mentions this fact with regard to his ministry. While the word "necessity" (*anagkē*) can mean a calamitous distress, it also carries the idea of basic needs, such as food and shelter.[24] It is difficult to ascertain which meaning Paul intends when he states that he was often in *anagkais* (2 Cor 6:4). Whatever Paul faced, he had learned to be "well content with distresses," because through his losses, he was driven to depend on Christ to meet his necessities (2 Cor 12:10). By using the similar word *hustereō*, Paul writes that he had suffered need (*hustereō*)—probably referring to hunger (Phil 4:12),[25] but such lack drove him to greater trust in God and harder work to meet his needs (2 Cor 11:9). Accordingly, the preacher ought not to be surprised if he finds himself in need, not because of his foolishness, but because he is under compulsion (*anagkē*) to preach the gospel (1 Cor 9:16).

---

yourselves know that we have been destined for this."

22. Schneider, "Tempt," *DNTT* 3:799.

23. BDAG § 5761 defines πειρασμός, first, as "an attempt to learn the nature or character of something;" and secondly, as "an attempt to make one do something wrong."

24. BDAG § 456 defines ἀνάγκη,
   1. "necessity;
   2. a state of distress or trouble; and
   3. compulsion by forcible means, *torture* (2 Cor 6:4; 12:10; 1 Thess 3:7).

25. BDAG § 7659 defines ὑστερέω in Phil 4:12 as experiencing deficiency.

Trials of Distresses

A similar word found in Paul's list of difficulties is *stenochoria*, a word meaning "narrowness of room," as if being caged in.[26] What comes to mind is the confinement of a small prison cell, which Paul had much time to experience, but it appears that he uses the word figuratively to describe the confining circumstances that thwarted his ministry. Perhaps a better example of constricting distresses would be the hindrances that Satan used to impede Paul's preaching (1 Thess 2:18).

The hardships that Timothy endured included these sorts of impersonal dangers, troubles, temptations, necessities and distresses that might be ordinarily labeled "bad luck." However, Paul's understanding of divine providence would not permit him to countenance any idea of impersonal luck, good or bad. He believed that his circumstances "turned out for the greater progress of the gospel" (Phil 1:12), even if that meant he was being squeezed under crushing pressures. Accordingly, the preacher must view the impersonal difficulties of everyday life as God's appointed means of advancing the preaching of the Word.

The Hardship of Personal Weaknesses

Paul readily admitted that his greatest hardship was his own inclination to sinful weakness—his frustration over indwelling sin is well documented in Romans 7. In his list of difficulties (2 Cor 6:4–5), Paul mentions several personal weaknesses, some that are physical, but others include the defects of his fallen nature. Such flaws are shared by every preacher of the gospel.

Circumstantial Weakness

The opposition and trials Paul encountered caused him to suffer severe physical deprivations. He mentions experiences of hunger (2 Cor 6:5; 11:27), and although the word *nēsteia* can imply voluntary fasting (as in Acts 14:23), the context in these lists of hardships suggests that he refers to hunger brought about by necessity.[27] This indication is verified when the apostle notes that he was also in famine (*limos*).[28] Thirst (*dipsos*) also had been Paul's lot (1 Cor 11:27), as had "many sleepless nights" (2 Cor 11:27; 6:5). Perhaps his most poignant admission of circumstantial weakness is found in 1 Cor 4:11, "To this present hour we are both hungry and thirsty, and are poorly clothed, and are roughly treated, and are homeless."

---

26. BDAG § 6812 defines στενοχωρία in "the literal sense, 'narrowness', fig. a set of stressful circumstances" (Rom 8:35; 2 Cor 6:4; 2 Cor 12:10).
27. BDAG § 5093.
28. BDAG § 4584.

Few western preachers can identify with Paul's plight, although preachers in many developing nations have experienced such personal destitution that was incurred by loyalty to the gospel. Such reality ought to serve as a sober reminder that the material blessings enjoyed by the American preacher are highly unusual and are not the expected norm!

Physical Weaknesses

It is interesting that a man who possessed the gift of healing frequently mentions his own physical weaknesses. Paul often refers to weakness, using the word *astheneia* as referring to "a state of debilitating illness,"[29] and plainly Paul uses it in that manner when he describes his own physical condition. For example, he reminds the Galatians that he preached to them the first time "because of a bodily illness" (Gal 4:13, *di' astheneian tēs sarkos*), which may have been an inflammation of his eyes, because he notes that his readers would have "plucked out your eyes and given them to me" (Gal 4:15). His detractors objected that Paul's letters were weighty and strong, but "his physical presence is weak and his speech is of no account." (2 Cor 10:10 NET)

Paul's evaluation of his physical weaknesses stands as a rebuke to the modern preacher, particularly when the apostle mentions that his weakness became the occasion for the preaching of the gospel: he preached to the Galatians "because of weakness" (*di' artheneian*), whereas the modern preacher might view his illness as an excuse not to preach! Similarly, when the Lord declined to rid Paul of his thorn in the flesh, Paul concludes, "Most gladly, therefore, I will rather boast about my weaknesses, that the power of Christ may dwell in me. Therefore I am well content with weaknesses . . . for Christ's sake; for when I am weak, then I am strong" (2 Cor 12:9–10). Likewise, the preacher needs to view his physical weaknesses as proving that the treasure of the gospel comes in earthen vessels (2 Cor 4:7).

Summary to the Preacher's Hardship

This chapter has examined the various difficulties that the preacher might encounter when he proclaims the gospel, hardships that comes from opposition, trials, and weaknesses. It might seem rather strange that one who serves the King of kings should receive such miserable treatment, but the preacher must remember that all these hardships were also faced by the King Himself ("He was crucified because of weakness," 2 Cor 13:4). It is in light of Christ's sufferings that Timothy—and every preacher—needs to take to heart Paul's command, "Endure hardship!"

---

29. BDAG § 1181.1.

CHAPTER 13

The Preacher's Work: "Do Work"

"Do Work," commands Paul to Timothy, specifying it as the work of an evangelist (2 Tim 4:5c); however, this imperative phrase, *ergon poiēson*, stands as a pointed reminder to the preacher that his task is that of active labor—even the word order emphasizes that fact, as Paul actually writes, "Work do!"

Besides using these two words, "working" (*ergazomai*) and "doing" (*poieō*), both Paul and Luke employ a plethora of similar verbs to describe the work of the preacher, including practicing (*prassō*), laboring (*kopiaō*), slaving (*douleuō*), serving (*diakoneō*), ministering (*hupereteō* and *leitourgeō*), striving (*sunathleō*), agonizing (*agonizomai*), building (*oikodomeō*), and soldiering (*strateuō*). The task of this chapter is to explore these concepts picturing how the preacher is charged to "Do work!"

As a Worker Working the Work (*ergatēs ergazetai to ergon*)

The preacher is to do the work (*ergon*[1]) of an evangelist because he is elsewhere described as a "worker" (*ergatēs*;[2] 1 Tim 5:18; 2 Tim 2:15; also Luke 10:2) whose task it is that he may "work the work of the Lord" (*to ergon kuriou ergazetai*;[3] 1 Cor 16:10). The Holy Spirit called Paul to a particular work (*ergon*, Acts 13:2), and the apostle calls his converts his "work (*ergon*) in the Lord" (1 Cor 9:1), because he knows that the risen Lord "gave . . . teachers for the equipping of the saints for the work (*ergon*) of service" (Eph 4:11–12).

Because Paul repudiates what he calls "works (*ergōn*) of law" as a means of obtaining righteousness (Rom 3:28),[4] one might find it surprising that he often places

---

1. L&N § 42.11 defines ἔργον as "that which is done, with possible focus on the energy or effort involved."

2. BDAG § 3109.1 defines ἐργάτης as "one who is engaged in work, worker, laborer."

3. BDAG § 3105.1 defines ἐργάζομαι as meaning, "to engage in activity that involves effort." Paul uses this verb at Rom 2:10; 4:4, 5; 13:10; 1 Cor 4:12; 9:6, 13; 16:10; 2 Cor 7:10; Gal 6:10; Eph 4:28; Col 3:23; 1 Thess 2:9; 4:11; 2 Thess 3:8, 10, 11, 12.

4. Paul uses the phrase "works of law" (ἔργων νόμου) in Rom 3:20 (twice), 27, 28; Gal 2:16 (thrice);

positive emphasis on "good works" as activities commanded by God's Word.[5] As a matter of fact, Paul never disparages works done out of faith and motivated by a desire to please God; especially, the labor of teaching the inspired Scripture is one such good work (2 Tim 3:16–17).

For that matter, preaching the Word is described as a "work," not only here in 2 Tim 4:5, but also in Rom 15:18, where Paul links his own speaking efforts with the pneumatic inworking of Christ, as he announces, "I will not presume to speak of anything except what Christ has accomplished (*kateirgasatō*) through me, resulting in the obedience of the Gentiles by word and deed (*ergo*)." As a workman (*ergatēs*), Timothy is to handle accurately the tool of his trade, the Word of the truth (2 Tim 2:15), because working and preaching are viewed as inseparable tasks, as Paul reminds the Thessalonians, "You recall, brethren, our labor and hardship, how working (*ergazomenoi*) night and day so as not to be a burden to any of you, we proclaimed to you the gospel of God" (1 Thess 2:9).

The fact that Paul describes preaching as a work ought to remove the popular notion that preachers "only work one day a week," a label that at times has been sadly deserved. Instead, the work of the Lord is a hard but necessary aspect of proclaiming the gospel, although the preacher, as a laborer in the Lord, should take courage in the thought that he can expect to fulfill his *ergon* only through the grace of God by which he has been divinely commended (Acts 14:26).

The Preacher's Work Relationship with Co-workers

Furthermore, the minister does not work alone: Paul names many of his co-workers, or "fellow workers" (*sunergoi*),[6] and he even describes all ministers as "all the ones working-together" (*panti tō sunergounti*, 1 Cor 16:16 AT), probably because he cannot conceive of a single person working alone at such a great task. The apostle uses the rather rare verb *sunergeō* to capture the idea of other believers working together

---

3:2, 5; and 10.

5. Paul uses "works" in a favorable sense in Acts 26:20; Rom 2:7; 13:3; 15:18; 1 Cor 3:13; 9:1; 15:58; 2 Cor 9:8; Gal 6:4; Eph 2:10; 4:12; Phil 1:22; Col 1:10; 3:17; 1 Thess 1:3; 5:13; 2 Thess 1:11; 2:17; 1 Tim 2:10; 3:1; 5:10, 25; 6:18; 2 Tim 2:21; 3:17; 4:5; Titus 1:16; 2:7, 14; 3:1, 8, 14). See Stout, "The Pauline Concept of Ethical *Erga*."

6. The noun συνεργός is a compound of the preposition σύν (BDAG § 7006, "a marker of accompaniment and association," generally translated "with") and the noun ἔργον (BDAG § 3110, as that "which displays itself in activity of any kind, deed"), thus meaning someone with whom another works, or a co-worker. The word is usually translated by "fellow-worker," and those who Paul describes as his fellow-workers (*sunergoi*) include Prisca and Aquila, "my fellow workers in Christ Jesus" (Rom 16:3); "Urbanus, our fellow-worker in Christ"(Rom 16:9); "Timothy my fellow-worker" (Rom 16:21; 1 Thess 3:2); Titus, my partner and fellow-worker" (2 Cor 8:23); Epaphroditus, "my brother and fellow-worker and fellow soldier" (Phil 2:25); Aristarchus, Barnabas' cousin Mark and Jesus who is called Justus (Col 4:11); Philemon "our fellow-worker" (Phlm 1:1); "Mark, Aristarchus, Demas, Luke, my fellow workers" (Phlm 1:24).

(1 Cor 16:16),[7] especially in the effort of others "joining in helping (*sunupourgeō*) us through your prayers" (2 Cor 1:11). Even more amazing is Paul's description of ministers as "fellow workers of God" (1 Cor 3:9), so that when preachers urge others "not to receive the grace of God in vain," God Himself actively works (*sunergountes*) with them in the work of preaching (2 Cor 6:1).

The Preacher's Work Relationship with Fellow-Elders

The NT indicates that the work of ministry in each congregation should be conducted by a plurality of elders, a *presbuterion* (1 Tim 4:14[8]), a corporate body of leaders who are responsible for the rule of the church.[9] This plurality is evidenced when Paul ordained "elders in each church" (Acts 14:23) and when he directed Titus "to appoint elders in every city" (Titus 1:5). The Jerusalem Synod was attended by "the apostles and elders" (Acts 15:2, 4, 6, 22, 23; 16:4), who jointly decided on a crucial doctrinal matter. When Paul was later hastening on to Jerusalem, he sent word to Ephesus and called to him— not a singular pastor, but "the elders of the church" (Acts 20:17), and upon arriving at his destination, Paul met with James "and all the elders were present. And after he had greeted them, he *began* to relate one by one the things which God had done among the Gentiles through his ministry" (Acts 21:18–19). When Paul writes to the Philippian congregation, he addresses his letter to "all the saints in Christ Jesus who are in Philippi, including the [body of] overseers and deacons" (Phil 1:1). In addition to Paul's writings, James instructs anyone who is sick to "call for the elders of the church, and let them pray over him, anointing him with oil in the name of the Lord" (Jas 5:14), and Peter, who identifies himself as a "co-elder (*sumpresbuteros*)," exhorts his fellow elders to shepherd the flock of God (1 Peter 5:1–2) and calls on younger men to "be subject to your elders" (1 Pet 5:5). For that matter, the noun *presbuteros* rarely appears in the singular form (in the NT, only in 1 Tim 5:17, 19; 2 John 1; 3 John 1); otherwise, its focus is usually on a plurality of elders who are ministering together.

In the historical development of Presbyterian church polity, the *presbuterion* (1 Tim 4:14) became the regional court of "Teaching and Ruling Elders" that represented congregations in a specified area (based on the model of the Jerusalem Synod); however, it is likely that the *presbuterion* of 1 Tim 4:14 is the original court of jurisdiction, or what is often called the session or consistory of the congregation. Regardless of which title is used, any gathering of elders, whether local or regional, consists of a *presbuterion*. The NT prefers another word for the largest (or highest) court of elders,

---

7. BDAG § 7071 defines συνεργέω to engage in cooperative endeavor. This verb appears only in Mark 16:20; Rom 8:28; 1 Cor 16:16; 2 Cor 6:1; Jas 2:22.

8. 1 Timothy 4:14, "Do not neglect the spiritual gift within you, which was bestowed upon you through prophetic utterance with the laying on of hands by the presbytery."

9. With all due deference to those denominations who title their officers as Trustees, Stewards, Deacons, or some other designation besides Elders, the point of agreement between each body is that the church should be governed by a body of leaders rather than just by one person.

sunedrion,[10] which is always used in the Gospels to describe the Jewish Sanhedrin (Matt 5:22; 10:17; 26:59; Mark 13:9; 14:55; 15:1; Luke 22:66; John 11:47). Because the Sanhedrin had unjustly condemned Jesus, the apostles avoided describing their own synods with that term, although the gathering of the apostles and elders in Jerusalem certainly would qualify as a biblical Synod. This gathering lends biblical warrant for elders from a larger region to "come together to look into the matter" (Acts 15:6) and decide on issues affecting the church at large (Acts 15:23–29).

So what is the relationship among elders in a particular congregation? When Paul writes in 1 Timothy 5:17 that some elders who "rule well" should be considered worthy of "double honor," he is not conferring upon one group of elders an exalted status above other elders but rather he is referring to remuneration for the work they perform. This meaning is confirmed in the following verse (1 Tim 5:18), where Paul alludes to Jesus' teaching now recorded in Luke 10:17, "The laborer is worthy of his wages."[11] Elders who may be paid for their labors are described as those who "work hard at preaching and teaching" (1 Tim 5:17), and from this distinction between "elders who rule well" and elders who especially work hard at preaching and teaching derives the distinction between ruling elders and teaching elders. Though the titles of ruling and teaching may be somewhat misleading because all elders fundamentally rule and teach by virtue of the office they hold, 1 Tim 5:17 implies that some elders are more gifted in the areas of teaching and preaching; therefore, they should be paid for their service to the church. This verse also suggests that the teaching elder may consider his duties of ruling, preaching, and teaching to be a "fulltime" vocation while serving his congregation.

Because one elder may be more apt in teaching than in ruling (or *vice versa*), this observation may help to determine the relationships elders share among each other. For example, Paul mentions the "three pillars" of the church in Jerusalem, James, Cephas (Peter) and John (Gal 2:9), and the name that appears rather unexpectantly is James, "the Lord's brother" (Gal 1:19), because he was not one of the original Twelve apostles as were the other two men. Yet, not long after Peter founded the church at Pentecost, when he was miraculously delivered from certain execution, he tells the startled prayer meeting to report his rescue "to James and the brethren" (Acts 12:17). One must wonder if Peter singles out James from the other leaders because the Lord's brother was already recognized as the presiding elder of the church, or what is called today the "senior pastor." Support for this view is bolstered when this same James summarizes the final arguments of the Jerusalem Synod (Acts 15:13), and when

---

10. BDAG § 7050 notes that συνέδριον is a combined word of the preposition σύν and ἕδρα 'a seat' of leaders who then "sit together" in judgment; thus, a governing board or council.

11. 1 Timothy 5:17–18, "Let the elders who rule well be considered worthy of double honor, especially those who work hard at preaching and teaching. For the Scripture says, 'You shall not muzzle the ox while he is threshing,' and 'The laborer is worthy of his wages.'"

Paul first reports "to James, and all the elders" upon his arrival in Jerusalem some years later (Acts 21:18).

In James then we see the beginnings of the proto-pastor as the presiding elder of a local *presbyterion*. In such a case, the designation, "Teaching Elder," has some biblical merit to describe a pastor as one of the elders who "works hard at teaching and preaching" (1 Tim 5:17). This recognition of leadership within the body of elders should not be viewed an office of higher status, and the one who occupies the presiding chair should remind himself that he is a fellow elder (*sumpresbuteros*) among the other elders, as even the apostle Peter describes himself (1 Pet 5:1).

Neither does Paul flout his apostolic authority when addressing other elders, as he reminded the Corinthians, "Not that we lord it over your faith, but we are workers with you for your joy; for in your faith you are standing firm" (2 Cor 1:24). In his address to the Ephesian elders, not once does Paul "pull rank" as an apostle in his reminders of his ministry among them—he speaks as an equal among equals. When it comes to describing his colleagues in ministry, Paul's favorite term is "co-worker." He credits a wide host of personalities as his *sunergoi*, including Prisca and Aquila, "my co-workers in Christ Jesus" (Rom 16:3); "Urbanus, our co-worker in Christ" (Rom 16:9); Titus, "my partner and co-worker" (2 Cor 8:23); Epaphroditus, "my brother and co-worker and co-soldier" (Phil 2:25); Aristarchus, Barnabas' cousin Mark and Jesus who is called Justus, "the only co-workers for the kingdom of God from the circumcision" (Col 4:11); Philemon "our co-worker" (Phlm 1:1); and Mark, Aristarchus, Demas, Luke, "my co-workers" (Phlm 1:24). The colleague mentioned most often is Timothy,[12] whom he singles out as "my co-worker in the gospel of Christ" (1 Thess 3:2). Paul not only recognized these workers as having equal ministry with him, but he actively sought to involve them in his own labors. Paul was not a ministerial loner—his apparent failure to establish a church in Athens may have been due to a lack of co-laborers to develop his initial evangelistic efforts (Acts 17:34), as his account in 1 Thessalonians 3 hints.

It is in the best interest of the preacher to surround himself with fellow elders who will share the ministry together as "fellow workers for the kingdom of God" (Col 4:11). Those honored as Teaching Elders need to impress this joint concept upon the Ruling Elders, so that the entire *presbuterion* will minister more effectively in both areas of teaching and ruling the congregation. A more experienced pastor should cultivate relationships with those whom Paul describes as "faithful men" in order to disciple them to teach others also (2 Tim 2:2) so they will—like Timothy of Paul—follow the "teaching, conduct, purpose, faith, patience, love, perseverance, persecutions, *and* sufferings" of the senior pastor (2 Tim 3:10–11). Such men will join together as "God's co-workers" (*theoū sunergoi*, 1 Cor 3:9) as they work together with Him (*sunergeō*) in urging others to receive the grace of God (2 Cor 6:1).

---

12. Paul mentions Timothy in Rom 16:21; 1 Cor 4:17; 16:10; 2 Cor 1:1, 19; Phil 1:1; 2:19; Col 1:1; 1 Thess 1:1; 3:2, 6; 2 Thess 1:1; 1 Tim 1:2, 18; 6:20; 2 Tim 1:2; Phlm 1:1.

Summary

In sum, the preacher needs to cultivate relationships with those who are his fellow workers so that together they may "steadfast, immovable, always abounding in the work of the Lord, knowing that [our] toil is not *in* vain in the Lord" (1 Cor 15:58). In his task as a worker with God, the preacher should exert all his energies to the work of preaching if he is to fulfill the command to "do work" (2 Tim 4:5)

As One Doing is Doing: *Ho Poiōn Poieī*

Although the word *poieō* is one of the most common verbs in the NT (*BibleWorks9* lists it 568 times), it is also one of the blandest in describing mere activity.[13] While *poieō* may carry ethical connotations ("Let us not lose heart in doing good," Gal 6:9), there are so many other words available that describe the work of preaching that it is not surprising that Paul rarely uses *poieō* in such contexts.

Other than commanding Timothy to "do (*poiēson*) the work of an evangelist" (2 Tim 4:5), Paul instructs him to pay attention to his doctrine, for "as you do (*poiōn*) this you will insure salvation both for yourself and for those who hear you" (1 Tim 4:16). However inexact may be this "doing" of the gospel (which would no doubt include preaching), it is stated as an imperative that ought to be done. So then, regardless of how imprecisely Paul uses the verb *poieō* in his letters, he finds good use for it when he states, "I do (*poiō*) all things for the sake of the gospel, that I may become a fellow partaker of it" (1 Cor 9:23). This assertion shows that all the conduct of the preacher must be controlled by his message—his "doing" (conduct) and his "becoming" (motives) are to meld into the one work of the gospel. He is to be one who is doing the gospel.

As One Practicing is Practicing: *Ho Prassōn Prassei*

The Greek verb *prassō* has come over into English in the noun "practice," a word that carries the idea of development and repetition, and so it became a good word to describe the ongoing practice of preaching.[14] Generally speaking, however, the NT uses the verb *prassō* in a pejorative sense of doing of evil works;[15] nevertheless, the verb

---

13. BDAG § 6015 describes ποιέω as a "multivalent term, often without pointed semantic significance, used in ref. to a broad range of activity." Paul uses the verb 83 times, in Rom 1:9, 28, 32; 2:3, 14; 3:8, 12; 4:21; 7:15, 16, 19, 20, 21; 9:20, 21, 28; 10:5; 12:20; 13:3, 4, 14; 15:26; 16:17; 1 Cor 6:15, 18; 7:36, 37, 38; 9:23; 10:13, 31; 11:24, 25; 15:29; 16:1; 2 Cor 5:21; 8:10, 11; 11:7, 12, 25; 13:7; Gal 2:10; 3:10, 12; 5:3, 17; 6:9; Eph 1:16; 2:3, 14, 15; 3:11, 20; 4:16; 6:6, 8, 9; Phil 1:4; 2:14; 4:14; Col 3:17, 23; 4:16; 1 Thess 1:2; 4:10; 5:11, 24; 2 Thess 3:4; 1 Tim 1:13; 2:1; 4:16; 5:21; 2 Tim 4:5; Titus 3:5; Phlm 1:4, 14, 21.

14. Schrenckenberg, πράσσω, *TDNT* 6:632, defines *prassō* as "an activity or industry directed to a specific goal."

15. Of the eighteen times Paul uses *prassō*, twelve usages have negative connotations (Rom 1:32, 32; 2:1, 2, 3, 25; 7:15, 19; 13:4; 1 Cor 5:2; 2 Cor 12:21; Gal 5:21), twice he uses it of doing good or evil (Rom 9:11; 2 Cor 5:10), and only three times does he use it of practicing something good (Eph 6:21;

itself does not necessarily imply doing bad deeds, because Acts 26:20 quotes Paul as declaring in his preaching that his listeners "should repent and turn to God, performing (*prassontas*) deeds appropriate to repentance."

Paul actually uses *prassō* once in a context clearly dealing with preaching: when he refers to the stewardship of preaching the gospel, he states, "If I do (*prassō*) this voluntarily, I have a reward" (1 Cor 9:16–17). Paul could have chosen other verbs, but perhaps he selected *prassō* because of the unlikely connection between obligatory practice ("I have to do this") and voluntary willingness ("I want to do this."). Preaching is a work that the preacher should perform voluntarily, but if not, then he must practice it habitually because of the divine stewardship entrusted to him. Whether the preacher preaches the gospel voluntarily or is paid to do so, believers should heed all the things "learned, received, heard and had seen" in the preacher—including preaching—and then practice those things (Phil 4:9).

As a Laborer is Laboring at Labor: *Ho Kopon Kopizei Kopos*

Not only does the gospel ministry consist of doing and practicing, but it is also a "laboring at a labor," as Paul often uses the words *koptō* and *kopos* to define his ministry.[16] The noun *kopos* is related to *koptein* (κόπτειν), a beating,[17] but eventually it came to mean any activity that leads one to exertion, toil, pain, and hardship, as Paul notes that his ministry put him "in far more labors" (1 Cor 11:23).[18] *Kopos* pictures the preacher as an everyday laborer, wearied by the burden of hard labor, and so it becomes a striking reminder of the difficulties that ministering involves.[19]

For example, Paul often compares his work of ministry to a labor (Phil 2:16; 1 Thess 2:9; 3:5), and He describes church leaders as "all the ones laboring" (*panti tō . . . kopiōti*, 1 Cor 16:16) and as those who are "laboring diligently among you" (*tous kopiōnta en humin*, 1 Thess 5:12). Elders who rule well are those who are especially "the ones laboring (*hoi kopiōntes*) among you in word and teaching" (1 Tim 5:17). Because the preacher is called to labor hard in exhortation (1 Thess 5:12), his toil must of necessity involve intense study of Scripture, followed by tireless endeavors to

---

Phil 4:9; 1 Thess 4:11).

16. BDAG § 4347 defines κόπος as an "activity that is burdensome." The noun appears eighteen times in the NT (Matt 26:10; Mark 14:6; Luke 11:7; 18:5; John 4:38; 1 Cor 3:8; 15:58; 2 Cor 6:5; 10:15; 11:23, 27; Gal 6:17; 1 Thess 1:3; 2:9; 3:5; 2 Thess 3:8; Rev 2:2; 14:13). BDAG § 4346 defines κοπιάω as 1. to "become weary/tired" (citing Matt 11:28; John 4:6; Rev 2:3); and 2. "to exert oneself physically, mentally, or spiritually, work hard, toil, strive, struggle" (citing Matt 6:28; Luke 5:5; 12:27; John 4:38; Acts 20:35; Rom 16:6, 12; 1 Cor 4:12; 15:10; 16:16; Gal 4:11; Eph 4:28; Phil 2:16; Col 1:29; 1 Thess 5:12; 1 Tim 4:10; 5:17; 2 Tim 2:6).

17. Thayer, *Lexicon*, §3043.

18. Seitz, "Burden," *DNTT* 1:262.

19. The concept of Christian laboring is found at Acts 20:35; Rom 16:6, 12; 1 Cor 4:12; 15:10; 58, 16:16; 2 Cor 6:5; 10:13; 11:23, 27; Gal 4:11; Phil 2:16; Col 1:29; 1 Thess 1:3; 2:9; 3:5; 5;12; 2 Thess 3:8; 1 Tim 4:10; 5:17; 2 Tim 2:6; Heb 6:10; Rev 2:2-3; 14:13.

proclaim the doctrines of the gospel. While the preacher may deem it undignified to compare himself to a manual laborer who works hard with his hands day and night, that is precisely how Paul describes his labors in the gospel ministry (Acts 20:34–35; also 1 Cor 4:12 and 2 Thess 3:8[20]). He even reminds Timothy that a model for ministry is the toiling of a hard-working farmer (2 Tim 2:6).

Because the first elders provided for their own needs, a fully salaried minister was probably quite rare in the apostolic days; however, Paul cites the Lord's direction that "those who proclaim the gospel . . . get their living from the gospel" (1 Cor 9:14), referring to Jesus' teaching now recorded in Luke 10:7, "The laborer is worthy of his wages." Paul actually quotes this saying in 1 Tim 5:18 where he gives Scriptural support for granting "double-honor"—remuneration—to hard-working elders.[21] While Paul supported himself by tent-making (Acts 18:3), he viewed his labor as only a means to an end—his purpose in laboring was not to make a profit but to show others that by working hard that they should help the weak (Acts 20:35)

Another noun used in tandem with *kopos* is *mochthos*, which more precisely refers to hard physical labor.[22] Paul uses the term three times, each in connection with the toil that accompanies ministry ("our labor and hardship"), as if emphasizing the difficulties that accompany the labor of the gospel ministry.[23]

These descriptions of the ministry as both a *kopos* and a *mochthos* indicate that preaching can be extremely tedious. How important then is Paul's statement. "I labor (*kopiō*), striving according to His power which works mightily in me" (Col 1:29). The strength for laboring comes from the grace of God ("I labored even more than all of them, yet not I, but the grace of God with me," 1 Cor 15:10), so the preacher needs to view himself as a laborer who must draw his strength from the One for whom he labors. Only then can he be assured that his "labor is not in vain in the Lord" (1 Cor 15:58).

---

20. Acts 20:34–35; "You yourselves know that these hands ministered to my *own* needs and to the men who were with me. In everything I showed you that by working hard (κοπιῶντας) in this manner you must help the weak and remember the words of the Lord Jesus, that He Himself said, 'It is more blessed to give than to receive'"; also 1 Cor 4:12, "We toil (κοπιῶμεν), working with our own hands"; and 2 Thess 3:8, "nor did we eat anyone's bread without paying for it, but with labor and hardship we *kept* working night and day so that we might not be a burden to any of you."

21. 1 Timothy 5:17–18, "Let the elders who rule well be considered worthy of double honor, especially those who work hard (οἱ κοπιῶντες) at preaching and teaching. For the Scripture says, "You shall not muzzle the ox while he is threshing," and, "The laborer is worthy of his wages."

22. L&N § 42.48 defines μόχθος as "hard work, implying unusual exertion of energy and effort."

23. The three occurrences of "labor and toil" appears as follows: "*I have been* in labor and hardship" (κόπῳ καὶ μόχθῳ, 2 Cor 11:27); "For you recall, brethren, our labor and hardship (τὸν κόπον ἡμῶν καὶ τὸν μόχθον), *how* working night and day so as not to be a burden to any of you, we proclaimed to you the gospel of God" (1 Thess 2:9); "with labor and hardship (ἐν κόπῳ καὶ μόχθῳ) we *kept* working night and day so that we might not be a burden to any of you" (2 Thess 3:8).

As a Servant is Serving the Service: *Diakonos Diakonei Diakonia*

Although one of the most common titles Paul assumes for himself is that of a minister (*diakonos*),[24] one who is involved in ministry (*diakonia*),[25] he apparently never uses the related verb *diakoneō* to describe preaching.[26] The reason is not hard to find, because *diakoneō* more properly applies to practical deeds such as waiting on tables (Acts 6:2) rather than to the preaching of the gospel;[27] thus, Paul uses *diakoneō* to describe the financial project he administered for the poor of Jerusalem (Rom 15:25–26; 2 Cor 8:19–20).

However, a Lukan reference to preaching as a ministry appears in Acts 6:4, where the apostles insist they must devote themselves "to prayer and to the ministry (*diakonia*) of the Word." In like manner, Paul uses the noun *diakonia* in contexts indicating that the primary duty of the minister (*diakonos*) concerns his application of the Word of God for the benefit of the church; for example, the *diakonos* is to be "nourished on the words of the faith and sound doctrine" (1 Tim 4:6); likewise, Paul was "made a *diakonos* . . . to preach to the Gentiles the unfathomable riches of Christ" (Eph 3:8), to proclaim "the hope of the gospel" (Col 1:23), and to "fully carry out the *preaching of the word of God*" (Col 1:25). These connections between Paul as a preacher and as a *diakonos* make the relationship to the Word of God patently obvious—a servant is to obey the word of his master and tell other servants to do so also.

The final chapter of this study will explore in further detail Paul's concept of ministry, because he concludes his challenge to Timothy with a charge to "fulfill your ministry" (2 Tim 4:5). A ministry requires a minister, so as a *diakonos*, the leader focuses on serving duties, and so the title applies more properly to those who "serve as deacons" (1 Tim 3:10, 13), but it is certainly not improper to liken preaching to ministering the Word. Paul links the ideas of ministry and preaching in Acts 20:24, when he tells the elders, "I do not consider my life of any account as dear to myself, in order that I may finish my course, and the ministry (*diakonia*) which I received from the Lord Jesus, to testify solemnly of the gospel of the grace of God." This connection shows that a significant part of the preacher's work is to be a servant who serves in the service of the gospel of "the Son of Man, who came not to be served, but to serve and to give His life as a ransom for many" (Mark 10:45).

---

24. BDAG § 1858 describes διάκονος as "gener. one who is busy with someth. in a manner that is of assistance to someone." Paul uses *diakonos* twenty-one times (Rom 13:4, 4; 15:8; 16:1; 1 Cor 3:5; 2 Cor 3:6; 6:4; 11:15, 15; 23; Gal 2:17; Eph 3:7; 6:21; Phil 1:1; Col 1:7, 23, 25; 4:7; 1 Tim 3:8, 12; 4:6).

25. BDAG § 1857 defines διακονία broadly as "service." Paul uses the word twenty-three times (Rom 11:13; 12:7; 15:31; 1 Cor 12:5; 16:15; 2 Cor 3:7, 8, 9; 4:1; 5:18; 6:3; 8:4; 9:1, 12, 13; 11:8; Eph 4:12; Col 4:17; 1 Tim 1:12; 2 Tim 4:5, 11).

26. BDAG § 1856 defines διακονέω, "generally to render service in a variety of ways either at someone's behest or voluntarily and freq. with suggestion of movement." Paul uses *diakoneō* only eight times (Rom 15:25; 2 Cor 3:3; 8:19, 20; 1 Tim 3:10, 13; 2 Tim 1:18; Phlm 1:13).

27. Thayer, *Lexicon* § 1313 compares διακονέω to "the Latin *ministrare*, to wait at table and offer food and drink to the guests." See also Hess, "Serve," *DNTT* 3:545.

As a Slave is Slaving: *Doulos Douleuei*

The preacher is also described as a *doulos*,[28] a slave who is to be "slaving" (*douleuō*) for the Lord.[29] Because the concept of slavery is quite offensive to modern sensibilities, most English versions temper (or tamper with!) the idea by translating *doulos douleuei* as a "servant serving" in favorable contexts (such as Rom 7:6, "We serve in newness of the Spirit.") and as a "slave slaving" in less favorable contexts (as in Titus 3:3, "We were once enslaved to various lusts."). However, there is no escaping the cultural practice of slavery that lies behind the biblical allusions, in that *doulos* appears often in the LXX as a translation of the Hebrew word *ebed*, which may describe either a servant or a slave,[30] although the Torah distinguishes between the status of the two positions ("If a countryman of yours becomes so poor with regard to you that he sells himself to you, you shall not subject him to a slave's service," Lev 25:39). Because God has purchased His church with a ransom price (Acts 20:28; Rev 5:9), the believer is, at the most basic level, a slave of God; however, what may well lie behind the idea of being a "servant of the Lord" (Jos 24:30; Jdg 2:8; 2 Kgs 18:12; Jonah 1:9) is the OT concept of the bond-servant, a man who is liberated by his master but then voluntarily chooses to serve his lord.[31]

Regardless of its derivation, a *doulos* describes someone who is under the authority of a lord (*kurios*), in the manner expressed by the centurion, "I say to my *doulos*, 'Do this, and he does it'" (Matt 8:9–10). Jesus not only commends this obedient soldier for his "great faith," but He frequently applies this *doulos/kurios* comparison to His followers: "A disciple is not above his teacher, nor a slave (*doulos*) above his master" (*kurios*; Matt 10:24); "Blessed is that slave (*doulos*) whom his master (*kurios*) finds so doing when he comes" (Matt 24:46); and, "His master (*kurios*) said to him, 'Well done, good and faithful slave" (*doulos*; Matt 25:23). Jesus modified this relationship between slave and master considerably by telling his disciples at the Last Supper, "No longer do I call you slaves (*doulos*), for the slave does not know what his master (*kurios*) is doing; but I have called you friends" (John 15:15). Even so, the apostles applied the title of *doulos* of themselves (Acts 4:29), and it even became a common designation Paul used of himself as a "bond-servant of Christ" (Rom 1:1; 2 Cor 4:2; Gal 1:10; Phil 1:1; Titus

---

28. Thayer, *Lexicon*, § 1476, notes that δοῦλος is "derived by most from δέω, to tie, bind; thus, a slave, bondman, man of servile condition." The minister is designated as *doulos* in Acts 4:29; 16:17; Rom 1:1; 2 Cor 4:5; Gal 1:10; Phil 1:1; Col 4:12; 2 Tim 2:24; Titus 1:1; James 1:1; 2 Pet 1:1; Jude 1; Rev 10:7; 15:3.

29. L&N § 35.27 defines δουλεύω, "to serve, normally in a humble manner and in response to the demands or commands of others," although L&N § 87.79 defines δουλεύω more basically, "to be a slave of someone."

30. BDB § 6712 defines עֶבֶד as either "slave, servant."

31. The law of the bond-servant is found in Exod 21:2–6, "If you buy a Hebrew slave, he shall serve for six years; but on the seventh he shall go out as a free man without payment. . . . But if the slave plainly says, 'I love my master, my wife and my children; I will not go out as a free man,' 6 then his master shall bring him to God, then he shall bring him to the door or the doorpost. And his master shall pierce his ear with an awl; and he shall serve (δουλεύσει) him permanently."

1:1). In like manner, the believer is "slaving to the Lord" (Rom 12:11). In particular, the preacher "slaves" under the authority of Christ as his *Kurios* so that he asserts with Paul, "We do not preach ourselves but Christ Jesus as Lord (*kurios*), and ourselves as your bond-servants (*doulous*) for Jesus' sake" (2 Cor 4:5).

Paul associates the verb *douleuō* with preaching in his address to the Ephesian elders when he reminds them that "from the first day that I set foot in Asia, how I was with you the whole time, serving the Lord (*douleuōn tō kuriōs*), . . . solemnly testifying to both Jews and Greeks of repentance toward God and faith in our Lord Jesus Christ" (Acts 20:18–21). He also reminds Timothy that in his status as a "slave of the Lord" (*doulon kuriou*), he "must not be quarrelsome, but be kind to all, able to teach, patient when wronged" (2 Tim 2:24). It is clear that Paul did not shy away from using the slave-master analogy as an appropriate comparison for the believer and especially for the minister.

For that matter, the verb *douleuō* seems to emphasize the obedience of service to Jesus as Lord despite any accompanying difficulties, as Paul recounts how he had "served the Lord with all humility and tears with trials" (Acts 20:19). Moreover, Paul uses "slaving" as part of the ministry when he reminds the Philippians how Timothy "served me in the gospel, as a son with the father" (Phil 2:22); notably, nearly half of the appearances of *douleuō* in the NT refer to serving God as an evidence of true faith and genuine conversion.[32] Clearly, this "slave/Lord" relationship is used so that the believer—and in particular the preacher—will consider himself to be a slave to his Lord who purchased him with His blood. As the Lord's slave," his primary duty is to work in obedience to the commands of his Master.

As a Minister is Ministering: *Hupēretēs Hupēretei*

The verb used to describe the work of the preacher as a minister is *hupēreteō*, which means to be "rendering service,"[33] usually as an "officer" (*hupēretēs*) in an official capacity.[34] Paul may well trace this function back to his original commission from the risen Lord, who appeared to him on the Damascus Road to appoint him as a *hupēretēs* (Acts 26:16). It was already a title Jesus had applied to His servants (John 18:36)[35] and

32. Of the twenty-five appearances of *douleuō* in the NT, twelve refer to serving God (Matt 6:24; 16:13; Acts 7:7; 20:19; Rom 7:6, 25; 12:11; 14:18; Eph 6:7; Phil 2:22; Col 3:24; 1 Thess 1:9), four refer to the proper service an inferior owes to his superior (Luke 15:29; Rom 9:11; Gal 5:13; 1 Tim 6:2) and nine refer to slaving in a negative manner (Matt 6:24; Luke 16:13; John 8:33; Rom 6:6; 16:19; Gal 4:8, 9, 25; Titus 3:3).

33. BDAG § 7590 defines ὑπηρετέω "to render service."

34. BDAG § 7591 defines ὑπηρέτης "frequently as a title for a governmental or other official for a governmental or other official; one who functions as a helper, freq. in a subordinate capacity." The Gospels and Acts use the word for "the officers of the Jews," officials of the Jerusalem Temple or local synagogues (Matt 26:58; Mark 14:54, 65; Luke 4:20; John 7:32, 45, 46; 18:3, 12, 18, 22; 19:6; Acts 5:22, 26; 13:5).

35. John 18:36, "My kingdom is not of this world. If My kingdom were of this world, then My

which Luke 1:2 applied to the apostles as "those who from the beginning were eyewitnesses and servants (*hupēretai*) of the word handed down to us." Paul embraces this term when he later asks that his readers regard him and his fellow workers "as servants (*hupēretas*) of Christ" (1 Cor 4:1).

Rengstorf notes that the *hupēretēs* differed from the *doulos* in that a *hupēretēs* was free and claimed wages for his services, and a *hupēretēs* differed from the *diakonos* in that he was dedicated with respect and zeal in his service for another.[36] Rengstorf adds, "The special feature of the *hupēretēs* is that he willingly learns his task and goal from another who is over him but without prejudice to his personal dignity."[37] Quite naturally, this term is most appropriate to describe the preacher who learns his task from the One who came to serve.

Paul uses the verb *hupēreteō* in its customary sense of "helping to the express will of another"[38] when he reminds the Ephesian elders, "You yourselves know that these hands ministered (*hupēretēsan*) to my *own* needs and to the men who were with me" (Acts 20:34). While he does not directly refer to preaching in this statement, Paul clearly shows that an aspect of ministry is for the preacher to be a willing worker, officially charged by the risen Lord to fulfill his ministry as a service to God and to others.

As One Liturgizing the Liturgy: *Latrueō ē Latreia*

A closely related term of the work of ministry but one that accents "the carrying out of religious duties" is *latrueō*,[39] which is the basis for the English word, liturgy. In the Bible, *latreuō* is translated occasionally as "worshipping" (Phil 3:3) but most often as "serving."[40] Paul confirms that "according to the Way . . . I serve (*latrueō*) the God of our fathers" (Acts 24:14) and that he "belongs to and serves (*latreuō*)" this God (Acts 27:23). Not only does Paul serve (*latreuō*) God "with a clear conscience the way my

---

servants (*hupēretai*) would be fighting, that I might not be delivered up to the Jews."

36. Rengstorf, ὑπηρετέω, *TDNT* 8:532.

37. Ibid.

38. Ibid., 540.

39. BDAG § 4524 states of λατρεύω, "in our lit. only of the carrying out of religious duties." The word is especially used in the LXX to translate עָבַד (*abad*) when it refers to "serving the Lord" (as in Deut 6:13, quoted by Jesus in Matt 4:10, "Worship the Lord your God and serve (*latreuseis*) Him only." The verb is particularly used in Hebrews in its comparison of OT liturgy (Heb 8:5; 9:9; 10:2; 13:10) with NT liturgy (Heb 9:14; 10:28).

40. The verb λατρεύω appears 130 times in the Greek Bible (Exod 3:12; 4:23; 7:16, 26; 8:16; 9:1, 13; 10:3, 7-8, 11, 24, 26; 12:31; 20:5; 23:24, 25; Lev 18:21; Num 16:9; Deut 4:19, 28; 5:9; 6:13; 7:4, 16; 8:19; 10:12, 20; 11:13, 16, 28; 12:2; 13:3, 7, 14; 17:3; 28:14, 36, 47-48; 29:17, 25; 30:17; 31:20; Jos 22:5, 27; 23:7, 16; 24:2, 14, 15, 16, 18-22, 24, 29; Jda. 2:11, 13, 19; 3:6-7; 10:6, 10, 13, 16; Jdg 2:11, 13, 19; 3:6-7; 2 Sam 15:8; 2 Kgs 17:12, 16, 33, 35; 21:21; 2 Chron 7:19; 1 Es 1:4; 4:54; Jdt. 3:8; 3 Macc 6:6; Odes 9:75; Sir 4:14; Ezek 20:32; Dan 3:12, 14, 18, 95; 4:37; 6:17, 21, 27; 7:14; Dat. 3:12, 14, 17, 18, 95; 6:17, 21; Matt 4:10; Luke 1:74; 2:37; 4:8; Acts 7:7, 42; 24:14; 26:7; 27:23; Rom 1:9, 25; Phil 3:3; 2 Tim 1:3; Heb 8:5; 9:9, 14; 10:2; 12:28; 13:10; Rev 7:15; 22:3).

forefathers did" (2 Tim 1:3), but more pointedly, Paul serves (*latreuō*) his God "in my spirit in the gospel of His Son" (Rom 1:9). He indicates in the following verses (Rom 1:10–15) that the various religious duties accompanying the Christian ministry include praying (Rom 1:10), imparting spiritual gifts (1:11), encouraging in the Faith (1:12), evangelizing (1:13), and of course, preaching the gospel (1:15). As the ritual of the Passover and the vessels of service for the house of the Lord are described in Exod 12:25 as aspects of the OT *latreia*, so the "logical liturgy" (*logiken latreian*, Rom 12:2) for the New Covenant church also includes the "rituals" of worship such as Baptism and Communion, matters for which the minister is responsible in leading the *latreia*. Such duties encompass the broad spectrum of worship that are part of the work commissioned to the pastor-teacher in his pastoral service in preparation for the time when the entire company of the saved "are before the throne of God; and they serve (*latreuousin*) Him day and night in His temple" (Rev 7:15).

As the One Striving: *Sunathleō*

On occasion, Paul uses several words to describe the work of the gospel as the exertion of extreme physical strength. One of those words is *sunathleō*,[41] which appears only twice in Paul's writing, both times in Philippians. First, Paul wants to hear that the believers are "striving together (*sunathlountes*) for the faith of the gospel" (Phil 1:27), and secondly, he commends Euodia and Syntyche, "women who have shared my struggle (*sunēthelēsan*) in the gospel" (Phil 4:3). The verb Paul uses—which he may have coined—consists of the preposition *sun* ("with") and the verb *athleō*.[42] While the word originally described arena sports such as boxing, the word has come over into English more generally in the word "athletics." Paul applies this athletic analogy to Timothy's discipleship ministry by reminding him, "If anyone competes as an athlete (*athlei*), he does not win the prize unless he competes (*athlesei*) according to the rules" (2 Tim 2:5), indicating that the work of the gospel includes tremendous physical striving.[43]

Naturally, the idea behind *sunathleō* is not that the minister strives contentiously with others but that he becomes like a well-trained athlete, exercising self-control in all things so that he may "run in such a way, as not without aim; (and) box in such a way, as not beating the air" (1 Cor 9:25–26, AT) but competing so as to win the prize (2 Tim 2:5). In order to remain in such good shape, the minister must discipline himself for godliness (1 Tim 4:7) so that he may "do the work of ministry" despite the physical energy expended to complete the tasks assigned to him by His Lord.

---

41. BDAG § 7010 defines συναθλέω, to "contend/struggle along with someone."
42. BDAG § 166 defines ἀθλέω, "to compete in a contest, *compete*, of athletic contests in the arena."
43. Stauffer, συναθλέω, *TDNT* 1:167.

As One Agonizing the Agony: *Agōnizomai ton Agōna*

Another term expressing physical effort in ministry is *agōnizomai*,[44] a verb originally used for a military *agōn*,[45] or combat (as in John 18:36, "my servants would be fighting"), but later it appears in Greek literature for sporting activities (as in 1 Cor 9:25, "everyone who competes in the games.").[46] Because the proclamation of the gospel invariably leads to conflict with opponents, Paul found in *agōnizomai* an apt description of the "agony" that every believer—and especially every preacher—must "agonize." For this reason, Paul explains to the Philippians that they are "experiencing the same conflict (*agōna*) which you saw in me, and now hear *to be* in me" (Phil 1:30).

Inasmuch as the gospel invites persecution, Paul recounts to the Thessalonians how "after we had already suffered and been mistreated in Philippi, as you know, we had the boldness in our God to speak to you the gospel of God amid much opposition (*agōni*)" (1 Thess 2:2). Likewise, Paul wants the Colossians to know "how great a struggle (*agōna*) I have on your behalf" (Col 2:1), no doubt referring to his imprisonment (Col 4:3). As a personal example, Paul mentions Epaphras, describing him as "one of your number, a bondslave of Jesus Christ, (who) sends you his greetings, always laboring earnestly (*agōnizomenos*) for you in his prayers" (Col 4:12). To suppose that the gospel ministry exempts the believer from spiritual striving patently ignores Paul's reminder to Timothy, "It is for this we labor and strive (*agōnizometha*), because we have fixed our hope on the living God, who is the Savior of all men, especially of believers" (1 Tim 4:10).

Just as a malevolent force must be counteracted by a benevolent force, so Paul proclaims Christ, "striving (*agōnizomenos*) according to His power, which mightily works within me" (Col 1:29). When Paul tells Timothy to "fight the good fight of the faith" (*agōnizou ton kalon agōna tēs pisteōs*, 1 Tim 6:12), he does not mean that physical force should be mustered in order to compel belief; instead, he reminds Timothy that the preaching of the gospel is an immense struggle against demonic and human opposition. In the face of such foes, Paul knows that "everyone who competes (*ho agōnizomenos*) in the games exercises self-control; therefore, . . . I buffet my body and make it my slave, lest possibly, after I have preached to others, I myself should be disqualified" (1 Cor 9:25, 27). By use of this imagery of a great struggle, Paul impresses on Timothy that for the preacher to "do work" (2 Tim 4:5), he must strive in his ministry in such a way that he can eventually state with Paul, "I have fought the good fight" (*ton kalon agōna ēgōnismai*, 2 Tim 4:7).

---

44. BDAG § 104 defines ἀγωνίζομαι "1. of a(n athletic) contest, lit. and fig. engage in a contest 2. gener. to fight, struggle." The verb appears in Luke 13:24; John 18:36; 1 Cor 9:25; Col 1:29; 4:12; 1 Tim 6:12; 2 Tim 4:7.

45. *VGNT* § 52; also BDAG § 101 defines ἀγών "1. the sense 'athletic competition' transfers to the moral and spiritual realm a competition, 2. gener. a struggle against opposition." The word appears in Esth 4:17; Isa 7:13; Phil 1:30; Col 2:1; 1 Thess 2:2; 1 Tim 6:12; 2 Tim 4:7; Heb 12:1.

46. Ringwald, "Fight," *DNTT*, 1:645.

As a Soldier Soldiering the Strategy: *Stratiotēs Strateuei Strateian*

Because Paul pictures the preacher as doing the work of combat, it is not surprising that he uses the analogy of soldiering: he describes Timothy as a "good soldier (*stratiotēs*) of Christ Jesus" (2 Tim 2:3),[47] and four times he compares the ministry to waging warfare (*strateuō*;[48] 1 Cor 9:7; 2 Cor 10:3; 1 Tim 1:18; 2 Tim 2:4) with weapons of warfare (*strateia*).[49] When he charges Timothy to "fight the good fight" (*strateuę̄tēn kalēn strateian*, 1 Tim 1:18), Paul clearly intends for his lieutenant to apply military strategy to his preaching ministry.

This soldiering imagery likens the work of the preacher to that of a warrior who has been enlisted by a commander (2 Tim 2:4).[50] While this military analogy seems to contradict the message of the gospel of peace, it reminds the preacher that there are times when he must do battle against deadly foes, Satan in particular. The believer does not wage this conflict with "weapons of warfare (*strateias*) of the flesh" (2 Cor 10:3–4) but rather by being armed "with the weapons of righteousness" (2 Cor 6:7); in other words, the military imagery lends no support for believers to evangelize by violent force of arms but by "taking every thought captive to the obedience of Christ" (2 Cor 10:5). Even so, the NT often commends professional soldiers for their piety (Matt 8:10: Acts 10:22), and Paul even dresses the Christian in Roman combat armor in preparation for spiritual warfare (Rom 13:12; Eph 6:13–17; 1 Thess 5:8). As a "good soldier of Christ Jesus" (2 Tim 2:3), Timothy must recall that "no soldier in active service entangles himself in the affairs of everyday life, so that he may please the one who enlisted him as a soldier" (2 Tim 2:4). It is his commission to "suffer hardship as a good soldier of Christ Jesus" (2 Tim 2:3). No doubt these principles also apply to all preachers, that they must be prepared for this aspect of "doing the work" of ministry with combat readiness.

As a Builder Building the Building: *Ho Oikodomōn Oikodomei tēn Oikodomēn*

If striving and combating emphasize the difficulties in doing the work of ministry, then building (*oikodomeō*) gives another analogy that emphasizes the edifying nature

---

47. L&N § 55.17 defines στρατιώτης as "a person of ordinary rank in an army." It appears only in the NT and usually describes of members of the Roman military (Matt 8:9; 27:27; 28:12; Mark 15:16; Luke 7:8; 23:36; John 19:2, 23, 24, 32, 34; Acts 10:7; 12:4, 6, 18; 21:32, 35; 23:23, 31; 27:31, 32, 42; 28:16); the lone exception is 2 Tim 2:3.

48. BDAG § 6846 defines στρατεύω 1. do military service, and 2. to engage in a conflict. The verb appears in Jdg 19:8; 2 Sam 15:28; Isa 29:7; Luke 3:14; 1 Cor 9:7; 2 Cor 10:3; 1 Tim 1:18; 2 Tim 2:4; Jas 4:1; 1 Pet 2:11

49. BDAG § 6844 defines στρατεία as "military engagement." It appears only twice in the NT, in 2 Cor 10:4 "the weapons of our warfare are not of the flesh, but divinely powerful," and in 1 Tim 1:18, "fight the good fight."

50. BDAG § 6851 defines the participle ὁ στρατολογήσας as "the one who enlisted." It appears only in 2 Tim 2:4.

of the gospel,[51] as Paul compares the preacher to a builder who builds a building (*Ho oikodomōn oikodomei tēn oikodomēn*). In speaking of his ministry as a "building (*oikodomē*) of God,"[52] Paul likens himself to an architect (*architektōn*[53]) who lays a foundation so that another may build upon it (*epoikodomeō*,[54] 1 Cor 3:9–10). The building being constructed is the church as the holy temple of the Lord (Eph 2:21), and the means by which it is built is by "the word of His grace" (Acts 20:32), implying, of course, the work of preaching the gospel (Rom 15:20). To this end, God gave "some *as* pastors and teachers, for the equipping of the saints for the work of service, to the building up (*oikodomē*) of the body of Christ" (Eph 4:11–12).

This picture of the work of building gives the preacher a very positive ministry of edification, as the word *oikodomē* is usually translated (as in Rom 15:2; 1 Cor 14:26). Like Paul, the preacher speaks "in the sight of God in Christ; and all for your upbuilding" (*oikodomēs*, 2 Cor 12:19), for as one who prophecies, he "speaks to men for edification" (1 Cor 14:3). While sin has destructive power, the power of the gospel builds up lives in Christ; that being the case, the preacher ought to view himself as Christ's builder, and through his preaching he should expect to see the church "being built up" (Acts 9:31) as the Risen Christ "causes the growth of the body for the building up of itself in love" (Eph 4:16).

Summary to the Preacher's Work

It has been the task of this chapter to examine the various words Paul uses to picture how he expects Timothy to "do work" (2 Tim 4:5) in fulfilling his charge to "preach the Word" (2 Tim 4:2). Synonyms for the words "working" (*ergazomai*) and "doing" (*poieō*) were surveyed, including practicing (*prassō*), laboring (*koptō*), serving (*diakoneō*), slaving (*douleuō*), ministering (*hupēreteō* and *latrueō*), striving (*sunathleō*), agonizing (*agōnizomai*), soldiering (*strateueō*), and building (*oikodomeō*). By use of these verbs illustrating the work of the preacher, Paul makes it quite clear that doing the work of the gospel involves the exertion of physical, mental, and spiritual energy in the most exacting sort in order to do the work of ministry. Obviously, Paul leaves no room for laziness in doing gospel work. Any man who distains manual labor needs to find an easier vocation, for the charge to the preacher is to "do work!"

---

51. L&N § 45.1 defines οἰκοδομέω "to make or erect any kind of construction–'to build, to construct.'" The verb appears 404 times in the BGT, but only nine times in Paul's letters (Rom 15:20; 1 Cor 8:1, 10; 10:23; 14:4, 4, 17; Gal 2:18; 1 Thess 5:11).

52. BDAG § 5219.2 defines οἰκοδομή as "a building as result of a construction process."

53. L&N § 45.10 defines ἀρχιτέκτων, "one who is a master or expert builder."

54. L&N § 45.5 defines the intensive verb ἐποικοδομέω "to build or construct something on some specified location." It is found at 1 Cor 3:10, 10, 12, 14; Eph 2:20; Col 2:7; Jude 1:20.

CHAPTER 14

The Preacher's Offices: "Do the Work of an Evangelist"

"Do the work of an evangelist," Paul charges in 2 Tim 4:5c; and with that admonition, the apostle reminds his fellow-worker of the particular office he holds as an evangelist of the gospel. But "evangelist" is only one of several offices the preacher occupies that deals with the proclamation of the gospel to the world: he also is called preacher, ambassador, and witness. He also holds offices relating to the preaching ministry to the church, including teacher, elder, overseer, shepherd, servant, leader, and steward. Furthermore, it needs to be asked how the modern preacher relates to the offices of prophet and apostle; therefore, it will be the task of this chapter to examine these various descriptions of the preacher.

The fact is, however, that despite the variety of titles Paul assigns to the Christian leader, one is struck by the infrequency by which he claims them for himself or even credits them to the preacher. For example, Paul uses the word "evangelist" (*euangelistēs*) only twice (here in 2 Tim 4:5 and Eph 4:11), whereas he uses the related verb *euaggelizō*, "preach the gospel" twenty-one times. It is apparent that preaching the message is more important than the messenger—the preacher should not become enamored with titles, but rather he should be more involved in the activities encompassed by these titles. Even so, on rare occasions, Paul does mention these titles, showing that the preacher does in fact occupy certain offices within the church. It is the task of this chapter to examine these titles and apply them to the modern preacher.

The Offices of Proclamation

The reference to "do the work of an evangelist" (2 Tim 4:5) serves as a reminder to Timothy of his responsibility to proclaim the gospel to the unsaved world, in which capacity he not only occupies the office of an evangelist, but also a herald, an ambassador, and a witness.

Proclaiming as an Evangelist

An evangelist (*euangelistēs*) is "one who announces the gospel,"[1] and the prototype of the evangelist is Jesus Himself, who was anointed by the Spirit of the Lord "to preach the gospel" (*euangelisasthai*, Luke 4:18) so that He asserted, "I must preach (*euangelisasthai*) the kingdom of God to the other cities also, for I was sent for this purpose" (Luke 4:43). To ensure that the good news will be announced throughout the church age, God gave some for the building of the body of Christ "*as* evangelists" (*tous de euangelistas*, Eph 4:11), although "Philip the evangelist" is the only man so designated in the NT (Acts 21:8). However, by extension of Paul's command to Timothy, every preacher is not only charged to "preach the Word" but also to "do the work of an evangelist" (2 Tim 4:2, 5). Although Paul only uses the title twice, there must be some compelling reason why the apostle chose 'evangelist' as a designation for Timothy instead of using any of the other titles at his disposal. Could it be that Paul wanted to impress upon Timothy's memory that the heart of his message is the *euangelion*, the gospel as outlined in the beginning of this letter, of how God "saved us, and called us with a holy calling, not according to our works, but according to His own purpose and grace which was granted us in Christ Jesus from all eternity, but now has been revealed by the appearing of our Savior Christ Jesus, who abolished death, and brought life and immortality to light through the gospel" (2 Tim 1:9–10; see previous studies on the Preacher's Content and Activity)?

In the Greek world, the *euangelos* was one who brought the message of victory or some other news that caused joy.[2] While the noun *euangelistēs* is not used in the LXX, the derived participle, "the one bearing good news" (*ho euangelizomenos*) is found, notably in Isa 52:7, "How lovely on the mountains are the feet of him who brings good news (*euangelizomenou*), who announces peace and brings good news (*euangelizomenos*) of happiness," a verse Paul quotes in Rom 10:15.[3] There, the apostle applies the word to an evangelist who is telling God's good news, so if a listener should "confess with your mouth Jesus *as* Lord, and believe in your heart that God raised Him from the dead, you shall be saved" (Rom 10:9). An evangelist, then, is one who proclaims the victory of Jesus as Lord over sin and death to all who believe in Him.

Because the verb "evangelizing" generally refers to initial contact with unbelievers, it appears that the preacher as an evangelist is called to present the facts of the Evangel as Paul outlines in 1 Cor 15:1–5[4] so that the light of the gospel will shine in

---

1. L&N § 53.76 defines εὐαγγελιστής as "one who announces the gospel–'evangelist.'

2. Becker, "Gospel," *DNTT* 2:107.

3. Romans 10:15, "How shall they preach unless they are sent? Just as it is written, "How beautiful are the feet of those who bring glad tidings of good things!"

4. Without much debate, (1) Cor 15:1–8 is the clearest presentation of the facts of the gospel in the NT: "Now I make known to you, brethren, the gospel which I preached to you, which also you received, in which also you stand, (2) by which also you are saved, if you hold fast the word which I preached to you, unless you believed in vain. (3) For I delivered to you as of first importance what I

the hearts of the blinded so that they hear of Christ as the image of God and then confess that Him as Lord (2 Cor 4:3–6).[5] The Book of Acts presents Paul as an example of an evangelist, as he often took the opportunity to evangelize unbelievers. He did so in open-air settings, such as when he led "Dionysius the Areopagite and a woman named Damaris and others with them" to faith in Christ after his address at the Areopagus (Acts 17:34); also, he introduced individuals to Christ in personal, one-on-one conversations, as when he led Lydia and the Philippian jailer to salvation (Acts 16:14, 31). With Onesimus, Paul uses birthing terminology to describe his activity as an evangelist, calling him, "my child, whom I have begotten in my imprisonment" (Phlm 1:10), a concept he also uses with the Corinthians ("In Christ Jesus I became your father through the gospel," 1 Cor 4:15). Timothy knew of Paul's work as an evangelist from first-hand experience, because Paul calls him "*my* true child in *the* faith" (1 Tim 1:2), suggesting that the apostle had been instrumental in leading Timothy to Christ. Now, in 2 Tim 4:5, he charges Timothy as the one he addressed as his "beloved son" (2 Tim 1:2) to carry on the same work as an evangelist in leading others to salvation.

Every preacher, then, by virtue of his calling to preach the gospel, occupies the office of an evangelist. While Paul teaches that God has given evangelists as gifts to the church (Eph 4:8, 11), he includes no specific gift of evangelism among the lists of *pneumatikōn* (Rom 12:6–8; 1 Cor 12:8–10; 28), suggesting that every believer should be "eager to evangelize" (Rom 1:15). In particular, every preacher needs to know how to present the gospel to unbelievers so they would have sufficient knowledge to put their faith in Christ as Savior; for that matter, every public sermon, at some point or another, should contain enough of the facts of the gospel (1 Cor 15:3–4, that Christ died for sins and was raised again) so that an unbeliever could make an informed response to "believe upon the Lord Jesus" and be saved (Acts 16:31). The preacher who desires to imitate Jesus as the supreme evangelist must "do the work of an evangelist" (2 Tim 4:5) and preach the gospel because, like his Lord, that is the purpose to which he was called (Luke 4:43).

---

also received, that Christ died for our sins according to the Scriptures, (4) and that He was buried, and that He was raised on the third day according to the Scriptures, (5) and that He appeared to Cephas, then to the twelve. (6) After that He appeared to more than five hundred brethren at one time, most of whom remain until now, but some have fallen asleep; (7) then He appeared to James, then to all the apostles; (8) and last of all, as it were to one untimely born, He appeared to me also. . . ."

5. 2 Corinthians 4:3–6 shows the dynamic of how the preached gospel effects regeneration: "Even if our gospel is veiled, it is veiled to those who are perishing, (4) in whose case the god of this world has blinded the minds of the unbelieving, that they might not see the light of the gospel of the glory of Christ, who is the image of God. (5) For we do not preach ourselves but Christ Jesus as Lord, and ourselves as your bond-servants for Jesus' sake. (6) For God, who said, "Light shall shine out of darkness," is the One who has shone in our hearts to give the light of the knowledge of the glory of God in the face of Christ."

Proclaiming as a Preacher

Related to the verb *kērussein* (as used in "Preach the Word!"), the noun *kērux* describes one who publicly announces official news as a herald of some authority.[6] Although *kērux* is used only of two named men in the NT, Noah (2 Peter 2:5) and Paul (1 Tim 2:7; 2 Tim 1:11), it has become what is arguably the most common title attributed to the Christian minister in its translation as "preacher." Paul's two references to himself as *kērux* are grammatically identical: "for this I was appointed a preacher" (*eis ho etethēn egō kērux*). He uses the related nominal participle *kērussontos* only in Rom 10:14, where most English versions translate it, "How shall they hear without a preacher?" This verse actually describes the activity of preaching rather than the office of a preacher (as rendered in the ESV, "How are they to hear without someone preaching?")

The scarcity of the noun *kērux* once again hints that the office of a herald is not nearly as important as the function of a herald, because the verb *kērussein*, "to be preaching," appears ninety-three times in the LXX and NT.[7] Friedrich suggests that *kērux* is a title of little account in the NT because there is only one true herald of God, the Lord Jesus, who is often pictured in His preaching ministry, but it must be noted that not even the noun *kērux* is used of Jesus.[8] Clearly the emphasis lies in the activity of heralding, but since the preacher is charged with "heralding the Word" (2 Tim 4:2), he needs to understand his office as a preacher, a *kērux* of the gospel.

The *kērux* in the ancient Greek world served as a royal adjunct whose primary function was to proclaim official news and decrees of the monarchy, thus necessitating that the herald possess a strong voice.[9] Besides being articulate, the herald must also have a reliable character, because his word was to be as good as the king's.[10] Since the king was sometimes considered to be divine (or to possess divine authority), the herald served as the mouthpiece for the divine, so that it was said of the Stoic philosopher, "Through him his God Himself speaks; his teaching is revelation, the preaching the

---

6. BDAG § 4231.1 defines κῆρυξ as "an official entrusted with a proclamation." The word appears only five times in the Bible, of the herald who rode before Joseph (Gen 41:43); of the herald who announced the worship of the image of Nebuchadnezzar (Dan 3:4); of Paul as Christ's appointed herald (1 Tim 2:7; 2 Tim 1:11); and of Noah, a herald of righteousness (2 Pet 2:5).

7. L&N § 33.206 defines κηρύσσω "to announce in a formal or official manner by means of a herald or one who functions as a herald." It appears in Gen 41:43; Exod 32:5; 36:6; 2 Kgs 10:20; 2 Chr 20:3; 24:9; 36:22; 1 Es 2:1; Esth 6:9, 11; 1 Macc 5:49; 10:63, 64; Prov 1:21; 8:1; Ps Sol 11:1; Hos 5:8; Mic 3:5; Joel 1:14; 2:1, 15; 4:9; Jonah 1:2; 3:2, 4, 5, 7; Zeph 3:14; Zech 9:9; Isa 61:1; Dan 3:4; Dat 5:29; Matt 3:1; 4:17, 23; 9:35; 10:7, 27; 11:1; 24:14; 26:13; Mark 1:4, 7, 14, 38, 39, 45; 3:14; 5:20; 6:12; 7:36; 13:10; 14:9; 16:15, 20; Luke 3:3; 4:18, 19, 44; 8:1, 39; 9:2; 12:3; 24:47; Acts 8:5; 9:20; 10:37, 42; 15:21; 19:13; 20:25; 28:31; Rom 2:21; 10:8, 14, 15; 1 Cor 1:23; 9:27; 15:11, 12; 2 Cor 1:19; 4:5; 11:4; Gal 2:2; 5:11; Phil 1:15; Col 1:23; 1 Thess 2:9; 1 Tim 3:16; 2 Tim 4:2; 1 Pet 3:19; Rev 5:2.

8. Friedrich, κῆρυξ, *TDNT* 3:696. The nominative participle κηρύσσων is used several times of Jesus "preaching" as a herald (Matt 4:23; 9:35; Mark 1:14, 39; Luke 4:44; 8:1).

9. Ibid., 3:686.

10. Mounce, *Essential Nature*, 13.

Word of God."[11] The LXX uses *kērux* to describe the royal courtiers who announced the king's decrees (Gen 41:43; see also 2 Chron 30:5–10), although the word is not used of the prophets as spokesmen of the Lord.

By no means was the *kērux* to be an innovator of the message, as Friedrich observes, "The essential point about the report which they give is that it does not originate with them. Behind it stands a higher power. The herald does not express his own views. He is the spokesman for his master."[12] As a mouthpiece, the herald had no authority to add to or subtract from the message entrusted to him.[13] He was always under the authority of another and thus conveyed only the message and intention of the master.[14]

The similarities between preachers of Stoic philosophy and early Christian evangelists have been long noted. Both spoke as messengers with a divine mission and brought to the hearers a new message that offered salvation.[15] The obvious difference is that the Christian preacher is appointed by Jesus Christ and delivers His message whereas the Stoic preacher had no true savior to offer. It is instructive to note that in the NT only Paul called himself a *kērux* and then only when he speaks of his apostolic commission, so that he always adds, "I was appointed a preacher and an apostle" (1 Tim 2:7; 2 Tim 1:1). Timothy, on the other hand, along with preachers that follow after him, cannot claim the apostolic office because they cannot meet specific requirement that an apostle must be an eyewitness of the resurrected Lord (Acts 1:22).

Because Paul links the office of preacher with that of apostle, one must wonder whether it is claiming too much to describe the preacher as a preacher! If he desired, Paul obviously could have used the term *kērux* to describe other preachers, but he chose not to do so. Paul's selection of words may be due to the association of the herald with delivering immediate revelation of the Master. Timothy is not to preach new revelation but to declare that which has already been heralded. Likewise, future generations of preachers coming after Paul occupy the office of herald only as those who deliver the previously delivered *kērygma* without adding or subtracting from it. Within these boundaries, they speak so authoritatively as royal courtiers that Paul can ask, "How shall [others] hear without heralding?" (Rom 10:14 AT). The weighty responsibility of the herald to proclaim the King's message exactly should be of far greater concern to the preacher than receiving any honor associated with the title. Only as he maintains this perspective will the preacher carry out the office of herald as he dutifully and faithfully proclaims the decrees of Jesus as King.

---

11. Friedrich, κῆρυξ, *TDNT* 3:693.
12. Ibid., 3:688.
13. Murphy O'Connor, *Paul on Preaching*, 50.
14. Coenen, "Preach," *DNTT* 3:49–50.
15. Friedrich, κῆρυξ, *TDNT* 3:693.

Proclaiming as an Ambassador

Closely related to the office of an elder (*presbuteros*) is the position of an ambassador (*presbeia*), who is defined as one who "has been given authority to communicate or to act on behalf of a ruler,"[16] in the manner that the king in Jesus' parable "sends an ambassage [*presbeian*] and asketh conditions of peace" (Luke 14:32 KJV). Likewise, when the preacher "functions as a representative of a ruling authority,"[17] namely King Jesus, he acts in the role of a royal ambassador. Paul describes himself as a *presbutēs* only one time (Phlm 1:9), and it is uncertain whether he intends the word to mean merely, "an old man" (as it is generally translated in the English versions),[18] or if he portrays himself rather ironically as "Paul an ambassador, now also a prisoner of Christ Jesus."[19] In any event, he does use the verb *presbeuō* two times, first in 2 Cor 5:20, "We are ambassadoring (*presbeuomen*) in behalf of Christ," (AT) and then again in Eph 6:20, "The gospel, of which I am ambassadoring (*presbeuō*) in chains." (AT) By using ambassadorial imagery, Paul indicates that the preacher occupies the office of an ambassador who represents the risen Lord and speaks on His behalf as a royal legate.[20]

The ambassador in the Greek world operated as a legal representative of the political authority that sent him so that he acted as a diplomat who delivered the official *presbeia* of a royal official.[21] As noted, the noun *presbeia* is used in Luke 14:32 and 19:14 of the official "ambassages" sent from one king to another; therefore, by applying this office to himself, Paul makes it evident that he, his fellow workers, and all succeeding preachers deliver the gospel as *presbeuoumen* of Christ, official delegates through whom God is entreating humanity to be reconciled to Him (2 Cor 5:21). Bornkamm adds that this verse ". . . very impressively sets forth the authoritative and official character of the proclamation; that is, the authority of the message rests in the fact that Christ Himself speaks in the word of His ambassador."[22]

Paul again applies the ambassadorial office to himself during his imperial imprisonment when he describes himself as "ambassadoring in chains" (AT) and prays that

---

16. L&N § 37.87 defines πρεσβεία as "a person who has been given authority to communicate or to act on behalf of a ruler–'representative, ambassador.'" It is found in the NT only in Luke 14:32 and 19:14.

17. L&N § 37.88 explains πρεσβεύς as "a derivative of πρεσβεία 'representative,' § 37.87; to function as a representative of a ruling authority–'to be a representative of, to be an ambassador of.'"

18. BDAG § 6140 defines πρεσβύτης as "old man, aged man."

19. NET *Notes* comments at Phlm 9, "Or perhaps 'an ambassador' (so RSV, TEV), reading πρεσβευτής for πρεσβύτης (a conjecture proposed by Bentley, cf. BDAG § 863 s.v. πρεσβύτης). NRSV reads 'old man' and places 'ambassador' in a note." The irony—even the outrage—of an ambassador being in held chains should not be lost on the reader, because the safety of a royal representative was considered as inviolate in the ancient world as it is in modern times.

20. *VGNT* § 3536 defines πρεσβεύω, "I am an ambassador," as 'the regular word in the Greek East for the Emperor's legate.'"

21. Bornkamm, πρεσβεύω, *TDNT* 6:681. He notes, "In general, one may say that the *presbus* acts more independently and that he is furnished with greater authority than the *kerux*."

22. Ibid., 682

he might proclaim the gospel boldly, as he is obligated to speak as an official legate (Eph 6:20). Every preacher needs to understand that he is the personal representative of Christ so that when he speaks, it is as if Christ Himself speaks (2 Cor 13:3). It is his duty as a preacher to deliver the *presbeia* on the basis of his office as a personal ambassador of the King of kings.

Proclaiming as a Witness

Although Paul never specifically designates the preacher as a witness (*martus*),[23] he does mention that the risen Lord called him to "be a witness (*martus*) for Him to all men of what you have seen and heard" (Acts 22:15) and that Jesus personally appeared to him "to appoint you a minister and a witness (*martus*) not only to the things which you have seen, but also to the things in which I will appear to you" (Acts 26:16). Like the term *kērux*, the noun *martus*, when used to describe an office in the church, is tied to the apostolic college as those who are immediate eyewitnesses of the resurrection of Jesus.[24] Although some preachers throughout church history have claimed to have seen the risen Jesus (such as Joseph Smith, the founder of Mormonism), neither Timothy nor preacher following after him can make a legitimate claim to be an eyewitness of the historical resurrection of Jesus. This fact may explain why the preacher is not designated as holding the office of a witness in the apostolic sense.

However, the verb *martureō*,[25] "to be witnessing," is used in the NT for another aspect of preaching, as when the risen Lord says to Paul, "Take courage; for as you have solemnly witnessed (*diemarturō*[26]) to My cause at Jerusalem, so you must witness (*marturēsai*) at Rome also" (Acts 23:11). A witness is someone who testifies to confirm certain facts, particularly in legal situations,[27] and for this reason the concept

---

23. L&N § 33.270 explains that μάρτυς is "a derivative of μαρτυρέω 'to witness' (§ 33.262), thus 'a person who witnesses.'"

24. Jesus addresses His apostles in the context of Acts 1:8, "You shall be My witnesses," and thus in mentioning the necessity to replace Judas in the apostolate, Peter states that ". . . of the men who have accompanied us all the time that the Lord Jesus went in and out among us—beginning with the baptism of John, until the day that He was taken up from us—one of these should become a witness (*martus*) with us of His resurrection" (Acts 1:21–22). It is this idea of eyewitness testimony of Christ's resurrection that comes to the forefront of being an apostolic witness ("This Jesus God raised up again, to which we are all witnesses (μάρτυρες)," Acts 2:32; also 3:15; 5:32; 10:39, 41; 13:31), as Peter describes himself as a "fellow elder and witness (μάρτυς) of the sufferings of Christ" (1 Pet 5:1).

25. BDAG § 4721.1 defines μαρτυρέω "to confirm or attest someth. on the basis of personal knowledge or belief, bear witness, be a witness."

26. BDAG § 1878 defines διαμαρτύρομαι as follows: "1. to make a solemn declaration about the truth of something; and 2. to exhort with authority in matters of extraordinary importance, freq. w. ref. to higher powers and/or suggestion of peril." The verb is used of Paul in Acts 18:5; 20:21, 23, 24; 23:11; 28:23; and in Paul's letters in 1 Thess 4:6; 1 Tim 5:21; 2 Tim 2:14; 4:1.

27. BDAG § 4725 defines μάρτυς as "one who testifies in legal matters, *witness*"; and 2. as "one who affirms or attests, *testifier, witness.*"

of bearing witness is closely tied to the covenantal structure of the Bible.[28] The scroll of God's Law is often called, "The Testimony" (the Hebrew *eduth* is generally translated in the Greek LXX by *marturion*,[29] beginning in Exod 16:34), and this scroll was placed beside "the Ark of the Testimony," the visible structure of God's presence, as a witness to Israel (Deut 31:36). God often invokes Himself as a *martus* to testify whether the nation is true to the covenant stipulations (1 Sam 12:5; Mal 3:5; Jer 29:23), and He calls upon His people to testify as His witnesses that He is God alone (Isa 43:12; 44:8).

Harris points out, "While in the OT the written words constitute the testimony, it is the proclamation of the gospel which is the essence of the testimony in the NT."[30] The concept of witnessing is especially prominent in the Johannine literature where it often refers to "bearing witness" to gospel truths (as in John 1:15; 3:11; 8:14; 15:27; 1 John 1:2; Rev 1:2).[31] Thus, the Father bears witness concerning His Son (John 5:37), who came into the world "to bear witness to the truth" (John 18:37) and who in turn promises the Spirit of truth who will then "bear witness" of the Son (John 15:26). Jesus extends this chain of witnesses to the apostles, telling them "you *will* bear witness also" (John 15:27) to that which is true, or more pointedly, to "the" truth (John 18:37; 19:35; 21:24; 2 John 1:3). As Jesus' apostles are *martures* to the truths of Scriptures "that the Christ should suffer and rise again from the dead the third day; and that repentance for forgiveness of sins should be proclaimed in His name to all the nations" (Luke 24:46–47), so, by extension, all who experience the "promised power from on high" of the Holy Spirit become *martures* of the risen Lord to those great saving events (Acts 1:8). For that matter, Paul describes the gospel message as "the witness of Christ" (*to marturion toū Christoū*, 1 Cor 1:6), so that to proclaim the gospel as true is to give legal testimony to the historical facts asserted by the work of Christ on behalf of sinners. Certainly, preachers should never be "found *to be* false witnesses of God" (1 Cor 15:15). Stott epitomizes the nature of witness bearing by noting, "We may summarize the biblical view of Christian witness by saying that it is borne before the world by the Father to the Son through the Spirit and the Church."[32]

Such witness bearing is especially true for the modern-day preacher. His life must stand as a testimonial to the truth of the message he proclaims. Obviously, he cannot

---

28. Coenen, "Witness," *DNTT* 3:1038–99. The truth-bearing in witness is shown in Isa 43:9, "Let them present their witnesses that they may be justified, Or let them hear and say, 'It is true.'"

29. *TWOT* § 1576g notes that תְּעוּדָה is "almost always used in reference to the testimony of God," designating the two tablets of stone upon which the Ten Words were written (Exod 24:12) as the "tablets of the covenant" (Deut 9:9). It adds, "The law of God is his testimony because it is his own affirmation relative to his very person and purpose" (ibid.).

30. Ibid.

31. The verb *martureō* appears forty-seven times in the Johannine literature (whereas only eight times in Paul's letters) in the following places: John 1:7, 8, 15, 32, 34; 2:25; 3:11, 26, 28, 32; 4:39, 44; 5:31, 32, 33, 36, 37, 39; 7:7; 8:13, 14, 18; 10:25; 12:17; 13:21; 15:26, 27; 18:23, 37; 19:35; 21:24; 1 John 1:2; 4:14; 5:6, 7, 9, 10; 3 John 1:3, 6, 12; Rev 1:2; 22:16, 18, 20).

32. Stott, *Preacher's Portrait*, 69.

give an eyewitness account of the resurrection of Jesus, as required of the apostles (Acts 1:22), but he is obligated to "make the good confession in the presence of many witnesses" (1 Tim 6:12) as one who is "not ashamed of the *marturion* of the Lord" (2 Tim 1:8). Grasso notes, "Preaching is the proclamation of a Good News which the herald has already experienced in his own life."[33]

Trites suggests three features by which the modern preacher fills the office of a *martus*:

1. he must be passionately involved with the case and be compelled to speak what he has heard;
2. he must realize that he is accountable to the truthfulness of the testimony, as Paul remarked four times, "God is my witness" (Rom 1:9; 2 Cor 1:23; Phil 1:8; 1 Thess 2:5); and
3. he must be faithful not only to the facts of the gospel but to its meaning as well.[34]

The preacher must always keep in mind that it is not the world that calls him to the witness stand, but it is God Himself who appoints him, like Paul, to "be a *martus* for Him to all men of what you have seen and heard" (Acts 22:15).

Due to this appointment, the preacher of the New Covenant should view himself as holding the office of a *martus*, a witness to the saving works of God in Christ Jesus. He is summoned by God Himself to bear witness to the truth of the gospel by which he is saved and which he now preaches.

Summary to the Offices of Proclamation

Because the preacher occupies the offices of Evangelist, Herald, Ambassador, and Witness, he speaks as the personal representative of the risen Lord to the unsaved, announcing the Good News by which the world might be reconciled to God. It is imperative for the preacher to fulfill these offices by constant involvement in outreach ministries to unbelievers, calling upon the lost to believe in Christ Jesus as Lord and Savior.

The Offices of Teaching

While the preacher acts as an evangelist in proclaiming the gospel (*euaggelizō*) to the unbelieving world, most of his speaking duties concern his responsibilities of teaching (*didaskō*) the truths of God's Word to the believing community. In this capacity, he serves in his office as Teacher (*didaskalos*), as well as functioning in the offices of Elder (*presbuteros*), Overseer (*episkopos*), Shepherd (*poimēn*), Servant (*diakonos, doulos, leitourgos, hupēretēs*), Leader *(ho Proistamenos)*, and Steward (*oikonomos*). By far,

---

33. Grasso, *Proclaiming God's Message*, 59.
34. Trites, "Witness," *DNTT* 3:1949–50.

these are the most common designations Paul uses to describe the offices appointed to the preacher by Jesus as the Head of the church, and each term is the focus of the following section as the offices of Teaching.

Teaching as a Teacher (*Didaskalos*)

An office that Paul credits to the preacher is that of a *didaskalos*, a teacher,[35] as he writes, "God appointed in the church first apostles, second prophets, third teachers" (1 Cor 12:28) By virtue of His ascension, Christ "gave some *as* apostles, and some *as* prophets, and some *as* evangelists, and some *as* pastors and teachers" (Eph 4:11). Paul also uses *didaskalos* of his own official calling, claiming that was "appointed a preacher and an apostle (I am telling the truth, I am not lying) as a teacher (*didaskalos*) of the Gentiles in faith and truth" (1 Tim 2:7), and that for the gospel he was "appointed a preacher and an apostle and a teacher" (*didaskalos*, 2 Tim 1:11).[36] Although Acts 13:1 labels the leaders of the church in Antioch as "prophets and teachers," Paul seems reluctant to apply the title of teacher regularly to church leaders. His hesitation may stem from the fact that Jesus was considered pre-eminently as "The Teacher"[37] who taught, "A disciple is not above his teacher . . . ; It is enough for the disciple that he become as his teacher" (Matt 10:24–25), and, "Do not be called Rabbi; for One is your Teacher" (Matt 23:8). Apparently, the office of teacher is of such high rank that James cautions, "Let not many *of you* become teachers, my brethren, knowing that as such we shall incur a stricter judgment" (Jas 3:1).

Despite this warning, the function of teaching (*didaskō*) was granted very high value in the early church,[38] as Paul describes the teacher as one who is gifted by grace as "the one teaching in the teaching" (*ho didaskōn en tē didaskalią*, Rom 12:7).[39] Even

---

35. L&N § 33.243 notes that διδάσκαλος a "derivative of διδάσκω 'to teach' (§33.224); 'one who provides instruction.'"

36. Paul uses the noun *didaskalos* only seven times, five being of Christian teachers (1 Cor 12:28–29; Eph 4:11; 1 Tim 2:7; 2 Tim 1:11), and once each of Jewish teachers (Rom 2:20) and false teachers (2 Tim 4:3). It also describes the office of the Christian teacher in Acts 13:1; James 3:1; and Heb 5:12.

37. Jesus is addressed as *Didaskalos* in Matt 8:19; 9:11; 12:38; 17:24; 19:16; 22:16, 24, 36; 26:18; Mark 4:38; 5:35; 9:17, 38; 10:17, 20, 35; 12:14, 19, 32; 13:1; 14:14; Luke 7:40; 8:49; 9:38; 10:25; 11:45; 12:13; 18:18; 19:39; 20:21, 28, 39; 21:7; 22:11; John 1:38; 3:2; 8:4; 11:28; 13:13, 14; 20:16. John 1:38 and 20:16 explain that *didaskalos* is a translation of the Hebrew *Rabbi*.

38. BDAG § 1957.2 defines the predominant use of διδάσκω to "provide instruction in a formal or informal setting." Of the sixteen times Paul uses the verb *didaskō*, twelve refer to the activity of Christian teaching (Rom 12:7; 1 Cor 4:17; Eph 4:21; Col 1:28; 2:7; 3:16; 2 Thess 2:15; 1 Tim 2:12; 4:11; 6:2; 2 Tim 2:2); once to Jewish teaching (Rom 2:21); to "natural" teaching (1 Cor 11:14); to teaching of men (Gal 1:12) and to false teachings (Titus 1:11).

39. Rengstorf, διδάσκαλος, *TDNT* 2:158, distinguishes the teacher from the other offices in that the "*didaskaloi* are non-pneumatics who edify the congregation by means of their own clearer understanding." This distinction seems rather tenuous, since "the one teaching" is plainly listed with the pneumatically gifted in Rom 12:6–8. In Rengstorf's defense, he may mean that the teacher is not a recipient of direct revelation in the way that the apostles and prophets are.

though Paul infrequently attributes the title *didaskalos* to the Christian preacher, he often applies the task of teaching not only to the entire congregation (Eph 3:16) but particularly to its leadership (Col 1:28; 1 Tim 4:11; 6:2; 2 Tim 2:2), who are charged with teaching the *didaskalia* and the *didachē*.[40]

If the offices of Evangelist, Herald, and Witness have reference toward proclaiming the gospel to the unbeliever, the office of Teacher primarily relates to the instruction of the believing community, illustrated when Paul and Barnabas "met with the church and taught considerable numbers" (Acts 11:26).[41] In his capacity as a teacher, the elder is to be "working hard in word and teaching" (1 Tim 5:17). It is not overstating the case to insist that the office of teacher is the primary office of the church, because the risen Lord commissioned his disciples with the primary task of "teaching . . . to observe all that I commanded you" (Matt 28:20). This assertion is not to insinuate that one office can be divorced from another, for while each office is distinct, each one works in conjunction with the others. For this reason, a leader cannot consider himself to be only an elder who teaches but not one who rules (or *vice versa*). The NT does not allow such fine distinctions, as the next section will argue.

This united view of the offices means that the preacher, when functioning as a teacher, needs to know first of all the content of the biblical *didaskalia*, the "sound words, those of our Lord Jesus Christ, and with the doctrine conforming to godliness" (1 Tim 6:3), and then he needs to devote himself to the actual delivery of that teaching by instructing the church, "teaching concerning the Lord Jesus Christ" (Acts 28:31). In so doing, the preacher will confirm his calling to the office of *didaskalos* "in the faith and truth" (1 Tim 2:7).

Teaching as an Elder (*Presbuteros*)

Another title that is inseparably linked to verbal proclamation of doctrine is that of the elder (*presbuteros*),[42] which appears originally in Scripture to refer to an older man (Gen 43:27). Eventually it came to signify those who were recognized as "the elders of Israel," the ruling officials of the tribes (Exod 17:5). These leaders were chosen as "able men who fear God, men of truth, those who hate dishonest gain" who were to "judge the people at all times" (Exod 18:21–22). Moses initially gathered these leaders

---

40. See the chapter studies under the Preacher's Content and Activity.

41. This distinction is not meant to imply that an inseparable wedge should been driven between the offices of proclamation to the world and teaching of the church, since obviously those outside the church need teachers to instruct them in the doctrines of salvation and those inside the church need evangelists to urge them make their calling sure.

42. L&N § 53.77 defines πρεσβύτερος, "a person of responsibility and authority in matters of socio-religious concerns, both in Jewish and Christian societies–'elder'. . . . In some languages πρεσβύτερος is best rendered as 'older leaders,' but in other languages the more appropriate term would be the equivalent of 'counselor,' since it would be assumed that counselors would be older than the average person in a group as well as having authority to lead and direct activities."

into a *presbuterion* of seventy elders (Exod 24:1) from those whom he "knew to be elders of the people," and the Lord "took of the Spirit on Moses and put Him" on these men (Num 11:16–17; 24–25), entrusting them with the instruction and rule of the law of the covenant (Deut 31:9). Even when Israel became a monarchy, the everyday governance of the nation remained with the elders (1 Chron 11:3), a practice that continued through the nation's exile (Ezra 6:14) and into the time of Jesus, when the "elders of the people" gathered with the priests and scribes as the ruling *sunedrion* of the Jews (Mark 14:53; 15:1)

Because this particular body of elders put Jesus to death, the church did not call its own council of elders a Sanhedrin, although James 2:2 does describe an early Christian gathering as a "synagogue" (*sunagogē*), a title the church quite naturally borrowed from Judaism. There is no question, however, that the designation of its ruling officers as "elders" derives from the OT. Coenen notes of New Covenant elders, "In a word, they continued the juridical role of elders in the synagogue in the form of a presiding group."[43] Although the church officer is in view only sixteen of the sixty-six times the word *presbuteros* is used in the NT,[44] it is evident from those citations that the elder is given the responsibility of spoken rule over the congregation.

The fact that elders must also be speakers is implied in the qualification for an elder to be "apt to teach,"[45] indicating that he should exhibit some ability in the spoken ministry of exhorting in sound doctrine (Titus 1:9). The speaking ministry is certainly confirmed in 1 Tim 5:17, where Paul refers to "elders who rule well be considered worthy of double honor, especially those who work hard at preaching and teaching." While the primary gift that distinguishes the elder is that of ruling (Rom 12:8),[46] Paul seems to

---

43. Coenen, "Bishop," *TDNT*, 1:199.

44. The noun *presbuteros* appears sixty-six times in the NT, once for the OT elders (Heb 11:2), six times for an older person (John 8:9; Acts 2:17; 1 Tim 5:1, 2; 2 John 1:1; 3 John 1:1); thirty-one times referring to the Jewish eldership (Matt 15:2; 16:21; 21:23; 26:3, 47, 57; 27:1, 3, 12, 20, 41; 28:12; Mark 7:3, 5; 8:31; 11:27; 14:43, 53; 15:1; Luke 7:3; 9:22; 15:25; 20:1; 22:52; Acts 4:5, 8, 23; 6:12; 23:14; 24:1; 25:15); twelve times of the twenty-four elders of heaven (Rev 4:4, 10; 5:5, 6, 8, 11, 14; 7:11, 13; 11:16; 14:3; 19:4); and sixteen times for the Christian elder (Acts 11:30; 14:23; 15:2, 4, 6, 22, 23; 16:4; 20:17; 21:18; 1 Tim 5:17, 19; Titus 1:5; Jas 5:14; 1 Pet 5:1, 5).

45. BDAG § 1953 defines διδακτικός as "skillful in teaching"; however, since the word appears only in the list of character qualities required of an elder (1 Tim 3:2) and of the servant of the Lord (2 Tim 2:24), an argument can be made that the word is better translated, "teachable," since the suffix -τικόν suggests a passive quality rather than an active ability; for example, when Paul uses the adjective πνευματικὸν (Rom 1:11; 1 Cor 10:3, 4; 15:44, 44, 46, 46), he does not mean one who is spiritually able, but one who has been spiritually enabled by the Holy Spirit. Thayer, *Lexicon* §1387, quotes a phrase from Philo, praem. et poen. sec. 4 (de congressu erud. sec. 7), in which διδακτικη ἀρετή refers to "the virtue which renders one teachable." Certainly all elders should be able to teach, but they must first show the quality of being teachable.

46. See the section on Teaching as Ruling. BDAG § 6214.1 defines προΐστημι "to exercise a position of leadership" with a secondary meaning of "showing concern." The word appears only in Paul's letters: Rom 12:8 ("he who leads"); 1 Thess 5:12 ("appreciate those who diligently labor among you, and have charge [προϊσταμένους] over you in the Lord and give you instruction"); 1 Tim 3:4–5 ("*He must be* one who manages [προϊστάμενον] his own household well, keeping his children under control with all

differentiate between elders who rule and those who "rule well." Such elders are distinguished by hard work "in word and teaching," evidencing that they have the additional gifts of teaching and exhortation (Rom 12:7–8). Sometimes this distinction is differentiated by the titles, "Ruling and Teaching Elders," in that a "Teaching Elder" is awarded the "double honor" of remuneration given to those who distinguish themselves in the toiling labor of preaching.[47] However, there is nothing in 1 Tim 5:17 prohibiting a "Ruling Elder" from receiving a salary for hard work in other ministries, nor does Paul suggest that a "Teaching Elder" is relieved from his responsibilities of ruling the congregation while he devotes himself to "prayer and to the ministry of the word" (Acts 6:4). Whether a man is called primarily to rule or to teach, his office as elder demands both duties, because the elder rules by teaching. The elder needs to demonstrate that the Holy Spirit has gifted him with the *charisma* of rule (which he should exercise with diligence, Rom 12:8) and also with the *charisma* of administration (*kubernesis*[48]) so he might maintain the order of the church. Yet he also needs to show in his speaking ministries of teaching (*didaskō*) and exhorting (*parakaleō*) that the Holy Spirit has granted him the *charismata* of *didaskalia* and *paraklēsis* (Rom 12:6–8).

Regardless of one's view on these distinctions within the eldership, the task is the same for both the Ruling and Teaching Elders: they are to rule over the congregation through the preaching of the Word and teaching of the *didachē*, whether in formal preaching, informal instruction, or in personal admonition. Certainly the elder is not to lord it over the flock (1 Pet 5:3), but as Paul exhorts Titus, he is to be "an example of good deeds, *with* purity in doctrine, dignified, sound *in* speech which is beyond reproach" (Titus 2:7–8), virtues befitting the office of a *presbuteros*.

---

dignity but if a man does not know how to manage [προστῆναι] his own household, how will he take care of the church of God?"); 1 Tim 3:12 ("Let deacons be husbands of *only* one wife, *and* good managers [προϊστάμενοι] of *their* children and their own households."); 1 Tim 5:17 ("Let the elders who rule well [προεστῶτες] be considered worthy of double honor, especially those who work hard at preaching and teaching."); Titus 3:8 ("This is a trustworthy statement; and concerning these things I want you to speak confidently, so that those who have believed God may be careful to engage [προΐστασθαι] in good deeds."); Titus 3:14 ("And let our *people* also learn to engage [προΐστασθαι] in good deeds to meet pressing needs, that they may not be unfruitful.").

47. The phrase "double honor" (διπλῆς τιμῆς) appears only here in 1 Tim 5:17, and Paul may have in mind the OT story when Elisha requested of Elijah, "Please, let a double (διπλᾶ) portion of your spirit be upon me" (2 Kgs 2:9). BDAG § 7367 points out that noun τιμή can not only mean "the manifestation of esteem" one bestows on another (as in 1 Tim 6:1), but also "the amount at which something is valued" (as in 1 Cor 6:20). As such, it refers to a remuneration for services, an "honorarium." Thus, Paul is directing Timothy that while all elders should be granted honor (as stated in 1 Thess 5:12, "We request of you, brethren, that you appreciate those who diligently labor among you, and have charge over you in the Lord and give you instruction."), some should considered worthy of the "double honor" of remuneration, because, "The laborer is worthy of his wages" (1 Tim 5:18).

48. BDAG § 4438 defines κυβέρνησις as "administration," thus requiring the ability to lead. See further discussion on the section, "Teaching as a Leader."

Teaching as an Overseer (*Episkopos*)

Another office that implies speaking is that of the overseer or "bishop," as the KJV translates *episkopos*.[49] Jesus described His visitation to Israel as an *episkopē* (Luke 19:44), meaning that He is the proto-typical "*episkopos* of the soul" (1 Pet 2:25). In like manner, the preacher is appointed by the Holy Spirit to be an *episkopos* of the church (Acts 20:28),[50] and the preacher's charge is defined as an *episkopē* (1 Tim 3:1).[51] His task is to "take the oversight" (*episkopountes*) of that responsibility (1 Pet 5:2) so he will be "looking over" (*episkeptomai*) the activities of the congregation (Acts 6:3), such as "visiting (*episkeptesthai*) orphans and widows in their distress" (Jas 1:27).[52]

Although the related verb *episkeptomai* is generally translated "to visit," the meaning is far deeper than dropping by to socialize. As an overseer, the preacher must take the oversight to see that the physical and spiritual needs of a person are being met ("I was sick, and you visited Me," Matt 25:36). In order to ascertain these needs, verbal interaction must take place, as when Paul planned to re-visit (*episkeptomai*) the churches he had previously established, his intent was to "see how they are," inquiring into both their physical and spiritual needs so that these churches were strengthened (Acts 15:36, 41; 16:1).[53]

The preacher, then, exercises the office of overseer not so much in public proclamation of the Word as in pastoral inquiry, visiting "from house to house" in order to discover spiritual applications of the Word in the lives of believers (Acts 20:20). While

---

49. BDAG § 3025 points out that in pre-Christian usage ἐπίσκοπος described "one who watches over, guardian," as it is used of Christ in 1 Pet 2:25 as "the guardian of the souls." It continues, "The term was taken over in Christian communities in ref. to one who served as *overseer* or *supervisor*, with special interest in guarding the apostolic tradition.... The ecclesiastical loanword 'bishop' is too technical and loaded with late historical baggage for precise signification of usage of ἐπίσκοπος and cognates in our lit., esp. the NT." When Paul directs Titus to "appoint elders in every city" (Titus 1:5), he then titles the *presbuteros* as an *episkopos* (Titus 1:7), indicating that elder and bishop are not two distinct offices but two different descriptions of the same office. Even the Anglican Bishop Lightfoot admits as much in his brief but important excursus, "The synonyms 'bishop' and 'presbyter,'" in his commentary on *Philippians*, 95–99. See also Merkle, "Do the Terms 'Elder' and 'Overseer' Represent the Same Office?" in *40 Questions About Elders and Deacons*, 76–83.

50. "Overseer" is about as near an equivalent to *episkopos* as possible, since the word is a compound of *epi* and *skopeō*, "to see over." The noun appears thirteen times in the LXX to describe various superintendents (Num 4:16; 31:14; Jdg 9:28; 2 Kgs 11:15, 18; 12:12; 2 Chr 34:12, 17; Neh 11:9, 14, 22; Job 20:29; Isa 60:17) and five times in the NT, once of Christ (1 Pet 2:25) and four times of the church administrator (Acts 20:28; Phil 1:1; 1 Tim 3:2; Titus 1:7). The duty of the *episkopos* is to be supervising (*episkopeō*, Deut 11:12; 2 Chr 34:12; Esth 2:11; Prov 19:23; Heb 12:15; with 1 Pet 5:2 having reference to the work of elders) within a specified ministry of oversight (*episkopē*, Acts 1:20; 1 Tim 3:1).

51. L&N § 53.69 defines ἐπισκοπή as "a religious role involving both service and leadership–'office, position, ministry as church leader.'"

52. L&N § 35.39 treats ἐπισκέπτομαι and ἐπισκοπέω as synonyms, each meaning "to care for or look after, with the implication of continuous responsibility–'to look after, to take care of, to see to.'" The idea is well illustrated when Paul said to Barnabas, "Let us return and visit (ἐπισκεψώμεθα) the brethren in every city in which we proclaimed the word of the Lord, *and see* how they are" (Acts 15:36).

53. Coenen, "Bishop," *DNTT* 1:191.

the idea of verbal ministry is not at the forefront of overseeing—it requires more of a personal presence, in the manner that God visits his people (Acts 15:14)—speaking is certainly part of exercising the office of overseer, as the preacher inquires into the needs of his congregation. By performing his duties as an overseer, the preacher demonstrates that it is the Holy Spirit who appointed him as an overseer of the flock, "to shepherd the church of God which He purchased with His own blood" (Acts 20:28).

Teaching as a Shepherd (*Poimēn*)

This connection Paul makes between the overseer and his task of shepherding (Acts 20:28) alerts the preacher of his office to be a shepherd (*poimēn*) who shepherds (*poimainō*) the flock (*poimnion*) of God. The prime example, of course, is Jesus, who is not only the "Shepherd of our souls" (1 Pet 2:25), but also "the great Shepherd of the sheep" (Heb 13:20), even the "Chief Shepherd" (*archipoimēn*, 1 Pet 5:4) who claimed, "I am the good shepherd" (John 10:11). When applied to church leaders, the term *poimēnas* is translated "pastors," a specific designation appearing only once in Paul's letters, although the concept of shepherding appears often throughout the NT;[54] in fact, an argument can be made that it is biblically primary for an elder to identify himself as a shepherd (a pastor) because the Holy Spirit appointed overseers, first of all, to shepherd or pastor the flock of God (Acts 20:28).

Furthermore, Paul indicates in Eph 4:11 ("He personally gave some to be apostles, some prophets, some evangelists, some pastors and teachers," CSB) that the principal designation of the gifted leader, after apostle, prophet, and evangelist, is "pastor-teacher." The grammatical structure of this verse suggests that Paul does not have in mind separate offices of pastor and teacher, but he unites the two spheres into one office, so it could be translated, "pastors, even teachers."[55] Even if "pastors" and "teachers"

---

54. The preacher is called a shepherd only at Eph 4:11, but the task of shepherding appears in John 21:16 ("Shepherd my sheep"); Acts 20:28 ("shepherd the church of God"); and 1 Pet 5:2 ("shepherd the flock of God"), and the church is described as a flock only in Luke 12:32; Acts 20:28–29; and 1 Pet 5:2–3.

55. The grammatical structure of Eph 4:11 is noteworthy, since Paul employs a parallelism among the first four offices of article + conjunction + noun but not so with the fifth noun, as follows:

Καὶ αὐτὸς ἔδωκεν
    τοὺς μὲν ἀποστόλους,
    τοὺς δὲ προφήτας,
    τοὺς δὲ εὐαγγελιστάς,
    τοὺς δὲ ποιμένας καὶ διδασκάλους.

This structure indicates that the fourth article τοὺς modifies both nouns and so unites them as "pastors-teachers." Wallace, *Greek Grammar*, 284, notes, "The uniting of these (last) two groups by one article sets them apart from the other gifted elders. Absolute distinction, then, is probably not in view. In light of the fact that elders and pastors had similar functions in the NT, since elders were to be teachers, the pastors were also to be teachers. Further, presumably not all teachers were elders or pastors. This evidence seems to suggest that the ποιμένας were part of the διδασκάλους in Eph 4:11.... Thus Eph 4:11 seems to affirm that all pastors were to be teachers, though not all teachers were to be pastors."

are used synonymously, it is an overstatement to insist that "Pastor-Teacher" is the only designation by which the preacher should be known, since this study has already noted the variety of titles Paul gives to the preacher, particularly when Eph 4:11 is the only time Paul ever mentions teachers as pastors. What does seem evident in Eph 4:11 is that the other offices listed are either foundational (as apostles and prophets are called earlier in Eph 2:20) or specialized (evangelists are mentioned only elsewhere in Acts 21:8 and 2 Tim 4:5), whereas the Pastor-Teacher is the "ordinary" office of leadership given to the church.

Jesus noted that the way a Palestinian shepherd led his flock was by his speaking voice, "The sheep hear his voice, and he calls his own sheep by name; . . . the sheep follow him because they know his voice" (John 10:3–4). Jesus even takes the analogy beyond what most shepherds would consider their duty by stating that He as the Good shepherd "lays down His life for the sheep" (John 10:15). Following the example of Jesus, the preacher who would be a good shepherd also lays down his life for his flock while shepherding them in such a way that the flock hears in his voice the voice of the Good Shepherd and follows Him (John 10:16).

Although Paul was a tentmaker, he uses the shepherding analogy on three recorded occasions: the first when he reminded the Ephesian elders, "The Holy Spirit has made you overseers, to shepherd the church of God which He purchased with His own blood" (Acts 20:28); the second when he defends his right as an apostle to receive remuneration by asking, "Who tends a flock and does not use the milk of the flock?" (1 Cor 9:7); and the third when he lists pastors as shepherds along with the other offices (Eph 4:11). Peter also uses shepherding imagery when he exhorts the elders to "shepherd the flock of God among you, . . . proving to be examples to the flock, and when the Chief Shepherd appears, you will receive the unfading crown of glory" (1 Pet 5:2–4). Peter's comments reflect his obedience to the final commands Jesus gave to him, "Tend My lambs; . . . Shepherd My sheep; . . . Tend My sheep" (John 21:15, 16, 17). Surely, both apostles knew that an effective shepherd leads by example and by voice, as Jesus taught, and so both encouraged the preacher to care tenderly for his appointed flock, lovingly speaking the Word of the Good Shepherd so that the sheep may hear His voice through the speech of the one who holds the office of the shepherd-pastor.

Teaching as a Minister (*Diakonos, Doulos, Leitourgos, Hupēretēs*)

Occasionally, Paul describes himself as a minister, a title that is the translation of several Greek words, including *diakonos, doulos, leitourgos,* and *hupēretēs,* all of which share the same basic meaning of a servant or an assistant. The most common of these designations in the NT is *diakonos*,[56] which many English versions transliterate as

---

56. BDAG § 1858 defines διάκονος most commonly as an "assistant." The *uses loquendi* of the thirty-four times *diakonos* appears in the NT falls into these categories:

"deacon" when the word refers to the church office (so identified by its connection with the overseer in Phil 1:1; 1 Tim 3:8 and 12).[57] The Diaconate seems to have originated when the Greek-speaking widows in the Jerusalem church were overlooked in the daily *diakonia*, and so the Twelve (the apostles who had been supervising this important ministry) summoned the congregation of the disciples and said, "It is not desirable for us to neglect the word of God in order to serve (*diakonein*) tables" (Acts 6:1–2). Both ministries (Word and Tables) need to be done, and so seven qualified men (all with Greek names!) were chosen and charged with the task of serving tables so that the apostles could devote themselves to prayer and the ministry of the Word (Acts 6:3–6). While these seven appointees are not specifically called Deacons (*diaconoi*),

1. The secular servant by vocation (Matt 22:13; John 2:5, 9);
2. The civil magistrate as a *diakonos* of God (Rom 13:4, 4);
3. The servants of Satan who disguise themselves as servants of righteousness (2 Cor 11:15);
4. Christ as a *diakonos* (Rom 15:8; Gal 2:17);
5. The Christian as a *diakonos*: "Whoever wishes to become great among you shall be your servant" (Matt 20:26; Mark 10:43); "The greatest among you shall be your servant" (Matt 23:11); "If anyone wants to be first, he shall be last of all, and servant of all" (Mark 9:35); "If anyone serves Me, let him follow Me; and where I am, there shall My servant also be; if anyone serves Me, the Father will honor him" (John 12:26); "I commend to you our sister Phoebe, who is a servant of the church which is at Cenchrea" (Rom 16:1); "What then is Apollos? And what is Paul? Servants through whom you believed" (1 Cor 3:5); "We are servants of a new covenant" (2 Cor 3:6); "in everything commending ourselves as servants of God" (2 Cor 6:4); "Are they servants of Christ?" (2 Cor 11:23); "The gospel of which I was I was made a minister, according to the gift of God's grace which was given to me according to the working of His power" (Eph 3:7); "Tychicus, the beloved brother and faithful minister in the Lord" (Eph 6:21); "Epaphras, our beloved fellow bond-servant, who is a faithful servant of Christ on our behalf" (Col 1:7) ; . . . the hope of the gospel . . . of which I, Paul, was made a minister" (Col 1:23); "Of *this church* I was made a minister according to the stewardship from God bestowed on me for your benefit, that I might fully carry out the *preaching of* the word of God" (Col 1:25); Tychicus, *our* beloved brother and faithful servant and fellow bond-servant in the Lord" (Col 4:7); "You will be a good servant of Christ Jesus, (1 Tim 4:6).
6. The church office of a *diakonos* (Phil 1:1; 1 Tim 3:8; 12).

57. The question arises whether Paul intends for Phoebe to be considered an officer by describing her as "a servant (a deaconess?) of the church which is at Cenchrea" (οὖσαν [καὶ] διάκονον τῆς ἐκκλησίας, Rom 16:1). The issue cannot be decided on grammar alone, since Tychicus is also described as a "faithful *diakonos*" without it being certain if Paul intends to identify him specifically as a Deacon or more generically as a servant. Support for the appointment of women as Deaconesses also appeals to 1 Tim 3:11 ("Women *must* likewise *be* dignified, not malicious gossips, but temperate, faithful in all things."), a list of qualifications sandwiched between the testing of deacons (1 Tim 3:10) and the directive to make sure deacons are "husbands of *only* one wife, *and* good managers of *their* children and their own households" (1 Tim 3:12). However, it is difficult to know if Paul uses Γυναῖκας in 1 Tim 3:11 to refer to the wives of deacons, as he surely does in the next verse (διάκονοι ἔστωσαν μιᾶς γυναικὸς ἄνδρες), or to women as a separate class of deaconess. A similar list of qualifications appears in Titus 2:3 ("Older women likewise are to be reverent in their behavior, not malicious gossips, nor enslaved to much wine, teaching what is good"), where it is applied to all older ladies irrespective of an official appointment, suggesting that the list in 1 Tim 3:11 similarly refers more generally to wives of deacons rather than specifically to a class of deaconesses. Regardless of whether she served as a Deaconess or as an assistant, Phoebe certainly is commended to all believers as a sister in Christ recognized for her service of the church, and as a helper of many.

the laying-on of hands by the apostles signals a distinction between the *diakonia* of the Word and a *diakonia* of Tables. What is certain is that by the time Paul established missionary churches, he appointed both overseers/elders and deacons (Phil 1:1) and provided the required qualifications for both of these offices (1 Tim 3:1–13).

Even if a man never receives the official title of a deacon, he is still called by Jesus to be a servant in the way He also came to serve (Mark 10:43–45), so that Paul even describes himself as a *diakonos* (Rom 15:8). The emphasis of the word *diakonos* clearly centers on the act of serving (*diakoneō*) rather than on the speaking of the servant;[58] however, in Col 1:25, when Paul describes himself as a *diakonos*, he explains how he carries out his ministry of the word of God, which is by proclaiming Christ (Col 1:25, 28). In the case of Timothy, Paul reminds him that when he points out the truths of the gospel, "You will be a good *diakonos* of Christ Jesus, *constantly* nourished on the words of the faith and of the sound doctrine which you have been following" (1 Tim 4:6). Quite obviously, the primary way Timothy—or any other *diakonos* of Christ— can display the office of a servant is by speaking the words of the Master to others; for that matter, deeds of *diakonia* cannot and must not be separated from the *diakonia* of the Word. The Christian servant is to minister in deeds as an application of the speaking ministry of the gospel (See chapter 13 on the Preacher's Work).

Another word Paul uses for the preacher as a minister, one closely related to *diakonos* yet implying a lesser status, is that of *doulos*, which describes "one who is a slave in the sense of becoming the property of an owner."[59] The analogy most likely originated when Jesus compared His followers to slaves of a master, by which He also implied Himself as a *doulos*.[60] Paul often introduces himself often as a "*doulos* of

---

58. BDAG § 1856 defines διακονέω as being "at one's service; one who renders assistance." The nominative participle ὁ διακονῶν ("the one serving") is used in Luke 22:26–27, "But not so with you, but let him who is the greatest among you become as the youngest, and the leader as the servant (ὁ διακονῶν); For who is greater, the one who reclines *at the table*, or the one who serves (ὁ διακονῶν)? Is it not the one who reclines *at the table*? But I am among you as the one who serves (ὁ διακονῶν)." Paul uses the verb eight times: Rom 15:25, "I am going to Jerusalem serving (διακονῶν) the saints"; 2 Cor 3:3, "You are a letter of Christ, cared for by us (διακονηθεῖσα), written not with ink, but with the Spirit of the living God, not on tablets of stone, but on tablets of human hearts"; 2 Cor 8:19, "[Titus] has also been appointed by the churches to travel with us in this gracious work, which is being administered (διακονουμένῃ) by us for the glory of the Lord Himself, and *to show* our readiness"; 2 Cor 8:20, "taking precaution that no one should discredit us in our administration (διακονουμένῃ) of this generous gift"; 1 Tim 3:10, "Let them serve a deacons (διακονείτωσαν) if they are beyond reproach"; 1 Tim 3:13, "For those who have served well as deacons (καλῶς διακονήσαντες) obtain for themselves a high standing"; 2 Tim 1:18, "You know very well what services he rendered (διηκόνησεν) at Ephesus"; Phlm 1:13; "I wished to keep with me, that in your behalf he might minister (διακονῇ) to me in my imprisonment for the gospel."

59. L&N § 87.76.

60. *Doulos* also refers to the Christian "slave" in Jesus' teaching (Matt 10:24–25, "A disciple is not above his teacher, nor a slave above his master. It is enough for the disciple that he become as his teacher, and the slave as his master"; Matt 20:26–28 || Mark 10:43–45, "It is not so among you, but whoever wishes to become great among you shall be your servant, and whoever wishes to be first among you shall be your slave; just as the Son of Man did not come to be served, but to serve, and

Christ Jesus" (Rom 1:1; Gal 1:10; Titus 1:1), and he uses the slave imagery numerous times in his letters (as in 1 Cor 9:19, that he has made himself as slave of all).[61] Some English versions attempt to tone down the offensive cultural implication of *doulos* by translating the word as "bondservant," which echoes the OT custom of a slave who voluntarily remained in his master's house after he was freed (Exod 21:5–6). Even voluntary slavery is quite repulsive to modern sensibilities, although it seems clear enough in 1 Cor 7:22 that Paul has the institution of slavery in mind when he reminds the one who "was called in the Lord while a *doulos*, (he) is the Lord's freedman; likewise he who was called while free, is Christ's *doulos*." Any degrading status of *doulos*, however, is removed when Paul reminds his readers that Christ Jesus took the form of a *doulos* (Phil 2:7), making the term a badge of honor to consider oneself "the Lord's slave" (2 Tim 2:24). Although the concept of being "enslaved to God" stresses the activity of slaving (*douloō*; Rom 6:18, 22), it also implies a speaking function when Paul declares, "We preach Christ Jesus as Lord and ourselves as your *doulous* through Jesus" (2 Cor 4:5). The slave speaks what he is commanded by his lord (Luke 14:22), so that "the *doulos* of the Lord must not be quarrelsome . . . but with gentleness correcting those who are in opposition" (2 Tim 2:24–25). The preacher will keep his ministry in proper perspective as he remembers that his office requires him to speak as a slave of Christ Jesus.

Another term related to the office of ministry is that of a *leitourgos*, "one who performs public service," but in biblical literature, it "always (appears) with sacred connotations."[62] Paul calls himself "a minister (*leitourgon*) of Christ Jesus to the Gentiles" (Rom 15:16), but he does not reserve the office for himself, as he describes Epaphroditus as "your messenger and minister (*leitourgon*) to my need" (Phil 2:25).[63]

---

to give His life a ransom for many"; John 13:16, "Truly, truly, I say to you, a slave is not greater than his master; neither *is* one who is sent greater than the one who sent him."). Jesus also uses *doulos* in a number of his parables with the referents to his disciples (Matt 24:45–50; 25:21; Mark 12:2–4; Luke 12:43–44; 14:17–23; 17:7–9; Luke 19:17–22; 20:10–11).

61. Paul uses *doulos* of the believer in these verses: Rom 1:1, "Paul, a bond-servant of Christ Jesus"; 1 Cor 7:22, "For he who was called in the Lord while a slave, is the Lord's freedman; likewise he who was called while free, is Christ's slave"); 1 Cor 9:19, "I have made myself a slave to all, that I might win the more"; 2 Cor 4:5, "For we do not preach ourselves but Christ Jesus as Lord, and ourselves as your bond-servants for Jesus' sake"; Gal 1:10, "If I were still trying to please men, I would not be a bond-servant of Christ"; Eph 6:6, "as slaves of Christ, doing the will of God from the heart"; Phil 1:1, "Paul and Timothy, bond-servants of Christ Jesus;" Phil 2:7, "Jesus . . . emptied Himself, taking the form of a bond-servant"; Col 4:12, "Epaphras, who is one of your number, a bondslave of Jesus Christ"; 2 Tim 2:24, "The Lord's bond-servant must not be quarrelsome, but be kind to all, able to teach, patient when wronged"; Titus 1:1, "Paul, a bond-servant of God"; and Phlm 1:16, of Onesimus, now "no longer as a slave, but more than a slave, a beloved brother, especially to me, but how much more to you, both in the flesh and in the Lord."

62. BDAG § 4539. *Leitourgos* appears in 2 Sam 13:18; 1 Kgs 10:5; 2 Kgs 4:43; 6:15; 2 Chr 9:4; Ezra 7:24; Neh 10:40; Ps 102:21; 103:4; Isa 61:6; Rom 13:6; 15:16; Phil 2:25; Heb 1:7; 8:2.

63. L&N § 35.23 notes that λειτουργός is a "derivative of λειτουργέω, 'to serve'" (L&N § 35.22), thus, "a person who renders special service–'servant.'" Paul uses the noun only three times, in Rom 13:6 of the civil magistrates as servants (λειτουργοί) of God; in Rom 15:15–16 of "the grace that was

While the related verb *leitourgeō* is used almost exclusively in the LXX regarding the Levites "serving as priests" in the Temple liturgy, in the one time Paul uses the word, he refers to Gentile believers ministering in material things (Rom 15:27)[64] not by way of priestly offerings but in a speaking ministry of the gospel of God (Rom 15:16). Likewise, in whatever liturgical ministry the preacher does, he should consider it his sacred duty to speak the mysteries of God as revealed in the gospel.

An additional term translated "servant" is *hupēretēs*,[65] which Paul uses once when he states, "Let a man regard us in this manner, as servants (*hupēretas*) of Christ, and stewards of the mysteries of God" (1 Cor 4:1). Paul no doubt applied the word to himself from his calling by the risen Lord, who said to him, "For this purpose I have appeared to you, to appoint you a minister (*hupēretēn*, Acts 26:16). While the Gospels often use *hupēretēs* of secular officers, it is Jesus who describes His disciples to Pilate as "My *hupēretai*" (John 18:36). Thus, when John (Mark) is called a *hupēretēs* of Paul and Barnabas, it is a term of highest compliment to the young man, in the manner that Paul applies the concept to his own hands as they "ministered (*hupēreteō*) to my *own* needs and to the men who were with me" (Acts 20:34). When Paul was held under custody, the centurion "did not to prevent any of his friends from ministering (*hupēreteō*) to him" (Acts 24:23), probably by deeds of generosity. Although the Greek and Roman world used *hupēretēs* of secular servants, it is more likely that the church borrowed the specific designation from the synagogue, because the attendant responsible for the repository of the Scrolls was called a *hupēretēs* (Luke 4:20). Luke also shows this connection of the *hupēretēs* to the written Word when he opens his gospel with an appeal to "those who from the beginning were eyewitnesses and servants (*hupēretai*) of the word" who handed down the written record of the life and teachings of Jesus (Luke 1:2). In this case, the preacher as a *hupēretēs* inherits a calling similar to one Jesus gave to Paul, to witness to the truths of the gospel so others may "turn from darkness to light and from the dominion of Satan to God, in order that they may receive forgiveness of sins and an inheritance among those who have been sanctified by faith in Me" (Acts 26:18).

In sum, Paul often refers to himself as a servant and in so doing attributes to himself the highest office in the church—according to the teaching of Jesus, "If anyone wants to be first, he shall be . . . servant of all" (Mark 9:35). It is in similar

---

given me from God, to be a minister (λειτουργὸν) of Christ Jesus to the Gentiles, ministering as a priest the gospel of God, that *my* offering of the Gentiles might become acceptable, sanctified by the Holy Spirit"; and in Phil 2:25 of "Epaphroditus, my brother and fellow-worker and fellow soldier, who is also your messenger and minister (λειτουργὸν) to my need."

64. Paul uses the related verb *leitourgeō* only once, in Rom 15:27, "For if the Gentiles have shared in their spiritual things, they are indebted to minister (λειτουργῆσαι) to them also in material things." While Acts 13:2 uses this verb of Paul and the Antioch teachers who were ministering (Λειτουργούντων) to the Lord and fasting, it is found ninety times in the LXX, where it describes the Levitical liturgy in the Tabernacle/ Temple, as it does also in its only other NT appearance in Heb 10:11, "Every priest stands daily ministering and offering time after time the same sacrifices."

65. BDAG § 7591 defines ὑπηρέτης as "one who functions as a helper, an assistant."

service to Him who came as Servant that the preacher ministers in word and in deed, teaching as a servant.

Teaching as a Leader (*Ho Proistamenos*)

Listed among the gifts given to the church in Rom 12:6–8 is "the one who is leading" *(ho proistamenos)*, with the verb *proistēmi* defined as "exercising a position of leadership."[66] Paul is the only NT writer to use the word, and in six of the eight appearances, it refers to the activity of a church leader, as when Paul states that an elder is to "rule well" *(proestōtes*, 1 Tim 5:17).[67] According to the list of officer qualifications (1 Tim 3:4–5), an obvious way a man knows (and the congregation confirms) whether he should occupy the office of an overseer in the church is whether he manages *(proistamenon)* his own household well. The same requirement is stated for the deacons also, that they are to be "good managers *(proistamenoi)* of their own households" (1 Tim 3:12). Paul asks rhetorically, "If a man does not know how to manage *(prostēnai)* his own household, how will he take care of the church of God?" The answer should be obvious: a man who cannot manage his home cannot manage the church, and thus a church leader should also possess the gifts of helps *(antilēmpsis*[68]) and administrations *(kubernesis*[69]) in order to be a good manager of the congregation.[70]

---

66. BDAG § 6214.1.

67. In the NT, προΐστημι appears only in Paul's letters, six times with the primary meaning, "to exercise leadership": Rom 12:8 ("he who leads"); 1 Thess 5:12 ("appreciate those who diligently labor among you, and have charge [προϊσταμένους] over you in the Lord and give you instruction"); 1 Tim 3:4–5 ("*He must be* one who manages [προϊστάμενον] his own household well, keeping his children under control with all dignity but if a man does not know how to manage [προστῆναι] his own household, how will he take care of the church of God?"); 1 Tim 3:12 ("Let deacons be husbands of *only* one wife, *and* good managers [προϊστάμενοι] of *their* children and their own households."); 1 Tim 5:17 ("Let the elders who rule well [προεστῶτες] be considered worthy of double honor, especially those who work hard at preaching and teaching."). The verb appears twice with the secondary meaning of "showing concern" (BDAG § 6214.2): Titus 3:8 ("This is a trustworthy statement; and concerning these things I want you to speak confidently, so that those who have believed God may be careful to engage [προΐστασθαι] in good deeds."); Titus 3:14 ("And let our *people* also learn to engage [προΐστασθαι] in good deeds to meet pressing needs, that they may not be unfruitful.").

68. L&N § 35.9 defines ἀντίλημψις as "the ability or capacity to help or assist." It appears in Ps 21:1, 20; 82:9; 83:6; 88:19; 107:9; 1 Cor 12:28.

69. BDAG § 4438 defines κυβέρνησις as "administration," but it is a derivative of κυβερνάω 'to steer a ship, to guide' (L&N § 36.3) by a κυβερνήτης, "one who commands a ship" (L&N § 54.28), so that κυβέρνησις refers to "the ability to lead."

70. Coenen, "Bishop," *DNTT* 1:198, notes how κυβέρνησις refers to a maritime helmsman (Acts 27:11; Rev 18:17), showing how the gift grants the elder the ability to direct the church. The word appears four times in the Greek Bible: Prov 1:5 ("A man of understanding will acquire wise counsel [κυβέρνησιν]."); Prov 11:14 ("Where there is no guidance [κυβέρνησις], the people fall, But in abundance of counselors there is victory."); Prov 24:6 ("For by wise guidance [κυβερνήσεως] you will wage war, And in abundance of counselors there is victory."); 1 Cor 12:28 ("And God has appointed in the church, first apostles, second prophets, third teachers, then miracles, then gifts of healings, helps, administrations [κυβερνήσεις], *various* kinds of tongues.")

While leading by example is important, it is also a rule by word, as the elder rules well by "working hard in word and teaching" (1 Tim 5:17). Thus, those who have charge over a congregation in the Lord do so by 'giving instruction" (*noutheteō*) in the ministry of admonishment (1 Thess 5:12).[71] The noun *nouthesia* describes a verbal reproof of improper conduct,[72] noting that for the preacher to fulfill his office as a leader, he must do so "with diligence" (Rom 12:8) by speaking the negative reproofs of Scripture as well as the positive encouragements it gives in "training in righteousness" (2 Tim 3:16).

Teaching as a Steward (*Oikonomos*).

Another office of management occupied by the preacher in the teaching ministry of the church is that of the Steward, as the Greek word *oikonomos* is usually translated, describing someone who was the manager of a household or municipality,[73] as Paul describes Erastus, the *oikonomos* of Corinth (Rom 16:23).[74] The analogy is appropriate, because the "church of the living God is the household of God" (1 Tim 3:15), and the Divine Owner has entrusted a stewardship (*oikonomia*) of grace to His officers (1 Cor 9:17; Eph 3:2; Col 1:15). Although Paul illustrates the historical progress of salvation with the common custom of placing a child "under guardians and managers" (Gal 4:2), it is likely that he derived the comparison from the question of Jesus, "Who then is the faithful (*pistos*) and sensible steward, whom his master will put in charge of his servants" (Luke 12:42). Paul echoes this saying of Jesus when he notes that "it is required of stewards that one be found trustworthy" (*pistos*, 1 Cor 4:2). When Paul directs Titus to appoint *presbuteroi*, he states that "the *episkopos* must be above reproach as God's steward" (*oikonomos*, Titus 1:7), for as a steward of God, the preacher has the duty of dispensing the grace of God to the church as he strives to "fulfill the Word of God" (Col 1:25).

The stewardship that the preacher has entrusted to him is the gospel itself, as Paul makes clear in 1 Cor 9:16–18 ("Woe is me if I preach not the gospel, for . . . I have a stewardship entrusted to me."). His responsibility causes him and his co-workers to be regarded "as servants of Christ, and stewards of the mysteries of God" (1 Cor 4:1), and previous study (chapter 3) has shown that the "mysteries" Paul refers to are the revealed doctrines of the gospel, so that the preacher as a steward dispenses the teachings of the Divine Houseowner to those who are servants (*oiketēs*) of His household.[75]

---

71. L&N § 33.231 defines νουθετέω, "to provide instruction as to correct behavior and belief." Paul uses the verb seven times in his letters (Rom 15:14; 1 Cor 4:14; Col 1:28; 3:16; 1 Thess 5:12, 14; 2 Thess 3:15), and Acts 20:31 quotes Paul as telling the Ephesian elders, "For a period of three years I did not cease to admonish each one with tears."

72. BDAG § 5138. The noun *nouthesia* appears in 1 Cor 10:11; Eph 6:4; Titus 3:10.

73. BDAG § 5225 defines οἰκονόμος as a "manager of a household or estate." The word appears twenty-two times in the Bible (1 Kgs 4:6; 16:9; 18:3; 2 Kgs 18:18, 37; 19:2; 1 Chr 29:6; Esth 1:8; 8:9; Isa 36:3, 22; 37:2; Luke 12:42; 16:1, 3, 8; Rom 16:23; 1 Cor 4:1, 2; Gal 4:2; Titus 1:7; 1 Pet 4:10).

74. As noted by Michel, "οἰκονόμος," *TDNT* 5:150.

75. BDAG § 5208 defines οἰκέτης as a "member of the household." Paul uses it in Rom 14:4 when

As God's steward, the preacher must be able to exhort in sound doctrine as he administers the truths of God's Word to God's family (Titus 1:7, 9). Because the chief responsibility of the *oikonomos* is to be faithful to his stewardship, so the preacher occupies his office as Steward by conscientious giving of the appropriate portions[76] of the Master to his servants (Luke 12:42). In particular, the preacher as Steward takes the message of the gospel and faithfully dispenses it to the household of God.

Summary to the Offices of Teaching

As Teacher, Elder, Overseer, Shepherd, Servant-Slave, Leader, and Steward, the preacher faces a wide variety of duties in the primary office of his calling, each of which involves the basic task of the vocal teaching of the gospel, primarily to the covenant congregation. Even more so, these offices would not exist apart from the proclamation of the gospel, for each is a description of a particular application of the gospel to the church. No man, then, should consider that he occupies these teaching offices unless he constantly points out the words of faith, so that whether in public preaching or in private conversation, he speaks the word of God in his office as preacher.

The Offices of Revelation

Some discussion needs to be given to the offices of apostle and prophet, which Paul designates as foundational to the church, which is ". . . built upon the foundation of the apostles and prophets, Christ Jesus Himself being the corner *stone*" (Eph 2:20). Their primary function was to be recipients of divine revelation, as the "mystery of Christ . . . has now been revealed to His holy apostles and prophets in the Spirit" (Eph 3:5). Quite naturally, the question arises if these offices can be assigned to the parish preacher, whether he also may receive and deliver divine revelation directly, in the manner God spoke personally to Samuel, causing him to respond, "Speak, for Thy servant is listening" (1 Sam 3:10). May the preacher claim with the prophet Micaiah, "As the LORD lives, what my God says, that I will speak" (2 Chron 18:13)? This matter demands careful study, as the implications are enormous, whether the preacher may occupy the office of apostle or prophet so that he becomes a receiver and deliverer of new revelation rather than being a messenger of revelation previously given and now recorded in Scripture.[77]

---

he asks, "Who are you to judge the servant of another? To his own master he stands or falls; and stand he will, for the Lord is able to make him stand." The word also appears in Gen 9:25; 27:37; 44:16, 33; 50:18; Exod 5:15, 16; 12:44; 21:26, 27; 32:13; Lev 25:39, 42, 55; Num 32:5; Deut 5:15; 6:21; 15:15, 17; 16:12; 24:18, 20, 22; 34:5; Jos 5:14; 9:8, 11; Prov 13:13; 17:2; 19:10; 22:7; 29:19, 21; 30:10, 22; Isa 36:9; Luke 16:13; Acts 10:7; Rom 14:4; 1 Pet 2:18.

76. L&N § 745.3 defines σιτομέτριον as "an appropriate portion or ration of food (a type of food allowance)." It is used only in Luke 12:42.

77. Most notably, the Roman Catholic Church elevates at least one parish priest to the office

Revealing as an Apostle (*Apostolos*)

The office by which Paul identifies himself most frequently is that of apostle,[78] which is a transliteration of the Greek noun *apostolos*. Derived from the verb *apostellō*, "to send away,"[79] an apostle in the Hellenistic world referred to an envoy who was "sent away" on an official mission and granted full authority to speak on behalf of the one sending him.[80] Lightfoot was one of the first scholars to recognize the link between the NT *apostoloi* and the OT *shaliach* (שָׁלוּחַ),[81] as God called His servants the prophets whom He sent (*shalach*/ *apostellō*) to Israel again and again (Jer 26:5). While Rensdorf developed this connection between *shaliach* and *apostolos* in his research,[82] Schmidthals challenged this association in his study on the apostles,[83] but he reached some dubious conclusions, because he read Gnostic ideas into the biblical concept. Muller, however, found the root of the NT apostle in the OT prophets, as both were men who received divine revelation and then were "sent out" to proclaim what they had heard.[84] Somewhat surprisingly, the noun *apostolos* does not appear in the Greek OT, yet it is Jesus Himself who links apostles with prophets, when he apparently summarizes the OT message by saying, "For this reason also the wisdom of God said, 'I will send (*apostellō*) to them prophets and apostles'" (Luke 11:49). What the office of prophet consists of in the First Covenant—being a spokesman for Yahweh—appears

---

of apostle in the See of Peter as the Pope, so that ". . . by divine right of Apostolic primacy the Roman pontiff is placed over the universal church, and . . . that none may re-open the judgment of the Apostolic See. . . . " ("The First Dogmatic Constitution on the Church of Christ," in *The Dogmatic Decrees of the Vatican Council,* chapter 3). Even some Protestant and Charismatic churches designate the preacher as an apostle or prophet, implying that he has the gift and authority to receive and deliver extra-biblical revelation.

78. Paul uses *apostolos* of himself fourteen times as follows: "Paul, a bond-servant of Christ Jesus, called *as* an apostle" (Rom 1:1); "As I am an apostle of Gentiles, I magnify my ministry" (Rom 11:13); "Paul, called *as* an apostle of Jesus Christ by the will of God" (1 Cor 1:1); "Am I not an apostle?" (1 Cor 9:1); "I am the least of the apostles, who am not fit to be called an apostle, because I persecuted the church of God" (1 Cor 15:9); "Paul, an apostle of Christ Jesus by the will of God" (2 Cor 1:1); "Paul, an apostle (not *sent* from men, nor through the agency of man, but through Jesus Christ" (Gal 1:1); "Paul, an apostle of Christ Jesus by the will of God" (Eph 1:1); "Paul, an apostle of Jesus Christ by the will of God" (Col 1:1); "Paul, an apostle of Christ Jesus according to the commandment of God our Savior" (1 Tim 1:1); "I was appointed a preacher and an apostle" (1 Tim 2:7); "Paul, an apostle of Christ Jesus by the will of God" (2 Tim 1:1); "I was appointed a preacher and an apostle" (2 Tim 1:11); "Paul, a bond-servant of God, and an apostle of Jesus Christ" (Titus 1:1).

79. L&N § 33.194 notes that ἀπόστολος is a "derivative of ἀποστέλλω, 'to send a message,'" or "to cause someone to depart for a particular purpose," as in John 13:16, "No messenger is greater than the one who sent him," and as in Acts 15:27, "Therefore we have sent Judas and Silas, who themselves will also report the same things by word *of mouth*."

80. Muller, "Apostle," *DNTT* 1:127.

81. Lightfoot, "The Name and Office of an Apostle," *Galatians,* 92–101.

82. Rengstorf, "ἀπόστολος," *TDNT* 1:407–45.

83. Schmithals, *The Office of Apostle in the Early Church,* 174, 230. See the critique of Schmithal's views by Muller, "Apostle," *DNTT* 1:133.

84. Muller, "Apostle," *DNTT* 1:135.

to be what the office of apostle consists of under the New Covenant—being a spokesman for the Ascended Lord.

Actually, the primary "Apostle of our confession" is Jesus Himself (Heb 3:1), as He was the One "sent away" from the Father into the world to accomplish the work of redemption (John 4:34). Jesus even explains His ministry in fulfillment of Isa 61:1 ("The Spirit of the Lord is upon Me, Because He anointed Me to preach the gospel to the poor. He has sent [*apestalken*] Me to proclaim release to the captives," Luke 4:18), making Him supremely "The Sent One" who claimed He was sent for this purpose, "to preach the Kingdom of God" (Luke 4:43).[85] In turn, He appointed twelve disciples whom He also named as the original apostles (Luke 6:13), "that He might send them out to preach" (Mark 3:14). Later, He also "appointed seventy others, and sent them two and two ahead of Him to every city and place where He Himself was going to come" (Luke 10:1).[86] After His resurrection, Jesus extends the same commissioning to His disciples, "as the Father has sent Me, I also send you" (John 20:21), appointing them as the original apostolate, to become known simply as "The Twelve" (Acts 6:2; 1 Cor 15:5).[87]

The importance of the Twelve cannot be overstated because Jesus delegated to the Twelve "... power and authority over all the demons, and to heal diseases; and He sent them out (*apesteilen*) to proclaim the kingdom of God, and to perform healing" (Luke 9:1–2). Not only did Jesus focus His ministry on these twelve men, that they would "be with Him" (Mark 3:14), but to these chosen apostles, "He presented Himself alive after His suffering, appearing to them over *a period of* forty days, and speaking of the things concerning the kingdom of God" (Acts 1:3). When the first believers gathered after the ascension of Jesus, the apostles are listed by name (Acts 1:13),[88] and Peter (whose name always heads the list) insisted that there was a scriptural necessity to fill the vacancy created by the death of Judas (Acts 1:21). For this reason, Matthias was chosen and then numbered with the eleven apostles, filling out the number of the Twelve (Acts 1:26; 6:2). There is no record that another such election was taken after the martyrdom of James (Acts 12:2), although Peter's biblical argument from Ps

---

85. The idea of Jesus being sent (*apostellō*) by the Father appears in Matt 10:40; 15:24; 21:37; Mark 9:37; 12:6; Luke 4:18, 43; 9:48; 10:16; John 3:17; 5:36; 6:29, 57; 7:29; 8:42; 10:36; 11:42; 17:3, 8, 18, 21; 23, 25; 20:21; Acts 3:26; 1 John 4:9, 10, 14. The concept of sending has profound implications toward the pre-existence of Christ, for when Jesus claimed to be sent into the world from heaven, His awareness of this sending requires that He was existent before His birth.

86. The following passages note that Jesus sent away (*apostellō*) His disciples: Matt 10:5, 16; 20:2; 21:34; Mark 3:14; 6:7; 11:1; Luke 9:2; 9:52; 10:1, 3; 19:29, 32; 22:8; 22:35; John 4:38; 17:18; 20:21.

87. Despite the plain assertions of the NT that Jesus founded the apostolate (Luke 6:13; Acts 1:2), critical scholarship insists that "...the darkness that lies of the beginnings of the primitive Christian apostolate can no longer be illuminated with certainty" (Muller, "Apostle," *DNTT* 1:134). Such skepticism seems rather needless, in light of the obvious connection Jesus makes to the twelve apostles as the judges over the twelve tribes of Israel (Matt 19:28; Luke 22:30). Revelation 21:12–14 confirms this connection by picturing the names of the twelve tribes of Israel and the twelve apostles of the Lamb on the gates of the New Jerusalem.

88. Acts 1:13 is actually the fourth list of the original apostles recorded in the NT. See the "Table Comparing the Lists of the Twelve Apostles" at the end of this chapter.

109:8 ("Let another take his office") might suggest that a precedent had been set. In that case, the custom of choosing replacements to the Twelve may have continued as long as qualified men could be found. Such qualifications are listed by Peter: "Of the men who have accompanied us all the time that the Lord Jesus went in and out among us—beginning with the baptism of John, until the day that He was taken up from us—one of these should become a witness with us of His resurrection" (Acts 1:21–22). Initially, at least two men qualified "to receive this apostleship" (*apostolēs*), and because Paul later mentions other *apostoloi*, it is conceivable that for some years there was an available pool of those who had been with Jesus and were eyewitnesses of His resurrection, a group Paul numbers at more than five hundred (1 Cor 15:6).[89]

It is certain that the newly-formed church, after receiving the promised Holy Spirit at Pentecost, were first of all "continually devoting themselves to the apostles' teaching" (*didachē tōn apostolōn*; Acts 2:42) as that which defined the doctrinal standard of this new fellowship. This significant observation marks the beginning of the NT canon as "the words that were spoken beforehand by the apostles of our Lord Jesus Christ" (Jude 1:17), who ministered, taught, and eventually wrote on behalf of the ascended Lord.

All this discussion raises the question, where does Paul fit into the Apostolate? He did not consider himself to be part of the Twelve (1 Cor 15:5); in fact, he calls himself, "the least of the apostles, who am (*sic*) not fit to be called an apostle, because I persecuted the church of God" (1 Cor 15:9). Others were not inclined to grant him the status of an apostle, as he admits, "If to others I am not an apostle, at least I am to you" (1 Cor 9:2). Even so, the Book of Acts 14:4 labels him as an apostle by the time of his first missionary journey, mentioning it as if his position was commonly accepted yet without explaining when and how the church recognized him as an apostle. Paul clearly did not meet the first requirement required of the Twelve (having been with Jesus, Acts 1:21), yet he insists he meets the second criteria as an eyewitness of His resurrection (Acts 1:22) when he asks, "Am I not an apostle? Have I not seen Jesus our Lord?" (1 Cor 9:1). The historical evidence for his claim is recounted three times in the Book of Acts,[90] with the crucial element being the commission given to Paul by

---

89. Besides himself, Paul refers to others as *apostoloi*, including "Andronicus and Junias, ... who are outstanding among the apostles" (Rom 16:7); "the rest of the apostles, and the brothers of the Lord" (1 Cor 9:5); "He appeared to James, then to all the apostles" (1 Cor 15:7); "our brethren, *apostoloi* of the churches" (2 Cor 8:23); "those who were apostles before me" (Gal 1:17); "I did not see any other of the apostles except James, the Lord's brother" (Gal 1:19); "Epaphroditus, ... who is also your *apostolon*" (Phil 2:25).

90. A comparison of the accounts of Paul's conversion (Acts 9; 22; 26) reveals the following (the particular elements of the individual verses are underlined):

Setting:

(Acts 9:1–2)   (Paul as persecutor and zealot of Judaism; Gal 1:13–14; Phil 3:3–5; and 1 Cor 15:8–10)

Event:

Preach the Word

the risen Lord, whom Paul quotes as telling him, "For this purpose I have appeared

(Acts 9:3)	"suddenly a light from heaven flashed around him." (Gal 1:15–17a)
(Acts 22:6)	"And it came about that as I was on my way, approaching Damascus about noontime, a very bright light suddenly flashed from heaven all around me."
(Acts 26:13)	"at midday, O King, I saw on the way a light from heaven, brighter than the sun, shining all around me and those who were journeying with me."

Effect:

(Acts 9:4a)	"and he fell to the ground,"
(Acts 22:7a)	"and I fell to the ground."
(Acts 26:14)	"And when we had all fallen to the ground,"

Voice:

(Acts 9:4b)	"(he) heard a voice saying to him, "Saul, Saul, why are you persecuting Me?"
(Acts 22:7)	"and (I) heard a voice saying to me, 'Saul, Saul, why are you persecuting Me?'"
(Acts 26:14)	"I heard a voice saying to me in the Hebrew dialect, 'Saul, Saul, why are you persecuting Me? It is hard for you to kick against the goads.'"

First Question:

(Acts 9:5)	"And he said, "Who art Thou, Lord?""
(Acts 22:8)	"And I answered, 'Who art Thou, Lord?'"
(Acts 26:15)	"And I said, 'Who art Thou, Lord?'"

Answer:

(Acts 9:5b)	"And He *said*, "I am Jesus whom you are persecuting."
(Acts 22:8)	"And He said to me, 'I am Jesus the Nazarene, whom you are persecuting.'"
(Acts 26:15)	"And the Lord said, 'I am Jesus whom you are persecuting.'"

Second Question:

| (Acts 22:10) | "And I said, 'What shall I do, Lord?'" |

Command:

(Acts 9:6)	"but rise, and enter the city, and it shall be told you what you must do."
(Acts 22:10)	"And the Lord said to me, 'Arise and go on into Damascus and there you will be told of all that has been appointed for you to do.'"
(Acts 26:16)	"But arise, and stand on your feet."

Companions:

| (Acts 9:7) | "And the men who traveled with him stood speechless, hearing the voice (ἀκούοντες μὲν τῆς φωνῆς = "sound," L&N § 14.74), but seeing no one." |
| (Acts 22:9) | "And those who were with me beheld the light, to be sure, but did not understand the voice [δὲ φωνὴν (= "voice," L&N § 33.103) οὐκ ἤκουσαν τοῦ λαλοῦντός μοι] of the One who was speaking to me." |

Condition:

| (Acts 9:8–9) | "And Saul got up from the ground, and though his eyes were open, he could see nothing; leading him by the hand, they brought him into Damascus. And he was three days without sight, and neither ate nor drank." |
| (Acts 22:11) | "But since I could not see because of the brightness of that light, I was led by the |

to you, to appoint you a minister and a witness not only to the things which you have seen, but also to the things in which I will appear to you; delivering you from the *Jewish* people and from the Gentiles, to whom I am sending (*apostellō*) you." Thus, as an eyewitness of the Resurrected Lord, Paul qualifies as an "apostle of Jesus Christ," although not as one of Twelve—an assertion he himself did not make.

His claim to the office of an "apostle of Jesus Christ" is quite important to Paul, because he recognizes that "God has appointed in the church, first apostles" (1 Cor 12:28; they are also listed first in Eph 4:11), leading Paul to ask rhetorically, "All are not apostles, are they?" (1 Cor 12:29), implying that indeed all are not called or gifted with apostleship. Paul bolsters his claim by noting, "The signs of a true apostle were performed among you with all perseverance, by signs and wonders and miracles" (2 Cor 12:12).[91] Most importantly, the mystery of the gospel has been "revealed to His holy apostles and prophets in the Spirit" (Eph 3:5), so that the church is "built upon the foundation of the apostles and prophets, Christ Jesus Himself being the corner *stone*" (Eph 2:20).

While the doctrine of apostolic succession insists that the apostolate continues to the present,[92] the description of the apostles as the foundation of the church logically implies that there is "no other foundation (than) that which is laid, which is Jesus

hand by those who were with me, and came into Damascus."

91. Various combinations of "signs and wonders and miracles" (σημείοις τε καὶ τέρασιν καὶ δυνάμεσιν) appear throughout the NT, borrowed from the OT record of the "signs and wonders" the Lord performed against Egypt (Deut 34:11; Neh 9:10; Jer 32:21). However, Jesus actually rebuked His listeners by telling them, "Unless you *people* see signs and wonders, you *simply* will not believe" (John 4:48), but Peter, in his Pentecost sermon, reminds the men of Israel that Jesus of Nazareth was "a man attested to you by God with miracles and wonders and signs which God performed through Him in your midst" (Acts 2:22). Many signs and wonders were done at the hands of the apostles (Acts 5:12), as well as by the deacon Stephen (Acts 6:8), and then later through the hands of Paul and Barnabas (Acts 14:3; 15:12), a fact to which Paul refers when he speaks to the Romans only of "what Christ has accomplished through me, resulting in the obedience of the Gentiles by word and deed, in the power of signs and wonders, in the power of the Spirit; so that from Jerusalem and round about as far as Illyricum I have fully preached the gospel of Christ" (Rom 15:18–19). One such sign is the gift of tongues (*glōssai*; 1 Cor 14:22), and another gift listed by Paul is the "effecting of miracles" (*dunamenōn*; 1 Cor 12:10, 28), yet he asks rhetorically, "All are not *workers of* miracles, are they?" (1 Cor 12:29). A modern reader of the NT may get the impression that every first-century disciple was gifted with signs and wonders, yet 2 Cor 12:12 indicates that "signs, wonders and powers" of such miraculous abilities are primarily "signs of a true apostle." While these signs were not exclusively given to apostles (Stephen in Acts 6:8 and Philip in Acts 8:6 being such examples), the writer of Hebrews reminds his readers that the word of salvation "was at the first spoken through the Lord (and) . . . was confirmed to us by those who heard, God also bearing witness with them, both by signs and wonders and by various miracles and by gifts of the Holy Spirit according to His own will" (Heb 2:3–4). In other words, signs, wonders, and miracles are means to an end: to confirm the preached word of salvation. Jesus warns of those who perform many miracles—even in His name—but they are cast from His presence because they do not do the Father's will or word (Matt 7:21–27). See the discussion in Graham Twelftree, *Paul and the Miraculous* (2013).

92. Higginson, "Apostolic Succession," *EDT* 73. Just how and by whom—presumably verified by other apostles—a man may be commissioned as an apostle if he is not an eyewitness of the resurrection of Jesus is a great obstacle to this view.

Christ," evidenced by the miracles and doctrines of the apostles (1 Cor 3:11). Also, Paul's insistence that the risen Lord appeared "last of all, as it were to one untimely born . . . to me also" (1 Cor 15:8) implies that he is not only the least of the apostles (1 Cor 15:9), but also the last of the apostles. It seems that the Holy Spirit willed to give the gift of apostle (as a foundational office) only to those who were eyewitnesses of the resurrected Lord. Accordingly, a modern preacher should not suppose that he has been appointed by God as an "apostle of Jesus Christ" (Rom 11:13; 1 Cor 1:1; 2 Cor 1:1; Eph 1:1; Col 1:1; 1 Tim 1:1; 2 Tim 1:1; Titus 1:1) in the sense that Jesus commissioned the Twelve or called Paul to be His apostle—not unless he can verify to the church at large that he too has seen the risen Lord (1 Cor 9:1). Apparently some in Paul's day made such claims, as Paul ironically (sarcastically?) refers to them as "most eminent apostles" (2 Cor 11:5; 12:11) whereas in reality they were "false apostles, deceitful workers, disguising themselves as apostles of Christ" (2 Cor 11:13). No true preacher of the gospel would cast this dubious mantle upon himself.

However, even if the office of apostle is not extended to the modern preacher, the function of an apostle as one who is sent by the Lord to speak authoritatively for Him is in fact bestowed on the preacher in Rom 10:15, when Paul asks, "How shall they preach unless they are sent (*apostalōsin*)?" It is not merely the church that sends those who proclaim: the sending must be initiated by the Spirit of Christ, as when He called "Barnabas and Saul for the work to which I have called them" (Acts 13:2). Knowing that he has been sent by Christ, the preacher can declare his message as a personal envoy of the Lord and of His personal legates, the original apostles, because, "The one who listens to you listens to Me" (Luke 10:16). That authority is valid, however, only when the preacher speaks the mystery of the gospel as it has been previously revealed to the holy apostles by the Holy Spirit and "remembered in the words spoken beforehand by the holy prophets and the commandment of the Lord and Savior *spoken* by your apostles" (2 Pet 3:2)—words now recorded in the prophetic Word written by "men moved by the Holy Spirit spoke from God" (2 Pet 1:21)—those who held the office of prophet.

Revealing as a Prophet (*Prophētēs*)

A very important consideration for the modern preacher is to ask whether he occupies the office of a prophet, one who receives and proclaims divine revelation,[93] perhaps best illustrated in Deut 18:15, "I will raise up a prophet from among their countrymen like you, and I will put My words in his mouth, and he shall speak to them all that I command him." The English word "prophet" is a transliteration of the

---

93. BDAG § 6373 defines προφήτης as "a proclaimer or expounder of divine matters or concerns that could not ordinarily be known except by special revelation." The word appears 280 times in the OT; fifty-three times in the Apocrypha, and 144 times in the NT, of those fourteen times in Paul's letters (Rom 1:2; 3:21; 11:3; 1 Cor 12:28, 29; 14:29, 32, 37; Eph 2:20; 3:5; 4:11; 1 Thess 2:15; Titus 1:12).

Greek noun *prophētēs*, describing in biblical literature one who "speaks forth" for God,[94] as captured in the question of Amos 3:8, "The Lord God has spoken! Who can but prophesy?" In the NT, the *prophētēs* invariably refers to an OT prophet or to the collection of their writings, "The Prophets" (Luke 24:44), although Jesus was recognized as "a prophet mighty in deed and word in the sight of God and all the people" (Luke 24:19), fulfilling the prophecy of Deut 18:15 (according to Acts 3:22). In his office as prophet, Jesus prophesied that God would send "prophets and apostles" (Luke 11:49), and in fulfillment, the early church was ministered to by those who occupied the office of prophet,[95] such those listed in the church at Antioch, including Paul (Acts 13:1).[96] While Paul never directly titles himself as a prophet, he does list the office of prophet as second in order of importance (1 Cor 12:28; Eph 4:11), subordinate to the apostle (1 Cor 14:37), probably because the prophet did not need to meet the stringent requirement listed in Acts 1:22 of being an eyewitness of the resurrection of Jesus. Even so, a prophet is verified as one who had been gifted by the Holy Spirit with *prophēteia* (Rom 12:6; 1 Cor 12:10), and although the great Pentecost prophecy of Joel 2:29 (quoted in Acts 2:18) predicts that "even on my male servants and female servants in those days I will pour out my Spirit, and they shall prophesy," not every believer is gifted as a prophet, shown when Paul expects a negative answer by asking rhetorically, "All are not prophets, are they?" (1 Cor 12:29). Paul imposes another boundary on prophets by stating that the gift should be used "in proportion to the faith" (Rom 12:6 NAB), not referring to the measure of the prophet's faith (as

---

94. Thayer, *Lexicon*, § 4549, notes that προφήτης derives from προφημι, "to speak forth," hence, a prophet is properly, "one who speaks forth."

95. In some academic circles, it is popular to assume that the early church was entirely pneumatic at its inception, with gifted participants receiving all their messages via direct revelations of the Spirit. Only after some passage of time did the worship gatherings devolve into liturgical forms under the tight control of authoritarian clergy. Although Paul does describe a pneumatic gathering in 1 Cor 14:26–33, he directs an order of worship that shows an early pattern of form, as conducted "in all the churches" (1 Cor 11:33). Plus, it is evident in the Book of Acts that the first gatherings of the church center around the apostle's doctrine (Acts 2:42) and the exposition of written Scripture (Acts 17:11). Peisker, "Prophet," *DNTT* 3:84, notes, "It must be assumed that at a very early stage this charismatic, impulsive prophecy became institutionalized, and prophets were then seen as holders of a spiritual office." There is no evidence of any such a transition in the NT: the incipient church was apparently both charismatic and institutional, in the sense that congregations chose officers (Acts 1:15–26; 6:3; 14:23; 15:6) and gathered for worship around the Word of God and breaking of the bread (Acts 2:42; 20:7).

96. The NT names the following prophets of the church: Agabus, who was one of "some prophets" in the Jerusalem church (Acts 11:27; 21:10); Barnabas; Simeon who was called Niger; Lucius of Cyrene; Manaen who had been brought up with Herod the tetrarch; Saul /Paul (Acts 13:1); and "Judas and Silas, also being prophets themselves" (Acts 15:32). Also, the four daughters of Philip are said to be "prophesying" (*prophēeuousai*), as 1 Cor 11:5 acknowledges that a woman may be "prophesying" (*prophēteuousa*).

it is commonly translated), but according to the "analogy[97] of the faith."[98] In such a case, one who supposed himself to be a prophet had to recognize that the teachings of the apostles were also the Lord's commands and could not therefore be superceded by contradictory revelation, according to the caution of Paul, "If anyone thinks he is a prophet or spiritual, let him recognize that the things which I write to you are the Lord's commandment" (1 Cor 14:37).[99]

An overview of Christian prophets indicates that they were men and women (Acts 21:9) who received and delivered particular revelations from the Holy Spirit, most likely given to meet specific needs, such as Agabus' prophecy concerning Paul's journey to Jerusalem (Acts 21:11). Like their OT predecessors, New Covenant prophets performed such functions as predicting future events (Acts 11:28), declaring judgments (Acts 13:11), and using symbolic actions (Acts 21:10–11). In his article on Christian prophets, Ellis notes a particular link between prophecy and biblical encouragement, so that the prophets were those of gifted abilities to proclaim to the church the New Covenant implications of Old Covenant texts and themes.[100] In this regard, the Christian prophet is also a preacher, as were "Judas and Silas, also being prophets themselves, (who) encouraged and strengthened the brethren with a lengthy message" (Acts 15:32). Similarly, Paul notes, "One who prophesies edifies the church" (1 Cor 14:4), no doubt by his activity of preaching the Word.

It is this function of the prophet, that of prophesying (*prophēteuō*), that Paul seems to extend to the preacher as "the one prophesying" (*ho prophēteuōn*). In such preaching, "one who prophesies speaks to men for edification and exhortation and consolation" (1 Cor 14:3). Because these terms are used elsewhere for preaching (Eph 4:29; 1 Tim 4:13; 1 Thess 2:11), one must wonder how prophesying can be

---

97. The noun *analogia* appears only here in the NT, making it difficult to define, but the adverb does appear in *Wisdom of Solomon* 13:5, "For from the greatness and beauty of created things comes a corresponding (ἀναλόγως) perception of their Creator" (RSV). Thus, while L&N § 89.10 defines ἀναλογία as "a relation of proportion," it acknowledges that it is "also possible to understand ἀναλογία in Rom 12.6 as meaning 'in agreement with,' but this meaning likewise involves a degree of isomorphic relationship." Since "isomorphic" is a mathematical term meaning "being identical in form" (Merriam's Webster's *Collegiate Dictionary*, 11th edition), Paul is apparently equating the *prophēteia* with "the faith," referring not to how much faith the prophet has, but to the way Paul has used "the faith" in Rom 10:8, "the word of the faith that we are preaching (τὸ ῥῆμα τῆς πίστεως ὃ κηρύσσομεν). In other words, prophecy must be in agreement with "the analogy of the faith," that which has already been revealed.

98. BDAG § 5941.3 acknowledges that πίστις in Rom 12:6 can be understood as "that which is believed, body of faith/belief/teaching," as in Rom 1:5, Gal 1:23, 1 Tim 1:19, 4:1, 6, 6:10, and 2 Tim 4:7, "I have kept the faith."

99. Peterson, *Engaging with God*, 196, makes an important observation that the words of the NT prophet do not carry the same weight as an OT prophet in that "the prophetic ministry given to certain members of the Corinthian church required assessment and evaluation, which implied the possibility of challenging and even rejecting such contributions (1 Cor 13:29; cf. 1 Thess 5:21–22)." Any prophecies given by a NT prophet had to agree with the "apostle's teaching" (Acts 2:42) that subsequently formed the basis of the NT canon.

100. Ellis, "The Role of the Christian Prophet in Acts," *Apostolic History and the Gospel*, 60.

distinguished from the regular ministry of the Word. Ellis states, "For Paul, prophecy apparently is a formal term embracing various kinds of inspired teaching."[101] If his observation is correct (and it seems so), then the modern preacher actually assumes the role of a prophet when he preaches the inspired Word of God.

Quite clearly, though, NT prophets were also preachers (Acts 15:32), and preachers were also "the ones prophesying" (1 Cor 14:3), yet it does not necessarily follow that modern preachers occupy the office of a prophet, at least, not in the sense of receiving direct revelation from the Holy Spirit. Although all NT prophets may also have been pastor-teachers (Acts 13:1), Paul never specifically identifies all those who hold the office of pastor-teacher as also being prophets.[102] It appears then that the preacher should not attribute to himself the office of a prophet, because the prophetic office is listed in Eph 2:20 as foundational, along with that of the apostles. With the completion of the prophetic word (the NT canon), the need for prophets diminished and ended. While this conclusion does not deny the ongoing need for prophetic utterances—what Peterson calls "spontaneous, verbal ministries of exhortation, comfort or admonition by congregational members"[103]—one must answer the question whether the Holy Spirit continues to gift preachers to the office of prophets with a guarded negative. Church history has invariably assessed post-apostolic prophets, more often than not, as *pseudoprophētai*, in that their so-called prophecies contradicted the true prophetic word as now included in the written prophetic word (2 Peter 1:19–21). So then, while the preacher should not consider that he is called to be prophet, he may speak in the ministry of prophesying the Word so that the church may receive edifying (1 Cor 14:5).

Summary to the Offices of Revelation

It appears that it is biblically accurate to say that the modern preacher does not occupy the offices of apostle and prophet, but rather he is one who is divinely "sent" (*apostellō*) to preach because he evidences that he is bestowed with the gift of *prophēteia* in the sense that he delivers the prophetic word (*ton prophētikov logon*, 2 Pet 1:19) of the Scriptures of the prophets (*graphōn prophētikōn*, Rom 16:26). Again, function takes priority over title, although in this instance, the titles associated with receiving revelation (apostles and prophets) are not extended to the modern preacher. He may in fact prophesy, but only in a sense restricted to "the words spoken beforehand by the holy prophets and the commandment of the Lord and Savior by your apostles" (2 Pet 3:2).

---

101. Ibid., 64

102. Ellis, ibid., 67, notes that "the role of the prophet may overlap that of the elder as it does that of the apostle and teacher," but the prophet does not seem to be incorporated into the organizational structure of the church.

103. Peterson, *Engaging with God*, 197.

Summary to the Preacher's Offices

"Do the work of an evangelist," exhorts Paul of Timothy (2 Tim 4:5). This exhortation prompted this chapter's study of the Preacher's Offices, in which the titles of proclamation to the unbelieving world were examined (Evangelist, Herald, Ambassador, and Witness), and then the offices relating to the speaking ministries to the church were surveyed (Teacher, Elder, Overseer, Shepherd, Servant, Leader, Steward), with a final excursus on the offices of revelation presented (Apostle and Prophet).

In these various offices of proclamation, the preacher fulfills their functions in the preaching of the gospel to the unsaved world. At the very least, the practice of these offices means that the preacher should know how to present the gospel so that he may be able to lead a person to Christ, just as Philip was able to do with the Ethiopian eunuch (Acts 8:35). The preacher who loses his evangelistic zeal has abandoned these offices, whereas the one who is truly called to these proclaiming offices will deepen his evangelistic skills.

The primary offices of the preacher are those that concern his teaching ministry regarding the church. In some aspect, each of these offices (Teacher, Elder, Overseer, Shepherd, Servant, Leader, and Steward) involves verbal participation with the congregation in the application of the gospel; in fact, the offices are empty apart from the message, so that the preacher who does not adhere to the truths of the gospel forfeits any claim to these offices. Also, the titles are empty apart from the function of the office, and for this reason ecclesiastical titles are surprisingly sparse amid Paul's writings (most notably absent is "Reverend"). The emphasis should be on the duty of the office, not on its label.

Interestingly, these ministerial titles are mentioned less frequently than the revelatory offices of Apostle and Prophet, which invariably refer to specified individuals. These offices are fairly well defined because of their importance in the formation of the early church and in the production of the canon of Scripture. While the preacher can consider himself "a sent one" endowed with the gift of prophecy, his function is not one of receiving and delivering new revelatory traditions; instead, he is called to deliver the apostolic and prophetic revelations now inscriptured in the written Word. For this reason, Paul commands Timothy, "Preach the Word," not, "Reveal the Word."

So then, as Timothy better understands his office, he will be able to "do the work of an evangelist," but at the same time, the magnitude of the task appears to be overwhelming. How is Timothy supposed to accomplish the work to which he is commanded? The answer lies in the next command, "Fulfill your ministry," and so this study now directs its attention to "The Preacher's Dynamic."

Table 1: A Comparison of the Lists of the Twelve Apostles

Matthew 10:2–4, "The names of the twelve apostles are these:	Mark 3:16–19 "He appointed the twelve:	Luke 6:13–16 "He called His disciples to Him; and chose twelve of them, whom He also named as apostles:	Acts 1:2, 13 "The apostles whom He had chosen . . . :	Order of the Disciples mentioned in the Gospel of John:
The first, Simon, who is called Peter,	Simon (to whom He gave the name Peter),	Simon, whom He also named Peter,	Peter	Andrew (1:40)
and Andrew his brother;	and James, the *son* of Zebedee,	and Andrew his brother;	and John	Simon Peter / Cephas (1:40, 42)
and James the *son* of Zebedee,	and John the brother of James (to them He gave the name Boanerges, which means, 'Sons of Thunder');	and James	and James	Philip (1:43)
and John his brother;	and Andrew,	and John;	and Andrew,	Nathanael (1:45)
Philip	and Philip,	and Philip	Philip	Thomas (11:16)
and Bartholomew;	and Bartholomew,	and Bartholomew;	and Thomas,	Judas *the son* of Simon Iscariot, one of the twelve (6:71)
Thomas	and Matthew (identified as 'Levi the *son* of Alphaeus' in Mark 2:14)	and Matthew	Bartholomew	First son of Zebedee (20:2; = James; Matt 10:2)

and Matthew the tax-gatherer;	and Thomas,	and Thomas;	and Matthew,	Second son of Zebedee (20:2; = John, Matt 10:2)
James the *son* of Alphaeus,	and James the *son* of Alphaeus,	James *the son* of Alphaeus,	James *the son* of Alphaeus,	The disciple whom Jesus loved (13:23; 19:26; 20:2; 21:7; 21:20; "This is the disciple who bears witness of these things, and wrote these things"(21:24)
and Thaddaeus;	and Thaddaeus,	and Simon who was called the Zealot;	and Simon the Zealot,	Judas (not Iscariot) (John 14:22)
Simon the Zealot,	and Simon the Zealot;	Judas *the son* of James,	and Judas *the son* of James."	First of two other disciples (John 20:2)
and Judas Iscariot, the one who betrayed Him."	and Judas Iscariot, who also betrayed Him."	and Judas Iscariot, who became a traitor."	Matthias (Acts 1:26).	Second of two other disciples (20:2).

Table 2: A Synthesis of the Twelve Apostles,[104] Following Matthew's Order

Matthew 10:2–4, "The names of the twelve apostles are these:	Mark 3:16–19 "He appointed the twelve:	Luke 6:13–16 "He called His disciples to Him; and chose twelve of them, whom He also named as apostles:	Acts 1:2, 13 "The apostles whom He had chosen . . . :	The Apostles mentioned in the Gospel of John:
The first, Simon, who is called Peter,	Simon (to whom He gave the name Peter),	Simon, whom He also named Peter,	Peter	Simon Peter / Cephas (1:40, 42)
and Andrew his brother	Andrew	and Andrew his brother	Andrew	Andrew (1:40)
and James the *son* of Zebedee,	James, the *son* of Zebedee,	James	James	First son of Zebedee (20:2; = James; Matt 10:2)
and John his brother	and John the brother of James	John	John	Second son of Zebedee (20:2; = John, Matt 10:2) (traditionally the beloved disciple)
Philip	Philip	Philip	Philip	Philip (1:43)
Bartholomew	Bartholomew	Bartholomew	Bartholomew	Nathanael (1:45)?
Thomas	Thomas	Thomas	Thomas	Thomas
Matthew the tax-gatherer	Matthew (Levi the *son* of Alphaeus in Mark 2:14)	Matthew	Matthew	First of Two other disciples (John 20:2)?

---

104. The "Twelve" are mentioned in John 6:67, 70, 71, as if the writer assumes the readers knows who they are. The mention of the Twelve in John 20:24 refers actually to eleven men, since Judas had died by then, showing that "the Twelve" was a technical title for the Apostolate.

James the *son* of Alphaeus	and James the *son* of Alphaeus,	James *the son* of Alphaeus	James *the son* of Alphaeus	Second of two other disciples (John 20:2)?
and Thaddaeus	Thaddaeus	Judas *the son* of James	Judas *the son* of James	Judas (not Iscariot) (John 14:22)
Simon the Zealot	Simon the Zealot	Simon who was called the Zealot	Simon the Zealot	
Judas Iscariot, the one who betrayed Him."	Judas Iscariot, who also betrayed Him."	Judas Iscariot, who became a traitor."	(deceased; replaced by Matthias, Acts 1:26)	"Judas *the son* of Simon Iscariot, one of the twelve" (John 6:71).

CHAPTER 15

The Preacher's Dynamic: "Fulfill Your Ministry!"

"Fulfill your ministry" (*tēn diakonian sou plērophorēson*) is the final command Paul gives to Timothy in this charge (2 Tim 4:5d). Clearly the urging is for Timothy to "finish the course" and not fall away as Demas did (2 Tim 4:7, 10). Apparently, there is no such thing as a retired preacher, as the final fulfilling of ministry comes as it did for Paul, at his death.

Before that inevitable event, how is Timothy to fulfill his ministry? The answer is found in the implications of the imperative *plērophorēson*, which means "to fully accomplish one's task."[1] By use of this word, Paul brings Timothy to one of his favorite themes, that of the biblical concept of fullness. It is God Himself who fills the church with the full knowledge of Himself (Eph 3:19), so that the fulfillment required of the preacher comes from the dynamic of the Word of the Speaking God. This chapter will examine the concept of this dynamic that empowers the preacher and enables him to fulfill his task. It will explore such subjects as the inherent power of the gospel, the pneumatic energy and gifting of the preacher, the duties of mediation, and the vitality of prayer.

---

1. L&N § 68.32 defines πληροφορέω "to fully accomplish one's task–to perform one's complete duty, to finish fully one's task, to accomplish satisfactorily."

Preach the Word

The Dynamic of Fulfillment

The rarely used verb *plērophoreō*[2] is a compound word combining the more common verb *plēreoō* (to make full[3]) with *phoreō* (to bear[4]); thus, the compound means to carry forth something to its fullest. In this instance, Timothy is to identify so fully with his ministry that he is to see it through to its conclusion.[5] Paul's command to Timothy is strikingly similar to the one he gave to Archippus, "Take heed to the ministry which you have received in the Lord, that you may fulfill it" (Col 4:17). Paul's intent in giving the same charge to both men is identical: to do as Paul declares in 2 Tim 4:7—finish the course!

The Fullness of Preaching

How is Timothy to fulfill his ministry? For that matter, how is any preacher to fulfill his divine commission to "preach the Word"? Paul does not leave Timothy wondering for long, because the same word *plērophoreō* appears a few sentences later in Paul's remark, "The Lord stood with me, and strengthened (*endunamoō*) me, in order that through me the proclamation (*kērugma*) might be fully accomplished (*plērophopēthe*) and that all the Gentiles might hear" (2 Tim 4:17). The fulfillment of the *kērugma* becomes another aspect of preaching whereby the Lord–Paul's usual designation for "Christ Jesus our Lord" (2 Tim 1:2)—empowers[6] the preacher to accomplish that which is divinely intended: that the nations would hear the message of the gospel.

Before Paul told Archippus to fulfill is ministry (Col 4:17), he had given himself as a pattern for fulfilled ministry when he wrote, "I was made a minister according to the stewardship from God bestowed on me for your benefit, that I might fulfill the

---

2. Paul uses *plērophoreō* five times of the seven it appears in the Greek Bible (Eccl 8:11; Luke 1:1; Rom 4:21; 14:5; Col 4:12; 2 Tim 4:5, 17), and he also uses the related noun *plērophoias* two of its four appearances (Col 2:2; 1 Thess 1:5; Heb 6:11; 10:22).

3. The basic meaning of πληρόω is "to cause something to become full." L&N § 159.37 note that the verb is a derivative of πλήρης ('full'). The verb *plēroō* appears 195 times in the Greek Bible, including twenty-three times in Paul's letters (Rom 1:29; 8:4; 13:8; 15:13, 14, 19; 2 Cor 7:4; 10:6; Gal 5:14; Eph 1:23; 3:19; 4:10; 5:18; Phil 1:11; 2:2; 4:18, 19; Col 1:9, 25; 2:10; 4:17; 2 Thess 1:11; 2 Tim 1:4). BDAG § 5979 insists that πληροφορέω a synonym of πληρόω, yet one must ask if that was the case, why then did Paul not use πληρόω again in 2 Tim 4:5 since he begins the letter with that word when he reminds Timothy how he longed to see him, "so that I may be filled with joy" (2 Tim 1:4).

4. BDAG § 7800.1 defines the primary meaning of φορέω "to carry or bear habitually or for a considerable length of time."

5. Delling, "πληροφορέω," *TDNT* 4:309–11 defines the word as "to bring to fullness."

6. BDAG § 2616.1 defines ἐνδυναμόω, "to cause one to be able to function." The verb appears only eight times in the Greek Bible, in Judges 6:34, "So the Spirit of the LORD came upon Gideon"; Acts 9:22, "But Saul kept increasing in strength"; Rom 4:20, that Abraham "was strengthened in faith"; Eph 6:10, "Finally, be strong in the Lord"; Phil 4:13, "I can do all things through Him who strengthens me"; 1 Tim 1:12, "I thank Christ Jesus our Lord, who has strengthened me"; 2 Tim 2:1, "You therefore, my son, be strong in the grace that is in Christ Jesus"; and here in 2 Tim 4:17, "But the Lord stood with me, and strengthened me." In each case, the word indicates a divine empowering.

word of God" (*plērōsai ton logon toū theoū*; Col 1:25). The context of this verse clearly shows that Paul fulfills the word by the verbal preaching of the gospel, when he is "proclaiming Christ, admonishing every man, and teaching every man in all wisdom" (Col 1:28), To emphasize this point, the NAS inserts "the preaching" into Col 1:25, "that I might fully carry out *the preaching* of the Word of God."[7] A similar cross-reference is found in Romans 15:19, where Paul writes, "From Jerusalem and round about as far as Illyricum I have fully preached the gospel of Christ" (*peplērōkena to euangelion toū Xristoū*). The NAS has again inserted the word "preached" into Rom 15:19 (only this time it was not italicized as it should have been, because the verb *kērussō* is not found in any Greek text), raising the question if Paul means that (1) he preached the whole content of the Word (as in Acts 20:27) or (2) if he blanketed the entire geographical region with the gospel, in accordance with his commission. The first option should not be questioned: Paul was always thorough with the content of his message. The second option, then, is the most likely interpretation: Paul has completed the task assigned to him by the risen Lord, fulfilling the Word.[8]

However, the idea of fulfilling is far broader than merely telling of a bare completion of a task.[9] This fact is shown in yet another instance where Paul uses *plērophoria* in the context of preaching: he reminds his converts that the gospel came to them not in word only—of course, it must come at least in word—but "also in power (*dunamei*) and in the Holy Spirit and with full conviction" (*plērophoria*, 1 Thess 1:5). Remarking on the use of *plērophoria*, Delling observes, "The declaration of the glad tidings of the apostle took place, not in mere words, but in great 'fullness of divine working.' The word [*plērophoria*] is thus one of the terms which Paul uses to try to define linguistically the great fullness of the divine work in the present life of Christianity."[10] If this divine fullness is the intent of *plērophoreō*, then the fulfilling of the gospel is not what the preacher says or how the hearer responds, but rather it is what the Word effects, because it comes in the power of the divine Fulfiller, the Holy Spirit.[11] Therefore, when Paul tells Timothy to "fulfill his ministry," he is not making primary reference to the preacher's ability to execute his commission to preach but rather reminding him of the energy that comes from the filling ministry of God the Holy Spirit. Only by such divine fulfilling will the preacher be enabled to accomplish what God has assigned to him.

7. The addition of "the preaching" has been questionable as a translation, and interpreters have wrestled with Paul's meaning. Eadie, *Colossians*, 91–92, gives an overview of the various opinions.

8. Delling, "πληρόω," *TDNT* 6:1297.

9. Eadie, *Colossians*, 92, decides, "Whether you regard [the word *phoreō* as showing] the purpose of its author, its own genius or adequacy, its unlimited offer, indiscriminate invitations, and tested efficacy; the apostle in preaching everywhere, and to all classes without reserve, labored, 'to fulfill the Word of God.'"

10. Delling, "πληροφορέω," *TDNT* 3:11.

11. The idea that the Holy Spirit fulfills His own Scripture is noted in Acts 1:16 ("The Scripture had to be fulfilled, which the Holy Spirit foretold by the mouth of David.") and in Rom 8:4 ("The requirement of the Law might be fulfilled in us, who do not walk according to the flesh, but according to the Spirit.").

The Filling of God

The concept of fullness (*plēroma*) plays a prominent role in Paul's theology: his understanding of fullness springs from the immensity of God, "who fills all in all" (Eph 1:23). Divine fullness is remarkably extended to His saints, that they may be "filled up to all the fullness of God" (Eph 3:19)—undoubtedly one of the most stupendous statements asserted in Scripture—so that each believer has been made full in Christ (Col 2:10). Significantly, the first result of the fullness of the Holy Spirit listed in Eph 5:18–21 is that believers are "speaking to one another in psalms and hymns and spiritual songs"; that is, the Holy Spirit causes believers to be filled with praises for God as derived from His Word.[12] The parallel reference in Col 3:16 ("Let the word of Christ richly dwell within you, with all wisdom teaching and admonishing one another with psalms *and* hymns *and* spiritual songs.") shows that filling by the Spirit and indwelling with the Word are one and the same, so to be filled with the Spirit is to be filled with the Word—and *vice versa*. This identity is certain because the written Word of the Spirit continues to be the speaking voice of the Spirit.

Because it is a mark of the true servant of God that his mouth speaks the Word of God through the enabling of the Spirit, it is of keen interest to the preacher that he experience the fullness of the Spirit in order to fulfill his ministry. This fullness is both subjective (as the pneumatic infilling by the Spirit in the heart of the believer) and also objective (as the nouetic infilling of the living God in the mind of the believer), so the preacher needs not only to understand the gospel but also to incorporate the dynamic of its message in order to preach it in the fullness of both the Word and the Spirit. As a practical application, the preacher should be meditating "day and night" on the Word of God (Josh 1:8; Ps 1:2) and always be memorizing portions of Scripture so that its words may indwell his mind, fill his heart and then come forth in his teaching (Deut 6:6–7).[13]

The Dynamic of the Gospel

The word *plērophoreō* would also remind Timothy that the fulfillment of his ministry is to be found within the fullness of the gospel message itself. When Paul states that he has "fulfilled (*peplērōkenai*) the gospel of Christ" (Rom 15:19), the phrase *to euangelion toū Xristoū* is generally understood as an objective genitive ("the gospel that

---

12. Without entering into the discussion on exclusive Psalmody in public worship, it does appear that Paul uses the adjective *pneumatikos* in Eph 5:19 (and elsewhere in Rom 1:11; 7:14; 15:27; 1 Cor 2:13, 15; 3:1; 9:11; 10:3, 4; 12:1; 14:1, 37; 15:44, 46; Gal 6:1; Eph 1:3; 6:12; Col 1:9; 3:16) to mean, "the things pertaining to the Holy Spirit," as in spiritual gifts, Law, words, body, and people. In that case, the reference in Eph 5:19 and Col 3:16 to "spiritual odes" would at the very least include the book of Psalms, as given by inspiration of the Spirit (Matt 22:43; Acts 2:25), and also the singing of other portions of Scripture. BDAG §5999.2 states that *pneumatikos* is used ". . . [i]n the great majority of cases in reference to the divine πνεῦμα."

13. An excellent habit is for the preacher to memorize the text of his next sermon and then mull it over throughout the week. That way, his thinking and speaking becomes more "bibline."

comes from Christ"), but it could also be taken as a subjective genitive, "the gospel that Christ speaks." If Paul means the latter, he would be emphasizing that the gospel comes with dynamic effect because it is the Ascended Christ Himself who confirms the preached message by His own power.[14] Paul makes note of this reality several times in his letters, as he does in 1 Thess 1:5, "Our gospel did not come to you in word only, but also in power (*dunamis*) and in the Holy Spirit and with full conviction," as well as in 1 Cor 2:4, "My message and my preaching were not in persuasive words of wisdom, but in demonstration of the Spirit and of power" (*dunamis*). The link of the Spirit's power with the Word of the message shows that the effectiveness of the gospel (to convert sinners and build up the sanctified, Acts 20:32) comes not from the persuasive ability of the preacher, but from the effective dynamic of the Spirit inherent within the gospel as His *logos* and *kērugma*.

Paul is convinced that this dynamic of the gospel pervades the entire process of his preaching. He is not ashamed of the gospel, for it is the power (*dunamis*) of God unto salvation (Rom 1:16) because it is God Himself who exhorts sinners through the preacher to be reconciled (2 Cor 5:20).[15] While "the word of the cross is to those who are perishing foolishness, to us who are being saved it is the *dunamis* of God" (1 Cor 1:18) because it has inherent efficacy to save "everyone believing" (Rom 1:16). Thus, the gospel "constantly bears fruit and increases" (Col 1:6) because of its power as the word of truth. In a similar vein, Paul commends the Ephesian elders to the Word of God's grace, "which is able (*dunamai*) to edify and give the inheritance" (Acts 20:32). Plainly, the efficacy of preaching does not depend on the ability of the preacher but in the power of the preached Word, so that even when Paul and Barnabas spoke boldly, their reliance was "upon the Lord, who was bearing witness to the word of His grace, granting that signs and wonders be done by their hands" in confirmation of their preaching (Acts 14:3). The most obvious evidence of the gospel dynamic is the effectual hearing and understanding of the grace of God in truth, so that sinners actually do believe in Christ when they learn it from faithful servants of Christ such as Epaphras (Col 1:4–7). Grundmann observes, "In the message of Christ we thus have the power of God which is the power of salvation. The power of God in the gospel consists in the fact that it mediates salvation, that by the gospel God delivers men from the power of darkness and translates them into the kingdom of His dear Son."[16] It

---

14. L&N § 76.1 defines the use of *dunamis* in such context as having "the potentiality to exert force in performing some function."

15. Grundmann, "δύναμαι," *TDNT* 2:309, insists, "The δύναμις θεοῦ, which is the Gospel, is not an empty word. It is grounded in the divine act of deliverance in the Christ event, which overcomes the rule of Satan and which works itself out in the continued, factual deliverance accompanied by the preaching of the Gospel." Grundmann, however, may come dangerously close to confusing the historical events of redemption—the crucifixion and resurrection of Jesus—with the existential encounter of preaching, but his point here is otherwise quite accurate: the reality of the Cross is brought to bear on sinners in the proclamation of the word of the cross (1 Cor 1:18).

16. Ibid., 2:309.

is indisputable that Paul believed that if there was any power in his preaching, it came from the Holy Spirit applying His Word to the hearts of hearers, not in the persuasiveness of the preacher.

It is in the preacher's comprehension of the dynamic of the gospel that his preaching becomes effective, for such awareness gives the preacher the optimism that his words will not fall on deaf ears due to God's assertion, "My word . . . shall not return to Me empty, without accomplishing what I desire, and without succeeding *in the matter* for which I sent it" (Isa 55:11). Of course, this sovereign declaration does not negate the preacher's responsibility to "preach the Word . . . with great patience and instruction" (2 Tim 4:2), but it is a reminder that the dynamic of preaching comes not from the preacher but rather, as James 1:21 advises, from "the word implanted, which is able to save your souls." It is not the preacher or the hearer who implants the Word, but it is the life-giving dynamic of the gospel that saves the soul.

The Dynamic Energy

When Paul states that "our gospel did not come to you in word only (*in logō monon*, 1 Thess 1:5), he makes it clear that the Word is not merely verbal, but it becomes dynamically energized when it "performs (*energeō*) its work in you who believe" (1 Thess 2:13). In Pauline thought, every believer is "energized" by "the surpassing greatness of His *dunamis* toward us who believe according to the *energeia* of the strength of His might" (Eph 1:19), the same "*energeia* by which God is able [*dunamai*] to subject all things to Himself" (Phil 3:21).[17] These terms describe the dynamic energy by which God "in-works" (*energōn*) in the believer, "both to will and to work (*energeōn*) for *His* good pleasure" (Phil 2:13), but what interests this study is that Paul uses these same words several times for the dynamic energy he received to fulfill his commission to preach the gospel.

For example, in Eph 3:7, Paul claims, "I was made a minister (of the gospel), according to the gift of God's grace which was given to me according to the *energeian* of His *dunameōn* . . . to preach to the Gentiles the unfathomable riches of Christ" (Eph 3:7–8). Paul clearly refers to his apostolic commission (Eph 3:5), a point he also makes in Gal 2:8 when he comments, "He who effectually worked (*energēsas*) for Peter in *his* apostleship to the circumcised effectually worked (*enērgēsen*) for me also to the Gentiles." This empowerment for service was given by "Christ Jesus our Lord," who strengthened (*endunamoō*) Paul when He entrusted him with "the gospel of the glory of the

---

17. Delling, "ἐνεργέω," *TDNT* 2:652, defines *energeō* by transliteration, "energy," and he notes that the NT uses it "almost exclusively for the work of divine or demonic powers, so that we almost have a technical use." Paul uses *energeō* eighteen times of the twenty-eight times it appears in the Greek Bible (Rom 7:5; 1 Cor 12:6, 11; 2 Cor 1:6; 4:12; Gal 2:8, 8; 3:5; 5:6; Eph 1:11, 20; 2:2; 3:20; Phil 2:13, 13; Col 1:29; 1 Thess 2:13; 2 Thess 2:7), plus he uses the noun *energeia* eight times of the sixteen times it is found in Greek Bible (2 Macc 3:29; 3 Macc 4:21; 5:12, 28; Wis 7:17, 26; 13:4; 18:22; Eph 1:19; 3:7; 4:16; Phil 3:21; Col 1:29; 2:12; 2 Thess 2:9, 11).

blessed God," an apparent reference to the appearance of the risen Lord on the road to Damascus (1 Tim 1:11–12).[18] While the modern preacher cannot claim an apostolic calling, he can rely on the same dynamic energy of the apostle, who asserts, when he proclaims Christ, that he admonishes and teaches by "striving according to His *energeia*, which works (*energoumenēn*) within me in *dunamei*" (Col 1:29). It is that same dynamic energy that the preacher must rely upon in order to "fulfill his ministry."

Unlike the spiritualist medium who manipulates the impersonal forces of spiritual energy, the preacher should realize that God's energy is exhibited in the speaking voice of the living God. Paul makes the connection between God's energy and His word in 1 Thess 2:13 when he reminds his readers how when they received from his preaching the "word of hearing, you received it not as the word of men but as it truly is, the word of God, which also energizes in you who believe" (AT). So, as the preacher fills his mind and heart with the written Word of God, it becomes energetic through the direct in-working of the Holy Spirit. The written Word then becomes incarnate in the preacher, and he is enabled to preach with effectiveness because God opens "a great and energetic (*energēs*) door for him" (1 Cor 16:9, AT). In this way, the Word of God is mediated to the congregation through the preacher, demonstrating that he "fulfills his ministry" through the dynamic energy given by "the same God who works (*energōn*) all things in all" (1 Cor 12:6).

The Dynamic of Mediation

Protestants have historically steered away from any mention of pastoral mediation, insisting that the Roman Catholic concept of a sacerdotal priesthood undercuts the NT emphasis that all believers are a "holy priesthood, offering up spiritual sacrifices acceptable to God through Jesus Christ" (1 Pet 2:5). Furthermore, nowhere does the NT describe any New Covenant minister as a priest or a mediator; instead, these titles are reserved for Christ Jesus as "a merciful and faithful high priest in things pertaining to God" (Heb 2:17) and as the "one mediator also between God and men, *the* man Christ Jesus" (1 Tim 2:5). The closest Paul comes to such language appears in Rom 15:15–16, where he writes of "the grace given me by God to be a minister of Christ Jesus to the Gentiles in the priestly service (*hierourgeō*) of the gospel of God, so that the offering of the Gentiles may be acceptable, sanctified by the Holy Spirit" (ESV).[19] Clearly, Paul uses the priestly terminology in a figurative sense, since he is not actually sacrificing Gentiles in the way a priest would offer a lamb, but the sacrificial language does indicate a mediatorial function of the preacher, of bringing the Word of God to

---

18. Murphy O'Conner, *Paul on Preaching*, 84, asks, "When is this supernatural aptitude for the office of preacher given? The reference is to the apparition on the Damascus Road, confirmed by the context of 1 Tim 1:12."

19. The only NT appearance of the verb ἱερουργέω is here in Romans 15:16, and it is a compound of *hiereus*, "priest," and *ergazomai*, "to work"; thus, the meaning is, "to work as a priest" (L&N § 53.85).

fellow-humans, and then bringing them to God. Grasso writes, "Preaching . . . is the vehicle through which the Word of God to man passes. He who speaks is God, but to make His voice heard He uses a human instrument, the Church in its preachers."[20] Since an edifying word of an individual believer "may give grace to those who hear" (Eph 4:29), how much more might grace be given to the preacher to evangelize with the unfathomable riches of Christ (Eph 3:8)!

In this sense, the minister does perform sacramental and mediatorial duties in that he administers the various means of grace in his preaching; for example, whenever he reads the God-breathed Scripture or preaches it, he mediates the Word of God, since faith comes by hearing the word of Christ (Rom 10:17), which is heard in "the word of faith that we are preaching" (Rom 10:8). However, one should not suppose that the Word is inert or ineffective apart from the mediation of a preacher, as some sacerdotalists would insist; rather, its effectiveness is found in the dynamic of the Holy Spirit, who combines the human words spoken by the preacher with words taught by the Spirit (1 Cor 2:14). Since the ministry of preaching the Word is especially given to elders who "work hard in word and teaching" (1 Tim 5:17), they should have a deeper understanding that the Word of God's grace edifies and gives inheritance to all being sanctified, and that mediation occurs in the dynamic of preaching (Acts 20:32).

Preaching as Mediation

Saving and sanctifying grace is mediated to the believer through the Word, especially the preached Word. Though somewhat neglected by Protestants leery of Roman Catholic influence, the concept of mediated grace is recognized in the Reformed creeds, no doubt because it is documented biblical truth,[21] best illustrated in Rom 15:18, where Paul states, "I will not presume to speak of anything except what Christ has accomplished through me, resulting in the obedience of the Gentiles by word and deed." Paul pictures himself as an agent of mediation, through whom (di[22] $emoū$) the Risen Christ works, by the words and deeds of the apostle, bringing about the obedience of those who hear. This same idea of mediation appears in the context of Paul's charge to Timothy to "fulfill his ministry," when the apostle spoke of the Lord's empowering "in order that through me (di' $emoū$) the proclamation might be fully accomplished" (2 Tim 4:17).

---

20. Grasso, *Proclaiming God's Message*, 56.

21. For example, the *Westminster Larger Catechism* Q. 154 asks, "What are the outward means whereby Christ communicates to us the benefits of his mediation?" It provides this answer: "The outward and ordinary means whereby Christ communicates to his church the benefits of his mediation, are all his ordinances; especially the word, sacraments, and prayer; all which are made effectual to the elect for their salvation" (citing as prooftexts Matt 28:19–20; Acts 2:42, 46–47).

22. L&N defines the preposition διά as "a marker of intermediate agent" (§ 90.4), as "a marker of the instrument by which something is accomplished" (§ 90.8), or as a marker of "the means by which one event makes another event possible" (§ 89.76).

Can the same mediation be assumed by the parish preacher? While Paul states that God's primary means by which salvation is mediated is "through (*dia*) the washing and renewal of the Holy Spirit" (Titus 3:5), it is "through the gospel" (*dia toū euangeliou*, 2 Thess 2:14) that God calls sinners to Himself. So, whenever the preacher faithfully preaches the apostolic message, the Holy Spirit calls His own unto "the possession of the glory of our Lord Jesus Christ" (1 Thess 2:14), communicating to them the benefits of salvation as He speaks through the written word of His prophets (Acts 28:25). Effectual hearing that leads to saving faith comes from "hearing through (*dia*) the word of Christ" (Rom 10:17), so that when the Lord gives opportunity, the unsaved hear His servants "through whom" (*di' ōn*) they believe unto salvation (1 Cor 3:5), making the preached word the primary means by which "the Lord opens the heart to respond to the things spoken" by the preacher (Acts 16:14).

Is it only through preaching that salvation is mediated to deafened sinners? While certainly the sovereign Spirit is free to work "just as He wills" (1 Cor 12:11), Paul addresses this question by asking, "How shall they believe in Him whom they have not heard?" (Rom 10:14b). The expected answer is that unbelievers will not believe if they have not heard, to which Paul follows with another question, "How shall they hear without preaching?" (Rom 10:14c). Although this question is usually translated, "How shall they hear without a preacher" (KJV, RSV, NAS), the ESV more accurately translates the participle *kērussontos*, "How are they to hear without someone preaching?" Whoever does the preaching is secondary to the process ("What then is Apollos? And what is Paul? Servants through whom you believed," 1 Cor 3:5), but what is essential for the conversion of a sinner is that the gospel is communicated by someone in some manner, whether in speech or in print.[23] The preacher should remember that he cannot regenerate anyone: it is in the exercise of the will of the Father of lights that He gives new birth by the word of truth (Jas 1:18). The evangelist is merely a "midwife" assisting in this birth, as Paul reminds his converts, "In Christ Jesus I begot you through the gospel" (*dia toū euaggeliou*, 1 Cor 4:15). Of course, just as babies can be born without the aid of a midwife, so individuals may (and do) come to Christ without a preacher being present, but not without the Word being present. A notable example is the conversion of the Ethiopian eunuch, who was initially informed and convicted through the reading of the prophet Isaiah, but he was still assisted to faith in Christ by the mediation of Philip, who "opened his mouth" (quite necessary for preaching!) and "from this Scripture he preached Jesus to him" (Acts 8:35). This process seems to show that the ordinary and normal means by which salvation is mediated to a lost sinner comes when the Holy Spirit confirms the message of the gospel when it is read

---

23. Friedrich, κηρύσσω, *TDNT* 3:711, claims, "The preaching of salvation has in itself an event of salvation," but this claim asserts too much, as it confuses the historical facts of redemption (the death and resurrection of Jesus) with its existential effects. Such a view seriously detracts from the uniqueness of the work of Christ. One can hardly imagine Paul confusing his work of preaching with Christ's work on the cross!

and/or spoken by someone preaching Jesus to him—thus showing why preaching is an essential mediation of the gospel.

The Preacher Mediates the Word

While Paul never calls the preacher a mediator, he does ascribe several functions to the preacher suggesting that he does mediate the realities of the New Covenant to others. Among these functions are "priesting," "stewarding," and "liturgizing," to coin some verbs from the related nouns.

Mediating the Word by "Priesting": Only once does Paul liken the ministry of the pastor to a priest, and even then only by using the verb *hierourgeō*, "to serve as a priest."[24] There Paul states, "Grace ... was given me from God, to be a minister of Christ Jesus to the Gentiles, ministering as a priest the gospel of God, that *my* offering of the Gentiles might become acceptable, sanctified by the Holy Spirit" (Rom 15:15–16). Although Paul pictures himself here as a priest, it is important to note that he is not offering sacrifices on behalf of the Gentiles but rather, he is offering the Gentiles as the sacrifice—no doubt as the "living sacrifice" he mentioned in Rom 12:2. Regardless, the use of this image of "priesting" indicates that the New Covenant minister does have some priestly functions. He is to present the people of his charge as a sanctified offering that shall be acceptable to God. The means by which he accomplishes this offering is by "the grace of God" given to him and by the "sanctification by the Spirit" (2 Thess 2:13). This priestly function raises the question of how this grace of holiness is brought to bear in the lives of believers.

Mediating the Word by "Stewarding": It is in the function of "stewarding" (*oikonomeō*) that the preacher dispenses the grace of God to the church. Previously, this study examined the office of the Steward, where it was seen that this office is specifically assigned to the elder when Paul states that "the overseer must be above reproach as God's steward" (*oikonomos*, Titus 1:7). The primary responsibility of a steward was to administer the possessions of the house-owner, which for the preacher is the gospel that God has entrusted to him (1 Cor 9:16–17). Because of that fact, Paul requests that "a man regard us in this manner, as servants of Christ, and stewards of the mysteries of God" (1 Cor 4:1). Assuming that this responsibility also applies to the parish preacher, then it shows that he has the duty to dispense God's mysteries so that he might further "the *oikonomia* of God which is by faith" (1 Tim 1:4).[25] As a steward speaks the instructions of the house-owner to the tenants, so the preacher as a steward mediates the commands

---

24. L&N § 53.92.

25. Michael, οἰκονομία, *TDNT* 5:152, notes that "there is room to doubt whether *oikonomia* denotes office or the divine plan of salvation." The two are closely linked because the knowledge of salvation is the stewardship entrusted by God to His stewards.

of the Lord to His people. To hear the steward is to hear the owner, so that the words of the master are in fact communicated to the church when the preacher acts as a faithful steward of the Lord Jesus.

Ministering by "Liturgizing": Another mediating aspect of Paul's ministry concerns the public worship of God, pictured when he gathered together with the church at Troas on the first day of the week to "break bread" and deliver to them a prolonged message (Acts 20:6). While the NT does not prescribe a specific liturgy in the manner that the OT mandated the sacrificial system, Paul does use OT liturgical terminology to describe the minister's duties, most notably the verb *leitourgeō* and the noun *leitourgia*.[26] For example, when Paul describes his journey to Jerusalem to offer the contribution for the poor Jewish saints, he notes that "if the Gentiles have shared in their spiritual things, they are indebted to minister (*leitourgēsai*) to them also in material things" (Rom 15:27)—an interesting irony in which formerly pagan Gentiles act as Levitical priests toward the Jews in what 2 Cor 9:12 calls, "the ministry (*diakonia*) of this *leitourgias*". The significance for Christian liturgy is that this material offering was presumably collected under the oversight of local church leadership, administered carefully by Paul's appointee Titus (2 Cor 8:16–24), delivered safely as a *diakonia* by Paul and other church designates (probably those named in Acts 20:4, Sopater of Berea, Aristarchus and Secundus of the Thessalonians; Gaius of Derbe, Timothy, Tychicus and Trophimus of Asia), and then disbursed by the elders in Jerusalem (Acts 21:18). The entire process shows the involvement of various church leaders in what Paul describes as a "liturgy," in the way that Acts 13:1–2 reports that the prophets and teachers of the church in Antioch "were ministering (*leitourgountōn*) to the Lord," presumably leading the gathered congregation in divine worship.

The apostle also uses the terminology of priestly functions to describe his own mediation when he calls himself a "minister (*leitourgos*) of Christ Jesus to the Gentiles,

---

26. The verb *leitourgeō* appears only three times in the NT (Acts 13:2; Rom 15:27; Heb 10:11), but ninety times in the LXX, with the vast majority describing the liturgical service of the priests and Levites. BDAG § 4536 thus correctly notes that λειτουργέω is used "in our lit. almost exclusively of religious and ritual services." Similarly, the noun *leitourgia* appears six times the NT (Luke 1:23; 2 Cor 9:12; Phil 2:17, 30; Heb 8:6; 9:21), but another forty-three times in the LXX, almost always for the "service in the tent of meeting" (Num 8:22) or for "all the service of the house of God" (1 Chron 28:21). Another verb used often of the OT sacrificial system is *propherō*, as a translation of *qorban*, "to bring an offering" (BDB § 8698), as used in Lev 1:2, "You shall bring your offering of animals from the herd or the flock." Hebrews 10:11 uses both verbs in describing the OT liturgy, "Every priest stands daily ministering (*leitourgōn*) and offering (*prospherōn*) time after time the same sacrifices." While *propherō* means primarily to bring someone or something to another (as in Matt 4:24, the disciples brought to Jesus all who were sick), when used in a religious context, it means "to bring an offering" (BDAG § 6349), as in Acts 21:26, when Paul "offered an offering," where the verb is used with the related noun *prosphora*. While the verb *propherō* is used twenty times in Hebrews (Heb 5:1, 3, 7; 8:3, 3, 4; 9:7, 9, 14, 25, 28; 10:1, 2, 8, 11, 12; 11:4, 17:2, 2; 12:7), it is not found in Paul's signed letters, and he uses the related noun *prosphora* only twice (Rom 15:16; Eph 5:2). Still, these NT references are sufficient to show that the concept of liturgy and offering are occasionally used to express NT worship.

ministering as a priest the gospel of God, that *my* offering (*prosphora*) of the Gentiles might become acceptable, sanctified by the Holy Spirit" (Rom 15:16). As a *leitourgos*, Paul performs the liturgy on behalf of other worshippers,[27] yet in an interesting twist, he is also "poured out as a drink offering upon the sacrifice and service (*leitourgia*) of your faith" (Phil 2:17), indicating that the preacher ought to consider himself to be like Paul's "brother and fellow-worker and fellow soldier" Epaphroditus, who was also a "messenger and minister (*leitourgos*)" to the needs of others (Phil 2:25). The testimony of this servant gives a sobering pattern for any preacher, since Epaphroditus "came close to death for the work of Christ, risking his life to complete what was deficient in the service (*leitourgias*)" of others (Phil 2:30).

Paul's use of liturgical terminology establishes a link between the worship of the Old Covenant and that of the New Covenant, as the apostle assigns the same mediating functions of the OT priests to the leaders of New Covenant worship services, although not in the offering of a sacrifice of blood but in the offering of service, which Heb 13:15 describes as "a sacrifice of praise to God, that is, the fruit of lips that give thanks to His name." Actually, the closest directive for conducting a first-century worship service is found in 1 Cor 14:26–33, where Paul instructs gifted men in the procedure for leading the assembly with an orderly speaking of "a psalm, a teaching, a revelation, a tongue, an interpretation" (1 Cor 14:26). Each of these activities refers to some form of public proclamation of divine prophecy, and since elders are elsewhere assigned to these duties (especially teaching, as in 1 Tim 5:17 and Titus 1:9), it is reasonable to assume that elders also serve as *leitourgoi* in leading the public gatherings for worship.

In this regard, Paul directs Timothy to "give attention to the *public* reading *of Scripture*, to exhortation and teaching" (1 Tim 4:13), a command applied by extension to every Christian minister, meaning that he serves as a mediator of the Word in public liturgy. When he reads the Scripture, exhorts in its directives, and teaches its doctrines, the preacher becomes the speaker through whom the Holy Spirit mediates His grace and truth to those who gather for worship.

Summary: Based on the examples found in Paul's writings, the preacher should view himself not as a mediator of grace–a title Paul reserves solely for Christ (1 Tim 2:5)—but certainly as one who mediates the Word of God to the people of God. While his voice is not indispensable to the communication of divine grace, his preaching is the normal means by which the Holy Spirit ministers to His people when they gather for public worship.

---

27. Strathmann, "λειτουργός," *TDNT* 4:229.

Preaching and Mediating the Signs

If the preacher serves to mediate the Word of salvation in his preaching, it is appropriate to ask what relationship a church leader has toward the outward signs of the New Covenant, variously called the ordinances or sacraments of Baptism and the Lord's Supper.[28] The Reformers reacted against Roman Catholic abuses in both practices by emphasizing that the duties of the minister are not only to preach the Word but also to administer the signs of salvation. This division of duty raises an unfortunate tension between sermon and sacrament that every preacher feels when he moves from the Pulpit to the Table or Baptistery, or *vice versa*.[29] Does he become a mediator of the grace of God when he administers the sacraments as Signs and Seals of that grace?

Without entering too deeply into this debate, several considerations ought to be noted. First, the Word and Sign go hand-in-hand with each other, illustrated when the original Christians "were continually devoting themselves to the apostles' teaching and . . . to the breaking of bread" (Acts 2:42). If a priority is to be considered, the Word must take precedence over the Sign, because a sign without an explanation remains nothing more than a basin of water, a cup of wine, or a loaf of bread—they have spiritual significance only when they are used within the context of Christian liturgy and when explained as signs of salvation. Furthermore, the reality to which a sign points is more important than the sign, in the way 1 Peter 3:21 announces, "Baptism now saves you"— an assertion sounding as if the sign is essential to salvation, as sacerdotalism insists—but then it continues, "not the removal of dirt from the flesh (as an outward sign), but an appeal to God for a good conscience (the inward reality)." The signs of the covenant have meaning only when tied to the historical realties of redemption, as Peter explains,

---

28. This study does not address the controversy of how to categorize Baptism and the Lord's Supper, the church ceremonies that historically have been called "ordinances" (in that Christ "ordered" them to be done) and "sacraments," the translation of *mustērion* in the Latin Vulgate (Eph 3:3; 5:32; 1 Tim 3:16). The closest biblical title for both rituals (for lack of a better term) might be "signs of the covenant," based on the description of the OT sign of circumcision in Gen 17:11, or "signs and seals," based on Rom 4:11. Even so, the NT is not concerned with a single label to hang on either Baptism or the Lord's Supper, since it pictures the "one baptism" (Eph 4:5) by numerous terms showing the application of water upon the believer, including cleansing (Acts 10:15; 11:19; 15:9; 2 Cor 7:1; Eph 5:26; Titus 2:14; Heb 9:14; 1 John 1:7, 9); washing (John 13:10; Acts 22:16; 1 Cor 6:11; Heb 10:22); purifying (1 Pet 1:22); sprinkling (Heb 10:22; 1 Pet 1:2); perhaps also pouring (Acts 10:45–48), and bathing (Eph 5:26; Titus 3:5). For that matter, the NT titles the Bread and the Cup not only as "The Lord's Supper" (1 Cor 10:20), but also as the "Breaking of the Bread" (*klasis*, Acts 2:42), "Communion" (*koinonia*, 1 Cor 10:16), "Eucharist" (for the "giving of thanks," *eucharisteō*, 1 Cor 11:24), "The Table of the Lord" (1 Cor 10:21), and perhaps even "The Blessing" (*eulogia*, 1 Cor 10:16). In light of this diversity, discussion in this section will use the terms Ordinance and Sacrament interchangeably but will prefer the biblical designation of a Sign.

29. One can see this tension in Christian church architecture, with sacerdotal sanctuaries placing the Table up front and center, with the pulpit located off to one side, whereas Reformed Churches moved the Pulpit behind and above the Table. The message is clear: the Word is to be pre-eminent, but it can be approached only through the Body and Blood of the Savior. One must wonder what it signifies when the Baptistery—historically placed in the entrance of the church building as the "door" to salvation—is often elevated above and behind the Table and the Pulpit.

"baptism now saves—through the resurrection of Jesus Christ" (1 Pet 3:21, AT), or as Paul notes that "as often as you eat this bread and drink the cup, you proclaim the Lord's death until He comes" (1 Cor 11:26). It is not that the elements savingly affect the Lord's death upon the participants but rather it is the participants who are proclaiming (*kataggellete*) through the elements the foundational event of salvation—the past historical death of Jesus on the cross—while announcing the completion of salvation at His future return. The following illustration pictures this relationship:

Historical Act →	**Explanation of Word**	→ **Sign of Covenant** →	**Reality of Salvation**
Baptism of Jesus →	Acts 1:5;[30] 2:18;[31] 2:33[32] →	Acts 2:41[33] →	1 Cor 12:13[34]
Death of Jesus →	1 Cor 11:26[35] →	1 Cor 11:24–25[36] →	1 Cor 10:16[37]

The above diagram shows that the most important aspect of the Sign is the historical event to which it points. Quite obviously, if there had been no cross at Calvary or no outpouring of the Spirit at Pentecost, then there would be no ceremonies designed to commemorate those events. However, historical events are quite unintelligible unless their significance is explained. After all, Jewish men often died on Roman crosses, so what is different about the crucifixion of Jesus of Nazareth? Foreign languages were heard daily on the streets of Jerusalem, yet the tongues heard on the day of Pentecost prompted the question, "What does this mean?" (Acts 2:12). Thus, the Word explaining the Event must take precedence over the Sign pointing to the Event, a fact Paul states emphatically when he insists, "Christ did not send me to baptize, but to preach the gospel" (1 Cor 1:17). It is in the preaching of the Word by which the signs become seals of salvation; otherwise, the signs remain nothing more than outward rituals.[38]

The practice of the apostolic church shows that the preached Word always accompanies the administration of the Signs (see Acts 8:12; 36; 10:47–48; 16:14–15; 16:31–33; 18:8; 19:4–5; 1 Cor 11:23–26), and due to this close tie between preaching

---

30. Acts 1:5, "John baptized with water, but you shall be baptized with the Holy Spirit not many days from now."

31. Acts 2:18, "I will in those days pour forth of My Spirit."

32. Acts 2:33, "Having received from the Father the promise of the Holy Spirit, He has poured forth this which you both see and hear."

33. Acts 2:41, "So then, those who had received his word were baptized."

34. 1 Corinthians 12:13, "For by one Spirit we were all baptized into one body."

35. 1 Corinthians 11:26, "For as often as you eat this bread and drink the cup, you proclaim the Lord's death until He comes."

36. 1 Corinthians 11:23–25, "The Lord Jesus in the night in which He was betrayed took bread; and when He had given thanks, He broke it, and said, 'This is My body, which is for you; do this in remembrance of Me.' In the same way *He took* the cup also, after supper, saying, 'This cup is the new covenant in My blood; do this, as often as you drink *it*, in remembrance of Me.'"

37. 1 Corinthians 10:16, "Is not the cup of blessing which we bless a sharing in the blood of Christ? Is not the bread which we break a sharing in the body of Christ?"

38. This argument is made by Reicke, "A Synopsis of Early Christian Preaching," in *Root of the Vine*, 148–49.

and sacrament, the church historically has reserved the right to administer the signs to those whom the church has ordained to preach. Thus, the preacher of the Word is to proclaim (*kataggellō*, 1 Cor 11:26) the significance of the Signs so that the recipient may experience the spiritual realities represented by the Signs, baptism by the Spirit (1 Cor 12:13) and communion in the blood and body of Christ (1 Cor 10:16).[39] It would seem that this duty of explanation falls within the stewardship of every elder who "works hard at preaching and teaching" (1 Tim 5:17), suggesting that there appears to be no biblical warrant for denying the privilege of administering the Signs to a ruling elder, since he is called to the same office as a teaching elder. Because the ruling elder must also "exhort in sound doctrine" (Titus 1:9), he should be able to explain the significance of the Signs as correctly as a teaching elder would do.

The historical reason that the church has entrusted the administration of the Signs to an ordained officer is that he is designated in Scripture as "a steward of God" (Titus 1:7), and the primary prooftext cited in support of this position is 1 Cor 4:1, "Let a man regard us in this manner, as servants of Christ, and stewards of the mysteries of God." The connection is made that the "mysteries of God" refer to the "sacred mysteries" of the sacraments, and perhaps somewhat surprising, this interpretation is the view of Calvin.[40] At first glance, this position appears to be exegetically suspect, because Paul tends to use *mustērion* for divine revelation, not for divine signs; however, by implication, Calvin's interpretation may not be ruled out. Certainly, the signs of the covenant are part of the revealed mysteries of Christ's covenant, and they certainly seem to be the means by which the Holy Spirit dispenses grace to the people of God through the mediation of the preacher. This duty of the preacher as a steward of God is an awesome privilege, yet it has been downplayed by Protestant theology in reaction to the Roman Catholic view that grants saving mediation to its priests. Protestant interpretation has rightly insisted that no mere man can thwart or manipulate the grace of God, but Paul indicates that a mere man can in fact mediate the grace of God in the moment of dispensing the Signs of the New Covenant in accord with the Word of God.

Summary to Mediation

This study has demonstrated that the preacher does in fact mediate the saving and sanctifying grace of God whenever he reads or preaches the Word of God. Preaching itself is the agency whereby God grants to those who hear to believe in Christ (Phil 1:29), so that the preacher of the Word becomes a mediator as a steward dispensing

---

39. The *Westminster Larger Catechism* Q. 161 asks, "How do the sacraments become effectual means of salvation?" and it provides this answer: "The sacraments become effectual means of salvation, not by any power in themselves, or any virtue derived from the piety or intention of him by whom they are administered, but only by the working of the Holy Ghost, and the blessing of Christ, by whom they are instituted" (citing 1 Pet 3:21; Acts 8:13, 23; 1 Cor 3:6–7; 1 Cor 12:13).

40. Calvin, *Institutes of the Christian Religion* 4.3.6.

the mysteries of God. This enabling also extends to the administration of the Signs of the Covenant, Baptism and the Lord's Supper, not in the sense of bestowing special grace but by demonstrating a visual representation of the kerygma.

In light of this awesome responsibility to mediate the Word of God's grace, no wonder Paul exclaims, "Who is adequate for these things?" (2 Cor 2:16). He answers his own question, "Not that we are adequate in ourselves to consider anything as *coming* from ourselves, but our adequacy is from God, who also made us adequate *as* servants of a new covenant" (2 Cor 3:5–6). This sufficiency comes from the dynamic gifting of the Holy Spirit by which Timothy—and every other preacher—is enabled to fulfill his ministry.

The Dynamic of Charisma

Paul credits his calling as a minister of the gospel to "the gift (*charisma*) of God's grace which was given to me according to the working of His power; to me, the very least of all saints, this grace was given, to preach to the Gentiles the unfathomable riches of Christ" (Eph 3:7–8). Likewise, he reminds Timothy "to kindle afresh the gift (*charisma*) of God which is in you" (2 Tim 1:6), bringing to his attention the divine source and dynamic power of fulfilling his ministry, the gift (*charisma*) of grace (*charis*). Because "to each one of us grace was given according to the measure of Christ's gift" (*charisma*, Eph 4:7), every preacher needs to understand how this same dynamic of *charisma* applies to him in fulfilling his own ministry to preach the Word.

The Nature of Charisma

It almost goes without saying that the gift (*charisma*) of the grace of God is one of Paul's favorite themes, as he scatters the noun *charis* an even one hundred times throughout his signed letters.[41] When he ties grace to ministry,[42] Paul is not referring

---

41. The noun χάρις (BDAG § 7895, "a beneficent disposition toward someone, favor, grace") appears 100 times in Paul's letters (Rom 1:5, 7; 3:24; 4:4, 16; 5:2, 15, 17, 20, 21; 6:1, 14, 15, 17; 7:25; 11:5, 6; 12:3, 6; 15:15; 16:20; 1 Cor 1:3, 4; 3:10; 10:30; 15:10, 57; 16:3, 23; 2 Cor 1:2, 12, 15; 2:14; 4:15; 6:1; 8:1, 4, 6, 7, 9, 16, 19; 9:8, 14, 15; 12:9; 13:13; Gal 1:3, 6, 15; 2:9, 21; 5:4; 6:18; Eph 1:2, 6, 7; 2:5, 7, 8; 3:2, 7, 8; 4:7, 29; 6:24; Phil 1:2, 7; 4:23; Col 1:2, 6; 3:16; 4:6, 18; 1 Thess 1:1; 5:28; 2 Thess 1:2, 12; 2:16; 3:18; 1 Tim 1:2, 12, 14; 6:21; 2 Tim 1:2, 3, 9; 2:1; 4:22; Titus 1:4; 2:11; 3:7, 15; Phlm 1:3, 25); plus the verb χαρίζομαι (BDAG § 8993, "to give freely") appears another sixteen times (Rom 8:32; 1 Cor 2:12; 2 Cor 2:7, 10; 12:13; Gal 3:18; Eph 4:32; Phil 1:29; 2:9; Col 2:13; 3:13; Phlm 1:22).

42. As in Rom 1:5, "we have received grace and apostleship"; Rom 12:6, "gifts that differ according to the grace given to us"; Rom 15:15–16, "the grace that was given me from God, to be a minister of Christ Jesus"; 1 Cor 3:10, "According to the grace of God which was given to me, as a wise master builder I laid a foundation"; 1 Cor 15:10, "But by the grace of God I am what I am, and His grace toward me did not prove vain; but I labored even more than all of them, yet not I, but the grace of God with me"; 2 Cor 12:9, "He has said to me, "My grace is sufficient for you, for power is perfected in weakness"; Gal 2:9, "recognizing the grace that had been given to me, James and Cephas and John . . .gave to me and Barnabas the right hand of fellowship, that we *might go* to the Gentiles, and they to

to saving grace whereby God declares a sinner to be righteous (as in Rom 3:24), but rather he refers to enabling grace by which the believer is empowered to do the will of God (1 Cor 15:10). Grace in such contexts stresses the vital dynamic of sanctification and service instead of the legal status that governs Paul's understanding of justification. Frankly, this aspect of grace tends to be neglected by Protestant theology in its reaction against Roman Catholicism, which has traditionally understood grace in its subjective and dynamic elements while minimizing grace in the legal relationship of justification. In actuality, Paul teaches both aspects of grace, the legal and the dynamic. While the preacher must ever assert justifying grace as the efficacious cause of salvation (Acts 15:11), he must also rely on charismatic grace to grant him the ongoing sufficiency to persevere in holiness and labor in ministry (1 Cor 15:10).[43]

The Preacher's *Charismata*

According to Eph 4:7, each believer is given grace according to the measure of Christ's gift (*dorea*) whereby each one is granted a gift (*charisma*) of service to others, "as good stewards of the manifold grace of God" (1 Pet 4:10). Similarly, Paul thanks God for His grace given in Christ Jesus to his Corinthian readers, "that in everything you were enriched in Him, in all speech and all knowledge, . . . so that you are not lacking in any gift" (*charismati*, 1 Cor 1:4–7), a sampling of which is given later in the letter (1 Cor 12:8–10).[44] Despite the variety of *charismata*, it is the same Spirit who gives them (1 Cor 12:4), so that not every believer has every gift, as Rom 12:6–8 makes clear, for "we have *charismata* that differ according to the grace given to us." These gifts include prophecy, service, teaching, exhorting, giving, leading and showing mercy—gifts that have special reference to church leadership, particularly the preacher and his speaking ministry. If he is to preach, he most certainly should evidence these speaking *charismata*.

No preacher can afford to forget that his gifts are endowed to him by the Holy Spirit. His labors, energies and abilities to "preach the Word" do not come from the force of his personality nor by the skillful use of his natural aptitudes (which is the secularized meaning of a "charismatic" leader, as if the man had gifted himself!), but rather from "the one and the same Spirit [who] works all these things, distributing to each one individually just as He wills" (1 Cor 12:11). Nothing is as important to a

---

the circumcised.; Eph 3:2, "the stewardship of God's grace which was given to me for you;" Eph 3:7–8, "I was made a minister, according to the gift of God's grace which was given to me according to the working of His power. To me, the very least of all saints, this grace was given, to preach to the Gentiles the unfathomable riches of Christ"; 2 Tim 2:1, "be strong in the grace that is in Christ Jesus."

43. Hughes, "Grace," *EDT* 479–82, lists these various aspects of grace: common, prevenient, efficacious, irresistible, and sufficient.

44. 1 Corinthians 12:8–10 reads, "For to one is given the word of wisdom through the Spirit, and to another the word of knowledge according to the same Spirit; to another faith by the same Spirit, and to another gifts of healing by the one Spirit, and to another the effecting of miracles, and to another prophecy, and to another the distinguishing of spirits, to another *various* kinds of tongues, and to another the interpretation of tongues."

minister than performing his duties with an utter sense of reliance upon the gifting of the Holy Spirit, so that he "fulfills his ministry" only by the enabling *charismata* given by the Spirit. When the preacher who has various gifts "according to the grace given" to him exercises them—particularly the gift of prophecy—"according to the analogy of the faith" (Rom 12:6, AT), the Spirit is pleased to make the Word of God effective for the salvation of sinners and sanctification of the saints.[45]

Preaching as a *Charisma*

This gifting by the Spirit means that every preacher is "charismatic" in the sense that his preaching ability is a gift from God. In particular, Paul lists the speaking gifts given as "the manifestation of the Spirit for the common good" to include a "word of wisdom, to another a word of knowledge, . . . to another prophecy (1 Cor 12:7–10). Because there seems to be perennial disagreement among interpreters as to the nature of these gifts, a brief discussion on each is warranted.

Preaching and Revelatory Charismata: All evangelical interpreters, presumably, would agree that the "word of wisdom, the word of knowledge, and prophecy" refer to divine revelation, God's immediate voice speaking to His church through His prophets. The current debate, however, concerns whether these revelatory *charismata* have ceased or still continue, and if they continue, are they extra-biblical revelations on par with God-breathed Scripture (2 Tim 3:16)? More pointedly, when the preacher preaches the Word, does he speak revelation that is mediated through Scripture as written prophecy, or does he speak immediate revelation, a direct word of God apart from the written Word?

The answer to the question whether the revelatory *charismata* have ceased or continue depends quite heavily on one's understanding of 1 Cor 13:8–10, which states that "prophecies shall be abolished; tongues shall cease, knowledge shall be abolished, for we know in part, and we prophesy in part; but when the perfect [*to teleios*] comes, the partial will be done away." This appearance of *to teleios* is the only occurrence of the word with a definite article, so the interpreter must ask, the perfect what? If "the perfect" (*to teleios*) refers to the final eschatological state, then the revelatory gifts have

---

45. For example, the *Westminster Larger Catechism* Question 156 asks, "How is the word made effectual to salvation?" It answers, "The Spirit of God maketh the reading, but especially the preaching of the word an effectual means of enlightening, convincing, and humbling sinners; of driving them out of themselves, and drawing them unto Christ; of conforming them to his image, and subduing them to his will; of strengthening them against temptations and corruptions; of building them up in grace, and establishing their hearts in holiness and comfort through faith unto salvation" (citing Neh 8:8; Acts 26:18; Ps 19:8; 1 Cor 14:24–25; 2 Chron 34:18–28; Acts 2:37, 41; 8:27–39; 2 Cor 3:18; 10:4–6; Rom 6:17; Matt 4:4, 7, 10; Eph 6:16–17; Ps 19:11; 1 Cor 10:11; Acts 20:32; 2 Tim 3:15–17; Rom 16:25; 1 Thess 3:2, 10–13; Rom 15:4; 10:13–17; 1:16).

not yet been abolished, but the word *teleios* is not used anywhere else in the NT of the final state but of completed maturity of character.⁴⁶

On the other hand, if "the perfect" refers to the perfection of revelation, then an argument can be made for the case that special revelation ceased when the initial agents of prophecy, the prophets and apostles, died off by the end of the first century; in other words, the Holy Spirit withdrew these revelatory gifts from circulation when there were no more apostles and prophets who needed these *charismata*. In the place of prophets and apostles, the church now has "the prophetic word made more sure" (2 Pet 1:19), which is the written Word of those "men moved by the Holy Spirit (who) spoke from God" (2 Pet 1:21). In the present age, the church "should remember the words spoken beforehand by the holy prophets and the commandment of the Lord and Savior *spoken* by your apostles" (2 Pet 3:2). This quotation defines the limits of the NT canon, which shows evidence of very early compiling and editing, according to Trobisch's important study, *The First Edition of the New Testament*.⁴⁷ Once the canon of the NT was completed, the need for immediate revelation ended. Fittingly, the NT concludes with a warning not to add to or take away from "the words of the prophecy of this book" (Rev 22:18–19) because, ostensibly, the perfection of revelation has arrived.

The suggestion that the revelatory gifts have ceased with the appearance of the most sure word of Scripture certainly avoids the thorny problem of how continuing revelation should be monitored. The weight of theological consideration may be on the side of cessation and canonicity, for it gives a tidy answer to the appearance of contradictory prophecies, that such revelation would certainly not come from the Holy Spirit. Also, the cessation view at best rescues the church from the tyranny of so-called prophets who produce supposedly new truths for the faithful to obey. However, the cessationist view banks on a slim insistence that "the perfect" of 1 Cor 13:10 refers to the completed NT when there is no other confirming Scripture stating this to be the case, so caution is in order, lest we "despise prophetic utterances" (1 Thess 5:20).

Even if the revelatory gifts continue to be given to the church, those who hold to such a view should insist that no contemporary revelation could ever contradict any previous revelation of the Spirit of truth, who obviously does not and cannot contradict Himself ("The Spirit of truth . . . will guide you into all the truth," John 16:13). All prophecy must be "according to the analogy of the faith" (Rom 12:6, AT), for the

---

46. The word *teleios* appears in the Greek Bible in Gen 6:9; Exod 12:5; Deut 18:13; Jdg 20:26; 21:4; 2 Sam 22:26; 1 Kgs 8:61; 11:4; 15:3, 14; 1 Chr 25:8; 28:9; Ezra 2:63; Ps 138:22; Song 5:2; 6:9; Wis. 9:6; Sir. 44:17; Jer 13:19; Matt 5:48; 19:21; Rom 12:2; 1 Cor 2:6; 13:10; 14:20; Eph 4:13; Phil 3:15; Col 1:28; 4:12; Heb 5:14; 9:11; Jas 1:4, 17, 25; 3:2; 1 John 4:18. In nearly every instance, it refers to meeting the highest standard of character and maturity (BDAG § 7298), not to an eschatological state.

47. Trobisch, *The First Edition of the NT*, points to these evidences of a first century official edition of the NT: the notation of the *nomina sacra* in all the early mms; the patterned arrangement and number of the writings; the consistent titles given to the books of the NT; and the title of the completed work, "ἡ καινὴ διαθήκη" (1 Cor 11:25).

Holy Spirit will not lead into any new truth that contradicts the truth He had previous given. Perhaps a better solution to this matter of revelatory *charismata* can be found by asking if the contemporary preacher also occupies the office of a prophet.

Preaching and the Charisma of Prophēteia: Previously, this study has examined the office of the prophet as defining someone who is an authorized spokesman for another (as Aaron was for Moses, Exod 7:1),[48] but in the Bible, the prophet almost always refers to a spokesman (or spokeswoman, in the case of Miriam, Exod 15:20) "who spoke in the name of the Lord" (Jas 5:10). Most NT references to the *prophētai* refer to OT prophets, as Heb 1:1 reports, "God . . . spoke long ago to the fathers in the prophets in many portions and in many ways," and in particular, "The Prophets" refer to the second part of the *Tanakh*, the *Nevi'im*, the written prophecies now contained in the OT (Rom 3:21), as Paul reports that "God promised the gospel . . . beforehand through his prophets in the holy scriptures" (Rom 1:1–2).

However, the office of prophet continued into the NT church, which is "built upon the foundation of the apostles and prophets" (Eph 2:20), to whom the mystery of Christ "has now been revealed to His holy apostles and prophets in the Spirit" (Eph 3:5). Because there are NT prophets (1 Cor 12:28; Eph 4:11), there obviously must also be the gift of *prophēteia*, whereby an individual is enabled by the Holy Spirit to receive and speak divine revelation—by definition, then, a prophet prophesies prophecies (*ho prophētēs prophēteuei prophēteias*).[49] Paul confirms this *charisma* of prophecy in Rom 12:6 and 1 Cor 12:10, so that in the formative period of the apostolic church, there might be several prophets in a local assembly, as Paul encouraged "two or three prophets to speak" (1 Cor 14:29). In his description of an apostolic worship gathering, Paul pictures the assembly as being led by those who speak "a psalm, a teaching, a revelation, a tongue, an interpretation" (1 Cor 14:26), but the primary speaker seems to be the prophet (14:29–32) "who prophesies (and) speaks to men for edification and exhortation and consolation" (1 Cor 14:3). These applications of prophecy were previously studied as aspects of the Preacher's Content and Activity, indicating that when the modern preacher preaches the inscripturated Prophecy of the written Word, he fills the role of the biblical prophet, and in that sense he is "a prophet prophesying the prophecies." The significant difference he has from the biblical prophet is that he is not receiving immediate revelation directly from the Spirit; instead, he is delivering mediated revelation, the inscripturated prophecies now consisting of what 2 Peter 1:19 calls "the prophetic word," the Scriptures of the Old and New Testaments.

What this investigation suggests is that while the preacher fills a prophetic role, his primary calling is not to receive and deliver prophecy but to "Preach the Word" (2 Tim 4:5). When Paul asks, "All are not prophets, are they?" (1 Cor 12:29), he implies

---

48. *TWOT* § 1277, "nâbî," states, "The essential idea in the word is that of authorized spokesman."

49. Rendtorff, "μυστήριον," *TDNT*, 6:812, observes, "In the LXX נָבִיא is always translated *prophētes*; there is not a single instance of any other word."

a limitation on the gift of prophecy in that while all prophets were preachers when they spoke "by way of revelation or of knowledge or of prophecy or of teaching" (1 Cor 14:6), not all New Covenant preachers are necessarily also prophets, at least not in sense of needing the gift of prophecy to deliver prophecies immediately received from the Holy Spirit–although they certainly should be teachers endowed with the gift of teaching. While it is entirely possible for the Holy Spirit to grant the *charisma* of *prophēteia*, Paul does state that *charismata* of *prophēteiai* will be done away because, at best, "we prophesy in part;" but when the perfect comes, the partial will be done away (1 Cor 13:8–10). If, as was suggested in the preceding section, "the perfect" refers to the completion of revelation with the closing of the NT canon of Scripture, then there is no longer a need for the gift of prophecy. However, there always remains the necessity for the gifts of teaching and exhortation, because these are the duties specifically required of the preacher (Rom 12:7–8).

This conclusion is not a categorical assertion that God would never again gift a preacher to prophesy in the manner Agabus did when he predicted a world-wide famine (Acts 11:28) or the arrest of Paul with the words, "This is what the Holy Spirit says" (Acts 21:11). Yet even in apostolic times, such prophecies seemed extraordinary rather than the normal expectation, which was that the one "who prophesies edifies the church" (1 Cor 14:4), presumably by expounding and applying "the word of His grace, which is able to build up" (Acts 20:32). In fulfilling his ministry, the preacher should focus not on seeking new revelations but rather on proclaiming the prophetic words "spoken beforehand by the holy prophets and the commandment of the Lord and Savior *spoken* by your apostles" (2 Pet 3:2). In this manner, the preacher comes close to being a NT prophet even if he has not been given the *charisma* of *prophēteia*.

The Preacher's Ordination as *Charisma*

Such a conclusion should not be construed to mean that the *charismata* are inconsequential to the preacher: he should be zealous for that which is spiritual, especially that he may be prophesying (1 Cor 14:1), so it is certainly in his interest to know whether he has received the *charismata* of teaching and exhorting—if God has in fact "called him to preach the gospel" (Acts 16:10). The usual procedure—at least among most evangelical circles—is that a man is called and gifted in a very subjective and individualistic manner, so that a congregation has little to say about the process until it calls him to be the pastor. To say the least, this is not the pattern of ordination found in the NT. Although the doctrine of ordination was previously discussed in chapter 1 under the Commission of the Preacher, further discussion is warranted on the relationship between the gifts of ministry and ordination to ministry.

Paul has not left Timothy in the dark about the reception of such gifts as being mediated—or at least being verified—by the leadership of the church. He reminds Timothy in both letters addressed to him about the significance of his ordination service, admonishing him, "Do not neglect the *charismatos* within you, which was bestowed upon you through *prophēteias* with the laying-on (*epithesis*) of hands by the *presbuterion*" (1 Tim 4:14).⁵⁰ Similarly in 2 Tim 1:6, Paul reminds his colleague "to kindle afresh the gift (*charisma*) of God which is in you through the laying-on (*epithesis*) of my hands." These verses clearly show that there is a connection between the receiving of ministerial gifts and the laying-on (the *Epithesis*) of hands by other elders. There is no indication that such a connection was only operative during the apostolic period or only by some type of apostolic succession, especially since Paul attaches his apostolic involvement with the participation of the eldership, the normal ruling body of the church throughout the church age. Assuming that Paul refers to the same event in both passages, these facts can be ascertained about that ceremony:

1. Timothy received a spiritual gift (*charisma*) at the time of his ordination;
2. it was mediated through (*dia*) the hands of the apostle and also through (*dia*) prophecy (*prophētesia*);
3. it was accompanied with (*meta*) a body of presbyters; and
4. it was symbolized by the imposition (*epithesis*) of their hands,⁵¹ evidently signifying the council's ratification of Timothy's call to preach.

These observations call for a brief discussion into the relationship between the *charismata* and the *epithesis*.

Ordination in Biblical History: The setting apart of a man for a sacred ministry by the covenant leadership is a biblical custom rooted in the Mosaic economy when the sons of Israel laid their hands upon the Levites for their ministry (Num 8:10). The ceremony is further explained when Moses laid his hands on Joshua in the presence of Eleazar the priest and before all the congregation, having been commanded by the Lord to "commission him in their sight, and you shall put some of your glory on him, in order that all the congregation of the sons of Israel may obey *him*" (Num 27:19–20). Clearly, the imposition of hands is intended to show the transfer of authority from one leader to another. The setting aside of officers for the New Covenant church is also displayed in the Book of Acts (6:6; 13:3),⁵² where a discernable pattern emerges. First,

---

50. The noun τὸ πρεσβυτέριον appears only three times in the NT, twice for the Jewish High Council of elders (Luke 22:66; Acts 22:5), and here in 1 Tim 4:14 "as a council in connection with administration of Christian congregations, including all the πρεσβύτεροι" (BDAG § 6138).

51. The noun ἐπίθεσις, which appears in 2 Chr 25:27; Ezek 23:11; Acts 8:18; 1 Tim 4:14; 2 Tim 1:6; Heb 6:2, derives from the commonly-used verb ἐπιτίθημι (271 times), to lay or place something on another or something (BDAG § 3059), in this case specified as the "laying-on of hands."

52. The selection of church officers is narrated in the Book of Acts in several accounts:
   1. The Office of Apostle (Acts 1:15–26)
      a. Gifts and Qualifications (1:21–22)
      b. Divine Calling: "which Thou hast chosen" (1:24)

men who are gifted by the Holy Spirit are divinely qualified to serve (Acts 6:3; 13:2); second, their calling is recognized by the selection of the congregation (Acts 6:5–6); third, they are set aside by other leaders in a solemn ceremony that involves fasting, prayer, and laying-on of hands; fourth, the newly appointed officers are commissioned to their various tasks (Acts 8:8); and fifth, they sent on to accomplish their ministry (Acts 13:4). In all likelihood, Paul assumes this process when he reminds Timothy of the same sort of ordination ceremony by which he was set aside to the gospel ministry (1 Tim 4:14; 2 Tim 1:6).

Ordination and Charismata: There is, however, more to the laying-on hands than participation is a mere ceremony—Timothy actually received a *charisma* through the *epithesis*, a biblical fact that many evangelicals have avoided, probably as a reaction against the sacerdotalist views of apostolic succession, Murphy-O'Conner, for example, in attempting to prove apostolic succession in the Roman Catholic sacrament of ordination, asks, "When is this supernatural aptitude for the preacher given? For Timothy, it was obviously the moment of the imposition of hands."[53] Evangelicals

---

    c. Nomination of Justus and Matthias (1:23)

    d. Election: by drawing lots (1:26)

    e. Ordination by Officers: prayer offered (1:24)

    f. Commissioning: "numbered with the eleven" (1:26)

2. The Office of Deacon (Acts 6:1–6)

    a. Gifts and Qualifications: "full of faith, etc." (6:3)

    b. Divine Calling: (implied)

    c. Nomination: Seven by name (6:5)

    d. Election: "the congregation chose" (6:5)

    e. Ordination by Officers: "after praying, the apostles laid their hands on them." (6:6)

    f. Commissioning: "put in charge of this task." (6:3)

3. The Office of Evangelist (Acts 13:1–4)

    a. Gifts and Qualifications: recognized already as prophets and teachers (13:1)

    b. Divine Calling: "I have called them" (13:2)

    c. Nomination: "Barnabas and Saul" (13:2)

    d. Election: appointed by the Holy Spirit (13:2)

    e. Ordination by Officers: "fasted and prayed and laid their hands on them" (13:3)

    f. Commissioning: "sent out by the Holy Spirit, they went down to Seleucia" (13:4)

4. The Office of Elder (Acts 14:23; 20:17–35)

    a. Gifts and Qualifications: outlined in 1 Timothy 3 and Titus 1

    b. Divine Calling: "the Holy Spirit has made you overseers" (Acts 20:28)

    c. Nomination: "they appointed elders" (Acts 14:23)

    d. Election: by "hand-raising" (Acts 14:23)

    e. Ordination by Officers: "prayer with fasting" (Acts 14:23)

    f. Commissioning "they commended them to the Lord" (Acts 14:23); "to shepherd the church of God" (Acts 20:28).

53. Murphy-O'Conner, *Paul on Preaching*, 64.

should admit that in Timothy's case, a supernatural *charisma* was bestowed through the laying-on of hands, because Paul mentions a spiritual gift given with a prophetic utterance (1 Tim 4:14). While Paul does not specify which *charisma* was given to Timothy during the laying-on of hands (teaching? exhortation?) nor does he give the content of the prophecy, evidently Timothy received an additional dynamic to fulfill his ministry at the time of the laying-on of hands. It seems apparent that as the Holy Spirit is pleased to grant healing when the elders of church anoint the sick with oil (Jas 5:14), so the same Spirit is pleased to grant a particular gift of ministry when the same elders lay hands on a man whom the Holy Spirit has set aside for a work to which He has called him (Acts 13:1).

It needs to be observed, however, that the laying-on of hands did not initiate Timothy's "supernatural aptitude" for ministry—when Paul first met him in Lystra, the young man was already described as "a certain disciple" who was "well spoken of by the brethren" (Acts 16:2). The same good report was said of the seven men chosen as deacons in Acts 6:3,[54] as they exhibited gifts of ministry and godly character some time before their ordination to the office, which is why Paul later tells Timothy, "Do not lay hands upon anyone too hastily" (1 Tim 5:22). He must make sure a candidate for office is well qualified before appointing him.

Even if the laying-on of hands does not miraculously change a man—it is, after all, not a regenerating ritual—it cannot be said that the *epithesis* conveys nothing more than a symbolic gesture, because Paul reminds Timothy to rekindle the *charisma* of God given to him through the *epithesis* (2 Tim 1:6). While Timothy's ordination was quite special in that it was attended by an apostle, one need not deduce some sort of apostolic succession from this fact, because apostleship was foundational (and no more candidates are yet living who were eyewitnesses of Christ's resurrection) whereas eldership is perpetual, thus suggesting that the *epithesis* of the *presbyteroi* provides the pattern for all future ordinations. Furthermore, the "theology" of *epithesis* taught in 1 Tim 4:14 and 2 Tim 1:6 suggests that the experience of Timothy serves as a precedent for the fact that the Holy Spirit may bestow additional gifts of ministry to future ordinands, mediated through the laying-on of the hands of the *presbuteroi*.

Obviously, abuses to the practice can creep in. A man may assume that the mere ceremony of *epithesis* will empower him for service, or the eldership may suppose that their own hands possess the power to dispense the Holy Spirit. Both parties must heed the warning Peter directed to Simon Magus when he attempted to purchase from the apostles the power to give the Spirit through the laying-on of his hands (Acts 8:17–24). No reception of the Spirit or giving of His gifts can be manipulated by any man, because "the Spirit works all these things just as He wills" (1 Cor 12:7) as the sovereign Lord who moves as mysteriously as the wind (John 3:8). Despite these

---

54. The passive verb *martureō* is used in both Acts 6:3 and Acts 16:2 to describe what others "were witnessing" about the reputations of Timothy and Stephen, as being "full of the Spirit and of wisdom" (Acts 6:3, 5).

possible abuses, the Spirit works through the means He has established; in this case, He grants gifts of ministry though the *epithesis* of the elders after they have thoroughly tested a candidate for spiritual maturity and doctrinal soundness (1 Tim 3:10). Once the candidate is selected by the calling congregation, he is appointed to his ministry by the eldership in a solemn ceremony of *epithesis*, accompanied with the prophecies of Scripture relating to the fulfillment of ministry (such as Paul gives after reminding Timothy of his ordination, "Pay close attention to yourself and to your teaching; persevere in these things; for as you do this you will insure salvation both for yourself and for those who hear you," 1 Tim 4:16). The participating elders at an ordination service should have a reasonable expectation that the Holy Spirit will confirm the ceremony by granting additional *charismata* for ministry, or certainly granting a greater infilling than had been previously demonstrated (as implied of Stephen in Acts 6:8). If such spiritual gifting was not a possibility, why would Paul remind Timothy not to neglect the gift he had received at that occasion?

Based on the pattern of Timothy's ordination, the preacher ought to remember his own ordination not only as the time of the church's approval of his calling, but also the time of the Spirit's granting of the gifts necessary for him to "fulfill his ministry." The elders involved in the laying-on of hands should keep in mind the solemnity of the ceremony, because the Holy Spirit may well use them to mediate His gifts and to speak through the prophetic utterances they make at that time.

Summary to the Dynamic of *Charismata*

Timothy can "fulfill his ministry" (2 Tim 4:5) only by the dynamic of the gifts granted to him by the Holy Spirit, and the same is certainly true of every preacher since Paul wrote this charge. When God appoints a man to minister, He also grants to him the *charismata* enabling him to be sufficient to complete his ministry. This section has examined the nature of the *charismata* of speech that are required of preachers to preach the gospel, particularly the gifts of teaching and exhorting. Some reservation has been suggested about the gift of prophecy, because it is so closely connected to special revelation required in the formation of the church, so that when Paul states that "prophecies shall be brought to an end" (1 Cor 13:8), it is possible that the Holy Spirit withdrew the gift of prophecy due to the passing of the founding generation of the prophets and apostles and because of the collecting of their prophecies into the canon of the New Testament.

Regardless of the nature of the gift of prophecy, it is certain for Timothy—and every other preacher—that to fulfill his ministry, he must receive the calling and gifting of the Holy Spirit, which is then verified by the hand-laying of the eldership, not merely by his personal desires. In this process, the preacher is not merely a passive recipient: he responds in the dynamic of prayer, which is the connecting communication with God by which the preacher is enabled to fulfill his ministry.

The Dynamic of Prayer

While it is the duty and privilege of every believer to spend time in prayer, Paul frequently mentions his own prayer ministry for his converts and friends,[55] following the example of the apostles who insisted that they must not "neglect the word of God in order to serve tables" but must "devote ourselves to prayer, and to the ministry of the word" (Acts 6:2, 4). It is not insignificant that the apostles list prayer even before the ministry of the Word, for apparently the preacher will not have much of a pulpit ministry if he does not first have a closet ministry.

What is of concern for this study are the prayers of others that Paul requests concerning the success of his preaching. In particular, he asks his converts to "*pray* on my behalf, that utterance may be given to me in the opening of my mouth, to make known with boldness the mystery of the gospel" (Eph 6:19). Similarly, he requests the Colossians to be "praying at the same time for us as well, that God may open up to us a door for the word, so that we may speak forth the mystery of Christ . . . in order that I may make it clear in the way I ought to speak" (Col 4:3–4). These requests are quite amazing, as Paul reveals his total inadequacy to preach apart from the prayers of God's people, whether he asks that they pray for God to open doors of opportunity or to grant him utterance and boldness to speak the Word. There is no presumption on Paul's part—he knows that he cannot fulfill his ministry apart from the prayers of the church.

Even the ministry of the Word preached to the church cannot be divorced from prayer, despite its sovereign dynamic to accomplish all that God intends. In this vein, Paul asks, "Pray for us that the word of the Lord may spread rapidly and be glorified" (2 Thess 3:1), meaning that the Word will proceed quickly and without hindrance only with the prayers of God's people.[56] It is obvious, then, that the preacher must have the prayer support of the church if his ministry of preaching is to be fulfilled. Paul's words will fall constantly on deaf ears if he and others are not praying for the gospel to enter the hearts and minds of those to whom the Word is preached.

This brief discussion on the dynamic of prayer has shown that the preacher needs to have both a private and a public ministry of prayer if he is to mediate the mysteries of God on behalf of those under his charge. It is in this ministry of prayer that the minister is most likened to a priest, because he bears the needs of others to the throne of grace so that the God of grace may fill them with the knowledge of His will.

Summary of the Preacher's Dynamic

How can the preacher obey Paul's command to "fulfill his ministry" (2 Tim 4:5d)? This chapter has studied the implications of the word *plērophoreō*, showing that the

---

55. See Paul's prayers in Rom 1:10, Eph 1:16; Phil 1:9; Col 1:3, 9; 1 Thess 1:2; 2 Thess 2:11; Phlm 4. A fine study on the prayers of Paul is that of Pink, *Gleanings from Paul*.

56. BDAG § 7427.3 defines τρέχω in 2 Thess 2:1, "to proceed quickly and without restraint."

concept of fulfillment speaks of the filling ministry of God, so that the inherent power of the gospel message and the indwelling energy of the Word and Spirit gives the preacher total adequacy to accomplish his task. He serves in the place of a mediator of the Word through which God calls his elect to salvation. The dynamic of the ministry is not in the man, but in the message of grace, which "is spreading to more and more people, causing the giving of thanks to abound to the glory of God" (2 Cor 4:15).

The actual power for this fulfilling comes from the gifts of the Spirit and the prayers of God's people on behalf of the preacher, all of which work together in concord to enable the preacher to do as Paul commands Timothy, "Make full proof of thy ministry" (2 Tim 4:5d, KJV). Through the dynamic of divine energy, it should be the goal of every preacher to say with the apostle, "I have finished the course" in completing his ministry, which is the subject of the next chapter.

CHAPTER 16

The Preacher's Ministry: "Your Ministry"

PAUL CONCLUDES HIS CHARGE to Timothy to "preach the Word" with the exhortation to "fulfill your ministry" (*tēn diakonian sou plērophēson*, 2 Tim 4:5d). The question must be asked, what is this *diakonia* Timothy is to fulfill?[1] Paul could be describing the activity of ministry in general, but by use of the definite article *tēn*, it is more likely that he refers to the specific task of Christian ministry to which Timothy has been called and commissioned, which presumably concerns the completion of his work at Ephesus to strengthen that congregation (1 Tim 1:3).

The mention of a particular *diakonia* indicates that the preacher ought to consider his work as a specific ministry, and he needs to examine the Scripture to discover what that ministry involves. This quest becomes all the more important because many have attempted to define the ministry apart from the Scriptures, as if the concept had suddenly vanished from the sacred pages. "Ministry" has become a by-word for any program designed to effect social change, and so church courts have issued endless resolutions on every conceivable and potential political injustice. Social crusading has replaced sanctification.

The perpetuators of this new definition of ministry are not merely "the liberals," for "conservatives" have also used the pulpit as a political platform, and while Christian ministry does carry the duty to address the social ills of the day, political reform is decidedly not the NT concept of ministry. In order to form a theology of Christian *diakonia*, this chapter will undertake an investigation of Paul's concept of ministry so that a biblical formulation of ministry can be determined. After noting Paul's description of ministry, his specific applications of *diakonia* will be outlined, followed by a discovery of the source and authority of ministry. Next, the proper spheres of ministry will be defined, and then the determination of proper attitudes of ministry will be suggested. After this thorough study of Paul's concept of ministry, a better understanding of his command to Timothy to complete his ministry can be ascertained.

---

1. L&N § 35.19 defines διακονία as a noun derived from διακονέω, "to render assistance or help by performing certain duties, often of a humble or menial nature."

Descriptions of *Diakonia*

The earliest appearances of the noun *diakonia* in Greek literature refer to waiting on tables, as it is used in Luke 12:37,[2] but generally the word means to perform unspecified routine services,[3] as when Martha was flustered with her meal preparations (Luke 10:40). As a word describing household chores, *diakonia* is an appropriate word for the church as the household of God (1 Tim 3:15), because it requires servants to perform menial but necessary tasks so that the work of the Master might be completed.

In this sense, the concept of Christian ministry pervades the pages of the NT, although the noun *diakonia* is found mostly in the letters of Paul.[4] A study of the various uses of the word, however, makes it quite possible to extract an accurate description of Christian ministry.[5] First of all, in his contrast between the Old and New

---

2. Luke 12:37, "Blessed are those slaves whom the master shall find on the alert when he comes; truly I say to you, that he will gird himself *to serve*, and have them recline *at the table*, and will come up and wait (διακονήσει) on them."

3. BDAG § 1856 διακονέω. See also Hess, "Serve," *DNTT*, 3:545.

4. The noun *diakonia* appears in the NT thirty-five times, once in Luke 10:40, eight times in Acts (1:17, 25; 6:1, 4; 11:29; 12:25; 20:24; 21:19) and once each in Heb 1:14 and Rev 2:19. The other twenty-three usages are found in Paul's letters (Rom 11:13; 12:7, 7; 15:31; 1 Cor 12:5; 16:15; 2 Cor 3:7, 8, 9, 9; 4:1; 5:18; 6:3; 8:4; 9:1, 12, 13; 11:8; Eph 4:12; Col 4:17; 1 Tim 1:12; 2 Tim 4:5, 11).

5. The various usages of *diakonia* are as follows:
   1. Practical Ministries:
      a. serving food (Luke 10:40; Acts 6:1)
      b. relief effort (Acts 11:29; 12:25)
      c. financial assistance (2 Cor 8:4; 9:1, 12, 13; 11:8)
   2. Descriptions of *diakonia*:
      a. ministry of death (2 Cor 3:7)
      b. ministry of condemnation (2 Cor 3:9)
      c. ministry of the Spirit (2 Cor 3:8)
      d. ministry of righteousness (2 Cor 3:9)
   3. Christian *diakonia* in general:
      a. Ministry to the saints (Rom 15:31; Cor 16:15; 2 Cor 8:4; 9:4)
      b. The work of ministry (Eph 4:12)
   4. The gift of *diakonia* (Rom 12:7; 1 Cor 12:5)
   5. The Gospel ministry
      a. of the Word (Acts 6:4)
      b. of reconciliation (2 Cor 5:18)
   6. Specific Christian ministries:
      a. The Apostolate (Acts 1:17, 25)
      b. Paul's ministry
         1. received from the Lord (Acts 20:24)
         2. among the Gentiles (Acts 21:19; Rom 11:13)
         3. He put me in ministry (1 Tim 1:12)
         4. the ministry (2 Cor 4:1; 6:3);

Covenants, Paul describes the old as being "the ministry of condemnation," whereas the new "ministry of righteousness" abounds in glory (2 Cor 3:9). While the old was a "ministry of death" (probably referring to the sacrificial system), the new covenant is "the ministry of the Spirit" (2 Cor 3:7–8), in that He gives life through Paul's "ministry of reconciliation," effected by the work of Christ reconciling the world by becoming sin on our behalf (2 Cor 5:18, 21). When the word of this "*diakonia* of reconciliation" is preached, God entreats sinners through His ambassadors to be reconciled to Him (2 Cor 5:18–20). These descriptions of New Covenant ministry show that it is primarily the verbal proclamation of the truths of reconciliation. While there are many practical and necessary ministries of church and secular agencies, only the church can fulfill the ministry of reconciliation—and that is accomplished through preaching the Word. From this broad definition of *diakonia*, Timothy—and the modern preacher—must apply the ministry to his primary calling to "preach the Word" (2 Tim 4:2).

Applications of *Diakonia*

The primary meaning of *diakonia* described a slave who waited on tables, so that *diakonia* in the first century was a term of menial service, not an activity anyone would eagerly desire.[6] Because the Lord Jesus came not "to be served, but to serve" (*diakonēthēnai alla diakonēsai*, Mark 10:45), that which was once a mark of servitude has become a badge of greatness among His disciples (Luke 22:26). He turned the concept of service on its head by noting in the Parable of the Watchful Slaves that the master will actually have his servants recline, and he would come and serve them (Luke 12:37). This act, of course, is precisely what Jesus did when He as "the Lord and Teacher" served as the foot washer and table waiter at the Last Supper, showing that service to others is a ministry of love and is not to be despised (John 13:14–15). For that matter, Jesus calls every follower to serve Him (John 12:26), so they toil not only for Him, but to Him with an unassuming attitude (Matt 25:44). Even more astounding is Jesus' remarkable prerequisite for leadership, that "the one leading shall be as the one serving" (Luke 22:26), providing the pattern for the preacher's service.

In the broadest sense of the word, *diakonia* came to include the entire scope of all service done in the name of Christ, so that God gives leaders for "the equipping of the saints for the work of *diakonia*" (Eph 4:12). Beyer notes, "Early Christianity learned to regard and describe as *diakonia* all significant activity for the edification of

---

c. Archippus is to "take heed to your ministry" (Col 4:16)
d. Timothy is to "fulfill your ministry" (2 Tim 4:5)
e. Mark is useful for ministry (2 Tim 4:11)
f. Ministry of angels (Heb 1:14)
g. Ministry of the church at Thyatira (Rev 2:19)

6. Beyer, διακονία, *TDNT* 2:82.

the community,"⁷ to which could be added, that even insignificant activities became sanctified when done in the pattern of the Servant-Lord. All believers should emulate the members of Stephanus' household, who "devoted themselves for ministry to the saints" (1 Cor 16:15), whatever that might entail. In another divine paradox, the Holy Spirit elevates *diakonia* to the level of a spiritual *charisma* (Rom 12:7; 1 Cor 12:5), especially by calling some to the office of *diakonos* (1 Tim 3:8–13). To these *diakonoi* are assigned the practical ministries of mercy, such as serving tables, caring for church widows (Acts 6:1–2), and collecting and distributing funds as "this grace of servicing" (2 Cor 8:19).⁸

From these practical applications of ministry, the word *diakonia* moves to a more specific application of the gospel ministry, as Peter announces that the apostles must devote themselves to "the ministry of the word" (Acts 6:4). Paul identifies the whole of his work as "the ministry (*tēn diakonian*) which I received from the Lord Jesus, to testify solemnly of the gospel of the grace of God" (Acts 20:24). Preaching then becomes the specific application of *diakonia* for the preacher, so much that Paul simply calls it "the ministry" (2 Cor 4:1; 6:3). More specifically, he narrows his *diakonia* to the proclamation of the gospel to the Gentiles (Acts 21:19; Rom 11:13).

In light of these specific applications, when Paul exhorts Timothy to "fulfill his ministry" (2 Tim 4:5), it would seem that he is telling him to continue his present assignment to its completion, which may not come until he, like Paul, has finished his course (2 Tim 4:7). Succinctly, New Covenant *diakonia* is "the ministry of the Word" (Acts 6:4), so that whenever and in whatever manner the inscripturated Word is applied to hearers so that they believe and obey the Incarnate Word, there New Covenant *diakonia* exists. Timothy will fulfill his ministry only so long as this goal governs the applications of his task.

In support of this interpretation, attention is directed to Paul's use of *diakonia* in contexts indicating that the primary ministry of the preacher concerns the application of the Word of God to the church; for example, the "good *diakonos* of Christ Jesus" is one who is "nourished on the words of the faith and of the sound doctrine which he has been following" (1 Tim 4:6). Likewise, if the "man of God" is another description of the preacher in ministry, then 2 Tim 3:16–17 gives a detailed job description of the application of *diakonia*. While this passage is rightly appealed to as a prooftext for inspiration, it more pointedly provides a breakdown of the various applications of the Word: "All Scripture is inspired by God and profitable for teaching (*didaskalia* as the content for the Preacher), for reproof (in the role as Elder), for correction (in the role as Pastor), for training in righteousness (in the role as Discipler); that the man of God may be adequate, equipped for every good work." To fulfill these applications, Timothy must "continue in the things he has learned and become convinced of," namely, "the sacred writings which are able to give (him) the wisdom that leads to

---

7. Ibid.
8. For practical examples of *diakonia*, see Acts 11:29; 12:25; 2 Cor 8:4; 9:1, 12, 13; 11:8.

salvation through faith which is in Christ Jesus" (2 Tim 3:14–15), and then he must take the things he has learned from Paul and entrust them to other faithful men (2 Tim 2:2). The success or failure of any preacher will be measured by his personal and ministerial obedience to the written Word of God. No person should undertake any ministry without this firm commitment to the Word of God as the only guidebook to the applications of *diakonia*.

The Source of *Diakonia*

There are many applications of *diakonia* for Christ because "there are varieties of ministries, and the same Lord" (1 Cor 12:5). Paul clearly teaches that the resurrected Lord who is the subject and head of all Christian ministry is also its source as the one who mediates all New Covenant ministry. Likewise, Christian ministry is "pneumatic" in that it flows as "the ministry of the Spirit " (2 Cor 3:8) who bestows to some the *charisma* of *diakonia* who in turn find application "in the *diakonia*" (*diakonian en tē diakonia*, Rom 12:7). This unusual repetition of terms indicates that one discovers and uses his (or her) gift of service only in the actual performance of loving service to others.

So who might have this particular gift of *diakonia*? Surely it ought to be a prerequisite for each one who is examined to fill the office of a *diakonos* (1 Tim 3:10), and it is not far-fetched to claim that every elder should also evidence the gift of *diakonia*, because his calling also involves ministry, as Paul exhorts Archippus (presumably also an elder), "Take heed to the ministry (*diakonian*) which you have received in the Lord, that you may fulfill it" (Col 4:17). Everyone who ministers in Christ's name should display the gift of ministry, as Paul describes *diakonia* as a *charisma* the ministers sovereignly "receives" from the Lord by virtue of his commissioning, as when Paul was "put" into ministry (Acts 20:24; 1 Tim 1:12).

The preacher should be aware that his ministry is heaven-sent—it is not a task he presumes upon nor one merely assigned by a congregation or by another minister. He must be able to affirm with the apostle, "Since we have this ministry, as we received mercy" (2 Cor 4:1). As surely as salvation is a gift of God's grace, so also the source of *diakonia* in that it has been "received in the Lord" (Col 4:17).

The Authority of *Diakonia*

Because God is the ultimate source of the preacher's ministry, it follows that the authority underlying a ministry lies not in the minister but in his office as a *diakonos* of God. As a servant, his calling requires of him not so much to give orders but to take orders from the Master, so that he locates any authority he may have in the word of the Master, not in his own words. This emphasis is certainly Paul's understanding when he affirms to the Ephesian elders that he "received the ministry from the Lord Jesus to testify solemnly of the gospel of the grace of God" (Acts 20:24). As one who serves to speak the gospel of his Master's grace, a *diakonos* is not at liberty to deviate from the direct orders of his Lord.

Timothy, and every succeeding preacher, needs such an understanding of his ministerial authority, for often he asks himself, who am I to tell others what they should believe and how they should live? Who indeed is the preacher? He is a *diakonos* of the *diakonia* given to Him by Jesus of Nazareth, who, by virtue of His obedience unto the death of the cross, has now been exalted to the right hand of God as Lord of all (Phil 2:8–10). Because all authority has been given to Christ Jesus (Matt 28:18), the preacher should speak to persuade others (2 Cor 5:11), because he speaks on behalf of the risen Lord to whom every knee shall one day bow (Phil 2:10).

Spheres of *Diakonia*

So where is the sphere of this ministry that Timothy is to fulfill? It is not unusual to find clergy proliferated in all sorts of professions, working as social workers, psychologists, politicians, etc., each with the approval of their respective courts of jurisdiction that consider such activities as valid ministerial callings. While it is certainly biblical for a believer to serve in these spheres as a "*diakonos* of God" (Rom 13:4), it is quite another matter for an ordained minister of the gospel to find his ministry outside the sphere of Christian ministry and particularly outside of the church.

Paul defines the sphere of ministry most pointedly when he notes that God gave some as "pastors and teachers for the equipping of the saints for the work of *diakonias*, to the building up of the body of Christ" (Eph 4:12); in other words, Christian ministry first of all serves the Christian church. One would be hard pressed to find Paul suggesting involvement in a ministry that fails to direct its focus "to the saints" (Rom 15:31; 2 Cor 9:1).

The account in Acts 6:1–6 sets a precedent for prioritizing spheres of ministry. The new church had inherited the OT mandate to care for widows (Exod 22:21), and so it had been feeding destitute widows, but apparently because of language difficulties, the Greek-speaking widows were being neglected, and the Twelve, acting as the presiding elders, summoned the congregation to address the complaint (Acts 6:1–2). Their explanation establishes an important priority: "It is not desirable for us to neglect the word of God in order to serve tables" (Acts 6:2b). They state the first priority of Christian ministry: "We will devote ourselves to prayer, and to the ministry of the word" (Acts 6:4). In this case, an important ministry of deed threatened to overwhelm the ministry of the Word, and the apostles recognized that unless all ministries of deed were directed by the ministry of the Word, the church would soon find itself doing many helpful activities but forgetting its first commission, and that is to make disciples by teaching all that Christ commanded (Matt 28:19–20). As the Word is taught to believers, they will soon enough suggest deeds of mercy to relieve human suffering, as Jesus went about "doing good, and healing all who were oppressed" (Acts 10:38). As the burdens increased, the apostles realized that delegation of these duties into workable spheres was crucial, and so they directed the congregation to select seven qualified men whom they would appoint to address this particular need, and thus the congregation chose what appears to be the first deacons. To these servants, the administration of ministries of mercy was delegated so that the apostles could devote themselves to the ministry of the Word. A wise church will follow the same precedent, selecting elders to teach the Word and appointing deacons to apply the Word.

These servants will also need to prioritize ministries according to the spheres Paul gives in Gal 6:10; first, "as we have time, to do good to all," but "especially to those of the household of the faith," as the relief ministries organized by Paul were intended so that "the ministry of this service is ... fully supplying the needs of the saints" (2 Cor 9:12). This sphere does not necessarily limit ministry only to one's own parish, but every ministry needs to focus first on building up the body of the church, first through evangelism (one cannot expect secular agencies to have any interest in spreading the gospel and starting churches!), and then by establishing particular ministries devoted to the relief of the congregation's poor and hungry. Such an approach follows the NT pattern in the way that the early church instituted a daily *diakonia* of food for its own impoverished widows (Acts 6:1) and as Paul took contributions for the poor saints in Jerusalem (Acts 11:29; Rom 15:26). In this manner, the leaders of a congregation, from the preacher to the elders and deacons, all serve as *diakonoi* applying the *diakonia* of the gospel in the various spheres of need within the church and community, "serving by the strength which God supplies; so that in all things God may be glorified through Jesus Christ" (1 Pet 4:11).

Sphere of *Diakonia* of the Pastor toward the Flock

As a good shepherd who lays down his life for the sheep (John 10:11), so the minister as a good pastor keeps watch over the souls allotted to him (Heb 13:17). Such watchfulness necessitates the establishment of a caring and loving relationship with each member of his flock. It is not unusual for Paul to use familiar terms to describe his ministerial relationships, such as designating his readers as "brothers and sisters."[9] He addresses his converts as his children,[10] even likening himself to a mother in child-

---

9. Paul uses *adelphos*, "brother," 133 times (Rom 1:13; 7:1, 4; 8:12, 29; 9:3; 10:1; 11:25; 12:1; 14:10, 13, 15, 21; 15:14, 30; 16:14, 17, 23; 1 Cor 1:1, 10, 11, 26; 2:1; 3:1; 4:6; 5:11; 6:5, 6, 8; 7:12, 14, 15, 24, 29; 8:11, 12, 13; 9:5; 10:1; 11:33; 12:1; 14:6, 20, 26, 39; 15:1, 6, 31, 50, 58; 16:11, 12, 15, 20; 2 Cor 1:1, 8; 2:13; 8:1, 18, 22, 23; 9:3, 5; 11:9; 12:18; 13:11; Gal 1:2, 11, 19; 3:15; 4:12, 28, 31; 5:11, 13; 6:1, 18; Eph 6:21, 23; Phil 1:12, 14; 2:25; 3:1, 13, 17; 4:1, 8, 21; Col 1:1, 2; 4:7, 9, 15; 1 Thess 1:4; 2:1, 9, 14, 17; 3:2, 7; 4:1, 6, 10, 13; 5:1, 4, 12, 14, 25, 26, 27; 2 Thess 1:3; 2:1, 13, 15; 3:1, 6, 13, 15; 1 Tim 4:6; 5:1; 6:2; 2 Tim 4:21; Phlm 1:1, 7, 16, 20) and the feminine noun *adelphē*, "sister," another six times (Rom 16:1, 15; 1 Cor 7:15; 9:5; 1 Tim 5:2; Phlm 1:2).

10. See Paul's use of *teknon* in Rom 8:16, 17; 9:7, 8, 8; 1 Cor 4:14; 7:14; 2 Cor 12:14; Gal 4:19, 27,

birth when he tells the Galatians, "My children, with whom I am again in labor until Christ is formed in you" (Gal 4:19). The gentle concern Paul and Silas felt for the Thessalonians was "as a nursing *mother* tenderly cares for her own children" (1 Thess 2:6), motivated by a fond affection by which "we were well-pleased to impart to you not only the gospel of God but also our own lives, because you had become very dear to us" (1 Thess 2:8). Switching to a paternalistic image, Paul reminds the same readers that "we *were* exhorting and encouraging and imploring each one of you as a father *would* his own children" (1 Thess 2:11). He speaks to the Corinthians as a betrothing father, "For I am jealous for you with a godly jealousy; for I betrothed you to one husband, that to Christ I might present you *as* a pure virgin" (2 Cor 11:2). Following Paul's example, the minister ought to think of his parish in terms of a family as he develops relationships with those under his pastoral care.

The preacher should also note how the Scripture recognizes differences in temperament and personality, in the manner that Paul tells Timothy not to rebuke sharply an older man but rather to appeal to him as a father; he is to treat younger men as brothers; older women as mothers, and younger women as sisters, "in all purity" (1 Tim 5:1-2). Also, Timothy is to serve as an example to believers "in speech, conduct, love, faith *and* purity" (1 Tim 4:12). He is to maintain his comportment "without bias, doing nothing in a *spirit of* partiality" (1 Tim 5:21), nor as the Lord's bond-servant should he be "quarrelsome, but be kind to all, able to teach, patient when wronged, with gentleness correcting those who are in opposition" (2 Tim 2:24-25).

All of these interpersonal issues indicate that the minister must develop relational skills in every sphere of ministry, striving to become a "people-person" so that his ministry does not become program oriented but remains centered around meeting the needs of his flock. Any man who has difficulty relating to others ought to reconsider his calling, because the ministry involves proclaiming Christ in such a way that it admonishes and teaches others in all wisdom so that the minister may "present every man complete in Christ" (Col 1:28). In this manner, a minister widens his sphere of ministry toward each one under his pastoral care as he follows Peter's exhortation to his fellow elders to "shepherd the flock of God among you, exercising oversight not under compulsion, but voluntarily, according to *the will of* God; and not for sordid gain, but with eagerness; nor yet as lording it over those allotted to your charge, but proving to be examples to the flock" (1 Pet 5:2-3).

Sphere of *Diakonia* of the Flock to the Pastor

The nature of *diakonia* is that it is selfless, and so it would be improper for a servant of Christ to demand the loyalty of the flock to himself. Even so, there is a reciprocal sphere of *diakonia* in that Paul calls upon the church to recognize "those who diligently

---

28, 31; Eph 2:3; 5:1, 8; 6:1, 4; Phil 2:15; Col 3:20, 21; 1 Thess 2:7, 11; 1 Tim 3:4; 5:4; Titus 1:6.

labor among you, and have charge over you in the Lord and give you instruction, that you esteem them very highly in love because of their work" (1 Thess 5:12–13). The practical outworking of this esteem is shown in the obedience of the congregation to its leaders, that their oversight might be done "with joy and not with grief" (Heb 13:17). This esteem is also evidenced with the "reaping of material things" from the congregation as it shares a "double honor" with elders who work hard in word and doctrine (1 Cor 9:11; 1 Tim 5:17). Because a worker is worthy of his hire (1 Tim 5:18, quoting Jesus in Luke 10:7), the congregation has a divine obligation to remunerate the leader, not only fairly but graciously.

Even though Scripture commands esteem and obedience from the congregation, a minister should not demand such treatment from his charge. Of course, he should preach on such texts as Heb 13:17, but he must allow the congregation to make its own application to their pastor. If he is faithfully developing Christ-oriented relationships with them, his flock will respond in kind with Christ-like love and care. In these ways, the spheres of the minister will be ever increasing as God will "supply and multiply the seed for sowing and increase the harvest of righteousness" (2 Cor 9:10).

Attitudes of *Diakonia*

Because Christian *diakonia* is of divine origin, it is important that the minister as the Lord's *diakonos* "give no cause for offense in anything, in order that the *diakonia* (should) not be discredited, but in everything commending ourselves as *diakonoi* of God" (2 Cor 6:3–4). The high calling of ministry necessitates that the servant must maintain the highest attitudes toward his ministry; for example, Paul commends the household of Stephanus because they have "devoted themselves for ministry to the saints" (1 Cor 16:15). The verb *tassō* indicates that this family understood that its ministry sprang from obedience to the authority of Christ;[11] likewise, every minister should have high devotion to and for his ministry. Also, Paul "magnifies (*dokazō*) his ministry," because of his belief that both Jews and Gentiles will come to Christ though his efforts (Rom 11:13), so he gives it highest honor.[12] In like manner, every minister needs to "take heed" to the ministry he has received in the Lord (Col 4:17),[13] for there is no higher calling than to be summoned by the Lord God to preach his Word. In whatever way the minister can enhance his attitude toward the ministry of Christ so that it will be glorified will bring even further praise to the abundant grace of our Lord, "with the faith and love which are in Christ Jesus," as Paul speaks of Christ placing him into *diakonia* (1 Tim 1:14).

---

11. L&N § 68.69 defines τάσσω in 1 Cor 16:15 as "to do something with devotion, with the possible implication of systematic, regular activity." See also Delling, "τάσσω," *TDNT* 8:28.

12. BDAG § 2078.1 defines δοξάζω in 1 Cor 16:15, "to influence one's opinion about another so as to enhance the latter's reputation."

13. BDAG § 1504.6.b. defines βλέπω in Col 4:17 as meaning "to direct one's attention to something."

Completion of *Diakonia*

Paul expresses a fear, "lest possibly, after I have preached to others, I myself should be disqualified" (1 Cor 9:27). Knowing what Paul teaches elsewhere that "nothing can separate us from the love of Christ" (Rom 8:39), it is not possible that he fears the loss of his salvation, but he does fear the loss of his ministry. For this reason, he tells the Ephesian elders that he does not "consider my life of any account as dear to myself, in order that I may finish (*teleiōsai*) my course, and the ministry which I received from the Lord Jesus, to testify solemnly of the gospel of the grace of God" (Acts 20:24). The verb *teleioō* has the idea of "bringing an activity to a successful finish,"[14] and Paul uses a similar idea when he urges Archippus to "fulfill"[15] his ministry (Col 4:17) and Timothy to "make full proof"[16] of his ministry (2 Tim 4:5).

The emphasis on fulfillment indicates that a minister should not leave an unfinished task but rather strive to "fulfill his ministry," as Barnabas and Paul finished their famine relief visit to Jerusalem (Acts 12:25). Their efforts completed a short-term ministry of a specific task, whereas the exhortations given to Archippus and Timothy refer to their life-long ministries. This idea of a completed ministry shows that it is proper for a minister to establish both short- and long-term goals he would like to accomplish for Christ during a specific charge as well as for the entire course of his ministry—God willing, of course. Some may object that if a man so predisposes, he robs the Spirit of His spontaneity, but such an objection cannot square with Paul's description of the ministry as a "course to be finished" (Acts 20:24, 2 Tim 4:5). Like his Lord, Paul was directed by a desire that insisted, "My food is to do the will of Him who sent me and to accomplish His will" (John 4:34), with the final intent that he could pray to his Lord at his last breath, "I glorified Thee on the earth, having accomplished the work which Thou hast given Me to do" (John 17:4).

Summary to the Preacher's *Diakonia*

Having examined all the texts in which Paul uses the word *diakonia*, one can formulate a suitable definition of what the apostle meant when he instructed Timothy to "fulfill his ministry" (2 Tim 4:5d). In the broadest sense, ministry is the practical application of the Word of God by the words and deeds of the Christian servant. When applied to a preacher like Titus, however, *diakonia* might refer to a commissioned task ("Set in order the things that remain and appoint elders in every church," Titus 1:5), or it could refer to the overall task of the preacher, as Paul says to Archippus, "Take heed to the ministry which you have received in the Lord, that you may fulfill it" (Col 4:17). Without exception, Paul uses *diakonia* to describe activity with reference to the

---

14. L&N § 68.22.
15. Delling, πληρόω, *TDNT* 8:81.
16. Schippers, "Fullness," *DNTT* 1:733.

church, as the preacher applies the Word of God to the congregation. This emphasis means that the primary ministry of the Christian preacher must have first application to the verbal proclamation of the Word of God, as Paul states in Acts 20:24, and then secondly, ministry refers to the actual demonstration of the Word in his conduct, relationships, and service. These two aspects (ministry of Word and ministry of deeds) must not be separated, but the ministry of Word must take precedence, for without the Word, the preacher has nothing to demonstrate. It seems then, that for Timothy—and any other preacher—to "fulfill his ministry," he must have a very clear idea of his *diakonia*, in that his calling is to testify solemnly of the gospel of grace. In so doing, he will continue to be as Mark was to Paul, "useful for ministry" (2 Tim 4:11).

CHAPTER 17

Conclusions and Applications

IT HAS BEEN THE thesis of this study that the central activity of the Apostle Paul was the preaching of the gospel of Jesus Christ, as he stated to the Ephesian elders, "I do not consider my life of any account as dear to myself, in order that I may finish my course, and the ministry which I received from the Lord Jesus, to testify solemnly of the gospel of the grace of God" (Acts 20:24). Even when he senses his time of departure has arrived, Paul intends that "through me the proclamation (*kerygma*) might be fully accomplished, and that all the Gentiles might hear" (2 Tim 4: 6, 17). So when the aging apostle looked for someone to carry on his preaching after his death, in the way that Elijah threw the mantle of his ministry upon Elisha (1 Kgs 19:19), he found a man already caring for his cloak—both actually and ministerially—his younger colleague Timothy (2 Tim 4:13).

Thus, Paul closes his farewell letter to Timothy with his final charge, pointedly commanding him, "Preach the Word" (2 Tim 4:2). While there are many beneficial ministries for which God gifts believers, the commission to preach the Word of God is the distinctive task of the preacher, and so he must devote himself to the fulfillment of this ministry, developing and following a "theology of preaching" based upon Paul's charge to Timothy as recorded in 2 Tim 4:1–5.[1] That task has been the purpose of this book.

Paul's solemn charge that the preacher "Preach the Word" is an important reminder when preaching can so easily be nudged aside by other aspects of ministry such as pastoring, counseling, organizing and leading a congregation. While such duties are necessary parts of the pastoral ministry, they soon lose their *raison d'être*

---

1. As a reminder, 2 Tim 4:1–5 reads, "I solemnly charge *you* in the presence of God and of Christ Jesus, who is to judge the living and the dead, and by His appearing and His kingdom: 2 preach the word; be ready in season *and* out of season; reprove, rebuke, exhort, with great patience and instruction. 3 For the time will come when they will not endure sound doctrine; but *wanting* to have their ears tickled, they will accumulate for themselves teachers in accordance to their own desires; 4 and will turn away their ears from the truth, and will turn aside to myths. 5 But you, be sober in all things, endure hardship, do the work of an evangelist, fulfill your ministry." (NAS)

if they are not viewed as extensions of the primary calling of the preacher, which is to "preach the Word."

In support of this thesis, this work has examined 2 Tim 4:1–5 word-for-word and in great detail, with the major concepts in each phrase analyzed and explained. The first chapter dealt with the importance of the commission of the preacher, asking the question, who gives any human being the authority to tell others what to believe about God and how to live for Him? The answer is found in the opening "solemn charge" Paul gives, implying an inherent authority in the preacher's message found in his commissioning from Jesus Christ as the risen Lord. This commission means that the old idea of a "call to the ministry" remains very relevant, but such a call is certainly not merely subjective: it is confirmed by a body of gifted elders. The preacher who is not under submission to some body of elders (a *presbuterion*) has overstepped the biblical bounds of authority. He must always subject his messages to those who can judge their truthfulness according to the written word, as Paul notes, "The spirits of prophets are subject to prophets" (1 Cor 14:32). At the very least, this commissioning accents the significance of ordination and installation to office, as it is in the highest interests of the church to appoint only qualified ministers to preach the gospel. In this regard, the *Westminster Larger Catechism* Q. 158 asks, "By whom is the word of God to be preached?" and then it answers, "The word of God is to be preached only by such as are sufficiently gifted, and also duly approved and called to that office." Furthermore, his commissioning reminds every preacher that his life and ministry must always remain accountable and in submission to his fellow elders in the Lord.

The second chapter discussed the theological and Christological reasons that undergird preaching, which Paul defines as the "presence of God and of Christ Jesus" (2 Tim 4:1b). The biblical revelation has become God's sermon to humanity, supremely heard in the preaching of Christ Jesus as the Son of God and in the ongoing preaching about Him as risen Lord who is "about to judge the living and the dead, even His appearance and His kingdom" (2 Tim 4:1c, AT). Even more dramatic is the significance Paul makes elsewhere, that in hearing the preaching of divine mysteries, Christ Himself is heard, although preaching does not become divine revelation. Mounce puts it this way, "Preaching allows God to talk in that He Himself is communicated."[2] Even the preaching of the kingdom hastens the coming of the end at the appearance of the King (Matt 24:14). The preacher should remind himself that he speaks in the presence of the One whom he proclaims. As the elders and deacons in past times used to sit on the "Amen" pew to agree with the sermon, so the preacher must preach as if the Lord Himself is seated to give confirmation to his preaching.

Chapter three explored Paul's definition of "the Word" by answering the question, what is the content of the message the preacher is charged to preach? In his letters, Paul pointedly defines "the Word" as inscripturated revelation, so that the preacher's exclusive text is the Bible as the holy and Spirit-breathed Scripture (2 Tim 3:15–16).

---

2. Mounce, *Essential Nature*, 154.

Conclusions and Applications

When such content is preached, Christ Himself is mediated to hearers, although only as He has revealed Himself within the framework of redemptive history (as crucified and resurrected) and as interpreted by the prophets and apostles; that is, according to "the word of the truth of the gospel" (Col 1:5 AT). A broad outline of the gospel was developed, showing that its central theme is reconciliation between God and humanity through Christ. Thus, the preacher should be convinced that each of his public sermons ought to present the primary facts of redemption with an appeal for repentance and faith, even though most of the sermon may actually be words of exhortation or edification addressed to a believing audience. As the preacher keeps in mind the needs of the hearers, the tone of the content of a sermon might be parakaletic (encouraging), parathumatic (comforting), didactic (teaching). parangelic (commanding), or apologetic (defending), with each of these terms being aspects of the Word mentioned by Paul. Plainly, no sermon can be considered Christian unless it expounds on some portion of the Word of God and applies it to the listeners. This deduction from Paul's charge to "preach the Word" is absolutely basic to a biblical theology of preaching.

The fourth chapter dealt with the activity of preaching by exploring the rich variety of Paul's vocabulary that showed preaching must be the predominant action of the preacher. Whether the activity concerns evangelizing the lost or edifying the saints, preaching is the vocal announcing and applying of the gospel. The type of preaching varies according to the audience and need, as the message should be tailored to fit the situation. In no way should the adaptation to the audience be construed as a compromise, because the message remains the same although the particular applications differ. Chapter four pointed out that the activity of preaching may indeed be multifaceted, as suggested by the way Paul uses the verbs "reproving, rebuking, and exhorting" (2 Tim 4:2c), so that the preacher will need to know when to apply these various aspects of the message to the listeners. A sermon may be distinctly comforting or evangelistic in tone, depending on the circumstances of the message and the text used in that situation; but in every case, the sermon remains the preaching of the Word. Packer insists, "The true idea of preaching is that the preacher should become a mouthpiece for his text, opening it as a word from God to his hearers only in order that the text itself may speak and be heard, making each point from his text in such a manner 'that the hearers may discern how God teacheth it from them' (*Westminster Directory*, 1645)."[3] Although it should seem self evident, the primary activity of the preacher is to preach the Word.

While the message is always the most important aspect of the activity of preaching, the preacher's motives were shown in chapter five to be quite crucial, as it explored Paul's instruction to Timothy, "Stand ready!" This command indicates that the preacher needs not only the motivation but also the eagerness to preach in a way to please God, flowing from a conviction of faith and a love for others. If a man is to be a

---

3. Packer, *God Hath Spoken*, 22.

genuine preacher, then he must feel as if he cannot help but preach, with such motives coming from an inward compulsion implanted by the Spirit of God.

By directing Timothy to stand ready "in season and out of season," Paul raises the question of the preacher's setting in which to preach the Word (chapter six). He is called to preach in formal worship settings, but also in very informal surroundings. A conscientious preacher will pray that God may "open to us a door for the word" (Col 4:3). Any location may become a pulpit, and so the preacher of the gospel should not confine himself to preaching only in the welcome environment of his own parish. He needs to show great willingness to seize any opportunity to proclaim Christ whether it is "in season or out of season," convenient or inconvenient.

In chapter seven consideration was given to the delivery of a sermon, based on Paul's directive to Timothy to "exhort with all great patience" (2 Tim 4:2d). This phrase implies that the preacher needs to develop a pleasing and effective ability to communicate. While the preacher is not an orator as such, he should become a wordsmith by skillfully selecting the words of his sermons. The discipline of writing out his sermons to find the best choice of words should prove helpful. He needs further to study the art of elocution so he may deliver his messages with heartfelt emotion. Luke even makes incidental note of the gestures Paul uses in his delivery, indicating that every action must intentionally draw attention to the message. The actual delivery of the sermon may be one of the more neglected considerations for modern preachers, but it behooves the preacher to hone his delivery skills because he will be compared (fairly or not) against the standards of multi-media personalities. Although the preacher as a servant of Christ should not strive to be a popular speaker, he should study the art of public speaking and analyze the delivery of popular orators into order to enhance his own communicative skills.

Chapter eight examined the structure of Paul's sermons, and an appeal was made for preachers to outline their sermons along the patterns found in the NT by which a particular text or passage is expounded within its setting in redemptive history and then by showing its fulfillment in Christ. On this basis, the promise of salvation is extended to all who believe, as shown in the sermons in the Book of Acts. Such structure would ensure that every Christian sermon will be evangelistic to some degree, meaning that an unbeliever who hears even a sermon intended for believers would depart knowing what it means to become a Christian. In planning for such a possibility, the preacher should carefully structure his messages, as the burden of imparting gospel information rests upon him. Of course, Christian sermons are not exclusively evangelistic: they are also to be exhortatory, encouraging believers to learn and apply the Word of God. A study of Paul's letters revealed a typical—but not ironclad—structure built around implications of the history of redemption. Such structure never permits a message to become moralistic: it has its roots in the person and work of Christ Jesus, calling the hearers to greater obedience to Him. If the preacher realizes that his sermon structure has become forced at times, then he needs to pay closer attention to the biblical context of his texts and frame the structure of his sermon around the text itself, so he truly is "preaching the Word."

Chapter nine explored the preacher's audience, as Paul warns Timothy of the antagonism he will encounter to his preaching (2 Tim 4:3–4). Regardless of opposition, the preacher must seek ways to adapt the message so that his audience will hear and understand. Despite the insurmountable barrier of the deafness of his hearers, the preacher must announce the gospel optimistically, believing that God will open ears to save sinners and edify saints through his preaching. It is to his advantage to know his audience, so he may apply the gospel to their felt needs (and even to unfelt needs, if they are real) that they might respond to Christ. In fact, Mounce insists that a revelation is incomplete without a response,[4] but it is more accurate to say that a sermon is incomplete without an appeal for a response; otherwise, the preacher might only preach for results and risk the danger of manipulating his hearers. He should certainly expect God to bring results; but if a positive response is not forthcoming, it cannot be said that the revelation is necessarily incomplete. Still, a wise preacher will study his audience in order to gain a greater sensitivity to the needs of his congregation and become better equipped to apply the gospel to the needs of his hearers.

In chapter ten, Paul contrasts Timothy with false teachers ("but you," 2 Tim 4:5a) and introduced the topic of preacher's character, having reminding him that the goal of Christian instruction is to come from a pure heart (1 Tim 1:7). As a type of Christ, the preacher is to incarnate the gospel by meeting the qualifications of the godly man in 1 Tim 3:1–15 and Titus 1:5–9. His character is to be tested by other elders to make sure that his life accords with his message; obviously, if a man is deficient in his ethical conduct, he ought not to be appointed in the first place, and those who persist in sin should be publicly rebuked (1 Tim 5:20) and then rejected after a second warning—presumably, being removed from ministry (Titus 3:10). The seriousness of such consequences should make every preacher realize the imperative of examining his own character to make sure that it is in accordance with the Word he preaches.

Chapter eleven discussed the manner by which the gospel is to be preached, as Paul directs Timothy to "be sober in all things" (2 Tim 4:5a). The *Westminster Larger Catechism* Q. 159 addresses the same issue when it asks, "How is the word of God to be preached by those that are called thereunto?" The answer provided by the Catechism follows six adverbial phrases and each one prooftexts Paul's works in preponderance[5] for support: "They that are called to labour in the ministry of the word, are to preach sound doctrine,

---

4. Mounce, *Essential Nature*, 153.

5. The *WLC* 159 cites thirty-nine total verses in this order: Titus 2:1, 8; Acts 18:25; 2 Tim 4:2; 1 Cor 14:19; 2:4; Jer 23:28; 1 Cor 4:1, 2; Acts 20:27; Col 1:28; 2 Tim 2:15; 1 Cor 3:2; Heb 5:12–14; Luke 12:42; Acts 18:25; 2 Cor 5:13, 14; Phil 1:15, 16; Col 4:12; 2 Cor 12:15; 2:17; 4:2; 1 Thess 2:4–6; John 7:18; 1 Cor 9:19–22; 2 Cor 12:19; Eph 4:12; 1 Tim 4:16–18. Thirty of them, more than three-fourths, come from Paul's letters.

1. diligently, in season and out of season;
2. plainly, not in the enticing words of man's wisdom, but in demonstration of the Spirit, and of power;
3. faithfully, making known the whole counsel of God;
4. wisely, applying themselves to the necessities and capacities of the hearers;
5. zealously, with fervent love to God and the souls of his people;
6. sincerely, aiming at his glory, and their conversion, edification, and salvation."[6]

Paul's injunction to Timothy, "be sober in all things," summarizes each of these phrases as it shows how the preacher should strive to speak in such a way that his manner of delivery attracts others to Christ rather than repels them from Him.

No matter how appealing a preacher may be, there will exist a scandal to the message he preaches that will embroil him in controversy, as chapter twelve shows, when Paul tells Timothy to "endure hardship" (2 Tim 4:5b). Whether through intentional opposition, impersonal trials, or personal weaknesses, the preacher must endure hardship and persevere in his commission to preach the Word. This persistence is reflected in the sixth ordination vow of the Presbyterian Church in America, "Do you promise to be zealous and faithful in maintaining the truths of the Gospel . . . whatever persecution or opposition may arise unto you on that account?" The preacher ought to be aware that lack of opposition is not necessarily a sign of God's blessing nor is affliction an indication of God's disfavor! He must continue to preach the Word in spite of all hardships.

In chapter thirteen, it was noted that Paul would not agree with the old adage that preachers only work one day a week; instead, he instructs Timothy, "Do work!" (2 Tim 4:5 AT), and the many verbal expressions Paul uses of the labor of ministry underscore the importance of hard work in preaching the Word. In order to preach the Scriptures, the preacher must study his Bible diligently and then exert himself in the delivery of the same. A homiletics professor of the author insisted that one hour of preparation should be invested for every minute of the sermon! While few busy pastors can meet that lofty goal, it does illustrate the importance of the careful devotion that one needs to spend in the study before entering the pulpit.

Chapter fourteen discussed the various offices that the preacher occupies, as Paul tells Timothy to "do the work of an evangelist" (2 Tim 4:5d ESV) by which he proclaims the gospel to the lost. The other offices emphasize specific aspects of the Word as proclaimed to the world (Herald, Ambassador, and Witness) or as taught to the church (Teacher, Overseer, Shepherd, Minister, and Steward). It was noted, however, that Paul minimizes the offices and exalts the activities of those offices, indicating that ministerial titles are not to be the quest of the preacher. Like John the Baptist, he must decrease while Christ must increase (John 3:30).

---

6. *Westminster Larger Catechism* Question 159.

Through this entire study, one theme dominates: preaching possesses an inherent dynamic, indicated by the last verb in this charge: "fulfill your ministry" (2 Tim 4:5e). Chapter fifteen explored this concept, finding it to be the basis of the Reformed idea of preaching as a means of grace, in that the *Westminster Larger Catechism* Q. 155 states, "The Spirit of God maketh the reading, but especially the preaching of the word an effectual means of enlightening, convincing, and humbling sinners." The *Westminster Confession of Faith* 14.1 adds, "The grace of faith, whereby the elect are enabled to believe to the saving of their souls, is the work of the Spirit of Christ in their hearts, and is ordinarily wrought by the ministry of the Word." These confessional statements find support in Paul's teaching of the dynamic of preaching as a gift of the Holy Spirit, so that preaching becomes a necessary if not an essential means by which a sinner is regenerated to new life and saving faith in Christ. Sadly, this dynamic of preaching has all too often been neglected among many preachers and needs desperately to be recovered, that it is the Holy Spirit who energizes the preacher that he may preach the Word so that it accomplishes the purpose to which God intends. Embracing of this concept should give the preacher a new confidence in his preaching, as he understands afresh that the power and results of preaching are not found in him nor in his ability but in the dynamic gifting and empowering of the Holy Spirit of God.

This study then concluded in chapter sixteen with an examination of the final word in Paul's charge to Timothy, "the ministry," where it was shown that the preacher is called to minister the Word of God to his listeners. As a servant of Christ, his first duty is to the "ministry of the Word" (Acts 6:4), thus bringing this study to its original thesis, that the primary responsibility of the man of God is to preach the Word of God—as Paul opens his charge to Timothy (2 Tim 4:2). This theme has been amply illustrated in the life, letters, and doctrine of the Apostle Paul, who commands preaching by every elder called to the teaching ministry. The preacher, first and foremost, is a man of the Word. His primary calling is to preach the risen Word from the pages of the written Word, so that all will hear and give praise to the God who speaks from heaven. The preacher becomes the mediating instrument in the delivery of the good news of redemption, so that the apostle asks, "How shall they hear without someone preaching?" (Rom 10:14 AT). Conversely, the listeners shall hear with and by a preacher, and for this reason, God entrusts the word of eternal life to those whom He calls to the highest duty, to preach the Word.

This study has presented a Pauline theology of preaching in an effort to help the reader discover how God uses what the apostle calls "the foolishness of preaching" (1 Cor 1:21) in order to bring the elect to faith. Amid all the various facets of ministry, the one element that links them all together is the verbal proclamation of the Word of God, thus justifying the Protestant and Reformed emphasis on true worship as centering on the preaching of the Scriptures.

The writer of this study has greatly benefited in his own ministry through this research, as it has helped him to bring his work into a more direct focus. It seems quite unbelievable that he was entering his eight year of theological studies and tenth year of pastoral ministry before being challenged to draft his own theology of ministry, an assignment that should have been given in his first year of study. That assignment served as the basis for this study; and the result, hopefully, will be a more effective preaching ministry for himself and anyone else who happens to read this work. The author is now much more aware of prayerful and careful preparation and delivery of his sermons. It is his prayer that this work will cause him to be a more faithful and more effective preacher of the Word of God, so that he might fulfill the commission of the Apostle Paul to his student and co-worker Timothy, "Preach the Word!"

Bibliography

Aageson, James W. *Paul, the Pastoral Epistles, and the Early Church*. Grand Rapids: Baker Academic, 2007.

Addley, W. P. "The Sayings of Jesus in the Epistles of Paul." ThM thesis. University of Edinburgh, 1971.

Adam, Peter. *Speaking God's Words: A Practical Theology of Preaching*. Vancouver: Regent College Publishing, 1996.

Aland, Barbara and Kurt, Johannes Karavidopoulos, Carlo M. Martini, and Bruce M. Metzger, eds. *Novum Testamentum Graece*. 27th Edition. Deutche Bibelgesellschaft, 2006.

Anderson, Janice Capel, Philip Harl Sellew, and Claudia Setzer, eds. *Pauline Conversations in Context: Essays in Honor of Calvin J. Roetzel*. London; New York: Sheffield Academic, 2002.

Andrews, Elias. *The Meaning of Christ for Paul*. New York: Abingdon-Cokesbury, 1949.

Aratus. *Phaenomena. Callimachus, Hymns and Epigrams. Lycophron, Aratus*, 380–473. Translated by A. W. Mair and G. R. Mair. Loeb Classical Library. Volume 129. London: William Heinemann, 1921.

Archer, Gleason L. and Gregory Chirichigno. *Old Testament Quotations in the New Testament*. Chicago: Moody, 1983.

Athanasius. "On the Incarnation." Pages 55–110 in *Christology of the Later Fathers*. Edited by Edward Hardy. Translated by Archibald Robertson. Louisville: Westminster John Knox Press, 1954.

Baird, William. "What is the *Kerygma*? A Study of 1 Cor 15:3–8 and Gal 1:11–17." *Journal of Biblical Literature* 26 (1957): 157.

Balz, Horst, and Gerhard Schneider, editors. *Exegetical Dictionary of the New Testament*. 3 vols. Grand Rapids: Eerdmans, 1993.

Banks, Robert, ed. *Reconciliation and Hope: New Testament Essays on Atonement and Eschatology*. Exeter: Paternoster Press, 1974.

Banks, Robert J. *Paul's Idea of Community: The Early House Churches in their Cultural Setting* Grand Rapids: Baker Academic, 1994.

Barclay, William. "A Comparison of Paul's Missionary Preaching and Preaching in the Church." In *Apostolic History and the Gospel*, 165–75. Edited by W. Ward Gasque and Ralph P. Martin. Grand Rapids: Eerdmans, 1970.

Barth, Karl. *Church Dogmatics*. Edited by G. W. Bromiley and T. F. Torrance. Four volumes, in twelve parts (one in two halves), plus index. Edinburgh: T. & T. Clark, 1936–1977.

Bartow, Charles L. *God's Human Speech: A Practical Theology of Proclamation*. Grand Rapids: Eerdmans, 1997.

Bassler, Jouette, M., editor. *Pauline Theology: Volume I: Thessalonians, Philippians, Galatians, Philemon.* Minneapolis: Fortress, 1994.

Bauckham, Richard. *God Crucified: Monotheism and Christology in the New Testament.* Grand Rapids: Eerdmans, 1999.

———. *Jesus and the God of Israel: God Crucified and Other Studies on the New Testament's Christology of Divine Identity.* Grand Rapids: Eerdmans, 2008.

Bauder, W. "Mimic." In *DNTT* 3:490–92.

Bauer, Walter, Frederick W. Danker, W. F. Arndt, and F. W. Gingrich. *Greek-English Lexicon of the New Testament and Other Early Christian Literature.* 3rd ed. Chicago: University of Chicago Press, 2000.

Bavernfeind, O. "νήφω." In *TDNT* 4:936–41.

Beale, Gregory K. *The Erosion of Inerrancy in Evangelicalism: Responding to New Challenges to Biblical Authority.* Crossway Books, 2008.

Beale, Gregory K., and D. A. Carson, eds. *Commentary on the New Testament Use of the Old Testament.* Grand Rapids: Baker Academic, 2007.

Beare, Francis Wright. *The Earliest Records of Jesus.* 1st ed. New York: Abingdon, 1962.

———, Peter Richardson; John Coolidge Hurd, editors. *From Jesus to Paul: Studies in Honour of Francis Wright Beare.* Waterloo, Ontario, Canada: Wilfrid Laurier University Press, 1984.

Becker, Jurgen. *Paul, Apostle to the Gentiles.* Translated by O. C. Dean. Louisville: Westminster/John Knox, 1993.

Becker, U. "Gospel." In *DNTT* 2: 107–14.

Behm, Johannes. "παράκλησις." In *TDNT* 5: 800–14.

Bernard, J. H. *The Pastoral Epistles.* Cambridge: University Press, 1899; rpt. Grand Rapids: Baker Book House, 1980.

Bertram, Georg. "ὕβρις." In *TDNT* 8:295–307.

Best, Ernest. *Paul and His Converts.* Edinburgh: T&T Clark, 1988.

Betz, Otto. "Word." In *DNTT* 3:1119–123.

Beaudean, John. *Paul's Theology of Preaching.* NABPR Dissertation Series. No. 6. Series Editor James McClendon, Jr. Macon, Ga., Mercer Press, 1988.

Beyer, Hermann. "διακονία." In *TDNT* 2:82–84.

———. "ἐπισκέπτομαι." In *TDNT* 2: 599–605.

———. "κατηχέω." In *TDNT* 3:638–640.

"Bibliography on Paul." *Journal for the Study of the New Testament* 27 (2005): 85–93; also *Journal for the Study of the New Testament* 28 (2006): 73–84; *Journal for the Study of the New Testament* 29 (2007): 79–88.

Bird, Michael F. *Introducing Paul: The Man, His Mission, and His Message.* Downer's Grove: IVP Academic, 2008.

Black, Matthew. "Jesus and the Son of Man." *Journal for the Study of the New Testament* 1 (1978): 4–18.

———. "The Son of Man Problem in Recent Research and Debate." *Bulletin of the John Rylands University Library of Manchester.* 45.2 (March 1963): 305–18.

Blaiklock, E. M. "The Acts of the Apostles as a Document of First Century History." In *Apostolic History and the Gospel,* 41–54. Edited by W. Ward Gasque and Ralph P. Martin. Grand Rapids: Eerdmans, 1970.

Blass, F., and Debrunner, A. *A Greek Grammar of the New Testament and other Early Christian Literature.* Translated and revised from the ninth-tenth German edition incorporating supplementary notes of A. Debrunner by Robert W. Funk. Chicago: University of Chicago Press, 1961.

Block, Daniel I. *For the Glory of God: Recovering a Biblical Theology of Worship*. Grand Rapids: BakerAcademic, 2014.

Blomberg, Craig L. *Can We Still Believe the Bible? An Evangelical Engagement with Contemporary Questions*. Grand Rapids: Baker Academic, 2014.

Blunck, Jürgen, "ἀναγιγνώσκω." In *TDNT* 1:245–46.

Boice, James Montgomery, ed. *Foundation of Biblical Authority*. Grand Rapids: Zondervan, 1978.

———. "The Preacher and God's Word." In *Foundation of Biblical Authority*, 123–135. Edited by James Montgomery Boice. Grand Rapids: Zondervan, 1978.

Bornkamm, Günther. *Paul*. Translated by D. M. G. Stalker. New York: Harper and Row, 1971.

———. "μυστήριον." In *TDNT* 4:802–28.

———. "πρεσβεύω." In *TDNT* 6:681–3.

Brown, Colin, ed. *Dictionary of the New Testament Theology*. 3 vols. Grand Rapids: Zondervan, 1975–1985.

Bowker, J. W. "Speeches in Acts: A Study in Proem and *Yellammedenu* Form." *New Testament Studies* 14 (October 1967): 96–111.

Bradley, David. "The *Topos* as a Form in the Pauline Paraenesis." *Journal of Biblical Literature* 42 (1953): 240.

Brauman, Georg. "παρακαλέω." In *TDNT* 5:569–71.

———. "Revelation in Contemporary Theology." In *DNTT* 3:325–37.

Brown, Francis, S. R. Driver, and Charles Briggs. *Hebrew-Aramaic and English Lexicon of the Old Testament*. Complete and unabridged. Oxford: Clarendon, 1906. Electronic edition is Copyright © 2001 by BibleWorks, LLC. All rights reserved. Significant Hebrew formatting modifications and improvements made by Michael S. Bushell, 2001, to conform to lemma and inflected Hebrew forms and typeface.

Bruce, Frederick Fyvie. "Jesus and Paul." *Theological Students Fellowship Bulletin* 46 (Autumn 1966): 21–26.

———. "Myth." In *DNTT* 2:643–47.

———. *Paul and Jesus*. Grand Rapids: Baker, 1974.

———. *Paul: Apostle of the Heart Set Free*. Grand Rapids: Eerdmans, 1977.

———. "Salvation History in the New Testament." In *Man and His Salvation: Studies in Memory of Samuel George Frederick Brandon*, 75–90. Edited by Eric John Sharpe and John R. Hinnells. Manchester: University Press; Totowa, N.J.: Rowman and Littlefield, 1974.

———. "The Speeches in Acts: 30 Years After." In *Reconciliation and Hope: New Testament Essays on Atonement*, 53–68. Edited by Robert Banks. Exeter: Paternoster Press, 1974.

Büchsel, Friedrich. "ἐλέγχω." In *TDNT* 2:73–76.

———. "παραδίδωμι, παράδοσις." In *TDNT* 2:169–173.

Buck, C. H., and Greer M. Taylor. *St. Paul: A Study in the Development of His Thought*. New York: Scribner's, 1969.

Budd, P. J. "Danger." In *DNTT* 1:419.

Buitenwerf, Rieuward. "Acts 9:1–25. Narrative History Based on the Letters of Paul." In *Jesus, Paul and Early Christianity: Studies in Honour of Henk Jan De Jonge*, 61–88. Edited by Rieuward Buitenwerf, Harm Hollander, and Johannes Tromp. Leiden: Brill Academic, 2008.

Bultmann, Rudolph. "Die Bedeutung des geschichtlichen Jesus für die Theologie des Paulus." In *Faith and Understanding: Collected Essays*, 220–46. London: SCM, 1969. Reprinted as "The Significance of the Historical Jesus for the Theology of Paul." Edited with an introduction by Robert W. Funk. Translated by Louise Pettibone Smith. Philadelphia: Fortress, 1987.

———. "New Testament and Mythology." *Kerygma and Myth: A Theological Debate*, 1–44. Edited by Hans Werner Bartsch. Translated by Reginald H. Fuller. New York: Harper and Brothers, 1961.

———. *Theology of the New Testament*. Two volumes in one. Translated by Kendrick Grobel. New York: Scribner's, 1951, 1955.

Bushell, Michael S., Michael D. Tan, and Glenn L. Weaver, programmers. *BibleWorks*™ Copyright © 1992–2008 BibleWorks, LLC. All rights reserved.

Cadbury, Henry. "The Speeches in Acts." In *The Beginnings of Christianity*. Vol. 5. 402–27. Edited by F. J. Jackson and Kirsopp Lake. Grand Rapids: Baker, 1979.

Calvert, D. "An Examination of the Criteria for Distinguishing the Authentic Words of Jesus," *New Testament Studies* 18 (1971–72): 209–19.

Calvin, John. *Institutes of the Christian Religion*. 2 vols. Edited by John McNeill. Translated by Ford Lewis Battle. Philadelphia: Westminster Press, 1960.

Carson, D. A., and John D. Woodbridge, editors. *Scripture and Truth*. Grand Rapids: Zondervan, 1983.

Catechism of the Catholic Church. New York: Image Books, Doubleday, 1995.

Ciampa. Roy E., and Brian S. Rosner. "1 Corinthians." In *Commentary on the New Testament Use of the Old Testament*, 695–752. Edited by G. K. Beale and D. A. Carson. Grand Rapids: Baker Academic, 2007.

Clowney, Edmund. *Preaching and Biblical Theology*. Nutley, N.J.: P&R, 1975.

Coenen, Lothar. "Bishop." In *DNTT* 2:188–201.

———. "Preach." In *DNTT* 3:49–50.

———. "Proclamation." In *DNTT* 3:48–57.

———."Witness." In *DNTT* 3:1038–1047.

Colquhoun, Frank. *Christ's Ambassadors: The Primacy of Preaching*. Philadelphia: Westminster Press, 1965.

Comfort, Philip W. *New Testament Text and Translation Commentary*. Carol Stream: Tyndale House, 2008.

Corley, Bruce. "Interpreting Paul's Conversion—Then and Now." In *The Road from Damascus: The Impact of Paul's Conversion on His Life, Thought, and Ministry*, 1–17. Edited by Richard N. Longenecker. Grand Rapids: Eerdmans, 1997.

Cullmann, Oscar. *Christ and Time: The Primitive Christian Concept of Time and History*. Translated by Floyd V. Wilson. Philadelphia: Westminster, 1950.

———. *Salvation in History*. Translated by Sidney G. Sowers et al. New York: Harper and Row, 1967.

———. *The Christology of the New Testament*. Translated by Shirley C. Guthrie and Charles A. M. Hall. Philadelphia: Westminster, 1959.

Danker, Frederick William, editor. *A Greek-English Lexicon of the New Testament and Other Early Christian Literature*. Based on Walter Bauer's *Griechisch-deutsches Wörterbuch zu den Schriften des Neuen Testaments und für frühchristlichen Literatur*. 6th ed. Edited by Kurt Aland and Barbara Aland, with Viktor Reichmann and on previous English Editions by W. F. Arndt, F. W. Gingrich, and F. W. Danker. Chicago, Ill.: University of Chicago Press, 2000. The edition cited is an electronic version of the print edition published by the University of Chicago Press accessed on BibleWorks™ Copyright © 1992-2008 BibleWorks, LLC.

Delling, Gerhard. "ἐνεργέω." In *TDNT* 2:652-54.

———. "καιρός." In *TDNT* 3:455-62.

———. "πληροφορέω." In *TDNT* 4:309-11.

———. "πληρόω." In *TDNT* 6:283-311.

———. "τάσσω." In *TDNT* 8:27-48.

Dibelius, Martin. *Studies in the Acts of the Apostles*, Edited by Heinrich Grennven. Translated by Mary Ling and Paul Schubert. London, SCM, 1956.

———, and Hans Conzelmann. *The Pastoral Epistles*. Translated by Philip Buttolph and Adela Yarbro. Edited by Helmut Koester. Philadelphia: Fortress, 1972.

———, and Werner Georg Kümmel. *Paul*. Translated by Frank Clarke. London: Longmans, 1953.

Dodd, Charles H. *According to the Scriptures: the Substructure of New Testament Theology.* London, Nesbit, 1953.

———. *The Apostolic Preaching and its Developments*. London: Hodder & Stoughton, 1950.

The Dogmatic Canons And Decrees: Authorized Translations of The Dogmatic Decrees of The Council of Trent, The Decree on The Immaculate Conception, The Syllabus of Pope Pius IX, and The Decrees of The Vatican Council. New York: The Devin-Adair Company, 1912.

Dungan, David L. *The Sayings of Jesus in the Churches of Paul: The Use of the Synoptic Tradition in the Regulation of Early Church Life.* Philadelphia: Fortress, 1971.

Dunn, James D. G. *The New Perspective on Paul: Collected Essays*. Tübingen: Mohr Siebeck, 2005.

———. *The Theology of Paul the Apostle*. Grand Rapids: Eerdmans, 1998.

Eadie, John. *A Commentary on the Greek Text of the Epistle of Paul to the Galatians*. Edinburgh: T. & T. Clark, 1869. Reprint, Grand Rapids: Baker, 1979.

———. *A Commentary on the Greek Text of the Epistle of Paul to the Colossians*. Edinburgh: T. & T. Clark, 1884. Reprint, Grand Rapids: Baker, 1979.

Ebel, G. "Persecution." In *DNTT* 2:805-807.

Ellicot, Charles. *Critical and Grammatical Commentary on the Pastoral Epistles*. Andover: Warren F. Draper, 1884.

Ellis, Earl. E. *Paul's Use of the Old Testament*. Grand Rapids: Baker, 1957.

———. "Role of the Christian Prophet." In *Apostolic History and the Gospel: Biblical and Historical Essays presented to F. F. Bruce on his 60th Birthday*, 55-67. Edited by W. Ward Gasque and Ralph P. Martin. Grand Rapids: Eerdmans, 1970.

Elwell, Walter A., ed. *Evangelical Dictionary of Theology*. Grand Rapids: Baker, 1984.

"Epimenides." http://www.princeton.edu/~achaney/tmve/wiki100k/docs/Epimenides.html. Cited June 20, 2014.

Faber, R. "The Apostle and the Poet: Paul and Aratus." *Clarion* Vol. 42, No. 13 (1993): 291-305.

Fairbairn, Patrick. *Commentary on the Pastoral Epistles*. Edinburgh: T&T Clark, 1874; reprint ed., Grand Rapids: Zonservan, 1986.

Fee, Gordon D. *Pauline Christology: An Exegetical-Theological Study*. Peabody, Mass.: Hendrickson, 2007.

———. *Paul, the Spirit, and the People of God*. Grand Rapids: Baker Academic, 1996.

Finkenrath, Gunter. "Secret." In *DNTT* 3:501-10.

Fitzmyer, Joseph A. *Paul and His Theology: A Brief Sketch*. 2d ed. Englewood Cliffs, N.J.: Prentice Hall, 1989.

———. "The Gospel in the Theology of Paul." In *To Advance the Gospel: New Testament Studies*, 149–161. New York: Crossroad, 1981.

Foerster, Werner. "κλῆρος." In *TDNT* 3:758–64.

———. "σωτήρ." In *TDNT* 7:1010–12.

Ford, D. W. Cleverley. *The Ministry of the Word*. Grand Rapids: Eerdmans, 1979.

Frame, John. "Inerrancy: A Place to Live." *Journal of the Evangelical Society* (March 2014): 29–39.

Franklin, Benjamin. *Autobiography: An Authoritative Text*. J. A. Leo Lemay and P. M. Zall eds. W. W. Norton & Co., 1986. Also available at http: //nationalumanitiescenter.org/pds/Becomingamer/ideas/text2/franklinwhitefield.pdf.

Freeman, Kathleen. *Ancilla to the Pre-Socratic Philosophers: A Complete Translation of the Fragments in Diels, Fragmente der Vorsokratiker*. Cambridge, Mass.: Harvard University Press, 1948.

Fridrichsen, Anton, ed. *Root of the Vine: Essays in Biblical Theology*. Intro. by A. G. Herbert. New York: Philosophical Library, 1953.

Friedrich, Gerhard. "εὐαγγελίζω." In *TDNT* 2:707–721.

———. "κηρύσσω." In *TDNT* 3:697–718.

———. "κῆρυξ." In *TDNT* 3:683–696.

Furnish, Victor. "The Jesus-Paul Debate." Pages 342–81 in *Paul and Jesus: Collected Essays*. Edited by A. J. M. Wedderburn. Journal for the Study of the New Testament. Supplement Series 37. Sheffield: Academic, 1989.

Fürst, Dieter. "διαλέγομαι." In *TDNT* 3:820–21.

Gaebelein, Frank E. *The Pattern of God's Truth*. Chicago: Moody Press, 1968.

"Gamaliel I." *Jewish Encyclopedia.com*. Cited 19 June 2014. Online: http://www.jewishencyclopedia.com/articles/6494-gamaliel-i.

Gartner, Burkhard. "ἐπιφάνεια." In *TDNT* 3:317–20.

Gasque, W. Ward. "The Speeches of Acts: Dibelius Reconsidered." In *New Dimensions in New Testament Studies*, 232–50. Edited by Richard Longenecker and Merrill F. Tenney. Grand Rapids: Zondervan, 1974.

———, and Ralph P. Martin, eds. *Apostolic History and the Gospel: Biblical and Historical Essays presented to F. F. Bruce on his 60th Birthday*. Grand Rapids: Eerdmans, 1970.

Gaussen, Louis. *Theopneustia*. Revised edition. Chicago: Bible Institute Colportage Association, n.d.

Gerhardsson, Birger. *Memory and Manuscript: Oral Tradition in Rabbinic Judaism and Early Christianity* with *Tradition and Transmission in Early Christianity*. Foreword by Jacob Neusner. Translated by Eric J. Sharpe. Grand Rapids: Eerdmans, 1998.

Getz, Gene. *The Measure of a Man*. Ventura: Regal Books, 1974.

Goetzmann, J. "House." In *DNTT* 2:247–56.

Goldsworthy, Graeme. *Preaching the Whole Bible as Christian Scripture: The Application of Biblical Theology to Expository Preaching*. Grand Rapids: Eerdmans, 2000.

Goppelt, Leonhard. *Jesus, Paul, and Judaism: An Introduction to New Testament Theology*. Translated and edited by Edward Schroeder. New York: Thomas Nelson, 1964.

———. *Theology of the New Testament*. Translated by John E. Alsup. Edited by Jürgen Roloff. 2 vols. Grand Rapids: Eerdmans, 1982.

———. "τύπος." In *TDNT* 8:246–59.

———. *Tupos: The Typological Interpretation of the Old Testament in the New.* Translated by Donald Madvig. Foreword by E. Earle Ellis. Grand Rapids: Eerdmans, 1982.

Gorman, Michael. J. *Apostle of the Crucified Lord: A Theological Introduction to Paul and His Letters.* Grand Rapids; Eerdmans, 2004.

Grasso, Domenico. *Proclaiming God's Message: A Study in the Theology of Preaching.* South Bend, University of Notre Dame, 1965.

Greenway, Roger S. *The Pastor-Evangelist: Preacher, Model, and Mobilizer for Church Growth.* Phillipsburg: Presbyterian and Reformed, 1967.

Grunden, Wayne. *The Gift of Prophecy in First Corinthians.* Washington: University Press of America, 1982.

Grundmann, Walter. "δύναμαι." In *TDNT* 2:284–317.

———. "χρίω, Χριστός, etc." In *TDNT* 9:493–589.

Guthrie, Donald. *New Testament Theology.* Downer's Grove, Ill.: InterVarsity, 1981.

Hagner, Donald A., and Murray J. Harris, eds. *Pauline Studies: Essays Presented to Professor F. F. Bruce on his 70th Birthday.* Exeter: Paternoster, 1980.

Hahn, Hans-Christoph. "Openness." In *DNTT* 2:734–37.

Harris, Laird, Gleason L. Archer, Bruce K, Waltke. *Theological Wordbook of the Old Testament.* 2 Vols. Chicago: Moody Press, 1980. BibleWorks, v.9.

Harris, Murray. J. "Prepositions and Theology in the Greek New Testament." In *DNTT* 3:1211–14.

Harrison, R. K. "Apostle." In *EDNT,* 70–72.

Hay, David, editor. *Pauline Theology: Volume II: 1 & 2 Corinthians.* Minneapolis: Fortress, 1993.

——— and E. Elizabeth Johnson. *Pauline Theology. Volume III: Romans.* Minneapolis: Fortress, 1995.

Hays, Richard B. *Echoes of Scripture in the Letters of Paul.* New Haven: Yale University Press, 1989.

———. *The Faith of Jesus Christ: The Substructure of Galatians 3:1—4:11.* 2d ed. Grand Rapids: Eerdmans, 2001.

Hawthorne, Gerald F. *Current Issues in Biblical and Patristic Interpretation: Studies in Honor of Merrill C. Tenney Presented by His Former Students..* Grand Rapids: Eerdmans, 1975.

———, and Ralph P. Martin, eds. *Dictionary of Paul and his Letters.* Downer's Grove: InterVarsity Press, 1993.

Hendricksen, William. *New Testament Commentary: Exposition of Ephesians.* Grand Rapids: Baker, 1967.

———. *New Testament Commentary: Exposition of the Pastoral Epistles.* Grand Rapids: Baker, 1957.

Hengel, Martin. *Acts and the History of Earliest Christianity.* Translated by John Bowden. Philadelphia: Fortress, 1980.

———. *Between Jesus and Paul: Studies in the Earliest History of Christianity.* Translated by John Bowden. Philadelphia: Fortress, 1983.

———. *The Son of God: The Origin of Christology and the History of Jewish-Hellenistic Religion.* Translated by John Bowden. Philadelphia: Fortress Press, 1976.

Hess, K. "Serve." In *DNTT* 3:544–49.

Higgins, A. J. B. "The Preface to Luke and the Kerygma in Acts." In *Apostolic History and the Gospel,* 78–91. Edited by W. Ward Gasque and Ralph P. Martin. Grand Rapids: Eerdmans, 1970.

Higginson, R. E. "Apostolic Succession." In *EDNT*, 73.
Hughes, Philip E. "Grace." In *EDNT*, 479–82.
Hunter, Archibald M. *The Gospel According to Paul*. Revised edition of *Interpreting Paul's Gospel*. Philadelphia: Westminster, 1978.
———. *Paul and His Predecessors*. New rev. ed. London: SCM, 1961.
Hurd, John C. "The Jesus Whom Paul Preaches (Acts 19:13)." In *From Jesus to Paul: Studies in Honour of Francis Wright Beare*, 73–90. Edited by P. Richardson and J. C. Hurd. Waterloo, Ont: Laurier University, 1984.
Jenni, Ernst, and Claus Westermann. *The Theological Lexicon of the Old Testament*. 3 Vols. Translated by Mark E. Biddle. Peabody, Mass.; Hendrickson, 1997.
Jeremias, Joachim. "θύρα." In *TDNT* 3:173–180.
Johnson, E. Elizabeth, and David M. Hay, editors. *Pauline Theology: Volume IV: Looking Back, Pressing On*. Atlanta: Scholars Press, 1997.
Johnson, Luke Timothy. *The Writings of the New Testament: An Interpretation*. Rev. ed. Minneapolis: Fortress Press, 1999.
Kaiser, Walter. *Toward an Exegetical Theology: Biblical Exegesis for Preaching and Teaching*. Grand Rapids: Baker, 1981.
———. *Uses of the Old Testament in the New*. Chicago: Moody Press, 1985.
Kent, Homer. *The Pastoral Epistles*. Chicago: Moody Press, 1958.
Ker, John. *Lectures on the History of Preaching*. Edited by A. R. Maceven. Introduction by William M. Taylor. New York: George Doran, 1889.
Kerr, High. *Preaching in the Early Church*. New York: Fleming H. Revell, 1962.
Kim, Seyoon. "Jesus, Sayings of." In *Dictionary of Paul and His Letters*, 474–92. Edited by Gerald F. Hawthorne and Ralph P. Martin. Downer's Grove, Ill.: InterVarsity, 1993.
———. *Origin of Paul's Gospel*. Eugene: Wipf and Stock, 2007.
———. *Paul and the New Perspective: Second Thoughts on the Origin of Paul's Gospel*. Grand Rapids: Eerdmans, 2002.
Kittel, Gerhard. "ἀκούω." In *TDNT* 1:216–25.
———, general editor. *The Theological Dictionary of the New Testament*. Translated by Geoffrey W. Bromiley. 10 vols. Grand Rapids: Eerdmans, 1964–76.
Klappert, Bertold. "King." In *DNTT* 2:372–84.
———. "Word." In *DNTT* 3:1087–1117.
Knox, R. A. *St. Paul's Gospel*. London: Sheed and Ward, 1953.
Koehler, Ludwig, and Walter Baumgartner. *The Hebrew & Aramaic Lexicon of the Old Testament*. Revised by Walter Baumgartner and Johann Jakob Stamm. Translated and edited under the supervision of M. E. J. Richardson. Study edition. 2 vols. Brill: Leiden, 2001.
Koester, Helmut. *Paul and His World*. Philadelphia: Fortress, 2007.
Köstenberger, Andreas J., and L. Scott Kellum, and Charles Quarles. *The Cradle, the Cross, and the Crown: An Introduction to the New Testament*. Grand Rapids: B&H Academic, 2009.
Kuiper, R. B. "Scriptural Preaching." In *Infallible Word: A Synopsis by Members of the Faculty Westminster Theological Seminary*, 216–262. Third revised edition. Nutley, Presbyterian and Reformed, 1946.
Kuist, Howard Tillman. *Pedagogy of Paul*. New York: George Doran, 1925.
Ladd, George Eldon. *A Theology of the New Testament*. Grand Rapids: Eerdmans, 1974.

Laertius, Diogenes. *The Lives and Opinions of Eminent Philosophers*. London: Henry G. Bohn, 1853.

Lau, Andrew Y. *Manifest in Flesh: The Epiphany Christology of the Pastoral Epistles*. Wissenschaftliche Untersuchungen zum Neuen Testament, 86. Hersausgegeben von Martin Hengel und Otfried Hofius. Tübingen: J. C. B. Mohr, 1996.

Lightfoot, J. B. *The Epistle of St. Paul to the Galatians*. Grand Rapids: Zondervan, 1957.

———, J. B. *St. Paul's Epistle to the Philippians*. Revised Text with Introduction, Notes, and Dissertations. Grand Rapids: Zondervan, 1974. Rpt London: MacMillan and Company, 1913.

Lindemann, Andreas. "Paulus und die JesusTradition." In *Jesus, Paul and Early Christianity: Studies in Honour of Henk Jan De Jonge*, 281–316. Edited by Rieuward Buitenwerf, Harm Hollander, and Johannes Tromp. Leiden: Brill Academic, 2008.

Lindsell, Harold. *The Battle for the Bible*. Grand Rapids: Zondervan, 1976.

Lischer, Richard. *A Theology of Preaching: The Dynamics of the Gospel*. Revised Ed. Eugene, Or.: Wipf and Stock, 2001.

Lloyd, R. R. "The Historic Christ in the Letters of Paul." *Bibliotheca sacra* 58 (1901): 270–93.

Longenecker, Richard N. *The Ministry and Message of Paul*. Grand Rapids: Zondervan, 1971.

———, editor. *The Road from Damascus: The Impact of Paul's Conversion on His Life, Thought, and Ministry*. Grand Rapids: Eerdmans, 1997.

———. *Studies in Paul, Exegetical and Theological*. Sheffield: Pheonox Press, 2004.

——— and Merrill F. Tenney, editors. *New Dimensions in New Testament Studies*. Grand Rapids: Zondervan, 1974.

Lüdemann, Gerd. *Paul: The Founder of Christianity*. Amherst, New York: Proetheus Books, 2002.

Louw, Johannes, and Eugene Nida, eds. *Greek-English Lexicon of the New Testament: Based on Semantic Domains*. 2 vols. 2d ed. New York: United Bible Societies, 1988. BibleWorks, v.9.

McDonald, James I. H. *Kerygma and Didache: The Articulation and Structure of the Earliest Christian Message*. Cambridge: Cambridge University Press, 1980.

McLuhan, Marshall. *Understanding Media: The Extensions of Man*. N.Y.: New American Library, 1964.

McNeill, John. *History of the Cure of Souls*. N.Y.: Harper Collins, 1977.

MacKinnon, James. *The Gospel in the Early Church: A Study of the Early Church Development of Christian Thought*. London: Longmans, Green and Company, 1933.

Martin, Ralph P. "The Christology of the Prison Epistles." In *Contours of Christology in the New Testament*, 193–218. Edited by Richard N. Longenecker. Grand Rapids: Eerdmans, 2005.

Mauer, Christian. "παρατίθημι." In *TDNT* 8:162–64.

Merkle, Ben. "Do the Terms 'Elder' and 'Overseer' Represent the Same Office?" In *40 Questions About Elders and Deacons*, 76–83. Grand Rapids: Kregel, 2007.

Merriam-Webster's Collegiate Dictionary. Eleventh Edition. Springfield, Mass., 2005.

Metzger, Bruce M. *A Textual Commentary on the Greek New Testament*. 2d ed. Stuttgart: Deutsche Bibelgesellschaft, 2002.

Meyer, Jason C. *Preaching: A Biblical Theology*. Wheaton: Crossway, 2013.

Michael, Otto. "οἰκονομία." In *TDNT* 5:149–153.

———. "οἶκος." In *TDNT* 5:119–158.

Michaelis, Wilhelm. "κακοπαθέω." In *TDNT* 5:936–38.

———. "προχειρίζω." In *TDNT* 6:862–864.

Moyise, Steve. *Paul and Scripture: Studying the New Testament Use of the Old Testament*. Grand Rapids: Baker Academic, 2010.

Montgomery, John Warwick. *God's Inerrant Word*. Minneapolis: Bethany Fellowship, 1973.

Morris, Leon. *The Apostolic Preaching of the Cross*. 3d ed. Grand Rapids: Eerdmans, 1965.

———. *New Testament Theology*. Grand Rapids: Zondervan, 1986.

Moulton, James Hope, and George Milligan. *The Vocabulary of the Greek Testament: Illustrated from the Papyri and Other Non-Literary Sources*. London: Hodder and Stoughton, 1930. Reprinted, Peabody, Mass.: Hendrickson, 1997. BibleWorks, v.9.

Moulton, W. F., and A. S. Geden. *A Concordance of the Greek New Testament*. 4th ed. Revised by H. K. Moulton. Edinburgh: T. & T. Clark, 1963.

Mounce, Robert H. *The Essential Nature of New Testament Preaching*. Grand Rapids: Eerdmans, 1960.

Mounce, William D. *Pastoral Epistles*. Vol. 46 of the *Word Biblical Commentary*. Edited by Bruce M. Metzger, et al. N. p.: Thomas Nelson, 2000.

Muller, Dietrich. "Apostle." In *DNTT* 1:126–135.

Mundle, Wilhelm. "Command." In *DNTT* 1:330–43.

———. "Hear." In *DNTT* 2:172–180.

Murphy-O'Connor, Jerome. *Paul: A Critical Life*. Oxford: Clarendon Press, 1996.

———. *Paul on Preaching*. New York: Sheed and Ward, 1963.

———. *Paul the Letter Writer: His World, His Options, His Skills*. Collegeville: Liturgical Press, 1995.

Neirynck, Franz. "Paul and the Sayings of Jesus." In *L'Apôtre Paul: Personnalité, Style et Conception du Ministère*, 265–321. Edited by Albert Vanhoye. Leuven, Peeters / Leuven University Press, 1986.

Oepke, Albrecht. "ἀκαταστασία." In *TDNT* 3:344–47.

———. "γρηγορέω." In *TDNT* 2:338–39.

Oesterly, W. O. F. *Jewish Backgrounds of the Christian Liturgy*. Oxford: Claredon Press, 1925.

Pache, Rene. *Inspiration and Authority of Scripture*. Translated by Helen Needham. Chicago: Moody Press, 1969.

Packer, J. I. "Determine." In *DNTT* 1:477.

———. *God Has Spoken: Revelation and the Bible*. London: Hodder and Stoughton, 1965.

Pate, C. Marvin. *The End of the Age Has Come: The Theology of Paul*. Grand Rapids: Zondervan, 1995.

Pattison, Harwood. *History of Christian Preaching*. Philadelphia: American Baptist Publishing, 1903.

Peisker, Herbert. "Prophet." In *DNTT* 3:74–84.

Peterson, David. *Engaging with God: A Biblical Theology of Worship*. Downer's Grove: InterVarsity Press, 1992.

Pink, Arthur. *Gleanings from Paul*. Chicago: Moody Press, 1967.

Porter, Stanley E. "Pauline Authorship and the Pastoral Epistles: Implications for Canon." *Bulletin for Biblical Research* 5 (1995): 105–23.

———. *Paul in Acts*. Grand Rapids: Baker Academic, 2000.

———. *The Paul of Acts: Essays in Literary Criticism, Rhetoric, and Theology*. Tübingen: J. C. B. Mohr (Paul Siebeck), 1999.

Reicke, Bo. "προΐστημι." In *TDNT* 6:700–03.

———. "A Synopis of Early Christian Preaching." In *Root of the Vine: Essays in Biblical Theology*, 128–160. Edited by Anton Fridrichsen. Intro. by A. G. Herbert. New York: Philosophical Library, 1953.

Rendtorff, Rolf. "μυστήριον." In *TDNT* 6:802–812.

Rengstorf, Karl. "διδασκαλία." In *TDNT* 2:148–59.

———. "ὑπηρετέω." In *TDNT* 8:530–44.

Resch, Alfred. *Die Logia Jesu nach dem griechischen und hebräischen Text wiederhergesestellt: ein Versuch*. Leipzig: J. C. Hinrichs, 1898.

———. *Der Paulinismus und die Logia Jesu in ihrem gegenseitigen Verhaltnis untersucht*. Leipzig: J. C. Hinrichs, 1904.

Ridderbos, Hermann. *Coming of the Kingdom*. Edited by Raymond O. Zorn. Translated by H. de Jongste. Philadelphia: Presbyterian and Reformed, 1976.

———. *Paul and Jesus: Origin and General Character of Paul's Preaching of Christ*. Translated by David. H. Freeman. Philadelphia: Presbyterian and Reformed, 1974.

———. *Paul: An Outline of His Theology*. Translated by Richard De Witt. Grand Rapids: Eerdmans, 1975.

———. *When the Time Had Fully Come*. Grand Rapids, Eerdmans, 1957.

Ringwald, A. "Fight." In *DNTT* 1:639–44.

Robertson, A. T. *A Grammar of the Greek New Testament in the light of Historical Research*. Nashville: Broadman Press, 1934.

Robinson, Haddon. *Biblical Preaching: The Development and Delivery of Expository Messages*. 3rd edition. Grand Rapids: Baker, 2014.

Robinson, John A. T. *Redating the New Testament*. Philadelphia: Westminster, 1976.

Robinson, Maurice A., and William G. Pierpoint. *The New Testament in the Original Greek: Byzantine Textform (2005)*. Southborough, Mass.: Chilton, 2005.

Rosser, J. *Paul the Preacher*. New York: American Tract Society, 1916.

Ryrie, Charles. *Dispensationalism Today*. Chicago: Moody Press, 1965.

Schattenmann, Johannes. "Fellowship." In *DNTT* 1:639–44.

Schippers, R. "Fullness." In *DNTT* 1:733–41.

———. "Right." In *DNTT* 3:349–51.

Schlier, Heinrich. "παρρησία." In *TDNT* 5:871–86.

———. "θλῖψις." In *TDNT* 3:139–48.

Schmidt, Karl. "βασιλεία." In *TDNT* 1:564–93.

———. "παραγγέλλω." In *TDNT* 5:761–765.

Schmithals, Walter. *The Office of Apostle in the Early Church*. Trans. John E. Steely. Nashville: Abington Press, 1969.

Schmitz, Otto, and Gustav Stählin. "παρακαλέω." In *TDNT* 5:773–99.

Schneider, W. "Tempt." In *DNTT* 3:798–808.

Schnelle, Udo. *Apostle Paul: His Life and Theology*. Grand Rapids: Baker Academic, 2005.

Schniewind, Julius. "καταγγέλλω." In *TDNT* 1:70–73.

Schreiner, Thomas R. *Paul: Apostle of God's Glory in Christ*. Downer's Grove, Ill.: InterVarsity, 2006.

Schrenk, Gottlieb. "διαλέγομαι." In *TDNT* 2:293–98.

Schrenckenberg, H. "πράσσω." In *TDNT* 6:632–38.

Schutz, John Howard. *Paul and the Anatomy of Apostolic Authority*. Society for New Testament Studies 26. Edited by Matthew Black. Cambridge: University Press, 1975.

Schweitzer, Albert. *Search for the Historical Jesus: A Critical Study of Its Progress from Reimarus to Wrede.* Introduction by James M. Robinson. Translated W. Montgomery. New York: Macmillan, 1968.

Schweizer, Eduard. "Concerning the Speeches in Acts." In *Studies in Luke-Acts: Essays Presented in Honour of Paul Schubert,* 208–16. Edited by L. E. Keck and J. L. Martyn. Nashville: Abingdon, 1966.

Seitz, M. "Burden." In *DNTT* 1:261–63.

Selywn, Edward C. *The Christian Prophets and the Prophetic Apocalypsis.* London: MacMillan and Company, 1980.

Stahlin, Gustav. "ἐγκόπτω." In *TDNT* 3:855–57.

Stanley, David M. "Pauline Allusions to the Sayings of Jesus." *Catholic Biblical Quarterly* 23 (1961): 26–39.

Stanton, Graham N. "Paul's Gospel." In *The Cambridge Companion to St. Paul,* 173–84. Edited by James D. G. Dunn. Cambridge: University Press, 2003.

Stauffer, Ethelbert. "συναθλέω." In *TDNT* 1:167–68.

Stevens, George Barker. *The Message of the Apostles.* New York: Scribner's, 1909.

———. *The Pauline Theology: A Study of the Origin and Correlation of the Doctrinal Teachings of the Apostle Paul.* Rev. ed. New York: Scribners' Sons, 1911.

Stewart, Alistair C. *The Original Bishops: Office and Order in the First Christian Communities.* Grand Rapids: Baker Academic, 2014.

Stonehouse, Ned. B. *Paul Before the Areopagus and Other New Testament Studies.* London: Tyndale, 1957.

Stott, John R. W. *Between Two Worlds: The Art of Preaching in the Twentieith Century.* Grand Rapids: Eerdmans, 1982.

———. *The Preacher's Portrait: Some New Testament Word Studies.* Grand Rapids: Eerdmans, 1961.

Stout, Stephen O. "Preach the Word: A Study of 2 Timothy 4:1–5 with particular application to the Principles and Practices of the Preaching Ministry of the Apostle Paul as the Primary Model for the Christian Preacher." DMin. Thesis, Covenant Theological Seminary, 1988.

———. *The Man Christ Jesus: The Humanity of Jesus in the Teachings of the Apostle Paul.* Eugene: Wipf and Stock, 2011.

———. "The New Testament Concept of Tradition." Th.M. Thesis, Westminster Theological Seminary, 1977.

———. "The Pauline Concept of Ethical *Erga*: Legalistic Works of Law and Evidential Good Works." MDiv Thesis, Grace Theological Seminary, 1976.

Strathmann, H. "λειτουργέω, etc." In *TDNT* 4:215–31.

———. "μαρτυρέω." In *TDNT* 4:510–21.

Thayer, Joseph. *A Greek-English Lexicon of the New Testament* (Abridged and Revised Thayer Lexicon). Ontario, Canada: Online Bible Foundation, 1997. BibleWorks, v.9.

Thielman, Frank. *Theology of the New Testament.* Grand Rapids: Zondervan, 2005.

Tice, Louis. *Investment in Excellence.* Seattle: Pacific Institute, 1983.

Thiele, F. "Work." In *DNTT* 3:1152–55.

Thiselton, A. C. "Truth." In *DNTT* 3:874–901.

Thompson, Claude W. *Theology of the Kerygma: A Study in Primitive Preaching.* Englewood Cliffs: Prentice Hall, 1962.

Towner, Philip. "1–2 Timothy and Titus." In *Commentary on the New Testament Use of the Old Testament*, 891–918. Edited by G. K. Beale and D. A. Carson. Grand Rapids: Baker Academic, 2007.

Trench, Richard Chenevix. *Synonyms of the New Testament*. Marshallton: National Federation for Christian Education, n.d.

Trites, A. A. "Witness." In *DNTT* 3:1047–50.

Trobisch, David. *The First Edition of the New Testament*. Oxford: University Press, 2000.

Turner, Nigel. *Syntax*. Edited by James H. Moulton. Vol. 3. *Grammar of New Testament Greek*. Edinburgh: T&T Clark, 1963.

Twelftree, Graham H. *Paul and the Miraculous: A Historical Reconstruction*. Grand Rapids: Baker Academic, 2013.

Vanhoozer, Kevin J., and Owen Strachan. *The Pastor as Public Theologian: Reclaiming a Lost Vision*. Grand Rapids: Brazos Press, 2015.

Vielhauer, Philip. "On the 'Paulinisms of Acts.'" In *Studies in Luke-Acts: Essays Presented in Honor of Paul Schubert*, 33–50. Edited by L. E. Keek and J. L. Martyn. Philadelphia: Fortress, 1980.

Vorlander, H. "Reconciliation." In *DNTT* 3:145–76.

Vos, Geerhardus. *Biblical Theology: Old and New Testaments*. Grand Rapids: Eerdmans, 1948.

———. *The Pauline Eschatology*. Phillipsburg, N.J.: Presbyterian and Reformed, 1991.

Wallace, Daniel B. *Greek Grammar Beyond the Basics: An Exegetical Syntax of the New Testament*. Grand Rapids: Zondervan, 1996.

Walter, Nicolas. "Paul and the Early Christian Jesus-Tradition." In *Paul and Jesus: Collected Essays*, 51–80. Edited by Alexander Wedderburn. Journal for the Study of the New Testament. Supplement Series 37. Sheffield: Academic Press, 1989.

Warfield, Benjamin Breckinridge. *Inspiration and Authority of the Bible*. Edited by Samuel Craig. Introduction by Cornelius Van Til. Philadelphia: P&R, 1970.

Watson, Francis. *Paul, Judaism, and the Gentiles: Beyond the New Perspective*. Rev. and exp. ed. Grand Rapids: Eerdmans, 2007.

Wegenast, Kurt. "Teach." In *DNTT* 3:759–81.

Weirsbe, Warren, and Lloyd Perry. *Wycliffe Handbook of Preaching and Preachers*. Chicago: Moody Press, 1984.

Wenham, David. *Paul and Jesus: The True Story*. Grand Rapids: Eerdmans, 2002.

———. *The Jesus Tradition Outside the Gospels*. Gospel Perspectives. Vol. 5. Sheffield: JSOT Press, 1984.

Westerholm, Stephen. *Perspectives Old and New on Paul*. Grand Rapids: Eerdmans, 2003.

Westminster Theological Faculty: *Infallible Word*. Nutley: Presbyterian and Reformed, 1946.

Wilckens, Ulrich. "σοφία." In *TDNT* 7:465–528.

Wilder, Terry L. *Pseudonymity, the New Testament, and Deception: An Inquiry into Intention and Reception*. Lantham, Md.: University Press of America, 2004.

Wiles, Maurice F. *The Divine Apostle: Interpretation of St Paul's Epistles in the Early Church*. Cambridge University Press, 1967.

Wilson, Walter T. *Pauline Parallels: A Comprehensive Guide*. Louisville: Westminster/ John Knox, 2009.

Winter, Bruce M., and Andrew D. Clarke. *The Book of Acts in Ancient Literary Setting*. Grand Rapids: Eerdmans, 1994.

Winter, Bruce M. *The Book of Acts in its Theological Setting*. Grand Rapids: Eerdmans, 2007.

Witherington, Ben. "Contemporary Perspectives on Paul." In *The Cambridge Companion to St. Paul*, 256–69. Edited by James D. G. Dunn. Cambridge: University Press, 2003.

Worley, Robert. *Preaching and Teaching in the Earliest Church*. Philadelphia: Westminster Press, 1962.

Wright, N. T. *Paul in Fresh Perspective*. Philadelphia: Fortress, 2006.

Young, Brad H. *Paul the Jewish Theologian: A Pharisee among Christians, Jews, and Gentiles*. Grand Rapids: Baker Academic, 1995.

Young, Edward J. *My Servants the Prophets*. Grand Rapids: Eerdmans, 1952.

———. *Thy Word is Truth*. Grand Rapids: Eerdmans, 1957.

Zetterholm, Magnus. *Approaches to Paul: A Student's Guide to Recent Scholarship*. Minneapolis: Fortress, 2009.

Ziesler, John. *Pauline Christianity*. Rev. ed. Oxford Bible Series. Oxford: University Press, 1990.

Author Index

Aageson, J., 1
Addley, W. P., 19
Aratus, 380–473
Athanasius, 15
Baird, W., 50, 52, 55, 59, 155
Banks, R., 115
Barclay, W., 130, 150
Barth, K., xx, 23
Bauckham, R., 14
Bauder, W., 175
Bavernfeind, O., 190
Beale, G., 48
Becker, U., 49, 221
Bertram, G., 198
Betz, O., 35
Beaudean, J., xvn1
Beyer, H., 6n16, 89, 286
Bird, M., 15
Black, M., 21
Block, D., 114
Blomberg, C., 48
Blunck, J., 87
Boice, J., 48
Bornkamm, G., 18, 25, 83, 225
Bowker, J., 132, 133
Bradley, D.., 131, 132, 137
Brauman, G., 61
Brown, C., 23, 54
Bruce, F. F., 128, 130, 131, 136, 137, 138, 140, 161
Buchsel, F., 45, 94, 102
Budd, P., 189, 200
Bultmann, R., 23, 45, 54, 161
Cadbury, H., 128
Calvert, D., 19
Calvin, J., 25, 85, 271
Carson, D., xviii
Clowney, E., 4, 5, 10, 38, 39, 57, 58
Coenen, L., 53, 69, 70, 73, 82, 101, 102, 105, 224, 227, 231, 233, 240
Comfort, P., 13

Cullmann, O., 21, 45,
Delling, D., 113, 258, 259, 262, 292, 293
Dibelius, M., 128, 129
Dodd, C., 28, 45, 52, 54, 55, 56, 59, 64, 140, 141
Dungan, D., 19
Dunn, J. D. G., 60
Eadie, J., 259
Ebel, G., 197
Ellis, E., 37, 39, 41, 44, 250, 251
Epimenides., 135, 136n36
Faber, R., 136
Fairbairn, P., 109
Fee, G., 15, 115
Finkenrath, G., 25, 36
Fitzmyer, J., 38, 39, 50, 60, 166
Foerster, W., 10
Ford, D., xvi, 39, 41, 42, 58, 69, 85
Frame, J., xviii
Franklin, B., 121n12
Freeman, K., 136
Friedrich, G., 50, 53, 54, 73, 133, 223, 224, 265
Furnish, V., 45
Furst, D., 79
Gaebelein, F., 47
Gamaliel I, 132n26
Gartner, B., 22
Gasque, W., 128
Gaussen, L., xviii
Gerhardsson, B., 19
Getz, G., 185
Goetzmann, J., 115
Goodwin, T., 17
Goppelt, G., 174
Gorman, M., 60
Grasso, D., 25, 26, 38, 50, 55, 86, 228, 264
Grundmann, W., 17, 261
Hahn, H-C., 81, 190
Harris, L., xviii, 227
Hay, D., 60
Hays, R., 39, 137

317

Author Index

Hawthorne, G., 60
Hendricksen, W., 30
Hengel, M., 14
Hess, K., 212
Higginson, R., 248
Hughes, P., 273
Hunter, A., 45
Jeremias, J., 116
Johnson, L., xv
Kaiser, W., 143
Kent, H., 183
Kerr, H., 141
Kim, S., 19
Kittel, G., 160, 167
Klappert, B., 27, 34, 36
Köstenberger, A., xviii
Kuiper, R., 32
Kuist, H., 39, 79, 114, 122, 123, 124, 163
Laertius, D., 136n36
Lau, A., 15
Lightfoot, J., 179, 233, 243
Lindemann, A., 19
Lindsell, H., xviii,
Lüdemann, P., 37
McDonald, J., xix, 32, 71, 119, 120, 128, 131, 132, 137
McLuhan, M., 118
Martin, R., 60
Mauer, C., 46
Merkle, B., 233
Metzger, B., 13
Michael, O., 266
Michaelis, W., 4, 195
Moyise, S., 39
Montgomery, J., xviii
Morris, L., 57, 59
Mounce, R., xx, 10, 42, 54, 55, 59, 64, 129, 162, 223, 296, 299
Mounce, W., xvi
Muller, D., 243, 244
Mundle, W., 51, 99, 160
Murphy-O'Connor, J., 194, 224, 263, 279
Neirynck, F., 19
Oepke, A., 93, 192, 199
Oesterly, W., 114
Pache, R., xviii
Packer, J., 4, 6, 297
Pate, C., 60,
Pattison, H., 136
Peisker, H., 249
Perry, L., xix
Peterson, D., 250, 251
Pink, A., 282
Porter, S., xix, 85

Reicke, B., 70, 102, 270
Rendtorff, R., 276
Rengstorf, K., 215, 229, 243
Resch, A., 19, 45
Ridderbos, H., 28, 57, 60
Ringwald, A., 217
Robinson, J., xv
Ryrie, C., 28, 159
Schippers, R., 293
Schlier, H., 190, 200
Schmidt, K., 29, 99
Schmithals, W., 3, 243
Schmitz, O., 60, 62, 65, 97, 98
Schneider, W., 201
Schnelle, U., 60
Schniewind, J., 77
Schreiner, T., 60
Schrenckenberg, H. 209
Schutz, J., 59, 74, 75
Schweitzer, A., 20
Seitz, M., 210
Stahlin, G., 60, 110
Stanley, D., 19
Stauffer, E., 216
Stevens, G., 141, 143
Stewart, A., 5
Stott, J., 46, 55, 59, 111, 166, 227
Stout, S., 12, 45, 53, 57, 137, 178, 205
Strachan. O, 68
Strathmann, H., 1, 268
Thayer, J., 80, 88, 210, 212, 213, 231, 249
Tice, L., 47
Thiselton, A., 48
Towner, P., 1
Trench, R., 95
Trites, A., 228
Trobisch, D., 47, 275
Turner, N., 14
Twelftree, G., 247
Vanhoozer, K., 68
Vorlander, H., 56
Vos, G., 28
Wallace, D., 14, 69, 118, 165, 234
Walter, N., 19
Warfield, B., xviii
Wegenast, K., 10, 64, 86
Weirsbe, W., xix
Wenham, D., 19, 45
Wilckens, U., 121
Wilder, T., xix, 1n1, 129
Woodbridge, J., xviii
Worley, R., xviii, 64, 128
Young, B., 15
Young, E., xviii, 16, 39

Subject Index

Abraham, 20, 41
Acts, Sermons in, 119, 127, 128, 129, 130, 148
Adam, 160
Affliction, 178, 195–96, 200, 300
Agabus, 43n41, 249–50, 277
Agony (*agōnizomai*), 217
Agrippa, Herod, 84, 90, 91, 123, 139, 166, 191
Akairōs (untimely), 113
Akoē (hearing, report), xx, 51, 163, 168
Allotment, 10, 290, 291
Allusions, 14, 29, 39, 57, 134, 137n43, 155, 213
Ambassador, xxii, 3, 16, 30, 83, 191, 220, 225–26
Ambassadoring (*presbeuō*), xxii, 83, 225
Anagnōsis (Reading), xxi, 66, 86–87, 132n27
Ananias, 138n46
Angel(s), 111, 123, 286n5
angellō, 75–77
Antioch in Pisidia, 6, 9, 57, 74n20, 88, 120, 134, 158, 197
Antioch in Syria, 7, 43n41, 85n59, 229, 239, 249, 267
Apologetics, 78, 90
Apologia, xxi, 60, 67–68, 90
Apologizing (*apologeomai*), 90–91
Apophthengomai, 80–84
Apostles, 3n7, 6, 16, 24, 30, 44–46, 64, 65, 129, 146, 212–213, 227, 243–48, 253–56, 275–76
Apostolicity, 23, 24, 243–248
Areopagus, 21, 47, 132, 135, 136, 222
Ascension of Jesus, 29, 42, 58, 229, 244
Atonement, 68, 144
Authority, ministerial, 4, 8, 71, 80–84, 94–96, 99, 150, 166, 181, 193–94, 213–14, 225, 243–44, 278, 284, 288–89, 292, 296
Baptism, of believers, 9, 25, 135, 142, 146, 156, 216, 269–72
of Jesus, 245
Barnabas, 3, 7, 9, 10, 62, 76, 84, 88, 230, 248, 261, 293

Beating, 196, 198, 210
Bebaiōsis, xxi, 67
Belief, Believing, xxiii, 35–36, 48, 51, 57, 84, 144, 145n65, 145n69, 146, 165
Benediction, 149n71, 155
Berating (*epiplessō*), 96
Biblical Theology, xiii, xvi, 118, 120, 297
Birth of Jesus, 244n85
Bishop, 5, 6, 102, 105n121, 233n49
Blood of Jesus, 28, 57, 138, 187, 214, 234, 271
Boldly Speaking (*parrēsiazomai*):, 80–81, 191
Burial of Jesus, 35, 50, 58
Calling, divine, 15, 146, 147, 165
Canon of Scripture, 245, 251, 252, 275, 277, 281
Catechizing (*katēchein*), 89
Cephas, 192n9, 207, 222n4, 253, 255, 272n42
Charisma, 272–281
Christos, 12, 17n23, 37
Christology, 13, 15, 120, 143, 296
Comfort (*paramuthia*), xxi, 63, 105
Comforting (*paramutheomai*), 105
Commanding (*parangellō*), 99
Commandment (*parangelia*), xxi, 65, 66, 68
Commending (*paratithēmi*), 9, 46, 99, 100
Communion (see Lord's Supper)
Compassion of Jesus, 194
Congregationalism, 5–7
Counseling (*noutheteō*), 70, 98–99, 241
Covenant, 27, 36, 140
Convert, conversion, 144, 145n68, 146, 185, 214, 265
Co-worker (*sunergos*), 173n7, 205–206, 208
Creed(s), 264
Critical scholarship, xv, 244n87
Cross, of Jesus, 20, 57, 197, 270, 289
Crucifixion of Jesus, 17, 18, 23, 28, 37, 53, 57, 59, 72, 143, 177, 203, 261, 270, 297
Cynics, cynic diatribe, 119, 131–32
Dabar Yahweh, 34, 36

Subject Index

Damascus (road), 3, 37, 79, 80n44, 112, 114n7, 138, 186, 191, 214, 246, 247, 263
David(ic), 27, 29, 40, 41, 90, 120, 133n29, 140, 164
Deacons, 6, 7, 170, 182n38, 185, 206, 212, 236, 237, 240, 279, 280, 289–290
Deaconess, 236n57
Declaring (*apophthengomai*), 82–83
Defense (*apologia* and *bebaiōsis*), xxi, 67, 78, 90
Deity of Jesus, 14, 22
Deposit (*Parthēke*), xx, 10, 46, 47, 67, 78, 100, 126
Dialectic Theology, 23, 25, 26
Diabebaioomai (authoritatively), 193
Diakonia, diakonos (service, servant), 212, 235–237n58, 284, 285n5, 287–92
Dialegomai (reasoning), 78–79
Diamarturomai (Solemnly witnessing) 81–82
Didachē (Doctrine), xxi, 52, 64, 65, 66, 84–86, 126, 155, 230, 232, 245
Didaktikos (teachable), 213n45
Didaskalia (Teaching), xxi, 64, 65, 68, 85–86, 155, 229, 230, 232, 286
Didaskalos (Teacher), 168, 229–30
Disciples of Jesus, 8, 17–18, 71–72, 88, 90, 95, 99, 185, 213, 230, 239, 244, 253–56, 286, 289
Discipling (*mathēteuō*), 88
Dispensationalism, 29, 159
Disputing (*suzēteō*), 80
Distress(es), 195, 200, 201, 202
Doctrine (*Didachē*), xxi, 52, 64, 65, 66, 84–86, 126, 155, 230, 232, 245
Double honor, 232n47, 292
Doulos, douleuō (slave, serving), 213, 237–238
Dynamic, 41, 222n5, 257–283, 301
Edification (*paraklēsis*), xxi, 59–67, 97–98, 155, 232
Ektithēmi (explaining), 77–78
Election, divine, 7, 164
Elder (*presbuteros*), 6, 101, 102, 179–180, 206, 230–33
Elegchō (reproving), 93–96
Encouragement (*paraklēsis*), 60–63
Encouraging (*parakaleō*), 60–63, 97–98
Energeia, 187, 257, 262–63, 283, 301
Epangelical theology, 143
Epiphany (of Jesus), 22, 23, 26
Episcopacy, 5–7, 105
Episkopos (overseer, bishop), 105, 179, 233n49
Epithesis (Laying on of hands) 278–81
Epistēthi, 108
Epitimeō (rebuking), 95–96
Eschatology, 13, 23, 24, 28, 42, 52, 77, 274
Eternal life, 15, 146–47, 175, 193, 199, 301

Ethics, 65, 130, 170n3, 171, 181
Euangelizō (evangelizing), 49, 74n18, 75, 220, 221
Euangelion (gospel), xx, 18, 39, 49, 50, 53, 56, 58, 68, 155, 260, 265
Eukairōs (timely), 113
Eucharist (see Lord's Supper)
Eutychus, 78n35, 115, 125
Evangelical Theology, 23, 28, 91, 130, 274, 277, 279
Evangelism, 4, 49, 71, 72, 75, 78, 80, 82–84, 135, 148, 290
Evangelist, 41, 74–75, 110, 112, 220–22, 234, 235, 265, 279
Evangelizing, 49, 74n18, 75, 220, 221
Exēgeomai (relating), 16, 88
Existentialism, 23, 161n10
Eyewitnesses of Jesus, 19, 129, 142–43, 224, 226, 228, 245, 247–49, 280
Ezekiel as a preacher, 158, 163
Ezra as a preacher, 40, 66, 87, 114, 231
Faith
   of Paul, 110
   saving, 142. 144, 146, 163–66, 265, 301
Fall, 161, 199, 200, 202
False Teachers/ Preachers, 161, 171–172
Felix, procurator, 71, 79, 90, 120, 129, 139
Festus, procurator, 83, 90, 129, 139n51
Forgive(ness), 55, 59, 77, 134, 144n64, 145, 147, 156, 227, 239
Form Criticism, 131
Free Offer, 57
Fulfill(ment), 27, 43, 54, 59, 120, 134, 139–48, 154, 156–57, 241, 257, 258–283, 287, 293–94
Gamaliel, 127, 129, 132
Gifts, spiritual, 7, 8, 9, 30, 43–44, 50, 186, 216, 222, 232, 240, 273–83, 295
Gnosticism, 243
God
   As Hearer, 110
   As Judge, 20
   As King, 27
   As Preacher, 15
   As Savior, 64, 54, 181, 217, 241, 261
   Grace of, 28n54, 81, 84, 101, 123, 137, 145n66, 164, 205, 208, 211, 266, 269, 271–73, 287, 293, 295
   Image of, 106, 222
   Nature of,, xviii
   Of Comfort, 61
   Oneness, 15
   Right Hand of, 21, 29, 30–32, 42, 58, 144, 289
Good works, 174, 178n27, 205, 287

320

Subject Index

Gospel (*euangelion*), xx, 18, 39, 49, 50, 53, 56, 58, 68, 155, 260, 265
Governing (*hēgeomai*) (governing), 102
Grace, 145n66, 264, 272–273
Granville Sharp Rule, 14
Graphē (Scripture), xx, 25, 38, 40–43, 65, 67
Great Commission, 30, 73, 81, 85, 86, 88
Grēgoreō (watching), 192
Haggadah, 120
Halachah, 120
Harusin, 132
Hearing, 48, 51, 86, 126, 160–69, 187, 261–265, 296
    Of faith, 162, 169
Heeding (*prosechō* and *epechō*), 92–93, 193
Hēgeomai (governing), 102
Herald, 4, 30, 39, 72, 223–24, 228, 230, 252
Herod(ian), 129
Hierourgeō (priestly service), 266
Holy Spirit, vi, 3, 4, 7–10, 25, 29, 46, 51, 61, 79, 94, 98, 102, 104–106, 141, 142, 144, 156, 164, 165n17, 181, 187, 194, 200, 227, 232–37, 239, 248–51, 259, 265, 273, 275–76, 277, 279, 280–81, 301
Homileō (converse), 71, 119
House Church, 115
Hubrizō (abusing), 197
Hupēretēs, hupēreteō (leading), 212–213, 240
Hupomimnēskō (reminding), 100
Hupotithēmi (pointing out), 100
Imprisonment, 198
Incarnation, 106
Inerrancy of Scripture, xviii, 48
Inspiration of Scripture, xviii, 16, 26, 87, 187, 205, 260n12, 287
Invitation, 4, 30, 146, 163, 168
James, brother of Jesus, 206–08
Jerusalem, 6, 10, 37, 67, 82, 124, 130, 138, 191, 208, 212, 226, 236, 250, 259, 267, 270, 290, 293
Jesus (see also individual entries)
    Appearances of, 13, 14, 19, 20, 22–26, 35, 36, 50, 58, 73, 139, 140, 296
    Ascension of, 29, 42, 58, 229, 244
    Baptism of, 245
    Birth of, 244n85
    Blood of, 28, 57, 138, 187, 214, 234, 271
    Burial of, 35, 50, 58
    Compassion of, 194
    Cross of, 20, 57, 197, 270, 289
    Crucifixion of, 37, 57
    Death of, 140, 141, 144, 145
    Deity of, 14
    Epiphaneia, 23
    Gentleness of, 97, 176
    Good Shepherd, 104, 166, 290
    Humanity of, 12n2
    Judge, 21, 22, 141
    King, 26, 27, 28
    Lord, 2, 141
    Love of, 194, 293
    Meekness of, 97
    Miracles of, 17
    Obedience of, 218, 289
    Prophet, 249
    Pontius Pilate, 103
    Preaching of, 16, 17, 18, 19, 141
    Pre-existence of, 15n15, 244n85
    Proclaiming, 75
    Raised third day, 35, 39, 30, 227
    Ransom, 212, 213
    Reconciler, 57, 58
    Redeemer, 77
    Resurrection of, 20, 21, 37, 58, 140, 141, 143
    Return of, 20, 28, 141
    Revealer, 22
    Righteous/Just One, 4n10, 151
    Sacrifice, 58,
    Savior, 142, 143
    Servant, 76, 212, 237n58, 240, 287
    Teacher, 85
    Sinlessness, 187
    Son of God, 37, 73, 80, 114n7, 173, 296
    Son of Man, 21, 27, 28, 212
    Sufferings of, 196
    Teachings of, 19, 137n43
Johannine literature and theology, 38, 98, 227
John the Baptist, 300
Judgment, 21, 22, 56, 141, 147,
Judas, 10, 159, 226n24, 245, 255n104
Justice, 20
Justification, 20, 57–58, 77, 144, 193, 273
Katallagē (reconciliation), xx, 55, 56, 57, 58, 59, 271
Katangellō (proclaiming), 77
Katēchein (catechizing), 89, 167
Kērux (Herald), 72
Kerussō (proclaiming), xxi, 18, 71, 72n13, 73, 133, 233, 259
Kērygma (Proclamation), xx, 15n18, 18, 52, 53, 54, 55, 64, 140, 141, 155, 223, 224, 258
Kērux (Herald), 223, 224
Kingdom (of God), 26, 27, 28, 42, 81, 115, 141
Koinonia, 155
Laleō (speaking), 70, 71
Law of God 79, 87, 193, 227n129
Laying on of Hands (Imposition), 7, 8, 9, 181, 206, 237, 278–81

321

Subject Index

Leading, leader (*proistēmi*), 240
Leitourgos (minister), 238–239
Liturgy (*leitourgeō*), 267–268
Logos (word), xx, 32–68, 33, 38, 43, 65, 70, 95, 174, 121, 261
Lord, 214
Lord's Supper/Table, 269n28
Love, of Jesus, 194, 293
Lydia, 79, 97, 116, 222
Lystra, 134
Martureō (witnessing), 91–92
Mathēteuō (discipling), 88
Mediator(s), 24, 137, 263, 264, 266, 268, 269, 271, 283
Message (*akoē*), xx, 51, 163, 168
Messiah (*mashiach*), Jesus as, 12, 15, 17, 29, 36, 37, 57, 78, 80, 103, 128, 141, 143, 147
Midrash, 120, 132
Miletus, 136
Minister, 10, 212–16, 235–40, 262–68, 288, 292
Ministry, 257, 284–294
Miracles (signs, wonders), 247n91
Mystery (*mustērion*), 24n44, 25, 36n14
Myth(ology), 161
Neo-Orthodoxy, xx, 36
New Covenant, 8, 15, 30, 35, 38, 40, 42, 43, 44–47, 79, 82, 85, 87, 101, 186, 216, 231, 244, 250, 263, 268–72, 277, 286–87
New Testament authorship, xviii
Noutheteō (counseling), 98, 241
Obedience of faith, 167
Old Covenant/Testament, 8, 36, 38, 39, 40, 41, 88, 79, 101, 141, 250, 268
One-woman-man, 183n50
Open Door, 116, 282
Opposition, 196
Ordination, 7, 8, 277–281
Paradosis (tradition), xx, 44–45, 67, 119, 126, 149, 167
Parakaleō (encouraging), 60–63, 68, 97–98, 232
Paraklēsis, xxi, 59–67, 97–98, 155, 232
Paramuthia (comfort), xxi, 63, 105–06
Parangelia (commandment), xxi, 65–66, 68, 297
Parangellō (commanding), 99, 297
Parathēke (tradition), xx, 46, 67, 100
Paratithēmi (commending), 9, 46, 99
Parrēsia (boldness), 190, 191
Parrēsiazomai (speaking boldly), 80–81, 191
Parousia (appearance), 20
Passover, 25, 216
Pastor (*Poimēn*), 104, 234, 290
Paul
    Apostle, 243n78, 245
    Author, 87, 119, 131
    Example, 175
    As Saul, 9, 10, 79, 88, 246
    As Teacher, 85n59
    Delivery of, 124
    Elocution of, 121
    Emotions of, 123
    Epistles as Sermons, 148—150
    Conversion, 245–247n90
    Commission, 3, 112
    Motives, 108, 111
    Rhetoric of, 120
    Settings, 114
Peithō (persuading), 83–84, 166
Persecution, 197
Persuading (*peithō*), 83–84, 166
Persuasion, 165
Peter, 3, 7, 10, 17, 62, 93, 95, 95, 104, 130, 161n10, 190, 192n9, 192n10, 206, 207, 208, 226n24, 235, 243n77, 244, 245, 253, 255, 262, 280, 287, 291
Pheobe, 236n57
Philip, 247n91
Philippi, 135
Pneumatikōn (spirituals), 50, 222, 260n12
Poimēn (Pastor, Shepherd), 234–235
Pointing out (*hupotithēmi*), 100
Prayer, 282
Preacher(s)
    Appointment of, 3
    As an Ambassador, xxii, 3, 16, 30, 83, 191, 220, 225–262
    As a Leader, 240
    As a Minister/servant, 235, 239, 287
    As a shepherd, 234–235
    As a type (*tupos*), 174
    As a steward (*Oikonomos*), 241, 266, 271
    As a witness 226
    Character of, 170, 177, 180, 197
    Commission of, 1, 9
    Conduct, 178
    Election of, 6
    Emotions, 177
    Enabling, 186–187
    Family, 183
    Finances, 184
    Gifts of, 273
    Manner, 189
    Motives of, 177
    Reputation, 182
    Suffering, 195
    Testing, 185–186
Preaching
    Activity of, 69–107
    Audience of, 158

Subject Index

Authoritatively (*diabebaioomai*), 193
Boldly, 80-81, 190
   and Prayer, 282
   and Sacraments, 25
   as a Gift, 30, 272-281
   as agonizing, 216
   as building, 218
   as doing, 209
   as encouragement, 60-63
   as laboring, 210
   as mediation, 263-264
   as ministering, 214m 239
   as practicing, 209
   as proclamation, 71-73
   as reasoning, 77-78
   as slaving, 213, 237-238
   as serving, 211-212
   as soldering, 218
   as speaking, 70-71
   as striving, 216
   as teaching, 229
   as working, 204-209
   of Jesus, 16, 17, 18n25, 19
   Energy, 262-263
   Reason for, 67, 68
   Soberly, 190
Presbyterianism, 5, 206
Presbeuō (ambassadoring), 83, 225
Presbuteros (Elders), 6, 101, 179, 206, 230, 278
Presbytery (*presbuterion*), 8, 206, 208, 278
Proclamation (*kērygma*), xx, 15n18, 18, 52, 53, 54, 55, 64, 140, 141, 155, 223, 224, 258
Proclaiming (*kerussō*), xxi, 18, 71, 72n13, 73, 77, 133, 233, 259
Proem, 132
Promise, 56n102, 57, 144
Prophecy, 8, 43-44, 249, 276-277
Prophet(s), 39, 43-44, 248-251
Propitiation, 57
Proving (*sumbibazō*), 79
Pseudonymity, xix, 1n1, 129n13
Ransom, 212, 213
Readiness
   (*epistēthi*), 108
   (*prothumos*), 109
Reading (*anagnōsis*), xxi, 66, 86-87, 268
Realized Eschatology, 28
Reconciliation (*katallagē*), xx, 55-59, 286
Regeneration, 165, 265
Redeemed, redemption, 42, 57, 68, 147, 148, 156, 178, 244, 269, 297, 301
Rebuking (*epitimeō*), 95-96
Reformed Theology, xx, 25, 57, 85
Relating (*exēgeomai*), 88-89

Reminding (*hupomimneskō*), 100
Repent(ance), 18, 49, 55, 59, 68, 82, 83, 94, 108, 136, 137, 141, 142, 144, 145n67, 146-148, 156, 172, 178, 210, 214, 297
Report (*akoē*), xx, 51, 163, 168
Reproving (*elegchō*), 93-96
Restoring (*katartizō*), 106
Rhēma, xx, 35-36, 67, 120
Resurrection
   of Christ, 2, 20-21, 37, 50, 52, 54, 58, 75, 90-91, 134, 136, 139, 140, 141-44, 156, 226, 228, 244, 245, 249, 270, 280
   of believers, 21, 62, 90
   of the dead, 20, 22, 140
Revelation, divine, xviii, 16, 241, 248, 274-275
Righteous One /Just One, 4n10, 151
Right Hand, 29-31, 42, 58, 289
Roman Catholicism, 25, 243n77, 263
Roman citizenship, 138
Roman world, 81
Ruling (*proistēmi*), 101, 102, 240
Sabbath, 132-33
Sacraments, 25, 269, 271
Salvation, 7, 23, 49, 51, 52, 57, 59, 74-75, 116, 126, 141-147, 224, 265-66, 269-70, 298
Sanctification, 164, 273-74, 284
Sanhedrin, 17, 29, 132n26, 139, 207, 231
Satan, 89, 96, 191, 202, 218, 239
Scripture, xx, 25, 38, 40-43, 65, 67, 251
   As Encouragement, 62
   Reading of, 66, 268
Sealing of the Spirit, 165n17
Sermonic Structure 155-156
   Of Romans, 150
   Of 1 Corinthians, 151
   Of 2 Corinthians, 151
   Of Galatians, 152
   Of Ephesians, 152
   Of Philippians, 153
   Of Colossians, 153
   Of 1 Thessalonians, 154
   Of 2 Thessalonians, 154
Service (*diakonia*), 212, 235-237n58, 284, 285n5, 286-92
Shepherding, 104, 234, 290
Signs (miracles, wonders), 247n91
Signs of the Covenant, 269-271
Sin(s), 35, 38, 50, 68, 94-95, 144-45, 184-85
Solemnly Testifying (*diamarturomai*), 81-82
Son of David, 27
Son of God, 37, 73, 80, 114n7, 173, 296
Son of Man, 21, 27, 28, 212
Sotēr; sotēria, sotērios; sozō (savior, salvation), 142n60

Subject Index

Sound doctrine, 167n22
Stephen, 247n91
Steward (*oikonomos*), 24, 266, 271
Stoicism, Stoics, 136
Striving (*sunathleō*), 216
Suffering, 195
Sumbibazō (proving), 79
Suzēteō (disputing), 80
Synagogue, 113
Synod, of Jerusalem, 7, 130, 206, 207
Symbol(ism), 8, 44, 250, 278, 280
Teacher(s), 85, 168, 229–30
Teaching (*Didachē* and *Didaskalia*), xxi, 52, 53, 64, 65, 84, 229
Teaching (*Didaskein*), 85–86, 229
Temptations, 112, 201
Tertullus, 120
Thematic preaching 138
Timothy, 86, 127
Topical preaching, 138
Topos, 132, 137
Type (*tupos*), 174–175
Tradition (*paradosis*), xx, 44–45, 67, 119, 126, 149, 167
Truth, xix, 47, 48, 81–84, 86, 91–93, 95, 100–01, 110–11, 121, 129, 143, 153, 161, 164–68, 170, 178, 190, 205, 227–30, 237, 252, 264, 275–76, 296–97, 300
Typology, 174–175
Vocation, 4
Watching (*grēgoreō*), 93
Weakness, 202, 203
Witness, 81, 226–228
Witnessing (*Martureō*), 91–92
Word, xx, 32–68, 33, 36, 38, 43, 65, 70, 95–96, 174, 121, 261
Working, 204
Wrath, of God, 20, 22

Scripture Index[1]

I. The Old Testament

Genesis
1:3	xviii, 15
3:8	160
3:15	41n34
15:1	120
17:11	269n28
18:25	20
21:10	41n34
21:12	38
21:12	38
41:43	223n7, 224
43:27	230

Exodus
4:1	158
4:15	16, 39
7:1	276
7:11	39
9:16	41n34, 76
12:25	216
15:18	27
15:2-	276
16:34	227
17:5	230
18:21–22	230
18:21	6n14
18:25	20
18:21	6
20:19	39
21:5–6	238
22:21	289
22:28	139
24:1	231
24:12	227n29

Leviticus
8:12	8
19:18	33n4, 38
25:39	213

Numbers
1:43	164
3:10	6
8:10	7, 278
11:16–17	231
11:24–25	231
22:38	16
27:18	181
27:19–20	278

Deuteronomy
1:11	39
4:2	40
4:25–26	133
6:6–7	260
6:7	89
6:13	215n39
9:9	227n29
12:32	40
18:15–18	39
18:15	249
18:18	17
19:15	36n12
25:4	41n34
30:14	36n12
31:9	231
31:36	227
32:4	20
34:9	7, 8

Joshua
1:8	260

Judges
2:8	213
6:34	258

1 Samuel
2:29	184
3:10	242
3:13	184
8:19–20	7
12:5	227
13:14	132, 133n29
16:13	8
16:18	134
16:34–35	192
17:34–37	90

2 Samuel
7:12–16	27
7:12	133
23:1	133n29

1 Kings
19:10	41n34
19:19	295

---

1. This Index does not include mere listing of verses but only verses that are quoted or discussed to some extent in either the body of the work or in the footnotes.

2 Kings

2:9	232n47
18:12	213

1 Chronicles

11:3	231
25:1	83

2 Chronicles

18:13	242
30:5–10	224
30:5	52n78

Ezra

6:14	231

Nehemiah

8:5–8	40
8:8	66, 87, 114
9:6	87

Esther

8:13	63

Job

12:10	135

Psalms

1:2	260
2:6–7	27
2:7	133, 134
16:10	133, 134
19:4	36
68:18	30
81:12	134
89:20	133n29
95:7	16
96:10–13	27
103:19	27
109:8	245
116:10	40
110:1	29
139:4	110
139:7	110
139:10	8
146:5	134

Proverbs

9:3	52n78
20:12	169
21:24	183n46
22:15	198
23:30	182n38

Isaiah

6:5	xx
6:9–10	140, 160
6:9	158
6:10	158
9:7	27
20:10	162
28:16	41n34
33:22	27
40:1	61
40:8	135
40:13	80n41
42:5	135
43:9	227n28
43:12	227
44:8	227
44:28	133
51:3	61
52:7	27, 30, 56, 74, 221
52:15	76, 165
52:16	41
52:17	39
53:1	51, 163
55:3	133, 134
55:6	135
55:11	16, 36, 165, 262
57:19	18
61:1–2	8, 17
61:1	18n26, 244
61:2	61

Jeremiah

3:13	167n27
4:19	108
6:10	161
7:13	15
17:9	111
26:5	243
29:23	227
32:21	247n91

Ezekiel

37:3	163
37:4	163
37:5	163
37:4–10	158
37:10	163

Daniel

3:4	223n6
7:13–14	21, 27, 29

Hosea

13:14	33n4, 38

Joel

2:28–32.	120
2:28	23
2:29	249
2:31	22

Amos

3:8	xviii, 249
4:13	17n23

Jonah

1:9	213
3:2	18n25, 52n78
4:10 (LXX)	195n2

Habakkuk

1:5	133, 134
2:4	150, 151
3:13	17n23

Zechariah

10:2	82n50

Malachi

3:5	227
4:5	22

II. Jewish Apocrypha and Pseudepigrapha

Sirach
2:6	145n69

III. The New Testament

Matthew
2:6	103
3:7	22
4:10	215n39
4:17	18
4:18	74
4:21	106
4:24	267n26
5:22	207
5:32	184n5
6:10	28
7:21–27	247
7:23	22
7:29	194
8:9–10	213
8:10	218
9:35	53
9:36	194
10:2–4	253, 255
10:5	99
10:17	198, 207
10:24–25	213, 229, 237
11:28	4
12:41	18n25, 52n78
13:2	200
13:11	17, 24, 36
13:14	51n75
13:13–23	160
13:21	197
13:24	99
16:16	192n9
16:18	159n2, 192n9
16:22	95
16:28	28
17:17	167
20:19	198
20:26-28	237n60
22:2–14	4
22:13	236n56
22:43	260n12
23:8	229
23:11	236n56
23:34	115, 198
24:10–11	159
24:14	29, 296
24:46	213
24:48	20
25:21	22
25:23	213
25:31–46	184n51
25:34	30
25:36	105, 233
25:44	286
26:59	207
26:63	37
26:64	21, 29
26:65	17
27:21	103
27:46	197
28:18	4, 289
28:19–20	81, 88, 264n21
28:20	4, 30, 81, 86, 230

Mark
1:14	17, 27
1:15	141
1:38	18, 72
2:14	253, 255
3:13	3
3:14	244
3:16–19	253, 255
4:3–9	163
4:11	24n44, 36n14
6:8	99
7:34–35	163
7:35	51
8:33	95
9:2	161n10
9:35	236n56.5, 240
10:43–45	237n60
10:43	236n56.5
10:45	212, 286
13:9	207
13:10	72
13:52	88
14:53	231
14:55	207
15:1	207, 231
16:8	18n25
16:20	52n78

Luke
1:1–4	xix
1:1	19
1:2	215, 239
1:4	128
1:37	16n20
2:9	108
2:38	108
4:16–21	17
4:18	72, 221, 244
4:20	239
4:28–30	158
4:39	95
4:40	8
4:43	17, 221, 222, 244
4:44	17
6:13–16	253, 255
6:13	244
6:47–48	167
8:10	24n44, 36n14, 169
8:24	95
8:50	145n69
9:1–2	244
9:42	95
10:1	244
10:2	204
10:7	41n34, 211, 292
10:16	2, 83, 164, 248
10:17	207
10:40	285

Luke (Continued)

11:32	18n25, 52n78
11:49	244, 249
12:3	72
12:11	90
12:32	234n54
12:37	285, 286
12:42	241, 242
14:22	238
14:32	83, 225
16:25	60
17:3	95
17:21	28
18:22	185
18:32	197
19:10	143
19:14	83, 225
19:44	233
21:14	90
22:26–27	237
22:26	103, 286
22:66	207
23:40	95
24:4	108
24:14–15	71
24:19	17, 249
24:25	181
24:26	29
24:27	143n61
24:44	249
24:46–47	73, 227
24:47	73
24:50–51	58

John

1:3	16
1:14	16, 38
1:15	227
1:18	16, 37, 88n67, 121
1:42	192n9
2:10	182n38
3:8	165n18, 280
3:11	227
3:16	145
3:30	300
3:36	145n65
4:25–26	37
4:34	244, 293
4:39	91
4:48	247n91
5:28–29	20, 21
5:25	164
5:27	21
5:37	227
6:60	162
6:63	71
6:67	255n104
8:14	227
8:43	162, 164
10:3–4	235
10:11	104, 234, 290
10:12–13	90, 192
10:15	235
10:16	235
10:24–25	37
10:27	165
10:36	37
11:19	63, 105
11:26	63
11:47	207
12:26	236n56, 286
12:39–40	160
13:14–15	286
13:16	238n60, 243n79
14:16	61
14:26	61
14:27	18
15:15	213
15:26	61, 227
15:27	227
16:2	115
16:7	61, 98
16:8	94
16:13	43, 275
16:33	18
17:4	293
18:20	190
18:36	214, 217, 239
18:37	166, 227
19:1	198
19:35	227
20:2	254, 255, 256
20:19	18
20:21	244
20:24	255n104
21:15–17	235
21:16	104, 234n54
21:23	20
21:24	227

Acts of the Apostles

1:3	129, 244
1:8	227, 228
1:13	244
1:17	10
1:20	105
1:21	245
1:22	224, 245, 249
2:4	83
2:18	249
2:20	23
2:21	145
2:29	190
2:32–36	29
2:32	129
2:38	144
2:39	146
2:40	62, 130
2:42	64, 245, 269
2:46	115
3:22	249
3:23	17
4:12	5
4:13	190
4:20	23
4:29–31	71
4:29	213
5:42	49, 115
6:1–6	6, 279n52.2, 289
6:2	212, 236, 244, 282, 287
6:3–6	8, 237
6:3	6, 10, 105, 233, 280
6:4	212, 232, 287, 301
6:6	7, 8, 181, 278
6:8	281
8:8	279
8:12	29
8:17–18	8
8:21	10
8:30	113
8:35	252, 265
9:15	112
9:17	8
9:20	37
9:22	37, 79
9:27	81, 191
9:29	80
9:31	219
10:22	218
10:36	17
10:38	290
10:42	3, 73
10:43	142, 144, 146

Reference	Pages	Reference	Pages	Reference	Pages	Reference	Pages
11:20	49	15:14	234	20:17–38	136, 279n52		
11:23	62, 63	15:22	6	20:17	101, 206		
11:26	230	15:23–29	130	20:18–21	214		
11:28	44, 250, 277	15:31	63	20:19	201, 214		
11:29	290	15:32	44, 62n121, 250, 251	20:20	76, 105, 115, 233		
12:2	245	15:35	86, 136	20:21	59, 82, 137, 146		
12:17	207	15:36	105, 233	20:23	200		
12:25	293	15:40	9	20:24	82, 112, 137, 212, 287, 288, 289, 293, 294, 295		
13:1–3	9, 10, 279n52.3	16:1–4	127				
13:1	8, 229, 249, 251, 267, 280	16:2	280				
		16:3	130				
13:2	3, 9, 10, 204, 239n64, 248	16:10	277	20:27	35, 76, 168, 181, 259		
		16:13	124				
13:3	7, 8, 181, 278	16:14	79, 116, 164, 165, 222, 265	20:28	4, 6, 10, 92, 104, 105, 138, 191, 193, 213, 233, 234, 235		
13:4	279						
13:9	124	16:17	77				
13:11	44, 250	16:18	96				
13:14–15	114	16:20	97				
13:14–43	134	16:22	198				
13:15	62, 66, 87, 132	16:23	198	20:29–30	90, 161		
		16:25–34	135	20:29	191		
13:16	39, 163	16:25	123	20:30	92, 192		
13:22	133n29	16:30	113	20:31	93, 99, 111, 123,		
13:26	49	16:31	4, 37, 142n60, 144, 146, 222	20:32	xxii, 60, 187, 192, 219, 261, 219, 26, 264, 277		
13:32	57						
13:38	77						
13:39	142	16:37	198				
13:42	84, 146	16:38	198				
13:43	84	17:2	38, 79	20:33–34	185		
13:45	39	17:4	146	20:34–35	211		
13:46	191	17:16–36	135	20:34	215, 239		
13:48	142, 146	17:18	58	20:35	19, 34, 36, 137, 211		
14:1	166	17:21	161				
14:3	105, 191, 261	17:30–31	147	21:9	2, 250		
14:4	245	17:31	21, 77	21:8	74, 221, 235		
14:5	198	17:34	208, 222	21:11	44, 250, 277		
14:9	124	18:3	211	21:18–19	206		
14:15–17	134	18:4	84	21:18	208, 267		
14:19	158, 162	18:5	82	21:19	287		
14:21	88	18:11	86	21:24	89		
14:22	62, 63, 97, 201	18:26	2n3, 80	22:1–21	138		
		19:6	8	22:1	67, 163		
14:23	6, 9, 10, 202, 206, 279n52.4	19:8	84, 191	22:3	132		
		19:12	65	22:8	37		
		19:18	142, 146	22:15	226, 228		
14:26	9, 49, 205	20:2	62n121, 98	23:1–6	139		
14:27	76, 114, 116	20:4	267	23:1	124		
15:2	206	20:6	267	23:6	15		
15:3	10	20:7–10	79, 115, 125, 130	23:11	82, 226		
15:6	207			23:25–30	129		
15:7	169	20:7	115, 137	24:1	120		
15:11	273	20:11	71, 110, 125	24:5	91		
15:13	207	20:12	98	24:10–21	139		

Acts of the Apostles
(Continued)

24:10	90
24:14	38, 144, 181, 215
24:23	239
24:25	71
24:26	71
24:27	79
25:24	191
25:25	129
25:27	198
26:1–29	139
26:1	90
26:3	163
26:9	37
26:16	4, 9, 81, 83, 214, 226, 239
26:18	144, 239
26:20	59, 210
26:22	91
26:23	90
26:24	90
26:25	83, 121
26:26	81, 191
26:28	84, 166
26:29	166
27:23	215
28:23–31	140
28:23	78, 82, 84
28:25	265
28:26–27	160
28:27	198
28:30–31	115
28:31	29, 30, 31, 42, 86, 190, 191, 230

Romans

	150
1:1–4	38, 150, 276
1:5	166, 167
1:9	216
1:10	216
1:11	216
1:13	177
1:14	112
1:15	109, 222
1:16	50, 56, 261
1:17	39
2:16	56
2:18	89
2:20	48
3:21	276
3:24	273
3:28	204
4:3	41n34
4:25	58
5:6	145
5:8	145
5:17–18	151
6:17	19, 64, 167, 169, 171n5
6:18	238
7:6	213
8:1	22
8:7	79
8:18–19	199
8:33–34	22
8:38–39	123, 293
9:2	123, 177
9:3	177
9:6–7	38
9:6	35
9:11	57
9:17	41
9:23–24	57
9:27	41
10:1	178
10:5	41
10:8	36n112, 73, 264
10:9	59, 221
10:11	41, 57
10:13	57
10:14–15	5
10:14	xx, 44, 70, 160, 223, 224, 265, 301
10:15	5, 39, 56, 74, 221, 248
10:16	41, 51, 163
10:17	36, 51, 66, 126, 160, 163, 264, 265
10:18	36n12
10:19	41
11:2	41
11:8	161, 162
11:9	41
11:13	287, 292
11:25	36
11:33	57
12:1	60, 97
12:2	102, 216, 266
12:6	43, 44, 248, 250n97, 274, 275, 276
12:6–8	50, 22, 229, 232, 240, 273, 277
12:7	44, 65, 85, 181, 229, 287, 288
12:8	61, 62, 98, 231, 232, 241
12:11	214
12:13	184
13:4	289
13:9	38
13:12	218
14:3	219
14:9	37
14:10	20
15:2	219
15:4	62, 63, 65, 97, 98
15:5	36, 61
15:8	237
15:12	41
15:15–16	263, 265, 266, 268
15:16	238, 239, 268
15:18	121, 168, 205, 264
15:19	10, 259, 260
15:20–21	166
15:20	74, 219
15:21	41, 76, 165
15:25–26	212, 290
15:27	239, 267
15:31	289
16:1	236n57
16:3–4	173
16:4	100
16:7	173
16:12	173
16:16	123
16:17–18	161
16:18	172n6
16:21	173
16:23	241
16:25	18, 38, 53, 151
16:26	25, 37, 167, 251

1 Corinthians 151

1:6	81, 227
1:9	146
1:10	97, 106
1:17	75, 120, 270
1:18	261
1:21	xxiii, 53, 59, 72, 166, 301
1:22	37
1:23	18, 50, 57, 72
2:1	36, 77, 91, 120
2:2	177
2:4	18n25, 53, 84, 121, 261
2:7	25, 70
2:9	41
2:11	108
2:13	25, 70
2:14	264
2:16	186
3:5	265
3:9–10	219
3:9	206, 208, 219
3:11	248
4:1	25, 46, 215, 239, 241, 266, 271
4:2	177, 241
4:6	40
4:9	176
4:11	98, 202
4:12	167, 211
4:13	98
4:14	99
4:15	222, 265
4:16	175
4:17	173, 174, 196
5:1	122
5:5	103
5:11	84
6:5	103
7:1	132
7:10	19
7:22	238
8:6	14n9, 15n13
9:1	204, 245, 248
9:2	245
9:11	292
9:14	77
9:16–17	266
9:7	218, 235
9:12	110
9:14	211
9:16–18	241, 266
9:16	47, 108, 111, 177, 201, 210
9:17	241
9:19	238
9:20–21	178
9:22	133
9:23	110, 209
9:25–26	216, 217
9:26	
9:27	178, 217, 293
10:11	40, 98
10:16	187, 270, 271
10:21	122
10:26	77
11:1	175, 187
11:2	45, 167
11:5	2
11:23–25	45, 270
11:23	210
11:26	270, 271
11:27	202
12:4	273
12:5	287, 288
12:6	263
12:7	280
12:8–10	222, 273, 274
12:10	43, 44, 249, 276
12:11	265, 273
12:13	270, 271
12:28	3, 8, 85, 102, 228, 229, 247, 249, 276
12:29	247, 249, 276
13:1	111
13:2	178
13:8–10	44, 274, 277
13:8	281
13:10	275
14:1	277
14:3	44, 63, 219, 251, 276
14:4	250, 277
14:5	43, 251
14:6	43, 44, 65, 277
14:9	160
14:19	89
14:24	94
14:26	65, 115, 219, 268
14:29	276
14:32	296
14:37	43n40, 249, 250
15:1–3	50, 75
15:1–8	45, 58, 211n4
15:2–5	20n31, 35, 37, 39, 45, 49, 58, 75
15:2	35, 167
15:3–4	39, 222
15:3	57, 68, 145
15:5	34, 38, 244, 245
15:6	19, 245
15:8	248
15:9	245
15:10	211, 273
15:11	73
15:12	58
15:14	18n25, 33, 54
15:15	91, 227
15:24	28
15:25	29
15:34	123
15:51	36
15:58	209, 211
16:9	116, 263
16:10	173, 204
16:15	287, 292
16:16	205, 210

2 Corinthians 151–52

1:3	61
1:4–6	63, 98
1:4	97
1:6	61, 62
1:11	206
1:12	178
1:19	73, 173, 196
1:20	120
1:23	228
1:24	208
2:6–8	103
2:4	178
2:7	97
2:12	116
2:14	23
2:16	272
2:17	31, 71, 109, 110, 172
3:5–6	186, 187, 272
3:7–9	286

2 Corinthians (Continued)		11:3	248	4:30	41n34
3:8	288	11:4	166	5:11	197
3:9	286	11:5	248	6:1	106
3:12	191, 194	11:6	121	6:4	205n5
3:14	66	11:9	201	6:6	89
4:1	287, 288	11:13	48, 172, 191	6:9	209
4:3–6	49, 56, 222	11:20	176	6:10	290
4:5	19, 37, 57, 58, 214, 238	11:23	198	6:12	197
		11:25	162, 198		
4:6	79	11:26	191, 200	Ephesians	152
4:7	203	11:27	202	1:3	7
4:13	xxiii, 40, 70, 110	12:9–10	198	1:13	34, 36, 48, 165n17, 166
		12:9	187, 203		
4:15	283	12:10	196, 201	1:19	58n106, 262
5:9	110	12:11	248	1:23	260
5:10	21	12:12	247	2:12	103
5:11	84, 121, 289	12:14	176	2:17	18
5:14	178, 194	12:19	71, 109, 219	2:19	101, 115
5:18–19	4, 286	12:21	178	2:20	44, 65, 86, 235, 242, 247, 251, 276
5:19	35, 55, 59	13:3	26, 226		
5:20	3, 16, 59, 83, 98, 164, 225, 261	13:4	203		
		13:9	106	2:21	219
				3:1	199
5:21	225, 286	Galatians	152	3:2	241
6:1	208	1:5	48	3:3	43
6:3	287	1:6	147	3:4–6	16
6:4–6	196, 202, 292	1:8–9	47, 75	3:5	24, 242, 247, 262, 276
6:4	200, 201	1:10	177, 213, 238		
6:5	198, 199, 202	1:11–12	25, 75	3:7	262, 272
6:7	218	1:12	43	3:8–9	25
6:11	178, 206	1:16	57, 75	3:8	57, 212, 264
7:4	178	1:18	186n57	3:11	30, 191
7:6–7	62	1:19	207	3:14	123
7:7	76	2:2	73	3:16	187, 230
7:11	91	2:4	172	3:19	257, 260
7:13	62	2:5	48	4:1	97
7:14	110	2:7–8	192n	4:5	9
7:15	173	2:8	262	4:7–10	30
8:3	91	2:9	207	4:7	272, 273
8:16	186	2:14	48, 93, 192	4:8	39, 41, 63, 222
8:19	6n15, 212, 287	2:16	204n4		
		2:17	236n56.4	4:11	10, 30, 44, 74, 85, 104n120, 146, 204, 219, 220, 221, 222, 228, 229, 234n55, 235, 247, 249, 276
8:20–21	178	3:1	23		
8:22	186	3:2	51, 162, 165		
9:1	132, 289	3:3	123		
9:10	292	3:8	41		
9:12	267, 290	3:11	39		
10:1	97	3:22	57		
10:3	218	4:2	241		
10:5	218	4:13	203		
10:10–11	150	4:15	91, 203	4:12	102, 219, 286, 289
10:10	203	4:19	176, 291		
10:16	74	4:20	122	4:14	64, 172
11:2	176, 291				

4:16	219	3:10	58, 197	4:12	10, 187, 217		
4:21	86, 165	3:17	174, 175	4:13	91, 173		
4:29	121, 251, 264	3:18	153	4:16	87, 119, 127, 148, 149, 153		
5:1	175	3:19	172				
5:6	121n11	3:21	262	4:17	9, 154, 258, 288, 292, 293		
5:11	94	4:1	123				
5:13	94	4:3	2, 216				
5:18–21	260	4:9	45, 168, 210	**1 Thessalonians**	154–55		
5:19	260n12	4:11	123	1:5	259, 261, 262		
5:26	36	4:12	201	1:6	200		
5:31	39			1:9	168		
6:12	89, 93	**Colossians**	153	2:2	71, 191, 198, 217		
6:13–17	218	1:5–6	28				
6:15	56	1:5	36, 34, 48, 297	2:3	61, 110		
6:16	36			2:5	110, 228		
6:17	36	1:6	48, 153, 159, 261	2:6	291		
6:19	36, 37, 81, 83, 116, 121, 191, 282			2:7	177		
		1:7	10	2:8	177, 291		
		1:13	28	2:9	205, 210		
6:20	71, 112, 225, 226	1:15	241	2:10	174		
		1:20	28, 57	2:11	64, 97, 105, 111, 251, 291		
6:22	63	1:23	72, 212				
		1:24	197, 200	2:12	28, 146		
Philippians	153	1:25	25, 153, 154, 200, 212, 237, 241, 259	2:13	xviiin7, 15, 26, 34, 36, 43, 45, 52, 168, 262, 263		
1:1	6, 206, 213, 236, 237						
1:7	67, 90, 91, 93	1:26–27	36				
1:8	178, 228	1:27	37	2:14	265		
1:12	114, 202	1:28	xx, 59, 77, 99, 111, 154, 230, 259, 291	2:16–17	97, 123		
1:13–14	199			2:18	202		
1:14	34, 71			3:2	97, 173, 208		
1:16	67, 77, 90	1:29	154, 211, 217, 263	3:3	200		
1:17–18	110			3:5	201		
1:17	172, 177	2:1	217	3:6	74n19		
1:18	48, 77	2:2	24, 37, 63, 123	3:10	106		
1:27	216			4:1	45, 97, 123, 154		
1:29	271	2:4	161				
1:30	217	2:6–7	45	4:2	65		
2:1	63	2:8	161	4:3–4	65		
2:7	238	2:10	260	4:6	2, 82		
2:8–10	289	2:22	64	4:9	132		
2:9–11	2	2:23	171	4:11	99		
2:10	289	3:12	164	4:18	62, 97		
2:13	262	3:16	35, 98, 154, 154, 260	5:1	132		
2:16	193, 210			5:8	218		
2:17	123, 268	3:17	121	5:11	97		
2:20	173	4:2	123	5:12	99, 101, 168, 210, 241, 292		
2:22	173, 214	4:3–4	71, 282				
2:25	10, 173, 208, 238, 268	4:3	37, 107, 116, 154, 217, 282, 298	5:13	169		
				5:14	63, 98, 105		
2:29–30	173, 268			5:18	218		
3:2	122	4:6	154	5:20	43, 275		
3:3	215	4:11	173, 208	5:21	167		

333

SCRIPTURE INDEX

1 Thessalonians
(Continued)
5:24   147
5:27   87

2 Thessalonians   154–55
1:8   166, 167
2:2   1n1
2:3   61
2:9   47
2:13–14   15
2:13   43, 45, 164, 266
2:14   147, 165, 265
2:15   45, 86, 119, 149
2:16   60, 61, 62
2:17   62, 63, 121
3:1   282
3:4   99
3:6   45
3:8   211
3:9   175
3:10   187
3:14   167
3:15   99
3:17   149n71

1 Timothy
1:2   222
1:3   93, 99, 161, 171, 192, 284
1:4   92, 161n10, 193, 266
1:5   65, 84
1:7   193, 299
1:10   64
1:11–12   263
1:11   3, 46n54
1:12   4, 288
1:14   292
1:16   175
1:17   26
1:18   9, 43, 46, 65, 100, 218
1:20   161
2:1   97
2:5   263, 268
2:7   xix, 1n1, 3, 4, 9, 43, 48, 72, 85, 129, 168, 223, 224, 229, 230
2:12   183n50
2:17   161
2:27   4n9
3:1–7   179
3:1   102, 105, 186, 233
3:2   6, 105n121, 182, 183, 184, 189
3:4–5   102, 240
3:3   184
3:5   184
3:7   70, 182, 183
3:8   182n38, 236
3:9   24, 181
3:10   185, 212, 281, 288
3:11   189, 236n57
3:12   236, 240
3:13   171, 191, 212
3:15   241, 285
3:16   23, 24, 36, 37, 73, 269n28
4:1   64, 159, 161
4:2   47, 172
4:6   64, 100, 195, 212, 237, 287
4:7   161n10, 216
4:10   217
4:11   86, 99, 230
4:12   171, 174, 291
4:13   61n122, 61–62, 62n122, 66, 65, 87, 92, 115, 193, 251, 268
4:14   3, 7, 8, 9, 43, 181, 185, 206, 278, 279, 280
4:16   92, 165, 193, 209, 281
5:1   96, 97, 291
5:7   99
5:9   181n
5:10   184
5:17   65, 103, 206, 207, 208, 210, 230, 231, 232n47, 240, 241, 264, 268, 271, 292
5:18   41n34, 204, 207, 211, 232n47, 292
5:19   186, 206
5:20   186, 299
5:21   14n8, 82, 291
5:22   8, 185, 280
5:23   1n1, 182n38
5:27   101
6:1   65
6:2   86, 97, 230
6:3   18, 64, 93, 171, 181, 230
6:4   172
6:11   170
6:12   146, 217, 228
6:13   91, 99
6:15   26
6:17   99
6:20   46, 47, 100, 172

2 Timothy
1:1   57, 224
1:2   222, 258
1:3   216
1:6   7, 8, 181, 272, 278, 279, 280
1:8   195n2, 196, 228
1:9–11   221
1:9   146
1:10   23
1:11   4n9, 43, 85, 223, 229
1:12   46, 100, 123, 174, 196
1:13   111
1:14   10, 46, 100
1:15   195
1:18   91
2:2   9, 46, 86, 88, 100, 127, 168, 208, 230, 288
2:3   218
2:4   218
2:5   216
2:6   211

2:7–8	189, 195n2	4:5	74, 170, 187,	2:1	64, 71
2:9	34, 196		188, 189,	2:2	189
2:11–13	100		192, 195,	2:3	64, 236n57
2:11	168		204, 205,	2:6	97
2:14	82, 100		209, 212,	2:7–8	64, 174, 232
2:15	34, 48, 204,		217, 219,	2:7	64, 178
	205		220, 221,	2:10	65, 181
2:16	172		222, 235,	2:13	14n8
2:21	178		252, 284,	2:15	71, 95, 96, 97
2:22	178		257, 276,	3:1	100
2:24–25	111, 214,		280, 282,	3:3	213
	238, 291		283, 284,	3:4	23
2:24	238		287, 293,	3:5	165n18, 265,
3:6	172		299, 300, 301		193, 197, 265
3:10	xv, 65, 158,	4:6	295	3:8	193
	174, 208	4:7	217, 257,	3:9	172
3:11	195, 197, 208		258, 287	3:10	99, 186, 299
3:15	xx, 24, 38,	4:10	195, 257	3:11	172, 186
	46, 288, 296	4:11	294		
3:16–17	xix, 16, 205,	4:13	47n58,	**Philemon**	
	287		62n122, 295	1:1	208
3:16	xixn9, 26,	4:14	195	8	191
	65, 62n122,	4:16	67, 91	9	225n19
	95, 96, 103,	4:17	54, 73, 166,	10	222
	241, 274, 296		258, 264, 295	21	149
3:17	178	4:18	28	24	208
4:1–5	xiv, xv, xvi,				
	xx, 65, 93,	**Titus**		**Hebrews**	
	158n1, 189,	1:1	164, 214,	1:1	276
	295, 296		238, 248	1:3	42
4:1–2	1, 12	1:2–3	15	2:3–4	247n91, 263
4:1	1n2, 3, 9,	1:3	15n17,	2:17	263
	12n4, 13n6,		18n25, 34,	3:1	244
	14n7, 17,		36, 54	3:7	16
	18n25, 20,	1:5–9	xxii, 179,	4:12	16, 26
	23, 26, 31,		187, 299	4:15	106
	42, 82, 109,	1:5	5, 10,	5:1	6
	296		182n44, 206,	5:2	106
4:2–3	64, 158		233n49, 293	5:4	3
4:2	32, 61, 63,	1:6	182, 183, 184	5:12	44
	64, 69n1, 73,	1:7	6, 184, 266,	6:2	7
	84, 94, 96,		233n49, 241,	10:11	267n26
	97, 108, 113,		242, 266	10:32	197
	118n3, 126,	1:8	184	11:3	16
	148, 169,	1:9	61, 64, 65,	13:2	184
	219, 221,		94, 96, 97,	13:7	102, 103, 176
	223, 262,		181, 231,	13:17	102, 290, 292
	286, 295,		242, 268, 271	13:15	268
	297. 298, 301	1:10	171	13:20	104, 234
4:3–4	xxi, 159, 161,	1:11	93, 172, 192	13:24	102
	166, 170, 298	1:13	95, 96		
4:3	118, 167, 168	1:14	92, 193		
4:4	xxi, 161n10				

James

1:18	265
1:21	185n55, 262
1:27	105, 233
2:2	114, 231
2:9	94
3:1	22, 171, 229
5:10	40, 195, 276
5:13	195n2
5:14	206, 280

1 Peter

1:11	40
1:12	76n26
1:21	xviii
2:5	263
2:9	146
2:25	104, 105, 233n, 234
3:13	197
3:15	91, 113
3:21	269, 270
4:9	184
4:10	273
4:11	290
5:1	206, 208
5:2	233
5:2–3	104, 235, 291
5:2	105, 233
5:3	7, 10, 102, 232
5:4	234
5:5	7, 186, 206

2 Peter

1:19–21	251
1:19	276
1:21	xviii
2:5	223
2:11	28
3:2	46, 252
3:8–9	20

1 John

1:2	227
1:5	76n26
2:18	159
2:20	165n18
5:20	14n8

2 John

1:1	2, 101n110, 206
1:3	227

3 John

1:1	101n110, 206
1:2	167n22
1:8	173n7
1:9	7
1:11	175n15

Jude

17	245

Revelation

1:2	227
1:17	8
2:7	160
3:8	116
5:9	213
6:16–17	20
7:15	216
20:11–15	21
21:6–8	21
21:12–14	244
22:18–19	44, 275
22:18	160

www.ingramcontent.com/pod-product-compliance
Lightning Source LLC
Chambersburg PA
CBHW082026300426
44117CB00015B/2365